Energy in America's Future

This book is a publication of the National Energy Strategies Project of Resources for the Future (RFF). The project was designed to study the technical, economic, institutional, environmental, and human health aspects of alternative energy systems for the future, and was financed through a special grant from the Andrew W. Mellon Foundation.

Sam H. Schurr, *Project Director*

Research Staff

Jos J. C. Bruggink
Joel Darmstadter
Harry Perry
William Ramsay
Milton Russell
Eliahu J. Salmon
Robert B. Shelton

Research Assistants

Elizabeth W. Cecelski
Christian P. Demeter
Rosamond Katz
Andrew McLennan
Sally S. Nishiyama

Consultants

Edward J. Burger, Jr.
Joseph Dukert
Marc H. Ross

University of Pittsburgh
Shiao-Hung Chiang
James T. Cobb, Jr.
George E. Klinzing

University of Texas, Center for Energy Studies
Herbert H. Woodson
Martin L. Baughman
John B. Gordon

Energy in America's Future
The Choices Before Us

By SAM H. SCHURR, Project Director
JOEL DARMSTADTER, HARRY PERRY
WILLIAM RAMSAY, MILTON RUSSELL

A Study by the Staff of the RFF
National Energy Strategies Project

Published for Resources for the Future
by The Johns Hopkins University Press
Baltimore and London

Library of Congress Catalog Card Number 79-2195
ISBN 0-8018-2280-7
ISBN 0-8018-2281-5 (pbk.)

Library of Congress Cataloging in Publication data will be found on
the last printed page of this book.

First Printing, July 1979
Second Printing, August 1979
Third Printing, January 1980

Contents

Detailed Contents

Part IV   Health, Safety, and Environmental Impacts

Figures and Tables

FIGURES

TABLES

Foreword

In 1976, with the generous support of the Andrew W. Mellon Foundation, Resources for the Future began a comprehensive study of the technical, economic, institutional, environmental, health, and safety aspects of alternative energy futures. There was no dearth of energy studies at that time, but most of them dealt only with selective aspects of the energy problem. Some focused on oil, some on coal, nuclear, solar, or other energy sources. Some were concerned with technological questions, or environmental issues, or other selected aspects of the problem. What was needed, we believed, was a systematic view of different energy supply possibilities, of demand projections, of the probable implications and consequences of different courses of action—all treated in a comprehensive framework that would facilitate the comparison of various strategies. By drawing on the wealth of special studies already completed and by supplementing them with additional studies that it commissioned, RFF sought to provide a comprehensive synthesis.

This book is the culmination of that National Energy Strategies Project, and it is indeed comprehensive. It includes energy demand, consumption, and the economy; all likely sources of supply; impacts on health, safety, and the environment; and their complex interrelations—long term and short. The capability for dealing with this range of subject matter required a diversity of disciplines—including economics and public policy analysis, physics and engineering, and public health and medical sciences—and RFF was fortunate in being able to assemble, as authors and consultants for the study, persons who are specialists in each. In my opinion, they succeeded in their objective of providing a synthesis. When facts from various sources were in conflict, they did their best to resolve them. Where the facts remain in doubt, no attempt is made to paper over the gap. The reader is made clearly aware that all relevant facts about energy are not known.

The study does not recommend a "plan" for "solving" the energy "crisis." That was never the intent. Indeed, the very concept is flawed. There is no *crisis* (although mismanagement could easily result in one or more). Rather, we face a set of *problems,* which will be with us for a long time. Liquid and gaseous fossil fuels are relatively benign and until recently were both abundant and cheap. How will we cope with their increasingly limited availability and unreliable sources of supply? How well can we adjust to their higher prices? Will we be able to mitigate the adverse environmental, health, and safety impacts of some of the new energy technologies? In short, will we be able to manage gracefully the transition to the abundant energy sources of the future?

But if there is no magic solution, there is in-depth analysis of policy alternatives; of the reasons why agreement on policies has proved so elusive and difficult; of the political and institutional factors that have immobilized our decision-making machinery; and of promising, hopeful directions for policy to take. Not too surprisingly, the first policy step is getting prices right, so that both consumers and producers of energy will treat it as the more precious stuff it has become. This will enormously facilitate both conservation and enhanced supply, not only from the dwindling supplies of oil and natural gas, but also, and more important, from alternative energy sources.

Among conservation possibilities, three were subjected to detailed analyses—automobile fuel economy, residential heating, and industrial cogeneration—and the conclusions in each case are encouraging. Among possible supply initiatives, four are examined in detail: expanded use of coal (no insuperable supply problems); continued development of nuclear (but put safety foremost); encouragement of the production of synthetic liquids and gases from coal and shale (the cleanest way to use our coal and the most reliable way to get our needed liquids); and support for solar (a serious barrier has been the underpricing of oil, gas, and electricity).

The main purpose of this volume is educational. It is written primarily for the general reader, for students, and for those in government who, while not expert in energy matters, still must wrestle with a process of policy formation in which energy issues play an ever-growing part. Most of the book is devoted to explaining the fundamental facts (broadly interpreted) of the energy problem. But even energy specialists will find fresh insights from the synthesis of all its facets. Everyone—perhaps most especially those who have staked out a position on the energy front—will benefit from its balanced perspective.

The important, reassuring (and unexpected) conclusions of the authors is that, despite differences in values and goals, Americans can reach consensus on the broad issues of energy policy if they understand the facts and are willing to settle for the hard core of their goals, sacrificing extreme positions in the recognition that everyone must give up at least a little. We can have a great deal of conservation and environmental improvement without imperiling economic health and growth, and at the same time we can reduce our dangerous dependence on OPEC imports. Pervasive uncertainties make absolute assurances impossible, but we probably can cap the increases in energy costs at about double the level of the 1978 real costs of imported oil. We will be poorer than we would otherwise have been—the adverse impact of increases in real costs, whether of imports or domestic materials, cannot be avoided—but not much poorer. Economists will recognize that the authors are pleading for a national policy based on what Nobel Laureate Herbert Simon calls "satisficing," instead of on "optimizing," which is not feasible when values diverge.

Washington, D.C.　　　　　　　Charles J. Hitch
June 1979　　　　　　　　　　President, Resources for the Future

Preface and Acknowledgments

During the three years this study was in progress, energy commanded the attention of the U.S. public and the country's leadership as never before. Yet, despite its front and center position on the domestic (and international) political stage, and such major initiatives as the establishment of the U.S. Department of Energy and the launching of President Carter's National Energy Plan, the country is not much closer to a national consensus on energy than it was before the feverish activities of the past several years.

Numerous factors have impeded progress, but two of the most important are (1) the pervasive lack of agreement—or even widespread ignorance—about the facts dealing with supply and demand, technological prospects, and the environmental, health, and safety impacts of energy production and use; and (2) the failure to realize that the energy future offers no ideal choices and that all of the alternatives carry a mixture of desirable and undesirable characteristics. There is no golden pathway to the future that is free of serious problems; nor is there any pathway that can magically avoid the short-term problems that are at the root of so many of the political squabbles that go on daily.

In undertaking this study our aim was to produce a report that would present the essential facts bearing on the energy future within a framework that highlights comparisons among the choices. We wanted to analyze and then compare the available alternatives in their various significant dimensions: economic, technical, environmental, and institutional. To do this we had to cover an extensive and highly diversified set of topics, with an emphasis on data evaluation and synthesis in order to throw new light on the major issues involved in making choices.

An effort of this kind places heavy demands on staff because it requires mastery of a wide variety of technical fields. To meet this need, the core staff of the project was much more diversified in its disciplinary composition than is usual for a typical RFF project. Even so, it could not include the entire range of professional expertise required, so that it was necessary to rely also on the services of consultants and on research done under contract at specialized university centers. The latter group consisted of the Center for Energy Studies at the University of Texas at Austin (electrical technologies); the Chemical Engineering Department at the University of Pittsburgh (synthetic fuels); and the Center for Environmental Studies at Princeton University (conservation).

The book is the result of the collaborative efforts of many individuals. Those who carried principal responsibility for the different sections are identified below sequentially.

Part I. *Overview*. The principal author of this chapter was Sam H. Schurr who conceived the study and was its director.

Part II. *Energy Consumption*. Joel Darmstadter was the principal author of these five chapters. Chapter 5, dealing with the technological approach to energy conservation, was adapted from a report prepared by Marc H. Ross, professor of physics at the University of Michigan, who was on leave to the Center for Environmental Studies at Princeton University during much of the time he devoted to this project; Robert H. Williams of the Center provided useful advice in defining the scope of the report prepared by Professor Ross.

Part III. *Energy Supply*. Jos J. Bruggink and Harry Perry were the principal authors of chapter 7 on mineral fuel resources. Chapter 8, dealing with synthetic liquid and gaseous fuels, was written principally by Harry Perry and William Ramsay, drawing upon a report jointly prepared by Professors Shiao-Hung Chiang, James T. Cobb, Jr., and George E. Klinzing of the Chemical Engineering Department at the University of Pittsburgh. The principal author of chapters 9, 10, and 11 was William Ramsay; for the analysis of central-station electricity technologies, he drew upon a report prepared under the co-direction of Professors Herbert H. Woodson and Martin L. Baughman at the Center for Energy Studies of the University of Texas at Austin.

Part IV. *Health, Safety, and Environmental Impacts*. William Ramsay was the principal author of these three chapters. The underlying research and writing of Eliahu J. Salmon, of the project's core staff, constituted a major input; Salmon's professional expertise is in the fields of environmental health and health physics. Edward J. Burger, Jr., M.D., served as a consultant.

Part V. *The Process of Making Energy Choices*. The principal author of these six chapters was Milton Russell. Underlying work on selected aspects was performed by Robert B. Shelton, a member of the project's core staff.

In such a collaborative effort all members of the professional staff played a part extending well beyond the individual chapters with which they were mainly associated. In his capacity as editorial coordinator, Joseph M. Dukert, in particular, had a hand in the final writing of all the chapters; he made a valuable contribution to the quality and content of the book.

The authors of the study benefited greatly from the participation of two advisory groups: the National Energy Strategies Forum, chaired by Charles J. Hitch, which met periodically to discuss major issues and to provide ideas, guidance, and criticism; and the Panel on Health Implications of Coal Liquefaction and Gasification, chaired by Edward J. Burger, Jr., which advised on a broad spectrum of health effects data.

We are particularly indebted to the following members of the Forum for their review of all or parts of the manuscript: John W. Anderson *(Washington Post),* Richard E. Balzhiser (Electric Power Research Institute), Jack F. Bennett (Exxon Corporation), John A. Carver, Jr. (University of Denver School of Law), Isaiah Frank (The Johns Hopkins University School of Advanced International Studies), J. Herbert Hollomon (Center for Policy Alternatives, Massachusetts Institute of Technology), Lester B. Lave (Carnegie–Mellon University), James W. McKie (University of Texas), Laurence I. Moss (consultant, and former president of the National Sierra Club), Robert H. Socolow (Princeton University), Alvin M. Weinberg (Institute for Energy Analysis, Oak Ridge Associated Universities), and Carroll L. Wilson (Massachusetts Institute of Technology). Their suggestions and criticisms are reflected in the book, but not necessarily to the extent that would satisfy each member of the Forum. Detailed criticisms of chapters 8 through 14, many of which are not reflected in the final draft, were also offered by Amory Lovins (Friends of the Earth).

Other members of the Forum who advised through participation in its meetings include Alfred E. Kahn (then chairman of the New York State Public Service Commission), Norton Nelson (New York University Medical Center), John F. O'Leary (U.S. Department of Energy), and Howard Raiffa (Harvard University).

On the difficult and controversial subject of health effects data, specialized technical advice and review were provided by the panel on health effects whose membership included A. Paul Altshuller (National Environmental Research Center, Environmental Protection Agency), Donald Borg (Brookhaven National Laboratory), N. Robert Frank (School of Public Health and Community Medicine, University of Washington), Gerald Rausa (Environmental Protection Agency), William L. Russell (Oak Ridge National Laboratory), Robert Scala (Exxon Research and Engineering Co.), Carl Shy (University of North Carolina Environmental Health Institute), Frank E. Speizer (Harvard University Medical School), and Gerald Wogan (Massachusetts Institute of Technology).

Valuable criticisms were received from numerous technical reviewers who read all or parts of the manuscript: Edward Allen (Institute for Energy Analysis, Oak Ridge Associated Universities), Jack Alterman (consultant, Resources for the Future), John Ashworth (Solar Energy Research Institute), James Beckerley (U.S. Nuclear Regulatory Commission), Douglas R. Bohi (Resources for the Future), Richard C. Corey (U.S. Department of Energy), Edward Davis (American Nuclear Energy Council), S. David Freeman (Tennessee Valley Authority), George Gleason (American Nuclear Energy Council), Lincoln Gordon (Resources for the Future), Reginald Gotchy (U.S. Nuclear Regulatory Commission), Christopher T. Hill (Massachusetts Institute of Technology), Eric Hirst (Minnesota Energy Agency and Oak Ridge National Laboratory), Charles J. Hitch (Resources for the Future), Robert T. Jaske (U.S. Nuclear Regulatory Commission), Alvin Kaufman (Congressional Research Service, U.S. Library of Congress), Henry Kelley (Office of Technology Assessment, U.S. Congress), Albert Kenneke (U.S. Nuclear Regulatory Commission), Richard R. Kolodziej (American Gas Association), George A. Lawrence (American Gas Association), Vincent E. McKelvey (U.S. Geological Survey), Arnold Moore (American Petroleum Institute), David B. Pariser (U.S. General Accounting Office), Allan G. Pulsipher (Ford Foundation), John J. Schanz, Jr. (Resources for the Future), Glenn Schleede (National Coal Association), Milton Searl (Electric Power Research Institute), Mark Sharefkin (Resources for the Future), Grant Thompson (The Conservation Foundation), Lee C. White (White, Fine, and Verville, former chairman U.S. Federal Power Commission), and Charles Whittle (Institute for Energy Analysis, Oak Ridge Associated Universities).

Although this book provides a comprehensive report on the work of the National Energy Strategies Project, more detailed findings are presented in a series of publications resulting from the research undertaken. Reports already published, or slated for publication, include the following:

William Ramsay, *Unpaid Costs of Electrical Energy: Health and Environmental Impacts from Coal and Nuclear Power* (Baltimore, Maryland, Johns Hopkins University Press for Resources for the Future, 1979).

Shiao-Hung Chiang, James T. Cobb, Jr., and George E. Klinzing, *Alternative Technologies for Producing Liquids and Gases* (in preparation).

Shiao-Hung Chiang, James T. Cobb, Jr., and George E. Klinzing, "A Critical Analysis of the Technology and Economics for the Production of Liquids and Gaseous Fuels from Wastes," *Energy Communications* vol. 5, no. 1 (1979).

George E. Klinzing, Shiao-Hung Chiang, and James T. Cobb, Jr., "Environmental Effect of Synthetic Fuel Production," *Energy Communications* (in press).

Marc H. Ross, *Energy and Innovation: The Impact of Technical Change on Energy Demand* (in preparation).

Eliahu J. Salmon, *Health and Environmental Implications of Various Energy Systems* (in preparation).

Herbert H. Woodson, Martin L. Baughman, and John B. Gordon, *Future Central Station Electric Power Generating Alternatives* (Austin, University of Texas Press, in preparation).

Sam H. Schurr, Joel Darmstadter, Harry Perry, William Ramsay, and Milton Russell, *An Overview and Interpretation of Energy in America's Future* (Washington, D.C., Resources for the Future, June 1979); this is a preprint of chapter 1.

We wish to thank those who provided us with assistance in performing the research: Elizabeth W. Cecelski, Christian P. Demeter, Rosamond Katz, Andrew McLennan, and Sally S. Nishiyama. Their efforts made it possible for the work to proceed with much greater efficiency than otherwise would have been the case.

Thanks are due also to members of the support staff who helped with typing the manuscripts and in other matters essential in getting the work done. Major responsibility was carried by Maybelle Frashure who was chief secretary to the project. Others who assisted in the work at various times were Debra A. Hemphill, Elizabeth Hines, Cassandra Madison, Adrienne D. Plater, Flora Riemer, and Helen-Marie Streich.

We also appreciate the assistance of the RFF editorial staff who cooperated in a joint effort to speed up the final editing and production of the book.

Financial support for the project was through a generous grant from the Andrew W. Mellon Foundation. John E. Sawyer, president of the Foundation, was very supportive and helpful throughout the project, and his wise counsel is greatly appreciated.

It is impossible to range across the underlying data and analyses feeding into the national energy debate without being impressed with the polarized positions that have emerged on the issues. The outlook on the future of energy has come to be a surrogate for other, more fundamental philosophical views on the future of industrial societies, and this has often led to the dead end of unresolved social conflict on energy issues.

Nevertheless, the substantive results of our study permit a guarded optimism on finding a way to break the deadlock. We believe that the facts support the view that an acceptable middle ground exists upon which a national consensus in pursuit of positive goals could be built. However, there is no denying the fact that achieving such a consensus will not be easy and that it will require vigorous, perceptive, and persevering national leadership. Some hopeful signs of a national awakening and a developing sense of purpose are now becoming visible following the traumatic effects of recent events in Iran and their aftermath, and the Three Mile Island nuclear accident. It is still too early to be certain, but a consensus approach to the nation's energy future may be beginning to coalesce. We hope this book will help in the process.

Washington, D.C.   Sam H. Schurr
June 1979

Part I

Overview

1 *An Overview and Interpretation*

There are many reasons why U.S. energy policy remains in dispute, but at least four underlying problems come to mind in explaining the specific motivations that gave rise to this book and the basis on which its contribution to policy dialog might be judged:

1. There is disagreement—and even widespread ignorance—about some fundamental facts.
2. There is great uncertainty about what results the most commonly suggested energy policies might produce.
3. It is painful to choose between short-term and long-term objectives. What is "best" for most of us this year may make things very unpleasant in 1990—and vice versa.
4. There is no clear national consensus on what the major long-term goals of U.S. energy policy should be.

The first and the last of these problems may well be the most serious, because they make even the discussion of the other two—energy strategies and time-tradeoffs—discouragingly more difficult.

In varying degrees, this book addresses all four of these general barriers to a workable, acceptable energy policy for our nation, but it deliberately stops short of concluding what the best policy might be. Instead we have concentrated on summarizing relevant and significant information as well as we could ascertain it. The confusion about basic data is a troublesome factor in the energy debate; and we believe that a public purpose can be served by presenting as simply—yet as objectively—as possible what we consider the most reliable information available about supply, demand, current and prospective technology, environmental and public health and safety impacts, monetary costs, equity issues, and the interrelationship of domestic energy questions with international affairs. We have tied these diverse elements together as best we could, and it is inevitable that cross-references among the various sections and chapters abound. Whenever our best efforts failed to determine the facts, we hope that we have been forthright about admitting uncertainty.

So far as energy policies are concerned, America's energy future is open to choice, but the combination of possible decisions is enormously complex and the menu before us is replete with dilemmas. We examined in this study both the limits within which some major choices might be exercised and the almost inevitable mixture of good and bad results which they might produce.

The task of reconciling actions in which the long- and short-term interests of the nation and its various subgroups might diverge was perhaps the one problem among the four which we addressed least specifically. This is an important gap because the tension between today's and tomorrow's energy welfare causes a great many of the political squabbles that go on daily. Yet this third problem might be considered an offshoot of the fourth—the fact that all of us are reluctant to make sacrifices at any time (whether these represent higher prices, lower profits, less comfort, more inconvenience, or any other sort of personal penalty) unless we know where energy policy is taking us and agree that we are satisfied with that ultimate destination. The desperate need for a national consensus of this sort emerged in the minds of the staff only after we began our study of energy facts and choices. The notion that such a consensus is *possible* came even later—and only gradually and haltingly.

In offering highlights from the chapters that follow, however, it seems appropriate to deviate from the expository order in which they will appear and to begin by stressing the overall need for consensus on goals. For a number of years, energy policies have been caught in a crossfire resulting from conflicting perceptions as to the nation's future path of development and energy's role in shaping that future. Failure to resolve these broad underlying differences in outlook has deprived energy policy of a sense of ultimate purpose.

A consensus on goals is essential, not only to provide a starting point for launching timely initiatives to meet long-term needs, but also to aid in coping with short-run problems. Realistic long-run objectives, which identify the nation's energy capabilities and the means for achieving chosen ends, can also dispel the pervasive feeling that this country can do no more than react passively to developments elsewhere in the world—actions and situations over which it has no control.

What are the attitudes that shape our national energy objectives? Until recently, continuous economic growth and continuous expansion in energy use to support such growth have been unquestioned aspects of U.S. life. An expanding economy provided the underpinnings for constant improvements in average living standards, upward social and economic mobility for the people, and the general aura of progress which has characterized American society. If energy (or any other resource) threatened to run short, the solution was sought in new discovery or new invention.

During the past decade or so, however, a fundamentally different view has gained increasing acceptance. Where energy is concerned, the essence of this new perception is the belief that the limits of the natural world are being approached, and that our outlook and social policy must change in order for American society to adjust to the imminent presence of such limits. Limits are perceived in (a) the natural resources of mineral fuels, (b) the restricted capacity of the natural environment to absorb the growing volume of residuals from energy processes, (c) the adverse effects on human health and safety of these same energy residuals, and (d) the growing risks of full-fledged catastrophe in an increasingly complex, centralized, and interdependent world. There is also a feeling that "more" is not necessarily "better," that technology itself may reach a point where it is seriously dehumanizing, and an associated belief that overuse or abuse of limited resources today represents an unfair diversion away from future generations.

Naturally, these two different perceptions lead to quite different basic positions on the major goals of energy policy. Whereas the "expansionist" view is oriented essentially toward policy designed to increase the availability of energy supplies to meet growing demands, the "limited" view places its major emphasis on the reduction of energy wants and on the preservation of environmental values. There is also, of course, a spectrum of views between these two polar positions; and the outlook of most people undoubtedly combines portions of each position in varying degrees.

As in all policy questions, the existence of such dissimilar views can be explained partly by differences in values. But in this case the disagreement reflects something more than matters of taste. Much of the conflict arises from a failure to agree on the underlying objective conditions of energy supply, demand, and environmental impacts; and this further colors the respective judgments of what certain policy actions are likely to accomplish. Disagreements over fact reflect the underlying conflict in perceptions; but in practice these two sources of hostility feed on each other.

In a case like this, it is important to seek answers to the specific factual questions which are critical to the debate; and that is one of the most important tasks this book sets out to perform. Its findings may not be totally pleasing to any individual reader, but energy problems are complex and offer no completely happy solutions. There is, however, as we shall see, ample room for substantial consensus. To form the basis for wise and effective action, a consensus does not have to please everybody—or anybody. The essence of consensus is that the overwhelming majority will consent to it.

Relevant Findings for an Approach to Consensus

The key questions in achieving a consensus on energy policies are these: (1) whether future energy use can be restrained so that it grows substantially less rapidly than does economic output; (2) whether domestic (and therefore secure) sources of energy can be available in the longer run to support the production of goods and services desired by consumers; and (3) whether the cost of that energy—including its environmental and health costs—can be sufficiently low as to not in itself disappoint expectations of a rising standard of living or force a dramatic shift in the way society is organized and decisions made. While many uncertainties remain, and the possibility of failure exists, it is the reassuring message of the findings of this study that, given proper policies, consumption *can* be restrained without endangering growth, domestic energy *can* be available in adequate amounts, and that energy *can* be provided at affordable costs—including acceptable environmental and health effects.

We leave discussion of prospects for consumption to a later section, but it is important here to highlight findings as to prospective energy availability and costs—monetary and nonmonetary—that bear on an approach to achieving a national consensus which will allow appropriate policies to be introduced.

Energy Availability and Cost

As to future energy supplies and costs, we find that there are serious short-run producibility problems for oil and gas (which have been at the root of the recurring crises of recent years) but that total domestic mineral fuel resources are adequate over a very long period to avoid overall physical shortages. There are qualifiers, however. Coal and uranium resources together offer this supply assurance; but only if we can assume the successful development of reasonably benign technologies for (a) converting coal into liquid and gas, two fuel forms which pose special resource problems, and (b) extracting substantially more useful energy from uranium than we do with present-day nuclear power technology. The abundance of some other "unconventional" resources of mineral fuels (such as oil shale) serves to reinforce this conclusion on the physical adequacy of domestic resources. So does the possibility of applying solar energy (and various other renewable resources) in certain practical uses.

The critical issue shifts then to the costs of producing useful energy from these abundant resources. In monetary terms, we find that liquids and gases from coal and oil shale appear to be producible at costs about twice the 1978 prices of petroleum and natural gas. These estimated cost increases might well be offset (at least partially) by improved efficiencies in energy use. An example is the likely doubling in miles per gallon for automobiles by the year 2000. Production costs of electricity from coal and uranium do not appear to be on a long-run rising trend (after adjusting for general price inflation), except for continued pressures arising from environmental, health, and safety concerns; but those pressures are impossible to predict.

A major influence on long-term costs will result from the fact that, in many of the new technologies, natural resource costs should become relatively less important while the costs of plant and equipment become relatively more important. Increasingly, fuels will shed the cost characteristics of an extractive commodity and take on those of a manufactured product. This would be particularly true of nuclear energy produced in breeder reactors, for which the costs of raw uranium could become a vanishingly small element per unit of energy production. In processes based on coal and oil shale the raw fuel component would continue to be significant; but even so, the cost of useful oil and gas produced from them will be determined less by rising extractive costs than would be the case for the petroleum and natural gas replaced. Costs for the synthetic and natural sources of oil and gas should tend to converge over time, and cost increases from that point on should be more gradual for the synthetics at equivalent output levels.

After technologies of this type mature, their long-run cost profiles are likely to take the general form of a plateau—now sloping upward with added environmental or raw material costs and now downward with technological advances—rather than a series of sharp steps upward. Thus, their very long-term cost behavior could depart sharply from the common expectations for industries based upon depletable resources. This outlook would of course be rendered even more favorable by commercial success with solar energy and other renewable resources.

Even if the long-run outlook for monetary costs is favorable, however, what about nonmonetary costs? Those may be measured in human lives lost to illness and accidents, in damages to the natural environment, and in possible catastrophic events that may affect large numbers of people. How serious do such impacts threaten to become?

To begin with, we should recognize that petroleum and natural gas are relatively safe and benign with respect to the environment and human health compared with some—but not all—of the energy sources that may replace them. Thus the prospect could be one of added nonmonetary costs if, as we expect, the contributions of petroleum and natural gas to total supply diminish over time. The size of these negative impacts may easily be overestimated, however, and the ability to lessen non-monetary costs by choosing less harmful technologies and by adopting appropriate policies is often overlooked. Future electricity supply—where oil and natural gas (and hydro) will be a progressively smaller input to generation—is a case in point.

Because coal technologies are a familiar, long-established component of modern industrial societies, we shall use them as a benchmark for assessing the comparative seriousness of nonmonetary impacts in future electricity production. We will look initially at human health.

If all the electricity generated in 1975 had come from coal, the total number of associated fatalities (including coal miners and members of the general public) would have ranged between about 200 and 4,000. (The wide range reflects the vast uncertainties in the scientific data relating pollutants from coal combustion to human health.) If, however, the electricity had been generated from nuclear sources, total fatalities which might have resulted have been calculated at between 60 and 900. (As chapter 12 points out, this includes an evaluation of accident proba-bilities which is 100 times higher than the controversial Rasmussen Report—partly because of subsequent criticisms of the margin of error assumed originally in that report and partly because of the accident in early 1979 at the Three Mile Island nuclear plant, which involved at least some problems that had not been anticipated.) Even without con-tinued improvements in nuclear technology and operating practices, which might be expected in the wake of the Three Mile Island accident, the range of estimates for health threats is substantially lower for nuclear than it is for coal—although the two overlap.

A reduction in likely adverse health effects (similar to that from replacing coal combustion with nuclear power plants, but not nearly as large) might also be made possible through the introduction of technologies which can use coal in clean ways. These include the production of synthetics, either to be used as power plant fuel or to be consumed directly in residential heating in place of electricity derived from conventional coal-fired plants.

Moving to a comparison of damages to the natural environment that result from the production of electricity by various technologies, land use is an aspect of disturbance which can be measured, and which might be roughly indicative of other such disturbances. In this case nuclear power shows a marked advantage over coal.

As chapter 13 explains, the most extensive land impacts result from the mining of fuels. For instance, mining for coal disturbs between 300 and 600 acres per electric power plant per year. For nuclear energy, as a result of its much higher energy content per unit, the land disturbed comes to only about 60 acres per power plant per year. Even for coal mining, however, the significance of land impairment could be substantially reduced in the future as a consequence of recent legislation requiring that surface-mined lands be restored to their approximate original contours— with vegetation renewed in most cases. Thus, the impacts on land environments from our major sources of electricity promise to be less in the future than in the past, in response both to new technology and new national policies. This should provide a significant offset to a growing level of energy use.

Not all new technologies would yield similar results in terms of land use. Some (like direct solar energy at the end-use site) would be better; others (like oil shale) would be worse. The main point is that there will be various choices, and at least some of them can be less destructive of land values than the technologies they replace.

The same general observation undoubtedly applies to the adverse impacts on air and water which might result from very large-scale reliance in the future on synthetic liquid and gaseous fuels derived from coal. Although the conclusions reached in chapters 12 and 13 suggest that such effects would be less than those from burning coal directly, those calculations are indirect and are based on projections made for an industry that is in its infancy. On the other hand, it is unlikely that the employment of synthetics could produce less disturbance to the overall environment than do the production and use of conventional petroleum and natural gas. Therefore synthetics may prove to be superior to the direct use of coal, but that is not to say that environmental problems in the near to mid-term future can be dismissed with the promise of any magic solution.

Catastrophic threats associated with energy technologies are a separate, special (and major) area of concern. What springs to mind immediately is the potential threat of major nuclear accidents and the possibility that the enhanced use of nuclear power—particularly with fuel reprocessing and nuclear breeder reactors—may increase the likelihood of nuclear war. The threat of catastrophic impacts is present also with fossil fuel technologies, however, particularly in connection with possible worldwide changes in climate due to the cumulative buildup of carbon dioxide in the atmosphere over a long period of time. That problem is quite distinct from the one that comes from using so-called "dirty" fuels; it arises from the combustion of any carbon-containing material.

There is no doubt that these possibilities pose huge *potential* dangers, but there are serious questions as to how *probable* their occurrence is. Nevertheless, concern is justified. Even if the probabilities are slim, the effects of the "worst case" could be devastating. The strongest possible efforts must be made to reduce to a minimum the threat of catastrophic impacts, particularly those connected with nuclear power. To get the job done in that case, we will need two types of responses: (1) technical improvements which reduce the probabilities of operational failures, and (2) institutional innovations which surround the technology with essential safeguards to thwart human malevolence and misadventure. We cannot afford any serious delay in devising effective approaches, *especially* where nuclear technologies are concerned. It seems reasonable to assume that nuclear technologies—which have compiled a historically excellent safety record, even allowing for Three Mile Island—can be made still safer by improving existing systems and developing other technologies. What we need to determine is whether it is possible to produce a national consensus on moving ahead with nuclear power or whether there is an alternate consensus on accepting the full consequences of a policy that does without it.

The need to make distinct choices as soon as they can be reached sensibly is implicit in an analysis of our findings. Regardless of our long-term wealth in energy resources, we stand to suffer serious disruptions if the necessary decisions are not made with full attention to the long lead times required to develop, demonstrate, and deploy new technologies. A great deal can be achieved by "getting prices right" and letting decisions be guided by the market place (although that draws fresh attention to problems of social justice which must also be faced). But we also need to make timely choices in regard to competitive new technologies, because a policy that does not face up to these choices can be counted on to get nowhere in time for anything. None of this will be easy.

Achieving a Consensus

We believe that our findings provide a measure of support for both the expansionist and limited perceptions of the future. The facts on the availability and costs of future energy supplies, and on the possibility of limiting routine human health and environmental effects resulting from energy operations, imply that we will be able to expand domestic energy production on relatively favorable terms for a long period into the future. The threat of catastrophic impacts, on the other hand, indicates the need to combine care and speed in fashioning technical, policy, and institutional safeguards. In addition, we conclude that—although energy consumption will continue to·grow (figure 1-1)—energy conservation measures can significantly reduce the rate at which consumption increases, while maintaining an overall rate of economic growth which is consistent with general expectations.

To be widely acceptable, we believe that an energy strategy for the long run must explicitly combine three broad goals:

1. An adequate energy supply, based chiefly on domestic resources, to meet the nation's requirements for future economic growth and development.
2. Conservation in energy use, both in the short and long run.
3. Protection against threats to the environment, defined to include human health and safety as well as the natural environment.

The hopeful message of this study's findings is that feasible, identifiable supply and conservation technologies can probably enable us to achieve major elements of these combined requirements over the long run. Not only are they not mutually inconsistent; they may indeed dovetail in significant respects. Still, practical outcomes would require numerous interrelated policy initiatives—some of them general, some specific; and we would need to begin some of them soon because of the very long lead times involved in producing results. Most important, there would have to be a will to seek a consensus, and to implement the supporting actions that can make it possible.

How might we go about achieving such a consensus? The National Coal Policy Project is perhaps the foremost example to date of an attempt to

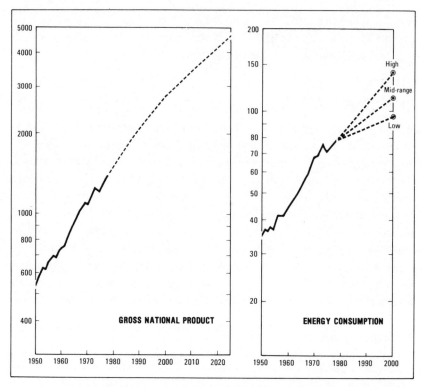

Figure 1-1. Historical and projected GNP (in billions of 1972 dollars) for the United States *(left)* is compared *(right)* with overall energy consumption (in quads—10[15] Btu). Historical data are from the U.S. Departments of Commerce and Energy; projections (including the range for growth in energy consumption) are discussed in chapters 4 and 6. A national consensus seems possible on energy policy goals seeking to provide the nation's long-term energy supplies primarily from domestic resources. We expect growth of energy consumption to be dampened because of slower economic growth and improved ways of utilizing energy to satisfy the demand for goods and services, and our analysis also indicates a relatively favorable outlook for domestic production.

reconcile conflicting attitudes toward environmental protection, resource conservation, and energy supply. It could be a prototype of what will be required if such reconciliation is to be achieved on the full range of energy policy issues. An analysis of what this disparate group agreed upon, and what it failed to agree upon, indicates both its promise and its limitations.

In the context of discussing a consensus on national energy policy, the National Coal Policy Project demonstrates at least that antagonists on important policy issues can reach agreement, if the conditions are suitable.

If their statements of common ground leave a good many issues still unresolved, we must admit at the same time that they are both broader and more specific than the areas of agreement the United States has staked out so far in connection with the overall energy picture.

The National Coal Policy Project has not been widely accepted as a "breakthrough," even with respect to coal. The participants have yet to convince the divergent groups from which they were drawn that the consensus reached is worth supporting. Nevertheless, it is a beginning.

Getting back to the triple base we suggested for a consensus on overall energy goals—domestic supply adequacy, conservation, and environmental protection—it is essential to point out that some policy decisions cannot be made by relying on precise calculations to compare benefits and costs of alternative choices and come up with a "best" solution. That technique works only when all major aspects of energy decisions can reasonably be expressed in terms of a common denominator.

Such cost–benefit analyses can yield valuable guidance where numerical precision is within reach; but they lead to the dead end of social conflict when the data are uncertain and controversial, and when the benefits and costs are so diversified as to defy expression in common units. For broad energy policy purposes, the trouble with using a cost–benefit calculus is even greater. Comparison among different goals brings value systems into conflict; and there can be profound disagreement over whether certain results are to be counted as benefits or as costs, not to mention the precise values to assign them. An approach which seeks a societal consensus acceptable to the mainstream of the American public is less exact, but at least it should be attainable.

We turn now to a summary of our analysis, beginning with the outlook for energy consumption. We examined consumption prospects within a long-run context, which would allow enough time for the economy to adjust to higher energy prices (and to other changes in energy supply conditions) through modifications of consumer behavior and the introduction of new and refitted energy-using and conserving equipment. In the short run, some individual regions and industries (and the people who live and work within them) could be seriously hurt—and others benefited. This might be brought about by energy conditions which changed suddenly as well as by those which unfolded more gradually. The processes of adaptation, and the stresses and strains to which they give rise, are outside the scope of this study. But, clearly, they could cause much pain; and they could also have a profound influence on the long-term adjustments which were finally achieved. By the same token, the problems of transition can be made easier if Americans understand what the ultimate destination might be, and how it is proposed that we get there. In seeking consensus, that is why we look first to the future—drawing lessons where appropriate from the past and present.

Energy Consumption in the Future

If there were reason to believe that market decisions reflecting all of the factors which influence consumer behavior would ultimately determine the level of energy supply and demand, the question of future energy consumption might be regarded as having no practical importance as a public policy issue. Whatever needed to happen would happen in response to market forces, and that would be that. But this does not appear to be the case. Instead, public policies are likely to have more and more influence on the broad setting within which individual choices will be made, if not in establishing actual targets or guidelines for energy consumption. Such policies, in turn, are strongly affected by how much energy the decision makers (including voters) believe our nation will use in the next two or three decades.

One of the most critical issues of energy policy thus turns on the question of how much energy the United States will consume in the future. Will energy consumption grow, as some believe, at essentially the same rate at which the broad economy grows? Or will the trend of energy consumption veer sharply away from general economic growth because of such factors as higher energy prices, the spread of conservation practices, and major changes in consumer habits?

Some Critical Issues

The energy problems of recent years have alerted the American people to the strong need for energy conservation and the real possibilities for achieving results. The drive to reduce energy consumption has become a major objective of national policy, advocated from the highest levels of government.

But what are the realistic possibilities for conserving energy? What constitutes waste? What can be learned from foreign experience? In what way does energy conservation bear on economic growth and the productivity of the American economy?

The difficulty of defining conservation. In its economic meaning, conservation of energy signifies the most economical application of energy —in its joint use with other inputs—in a given process or activity. This may be in the production of other goods and services or in the direct use of energy resources by the ultimate consumer. For example, a homeowner practices conservation in this sense when he reduces heat losses through improved insulation at a cost below the savings realized on the home-heating bill—that is, at a net financial gain. To achieve conservation that is cost-effective, saving energy alone is not sufficient; the cost involved in saving the energy must be no greater than the cost of the energy that is saved.

This oversimplified example could be misleading by itself, however. Not all cost savings that are germane from a societal standpoint can be calculated within a private financial accounting system. Legislating fuel economy standards for private automobiles illustrates an alternative approach. In this instance, Congress decided that the broad social benefits to be achieved would justify removing much of the choice about automobile fuel efficiency from the domain of individual decision makers. Even here, however, such mandated changes in energy efficiency probably must not be divorced too far from cost effectiveness as an individual might calculate it (taking loss of amenities into account). A law that blatantly ignores individual costs and benefits runs the risk of citizens' protests, which could lead to subsequent modifications in standards.

There are other ways of looking at conservation too. From a thermodynamic standpoint, energy conservation and efficiency are measured against ideal limits set by physical laws and processes. Such standards can be useful in defining goals for improving technical performance, but their practical application would require that the cost of achieving the higher level of performance also be taken into account. That takes us back to the economic definition.

Frequently, conservation is also considered in its ethical, equity, or environmental dimensions. In these contexts, it pertains to moderation as an inherently worthy value—or as an act dedicated to distributive justice or other social goals in the face of resource and environmental limitations. The practical difficulty in applying standards like these is that they easily lead to prescribing behavioral norms that reflect one particular set of value judgments as to what constitutes an "essential" use of energy. Yet it is as difficult to determine essential energy consumption as to determine what is essential in any other phase of consumption, whether it involves food, clothing, shelter, or recreation.

Lessons from foreign experience.   In public discussions, energy efficiency in the United States is often matched against the superior energy
performance of other countries. In relationship to levels of income, energy
consumption in a number of other advanced industrial societies falls considerably below that in the United States. (Canada, even adjusting for its
more severe climate, is the major exception.)

Could the United States conserve energy appreciably by adopting the
energy practices of other countries? About 40 percent of the difference
between the higher overall intensity of energy use in the United States and
the lower foreign intensities can be explained by "structural" and geographic characteristics. Two factors of major significance are: (1) the
large size of the United States and its dispersed population patterns, which
give rise to long-distance transportation of goods and people; and (2) the
preference of Americans for comparatively large, single-family homes.
These are deeply rooted features of American society, abetted no doubt
by the past availability of cheap energy. Some of these factors could be
changed, but not easily (and certainly not quickly).

The remaining (60 percent) difference in energy intensity between the
United States and other advanced countries is explained mainly by the
fact that we do use energy less efficiently in essentially the same applications. Thus, even adjusting for the size of American houses and the climatic conditions in the United States, we spend more energy per person
(at given income) on heating, cooling, lighting, and appliances. Of course,
much has been said also about our automobiles' low efficiency in gasoline
mileage, and this is a major source of difference between energy use in
the United States and other countries. As such, it deserves a large conservation effort.

In a wide range of industrial operations leading to the same products,
energy consumption per unit of output is also still distinctly higher in the
United States than in Europe, although that fact need not in itself signify
an economically inefficient production process. Traditionally higher energy prices in Europe—partly reflecting taxation on fuels—undoubtedly
provide a large part of the explanation for these differences. As relative
energy prices in the United States approach European levels (and as the
gap in nonenergy costs narrows simultaneously), production operations
in this country are almost bound to shift more toward reduced energy
intensities. In fact, the U.S. industrial trend in that direction began well
before the oil embargo of 1973–74.

To the extent that differences in energy practices between the United
States and other countries are organically related to economic, geographic,

and social features that also differ, it takes very careful analysis of specific circumstances to begin to apply another country's experience to the American situation. Detailed appraisals of energy conservation technologies, such as those outlined in chapter 5, are indispensable in determining which technological changes or transfers of energy practice from other countries are feasible in the U.S. setting. For the three cases considered in detail in that chapter (residential heating, automobile transportation, and cogenerating process steam with electricity at industrial sites), the prospects for conservation are good between now and the end of the century. But all tend to *adapt* foreign models to U.S. circumstances rather than *adopt* them directly; and the idea of adaptation might well be a general principle in such cases.

Energy and economic growth.   Much of the debate on energy consumption for the future focuses on the question of how much energy is required if economic growth is to continue. Although some social critics question the significance for human welfare of conventional concepts of economic growth, we do not address that subject in our analysis. On the contrary, we assume that there is a consensus for the idea that sustained real growth is essential if the United States is to meet the many domestic and international demands that press for attention. Even among those who accept the need for overall economic growth, however, there is no clear agreement on how much (if any) accompanying growth we need in energy consumption.

Historical analysis can throw some light on the relationship of energy use to national output. The record, back to the latter part of the nineteenth century, is traced in figure 1-2. Over the long historical period—almost a century—there are distinctly different subperiods:

1. An early period—from the last part of the nineteenth century approximately through the second decade of the twentieth century—in which energy consumption grew at a markedly faster rate than GNP.
2. A middle period—from about the end of World War I to the end of World War II—during which energy consumption grew persistently at a slower rate than GNP, with the ratio falling by about one-third over the entire period.
3. The most recent period—the past thirty-five years or so—in which there have been numerous short-term fluctuations, but no definite trend either up or down in the energy–GNP ratio. There is a good possibility that a new long-term downward trend has begun during the 1970s, but it may be too early to say conclusively.

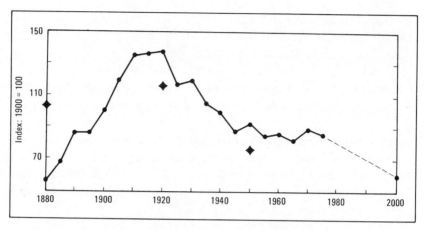

Figure 1-2. An index (1900 = 100) of energy consumed per dollar of real GNP for the United States from 1880 to 2000 shows successive trends of rising, declining, stable, and—for the projected years 1975–2000—once again falling energy intensity, as discussed in chapters 3 and 6. This plot excludes fuelwood, whose consumption exceeded that of coal into the 1880s. Single-year points that do include fuelwood are indicated for 1880, 1920, and 1950. [Sources are the same as for figure 3-1, with reference points including wood based on Sam H. Schurr and Bruce C. Netschert, *Energy in the American Economy 1850–1975* (Baltimore, Md., Johns Hopkins University Press for Resources for the Future, 1960).]

When people speak of a close relationship between energy and GNP growth in the United States, they are usually referring to the most recent of these three historical phases. Yet this period contrasts sharply with the two periods before it. Very likely the contrasting behavior of the ratio at different stages in the nation's history is related in some degree to structural changes in the American economy. Basic industrialization could have set the dominant trend of rising intensity during the early period; and the emergence of less energy-intensive lighter industries and services might help to account for the period of declining intensity (and subsequent stability).

But fundamental changes within the energy sector have also been at work: the replacement of wood by coal during the first period, and the rapid growth later in the use of electricity and liquid and gaseous fuels. These energy sector changes have been instrumental in altering the efficiency with which energy itself is used (for instance, fuel efficiencies were improved in the substitution of diesel for steam locomotives). Technological changes also affected overall efficiency in certain productive functions; the heightened efficiency of manufacturing operations as a result of electrification is one important example of that.

The overall efficiency with which energy will contribute to GNP in the future cannot be determined without a detailed examination of the expected structure of future national output (the basket of goods and services to be produced) and the technological processes that might be used in their production. These matters constitute a pervasive theme of Part II of this book, although they still have not been investigated in sufficient depth to support firm conclusions.

Productivity. The productivity question, important at all times, is vitally important today as the American economy finds itself straining—and failing—to meet a variety of national objectives. The annual dividend yielded by economic growth has been dwindling in recent years, and the decline of productivity growth is a root cause.

In evaluating the connection between energy use and the efficiency of productive operations, it helps to divide energy consumption into two broad categories: (1) energy as a consumer good, as in the heating of homes and the fueling of private automobiles; and (2) energy as an input into the productive sectors of the economy, such as industry, agriculture, and services. Although these two broad categories overlap (private automobiles do, after all, transport people to their jobs and to stores and other places of business), the general distinction is useful.

Where energy is clearly a consumer good in itself, it is difficult to argue that reducing its use (particularly where guided by the cost-effective basis mentioned earlier) would jeopardize productivity gains. Energy used for personal purposes is primarily one of the proceeds of the productive economy, rather than a factor in national output. This does not mean, however, that consumer use of energy can be dealt with cavalierly. Questions of welfare and equity are involved, particularly for those who are just beginning to enjoy comforts that were previously beyond their means.

Energy as an input into productive operations is an essentially different matter. There the quantity and form of energy used can decidedly affect the efficiency with which labor and capital are combined to produce output. Even when it is cost-effective to substitute other productive factors for energy, we may wind up with reduced productivity. If energy costs rise, production may be optimized by using more labor and less energy; but total output may still be lower than it would have been under earlier circumstances, when energy was used more freely because of its lower price. Reducing energy use even further—by imposing taxes on its use or through other policy instruments which might be considered desirable—may compound the problem of losses in productivity.

Another, less visible strand connecting energy with productivity merits attention. It is the dynamic impulse to economic growth and development provided in the past by forces originating within the technology of energy supply and of the capital equipment that uses energy. As noted above, this can be seen clearly in the emergence of electricity and liquid fuels as major components of the energy-supply stream during the twentieth century.

The electric motor removed limitations imposed on the layout and sequencing of factory processes by the earlier mechanical energy systems, which used shafts and belting to transmit power from the in-house prime mover. By permitting fundamental reorganization of factory production, electricity paved the way for large-scale productivity increases in manufacturing. Similarly, liquid fuels and the tractor helped farmers to increase their individual productivity sharply, so that agricultural workers were freed to move into other sectors of production. It is hard to overestimate how much these developments in manufacturing and agriculture have meant to the growth of overall productivity in the American economy.

Our probe of the energy–productivity connection may be carried one step further. In figure 1-2, there is one long period of sustained decline in energy use in relation to national output—the quarter century beginning around 1920. Energy was abundantly available during this period, and its price was falling. Simple economic reasoning would tell us that the intensity of energy use should have risen under these conditions. Instead it declined. Did the decline take place in spite of low energy prices, or somehow because of them? We cannot really know. Of course, it is quite possible that rising energy prices (or prices that fell less rapidly) would have led to even more restrained energy use than actually occurred. But it is an interesting and at least plausible hypothesis that easy conditions of energy supply encouraged imaginative developments (which otherwise would not have occurred) in the way energy was applied to production. Such a schema is consistent with our record of higher overall efficiency of production—rising output per unit of labor and capital. Also, in a roundabout, completely unplanned (and unnoticed) fashion, it could have resulted in greater national output per unit of energy consumed. Paradoxically, we may have learned how to get more from a resource (energy) precisely *because* we had plenty of it then.

In our view, it is more important to focus on the broader effects which energy consumption has on economic efficiency than on the narrower

question of energy efficiency as such. As a first approximation in projecting conservation potentials, we considered the cost-effectiveness of
energy-saving technologies (rather than their energy savings alone) in
judging feasibility. As we have already suggested, however, even this is an
inadequate guide from a broad social standpoint. We can say what the
proper guide should be, but we simply do not have all the data we would
need to implement it fully. Cost effectiveness really needs to capture all of
the externalities connected with energy use which are not covered in the
market price of energy—the negative externalities such as detrimental
impacts on the environment and also positive externalities such as enhanced overall productive efficiency which results from technical and
organizational innovations related to energy.

Estimated Levels of Future Consumption

Total U.S. energy consumption in 1976 came to about 75 quads (10^{15}
Btu).[1] For the year 2000, this study estimates consumption of about 115
quads for an economy that grows at a rate consistent with current expectations. This implies an annual average energy growth rate of 1.8 percent
compared with an estimated GNP growth of 3.2 percent per year. In
other words, we suggest that the total economy can grow at a substantially
higher rate than the use of energy.

Our estimated level of energy consumption for the year 2000 is considerably less than such an estimate would have been prior to the energy
upheavals of the past few years. Without taking into account the new
realities of energy prices and conservation that have surfaced in recent
years, estimated energy consumption in the year 2000—within the same
economy-wide assumptions—might have been about 135 quads, instead
of 115. The estimated amount of energy saved (20 quads) is equivalent
to all of the natural gas consumed in the United States in 1976, or about
one and one-half times the coal consumed in that year.

The detailed assumptions that underlie our estimates of reduced
future consumption are presented in chapters 5 and 6. We illustrate here
a few key points for three important energy uses in which conservation

---

[1] For the sake of comparison, one quad is roughly equivalent to the amount of
energy released by burning just under one-half million barrels of oil (or its equivalent) daily for a full year. The term is used extensively throughout this book as a
convenient means of comparing diverse energy inputs and outputs, but—as the discussion of uranium's heat content in chapter 7 brings out—some comparisons risk
oversimplification unless the underlying assumptions are spelled out.

may have a dramatic effect. Two of these use sectors—automobiles and residential heating—accounted for about one-fourth of all the energy consumed in this country in 1976. The third conservation example, potentially applicable to about 14 percent of total energy consumption in that same year, is an industrial technology known as cogeneration, which produces usable steam and electricity simultaneously and applies one or the other as a sort of bonus by-product. Thus, our projection of nationwide energy consumption includes an intensive analysis of approximately two-fifths of all energy use in the country, with somewhat less detailed examination of others. Here, and in figure 1-3, are highlights of what we found.

- With the number of automobiles expected to increase substantially between 1976 and the year 2000, it is nevertheless reasonable to estimate that automotive transportation will consume less fuel in the year 2000 than it did in 1976—dropping by about 30 percent, from slightly over 10 quads to about 7 quads. Our estimates are for about 150 million vehicles by the end of the century (up from about 110 million now). There are various indications that we are approaching substantially slower growth in the total number of vehicle miles travelled, and the projected rise in that crucial figure is more than offset by estimated improvements in gasoline mileage. We estimate the average fuel efficiency of the total fleet of automobiles on the road in the year 2000 at 27.5 miles per gallon, the standard mandated for cars to be produced in the 1985 model year. (The 1976 fleet average was about 14 miles per gallon.)

- Housing units are also expected to increase substantially between 1976 and the year 2000, from about 70 million to roughly 115 million. Nevertheless, the fuel consumed in residential space heating is estimated to decline from just over 8.5 quads to about 8. Our housing estimates imply more commodious occupancy levels of 2.3 persons per dwelling unit in the year 2000, compared with 3 per unit in 1976, and more floor space per dwelling in new houses, in line with recent construction experience. Even with 45 million more dwelling units and improved space standards, however, we estimate that thermal improvements in the housing shell (including the use of passive solar techniques in new construction) and increased efficiency in heating systems (including a shift away from electrical resistance heating because of higher energy costs) might actually diminish the total fuel consumed. It cannot be emphasized too strongly that all of the increases in efficiency we discuss could be

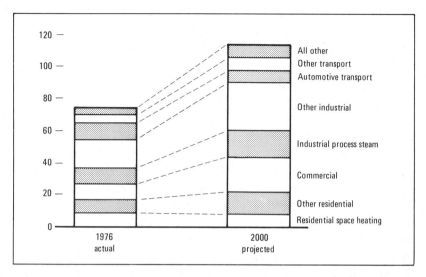

Figure 1-3. A mid-range projection of U.S. energy consumption to the year 2000, based on the data presented in this book, shows a rise to about 115 quads—with some sectors actually declining.

achieved through improvements which, on balance, result in cost savings to consumers. (Public policies could assist the process, as noted on pages 52–54.)

- There are several methods of generating electricity from fossil fuel, including steam turbines, gas turbines, and diesels. Each of these technologies offers different prospects for the cogeneration of industrial process steam. Overall efficiencies vary, as do output capacities and the electricity-to-steam ratios in the output; and all of these factors affect the prospects for penetrating the large market for industrial steam (representing 14 percent of U.S. energy use). There are also institutional barriers to the widespread introduction of cogeneration, which we will return to in our discussion of public policy. Still another difficulty is that the cogeneration systems which show great promise on some grounds are simply not ready yet to use coal as fuel. Nevertheless, reasonable success in technical development and a certain measure of public policy support could permit cogenerated steam to account for a significant portion of all steam used in industry by the end of the century. If the current trend in improving industry's efficiency in the basic use of fuel per unit of output also continues, the United States might be able to achieve the increased industrial production we would expect by that time while consuming virtually no more fuel for the generation of process steam than in 1974. However, with allowance for some slippage in these targets, our most probable projection points to total industrial steam demand for raw energy rising at about 2 percent annually.

We believe that some substantial economies in energy use can be achieved without sacrificing personal comfort and without increasing the combined costs of fuel and equipment (for example, in residential heating). In other cases, the energy savings would entail a minor reduction in amenity levels. For example, improved mileage standards for automobiles thus far have been mainly achieved through lighter, smaller, and less powerful vehicles, but without any significant reduction in the interior size. Of course, this does not imply that adjustments to our new energy situation over the next couple of decades can take place without some loss in comfort and convenience, or without an absolute monetary cost. Conservation—like every other energy policy we might consider—has limits in what it can accomplish painlessly.

For components of energy use (beyond the three discussed above) we did not, in general, undertake detailed analyses comparable to those for automobiles, residential heating, and cogeneration. In the absence of detailed study, we were somewhat more cautious regarding the conservation opportunities that might be realized. Furthermore, some of the other energy-consuming categories (like commercial activities and airline transportation) face a still rapidly expanding demand for the products and services which they offer. Such factors are reflected in our projection of a more rapid rate of increase in estimated energy consumption for the remaining categories compared with those activities we analyzed in more depth.

Even though the conservation practices built into our estimates yield substantial energy savings, we anticipate a 40-quad increase in the level of energy consumption in the year 2000 compared with 1976. This change implies cumulative consumption over the intervening quarter century of around 2,400 quads, which, we will see, is equivalent to considerably more than we could get from *all* our domestic resources of conventional oil and natural gas (see pages 25–26).

Although a 40-quad increase (from about 75 to 115 quads) is our best judgment, we have bracketed our projection for the start of the next century by higher and lower estimates—140 quads and just under 100. We regard these as less likely; but they indicate possible outcomes depending on policy choices that might be made. All three estimates are meant to be consistent with the same overall economic growth rates; the major variable is the degree to which energy conservation is judged feasible. Thus, whereas we assumed 27.5 miles per gallon as the most likely fleet average, and used this as a component in calculating the 115-quad total, the lower-end estimate assumed 37 miles per gallon. (The judgment here turned on the comparative feasibility of achieving alternative miles-per-gallon standards; 37 miles per gallon would require more stringent standards than those already legislated, and probably presupposes a significant down-sizing of vehicles beyond 1985.)

On a more casual basis, we extended our estimates to the year 2025 in order to glimpse the longer-run demand prospects. On the combined assumptions that the annual GNP growth rate for the United States between the years 2000 and 2025 were to decline to 2.2 percent (from the 3.2 percent rate assumed for 1976–2000), and that the intensity of energy consumption per unit of GNP fell to the level implied in the low end of our estimated range of consumption for the year 2000, we obtained an energy total for the year 2025 of 143 quads. That would mean an increase of just under 30 quads above the most likely estimate for the year 2000. A marked acceleration in the increase of real energy prices over the long run (which we do not expect) could render this figure too high; a continued outpouring of new energy-using goods and services in response to higher income levels (including, as an example, the widespread use of inside climate control) could render this figure too low.

Domestic Mineral Fuel Resources

The United States is not now producing enough fuels from domestic resources to meet its own consumption, and we are slipping into progressively larger deficits. Yet the potential exists to do far better, and even to achieve a high degree of energy self-sufficiency if the nation should choose to do so.

The resource analysis in chapter 7 distinguishes between the total base of natural fuel resources which exists in the United States and that portion which is now commercially available; but it also considers technological advances which would tap presently unconventional sources or would permit substitutions among fuel resources to produce the energy *forms* which are ultimately consumed. Oil shale is a typical unconventional source. An example of substitution is the possible future use of coal as a source of liquid and gaseous fuels, in addition to its current uses as a solid fuel and in the generation of electrical energy.

There are several gradations in the classification of natural resources—ranging from the total resource base at one extreme to commercial reserves at the other; but the broad distinction between resources and reserves is of basic importance for our purposes. "Resources" are that portion of the total resource base that has been estimated with some degree of certainty and which various prudent assumptions lead us to believe might be recoverable some time in the future. Only that portion of resources which has been located with considerable certainty and that can be recovered with present technical and economic means is called "reserves." Resource estimation is performed in various ways. It generally relies upon analytical models which draw upon geologic, economic, and historic evidence. Reserve data usually depend on the physical evidence of drilling data. Data on reserves most usefully serve near-term, commercial purposes, but resource estimates are far more useful in appraising long-range prospects for fuel supplies. Resources indicate the amounts that might become economically available in the future, with altered conditions of costs, prices, and technologies, and with the help of changes in public policies.

Data on both the reserves and resources of coal, oil, gas, and uranium are collected by different agencies (both governmental and private) and are meant to serve various purposes. Neither the terminologies nor the underlying definitions employed by the various agencies are uniform. In chapter 7 these estimates are assembled and documented, and an effort is made to achieve a degree of comparability among them, but there is no way completely to overcome the lack of underlying agreement on terminology, definitions, and numerical estimates.

Here we will focus on the recoverable resource estimates only. These are depicted graphically in figure 1-4, alongside the estimate of cumulative energy consumption summarized above. The combined resource total for all mineral fuels used in today's commercial technologies—oil, gas, coal, and uranium—ranges from about 40,000 to 110,000 quads, depending on whether the energy content of uranium is measured with or without "breeding" (see page 31). If all energy sources were readily interchangeable and there were no concerns about public or environmental health, there would clearly be no near-term danger of running out of domestic resources to satisfy future U.S. consumption (although there could be problems in gearing up production in a timely fashion, as well as some additional monetary costs). Assuming, for instance, that energy

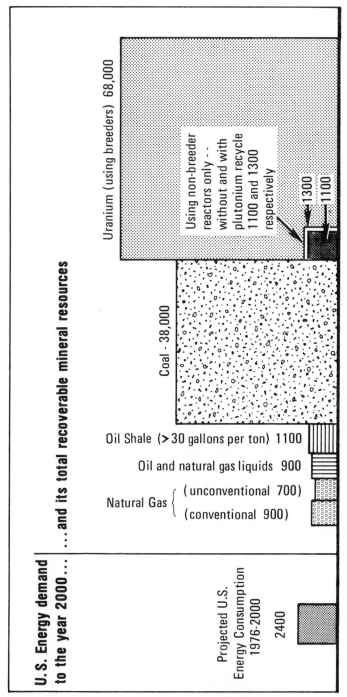

Figure 1-4. Except for coal and uranium (as extended by breeders), domestic mineral resources seem small when compared with cumulative energy consumption for the rest of this century. However, with coal as a source of liquid and gaseous fuels—and both coal and uranium as a basis for generating electricity—the long-term domestic outlook for mineral energy is good. Costs (in the broadest sense) are the major constraints. Recoverable resource estimates are based on data presented in chapter 7 and are expressed in quads. Consumption estimates are developed in chapter 6.

U. S. Energy demand to the year 2000... ...and its total recoverable mineral resources

Uranium (using breeders) 68,000

Using non-breeder reactors only -- without and with plutonium recycle 1100 and 1300 respectively

1300

1100

Coal - 38,000

Oil Shale (> 30 gallons per ton) 1100

Oil and natural gas liquids 900

Natural Gas { (unconventional 700) (conventional 900)

Projected U.S. Energy Consumption 1976-2000

2400

consumption grew at a 2 percent rate annually (which is slightly more than we projected above), the smaller total would still "last" for about 125 years, and the larger (with nuclear breeders) for about 175 years. Since, in the long run, other factors would limit such steady compounding of consumption growth, and much lower grades of resources could become economic, even longer periods of sufficiency are likely.

However, such a conclusion holds only for energy resources in the aggregate, and the aggregate is obviously dominated by coal and uranium. Both are useful today principally in generation of electric energy, which makes up about 30 percent of total fuel consumption. Of the remaining 70 percent, more than nine-tenths is consumed in the form of oil and gas; and the natural resources of petroleum and natural gas present an altogether different picture. To illustrate: even if imports of oil were maintained at the 1976 level of about 40 percent, and oil and gas consumption grew at an annual rate of 2 percent, conventional domestic oil and natural gas resources would last not much beyond the year 2000.

It is precisely because of this relative scarcity of oil and gas resources that we must also take into account the additional domestic potential associated with unconventional raw materials, such as oil shale, and with the liquefaction and gasification of coal and biomass. Chapter 7 also estimates the additional unconventional resources of natural gas contained in formations such as tight sands, coal seams, and geopressured zones, but these all require unusual measures to tap and the margins of uncertainty about their eventual yield are large.

It cannot be stressed too strongly that calculations measuring the life expectancy of resources under hypothetical conditions of demand are no more than a device to demonstrate the major dimensions of the long-run mineral fuel situation confronting the United States. At least three oversimplifications should be kept in mind:

1. We do not really know the true ultimate dimensions of our resources. Future discoveries, and the economic extraction of resources we now recognize, will be influenced by new geological knowledge, as well as by price and technological developments. The amounts may be higher or lower than the estimates used here.

2. Demand and supply for any particular fuel will not grow exponentially to a point where resources are suddenly exhausted. Instead, production will peak long before exhaustion; then it will fall gradually while substitutes take over the market as the price of the

original fuel rises. It is widely believed that the domestic production of oil and natural gas may already have peaked.

3. Regardless of resource availability, a number of physical and economic constraints will limit the maximum amount of energy to be produced from any source within any particular time period. This producibility problem applies not only to the output of fuels, but may also be especially important for central-station generating plants and synthetic fuels, both of which require huge amounts of risk capital and skilled labor as well as long development and construction times.

Nevertheless it appears that, among the current mineral fuel resources, coal and uranium both offer long-lasting supply. Furthermore, the resource estimates for uranium are likely to be conservative because the uranium mining industry is still in its infancy compared with the search for coal, oil, and natural gas. Extended exploration efforts in response to commercial forces might be expected to combine with improved geological knowledge in increasing recoverable uranium resources over time. Another factor which tends to make the uranium estimates conservative is the comparative insensitivity of nuclear power prices to the costs of raw ore. The cost per ton of mined uranium could increase very steeply, to allow tapping of lower-grade ores, without having much effect on the cost per unit of electricity produced. Using uranium in breeder reactors (which eventually derive 60 times or so as much energy as light water reactors do from each ton of ore) could make it economical to recover extremely low-grade resources not considered in the estimates presented here, and that would extend the lifetime of nuclear resources even further.

Comparing Energy Supply Alternatives

If our domestic resources are adequate to provide the energy we consume over the long term, the next crucial question is how much it will cost to use them. "Cost" includes both dollar costs of production *and* other penalties associated with the production and use of energy, such as impacts on health, safety, and the environment. Much of the debate about the nation's energy situation and outlook reflects sharply differing beliefs about these costs; our findings and evaluations regarding this issue constitute the bulk of chapters 8 through 14. We will try to summarize those findings here.

Monetary Costs

We have pointed out how heavily the nation now relies on oil and natural gas, as well as the steadily growing significance of electric power in our economy. Among "renewable" energy sources for the future, perhaps none has captured the public imagination more thoroughly than that of the sun. Thus, the conclusions we have reached about future monetary costs for liquid and gaseous fuels, electricity, and solar energy deserve to be treated as highlights.

Liquid and gaseous fuels.   Many of the nation's most serious energy difficulties today, and those projected for the near future, result from the declining domestic reserves and production of oil and gas. Imports of oil have grown in importance in recent years, while imports of natural gas, either overland or by sea, have emerged as a source that may become important in the near future.

Imports do not, however, appear to be a promising approach to meeting the nation's long-term needs for liquid and gaseous fuels. The grave economic, political, and strategic difficulties that massive imports create have been evident in recent U.S. experience. We have faced insecurity of supply, substantial price rises, and balance of payments difficulties since 1973.

Even on the optimistic assumption that these difficulties could somehow be managed, world production of conventional petroleum and natural gas, although based on comparatively much more plentiful resources than those in the United States, also threatens to have trouble keeping up with worldwide demand by about the turn of the century. There is considerable controversy about the dimensions of remaining recoverable world oil and gas resources and their geographic distribution, and thus about how soon the effects of global supply stringency might begin to be felt; but the weight of the evidence indicates that long-term import dependence would carry risks in resource availability and the threat of constantly rising prices. There seems to be no doubt, of course, that we will require substantial imports for an extended period in any event, because the development of adequate substitute sources would require long lead times. We will come to some policy issues raised by that interim import dependence a little later (pages 50–52).

Fortunately, liquid and gaseous fuels can be derived from resources that are abundantly available in the United States. Domestic resources of coal and oil shale are adequate to permit large-scale production of liquid and gaseous fuels for a long period into the future, and these products could well handle the functions now performed by conventional sources. Liquids and gases could also be derived from wood, from agricultural wastes, and from other biomass resources, including municipal wastes. The critical questions for all of these alternative sources concern costs (of all kinds) and the length of time it might take for research and development and the buildup of productive capacity.

We still have no domestic experience with commercial-sized plants for these technologies, and that lack of experience results in widely varying cost estimates. The situation is further complicated by the tendency of proponents to make the best possible case for their own technological approaches. Taking into account the improvements which may be expected as operating experience expands, our own evaluation of the estimates yields cost figures which may be expected to be about twice as high for synthetic fuels (in constant dollar terms) as the prices we paid in 1978 for their conventional counterparts. It is important to recognize, however, that because of the comparative scarcity of petroleum and natural gas resources, their future costs are likely to rise more steeply than the costs of the coal and shale oil resources from which some of these synthetics would be derived. Furthermore, international petroleum is particularly vulnerable to monopoly pricing. So, all in all, we expect conventional and synthetic fuel prices to converge gradually in the future.

Moreover, the costs of naturally produced oil and gas at the end-use point are influenced more by raw material costs than will be the case for the synthetics. Only a small portion of the cost of producing synthetic oil and gas is accounted for by the raw fuel (in the neighborhood of one-third). Thus a smaller element of the final fuel price would be subject to the long-term cost rises associated with resource depletion. Even if the cost of extracting coal doubled, this would mean only a one-third increase in the cost of producing synthetic oil or gas from coal. In this respect (although not to the same extent) synthetic oil and gas technologies resemble nuclear power from breeders, which we will consider in the next section. The use of either synthetics or breeders (or both) could strongly dampen the long-term effects of natural resource depletion on the costs per unit of useful energy produced.

What can be said about the rate at which a commercial synthetics industry might develop? Under a "business as usual" philosophy, the industry would be a nonstarter at present price levels because its products would be more costly than natural sources of oil and gas by a wide margin. As the prices of natural products increased, however, an industry could develop. Special steps, discussed below (see pages 56–58) could hasten the development of such an industry.

Electricity from coal and uranium.   Among the fuels now used to generate electricity, only coal and uranium are potentially available as domestic resources in large quantities. Thus it is important to develop accurate economic comparisons between the two. Estimated generation costs, like all other aspects of coal and nuclear energy comparisons, are surrounded by controversy. In the research done for this study, total dollar costs per unit of electrical output for new power plants that could be constructed for operation in the mid-1980s were estimated to be lower for nuclear power in some regions of the United States and lower for coal in others. On average, nuclear was found to be cheaper than coal, with its cost advantages greatest in those places to which coal needs to be transported over long distances—such as New England and the coastal areas of the western states.

Looking to the more distant future, it is less important to try to make precise estimates of costs (which are unlikely to be on target in any event) than to understand the underlying factors that will determine comparative cost behavior over the long run. For this purpose the difference in cost structure between these two technologies is crucial, as is the outlook for technological advances.

The price of coal-generated electricity is much more dependent than that of nuclear power on the cost of the raw fuel. Coal plants require large quantities of fuel (several million tons of coal per year for a "standard size" plant of 1,000 MW); and the fuel bill at such a plant accounts for one-third or more of the costs of the electricity generated. Uranium, by contrast, is required in comparatively small amounts at nuclear power plants; and most of the cost of nuclear fuel elements is due in any case to enrichment and other processing and fabrication, rather than the costs of the raw uranium. As a result, raw uranium fuel constitutes less than 10 percent of the cost per kilowatt hour in today's nuclear power plants.

Thus, if other factors remain the same, the price of coal-generated electricity is potentially three times as sensitive to the cost pressure of resource depletion as the price of nuclear power is. Because such pressures on uranium now appear to be greater than those on coal, the differences might balance out in the case of nonbreeding reactors; but for breeders this relative insensitivity to price rises in the mineral fuel base is a distinct economic plus. In the event of large additional demands for coal as a source of synthetic liquids and gases, the comparative fuel-cost advantage for nuclear plants might grow over time.

On the other hand, nuclear energy is more capital-intensive than coal-generated electricity, and the costs of nuclear power plants have tended to grow more rapidly over time than the general price level. New safety systems and extended delays resulting from safety and environmental reviews (which add to interest charges) have been important factors in these cost increases. There are continuing uncertainties about the future costs of safety systems and liability insurance for nuclear plants (particularly in the aftermath of Three Mile Island) and also about the costs of new pollution control systems for coal plants. If the costs of building and equipping all power plants happened to rise more rapidly than the general price level, this would tend to favor coal plants over nuclear facilities.

New technologies for generating electricity from coal and uranium carry some significant implications for the long-run costs of electrical energy in the United States. If it is possible to solve the technical problems of fluidized-bed coal combustion (in which coal is burned in the form of a powder suspended in a stream of compressed air) this technology appears to promise cleaner energy from coal at costs lower than those with existing techniques (taking all pollution control costs into account). If this promise should be realized, it would constitute a significant reversal in the upward cost trend of producing electricity cleanly from coal. On the other hand, the gasification of coal (to produce a relatively cleaner power plant fuel from this abundant resource) is likely to involve higher overall costs than burning coal in conventional plants equipped with scrubbers.

For nuclear power, new technology holds the possibility of breeding new fissionable fuel from the uranium 238 component of natural uranium (which is 140 times more abundant than the component occurring as naturally fissionable uranium 235); but this presupposes that we can resolve satisfactorily the technical, economic, and public attitude questions that surround the U.S. breeder program. Much of the research and development work for the liquid metal fast breeder reactor is now complete, but future costs are not easy to pin down. Our estimates indicate that the eventual costs of electricity from commercial breeders in the country might not differ greatly from those for reactors of current design.

The long-run implications of the breeder reactor are of great importance, assuming that capital costs prove to be attractive. Although uranium supplies could be stretched significantly in the medium term by using improved converter reactors, the breeder could dramatically expand the life expectancy of uranium in meeting energy needs. Equally important is the fact that breeder technology could reduce the raw fuel component to an altogether negligible element in the cost of electrical power. This certainly does not match the careless claim of some years ago that nuclear-based electricity would be "too cheap to bother metering," but it should not be dismissed either. In effect, breeder technology could effectively emancipate nuclear electricity production from any threat of cost increases arising from resource depletion—the perennial nemesis of the mineral industries.

Solar energy.   The technological alternatives analyzed in this study include a number of renewable energy sources which are not used much now in the United States but which could possibly find wider commercial use in the future. Many of these (such as geothermal steam, the tides, and small-scale water power) have a restricted potential because they are tied to resources which are available only at certain sites or under conditions which vary sharply from site to site. In this respect they resemble energy sources used much earlier in the nation's history, like the waterwheel (which was rigidly tied to a specific location) or fuelwood (which had to be used close to the point of origin because the heat value per unit of weight and volume did not allow economical transportation over long distances).

Because sunlight is ubiquitous, it carries more potential than any other renewable resource for going beyond mere local or regional importance within the United States. However, its future importance as a commercial energy source will depend heavily on the costs associated with the equipment needed to put it to use.

Active applications of solar energy to space heating and to providing hot water appear to have near-term potential for broad use. The sun's natural contribution to the space heating of homes can also be substantially enhanced through the use of such "passive" measures as appropriate building design—particularly in new structures. Whether this last technology should be regarded as a commercial use of solar energy or as another fuel conservation measure is simply a question of semantics.

Although it is a short step *conceptually* from the passive use of the sun's energy to the active collection of the sun's heat in equipment designed to provide for space heating or hot water, such active applications must overcome some special problems. Because solar energy is a relatively diffuse source compared with the concentrated energy stored in fossil fuels, a large physical system for collecting it is required; and this can be expensive.

Storage of solar energy adds further complications. Some long-term storage is a necessity if completely independent solar systems are to supply peak winter heating needs, but typical storage systems of adequate size are relatively expensive.

Another possibility—the most common one in actual practice—is a hybrid system, which includes a backup system using another energy source (most commonly electricity or natural gas). With such backup systems, smaller and relatively cheaper storage systems can take care of daily variations; and there is no need for the disproportionately more expensive systems used for seasonal storage. In this case, however, fair cost accounting requires that the capital costs of a greatly underutilized conventional home heating system be added to the cost of the solar energy system.

Generally, capital costs for solar household systems tend to be relatively high compared with the costs of conventional home heating technologies, but the extra costs vary by type of application. The cost problem is least bothersome for hot water heating, because such systems already have a built-in storage facility (the hot water tank itself) and because demand for hot water remains fairly steady on a year-round basis.

We have examined a range of cost estimates for a practical solar household system for representative conditions in different parts of the United States. (Isolated examples can be misleading, because they may involve ingenious but atypical techniques or a considerable amount of householder labor which isn't always factored in.) Even under favorable assumptions, we found that broadly applicable costs would apparently be no lower than about $12 per million Btu. This means that active household solar energy systems would not be generally competitive unless crude oil prices were to reach the equivalent of about $35 per barrel (in 1975 dollars). These prices are not only much higher than today's oil and gas prices, but, more significantly, they equal or exceed the upper part of the range of estimated costs of synthetic oil and gas from sources which could become available over the long term. Solar systems could compete in cost with electric resistance heating under some conditions, but probably not with electric heat pumps, if continued experience with those devices proves the relatively high efficiency claimed for them when they are properly designed and used.

Our conclusion is that, unless there is a breakthrough in the use of cheaper materials, home solar heating systems will only be able to compete widely with most future technologies if solar heating is assigned a social benefit not reflected in its monetary costs. If solar technologies were to be regarded as sufficiently advantageous from a health and environmental standpoint when compared with fossil and nuclear-based alternatives, such an allowance might be deemed an appropriate public policy (see pages 54–55).

Solar energy is also a potential source of central station electricity, but in that role it would be at a larger cost disadvantage than in household heating. The cost problems associated with collector systems and storage arise again here, but the cost of a conversion system must be added. Whether a large-scale solar power station were to collect heat and generate electricity in the usual way, through a steam turbine, or employ photovoltaic methods of direct conversion to electricity, the estimated costs are well above those in conventional power technologies.

Because of the engineering simplicity of the photovoltaic approach, it is natural to ask whether this system could not become economical if cell costs were to fall far enough, as suggested by proponents of photovoltaic technology. This seems doubtful for central station use, if only because the costs of the structure and framework to support the necessary array of cells appear to be high enough to render the technology noncompetitive even if very inexpensive structural materials were used. On the other hand, this conclusion may not hold for decentralized generation of electricity, because in rooftop installations the structural materials could easily be integrated into the building design.

Health, Safety, and Environmental Impacts

The public today is acutely aware that many activities of modern society result in damages to human health, safety, and the environment. Energy processes have been a special object of concern in this regard, influencing both policy debate and action. Unfortunately, the scientific data and analyses needed to measure and evaluate such impacts are often not well established; but careful use of existing data within a consistent framework of comparative analysis can still narrow the issues and make them more comprehensible.[2]

Risks to human health. To begin with, it is important to recognize that we are talking about *comparative* risks. All energy systems involve some elements of hazard to human well-being (see figure 1-5). We need

---

[2] In fact, a separate report of this project has treated in detail these health and environmental problems for coal and nuclear power (see William Ramsay, *Unpaid Costs of Electrical Energy: Health and Environmental Impacts from Coal and Nuclear Power*, Baltimore, Md., Johns Hopkins University Press for Resources for the Future, 1978).

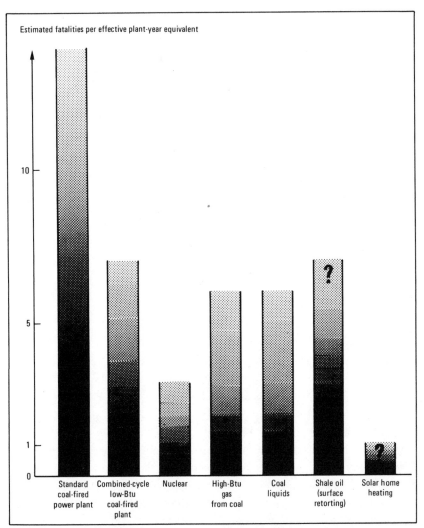

Figure 1-5. The range of estimates is shown for fatalities among workers and the general public from all accidents and illnesses related to the production of a given amount of energy by various energy technologies. The "effective plant-year equivalent" represents an amount of energy equivalent to that derived over the course of a year from a 1,000 MW generating plant with a capacity factor of 75 percent, with the energy delivered for use in electrical resistance heating. For other energy technologies, such an amount of delivered end-use energy may require more or less original energy input (see table 12-2, notes a and c).

The variable shading on the bars (and the fact that all are opened-ended at the top) suggests uncertainty in the estimates. The main contributors to the darkest portions of the bars are occupational accidents and directly traceable illness (and coal transportation accidents, for the coal-related technologies). The upper range is mostly from air pollution for coal-related technologies and from statistically projected nuclear reactor accidents for that technology. The question marks for shale and solar represent even greater uncertainties about patterns of mining accidents and home repair accidents, respectively. The information in this graph was taken from tables 12-5 and 12-6; the methodologies used are discussed in chapter 12.

35

to examine how the levels and patterns of risk compare among the different energy technologies, and (in a full accounting) how high the benefits (including health benefits) are from the additional goods and services made possible by using energy.

Coal and uranium, as we have seen, could continue to supply useful energy well into the distant future. But both have also aroused substantial concerns because of dangers to human health. What is the comparative magnitude of these health risks?

A substantial amount of uncertainty surrounds the estimates of deaths and illnesses associated with energy processes. Apart from the familiar debate over low-level radiation effects, chapter 12 notes the questionable validity of the scientific data underlying the connection between health effects and air pollution resulting from coal combustion—with high and low estimates of related illness varying by several orders of magnitude. Instead of being able to compare firm values for coal versus nuclear power, we are reduced to citing a wide range of possible outcomes from each.

Despite the wide ranges in the estimates, however, it appears that the year-in and year-out fatalities and illnesses expected to be associated with electricity from coal power stations may well be larger than those from nuclear power plants. Estimated coal-associated fatalities per plant-year (for the entire chain of supply operations beginning at the coal mine) range from about 1 to 14, while for the nuclear plant the range is from 0.2 to 3—even including our conservative reevaluation of the Rasmussen Report's estimates regarding reactor accident probability noted above (see page 6). Thus, although the high end of the range of estimated nuclear fatalities overlaps the low end of the range for coal, the high end of the coal range is about 5 times that for nuclear.

Let us examine some of the factors inherent in the two technologies that lie behind these results. The *maximum* estimated fatalities for coal-based power is made up of the following components (per power plant-year):

· Air pollution	8
Coal transportation	1
Coal mining (including black lung estimates)	5
Approximate total	14

The last two elements in the breakdown, which add up to almost half of the total, reflect the unalterable fact that a large amount of coal needs to be mined and transported to supply the needs of a power station that burns coal. Nuclear fuel, by contrast, is required in comparatively small amounts. Human exposure to the risks of mining and transportation naturally tend to weigh heavily against coal in such a comparison.

The specific breakdown for the *maximum* of the nuclear fatality estimate (per power plant-year) is:

Routine radiation	0.005
Gaseous wastes	0.3
Reactor accidents	2
Occupational	0.4
Approximate total	3

A very large proportion of the high-end estimate for nuclear fatalities is accounted for by low-probability large accidents; but because such reactor accidents are not a "routine" risk in the same sense as continuing emissions or mining accidents, we will also discuss them later under catastrophic threats.

As for air pollution, although the routine release of radioactive atoms into the environment may be regarded as the nuclear counterpart to the products of coal combustion, the radiation levels are very low in normal operations, and have minor impacts on health. The doses are much smaller than those from the natural background everyone receives from uranium-bearing rocks on the surface of the earth or the average doses from medical X rays. If the higher level of the range of estimates for fatalities and illnesses associated with coal combustion emissions is judged to be valid, the weight of any health comparison seems favorable to nuclear.

The comparative position of coal-based processes would improve somewhat if solid coal could be converted entirely into a gaseous or liquid form. This would be true, for example, whether coal were gasified and then used as a fuel in electric power plants, or (assuming gas of high quality) if it were piped long distances—as natural gas is today—to be used in high-value applications such as residential heating. The gaseous fuel itself would be much cleaner to burn than the coal from which it was derived, and the process by which it was converted to gas would produce a smaller volume of pollutants than the combustion of coal in a power plant. Even so, the upper estimates for coal used in this less harmful form would continue to be more damaging to health than the upper estimates for the nuclear alternative. (All these comparisons are for equivalent amounts of useful energy delivered to a typical end use such as home heating.)

Risks associated with solar energy are different from the risks created by mining and using mineral fuels, but solar energy does impose some health and safety risks too. The fairly dangerous rooftop work involved in installation and repair of solar collectors forms a potential source of injuries and deaths. In addition, the production and transportation of the relatively large amount of glass and metal contained in solar equipment per unit of energy produced offer some opportunity for industrial and transport accidents. Of course, technologies based on mineral fuels also carry these types of risks. Electric repair work is far from risk-free, and the production and transportation of electric generating and end-use equipment is also responsible for accidents. In general, all capital-intensive technologies carry substantial risks which are embodied, so to speak, in the materials used. In this study, we chose to concentrate on those risks peculiar to energy production, and under this more narrow conception of risk accounting, the health effects of solar energy can be considered minimal.

Land use and other environmental impacts.   This section concerns the direct environmental impacts of energy supply technologies on land, water, and air. Despite the fact that the amounts of land involved could be considered small relative to total U.S. land areas, we highlight land impacts because they appear to be of greater concern than the other direct environmental impacts. With water impacts involving thermal and chemical pollution, the major questions now concern compliance, not the types of regulation required. The human health effects of air pollution, a major environmental concern, have already been covered.

The most extensive impacts on land use result from the mining of fuels, especially by surface operations. This is a particularly serious problem for coal, for which the land disturbed in mining averages out to between 300 and 600 acres per electric power plant-year, depending on ratios of surface to underground mining. For nuclear energy, the disturbed mining acreage comes to about 60 acres per power plant-year, and there is the potential for further substantial reduction if the breeder reactor and fuel reprocessing are introduced. As in previous comparisons between coal and nuclear fuels, the substantial difference in their comparative damages can be traced to the fundamentally different energy densities of the two fuels.

The long-term significance of land disturbances as an environmental problem will depend on the success of land reclamation efforts. The law now requires that surface-mined lands be restored to their approximate original contours, and, in most cases, that vegetation be regrown. However, it is too early to be sure whether reclamation techniques for the recreation of the landscape will yield "satisfactory" results, especially in arid areas.

Converting coal to liquids and gaseous fuels for direct combustion, instead of using it to generate electricity, could significantly reduce air pollution impacts but would reduce land use impacts only slightly. This is because those technologies would have little effect on the coal tonnages that had to be mined.

Waste disposal areas and plant sites also take up space, whether coal or uranium is the basic fuel. These impacts are relatively minor for coal (less than 20 percent of the mining total), but relatively large for nuclear (up to 70 percent of the total). Nevertheless, even under the most unfavorable conditions for nuclear (assuming large exclusion areas and cooling lakes instead of towers), the total nuclear land use impact is less than half that from coal.

In addition, however, some qualitative factors have to be taken into account. Some of the land uses required by nuclear processes, such as the disposal of uranium mill tailings, represent a permanent removal from other uses because the sites must remain undisturbed to prevent emissions of radioactive gases. Similar considerations will apply to the sites of decommissioned reactors, and to the repositories used for the disposal of high-level reactor wastes. A satisfactory solution to the latter problem, although apparently attainable from a technical standpoint, has yet to be achieved; but the size of its impacts would be unimportant as a land-use factor because the overall volume of all high level wastes from commercial U.S. power reactors up to the year 2000 is small—estimated to be less than 100 acre-feet. The difficulty in waste disposal lies in winning acceptance for a site or sites.

Some of the newer energy technologies may have even larger land-use requirements than coal. This is true of oil shale, which would require between 2,000 and 3,000 acres per equivalent power plant-year in surface mining operations, although only 7 acres or so would be involved if in situ methods could be used entirely. Biomass, too, would have very large land requirements—an averaged-out rate of about 10,000 acres per plant-year (equivalent to hundreds of thousands of acres of forest dedicated to support each single power plant).

Social attitudes will be important in assessing the impacts resulting from biomass operations. While new lumbering operations in established forests to gather wood for energy conversion might be considered environmental degradation, the planting (and periodic harvesting) of new biomass fuel forests and farms might be considered beneficial overall.

Large-scale solar electricity, an unpromising technology from a commercial standpoint, would also involve a great deal of land. A standard-sized central power plant might use 70 to 300 acres per plant-year, averaged out over its lifetime. This land (equivalent to a dedicated area of somewhere between 2,000 and 10,000 acres) would have to be cleared and covered with arrays of solar collectors. If the plant were to be decommissioned at a later date, however, the land presumably could be restored with less damage than for surface-mined land and at less cost than land occupied by a nuclear power plant.

Space and water heating applications provided by solar collectors at the site, which we cited above as the most promising solar technology from a cost standpoint, are also attractive because they use little land. The site would already be occupied by housing, so the added environmental impacts would be primarily visual. Some collectors might be regarded as unsightly, and their use might also reduce the amount of overhanging foliage allowable in a neighborhood.

Environmental impacts, whether to land, water, or air, depend greatly on local conditions. Relatively high water-use rates (for instance, nuclear power plants generally are heavier users than coal plants) may be acceptable in water surplus regions, yet relatively low water-use rates (as in shale oil and coal conversion plants) may be unacceptable in water deficient regions. If ambient air quality is already low, additional air pollution may be unacceptable; if it is still unusually high (as in a pristine area) any air pollution at all may be unacceptable. Visibility standards may not matter much in urbanized regions, but they may be essential in scenic regions. Thus, to compare environmental impacts without paying attention to regional differences could be seriously misleading.

With this important qualification in mind, it is still safe to draw some generalizations. First, conventional coal power plants put a heavy burden on land, air and water, although impacts on one or the other may be heavier for other technologies. Surface-mined shale would require more land than coal, and nuclear power plants more water. Second, higher water usage by nuclear plants seems to be more than balanced by their lesser impacts on air and land; so nuclear power appears to be less damaging environmentally than coal, unless one puts special emphasis—as many of its staunchest opponents do—on the length of time some of its specialized land-use impacts involve. Third, solar energy and biomass compare favorably with mineral resources from the standpoint of environmental effects. For solar heating at the site, this conclusion is almost unconditional; in other cases it depends on whether one is willing to assign positive values to the multiple-purpose aspects of biomass or the easier reclamation that is possible with large-scale solar-electric plants.

Catastrophic threats.   A major concern about energy technologies— *the* major concern, according to some observers—is that the use of some of these technologies may lead to events of a catastrophic nature. In the public mind, the danger of energy-related catastrophes appears to be linked mainly with nuclear energy because of the almost automatic mental connection among nuclear fuels, nuclear explosives, and radiation. The Three Mile Island accident undoubtedly heightened conscious concerns about the consequences if a major reactor accident were accompanied by a breach of the containment system that is designed to retain most of any emitted radioactivity.

Catastrophic threats are not confined to nuclear technologies. Despite recent controls, emissions produced by the burning of fossil fuels could still conceivably produce what we define as health catastrophes—namely, events that might cause severe damage or death to a large segment of the population. Residuals from air pollution in the form of acid rainfall might also in the future lead to widespread regional ecological damage; but more threatening (because it would be less reversible) is the possibility of worldwide changes in climate due to the cumulative buildup of carbon dioxide in the atmosphere over a long period of time. It is true that major coal mining accidents also kill and injure large numbers of people, but they occur with enough frequency to be classified as routine risks and that is why we covered them in our earlier discussion of risks to human health and do not give them additional attention here.

Catastrophes, no matter how improbable their occurrence, are regarded with special apprehension by the public. In part it may be precisely *because* their occurrence is rare, or even unlikely by any normal measuring stick. At any rate, it is an indisputable fact that more emotion and concern is generated over the possibility that a single event could cause thousands of deaths than over the reality that automobile accidents in this country cause tens of thousands of deaths every year. That is just the way it is, so we had better consider catastrophic threats as a separate category, even though, in the case of nuclear accidents, their statistical danger (that is, averaged-out illnesses and fatalities) has already been included in our earlier estimates of risks to human health.

As poor as the data base is for analyzing some of the impacts already considered, particularly those dealing with the health effects of fossil fuel combustion, data and analytical concepts are even poorer for assessing possible catastrophic impacts. And the factual and conceptual base is perhaps weakest in connection with the possible tie between nuclear war and the productive use of nuclear energy—the subject to which we now turn.

Catastrophic threats: Nuclear.   Nuclear war has been an overhanging global threat since the development and use of nuclear weapons in the final stages of the Second World War. Although such weapons now exist in great numbers, mainly in the hands of a few large nations, there is a fear that expanding the international use of nuclear fuels in a civilian power industry could lead to the proliferation of nuclear weapons capability among many countries.

The key points here are that (1) the same process that enriches fuel for use in conventional light water reactors can, if carried far enough, be used to produce weapons-grade materials; and (2) that all power reactors regularly produce the element plutonium (by transmutation of nonfissionable U238), and that if plutonium can be extracted from the "spent" reactor fuel and purified it can also be used in weapons. The breeder reactor economy, in particular, will depend upon the routine recovery and reprocessing of fissile plutonium. Thus, development of a large breeder reactor industry (or the substantial use of reprocessing even without breeders) could greatly increase the quantities of potential weapons materials that are available and might indeed result in their becoming fairly common items of international commerce.

How can anyone truly evaluate the significance of this threat? Nations can always acquire nuclear warfare capability through special weapons programs or through other deliberate means. A major concern is that a commercial nuclear energy industry involving the use and reprocessing of plutonium could encourage countries which do not now have nuclear weapons to build up an inventory of nuclear fuels (convertible to weapons use) in a casual, unplanned way. If the inventory existed, a decision to build nuclear weapons might be reached in response to newly perceived strategic objectives—or changes in national leadership. On the other hand, simplified techniques for uranium enrichment are also in the offing, and these might provide an equally easy alternative route to the feared weapons capabilities.

Suppose that the United States, out of concern for possible weapons proliferation elsewhere in the world, were to forgo particular aspects of nuclear technology, including breeder reactors and nuclear fuel reprocessing. Would other countries follow our lead? The response to U.S. initiatives so far has been mixed. Some other countries have different perceptions of the benefits to be gained by pursuing a broad range of nuclear energy technologies. They may also judge differently the added risks of nuclear warfare due to making nuclear fuel more widely available internationally. There are many links in the theoretical chain that connects a U.S. decision about commercial nuclear energy technology with an increased likelihood of nuclear warfare, and there are wide differences of opinion about how strong those links are.

There could even be possibilities for mitigating the threats of weapons proliferation via certain types of international control of the nuclear energy industry. Multinational approaches to the supervision of the nuclear fuel cycle have been proposed. Just after World War II, there was an American initiative at the United Nations to institute international ownership and management of dangerous nuclear facilities. Institutional innovations of this sort, along with technical approaches to making weapons materials relatively inaccessible (for example, through in-plant schemes for fuel reprocessing) may point to eventual solutions for dealing effectively with the legitimate concerns about weapons proliferation.

Another threat arises from the possible diversion of nuclear weapons to groups of criminals and terrorists. Up to now terrorists have not used nuclear weapons, perhaps because of the difficulties of getting nuclear explosives or fear of the dangers to themselves of handling such materials. Nevertheless, we ought to consider the degree to which various forms of nuclear fuel might be vulnerable to that type of diversion.

Existing nuclear facilities are protected in various ways against theft or embezzlement of dangerous nuclear materials. To steal bomb-grade material from a protected installation by overt means probably would require a fairly large force and the use of heavy weapons, such as rockets and tanks. Protection against materials diversion would probably become less effective, however, if plutonium were to become an item of worldwide trade as part of the breeder reactor economy.

There is a strong irrational element in many terrorist activities; and the fact that these activities often appeal to real, if sometimes exaggerated, public fears makes the terrorist problem a real concern. It is one that must be considered in assessing nuclear energy options, especially the breeder strategy. Technical schemes to make weapons materials more inaccessible (such as co-located power and fuel cycle facilities or in-plant reprocessing for liquid-fueled reactors) could be critically important in dealing with this problem.

Aside from concerns about nuclear warfare and terrorism, there is also a persistent anxiety about the possibility of accidents at nuclear power plants. As emphasized by the recent accident at Three Mile Island, which

involved releases of some radioactivity, some possibility of a large accident does exist despite backup safety systems. In a major study done
on this problem several years ago (the Rasmussen Report), the chances
of such accidents were calculated as very small—only a few chances in a
billion plant-years. The calculation was quite difficult to make, depended
on incomplete data, and may have omitted or misevaluated certain possible accident sequences (especially involving human error). This was
compensated for in part by extreme—possibly unrealistic—conservatism
in other assumptions; and we have introduced still more caution by multiplying the Rasmussen-calculated risks by 100. Nevertheless, the results
must be used with care. They clearly involve a high degree of uncertainty.

   Although the probability of a major accident appears very small, it is
always possible that new studies prompted by the Three Mile Island occurrence might lead to revised estimates of the probable frequency and
severity of accidents. And even if the revised probability estimates for a
major accident were still slight, the "worst possible accident" could still
result in as many as 3,000 relatively quick deaths from radiation sickness
plus 45,000 later deaths from induced cancers—*if* it ever happened.

   This leads to another aspect of the health and safety question which
needs to be confronted. What is society's attitude toward catastrophic
events? Despite the fact that the annual number of fatalities from a catastrophic accident could turn out to be small when averaged out over time,
the remote chance of such an accident's happening might be viewed with
greater concern than those impacts which occur with great regularity and
which add up to high cumulative totals. It is a question on which universal
agreement is obviously not going to be found—and for which even a consensus may be difficult, if not impossible.

   Catastrophic threats: Fossil fuels.   The fact that burning fossil fuels
(or even wood and agricultural wastes) produces carbon dioxide as a
combustion product leads to the concern that over time there may be a
sufficiently large carbon dioxide buildup to increase average global temperatures. Such air temperature increases, in turn, could affect the growth
and melting of the polar ice caps, heat up ocean waters, and change rainfall distribution and associated agricultural patterns.

   The only things that are certain about this line of speculation are that
carbon dioxide is produced as a combustion product and that there have
been significant increases in the average atmospheric content of carbon
dioxide over past decades. Beyond that, it is reasonable on general physical grounds to expect that such increases might lead to a rise in global
temperatures.

The extent and timing of the problem is controversial. Crude mathematical models estimate that the cumulative impact from U.S. fossil fuel energy use until the end of the century might contribute as much as $0.1\,^{\circ}C$ to a rise in global temperature. However, as far as is known, the effect could continue to add up almost indefinitely. Thus, levels of emissions corresponding to several degrees Celsius could be reached by the middle of the twenty-first century on the basis of rough global extrapolation of fossil energy use.

Although many questions of scientific fact and theory have yet to be resolved, the threat inherent in carbon dioxide buildup is regarded as critically important by some climatologists. However, even if this is a real threat, it is a distant one, and it might be possible to develop counteractive measures to reduce or negate the impacts. At the moment this particular threat is hardly a major public concern; but as one looks toward an energy program for decades in advance it must be considered.

The same consideration of potential reversibility applies to the more localized problem of acid rain resulting from fossil fuel emissions. We considered this danger even more remote on a truly catastrophic scale. Threats to plants and animal communities would probably be detected initially on a relatively small scale. Natural corrective processes could presumably be aided by human intervention, so ecosystems should be able to recover before the damage extended to the point of massive species endangerment.

In comparing the possible catastrophes associated with fossil fuel and nuclear technologies, an important distinction involves this question of reversibility. Presumably, climate modification and ecological damages can be monitored over time and adverse impacts noted (and perhaps reversed) before they become disastrous. Catastrophic nuclear threats, if they should materialize, could happen suddenly. They do not appear to offer the same opportunity for phasing in needed adjustments, so they call for the development of effective preventive measures which can be implemented as the technologies carrying such threats are being deployed. Those measures also need to be kept under continuous review, to allow improvement as required by new knowledge and changing circumstances (see pages 62–64).

Energy Policies

From among the various policy issues considered in chapters 16 through 19, we will turn first to two broad matters of overarching importance—

matters on which the nation needs to make early decisions. These matters are energy pricing and the degree of U.S. dependence upon foreign supplies.

More specific policy initiatives will then be the subject of the rest of this section. We will consider, in particular, those policy areas where action is necessary to achieve the future supply and demand conditions which underlie our belief that a national consensus on broad energy goals is feasible. Policy actions, including reform of energy pricing, can have substantial effects on the future sources and uses of energy, the 1976 pattern of which is shown in figure 1-6.

The Broad Policy Setting

Energy pricing. Effective energy policy is best served by a pricing system that tells each consumer accurately and directly what it costs our economy to use more energy, as well as each producer or importer how much those additional supplies will contribute. In such a system, energy prices reflect the full marginal costs of the energy supplied.

The incremental source of energy in the United States is imported crude oil, so its cost is the basis for the marginal value of all energy used in this country. While the price of imported oil does not reflect a competitive market price, it represents what must be surrendered in economic value (in the form of exports or debts to foreigners) for each imported barrel we use.

In major ways, energy prices in the United States do not now reflect marginal costs. Consequently, as compared with a regime of marginal cost pricing, more energy is being consumed, less energy is being produced domestically, more energy (mainly oil) is being imported, and both our energy production and consumption are allocated inefficiently as to form and location. The most important action required to reconcile prices with marginal costs is to remove existing price controls on domestic petroleum and natural gas—which means that the prices of both would rise. Reform also is needed in electric and natural gas utility pricing. Present rate structures generally do not confront consumers with the marginal costs of the energy they use, even though there have been some moves in that direction (at least in seasonal rates and experiments with time-of-day pricing for electricity).

Different pricing categories now exist for oil at the wellhead, so that oil may flow at prices ranging from about one-third the imported oil price to

WHERE U.S. ENERGY CAME FROM AND HOW IT WAS USED IN 1976

(All values in quadrillion Btu—"quads")

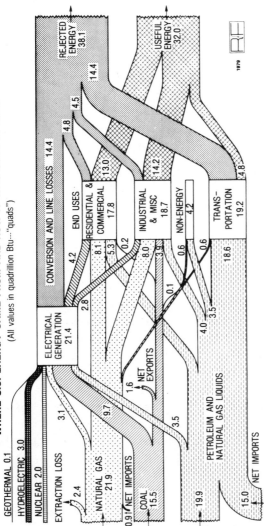

Figure 1-6. This updated version of a chart widely reproduced during the national energy debate in the early 1970s uses the statistics upon which the analysis in this study was based. A quad is roughly equivalent to the energy content released by burning about one-half million barrels of oil per day for a year. Total national energy consumption in 1976 showed only a modest increase over 1970 (increasing from 71.6 to 74.3 quads), but the composition of supply and end use changed significantly. There is, compared with the first date, greater national dependence than ever on oil—with net imports of petroleum having doubled in the six-year period. Coal use barely increased, while natural gas consumption declined. Electricity use increased by about 30 percent, with the relative share of coal-fueled generation remaining about the same (at 55 percent), while that fueled by oil and natural gas fell from 43 to 35 percent. Nuclear generation increased eightfold. Modest changes occurred also in energy use by sector; transportation energy use increased by nearly 20 percent—much faster than either of the other two major sectors. However, industry continues to be the leading energy-consuming sector (followed by residential-commercial) when the nonfuel uses of energy resources and the losses occurring in electricity generation are allocated among the major sectors.

(U.S. Bureau of Mines, "Annual U.S. Energy Use Up in 1976," news release, March 14, 1977. The end-use efficiencies used were calculated from Jack Alterman, *The Energy/Real Gross Domestic Product Ratio: An Analysis of Changes During the 1966–1970 Period in Relation to Long-Run Trends*, BEA Staff Paper No. 30, U.S. Department of Commerce, Oct. 1977, p. 71.)

the full price. When President Carter announced his intention in the spring of 1979 to move administratively toward oil price decontrol, various estimates were made of how much decontrol would raise the prices of different products. Precise calculations are complex (and they depend on various debatable assumptions about future OPEC pricing, the nature of competition, the rate at which decontrol might take place, and so on), but a simple, straightforward measurement of crude price differentials and the amount of petroleum affected can give us a general idea of the impact involved. We estimate that instantaneous, full decontrol at the time of President Carter's speech in April would have added about 5 to 7 cents per gallon to average petroleum product prices.

Natural gas prices at the wellhead have been held below free market prices for more than a decade. Although legislation passed in 1978 allowed the overall price of gas to rise closer to its replacement cost and promised deregulation of most gas by 1985–87, the new prices still do not meet the criteria for marginal cost pricing. In fact, more gas is controlled now (1979) than before; and different prices are assigned to various categories of the fuel with identical energy values. If all price controls at the production stage were dismantled, the short-run effect might be to raise natural gas prices in the field 20 percent or so above the regulated level.

From the standpoint of acquiring and using energy efficiently, the earlier that price controls on oil and gas can be removed the better; but other major concerns, such as inflation control and equity considerations, probably require a gradual approach to the dismantling of regulations.

These concerns were reflected in the president's energy message of April 5, 1979, in which he announced that he would gradually decontrol domestic crude oil prices starting June 1, 1979, which was as soon as existing legislation gave him authority to do so. His program was to first decontrol oil from sources where price incentives would be most effective, including production from new and marginal wells. Then other phases of decontrol were to take place at six-month intervals, until September 30, 1981, when all controls would have been dismantled. This schedule provides smaller price increases in the early stages of the program than in the later part, lessening the short-run inflationary effect and giving Congress an opportunity to enact a windfall profits tax. The particular tax suggested by the president had the stated objective of taxing away 50 percent of those producer revenues attributable to decontrol of production which had previously been controlled. It would also absorb 50 percent of any additional revenues from the sale of uncontrolled oil which might accrue from future OPEC price increases.

Even with the abolition of controls on petroleum and natural gas at the wellhead, prices would not adequately reflect costs because some unpaid costs which energy production and consumption impose on the economy are not now reckoned into the decisions of producers and consumers. Two forms of such costs are particularly relevant: the supply insecurity and other nonmonetary costs to the United States of importing oil, and the damages to the environment, human health, and safety that are imposed by energy production and use. In principle, such costs should be internalized within energy prices, though some costs are difficult, if not impossible, to quantify.

Unfortunately, "getting energy prices right" would add to inflationary pressures. This effect might be smaller than generally feared, however, because the value of the raw energy we use still constituted only about 6 percent of our GNP in 1978 (although this was up somewhat from the data base we used in the major part of our analysis). If the full effect of reform were to increase energy prices by an average of 20 percent, we can make the rough approximation that the overall price level would end up about 1 to 1.5 percent higher than it otherwise would be. Reductions in energy consumption could lessen this impact, and some other factors might increase the contribution to inflation. Still, if pricing reform took place in stages (as it very likely would) the economic shock effect would be much smaller than that of 1973–74. The great problem is that this would be one more straw on the camel's back—and one to which the public is understandably sensitive.

All energy price increases raise concerns about "fairness." Price reform might face less opposition on equity grounds if the public realized that price rises were mainly the result of processes beyond our own control, either imposed by foreign sources or the result of resource depletion. But credible information bearing on costs and prices is an especially scarce commodity in a field where mistrust is already intense, and where information is hard to come by at all. Fuller disclosure of financial data for energy companies might help, along with more government effort in data collection and dissemination.

Another complicating factor is that it is wasteful to try to build "fairness" into each individual element of energy policy. For example, energy price controls benefit rich and poor consumers alike, producing very little relative assistance to the poor (see chapter 17); yet they cause all consumers to use energy (wastefully) as if its real costs were lower than they are. Price controls aimed at preventing windfall profits (and even taxes to achieve the same result) lead in part to less energy being produced domestically, so that more oil is then imported—at still higher overall cost.

Instead of trying to use energy policy itself to achieve equity, we would increase our chances of assuring an efficient and equitable outcome by concentrating on general instruments which affect the distribution of income. Improving those instruments—the tax system, income maintenance programs, and the like—would simplify the problems of energy policy by relieving the pressure to make each individual energy outcome fair in itself.

Energy imports. The increase in consumption and the decline in domestic reserves of oil and natural gas have led to rapid growth in the importance of imports in recent years. While U.S. production has grown, it has been outpaced by increases in energy use (figure 1-7). Oil has been the dominant source of imports by far, but natural gas may become important in the near-term future. As we said earlier, we do not regard the expansion of imports as a promising approach to meeting the nation's long-term needs, partly because of the grave economic, political, and strategic difficulties and partly because world resources of relatively low-cost petroleum and natural gas may also be in short supply around the end of the century (see page 28 and chapter 7).

Although no short-term means are available for substantially reducing imports (and although, as chapter 16 shows, there are some benefits as well as drawbacks from continuing them), we believe it is essential that the nation assign great importance to the goal of assuring domestic ability to produce adequate supplies of liquid and gaseous fuels, either from natural sources or through synthetics derived from coal, oil shale, or other sources. Decontrol of prices would serve to encourage domestic supplies, particularly from natural sources; but that alone appears to be far from sufficient to meet future needs. It is likely that synthetic sources ultimately will be needed too, and this could require an early national commitment to both a program of sustained RD&D (research, development, and demonstration) and some assurance of an eventual domestic market for such supplies (see pages 56–58). Although synthetic oil and gas will be more costly at the outset, they appear to offer the prospect for ample supplies along with comparative stability in long-run costs.

As always in matters of large-scale national expenditures, avoiding excessive costs is crucially important. One of the most critical judgments in the entire energy policy field involves the decision as to what costs are worth incurring to reduce our dependence on imports. It will require serious and careful consideration by U.S. policy makers and the American public (see pages 57 and 61).

Imported oil will inevitably continue to be an important element in U.S. supply for some years. We need policies to see our way safely through

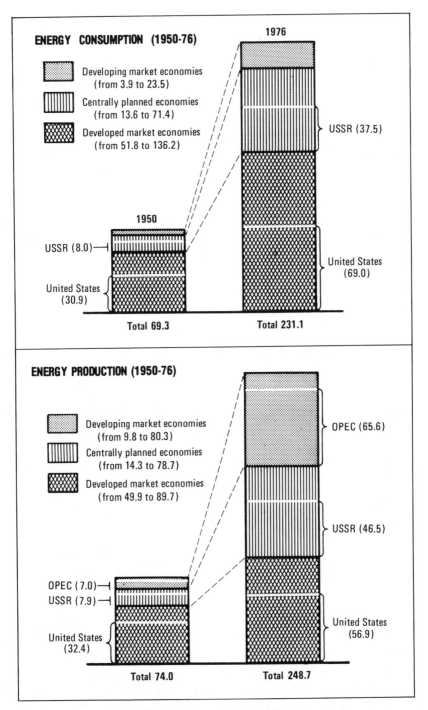

Figure 1-7. There were regional shifts in both the consumption and production of commercial energy during the third quarter of this century. The U.S. relative share of each has declined; but the United States has also changed from a net exporter to a net importer of major significance in the global market. Numbers (in quads) are drawn from the discussion in chapter 16.

this period, however long it may turn out to be. Beyond the balance of payments and other economic costs, it is necessary to guard against economic harm from interruptions in imports like those we have already experienced, most recently as a result of the political troubles which started in Iran in 1978. Such interruptions could vary in duration, up to the extreme case of permanent cutoff or permanent diminution in major sources of imported supplies.

Fortunately, the economy can be insulated against some of the harmful effects of import dependence through strategic oil storage, which can be drawn upon if oil imports should be interrupted. Such a stockpile would provide an interval during which diplomacy could work, domestic energy consumption could be dampened in an orderly way, and alternative foreign and domestic supplies could be brought onstream. Strategic storage might even reduce the temptation of oil exporters to make demands, because they would know that an interruption would need to go on for a long time (perhaps at high costs to some of the exporting countries) before resulting in significant harm to the United States.

How should we pay for the costs of the strategic oil storage program, and of other actions required because of the costs and risks associated with oil importation? Chapter 16 suggests a separate "security fee" on imports. By raising prices, the fee would serve not only to help pay for the programs required, but also to dampen additionally the demand for imports.

Specific Supporting Policies

The broad policy setting needs to be right, but this alone would not be enough to develop the national consensus we are seeking on broad energy goals. Our belief in the feasibility of substantially reconciling the diversity of attitudes toward America's energy future hinges largely on certain factual findings in this study, namely that: (1) specific conservation prospects can lead to a significant dampening in the growth of energy demand consistent with the expanding requirements of a growing economy; and (2) particular supply technologies present favorable long-term prospects for both monetary costs and health and environmental impacts. But the particular supply and demand developments needed to achieve these conditions will not be realized unless certain supporting policies are implemented in a timely fashion. So we will now consider some of those necessary policies.

Conservation. As we said above, the findings of this study show a significant energy-saving potential in the United States—judged by both economic and technological criteria. The adoption of techniques for conserving energy would be hastened by pricing reforms which lead to more realistic costs to consumers for the energy they use. The case studies in chapter 5 focus on improved residential heating practices, better automotive fuel economy, and combined production of electricity and process steam in industry; but opportunities exist in many other instances as well.

Policy and institutional initiatives would be needed to assure that we realized the full measure of feasible energy savings. In the major area of automotive transportation, for example, federal fuel-efficiency standards have already been imposed upon manufacturers as the means of achieving improved gasoline mileage. This approach will no doubt be carried forward in the future.

In the residential sector, the most serious impediments to improved efficiency seem to arise from consumers' tendencies to minimize initial capital costs. As a result they forego the energy-saving attributes of more expensive appliances or equipment, even though their use would save money over time.

Easily understood information on comparative economics is one means of reducing the obstacles posed by initial capital costs; it can help to steer people toward choices that save both energy and money. Furthermore, lending policies would inhibit conservation initiatives less if energy-efficient homes or appliances could qualify for more lenient down-payment terms because of the lower fuel charges expected over their lifetimes. Performance standards (such as minimum insulation requirements for homes) might be imposed too, but the danger here is that extensive regulatory intervention invites bureaucratic complexity and could stultify product innovation.

Even with all these policies in effect, however, the high initial capital cost of energy conservation equipment would continue to pose a serious problem for many. Many consumers, especially in lower-income groups, prefer to limit expenditures *now,* rather than over a number of years in the future. In addition, capital markets (and the tax system) make it far easier and cheaper to get money for large-scale energy *production* uses than for numerous small-scale energy *conservation* items. As a result, residential and commercial energy conservation initiatives may be denied funds while capital is available to support supply efforts whose costs per Btu are higher. A similar problem appears when you compare the energy-supply decisions of a regulated utility and the energy-conservation decisions of a manufacturer. The rate of return on investment prescribed for the utility is much lower than that targeted by the manufacturer, so it may take a lower rate of return to stimulate the production of energy than to stimulate the production and use of devices that conserve energy. Serious effort ought to go into finding ways to offset such subtle but energy-wasteful factors in existing institutional arrangements.

Other institutional barriers surround the prospective adoption of energy-sparing practices in industry. For example, joint production of electricity and process steam is frequently technologically feasible and economically promising, at least under marginal-cost pricing. But the complications of utility regulation may allow this cogeneration option to stand or fall on the question of whether the generating equipment itself is to be owned by the industrial enterprise, by utilities, or by independent parties.

Government may also encourage energy conservation through exploiting its role as a massive energy consumer. Federal, state, and local government units could acquire and operate buildings, motor vehicle fleets, and other equipment in a way that emphasizes energy conservation. Government installations could become show windows of cost-effective energy conservation, and training grounds as well.

Supply technologies: Solar.   For the long term, the supply technologies which look most promising for wide-scale application are: (1) solar energy, especially for household heating and providing hot water; (2) synthetic oil and gas based on coal and oil shale; and (3) nuclear technologies for producing electricity. These technologies have attractive long-term cost or supply potentials, or both; and in certain major respects they may offer significant comparative advantages from a health and environmental standpoint. What supporting policies could be undertaken, then, to enhance the prospects that they will be developed, used, and accepted by the public?

Home heating based on the type of solar collector systems now available represents one of the more promising "active" solar applications. Nevertheless, our findings suggest that it will not compete with alternative future technologies in most areas unless solar processes are assigned a social benefit which is not measured in monetary costs but which reflects superior health and environmental characteristics. If such advantages exist, what level of subsidies to solar energy would they justify? This question calls for early and serious attention; our own findings so far are inconclusive.

Even in the absence of subsidies, however, numerous policy steps could make solar household applications more attractive economically. Setting other energy prices at their correct cost levels, as proposed above, would help. Solar energy would then be competing with alternative sources such as oil, gas, and electricity priced at their true costs to society, rather than at some fraction of those costs as has been the case.

The uncertainty which now exists about the prospective performance of solar devices could be reduced if standards were developed, promulgated, and enforced by which performance (adjusted for local conditions) could be judged. Then consumers would have greater assurance that installed equipment would work as advertised and last as long as promised. This might also have the important side effect of reducing costs of solar equipment, because firms would be designing equipment to known specifications, assured that competitors faced the same performance tests.

Just as in conservation practices, various governmental installations could be the site of large-scale federal demonstrations of solar technology equipment. Widespread test sites would offer information and examples to local residents. They would also provide a training ground for the large numbers of building-trades professionals required for a major commitment to solar energy. Experience from such a demonstration program could feed into follow-on research and development activities. The result ought to be better products as well as better techniques for integrating them into new and existing structures.

Use of solar energy faces its own set of significant institutional barriers which could be eliminated or reduced. These include legal questions about "sun rights," mortgage policies which directly or indirectly discriminate against using solar technologies, and utility policies which limit availability of back-up service or make it excessively expensive. Chapter 19 discusses possible approaches to dealing with these problems, primarily through federal encouragement of actions which are best taken at the state or local level.

Supply technologies: Liquids and gases. Perhaps no aspect of this country's energy future causes more concern than the matter of providing reliable and reasonably priced supplies of liquid and gaseous fuels. Problems with the supply of these fuels have been at the root of the recurring energy "crises" of recent years, and the terms of their future availability—whether in the near or distant future—are a subject of much anxiety and controversy.

The factual materials examined in this study support the view that adequate near-term supplies of oil can only be provided through an absolute and relative growth in imports, but that domestic supplies of synthetics from coal and shale could assure the long-term future for both liquids and gases. The synthetics appear to promise ample substitutes, at real costs about double 1978 prices of imported crude oil, but, for reasons explained earlier, with the significant prospect that further cost rises over the long term could be moderate.

Research and development efforts on various processes for producing synthetic liquids and gases have been going on for many years, and some firms have announced projects on their own, but no commercial-scale liquid or gas project is anywhere near completion yet in the United States. Even aside from what seem like excessive costs, the environmental impacts of such programs remain uncertain, federal involvement has looked overwhelming to commercial interests, and even the states and localities in which such facilities would be placed are unenthusiastic because of concern about pollution and a number of socioeconomic problems (particularly the "boomtown" syndrome). In dealing with these specific problems, chapter 19 suggests a variety of possible measures that amount to spreading both costs and benefits among larger groups than would ordinarily be the case.

In general, there does not seem to be any difficulty in providing raw materials for synthetic fuel plants, but there is some possibility that shale oil technology may lack the inputs of oil shale and water it needs—oil shale because of leasing uncertainties and water because most of the supply in the shale regions is subject to prior appropriation. And, although coal supplies appear to be adequate to support an extensive synthetics industry, federal initiatives might reduce the costs of coal required for this industry (as well as for electricity generation). The major opportunities for federal encouragement, detailed in chapter 18, lie in improving the prospects for coal transportation and widening access to coal deposits on federal lands.

The overriding negative factor, though, is economic. There is still uncertainty as to whether the new technologies will work at commercial scale, and what their actual costs will be. Our best estimate is that the costs of synthetics will be higher than the prices expected for natural fuels at the earliest time such plants could go into production, and probably for some years beyond. This obviously constitutes a major impediment to development.

Under the anticipated circumstances, some policy instrument directed toward subsidizing synthetics would be required. Purchase guarantees illustrate one approach that might be successful. Bids could be solicited for fuels that met agreed-upon specifications. The government would pledge to buy the product (at the successful bid price, but for resale at market prices), and the firm would remain free to sell the fuel on the open market if it could get a higher price. The government's maximum obligation would be for the difference between the guarantee price and the market price. The firm, in turn, would lose if the price guarantee it offered to accept turned out to be too low in relation to actual production costs. The possibility of profits would encourage bids, but the mechanism would give potential fuel producers a strong incentive to bid realistically and to produce efficiently. Depending on its size, even if this program were operated efficiently, it could still prove quite costly.

One way to minimize federal outlays could be to limit national goals for a synthetics program to: (1) learning whether it would be technically and economically feasible in the future to rely substantially on synthetics, and (2) reaching a stage of development from which a large number of synthetic plants could be brought on line in a relatively short time in case of an unexpected increase in the price of oil and gas (caused by, say, disruptions abroad). Such a focus on information and insurance would limit the potential expenditures because these purposes could be fulfilled with one-of-a-kind installations, and there would be no open-ended commitment to purchase large amounts of fuel. The direct benefits from such a limited governmental commitment might overcome an understandable reluctance to underwrite a technology that, on narrow economic terms, promises to be a drain on the nation's resources.

But are information and insurance sufficient objectives to meet national needs? There is a strong case for going beyond this to encourage and expedite commercialization, but would it be worth the substantially greater costs? This depends to a major extent on the outlook for natural supplies, and whether we can obtain these supplies from abroad on acceptable economic, political, and strategic terms. Optimism on the latter issue does not square with the steadily accumulating evidence of recent years.

Failure to commercialize synthetics at a more rapid rate than would be determined by strictly private considerations (even allowing for the information provided to producers through a government-guarantee program), could be seriously destabilizing from an economic and political standpoint if oil supplies were not available on acceptable terms. On the other hand, adopting a cautionary stance and forcing commercialization seems to imply at worst that the investments would be made earlier than required. Sooner or later (but probably well before the close of this century, given the recent trend of international events) synthetic oil and gas supplies will apparently be required. Which is preferable—to incur the extra costs of being too early with synthetic plants, or to risk the potential economic, political, and strategic consequences of being too late? This is a critical question to which we will return in connection with a similar issue affecting the development of nuclear breeder reactors.

Supply technologies: Nuclear.   No technology shows more potential than nuclear power for long-run supplies of electricity at reasonable costs, nor does any other technology pose issues of public policy that are more complex and unyielding to solutions with wide public acceptance. We must do our best to resolve these problems, because the development and use of nuclear power could contribute greatly to the nation's long-term energy supplies. Prospects for nuclear power have deteriorated during the 1970s despite sharply rising prices of fossil fuels and intensified concern about the environmental consequences of using coal. Estimates of installed nuclear capacity by the end of this century have fallen sharply, and the decline in new orders for light water reactors has reached the point that questions have been raised as to whether the reactor manufacturing industry can survive.

Several factors account for the declining fortunes of nuclear power, but a major underlying reason is that significant doubt exists as to whether, and on what terms, nuclear power will ever prove acceptable to the American public. A few of the major issues involved in public acceptance—the fear of diversion of fissionable materials, accidental releases of radioactivity, and problems in waste disposal—are discussed on pages 62–64.

From among the various policy questions involved we will focus on two sets of issues which are of particular importance to the broad energy goals upon which a national consensus might be built: (1) those related to research, development, and demonstration of advanced nuclear technologies, particularly the breeder reactor; and (2) those related to public acceptance of the more widespread commercial use of nuclear processes that are already in place. Although the two matters are conceptually separable, public concern with the unique risks of nuclear power has been a major factor affecting decisions on both advanced RD&D and the broader deployment of existing nuclear technologies.

1. At least one class of concerns arises not so much from problems connected with existing technologies employing light water reactors (LWRs) as from problems anticipated for the liquid metal fast breeder reactor (LMFBR) or other breeders. Yet breeders are the advanced technology with the potential for stretching nuclear fuel supplies into the far distant future. While the LWR reactor does not require (but may benefit from) the reprocessing of spent fuel rods which yield plutonium, reprocessing

is essential if breeders are to be used. The fear of making bomb-grade material more accessible through acceptance of the "plutonium economy," and with it the potential proliferation of nuclear weapons based upon that material, might thus be allayed if the development of the LMFBR were terminated, or at least postponed. This has led to some support for a strategy meant to assure the continued growth of the LWR industry by instituting at least a temporary moratorium on breeder reactor development.

The importance of continued deployment of LWRs is measured by the fact that even the minimum of 225,000 MW in nuclear generating capacity that is still projected for the year 2000 represents an enormous fossil fuel saving that is already being counted on—equivalent annually by then to about 80 percent of our 1978 oil imports or 90 percent of our 1978 coal production. A U.S.-developed breeder, on the other hand, has no importance as a near-term energy source. Very long lead times, ranging from two to three decades or more, will be required for its further development and commercial deployment. Its major potential energy contributions must inescapably be targeted for the twenty-first century.

From this standpoint, therefore, it could be sensible to trade off the development of the breeder in order to continue to expand the use of LWRs. But if the breeder is to begin to feed into U.S. energy supply, say by the year 2000, commitment to a full-fledged program of development must also come soon. And therein lies the dilemma.

The critical question in all this is how significant a U.S. decision on breeder development could be to the prospects for nuclear weapons proliferation and nuclear war. Putting aside doubts as to the strength of the relationship between nuclear weapons proliferation and the spread of breeder reactors, there remains the question of the connection between a U.S. decision on the development of breeder technology and the decisions of other countries on the same matter. If the United States announces a decision to develop breeder technology, it may be impossible to convince other nations that they should behave differently. If, on the other hand, the United States should refrain from developing the breeder—as at present—it could argue more convincingly against foreign development. However, other nations could still choose to proceed with the breeder if it appeared to be in their best interest to do so. France and the Soviet Union already have breeders in operation at an incipiently commercial level, and they are also being developed in West Germany and elsewhere.

Under these circumstances, can proliferation control be significantly influenced by the unilateral actions of any one country, or does it depend upon concerted international action? As far back as the early post-World War II years (when the leverage of the United States was much stronger), our government proposed international solutions encompassing multi-national approaches to the control of the nuclear fuel cycle, along with technological adaptations to maximize the resistance of fuel processes to the diversion of potential weapons materials. International efforts have continued, with some interruption, down to the present day, most recently with the on-going International Nuclear Fuel Cycle Evaluation Study (INFCE). This study seeks to provide information on possible multi-national control at key stages in the fuel cycle, and to examine other tech-nical and institutional measures to resist diversion.

A possible way out of the current domestic policy stalemate on breeder development could be to make a clear separation between any decision to proceed with *development* of the LMFBR and its supporting technology, and a decision to be taken at a later date as to whether or not breeder reactors should be *introduced* commercially into the U.S. energy supply system. Deployment is a long way off at best, leaving a lot of time for international efforts to proceed and progress. Still, any future deployment of breeders should require an explicit decision at that time—one which would be fully debated in all respects—and should not be just another step in a line of incremental decisions with a predetermined outcome.

If the breeder reactor could be made available on acceptable terms, this would be a major step towards assuring long-run energy supply for the United States. No other nonfossil fuel option is as certain to be able to provide electricity at reasonable costs into the distant future. Its im-portance is such that serious consideration should be given to a develop-ment program designed to demonstrate as quickly as possible (at a minimum by the end of this century) whether the breeder reactor is com-mercially feasible.

Such a program might be strictly domestic in nature, or it could involve cooperation with other countries—for example, with the French, who have achieved a relatively advanced breeder technology. The small Phénix reactor now supplying power commercially in France and the Super Phénix reactor now being developed there could be used as a source of data and technological expertise. To be sure, differences in plant design from the LMFBR might require modifications in approach to correspond to American safety or environmental standards. Any such international exchange of technology could also introduce difficulties of both a technical and political nature.

Past planning for the LMFBR has been based on the assumption that the government will support a progressively smaller proportion of the costs as technologies come closer to commercial scale, with commercial plants being totally the responsibility of the private sector. This is generally a sound approach, because the involvement of private firms serves to introduce commercial criteria into research and development decisions, minimize technology transfer problems, and decrease subsidies (because at least some of the costs are borne by investors and electricity consumers).

Today, however, general uncertainty grips the nuclear industry, and confidence in the future of the breeder has been sapped by a series of recent governmental actions. Firms are less ready to invest than they were only a few years ago. If the development program is divorced from all subsequent decisions concerning commercialization and deployment, commercial incentives will be weakened even further.

It is likely, therefore, that unless the federal government accepts the lion's share of the financial risks, the development program will be substantially delayed. If we are to move ahead, an institutional arrangement probably is required whereby the private sector can have a large measure of managerial and operational control (with responsibility to meet performance goals) but without the level of financial responsibility that seemed reasonable only a few years ago.

If a decision were taken to try to reduce lead times by overlapping development and demonstration of the LMFBR, as discussed in chapter 18, this would be an additional reason for heavier federal financial involvement. The amount of money at risk would be greater at certain times, compared with a more deliberate staging of the developmental sequences, but this approach would have some advantages. It would not only speed the time when deployment would be possible, but also permit earlier abandonment of the breeder concept if unacceptable safety and environmental problems were discovered. As indicated above, cooperation with other countries (such as France) who are ahead of the United States in LMFBR technology could also be pursued as a means of achieving greater speed and lower costs. This option gains in attractiveness as the possibility grows that increasingly massive government funding for RD&D will be needed.

The issues associated with an increased level of federal support to hasten the development of breeder reactors during a period of budgetary stringency are like those posed earlier in connection with technologies for producing synthetic liquid and gaseous fuels. In both cases it will be important to weigh the additional costs of speed in achieving the particular objectives against the losses (not easily expressed in dollar terms) that would result from failure to undertake appropriate actions on a timely basis. It is important to avoid excessively costly solutions, but the truth is that we can (and often do) absorb substantial inefficiencies in such "hedging of our bets." We may not be able to afford mistakes (even of economic caution) which pose potentially serious threats to an independent foreign policy, domestic stability, and international order. The choice between two such imperfect options is up to the American people; but it is vital that it be a conscious and informed choice.

2. There is, finally, the important issue of public acceptance. All energy alternatives, as we have seen, carry risks; but concern over the unusual risks of nuclear power is especially strong. Of particular importance are such matters as the linkage between nuclear power and the proliferation of nuclear weapons, the disposal of long-lived wastes, and possible reactor accidents. The topic of nuclear risks was dealt with earlier, but we return to it here because concerns about these three specific problem areas can determine the fate of nuclear power in this country.

Proliferation is a problem requiring international solutions. Americans cannot escape the risks of nuclear proliferation by adopting restrictive nuclear development policies at home, if other countries do not follow our lead. It is true that U.S. rejection of the breeder might form an important part of an antiproliferation foreign policy. However, all feasible international initiatives should be pursued as an integral part of any breeder program. Technical approaches to making fissionable materials diversion-resistant would also help to minimize the danger that domestic and international terrorist groups might acquire nuclear weapons.

The nuclear waste disposal problem, to turn to another major concern, would need to be dealt with even if the United States had never undertaken a commercial nuclear power program at all—because of the large military program conducted since the Second World War. This problem displays a history of proposed technical solutions, but none that has gained general acceptance. Early AEC policy was that highly radioactive wastes from commercial nuclear power plants (like those from the reprocessing of "production reactor" fuel elements to yield plutonium for weapons) should be stored as liquids in underground tanks. Some such storage actually took place at the one commercial reprocessing plant that operated briefly in upstate New York. Later, the policy shifted toward permanent underground storage (most probably in solid form) in stable geological formations, particularly in salt deposits. However, increasing public concern about this solution, probably combined with increasing caution on the part of government energy planners, led to delays in the development of pilot projects. In the intervening years, government policy has veered first to retrievable storage systems above ground, and now back to considering geologic storage again. Furthermore, some critics have raised new questions recently about the possible migration of radioactive materials through underground salt deposits; and these will have to be considered before the matter can be considered fully resolved. At the present time there is a proposed Waste Isolation Pilot Project (WIPP) in Carlsbad, New Mexico, which is not yet operative, but no system of established waste disposal facilities exists.

The prospects for a reasonable technical solution to the nuclear waste problem seem good; but finding locally acceptable sites for waste disposal is difficult in practice because, in the present climate of public opinion, strong doubts exist as to the safety of such facilities. Experiments such as the WIPP should help settle the matter. Since any contamination from future nuclear wastes is apt to be at very low levels, another approach would be to carry out extensive laboratory studies on the effects of low level radiation on health. Such studies, while quite expensive because of the scale of experimentation involved in coming to fairly definite conclusions, might well be worthwhile considering the stakes.

In reactor accidents, as in the matter of waste disposal, there is a long history of government action but a failure to satisfy public concerns. The Atomic Energy Commission was given explicit power in the Atomic Energy Act of 1954 to regulate the operation of (and hence establish the safety requirements for) commercial nuclear power plants. Added authority for regulation came under the National Environmental Policy Act. Subsequently, a large independent regulatory agency, the Nuclear Regulatory Commission (NRC), was established. It was completely separated from the nuclear energy development function to insure its single-minded concern for health and safety. The NRC has set up a multiplicity of regulations and guidelines for the safety of nuclear power plants.

In addition to performing detailed safety reviews for each proposed nuclear plant, the NRC sponsored a massive Reactor Safety Study—the Rasmussen Report—to establish the probability of serious nuclear accidents and their effects. More recently the NRC has released a critique of the Rasmussen Report which casts serious doubts on the numerical accuracy of its findings but which does not necessarily invalidate general conclusions about the expected low risk of nuclear accidents. The accident at Three Mile Island has also contributed to concern about safety, and to doubts about the completeness of the coverage of potential accident sequences in the Rasmussen Report.

Continued uncertainties about safety could be a key obstacle in the way of new policy moves to expedite the licensing of nuclear power plants, even though the shortening of licensing time has become a recognized condition for encouraging utilities to exercise the nuclear option. Legislation has been proposed repeatedly in recent years to simplify licensing by standardizing plants and predesignating sites. However, if basic safety concerns are not satisfied, there seems to be little chance that the shortening of licensing time (which could lead to a concomitant reduction in opportunities for judicial review of health and safety matters) will be realized. It seems safe to assume that the commercial nuclear power industry will not be able to grow unless the conclusions of the Rasmussen Report are either validated, revised, or replaced in the light of the Three Mile Island accident. President Carter's appointment of a blue ribbon committee to investigate that accident is a part of this sequence. Chapter 18 suggests that safety might be increased by adopting an even sterner attitude toward the question of accident avoidance and by changes which would strengthen incentives to avoid situations which might prove risky. It also notes that limitation of the size of the population at risk from any one accident is important to any "defense in depth," and points out that several possibilities—including siting and reactor size restrictions—have been proposed to achieve this end.

Resolution of controversies on the role of nuclear power depends ultimately upon public understanding of the facts and their bearing on the *comparative* advantages and disadvantages of this technology and alternative energy sources. In turn, this requires a total effort by the government and the industry to make the critical facts publicly available. Legitimate concerns stand in the way of broad acceptance of the development and use of nuclear power. We need more thoughtful and determined efforts to inform the public as to the threats posed by (and the means available for dealing with) problems of deep and continuing concern, such as reactor safety, weapons proliferation, and the disposal of long-lived radioactive waste.

We began this study with the conviction that concern about America's energy future is so pervasive and that beliefs about the realities underlying the nation's energy problems are so divergent that it would help immeasurably to clarify the factual and analytical bases for future public discussion. It seemed almost equally important to review the most likely consequences of various policies that might be considered in trying to resolve these energy problems. Yet even agreement on the consequences of policy choices and on major matters of fact might not enable the United States to evolve a publicly acceptable national energy policy that would accomplish what needs to be done in time. We still would need a consensus on long-term goals and agreement on the tradeoffs between near-term and more distant objectives.

National consensus cannot be established in a book. The chapters that follow will have succeeded if this book's readers decide that such a consensus can and should be reached—and work at it. We have presented here an internally consistent framework which will support and encourage such efforts at broader reconciliation. Deciding whether or not to press the effort on energy consensus is one of the critical choices before us. It could be as important as the actual policy strategies that evolve in shaping America's energy future.

Part II

Energy Consumption

2 Measuring Energy Flows in Today's Economy

Energy Inputs into the Economy

There are different ways of measuring overall energy consumption and of breaking down that total into its various components. The most widely employed present-day yardstick of U.S. energy use is the summed total, expressed in a common measurement unit, of gross energy inputs entering various energy-using sectors of the economy. The term *gross* signifies the inclusion of losses occurring when primary energy sources are converted into the secondary, or *net,* energy forms that are delivered to ultimate consumers. Under current measurements, the difference between gross and net energy consumption arises almost exclusively from electric power generation. That is, gross energy inputs include the thermal content of fuels delivered to power stations; while net energy consumption includes only the thermal equivalent of the electricity being sent out. (Typically, some two-thirds of a utility's energy inputs are dissipated in the form of waste heat; even in the most modern conventional power plants, losses of around 60 percent are unavoidable.)

Currently, the primary energy sources which are quantitatively relevant include coal (mostly bituminous), natural gas, oil (including natural gas liquids), water power (hydroelectricity), and nuclear energy. Geothermal sources are used to generate modest amounts of electric power in the far West but are often hidden in, or missing from, published energy data. Productive use of wood wastes and products as energy sources is another, quantitatively minor, example of unmeasured energy consumption. In all, these unrecorded items might, at most, add 2 percent to measured energy consumption in the United States. In principle, of course, solar energy also belongs to the array of primary energy sources; as its application grows from the infinitesimal level of today, solar will no doubt begin to be statistically recorded.

In order to compare or total the different energy sources and forms it is necessary to use a common unit of measure. For that purpose, the British thermal unit (Btu) has emerged as the most widely used measurement in the United States. (The Btu measures the amount of energy needed to heat one pound of water to one degree Fahrenheit.) American energy consumption is usually recorded, and often cited, in quadrillion Btus (that is, 10^{15} Btus), or *quads.*

In 1976 the nation's gross energy consumption reached 74 quads.[1] Table 2-1 and figure 2-1 summarize the composition of the primary resources that made up this total. Well over 90 percent come from fossil fuels: somewhat under one-fifth is derived from coal and three-quarters from oil and gas. Waterpower contributes 4 percent, and nuclear a bit under 3 percent. Of course, these current proportions have been preceded, in the course of the last 125 years, by shifts in the nation's energy balance that are as fundamental as those accompanying the changing character of the American economy itself—from an agrarian-rural profile to an industrial-urban one. It was not until the closing decades of the nineteenth century that coal surpassed wood as America's predominant energy source; and not until the end of World War II that petroleum began to outrank coal.

Distribution of Gross Energy Inputs by Sector and End Use

A broad picture of energy flows—in the aggregate and by source—to the three major consumption sectors of the economy appears in table 2-2 and figure 2-2. The percentage distribution shows the combined household–commercial sector and industry to occupy roughly the same proportionate standing in nationwide energy use, each accounting for about 37 percent of the total. The prevailing household—commercial share, however, is higher than the proportion of a quarter century earlier—it was 30 percent

---

[1] By the time this chapter was completed, slightly revised and more recent energy-consumption data than the 1976 figures relied upon here and in ensuing chapters had been issued by the Department of Energy's Energy Information Administration (see successive editions of the *Monthly Energy Review*). Nonetheless, it made sense to stick with 1976 for our base year statistical framework. The *detailed* components of total energy use to which we refer periodically in most cases have not been estimated beyond 1976—indeed, some of these subaggregates are not even available for 1976. Also, 1976 reflected a more "representative" pattern of energy-resource usage than 1977, owing to the drastic drought-induced reduction in hydropower consumption which occurred in 1977.

Table 2-1. U.S. Gross Energy Inputs for 1976, by Source, Given in Physical Quantities and Btus

Source and unit	Physical quantity	Quadrillion Btus	Percentage distribution
Coal, million short tons	602.4	13.75	18.6
Anthracite	5.2	0.13	0.2
Bituminous	597.2	13.62	18.4
Natural gas, trillion ft³	19.8	20.22	27.3
Petroleum, billion barrels	6.35	34.94	47.2
Hydropower, billion kWh	295.1	3.06	4.1
Nuclear power, billion kWh	190.6	2.03	2.7
Gross energy inputs		74.00	100.0

Notes: Conversion factors for equating physical quantities to energy units, are shown below. These conversion rates are, to some extent, implicit averages reflecting underlying energy products (for example, gasoline and residual fuel oil are included in "petroleum") which may vary from each other in energy content. The factor for hydropower represents the nationally averaged conversion efficiency, the so-called heat rate at fossil-fueled steam electric plants. Conversion factors are coal (22.8 million Btu per ton); natural gas (1,021 Btu per ft³); petroleum (5.5 million Btu per barrel); hydropower (10,383 Btu per kWh); and nuclear power (10,660 Btu per kWh).

These consumption estimates represent domestic production plus (minus) imports (exports) plus (minus) stock withdrawals (additions). A balancing adjustment factor, representing processing losses or gains and statistical discrepancies, serves to equate consumption, as just defined, with consumption derived as the sum of sectoral energy demands. Shipments into and out of the country of electric power, which are small, are included with hydropower. For nuclear electric power, production and consumption are identical by definition.

Source: U.S. Department of the Interior, Bureau of Mines Release (March 14, 1977).

in 1950; while industry's share has fallen from a figure of 44 percent twenty-five years ago. Transportation—with an essentially constant share —makes up the balance of 26 percent.

The horizontal breakdown in the table allows us to differentiate between how much energy is consumed in the form of electricity and how much is consumed directly in the form of fossil fuels (largely oil products and natural gas, with coal also being used in industry). Thus, the use of electricity accounts for over 22 percent of net energy consumption by the household–commercial sector, a considerably larger share than the 13 percent used by industry. Transportation obtains minimal quantities of its energy in the form of electricity. Keeping in mind the gross–net distinction noted on page 69, we find that, for the economy as a whole, electricity comprises around 12 percent of net energy consumption. On a gross-consumption basis, delivered electricity accounts for approximately 10 percent of the total; but—counting the associated heat losses of 20 percent—this means roughly 30 percent of the nation's gross use of energy resources are channeled through electric utilities.

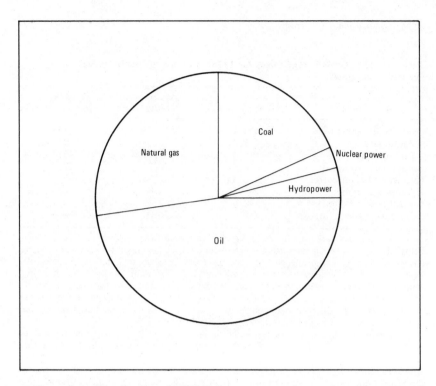

Figure 2-1. Distribution of 1976 U.S. gross energy inputs, by source. (Based on data from table 2-1.)

Table 2-2. U.S. Gross and Net Energy Inputs for 1976, by Source and Major Consumption Sector

(in quads)

Consumption sector	Fossil fuels[a]	Elec- tricity	Net energy consump- tion	Electric utility- generation losses by sector	Gross energy consumption	
					Quads	%
Household–commercial	14.69	4.14	18.83	8.56	27.39	37.0
Industry	18.40	2.81	21.21	5.80	27.01	36.5
Transportation	19.32	0.02	19.33	0.03	19.36	26.2
Total, quads[b]	52.63	6.97	59.60	14.40	74.00	100.0
Total, %	71.1	9.4	80.5	19.5	100.0	—

Source: U.S. Department of the Interior, Bureau of Mines Release (March 14, 1977).

[a] Bear in mind that the fossil fuel total applies only to what is consumed as a result of direct shipments to the sectors shown; fossil fuels converted into electric power are implicitly reflected in the sum of the columns "Electricity" and "Electric utility-generation losses by sector."

[b] This total includes a miscellaneous and unaccounted for category, not shown separately.

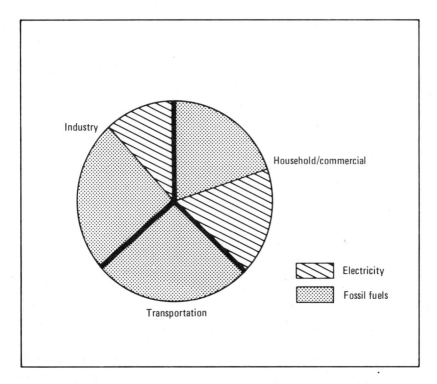

Figure 2-2. Distribution of 1976 U.S. gross energy inputs, by consumption sector. Note that the electricity (shaded) portions represent gross energy inputs required to meet sectoral electricity consumption. (Based on data from table 2-2.)

The net–gross relationship is sometimes used as a very crude kind of overall efficiency measure reflecting the "efficiency" of the U.S. energy system. (The "net energy consumption" column in table 2-2 shows such an efficiency figure to be around 80 percent.) As a representation of how much of the primary energy input is dissipated as electric-generation losses, such a figure may have some informational value, but for the most part it is an arbitrary designation. Where electricity has a unique role to play—as in powering electric motors or in the electrolytic reduction of metallic ores—it is, after all, misleading to equate inefficiency with the degree of dependence upon the electric form of energy.

In any case, there are other nonelectric losses in the system of energy flows from primary source to ultimate user *not* captured in the statistical schema of table 2-2—for example, losses in petroleum refining or in coal handling and processing. Then, too, there are losses associated with par-

ticular kinds of energy-using equipment (say, oil furnaces). These losses,   •
which may be inherent in the thermodynamic characteristics of the equipment or be a result of its improper use or maintenance, will cause effective
use of energy to be lower still. This aspect will be considered a little later
in the chapter.

The threefold breakdown that we have been discussing is, of course,
exceedingly broad, with each sector covering a multitude of different activities. To address the question of future trends in energy consumption
and conservation potentials, it is necessary to probe further into energy
consumption patterns (table 2-3). In addition to providing *intra*sectoral
detail, table 2-3 also shows a separation between what is shown in table
2-2 as a consolidation of the residential and commercial sectors. Unfortunately, however, the data in table 2-3 apply only to the year 1973, since
the energy statistical system maintained by the federal government has not
routinely included these specifics. One can nevertheless gain considerable
perspective on the principal purposes for which energy is used in the
United States.

Certainly, it is not difficult to identify the components which deserve
particular attention when one is concerned with future energy demand
and conservation opportunities. For it becomes quickly apparent that in
each of the major sectors of the economy, one or two items dominate the
entire sector: space conditioning in the residential as well as in the commercial sector; process steam- and direct-heat applications in industry;
and automobiles and trucking in the transport sector. In fact, the foregoing small number of identifiable end uses accounts for 62 percent of
the nation's gross energy consumption. The addition of water heating in
households and commercial buildings and energy to run motors in factories brings the share thus accounted for to nearly 70 percent. It is
somewhat surprising perhaps that a wide range of applications—air conditioning, lighting, cooking, clothes drying, and refrigeration—adds only
another 13 percent to the total. Granted, certain end uses—notably air
conditioning and air transport (the latter still swamped by automotive
energy use)—have tended in recent years to record the fastest annual
growth rates among energy uses, even though these categories continue
to represent relatively modest portions of nationwide energy consumption. These and other trends, such as a persistently faster historic growth
of electricity than of total energy consumption, need to be kept firmly
in mind when one looks at the dynamics of future energy demand.

The categories listed in table 2-3 refer to functions for which energy is
consumed. For the industrial sector, it is possible also to identify the par-

Table 2-3. Gross Energy Consumption, Estimated Distribution by Sector, and Detailed End Use, 1973

Sector	Quads	Percentage distribution
Residential, total	*15.3*	*20.5*
Space heat	7.8	10.4
Water heat	2.3	3.1
Air conditioning	1.1	1.5
Refrigeration	1.3	1.7
Cooking	0.7	0.9
Lighting	0.9	1.2
Clothes drying	0.4	0.5
Other	0.8	1.1
Commercial, total	*10.8*	*14.4*
Space heat	3.8	5.1
Water heat	0.5	0.7
Air conditioning	1.5	2.0
Refrigeration	0.8	1.1
Cooling	0.1	0.1
Lighting	2.9	3.9
Road surfacing (asphalt, road oil)	1.1	1.5
Industrial, total[a]	*29.6*	*39.7*
Process steam	10.5	14.1
Direct heat	7.1	9.5
Electric drive	6.5	8.7
Electrolysis	0.9	1.3
Feedstocks	4.0	5.3
Other	0.6	0.8
Transportation	*19.0*	*25.4*
Automobiles	9.8	13.1
Trucks	3.9	5.2
Aircraft	1.3	1.7
Rail	0.6	0.8
Pipelines	1.8	2.4
Ships	0.3	0.3
Buses	0.2	0.2
Other	1.1	1.5
Total	74.7	100.0

Source: Amory B. Lovins, "Scale, Centralization, and Electrification in Energy Systems," in Oak Ridge Associated Universities, *Future Strategies for Energy Development* (Oak Ridge, Tenn., Oak Ridge Associated Universities, 1977) p. 101. Since data presented by Lovins are an extrapolation of estimates for an earlier year, they have been somewhat modified here on the basis of figures contained in U.S. Department of Energy, Energy Information Administration, *End Use Energy Consumption Data Base: Series I Tables* (Washington, D.C., Department of Energy, 1978).

[a] The industrial sector, as defined here, is dominated by manufacturing (82 percent) but also comprises mining (7 percent), construction (6 percent), and agriculture (5 percent).

ticular industrial groups accounting for the bulk of the sector's energy inputs. For even though industrial energy use is concentrated among a handful of applications, whether these applications are widely dispersed among many industrial segments or limited to a few can be a factor in the success with which new end-use energy technologies can infiltrate the industrial economy. As it turns out, the bulk of industrial energy consumption that occurs is explained by a small number of manufacturing activities. To be specific, six manufacturing groups accounted for nearly two-thirds of total industrial energy consumption in 1974[2]: chemicals (21 percent); iron and steel (13 percent); petroleum refining (12 percent); paper (10 percent); aluminum (5 percent); and cement (2 percent). These groups total 63 percent, while all others account for the remaining 37 percent. Most of the end-use functions in industrial energy utilization (as shown in table 2-3) are represented; electrolytic processes are preeminent in the case of aluminum; process steam, in the case of paper; and direct heat, in the blast furnace and steel-making stages of iron and steel production.

In addition to accounting for disproportionately large shares of industrial energy consumption, these are also industries whose typical ratio of energy input (expressed either in dollars or Btus) to the value of industrial output is conspicuously above the industrywide average. For example, if we set the 1975 ratio of energy purchases per unit of value added for all manufacturing industries at an index of 100, the corresponding ratio for aluminum is 1,350; blast furnaces and steel mills, 490; petroleum refining, 760; cement, 870; paper in the aggregate, 190, and papermills, 360; all chemicals, 190; and industrial inorganic chemicals, 500.[3]

Other Dimensions of Energy Flows Through the Economy

As we have seen, prevailing pattern of energy consumption can be represented in a number of alternative ways. In the following paragraphs we will depict briefly some other ways of characterizing energy use. Elsewhere we will indicate how each representation provides a firmer basis

---

[2] Federal Energy Administration, "1977 National Energy Outlook" (January 1977) tab. IV-6.

[3] John G. Myers and Leonard Nakamura, *Saving Energy in Manufacturing: The Post-Embargo Record* (Cambridge, Mass., Ballinger, 1978).

for understanding the nature of energy–economy interrelationships (see chapters 3 through 6).

Energy in Nonfuel and Power Uses

The preeminent application of energy resources—and that which the public is most aware of—is in their capacity for work, either by means of fuel combusion or in conversion to electric power. The routes by which this potential for work is realized are too widely known to require elaboration: the creation of mechanical energy, using electric motors or internal combustion engines; the creation of heat, using industrial or residential furnaces, or via electric-resistance elements; incandescent or fluorescent lighting by means of electric current; as well as other common examples. Less widely appreciated is the fact that a growing, and quite important, share of primary energy resource consumption is accounted for by uses involving the inherent raw material properties of energy resources rather than their combustible features or electricity-producing characteristics. In 1976, around 6 percent of gross energy inputs involved such raw materials consumption; for industry alone, the share was close to 10 percent. Typical examples of nonenergy applications include such crude oil derivatives as naphtha or benzene as petrochemical "feedstocks," used for the production of synthetic fibers, plastics, pharmaceuticals, and many other products; asphalt for road surfaces; lubricating oil for car engines; and natural gas in fertilizer production. Over 80 percent of these nonenergy materials are derived from oil as the basic resource; the balance involves products derived from natural gas and coal. Industry is the main consumption sector. What gives energy as a raw material prominence in an era of perceived energy scarcity is its nonsubstitutable character in many of the uses illustrated above. Plastics and synthetics require liquid or gaseous hydrocarbon as feedstocks. Coal (conventionally burned) or electricity will not do, although feedstocks *can* be derived from coal at a severe economic penalty. There is far greater scope for interfuel substitution in energy consumption per se. Recognizing these indispensible attributes of oil and gas as petrochemical feedstocks, we find a growing acceptance of a prudent long-term energy strategy which advocates a shift away from these sources in uses where they are replaceable and for their eventual preemption for purposes where they are irreplaceable. Such a course may enable the petrochemical producer to escape—or at least, delay facing—costly penalties of substitution.

"Intermediate" Versus "Final Demand" Energy Deliveries

A useful differentiation can be made between the energy consumed in the final demand sectors of the domestic economy and that consumed in intermediate economic activities. By *final demand,* we mean direct purchases of fuels or power by ultimate consumers—overwhelmingly the consumption by persons and families as part of their household and personal transportation expenditures, but also, to some extent, involving energy use by different units of government. Typically, we are talking about such items as gas and electric utility sales to residential customers, expenditures for home-heating oil, or motor gasoline purchases. Unlike the energy used by the business sector in production of goods and services, these are direct energy purchases insofar as they are not subject to further processing and not embodied in other commodities. Their consumption, of course, is very closely tied to other expenditures, such as those on cars, television sets, or air conditioners. By contrast, *intermediate* energy consumption occurs at a prior stage of economic flows where energy, along with other resources, constitutes an input into the production of goods and services, either destined for still further processing or for subsequent delivery to ultimate consumers. One such example is coking coal used to produce iron and steel, which in turn is used to manufacture cars sold to the public. Another is electricity consumed by an aluminum smelter in electrolytic reduction. Diesel or jet fuel purchased by a bus system or airline, both of which sell services to final consumers, is yet another example.

For 1975, it can be estimated that gross energy inputs into the economy can be broken down approximately as follows[4]:

Consumption sector	Percentage
Consumption by final demand	35
Households	30
Government	5
Consumption by intermediate sectors	65

A recognition of this breakdown is important because of the distinctly different character of energy utilization in the two categories. Intermediate

---

[4] Based on U.S. Bureau of Mines data, shown in Sam H. Schurr and Joel Darmstadter, "Some Observations on Energy and Economic Growth," in Oak Ridge Associated Universities, *Future Strategies for Energy Development* (Oak Ridge, Tenn., Oak Ridge Associated Universities, 1977).

energy use—that is, consumption by industry and other business enter-prises—reflects energy consumption that is especially significant as a *contributor* to production and to economic growth. Here, energy takes its place along with other resources (labor, capital, land, and nonenergy materials) to produce the goods and generate the national income which, in turn, constitute the springboard for further growth. It is not difficult to appreciate that severe constraints on energy availability in the business sector might encroach on output (in spite of greater or lesser latitude for substitutability with nonenergy factors of production). In the final demand sector, on the other hand, energy consumption reflects more the *proceeds* of economic growth, with rising income being used to provide for both energy-associated necessities and creature comforts. As a factor in eco-nomic growth, it has more of a discretionary than preemptive character, and this is analogous in a crude way to the contrast between personal con-sumption and capital investment—the latter helping to generate the in-come that paves the way for the former. Curtailed energy supplies to consumers undoubtedly create—or are perceived as creating—occasion-ally severe hardships: gasoline is vital for those having to commute to work in automobiles. Yet, economically at least, the negative impact of constrained energy in the final demand sector is essentially of a different character from the effects of shortages in production activity.

The Dollar Value of Energy Inputs into the Economy

The proportionate importance of energy consumption in the national economy is not adequately captured when expressed only in physical units (such as barrels of oil or tons of coal) or in calorific terms (such as Btus). To help probe the interconnections between energy and the econ-omy, it is also instructive to have some idea of energy consumption in dollar terms. Energy can then be expressed as a component of the gross national product (GNP). And whether it is a minor or ranking compo-nent of the GNP can obviously influence the extent to which shocks aris-ing in the energy sector can reverberate within the broader economic scene, although it is not the dollar value alone which measures this in-fluence.

Table 2-4 shows that the estimated value of gross energy inputs into the economy came to around $89 billion in 1976—or to 5.2 percent of that year's GNP of $1,706 billion. (For the different primary energy sources combined, this works out to about $1.20 per million Btu.)

Table 2-4. Value of Gross Energy Inputs at Point of Primary Production or Import, 1976

Source	Quantity	Representative price	Value (billion dollars)
Coal, million short tons	602.4	$20 per ton	12.05
Natural gas, trillion ft³	19.80	58 cents per 1,000 ft³	11.48
Petroleum, billion barrels	6.35	$8.11 per barrel	51.50
Hydropower–nuclear, billion kWh	485.7	2.9 cents per kWh	14.09
Total			89.12

Note: Coal is priced at the mine; gas and oil at the wellhead (or point of importation); electricity price is unit revenues received by utilities from all classes of customers.

Sources: Quantities have been taken from table 2-1. Representative prices for coal, gas, and oil are taken from U.S. Department of the Interior, Bureau of Mines, *Minerals & Materials/A Monthly Survey* (Washington, D.C., September 1977); and those for electricity are from Edison Electric Institute, *Advanced Release of Data for the Statistical Yearbook of the Electric Utility Industry, Year 1976* (New York, Edison Electric Institute, May 1977).

If the 5 percent GNP share seems modest, note that it was a mere 3 percent in 1972, prior to the sharp relative increase in energy prices. More important, the 5 percent share reflects a valuation of energy inputs at their primary, preprocessed stage of production or at their point of importation. That is, the upgraded value of energy inputs that occurs as domestic petroleum is converted into refinery outputs (including specialty items for the petrochemical industry), or as coal is converted into electricity (with a vastly higher unit value in Btu terms), is not reflected in the value estimates in table 2-4. We estimate that (in terms of purchasers' prices) the stepped-up value of end-use energy products or services consumed amounted, very approximately, to $200 billion, or 12 percent of the GNP in 1976.[5] This, of course, represents quite a significant share of national output. On the basis of the energy content of fuels and power delivered to users (the 59.60 quads shown under "Net energy consumption" in table 2-2), this works out to roughly $3.50 per million Btu. When related to the larger total gross input total of 74 quads, the figure falls to $2.75 per million Btu. A calculation can also be made about the relative importance of expenditures for household fuels and power, along with gasoline and oil for personal transportation, within the aggregate of personal consumption expenditures for all goods and services.

---

[5] The quantities used in the calculation came from the U.S. Department of the Interior, Bureau of Mines Release (March 14, 1977). Prices were taken from a variety of publications, including those of the National Coal Association, the Edison Electric Institute, and the Federal Energy Administration.

For 1976, this share worked out to between 8 and 9 percent—the precise figure depending on the different definitions of personal consumption that one can employ.

Measures of Effective Energy Use

A final dimension of energy-use measurement concerns the extent to which gross energy resources absorbed by the economy actually remain, after successive stages of transformation and handling, to provide effective heat or power at the ultimate point of end-use application. Although we shall revert to this topic, in both its macro and micro aspects, in ensuing parts of this book, a few initial remarks may be helpful.

The main point to be made is that, except for the restricted domain of thermodynamics, there is no clear-cut measure of energy efficiency. By "efficiency" we are here referring to a relationship (energy in divided by energy out) indicating how much energy is squeezed out of every unit of energy input. (The broader question of how much energy is needed to provide a given quantity of useful services or economic output is discussed in chapters 3 and 5.)

A few examples illustrate how different stages of energy use can give rise to different estimates of energy efficiency. Consider the time when coal predominated as a domestic heating fuel. Under those conditions, relatively few of the "gross" Btus survived the losses that were associated with handling and burning coal in open grates to provide effective comfort heating. Many homes constructed in recent years feature electric heating. In these, there is a virtually 100 percent effective conversion of that electricity into space heating, but only after large losses have occurred in the conversion of power-plant fuel inputs into electricity, and additional losses have been incurred in the transmission and distribution of that electricity.

In that connection, we have already introduced the notion of net energy consumption, which differs from gross energy inputs by the subtraction of losses associated with electric-power production. In table 2-2, for example, we saw that in 1976 gross energy inputs required a downward reduction of 20 percent to reflect this adjustment. It is thus no accident, incidentally, that conservation strategists single out dampened electric-power consumption (so as to avoid the huge associated thermal losses) as a prime objective. Where functions frequently served by electricity— such as in the heating of buildings or the providing of low-grade heat for industrial activities—can be technically and economically met by more efficient substitute means, that conservation goal is legitimately given particular emphasis. Lovins's surmise that only around 65 percent of current electricity usage in the United States involves functions whose dependence is "obligatorily electrical" bears on that issue, although the basis for that minimum electricity estimate is open to doubt and the feasibility of approaching it is questionable.[6] Another proposed means of reducing the prevailing inefficiency in electricity conversion is through cogeneration schemes making productive use of the waste heat released, as will be discussed in chapter 5.

For a more thorough accounting of the relationship between gross inputs and effective use of the different energy forms—solids, gases, liquids, electricity—in principal applications, just consider the use of liquids for transportation, where less than 25 percent of the primary energy input is realized as work output. For natural gas in industrial activity, the effective end-use energy factor averages much higher—approximately 80 percent. Petroleum and natural gas in residential activities (largely space and hot-water heating) show efficiencies ranging from 60 to 70 percent. A recent attempt to quantify the rate of effective energy use for the year 1975 suggests that, overall, approximately 40 percent of the raw energy resources absorbed by the economy are ultimately transformed into effective work. For the household–commercial sector, industry, and transportation, the respective figures are 42, 44, and 23 percent.[7]

There is no way, in this brief account, to have spanned all economic and thermodynamic concepts of energy efficiency. For example, another recent calculation of nationwide energy consumption puts the rate of effective use at the lower figure of about 33 percent.[8] While the higher effective-use rate of 40 percent is a kind of engineering standard which, in homes, for example, reflects the operating characteristics of a properly maintained oil furnace, the lower figure tries to reflect the prevalence of poor maintenance or losses through leaky walls. Or, for cars, it reflects

[6] Amory B. Lovins, "Scale, Centralization, and Electrification in Energy Systems," in Oak Ridge Associated Universities, *Future Strategies for Energy Development* (Oak Ridge, Tenn., Oak Ridge Associated Universities, 1977) p. 101.

[7] Jack Alterman, *The Energy/Real Gross Domestic Product Ratio—An Analysis of Changes During the 1966–1970 Period in Relation to Long-run Trends,* Bureau of Economic Analysis Staff Paper No. 30 (Washington, D.C., U.S. Department of Commerce, October 1977).

[8] Earl Cook, "The National Energy Future: Problems and Policy Issues," in *Middle- and Long-term Energy Policies and Alternatives,* Part I, Hearings before the Subcommittee on Energy and Power, House Committee on Interstate and Foreign Commerce (Washington, D.C., GPO, 1976) app. sect., p. 13.

not only the energy conversion characteristics of an engine and associated equipment (as in the higher figure) but also attempts to account for additional energy lost between the drive shaft and actual motion of the car.

Still another recent analysis is conducted in terms of "second-law" efficiency,[9] where the prevailing consumption of energy is compared to the amount needed if identical tasks were met with feasible, but more energy-efficient, technology. Substitution of heat pumps for electric-resistance elements in space heating is one such example. For the economy as a whole, the authors' estimates suggest an overall second-law efficiency of around 15 percent. Since, in this particular analysis, certain characteristics describing the task in question are not altered, a redefinition or modification of the task itself, for example, heating a tightly rather than a poorly insulated home, would lower the figure to even below 15 percent. Part of the challenge for conservation is to explore ways of raising such estimates of poor energy performance.

[9] Marc Ross and Robert Williams, *Energy and Economic Growth,* a study prepared for the Subcommittee on Energy, Joint Economic Committee, 95 Cong., 1 sess. (Washington, D.C., GPO, 1977).

3 The Interrelationship of Energy Consumption, Economic Growth, and Conservation

The Key Issues

Energy use and economic activity are inescapably connected. Energy utilized in productive activity is clearly an essential ingredient in economic growth; and, in turn, the proceeds of growth and rising income permit the consumption of energy-associated creature comforts and other services. Fuels and power are involved in mechanized industry or farming, in the transport of freight or passengers, and in the illumination and heating of commercial and residential structures; in short, energy is clearly indispensable to the welfare of a modern industrial society. Energy is related both to levels of economic development and to changes over time. A more difficult question remains as to whether that relationship is intractable or elastic. Specifically, could we accommodate our country's present gross national product (GNP)—both in size and composition—with a substantially lower energy consumption? How much lower—and under what circumstances? What are the promises and pitfalls of energy conservation? And even more pertinent to the current debate, what range of growth rates for energy consumption might accompany an assumed growth rate for the GNP in the decades ahead? In this chapter, we want to provide the broad historical, conceptual, and comparative international setting within which to illuminate these issues. The discussion paves the way for the projections found in chapters 5 and 6.

A Review of Historical Trends

National output and energy demand may be highly correlated in the sense that movements in the latter are strongly associated with changes in the former. Nevertheless, a given rate of GNP growth need not signify an equivalent or even a near equivalent growth rate in energy demand. That quantitative relationship describes what, in statistical language, is referred to as the *regression coefficient*. In the relationship between energy and the GNP, a regression coefficient of 0.8, for example, means that—with other things unchanged—an 8 percent increase in energy demand accompanies a 10 percent increase in the GNP.

In order to give some real life content to these thoughts, suppose that one is probing the range of future expansion paths for fuel and power that might accompany growth of the overall economy. It is decided, based on an awareness of past trends, that at the very least the growth rate for consumption of energy resources will match the prospective rate of growth for the nationwide economy. These speculations, which took place in the mid-1920s, have turned out—forty years later—to have been noticeably off the mark. The GNP increased at an average annual rate of 3.1 percent; energy consumption increased only 80 percent as fast, at 2.5 percent per year. That is, there was a yearly decline in the level of the energy–GNP ratio of 0.6 percent (see figure 3-1). Had the economy and energy use grown commensurately, the country, toward the end of the 1960s, would have been consuming 17 quads more than it consumed in the 1920s, or 8.5 million barrels of oil equivalent per day. This raises the interesting question of whether conservation impulses (and results) are an entirely unprecedented phenomenon. Certainly, to the extent that more productive use of energy resources contributed to this degree of energy–GNP "decoupling," this would have been a conservation effect. The reasons for its realization, however, need not have stemmed from "conscious" conservation impulses. (See pages 96–101 for further discussion on conservation and its meaning.)

This momentary and obviously much compressed excursion into economic history is instructive. It serves as a useful reminder that there has hardly ever been a lockstep relationship between energy and the GNP—either at the time when energy growth was rising relatively fast, as it was toward the end of the nineteenth and first two decades of the twentieth century; or when its growth was disproportionately less, as has been characteristic of much of the ensuing period. Figure 3-1 tracks this long-term development.

Apparently failing to recognize this clear-cut evidence of at least some flexibility in the relationship between the growth of energy consumption and aggregate economic growth, some persons see no possibility of energy growth trailing the growth in national output in the years ahead. One ex-

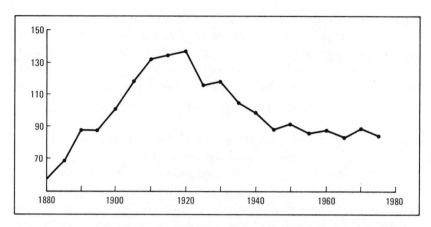

Figure 3-1. The Energy–real GNP ratio, 1880–1975 (index numbers, 1900 = 100). Fuelwood is excluded from the energy series. Its inclusion would produce a much more flattened trend during the first several decades plotted. This figure is based on data from Sam H. Schurr, Bruce C. Netschert, Vera F. Eliasberg, Joseph Lerner, and Hans H. Landsberg, *Energy in the American Economy, 1850–1975: Its History and Prospects* (Baltimore, Md., Johns Hopkins University Press for Resources for the Future, 1960); and from Jack Alterman, "The Energy/Real Gross Domestic Product Ratio," Bureau of Economic Analysis Staff Report (U.S. Department of Commerce, 1977). [Figure courtesy of Sam H. Schurr, "Energy, Economic Growth, and Human Welfare," *EPRI Journal* (May 1978) p. 16.]

pression of the view that energy consumption and output are activities almost rigidly linked emerges from a publication of the Chase Manhattan Bank. Ignoring the progressive long-term decline in the U.S. energy–output ratio after the mid-1920s, the bank not long ago asserted that the roughly parallel trend of more recent years augurs an enduring constancy in this relationship. The report states that "There is no sound, proven basis for believing a billion dollars of GNP can be generated with less energy in the future."[1] Nor is the bank's view an isolated one. In a more recent statement Philip Powers, then professor of nuclear engineering at Purdue University, writing in the newsletter of the Energy Engineering Center, makes the assumption that the ratio of energy consumption to national output will not change. He adds (inaccurately, as is clear from the foregoing) that "It is a remarkable fact that a change in GNP (measured in

[1] John G. Winger and Carolyn A. Nielsen, "Energy, the Economy, and Jobs," *Energy Report from Chase* (New York, Chase Manhattan Bank, September 1976) pp. 2–3.

constant price) is accompanied by almost an identical change in energy consumption."[2]

The behavior of the energy–output ratio since the 1920s is particularly illuminating from a conservation perspective. For the downward trend in the ratio occurred in spite of the steady decline in real energy prices which, all other things being equal, would have prompted an intensification of energy use rather than the reverse. But clearly, all other things were not equal. This was a period during which a number of forces acted, in their net effect, to dampen the U.S. aggregate energy growth rate. There are three factors which are worthy of our particular attention: (1) the composition of national output; (2) trends in energy intensity; and (3) the significance of changing energy forms. In the first case, energy consumption per unit of GNP is affected because the nation shifts its emphasis among energy-using activities. In the second instance the variation in consumption results from an increase or decrease in the respective energy requirements of some important components of the national product. The final factor relates to changes in the role of energy itself which follow from the form in which it is being used. Even though there are overlapping strands among these three factors, each has enough distinctive features to justify its individual treatment. Any one of the three may result in either an increase or a decrease in energy consumption per unit of GNP—which is why their net combined effect during any period of interest should be considered after each has been analyzed by itself. Then we can devote special attention to a fourth interrelated factor in the complex equation— price developments—and go on to ponder the meaning of all these lessons from history.

Composition of National Output

What have been the energy-use implications of the changing U.S. economy during roughly the past century?

In an RFF study published some years ago, this was addressed in some depth.[3] During the first half century, the relative shift from an agrarian

---

[2] "A letter from the Director of the Energy Engineering Center," Purdue University (February 1978).

[3] Sam H. Schurr, Bruce C. Netschert, Vera F. Eliasberg, Joseph Lerner, and Hans H. Landsberg, *Energy in the American Economy, 1850–1975: Its History and Prospects* (Baltimore, Md., The Johns Hopkins University Press for Resources for the Future, 1960).

society to one establishing a heavy industrial base signified a proportionately rapid growth of sectors heavily linked to using a lot of energy.
Although this trend coexisted with other forces whose separate effects
cannot be entirely sorted out, its presence was pronounced enough to give
rise to the increasing energy–GNP ratio during the last quarter of the nineteenth century and first several decades of the twentieth.[4] By contrast, the
decades following World War I, during which the ratio declined, spanned
a period during which America's heavy industrialization phase was beginning to subside—a process implying some moderation in energy use.

Although the observed long-term development in the energy–GNP
ratio is in accord with this gradual structural transformation of the American economy, our understanding of economic history is not so complete
as to depict these connections in a clear-cut fashion. For example, the
fact that the ratio of manufacturing growth to overall economic growth
was greater in the first half century than in the ensuing period would have
been as consistent with a mere slowdown in the rise of the energy–GNP
ratio as with the reversal that actually occurred. Another common, and
perhaps overdrawn, supposition is that in recent decades there has been
an "explosion" of the services sector of the economy and a consequent
suppression of the extent of energy demand. Thus, the services component of national output has risen—from a 40 percent share in 1929 to
around 46 percent in the last few years.[5] But most of that relative increase
dates from the mid-fifties when, paradoxically, the long-term decline in
the energy–GNP ratio began leveling off (see figure 3-1). This observation points up the need to probe into the variety of activities that comprise
the services aggregate. Some of these—say, hotel bookings and visits to
Disney World—are clearly allied to activities (motoring, airplane trips,
and so forth) that are very energy intensive. Other services components
(for example, education, repair functions, and certain types of entertain-
ment) are clearly less demanding of energy.

Our discussion underscores the importance of considering the structural or compositional phenomena shaping the long-term relationship
between energy consumption and economic growth. That perspective
offers a useful but, at best, limited insight. It is necessary to probe other
explanatory factors as well.

---

[4] This trend is based on energy data excluding fuelwood. Inclusion of fuelwood
would noticeably dampen the trend in the ratio to the 1920s.

[5] Executive Office of the President, *Economic Report of the President* (Washington, D.C., GPO, January 1978) p. 265.

Trends in Energy Intensity

A variety of factors can bring about changes in the amount of energy that underlies a specified final product entering the marketplace. Technological advance in a particular production process, say, steel making, may permit economizing on the energy needed to yield a unit of output. But it is also possible that a change in energy transformation itself—that is, economies realized as energy is converted from one form to another or as it undergoes successive stages of processing—contributes to overall changes in energy intensity.

History illustrates the operations of such forces at work. Perhaps the preeminent case is that of electricity, whose "thermal efficiency" (or "heat rate") improved substantially over the years. In the early 1960s, it took less than half as much coal to generate a kilowatt-hour of electric power as it had taken in 1925. Such an improvement in efficiency substantially blunted the effect of the steadily rising share of primary energy consumption converted to electricity. That share has grown from around 8 percent in 1920 to approximately 30 percent in recent years. In other words, in spite of the "penalty" inherent in converting (at today's heat rate) three units of raw energy resources into one unit of electricity, the doubling in efficiency over the years—cushioned the effect of increased dependence on electricity. This cushioning was apart from the unique properties of electricity as an energy form, a topic which will be discussed below.

Progressively rising efficiency in electricity generation thus supported or reinforced the long-term decline in the energy–GNP ratio. Interestingly, a leveling off in that improvement, dating from the early 1960s, was followed, within several years, by the start of a five-year *upswing* in the energy–GNP ratio.

Again, however, diverse trends and crosscurrents complicate the job of analysis. In the industrial sector of the economy, for example, even as the long-term decline in the nationwide energy–GNP ratio gave way to a sidewise movement in the mid-1950s and increased in the latter part of the 1960s, and as improvements in electricity-conversion efficiency became stalled, energy intensity within numerous manufacturing branches moved unmistakably downward.[6] Chemicals and paper are clear-cut cases in point. During the twenty-five years following World War II, the energy

---

[6] The Conference Board, *Energy Consumption in Manufacturing,* A Report to the Energy Policy Project of the Ford Foundation (Cambridge, Mass., Ballinger, 1974) pp. 20–21.

consumed per dollar of value added in all manufacturing declined at the rate of about 1.5 percent per year.

The Significance of Changing Energy Forms

In addition to the dual questions of compositional characteristics and energy-intensity factors, one needs to pay explicit attention to surrounding developments which bear closely on both questions. One such development has to do with the changing distribution and functional role of the different energy forms being utilized—solids, liquids, gas, and electricity. The shift from coal to oil, for example, did not merely signify that given energy-using functions—say, operation of steam boilers—could now be fueled by an alternative energy source. Insofar as it supported the development of an entirely new industry—motorized transport—the emergence of petroleum as a widely available new energy form in a sense helped generate its own demand. Growth of motorized transport illustrates a major change in the pattern of economic and social activity which was not simply an autonomous force with important energy consequences; it was itself very much impelled by energy-resource developments and energy-related technological change.

The importance of the form in which energy is delivered is graphically illustrated, once again, by the historical example of electricity—a form of energy whose development permitted economies of operation which pre-existing energy forms could not come close to matching.[7] A significant, but not well-recognized, aspect of electrification was in its effect on the overall productive efficiency of the economy, particularly in the manufacturing sector. Historical examination of the organization of production within manufacturing shows that the growth of electrification permitted the laying out and organization of productive processes within the factory in a manner that would have been altogether impossible during the period when factories were powered by prime movers, with shafts and belting carrying mechanical power to the various points of use. Electricity, which made possible the use of electric motors to which the power was delivered by wire, paved the way for a major reorganization of the sequence and layout of production. The new arrangements—situating heavy energy uses

[7] Much of the following discussion is adapted from Sam H. Schurr and Joel Darmstadter, "Some Observations on Energy and Economic Growth," in Oak Ridge Associated Universities, *Future Strategies for Energy Development* (Oak Ridge, Tenn., Oak Ridge Associated Universities, 1977) pp. 280–297.

close to the prime mover—were more in keeping with the logic of the productive process than were the more rigid locational requirements imposed by a system of shafts and belting. This was a factor of enormous importance in the growth of manufacturing productivity and thereby in the productivity of the total economy—resulting in the greater output of goods and services per unit of *all* input factors; labor, capital and energy. Although the increases in labor and capital productivity have been well recognized and are critical aspects of U.S. economic development and growth, the concurrent improvement in the overall efficiency of energy consumption is commented on far less frequently.

Together with thermal efficiency improvement in generation of electricity, general improvements in production efficiency contributed to the decline in the amount of raw energy required per unit of national output. This occurred despite the heat losses involved in electric generation, already referred to, and despite the fact that electricity is, in certain particular applications, less efficient thermally than alternative energy forms.

Analogous to electricity, the internal combustion engine, powered by liquid fuels, permitted the substantial mechanization of agriculture, which played so great a part in the rising productivity of the U.S. economy. Similarly, the growth of truck transportation made it possible for industry to move away from sites dictated by the location of railroad facilities or waterways—another development which served to broaden the opportunities for enhanced productive efficiency.

Railroad operation, itself, was another major beneficiary of the era of liquid fuels. The virtual elimination of coal-burning steam locomotives and their replacement by much less energy-intensive, diesel-driven units signified another major step toward reducing the ratio of energy to national output. In railroad freight operations, diesel oil was utilized about six times as efficiently as coal, and it has been estimated that the coal-diesel substitution in railroad freight traffic alone meant a "saving" in energy consumption that accounted for roughly 4 percent of national energy use in 1955.[8]

Finally, the liquid fuels era led to the widespread use of the automobile. In this case, however, the dominant consequence was the effect on lifestyles and residential patterns—fundamentally altering the patterns of life of ordinary people through far greater mobility—rather than the overall energy-economy relationship. Indeed, for many years fuel performance of automobiles deteriorated steadily, while substantial environmental

---

[8] Schurr and coauthors, *Energy in the American Economy*, pp. 178–179.

damage was resulting from use of the automobile. (The future automotive outlook will be discussed in chapter 5.)

In summary, the important changes in the composition of energy output toward the more flexible forms of electricity and liquids have tended to transcend thermal efficiency considerations. These changes have made possible shifts in production techniques and locations within industry, agriculture, and transportation that greatly enhanced the growth of national output and productivity. In enhancing the growth of productivity for the overall economy—that is, the efficiency with which labor and capital are employed—the changes in the composition of energy output have, in a roundabout way, also enhanced the efficiency with which energy itself has been employed as a factor of production, and so constituted a force toward a declining energy–GNP ratio.

Price Developments

Another element in the historical record which deserves review concerns long-term trends in the price of energy and energy-associated products. As mentioned earlier, the decline—over some three decades—in the national energy–output ratio occurred even while most energy prices moved steadily downward in real terms. The usual economic expectation is that energy intensity would rise, not decline, when prices are falling. This does not, of course, prove that trends in energy use do not accord with ordinary economic expectations. Intensity of energy use (relative to the GNP) might have diminished still further (that is, greater improvement in energy efficiency might have been encouraged and achieved) if relative energy prices had declined less or had risen.

It is also conceivable, however, that a less drastic energy price decline might have been accompanied by a more slowly falling energy–GNP ratio than occurred—rather than the more rapidly falling ratio which economic logic would dictate. To appreciate that hypothetical outcome, consider the possibility that the price-induced encouragement of energy use which actually took place resulted in productivity increases which were related to energy-based technology.

For quite apart from energy prices, technology developed its own momentum. Even a precipitous fall in coal prices could not have sustained steam railways, given the virtues of diesel fuel and technology. A constant or rising gasoline price might have dampened—but could not have arrested—the growth of motorization, given the wider perceived benefits

Table 3-1. Trends in Real Energy Prices, Selected Items and Years, 1925–77
(index numbers, 1967 = 100)

| Year | A. Prices to personal consumers | | | | B. Composite fossil fuel price at primary stage |
	Electricity	Gas	Fuel oil	Gasoline	
1925	262.1	NA	NA	NA	
1930	248.8	NA	NA	NA	
1940	227.9	168.8	96.4	114.5	
1950	125.9	101.4	100.7	99.6	130.0
1955	118.7	101.0	107.2	104.2	123.9
1960	112.5	110.1	100.3	104.3	115.1
1965	104.9	105.4	99.9	100.4	102.1
1970	91.3	93.3	94.0	90.8	88.3
1971	80.2	95.8	95.7	87.6	98.7
1972	94.9	97.6	93.1	85.9	96.8
1973	93.8	96.1	101.1	88.7	105.0
1974	99.9	97.4	144.2	108.3	172.4
1975	103.6	108.7	143.1	106.0	184.6
1976	104.2	118.0	145.0	104.3	
1977	104.3	131.8	154.4	103.7	

Sources: The panel A series are all components of the Bureau of Labor Statistics (BLS) consumer price index (CPI). The figures shown were deflated by the overall CPI. Data were obtained from Bureau of the Census, *Historical Statistics of the United States: Colonial Times to 1970* (Washington, D.C., GPO, 1975); BLS, *Handbook of Labor Statistics* (Washington, D.C., GPO, 1975 and 1977 editions); and directly from the BLS. Note that apart from underlying price changes, electricity and gas price movements may result from consumers shifting between rate classes depending on volume purchased. Gasoline data refer to a weighted average of premium and regular and include taxes.

The panel B series was obtained from U.S. Department of the Interior, *Energy Perspectives 2* (Washington, D.C., GPO, 1976). The data, referring to point of production or importation, represent current values converted to constant 1972 price levels by means of the implicit GNP deflator, subsequently shifted to a base of 1967 = 100 for consistency with panel A.

conferred by its availability to society. Had it occurred, such a lessening demand for gasoline (spurred, conceivably, by an earlier concern with more fuel-efficient cars) would have disclosed a "price effect," even while demand growth dominated the picture. More paradoxically, a rising trend in electricity prices might not have provided the same encouragement to electrification of industrial processes as did falling prices, and thus price rise might have yielded a higher energy–GNP ratio than was the case historically. It is, of course, one of the vexing tasks of energy projections to extract from a history of price declines the basis for judging the demand response to possible price increases in the future.

A brief look at that history is in order. Selected data appear in table 3-1 and are plotted in figure 3-2. One panel of figures relates to prices of various energy forms delivered to consumers; the other, to fossil fuels at

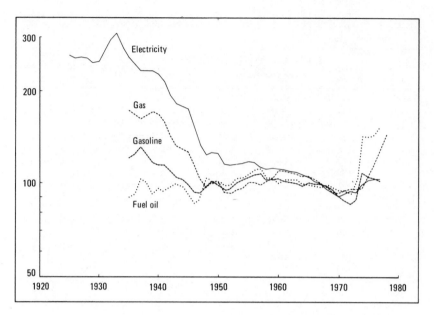

Figure 3-2. Trends in real energy price to personal consumers, 1925–77 (index numbers of energy prices deflated by consumer price index, 1967 = 100).

point of production (or importation). In both cases, the series of figures refers to relative (or real) energy prices, that is, after correction has been made for changes in the overall price level. Note how, in the last full preembargo year (1972), real energy prices at retail were below pre–World War II levels—substantially so in the case of electricity, gas, and motor gasoline. The index of real fossil fuel prices recorded an annual rate of decline of 1.3 percent yearly between 1950–72.

No one desires energy per se, of course, but only as the wherewithal for satisfying one or another amenity. Thus, even a pronounced fall in real energy prices could have accompanied restrained energy use if the real price of energy-associated goods and services rose sharply. (In Western Europe, low gasoline consumption is conditioned not only by high fuel taxes, but also by steep levies on car purchases, weight, and registration.) In fact, however, prices for such important energy-using consumer durables as autos and household appliances show a long-term trend no higher, and in some cases, even lower than the price of consumer purchases overall. Between 1950 and 1976, the average annual percentage change in real price (that is, deflated by the price index for all consumer purchases) was motor vehicles, -0.5; household appliances, -2.9; and radios and TVs, -4.3.[9]

Most of the 1960–70 decade was still marked by stability in real energy prices. That situation began to change toward the end of the decade for some energy forms and, of course, changed drastically following the sharp rise in OPEC oil prices in 1973–74. In the latter period real gasoline prices rose 22 percent and heating oil by 43 percent. Residential natural gas prices rose sharply after 1974, while electricity prices have risen moderately throughout the period. Thus, the last decade has seen a dramatic turnabout from earlier, long-term price experience. Note, however, that following the big increases in 1974, real gasoline prices proceeded to drop slightly, and heating oil prices have risen just a bit. One can conjecture about how the postembargo stimulus toward conservation might have been reinforced by *sustained* price pressures. Overall, as table 3-1 shows, price increases at the consumer level have been more muted than at the primary level.

Pondering the Lessons of History

Our reconnaissance of historical developments, though far from exhaustive, leaves little doubt that the long-term aggregative relationship between energy and economic growth evolves from the interplay of diverse and complex underlying forces—operating both within the energy sector and the economy as a whole. The picture is replete with paradoxes: for example, a long-run decline exists in the energy–output ratio even while declining real prices and the dual processes of electrification and motorization might have been expected, in the absence of more subtle factors at work, to increase the ratio.

If, with all these underlying crosscurrents, the overall energy–output ratio nevertheless shows some fairly smooth and systematic behavior, that fact may be useful in speculating on future energy–economy developments. If a given level and compositional content of the national product can be economically accommodated with *less* energy rather than more, that possibility very likely spells a social benefit to the country. However, energy–output ratios—abstractions, after all—can easily mask the pro-

[9] Data from U.S. Department of Commerce, *The National Income and Product Accounts of the United States 1929–1974* (Washington, D.C., GPO, 1977); *Survey of Current Business* (July 1977); and *Economic Report of the President* (January 1978).

found role played by changing energy systems in shaping the economic character of the country and society.

Energy developments, as we have seen, have been a dynamic historical influence in the economic growth and development of an industrial economy. Many of the fundamental features of contemporary Western society have had their origins, at least in part, in developments of unique energy systems. To be sure, numerous effects that have been produced are negative rather than beneficial in nature, making it essential that no future effort is spared to achieve environmentally benign energy technologies. But it is essential also that we not lose sight of the benefits in terms of improved living standards, decreased drudgery at work and at home, and greater mobility of all kinds—not just physical but also societal—that are the result of the dynamic thrust given by energy technology to socio-economic conditions in the industrialized world.

The Role of Conservation

Our historical review confirms that there is no defined, ironclad linkage, over the long run, between energy and economic growth. Changes in this relationship were seen to be rooted in a variety of factors. Some of these had to do with basic transformation of the economy. Others involved more productive use of energy resources, as in enhanced electricity-generating efficiency. Still others straddled multiple factors; in a sense improved rail freight ton mileage per Btu, while of course representing more productive energy use, resulted not so much from conservation impulses as from the wider confluence of two historical phenomena—large-scale development of liquid fuel resources and development of diesel technology.

As we proceed to hypothesize alternative energy consumption paths for the future (see chapters 5 and 6), the diversity of interacting factors that have influenced past energy demand growth ought to remind us that it will be impossible to anticipate the many influential circumstances which are going to occur within the energy sector or the surrounding economy. But, even if we cannot hope to comprehend all of the possibilities which will turn out to have been important, one key element in the analysis of future growth of energy demand deserves more disciplined and focused attention than it is commonly accorded. And that is the topic of energy conservation.

Defining Conservation

Contemporary discussions of conservation arise in a number of contexts. In its ethical, equity, or environmental dimensions, conservation has to do with moderation as an inherently worthy value or as an act dedicated to distributive justice in the face of resource limitations and environmental constraints. A thermodynamicist views energy conservation and efficiency within the bounds of physical laws and processes. In its economic meaning, with which we are largely concerned in this chapter, conservation of energy signifies just that: the most economic application of energy—in its joint use with other resources—in a given process or activity, whether in the production of goods and services or in their use by ultimate consumers. An aluminum manufacturer may be able, on balance, to lower costs by introducing a process that lowers the energy requirement of an ingot produced. A homeowner may succeed in reducing heat losses through beefed-up insulation whose amortized cost is less than savings on the utility bill. Both instances satisfy the definition of conservation. It is important to emphasize that, in order to achieve conservation, it is not sufficient to point to reduced energy use per unit of output or activity. It is necessary to show how such a change conforms to overall cost-effectiveness—a calculation depending on the joint use of all input factors (energy and nonenergy) and their cost in a given task.

It is not essential to this formulation that conservation occurs exclusively within the domain of private markets, although that is undoubtedly the predominant context. Legislated fuel-economy standards for passenger automobiles illustrate an alternative to purely private decision making (or to the tax route, another form of public intervention). But even mandated energy-use characteristics cannot, without subordinating welfare effects, ignore cost-effectiveness criteria. A provisional fuel economy standard (since revised) for light-duty trucks and vans by the National Highway Traffic Safety Administration was criticized by the President's Council on Wage and Price Stability as necessitating truck weight reductions that could imperil profitability for many truckers.[10]

On a nationwide level, as we saw earlier, energy consumed per unit of the GNP can, of course, decline both because important components of the GNP require less energy per unit output or because the nation shifts

---

[10] See Comments of the Council on Wage and Price Stability, Executive Office of the President, Docket No. FE-77-05, Proposed Fuel Economy Standards for Nonpassenger Automobiles (31 January 1978).

away from energy-intensive activities, such as less heavy manufacturing or more of certain kinds of personal services. Many such shifts, however, occur obviously for reasons unrelated to conservation impulses. Cultural activities, for example, are desired independently of the fact that their low energy content makes them a "good buy." Other shifts may be more directly attributable to the conservation-induced effect of higher real energy costs. For example, higher prices for those products of the petrochemical industry whose energy-resource content is not easily altered may impel users to seek out substitute products.

Economic Effects of Energy Constraints

In short, conservation, representing monetary savings which would be forgone by doing nothing, ensures a level of welfare above that implied in its absence. But it *does* seem likely that, even with conservation, welfare tends nonetheless to be less than it was before an event, such as a drastic price increase, that prompted a change in an energy-using activity. (An exception would be a price rise brought about by a previously "uncosted," welfare-eroding externality—say, lead emissions in gasoline consumption.) A warehousing operation conducted under economically optimal conditions may face new choices in the balance of advantage between, say, the use of forklift trucks and conveyers, on the one hand, and the use of laborers, on the other, once increased energy prices shift the cost relationship between these two inputs. The enterprise may conceivably conclude that the new circumstances argue for employing more labor, less energy. But the economic attractiveness of the operation, while maximized at the new conditions, may be below its preexisting level. To the extent that demand for the resource being substituted in place of energy creates a scarcity of its own, the costs of adjusting to energy constraints may be compounded.

Thus, the process of adjusting to higher energy costs *will* occur at the expense of at least some decline in the level of output. The relevant consideration is whether more economic resources are sacrificed by attempting difficult substitutions of nonenergy for energy resources or by attempting to absorb higher real energy costs.[11]

[11] Consider the extreme case where higher real energy costs must be fully absorbed. In chapter 2, we noted that consumption of primary energy resources, in 1976, amounted to approximately 5 percent of the GNP. If, in order to meet, say, a 100 percent rise in energy prices, resources had to be shifted from nonenergy sectors of the economy, the country would suffer a 5 percent loss in the GNP.

Therefore, the point is not to establish definitively whether energy is or is not substitutable. That would lead, at best, to a highly idealized picture. We can all think of processes and activities that veer toward one or the other camp. A person's relationship to his power mower, if not intimate, is virtually fixed; indeed, two individuals coupled to one mower will not make an easier assault on the lawn. (A more fuel-efficient engine might, however, make a difference; that would be a case of substituting capital for energy.) Near the other end of the spectrum, there is our earlier ware-housing example, which at least raises the possibility of choice as to an energy-labor tradeoff. The uncertainty centers on how, on balance, these countless instances work out for the economy as a whole.

In their treatment of this issue, economists focus particularly on a parameter known as the "elasticity of substitution." Technically, the elasticity of substitution describes what happens to the ratio of nonenergy inputs to energy inputs when there is a specified change in the ratio of energy prices to other prices. In effect, this measure—which, in simplified terms, is commonly equated to the price elasticity of demand for energy—provides a basis for judging the relative ease or difficulty of substituting other resources for energy in economic activity. A high elasticity of sub-stitution implies that a shift away from energy to other inputs may be achieved with relatively little loss of real output. A low elasticity reflects a much stickier situation, where substitution for energy is difficult and where higher energy prices or energy supply constraints may inflict meas-urable damage to the economy.

Although we do not operate in complete ignorance about these rela-tionships—mid-range assumptions being probably more realistic than extremes—little empirical research has been performed to estimate elas-ticities of substitution that could impart confidence to those making energy projections and those engaged in energy policy making. Engineering, combined with economic analyses (such as those found in chapters 5 and 6) go some distance in strengthening our ability to judge the degree of economic resiliency to changes on the energy side.

Why is it important to keep this aspect of energy-economy interactions in mind when speculating on the future course of energy demand and on the economic environment within which that demand takes place? Con-ventionally, one leads up to a projection of future energy consumption by first specifying the GNP and its principal underlying, macroeconomic building blocks: population, labor force, employment, and productivity. A subsequent step is to analyze and calculate the amount—or ranges—of energy demand consistent with that initially postulated level of national output. However, this approach neglects consideration of whether that specified level of output is itself attainable given a constraint in energy such as to make it difficult to realize, say, the assumed rate of productivity growth. In other words, simply to assume the future national product as a given risks ignoring the *reverse feedback* effect of energy upon economic activity. Keeping in mind the elasticity of substitution at least alerts us to the fact that energy-economy interrelationships should be viewed as a two-way, rather than simply unidirectional, process.[12]

What emerges from this discussion, with respect to conservation, is that *some* negative economic impact resulting from energy constraints (induced through higher costs or other reasons) is almost inescapable. Thus, conservation does not justify indifference to higher real energy costs or to energy rationing or curtailment policies since it principally cushions the severity of their impact. The task for economic and technological research is to improve our ability to establish reasonable bounds to those effects.

In this context, finally, one must express skepticism of ideas—sometimes made on this issue—seeking to promote labor substitution for energy as if that were almost an end in itself. To be sure, if one were to assume long-run, chronic unemployment in the United States, a policy to deliberately replace energy with labor might represent a defensible social program, in spite of the price paid in lost productivity and potential economic output. Under most other circumstances, however, such a strategy seems mildly bizarre, ignoring, as it does, the bedrock importance of labor productivity growth to the growth in overall economic well-being. It is as if an agricultural energy policy appropriate, say, to China's condition of capital scarcity and labor abundance (that is, encouragement of muscle power relative to inanimate energy per unit of output) was also the proper model for U.S. farming. (A related sort of confusion surrounds frequent discussions of "appropriate" energy-supply systems: the labor-intensive system that is sometimes favored can be an economic loser.)

Conservation and Life-styles

A discussion of the economic effects of conservation should recognize the demonstrable proposition that there are adaptations—mostly behavioral —that save energy with virtually no negative effects. This has "good

---

[12] For a fuller discussion, see Sam H. Schurr, "Modelling Energy-Economy Interactions," *Energy Policy* (June 1978) pp. 160–162.

news–bad news" aspects. The good-news part arises from the fact that a significant portion (nearly 30 percent) of U.S. energy demand occurs in the form of direct consumption for personal use—that is, for such things as passenger transportation and household fuels and power (see chapter 2). In this segment of energy consumption, one cannot really argue that any deceleration in the growth of energy use not governed by cost-effective criteria necessarily jeopardizes welfare and the economy. To be sure, there are gradations in the ease with which people comfortably change their way of doing things (and it is these blurred lines of demarcation that give rise to the problem noted below). Turning off lights in unoccupied rooms is no doubt regarded as less burdensome than, say, avoiding all automobile trips of less than one mile. Also, obviously some portion of personal energy use—for example, commuting to work—*is,* in a certain sense, a productive input into economic activity. Still, it is important to recognize that energy use in this sector is more nearly a proceed of income growth than it is a springboard for growth through its role in the productive process. Thus, energy constraints are potentially much more damaging to the business sector, whose 65 percent of yearly energy use goes to industry, freight transportation, agriculture, and commercial enterprises. (The balance of 5 percent goes to government.)

The bad-news side of the picture is that the personal segment of national energy use makes a very tempting target for the assertion of value judgments—that is, for prescribing "innocuous" behavioral and life-style changes that save energy. Cost-effective adaptation to the new energy price realities—through better insulation, use of heat pumps, more efficient appliances, and attention to solar possibilities—is one thing, but energy agendas that guarantee human satisfaction are quite another matter. These are probably as useful, or mischievous, as demonstrating that, nutritionally, the individual can thrive very nicely on a diet of cottage cheese and kidney beans. Self-indulgence in energy use, no less than in other pursuits, ought not to be denied the individual willing to incur the cost. Automatic transmissions in automobiles are about as necessary or unnecessary as beef, chicken, or strawberry cheesecake.

Intercountry Comparisons of Energy Use

Whether it is related to levels of per capita income, GNP or GDP, per capita energy consumption in a number of other advanced industrial societies falls considerably below that in the United States (see table 3-2

Table 3-2.   Per Capita Energy Consumption and Per Capita Gross Domestic Product in Nine Developed Countries, 1972

Country	Per capita			Index numbers ($U.S. = 100$)		
	GDP ($)	Energy (million Btu)	Energy–GDP ratio (thousand Btu/$)	Per capita		Energy/GDP ratio
				GDP	Energy	
United States	5,643	335.5	59.5	100	100	100
Canada	4,728	336.6	71.1	84	100	120
France	4,168	133.1	31.9	74	40	54
Germany	3,991	165.6	41.5	71	49	70
Italy	2,612	95.7	36.6	46	29	62
Netherlands	3,678	188.1	51.1	65	56	86
United Kingdom	3,401	152.9	45.0	60	46	76
Sweden	5,000	213.4	42.7	89	64	72
Japan	3,423	116.6	34.1	61	35	57

Note: The primary electricity (hydropower and nuclear) component of primary energy consumption is converted into Btus on the basis of fuel inputs that would have been required to generate the same quantity of electricity in fossil-fueled power plants, assuming a 35 percent efficiency rate. Foreign gross domestic products are expressed in dollars, by means of purchasing power basis of comparison rather than market exchange rates. The GDP, which excludes that portion of a country's GNP originating as investment income and other earnings within other countries, is the preferred basis for intercountry comparisons of energy and output. While the U.S. GDP is virtually identical to GNP, for some other countries, it may range up to 5 percent or so below GNP.

Source: Joel Darmstadter, Joy Dunkerley, and Jack Alterman, *How Industrial Societies Use Energy: A Comparative Analysis* (Baltimore, Md., Johns Hopkins University Press for Resources for the Future, 1977).

and figure 3-3). This phenomenon has prompted some persons to suggest that the United States could shift to drastically reduced levels of energy use without impinging on economic activity. A recently completed study at Resources for the Future found that intercountry variability in energy–GDP ratios is a much more complex affair than is implied in such assertions.[13] At the very least, any effort to probe into the reasons for differences in energy–GDP ratios benefits from a clear-cut differentiation between (1) the compositional and structural differences among countries; and (2) the energy-intensity differences that characterize the same (or similar) energy-using processes in the various countries. About 40 percent of the difference between the higher U.S. energy–GDP ratios and the lower foreign ratios can be attributed to such U.S. characteristics as the large size of the country and dispersed population patterns—both of

[13] Joel Darmstadter, Joy Dunkerley, and Jack Alterman, *How Industrial Societies Use Energy: A Comparative Analysis* (Baltimore, Md., Johns Hopkins University Press for Resources for the Future, 1977). For a discussion of the relationship between the GNP and the GDP, see note to table 3-2.

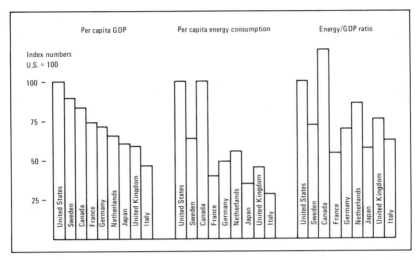

Figure 3-3. Energy-output relationships for nine selected countries, 1972.

which give rise to the long distances over which goods and people move —or our preference for large, single-family homes. It is a moot point whether these should be considered "energy-inefficient" attributes of U.S. life. Certainly, the availability of low-cost energy, compounded by governmental policies designed to keep certain energy prices *artificially* low, facilitated these evolving patterns. However, it is clear that they are by now deeply rooted features of American society that are not easily changed—at least not until current housing stock and settlement patterns have been replaced.

Parenthetically, the structural differences among countries can be illustrated by the fact that Canada, even allowing for its cold climate, uses more energy relative to income than we do. This comes about largely because of the country's specialization in such energy-intensive activities as metallurgy, pulp and paper manufacturing, and chemicals production, which in turn are based upon historically cheap hydropower and abundant natural resources.

About 60 percent of the energy–GDP difference between the United States and the typical Western European country arises from energy-intensity differences in particular applications. For example, the fuel economy of American automobiles has historically been very much poorer than that of European models, and the energy consumption per unit of output in a wide range of manufacturing enterprises is distinctly higher in the United States than in Europe. These contrasting energy intensities immediately force us to recognize that foreign energy prices—particularly for motor fuel as well as for other products—have traditionally been much higher. In part, these cost differences arise because European prices are held above the market level through taxation of energy (as well as of energy-using equipment); while in the United States, they have been held down through the use of controls. In both cases, social policy has intruded to help shape energy patterns, by deterring energy use in the first case and encouraging it in the second. When one takes account of these cost differences, high U.S. energy intensities need not, and frequently do not, imply *economically* inefficient or wasteful practices by a particular user or business enterprise, even though the country as a whole may suffer a resource loss through misguided pricing.

Incidentally, even where the data point to one country's energy use as being more effective than another's, that fact need not define the best attainable practice. Overall, U.S. freight transportation is less energy-intensive than Western Europe's. Yet, U.S. energy intensity in freight might be even lower if, for example, Interstate Commerce Commission regulations did not dictate an empty backhaul for a northbound trucker of Georgia pecans. Similarly, Swedish heating practices, impressive as they are, could be still further enhanced if overheated occupants of unmetered apartments served by district heating turned down the heat rather than using open windows to maintain their comfort level.

Do international comparisons point to the potential for significantly reduced energy consumption without sacrifice of economic welfare? It would certainly be presumptuous to conclude that we have nothing to learn from foreign energy-using practices, especially where these represent an adaptation to the high energy costs which, at least selectively, are now beginning to confront Americans. But we would delude ourselves if, in looking at aggregate energy–output ratios in other countries, we were to conclude that these provide a formula for painlessly lowered energy consumption in the United States.

Conclusion

One's reading of historical trends and intercountry comparisons does suggest that there is scope for long-term flexibility in the relationship between energy consumption and economic activity; and it may not be unreasonable to suppose that an upward course for relative energy prices, gradual changes in the socioeconomic complexion of the country, and technological developments might all contribute to depressing the energy growth rate below the economic growth rate, perhaps even substantially so. Conservation, properly defined, has a clear-cut role to play in this unfolding process, and its consequences are much more apt to be beneficial than harmful to society's economic welfare. But the basis for these thoughts—historical evidence, inference, and intuition—needs to be strengthened with more solid quantitative analysis. That will be the task of chapters 5 and 6.

4 How Will the U.S. Economy Develop?

Analyzing Energy Demand Within an Economic Perspective

Future energy-consumption trends and conservation potentials must be cast within a disciplined analytic and quantitative setting. An obvious and logical framework for establishing reasonable outer bounds to prospective energy-consumption levels and rates of change lies within the unfolding economic environment that will, in the decades ahead, confront the business community, households, and the public sector.

To link the possible range of future energy demands to the economic activity of the country does not mean that energy-consumption decisions are exclusively a matter of economic calculation—particularly among consumers responding to a variety of impulses and influences. Specifying a set of economic assumptions and projections as a way of approaching our task does not imply any unique and predetermined consequence for energy consumption. But those who wish to project future energy use can best do so in an economic framework (and more specifically, a social accounting framework) that includes consideration of income, expenditures, prices, and production. Such an economic framework, in turn, can only be constructed by considering more basic factors such as the future size of the population, size of work force, and some measure of productivity per worker. In other words, consumption of energy occurs within the context of an economic system that generates a flow of income and permits an objective expression of market preferences for goods and services—energy and otherwise.

To embody energy-demand futures within a gross national product (GNP) framework does oblige us to note one important caveat. To assume that income equals $100 and that this sum can be spent on $100 worth of goods and services (including energy) is to ignore the question of whether conditions of energy supply may be such as to preclude that level of economic activity from occurring in the first place. This issue of two-way energy-economy interactions is dealt with elsewhere (see pages 98–100 and 201–203). For now, however, we must be concerned with that first indispensable, if incomplete, step of depicting alternative, but credible, future pathways for the American economy.

The Procedure for Projecting the GNP

It is worth underscoring the caution with which one ought to use projections and the reliance that one can afford to put in them. Projections depict the estimated consequences of specified assumptions. Accept or reject the assumptions, and you accept or reject what flows from those assumptions. Assumptions can involve judgments regarding future policy decisions, they can refer to behavioral factors, or they can be technological in character—for example, as an element in projected productivity changes. To specify assumptions is not to buy the likelihood of the assumed event happening; rather, it is to explore what follows from the possibility that it does happen.

The way in which we depict the range of possibilities for the future economic environment of the United States conforms very much to traditional broad, macroeconomic approaches. Alternatives for the total GNP are projected on the basis of the two key factors which, when multiplied, equal the GNP. These are the growth and projected levels of, first, the employed work force of the country; and second, the amount of the GNP per employed worker, a measure of aggregate labor productivity. We will also speculate on the extent to which the national "market basket" of goods and services which constitute the GNP—that is, consumer purchases, capital investment, housing, and government expenditures—will shift in the years ahead, in order to ponder the consequences for energy consumption.

What has happened, and may happen in the future, to each of these two separate and major determinants of GNP growth depends obviously on a large number of underlying developments. Projected trends in the volume of employment reflect explicitly or implicitly one's judgments or assumptions about fertility characteristics, the labor-force participation patterns of different age and sex groups within the population, trends in the length of the workweek, and unemployment rates. Productivity, for its part, is heavily influenced by trends and expectations regarding, among other things, technological change, the volume and nature of the capital stock, the qualitative characteristics of the labor force, and, more speculatively, environmental control requirements.

Population, Labor Force, and Employment

Population

Assumptions about U.S. population growth—rates of change, future aggregate levels, age-sex characteristics, family formation patterns—are an indispensable element in any consideration of the nation's long-term economic profile. The demographic outlook shapes the economic outlook both on the supply and demand side of the social accounting ledger. The number of future entrants into the labor force is closely, though, of course, not solely determined by changes in the size and age-sex composition of the population. This is particularly true for the period *after* the year 2000, for the labor force in 1990 will be almost entirely drawn from among persons now living, while some 85 percent of the labor force in the year 2000 are similarly already alive. The volume and pattern of demand for goods and services are likewise impossible to project without recourse to demographic trends. For example, additions to the housing stock are decisively influenced by the extent of growth among younger population cohorts and their disposition to set up households. An aging population—which, as we shall see, occurs with even the highest fertility case included in recent Census Bureau projections—affects housing characteristics and expenditure patterns in different ways.

The mid-1977 U.S. population numbered nearly 217 million persons. Our population growth rate has undergone a progressive historical decline from around 3 percent annually, early in the nineteenth century, to 0.7 percent in recent years. Of course, some sharp, intermittent fluctuations have accompanied this long-term trend. The growth rate dropped by more than half during the Depression decade of the 1930s and then, with the postwar baby boom, rebounded to above its pre-Depression rate. Also, the contrast between the relatively high population growth rates of the nineteenth century and those of today is less sharp when the influence of immigration is removed. For in the latter part of the nineteenth century, immigration accounted for approximately one-third of overall population growth, while during recent years, its influence has been only half as much.

The steadily declining rate of population growth over the past several decades and prospective trends for the future are most closely related to what has happened, and what is assumed to happen, to fertility. (Mortality rates have, it is true, continued in a slight downward direction and are projected to continue this trend; but this development has exerted a subsidiary influence on overall population growth and, moreover, is susceptible to being accurately projected with greater confidence than birthrates.) The total fertility rate, spanning American women in all child-bearing age groups, was 1,771 births per 1,000 women in 1975.[1] This figure means that if the age-specific fertility experience of 1975 became, henceforth, the norm for women to the end of their child-bearing period, each woman would, "on the average," bear a total of 1.7 children. Since 2.1 children ultimately leads to zero population growth, recent fertility experience, if sustained, implies an eventual population decline.

Census population projections to the middle of the next century comprise three alternatives, two of which reflect the possibilities just mentioned. The highest Census projection (Series I), assuming a long-term fertility rate of 2,700, reverts to the experience of the earlier postwar years. The lowest projection (Series III) essentially carries forward the recent 1,700 rate. A middle-of-the-range projection (Series II) assumes a renewed increase in fertility, but one leveling off at the 2,100 replacement figure (see table 4-1 and figure 4-1). Each alternative assumes a constant annual immigration level of 400,000 persons—about the same as the nominal estimate for recent years.

While the Series I assumption leads to steadily rising population levels, reaching 488 million in the year 2050, and reflecting average annual growth rates of 1 percent or more, the Series III projection is in marked contrast. In the latter case, population growth levels off at 253 million around the year 2020 followed by absolute yearly declines. (Continued absolute growth over present levels occurs for some decades because of the preponderance of women in their child-bearing years.) In mid-century, the population will revert to 230 million and decrease annually at 0.4 percent. Under the Series II assumptions, reflecting fertility below ultimate replacement level, population would nonetheless continue to grow in absolute terms. But annual growth rates would decline from 0.8 percent during the next fifteen years to 0.2 percent by the middle of the

[1] Past and projected demographic data come from the U.S. Bureau of the Census, *Projections of the Population of the United States: 1977 to 2050,* Current Population Reports, Population Estimates and Projections, Series P-25, no. 704 (Washington, D.C., GPO, July 1977).

Table 4-1. Population of the United States: Actual 1900–77 and Projected to 2050 (in millions, as of July 1)

Year	Series I	Actual and Series II	Series III
Actual			
1900		76.1	
1920		106.5	
1940		132.6	
1950		152.3	
1960		180.7	
1970		204.9	
1975		213.6	
1976		215.1	
1977		216.8	
Projected			
1980	224.1	222.2	220.7
1985	238.9	232.9	228.9
1990	254.7	243.5	236.3
1995	269.4	252.8	242.0
2000	282.8	260.4	245.9
2005	297.6	267.6	248.6
2010	315.2	275.3	250.9
2015	334.7	283.2	252.5
2020	354.1	290.1	253.0
2025	373.1	295.7	251.9
2050	488.2	315.6	231.0

Note: The principal assumptions governing the projections follow:

The ultimate levels of completed cohort fertility (average number of lifetime births per woman) are Series I (2.7), Series II (2.1), and Series III (1.7).

The average life expectancy at birth rises from 69.1 to 71.8 for males and from 77.0 to 81.0 for females.

The annual level of immigration holds at 400,000 persons. (A variant to Series II, called II-X, assumes zero future immigration; the result is a population level of 248 million in the year 2000 and 267 million in the year 2025.)

See also the accompanying text remarks.

Sources: Actual data are from U.S. Bureau of the Census, *Statistical Abstract of the United States 1976* (Washington, D.C., GPO, 1976); and *Estimates of the Population of the United States to September 1, 1977,* Current Population Reports, Population Estimates and Projections, Series P-25, no. 713 (Washington, D.C., GPO, October 1977); projections are from U.S. Bureau of the Census, *Projections of the Population of the United States: 1977 to 2050,* Current Population Reports, Population Estimates and Projections, series P-25, no. 704 (Washington, D.C., GPO, July 1977).

next century when the projected size of the population reaches 316 million. Even though *natural* increase of the population will thereafter drop rapidly to near zero, some small annual increments in population size would occur as long as the assumed annual immigration flow of 400,000 persons continued. (A leveling off in population growth might be further impeded by inflow of illegal immigrants.) A summary of the projections which have been discussed can be found in table 4-1.

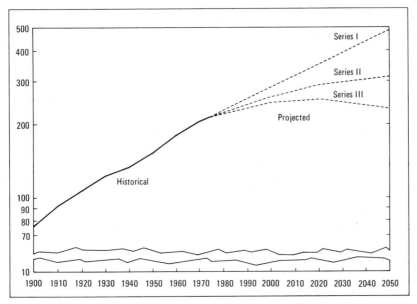

Figure 4-1. U.S. population growth, 1900–2050 (in millions).

One could debate at length the question of which of the three fertility assumptions carries the greatest probability of occurrence. Preferences for the lowest fertility case could be backed by the observation that each successive years' fertility experience since the early 1970s has established a new historic low. (In a sense, the 1,700 Series III projections thus actually represent a break of trend.) The Series III case might be further justified by pointing to the diffusion of contraceptive knowledge and the eagerness of women for occupational parity and rejection of the "housewife" role, both being reinforced by the social "respectability" of small families.

The middle projection—conforming to recent survey data on *future birth expectations* of young married women—would appeal to one who perceives a genuine basis for at least some turnabout from the trends of the past decade, when fertility dropped by about 40 percent. For example, an improved economic climate might overcome anxiety over the cost of child-rearing, and some of the recent fertility decline may reflect postponed, rather than forgone, births. In a broader historical perspective, one can recall periods when what turned out to be an ephemeral demographic trend was invested with more enduring properties. For example, when compared with what subsequently happened, the experience of the

Depression's fertility decline for a long time produced overly conservative population projections, while the postwar surge produced excessive ones.

The Series I projection involves plausible, but less easily defensible, premises. These, it is true, involve fertility rates substantially below the postwar highs. But the turnabout that this case assumes signifies a 60 percent rise in fertility rates above recent levels—that is, back to the mid-1960s experience.

In the ensuing discussion, we will mostly apply the middle set of population projections. This is largely for reasons of convenience, although it seems to us not unreasonable to accord major emphasis to Series II: its fertility-rate assumption stops short of the low level to which the rate has dramatically fallen in the past few years; and, as noted earlier, it conforms to expectations disclosed in survey approaches to the issue. Still, the test of reasonableness and, therefore, the choice of a particular projection, depend on use. If the consequences of an assumed rate of low population growth were to give rise to lower expectations regarding energy demand than turns out to be the case, the implications of that misjudgment—for an industry or the nation—can be compared to risks associated with an overestimate.

Finally, a word on the changing age characteristics of the projected population. To some extent, the population grows older no matter which of the three variants is adopted. In the Series-II case, the population's median age—which has hovered around thirty years or a bit younger during the past quarter century—rises to about thirty-six years by the year 2000 and to thirty-eight years by 2025. The proportion of persons aged sixty-five and over rises steadily throughout this period, from 11 percent in 1976 to 17 percent in 2025. These are not trivial changes. They have implications in a number of areas, for example, the growth of what demographers call the dependency ratio and the effect on the productivity of the work force. In the somewhat narrower energy context, the location and types of future housing demand and mobility characteristics are age-related topics that deserve consideration.

Labor Force and Employment

Long-term labor-force growth rates conform closely to population trends, varying principally by the effect of the steadily rising share of women who work. Thus, labor-force growth averaged 1.6 percent yearly, as compared with 1.4 percent for population in the years since 1947, a period during

Table 4-2. Labor Force and Employment, Actual 1955–76 and Projected to 2025 (in millions)

	Total labor force			Total employment		
		Actual and			Actual and	
Year	Series I	Series II	Series III	Series I	Series II	Series III
1955		68.1			68.6	
1968		82.3			83.8	
1972		89.0			88.2	
1976		96.9			93.2	
1985	108.9	110.2	112.1	108.7	110.0	111.9
1990	113.5	115.6	116.8	113.8	115.9	117.0
2000	129.5	127.2	127.6	129.8	127.5	127.9
2010	141.1	133.1	130.3	141.3	133.3	130.4
2020	155.1	139.3	131.6	155.1	139.2	131.6
2025	161.9	141.7	131.0	161.8	141.6	131.0

Note: The projected employment estimates assume (in all three cases) the 1976 armed forces level of 2.1 million persons and an unemployment rate declining from the recent rate of around 7 percent to 5.7 percent in 1980, 5.2 percent in 1985, and 4.8 percent in 1990 and thereafter. (The unemployment rate is applied to the *civilian* labor force in order to derive *civilian* employment. These two series are not shown separately here.) A projected adjustment factor necessary to relate jobs to persons was reduced gradually from its recent implicit level, on the assumption that the incidence of multiple-job holding would not figure as importantly in the future. But dual-job holding is likely to persist to some degree, as workweek reductions will facilitate holding second jobs for those who want them. Nationwide hours averaged 36 hours per week in 1976. They are projected to 33.5 in the year 2000 and 31 in the year 2025. See text for additional discussion of these projections.

Sources: Historical data on total labor force and employment appear in Executive Office of the President, *Economic Report of the President* (Washington, D.C., GPO, January 1977). The employment series shown here, and provided by the U.S. Bureau of Labor Statistics, actually refers to number of jobs rather than employed persons. The "jobs" series includes the activity of the multiple-job holders. Alternative labor-force projections to 1990 appeared in H. N. Fullerton, Jr., and P. O. Flaim, "New Labor Force Projections to 1990," *Monthly Labor Review* (December 1976) pp. 3–13. The labor-force participation rates assumed in those projections have here been applied to the three series of population projections, as shown in table 4-1. Using 1990 as a benchmark, we projected the size of the labor force for the years beyond on the basis of the rates of change assumed in Ronald K. Ridker and William Watson, "To Choose a Future: Resource and Environmental Problems of the U.S., A Long-Term Global Outlook," an RFF study sponsored by the National Institutes of Health (in preparation).

which the female "participation rate" (that is, the proportion of women in the labor force) went from 30 to 46 percent at the same time that the participation rate for men declined from around 90 to 78 percent. The latter change reflects another distinct post–World-War-II trend: the later entry into the labor force as years of schooling lengthened, reinforced, in later years, by earlier retirements.

Net labor-force additions for the balance of this century are projected to number around 30 million persons, with relatively little variability among the three population series (see table 4-2). This is to be expected

Table 4-3. Percentage of Working-Age Population in the Labor Force, 1960 and 1990

Population	1960	1990
Men	82	77
Women	37	51

Sources: U.S. Bureau of the Census, *Statistical Abstract of the United States 1976* (Washington, D.C., GPO, 1976); and H. N. Fullerton, Jr., and P. O. Flaim, "New Labor Force Projections to 1990," *Monthly Labor Review* (December 1976) pp. 3–13.

since a preponderant number of the year 2000 labor force is already alive. Some variability in labor-force growth is, however, related to near-term fertility trends, insofar as child-bearing and child-rearing conflict, at least in part, with labor-force membership. After the turn of the century, at which point the size of the labor force may range between 127 million and 130 million, the sharply disparate rates of labor-force change mirror more nearly the correspondingly disparate fertility alternatives.

If we concentrate on the Series II projections shown in table 4-2, we find a progressive deceleration of labor-force growth. During the past decade, the labor force has grown at about 2 percent yearly. Between 1976–85, the rate will very likely be about 1.5 percent. It will decline thereafter to around 1 percent per year for the final five-year period of this century. Of course, sizable net additions to the labor force, averaging, in absolute terms, about 1.5 million persons to 1985, continue to reflect the consequences of the large number of births in the 1950s and early 1960s. Beyond that, they reflect the sustained tendency toward rising labor-force participation rates among women.

That longer-term phenomenon deserves to be singled out. As we mentioned earlier, women's labor-force participation rates for a long time have been rising faster than the rate for men has been declining, and that trend is expected to endure in the decades ahead, albeit in a progressively more modest fashion. By 1990, the U.S. Bureau of Labor Statistics assumes that over half of working-age females will be in the labor market.[2] The contrast with as recent a year as 1960 is shown in table 4-3.

Another RFF project undertook a detailed age- and sex-specific analysis of labor-force trends beyond 1990.[3] It assumed that, soon after the turn of the century, changes in both male and female participation rates will level off and approach zero change around the year 2020. Within the first several decades of the twenty-first century, as a consequence of

[2] H. N. Fullerton, Jr., and P. O. Flaim, "New Labor Force Projections to 1990," *Monthly Labor Review* (December 1976) pp. 3–13.
[3] Ronald G. Ridker and William Watson, "To Choose a Future: Resource and Environmental Problems of the U.S., A Long-Term Global Outlook," an RFF study sponsored by the National Institutes of Health (in preparation).

this assumption and the age composition of the population, labor-force and population growth rates will conform closely to each other. Thus, for the five-year period 2020–25, both population and labor-force growth work out to between 0.3 and 0.4 percent per year. For the year 2025, the projected size of the Series II labor force is 142 million persons.

What do these labor-force projections portend for the number of future jobs? Table 4-2 contains employment estimates. What one assumes about factors governing future unemployment rates is, of course, crucial. Ten or fifteen years ago, it was commonplace in long-range projection efforts to hypothesize a "full-employment" unemployment rate of 4 or even 3.5 percent as a figure both consistent with the federal government's perceived policy imperatives and attainable without an unacceptable degree of inflation. It is fair to say that thinking in this area has changed rather significantly. "Structural" characteristics accompanying recent and prospective labor-force growth are thought to generate higher unemployment rates. Policy constraints arising from fear over inflation is another reason for modifying past unemployment-rate assumptions. Recently, for example, a congressional staff report exposed what it saw as fundamental conflicts between President Carter's objective of reducing unemployment to 4.75 percent by 1981 amid an inflation ceiling of 4.3 percent per year.[4] In the light of these considerations, we have adopted an assumed unemployment rate of 5.6 percent for 1980, of 4.8 percent for 1985 and for the subsequent years shown in table 4-2.

Even a lower unemployment-rate assumption does not alter the long-term likelihood of sharply decelerating labor force and, consequently, employment growth. That outlook is rooted in basic demographic phenomena. An energy-related question arises from this prospect. Long-term strategies concerning development of alternative energy systems are sometimes deemed to focus inadequately on their comparative job context. Our projections remind us that, irrespective of current labor-market conditions, one must be circumspect in designing future options too simplistically around assumptions of a chronic overabundance of job seekers.

Productivity and the Total GNP

Productivity occupies a critical place in any effort to probe the range of economic futures for the United States. Productivity growth, the mainspring of advancing living standards, commands further interest because

[4] Joint Economic Committee, *The Macroeconomic Goals of the Administration for 1981: Goals and Realizations,* 95 Cong., 1 sess. (Washington, D.C., GPO, 1977).

of its dramatic slowdown in recent years and heightened uncertainty regarding its future course.

The starting point for any speculation about prospective productivity trends must include the recognition that there has been an unmistakable and prolonged slowdown in productivity advance. Already, in the mid-1970s, Kendrick pointed to a number of factors which, he believed,[5] contributed to the slowdown. One was a government cutback in R&D spending, and a dampening in business R&D outlays. Historically, R&D—along with other intangible investments, such as education —are widely believed to have been an important source of productivity growth. Another element in the productivity slowdown to which Kendrick ascribes some significance is the retardation in *total output* growth in the latter part of the 1960s. This conviction derives from the observed tendency—stemming from the scale economies of expanding markets—of productivity to advance faster with rapid rather than sluggish growth in real output. A third reason for the slowdown in productivity growth was the disproportionately large jump of labor-force entrants (youths, women) whose value added falls below the economywide average. Finally, Kendrick cites the unfavorable impact on productivity—at least as measured—of business spending having to be diverted in large amounts to meet environmental and occupational health and safety objectives, a viewpoint strongly reinforced by recent work of Edward Denison, performed at the Brookings Institution.[6]

Kendrick might have cited still one other source of productivity growth deceleration in the last decade or so, that is, the progressive slowing down in the movement of workers from farming into the nonfarm sector of the economy. When the shift was in full swing, the effect was to raise economywide productivity growth rates, because of the higher *level* of output per worker in the nonagricultural sector. A Bureau of Labor Statistics analysis suggests that unlike the productivity-decelerating impact of a slowed out-migration from farming, other sectoral employment shifts (for example, the movement toward services) has had minor consequences for nationwide productivity growth.[7]

[5] John W. Kendrick, "Productivity and Growth Trends and Their Implications," *Pittsburgh Business Review* (Fall 1975) pp. 4–11.

[6] Edward F. Denison, "Effects of Selected Changes in the Institutional and Human Environment Upon Output Per Unit of Input," *Survey of Current Business* (January 1978) pp. 21–44.

[7] Ronald E. Kutscher, Jerome A. Mark, and John R. Norsworthy, "The Productivity Outlook to 1985: A Summary of the BLS Productivity Projections." Paper prepared for Symposium on the Future of Productivity, November 16–17, 1976, Washington, D.C.

A final point concerns the consequences of the drastic increase in energy prices dating from 1973–74. Few dispute their significant one-time contribution to the decline in real output and rise in unemployment which characterized the ensuing and prolonged recession. But will higher energy prices signify an enduring slowdown in productivity advance and growth of potential output even under postrecessionary circumstances? A fuller discussion of that issue appears elsewhere (see chapters 3 and 5), though even here we can note that the long-term implications of higher energy costs are at best speculative and dimly seen. Some economists, notably Hudson and Jorgenson,[8] perceive already a process of labor substitution for energy, implying, at given levels of employment, lower labor productivity and national output. Irrespective of ultimate effects, one may, however, question whether the limited data represented by developments since 1973–74 can so soon convey a clear-cut message. Another effort to unravel post-1973 trends has been made by George Perry of the Brookings Institution.[9] He deems it unlikely that higher energy prices have caused more than a 0.2 percent reduction in the annual labor-productivity growth rate or that in potential GNP between 1973–76.

The judgments underlying the productivity projections shown in table 4-4 and figure 4-2 have been guided by the preceding discussion relating to recent developments, as well as by analysis and projections prepared elsewhere.[10] As can be seen from table 4-4, even the highest productivity projection involves an average annual rate of growth of around 1.9 percent—somewhat below the trend preceding the deceleration dating from a decade ago.

Our reasons for projecting productivity advances exceeding those of the past decade are threefold:

1. The depressing effect of the low value-added cohort of labor-force entrants will gradually subside, removing that cause for deceleration.

2. The negative impact of sudden and large investment diversions into pollution controls and health and safety programs can likewise be expected to move along much more gradual lines. Moreover,

[8] Edward A. Hudson and Dale W. Jorgenson, "Energy Prices and the U.S. Economy, 1972–1976," Discussion Paper no. 637 (Cambridge, Mass., Harvard Institute of Economic Research, Harvard University, 1978).

[9] George L. Perry, "Potential Output: Recent Issues and Present Trends," in *U.S. Production Capacity: Estimating the Utilization Gap*, Working Paper 23 (Saint Louis, Mo., Center for the Study of American Business, Washington University, December 1977).

[10] Ridker and Watson, "To Choose a Future."

Table 4-4. Historical and Projected Average Annual Percentage Rates of Change in Employment, Productivity, and the GNP, for Various Periods from 1955 to 2025

	Historical				Projected				
	1955–68	1968–72	1972–76	1968–76	1976–85	1985–2000	2000–25	1976–2000	1976–2025
Employment									
Series I					1.7	1.2	0.9	1.4	1.1
Series II	1.6	1.3	1.4	1.3	1.9	1.0	0.4	1.3	0.9
Series III					2.0	0.9	0.1	1.3	0.7
GNP per employee									
High					2.1	2.0	1.9	2.1	2.0
Medium	2.1	1.4	0.7	1.1	1.9	1.8	1.7	1.9	1.8
Low					1.7	1.6	1.5	1.7	1.6
GNP									
Series I									
High					3.9	3.2	2.8	3.5	3.2
Medium	3.7	2.7	2.1	2.4	3.7	3.0	2.6	3.3	3.0
Low					3.5	2.8	2.4	3.1	2.7
Series II									
High					4.0	3.0	2.4	3.4	2.9
Medium					3.8	2.8	2.2	3.2	2.7
Low					3.6	2.6	2.0	3.0	2.5
Series III									
High					4.2	2.9	2.0	3.4	2.7
Medium					4.0	2.7	1.8	3.2	2.5
Low					3.8	2.5	1.6	3.0	2.3

Note: Future rates of change in productivity, discussed further in the text, were initially specified for somewhat different subperiods, as follows:

	Percentage		
Years	High	Medium	Low
1976–90	2.1	1.9	1.7
1990–2010	2.0	1.8	1.6
2010–25	1.9	1.7	1.5

Sources: Employment data from which rates of change are calculated appear in table 4-2. The GNP data (reflecting the constant dollar, 1972 price series) necessary for calculating the GNP per employee can be found in Executive Office of the President, *Economic Report of the President* (Washington, D.C., GPO, January 1977); and U.S. Department of Commerce, *Survey of Current Business,* National Income Number (Washington, D.C., GPO, 1977).

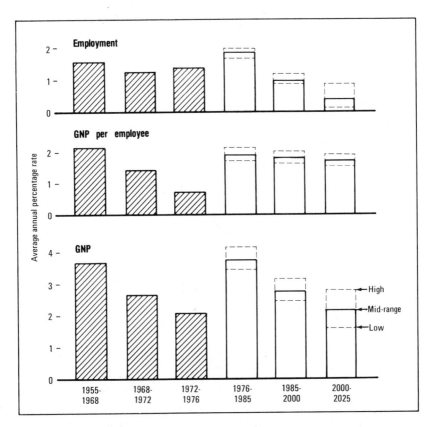

Figure 4-2. Growth rates in employment, productivity, and the GNP, 1955–2025.

as environmental protection becomes more and more integrated into the design and production process of new capital facilities, rather than being grafted onto existing facilities, the encroachment, if any, into productivity advance should be much milder. (Negative impacts on productivity may also be cushioned by economic use of by-products because of pollution-control charges.)

3. The declines in R&D expenditures are assumed to level off and capital investment rates to rise. Recent evidence lends some support for these judgments.

While we are thus projecting a speedup in productivity growth, we do not, in our medium projection, look to a restoration of the longer-term historical rate. Of particular importance, as well, we do not allow our

Table 4-5. Real GNP, Actual 1955–76 and Projected to 2025
(in billion 1972 $)

| Year | Actual | Productivity | | | | | | | | |
| | | Population Series I | | | Population Series II | | | Population Series III | | |
		High	Medium	Low	High	Medium	Low	High	Medium	Low
1955	654.7									
1968	1051.8									
1972	1171.1									
1976	1274.4									
1985		1792.6	1761.0	1730.3	1814.0	1782.1	1751.0	1845.3	1812.9	1781.2
1990		2082.2	2025.6	1970.7	2120.6	2063.0	2007.0	2140.7	2082.6	2026.1
2000		2895.1	2761.8	2634.4	2843.8	2712.8	2587.7	2852.7	2721.3	2595.5
2010		3841.7	3593.5	3361.6	3624.2	3390.1	3170.8	3545.3	3316.3	3101.8
2025		5834.2	5298.6	4811.6	5105.8	4637.1	4210.9	4723.6	4290.0	3895.7

Sources: 1955–76 data are from the Executive Office of the President, *Economic Report of the President* (Washington, D.C., GPO, January 1977) and 1985–2025 projections are calculated from percentage growth rates given in table 4-4.

productivity projections during the next decade to reflect the catching up that has traditionally characterized the emergence of the economy from recession. (Such catching up would mean temporary productivity growth rates of, say, 4 percent or more.) Simply too much time has passed during this recovery phase for the experts to believe that historical experience will recur.

Charting productivity pathways into the next century stretches conjecture still further. We are content with the qualitative thought (to which table 4-4 gives symbolic expression) that successive long-run intervals into the future may witness a gradual and slight slowdown in productivity advance. We have in mind the progressive relative shift away from material goods production and greater concern with the quality-of-life characteristics of the GNP: relatively more public goods consumption and cultural activities, for example, imply lower measured productivity levels and slower measured productivity growth. But, as is clear from our earlier discussion, the factual basis for such a projection remains quite limited.

When coupled to the projected rates of change in employment, the projected productivity trends produce a range of GNP growth rates between 3.0 and 3.5 percent per year for the period 1976–2000, and between 1.6 and 2.8 percent during 2000–25. (See table 4-4 for rates of change for all three indicators; and table 4-5 for absolute levels of the GNP.) For convenience, we might focus especially on the GNP implications of the Series II population–medium productivity assumptions. The GNP growth is expected to be highest (near 4 percent) during the next decade, both because of a pick up in productivity growth and a reduction in the unemployment rate. The deceleration in the GNP growth rate that is assumed to occur during the last fifteen years of this century and, subsequently, the first twenty-five years of the next one, stems largely from the effect of demographic factors, which explain roughly 90 percent of the projected slowdown.

Absolute numbers begin to leave numbing impressions as the effect of compounding over a long time path registers, even with slower growth. In the mid-set of projections referred to in the preceding paragraph, the GNP (expressed in 1972 prices) would increase from $1.3 trillion in 1976, to $2.7 trillion in 2000, and to $4.6 trillion in 2025. On a per capita basis, this would mean levels rising from $5,755 in 1976, to $10,418 in the year 2000, and to $15,681 in the year 2025. The corresponding per-annum growth rates are 2.5 percent during the first interval and 1.6 percent during the second one.

Distribution of National Expenditures

Different expenditure categories within the GNP are associated with different energy intensities. Certain services, for example, finance or repair, typically involve far less consumption of energy than is required in the production of, say, food or of heavy equipment. Thus, even if one were to assume unrealistically that the energy needed to deliver a dollar's worth of a particular product or service to a consumer would undergo no future change, one would still want to know something about the impact on aggregate energy consumption stemming from a shift in the pattern of expenditures. As one tries, additionally, to account for the prospect of energy-intensity changes in given economic activities, the changing importance of that activity within the GNP becomes doubly significant.

Unfortunately, projecting changes in the pattern of national expenditures in a realistic, analytically sound, and internally consistent fashion is a difficult task indeed. Suppose one assumes that a diminishing proportion of the consumer's dollar will be spent on automobiles. This is bound to have at least some specific effect on spending for automobile repair services. How is one to ensure that the logical connection between these two items is preserved? And if this example is among the simpler ones to deal with, what of the myriad other interrelationships in expenditure clusters that an assumed change in any *given* item is likely to upset?

This problem can be partially swept aside by dealing only in highly aggregative components of the GNP. But the greater the degree of aggregation the more limited the scope for deducing energy insights. Two lines of attack have made meager progress—the simulation of future spending patterns by using the *prevailing* experience of different income groups, or, where spending habits differ substantially from those of the United States, by using the pattern of expenditures of other countries.

Another major difficulty relates to the consistency between the aggregate GNP and certain key components upon which attainment of the aggregate is dependent. This is obviously the case with capital investments for these are critical to achieving the productivity projections, and hence the total GNP, and thus occupy almost a unique quantitative place amid the various expenditure components which make up the GNP. Such consistency is handled in the construction of projection models,[11] by making the ultimate solution the explicit result of feedbacks between the capital goods sector and total output.

[11.] Ibid.

Table 4-6. Expenditure Components of the GNP, for Selected Years 1950–76
(percentage distribution based on constant 1972 $)

Expenditure components	1950	1960	1970	1976
GNP	100.0	100.0	100.0	100.0
Personal consumption	63.4	61.5	62.2	64.4
Durables	8.1	7.1	8.3	10.0
Nondurables	30.3	28.3	26.3	25.2
Services	24.9	26.1	27.6	29.2
Gross private domestic investment[a]	17.6	14.3	14.4	13.6
Structures	3.6	3.9	4.0	2.9
Equipment	5.8	5.1	6.3	6.3
Housing	6.2	4.7	3.7	3.7
Net exports	0.7	0.7	0.1	1.3
Government purchases	18.3	23.5	23.3	20.7

Sources: U.S. Department of Commerce, *Survey of Current Business,* National Income Number (Washington, D.C., GPO, July 1977); and *The National Income and Product Accounts of the United States 1929–74* (Washington, D.C., GPO, 1977).
[a] Including changes in business inventories, not shown separately.

Formidable as these problems are, one's judgment about future energy demand does not need to reflect not only total GNP growth but changes in the composition of the GNP as well. At the very least, clear-cut trends need to be considered. As table 4-6 indicates, for example, the role of expenditures on nondurable items is clearly downward; while the proportionate share of consumer spending for durable goods seems, without much doubt, to be modestly upward. Consumer purchases of services also show an unmistakable relative increase. However, lest that trend be too readily viewed as spelling dampened future energy demand—owing to the relatively low energy intensity of numerous services—an important point needs to be made. Energy items themselves (utility purchases and transportation services are an important reason for the expanded role of services, while another rising component (an accounting adjustment reflecting the imputed rental value of owner-occupied housing) is neutral in its energy implications. Excluding these items, we find that services are essentially a constant share of consumer expenditures and of the GNP. As in chapter 3, we emphasize here that one must exercise caution in ascribing too significant a portion of future energy-demand restraint to the influence of the consumer services sector.

In the case of investment, the past may be a poor guide to the future. That is, the falling investment rate and its depressing effect on productivity would need to be reversed if the productivity and overall GNP projections are to materialize. A 15 to 16 percent figure for the year 2000 (compared with 13.6 percent in 1976) may be the approximate investment share fulfilling this necessary condition. Most of that rising share would originate with the business equipment component of investment.

A number of analysts see the government share of the GNP continuing to decline somewhat and the proportionate role of the housing sector to follow a level or modestly rising direction.

Conclusions

Decisions by households and business firms regarding their consumption of energy are strongly influenced by the surrounding economic environment. Energy-consumption trends are, of course, governed by factors other than overall economic growth—factors, as seen in chapter 3, which may prompt energy use to proceed faster or slower than the pace of the general economy. But the outlook for national economic growth remains, obviously, one important consideration in assessing future energy demand.

Our mid-range set of projections suggest that, compared to the quarter century that followed World War II, the next twenty-five years are likely to see a slowdown—by at least half a percentage point—in GNP growth. That prospective deceleration is somewhat more decisively conditioned by the expected slowdown in population and, hence, labor-force growth, than the projected reduction in the pace of productivity advance, though both elements deserve to be recognized.

Near-term policy concerns need to be distinguished from longer-term prospects. For example, the scope for considerably higher female labor-force participation, the entry into the labor force of persons who were the product of the earlier, high-fertility postwar years, and the fact of high levels of unemployment all signify a potential for fast employment growth in the years immediately ahead. In another decade, however, significantly slower growth of labor force and employment may be anticipated. The productivity situation is a bit different insofar as the long-term slowdown in growth that we have in mind is not in comparison with the disappointing performance record in recent years (which is assumed to be improved upon in the future), but, rather, relative to longer-run experience during the past quarter century.

We touched briefly on the nature of changes in the composition of the GNP. This subject has potentially significant energy-use implications, for proportionately fast- or slow-rising components of the national product may be associated with different quantities of energy. Much more rigorous analysis needs to be conducted in this area. The energy consequences of a rising services component, in particular, may not signify as much energy dampening as is sometimes ascribed to it.

5 The Technological Approach to Energy Conservation—Prospects in Three Major End Uses

How Much Energy Can Technology Save?

It is clearly preferable to dampen the growth rate of energy demand by applying feasible cost-effective technologies to given activities rather than to achieve that dampening by curtailing the activities. Energy savings achieved through, say, improved automotive fuel economy preserve the mobility that is such a widely assumed amenity as to represent an expression of national values. Disrupt the amenity and you tamper with those values.

Nevertheless, technological approaches to energy conservation are not without limits in what they can accomplish; and a feeling for these bounds is a prerequisite to the development of sound policy choices whose effects might be anticipated.

This chapter[1] explores the energy demand implications of different technologies—routine as well as innovative—in three selected (but disproportionately important) segments of national energy use: residential space heating (about 10 percent of U.S. consumption), automotive transport (between 13 and 14 percent), and industrial process steam (also roughly 10 percent). Aside from the central concern with the outlook for energy-saving technologies, each of the three case studies has a three-fold emphasis: (1) the factors underlying the demand for the respective good or service giving rise to requirements for energy; (2) the economic

[1] This chapter represents a considerably shortened adaptation of a study, *Energy and Innovation: The Impact of Technical Change on Energy Demand,* commissioned by RFF and written by Marc H. Ross, Professor of Physics, University of Michigan. Data or factual information lacking a specific reference in the present condensation are fully documented in the complete paper, slated for separate publication by Resources for the Future.

and noneconomic elements (including policy and institutional issues) affecting the potential adoption and penetration of the technologies being considered; and, (3) a judgment about the range of primary energy demands that, on the basis of the preceding factors, is apt to materialize over the next twenty-five years. In the next chapter, these projections will be used along with a broader review of possible future trends in other categories of energy use to develop overall projections of U.S. energy consumption.

One measure of technology-based conservation lies in the degree to which energy consumption can be made more *efficient;* but this term in itself calls for some analysis. In the case of a heating system, for example, efficiency is measured conventionally by the following ratio:

$$\text{conventional efficiency} = \frac{\text{heat energy delivered to living space}}{\text{total energy consumed}}$$

Thus, if a heating system consists of a gas furnace plus hot-air duct system, the conventional efficiency of, say, 55 percent describes limits to potential improvements as one approaches an optimal gas-furnace plus hot-air-duct system.

Recently, however, a different notion of efficiency has gained interest; and it is one that suggests a broader scope for conservation potential. This so-called second-law efficiency[2] compares any system actually being used for heating a home to an ideal system—for example, an optimal heat pump. A second-law efficiency of, say, 5 percent signifies that converting from a gas furnace to an *ideal* heat pump could accommodate the task in question with one-twentieth the overall energy requirement. The pertinent ratio is:

$$\text{second-law efficiency} = \frac{\text{absolute minimum energy required for given task}}{\text{total energy consumed}}$$

Clearly, there may be some disagreement when one tries to determine "absolute minimum energy." In particular, ambiguities can easily arise over defining the "given task." In the case of heating a house, is the requirement simply that the heating system provide air at a certain tem-

[2] "Second-law efficiency" is so named because the fuel consumed by a thermodynamically ideal system is determined by the second law of thermodynamics. Background on this topic can be obtained in the 1974 American Physical Society Summer Study, "Efficient Use of Energy: A Physics Perspective," *American Institute of Physics Conference Proceedings* vol. 25, or available separately from NTIS (PB-242-773). In that study and in this chapter, second-law efficiency numbers relate to strictly limited definitions of task (for example, to the task of a household heating system in providing warmth at a specified temperature).

perature to warm the entire living space—or is it the more general assignment to keep the occupants "comfortable"? In the instance of personal transportation systems, is the object merely to bring about someone's change in location—a change that might be achieved by walking? For transportation tasks, how much of a factor is speed? Or to take an even more extreme view, could electronic communication accomplish the task by eliminating the need to travel altogether in certain circumstances? For all its shortcomings, however, second-law efficiency is a provocative and useful tool in examining the potential for technological conservation; and it will be applied as seems appropriate in this chapter.

Residential Comfort Heating

Space heating dominates household energy use, accounting for over half of the residential energy total and, as noted above, one-tenth of nationwide energy consumption. We hope, in the course of this discussion, to demonstrate that (1) the economically justified potential for improved energy performance in this important category of energy use is very great; (2) barriers inhibiting rapid realization of this potential are, however, formidable; (3) an effective means to help reduce these barriers may be "information technology," enabling consumers, designers, builders, and regulators to evaluate the energy efficiency of buildings; and (4) primary fuel use for an expanded stock of residential structures in the year 2000 can remain close to recent levels (8.6 quads) with just moderately improved energy performance, although projections both significantly lower and moderately higher are also considered.

Although much remains to be learned about the thermal performance of housing, the commercial standing of new technologies, and the potential impact of policies to improve space heating performance, our understanding of these issues has been greatly strengthened by the work of such groups as the Lawrence Berkeley Laboratory,[3] the Princeton Center for Environmental Studies,[4] and the Oak Ridge National Laboratory (ORNL). What follows makes recurrent use of studies by these organizations. In particular, the development of the projections owes a good deal to Hirst and Carney's ORNL analysis,[5] although in two respects—

---

[3] See, for example, *Energy and Buildings* (Switzerland) vol. 1, no. 3 (1978).
[4] Ibid., vol. 1, no. 1 (1977).
[5] The ORNL research in question is described in Eric Hirst and Janet Carney, *Residential Energy Use to the Year 2000: Conservation and Economics* (Oak Ridge,

in our assumption that future electricity prices may exceed the projections from the U.S. Department of Energy used by ORNL and in our consideration of new, technical developments—we push our examination still further.

The Current State of Affairs

Housing units in the United States in 1975 numbered 70 million, of which single-family homes accounted for two-thirds and apartments for approximately three-tenths. (Mobile homes made up the balance.) On the average, the occupants of these 70 million residences consumed space-heating energy at the annual rate of 122 million British thermal units (Btu) per dwelling unit and 110 thousand Btu per square foot of living space. As one would expect, significant variability surrounds these averages. Thus, in a multifamily dwelling unit (whose energy use per square foot tends to be around 40-percent lower than in a single-family home) the lower heat losses through the shell more than compensate for the lack of control that individual families have over the heating system of the building. There is obviously geographic variability as well, although not to the extent that climatic differences would suggest: presumably, the potential for fuel saving has been large enough in the North and small enough in the South to have induced and deterred significant conservation measures in those respective regions. Then, too, more recently built housing, embodying more insulation, uses less fuel than comparable units of earlier vintage.

There is also surprising variability in the amount of energy used to heat given housing types, even with adjustment for climate; and this is perhaps most noteworthy from the standpoint of this study. Consumption by typical single-family housing in central United States varies perhaps from 50,000 to 200,000 Btu per square foot. The presence or absence of adequate insulation plays a major role in explaining such differences, but it is not the only factor at work. Variations in the use of space, in

Tenn., Oak Ridge National Laboratory, September 1977) (Report ORNL/CON-13). Hirst and Carney assume the following modestly rising 1976 to 2000 price trajectories: gas, 2.3 percent yearly; oil, 1.2 percent; and electricity, 0.9 percent. To test conservation potentials, we shall here assume an electricity price rise (2.4 percent) such that residential customers in the year 2000 pay *today's* estimated long-run marginal cost to residential customers of about 6 cents per kWh. (The actual recent residential electricity price has been approximately 3.2 cents per kWh.)

control of heating systems and windows, and in construction and equipment all play their part.

Concern over adequate insulation is a fairly recent phenomenon in the United States. (Of course, a history of declining real energy prices—discussed in chapter 3—weakened economic incentives for improved performance until the past few years.) The 1975 Annual Housing Survey by the Bureau of the Census disclosed that 16 percent of U.S. housing lacked attic insulation; and before 1939, it was a rarity altogether. Wall insulation as a general practice did not appear until the late 1950s.

Even before the fuel price increases of the 1970s, substantial retrofit outlays in existing housing and investment for enhanced energy performance in new structures would have been justified by net life-cycle savings associated with reduced fuel costs. There were, however, important barriers to realizing the economically justified level of building and heating system technology. A recent study[6] discussed five such barriers: (1) New equipment and materials are purchased primarily by builders rather than by building owners or users. (2) Building codes are based mainly on detailed specifications, rather than on performance standards. (3) The building industry is more sensitive to initial costs than to life-cycle costs. (4) The building industry is fragmented and horizontally stratified. New technology must fit the existing distribution, sales, and service system or—alternatively—be capable of establishing a parallel, equally effective system. (5) The industry is largely craft based, with workers in each union applying separate skills to the construction process, and this tends to keep the industry oriented toward traditional ways of doing things.

Technology

Available technology. It is useful to draw a distinction between the performance—and potential improvements therein—of heating systems on the one hand and the thermal properties of the building shell on the other. Second-law efficiency considerations apply directly to the heating systems only.

In fairness to both suppliers and users of heating systems, it must be said that anything approaching the twenty-to-one improvement in heating

---

[6] See Richard Schoen, Alan S. Hirshberg, and Jerome Weingart, *New Energy Technologies for Buildings* (Cambridge, Mass., Ballinger, 1975) chap. 4.

efficiency that second-law analysis suggests may not be defensible financially in new structures, let alone in existing ones. In the case of heat pumps, practical energy savings accrue primarily in comparison with electric resistance heating; taking power plant losses into account, present electric heat pumps are far from ideal and do not improve significantly upon gas furnaces.

But even conventionally measured efficiency (of about 55 percent) can be improved upon with demonstrated retrofit techniques. In regard to the heating system, for example, installation of an electric pilot for a gas furnace saves about 6 million Btu per year, or 5 percent of typical annual fuel use for space heating. The simple modification of reducing fuel flow, thereby increasing the length of time the furnace is on and reducing the number of times it turns on and off, reduces losses (from the flue and distribution system) associated with the on-off cycling of the furnace. Tests by Michigan Consolidated Gas Company suggest 12-percent savings via this technique in its service area. A flue damper that closes when the furnace is turned off can also result in significant savings.

The sum of such savings (achievable at relatively low cost) may conservatively be assumed to reduce fuel needs by 20 percent. In other words, if a typical heating system efficiency is 55 percent, steps such as those described can bring the efficiency to 69 percent ($0.55/0.8$).

Although large improvements can be made in heating systems, even greater improvements can be made by reducing losses through the building shell. The "lossiness" of a building depends on air infiltration and also on conductance (that is, direct passage of heat through wall, ceiling, and floor surfaces as well as through windows and doors). The major existing retrofit technologies include insulation, installation of storm windows and doors, and caulking and weatherstripping. For new buildings, such practices can be reinforced by devices such as south-facing windows, infiltration seals for fixed parts of the shell, and more thickly insulated walls.

The use of ceiling, wall, and floor insulation is widely appreciated, if less widely practiced. Much less understood is the fact that many houses have important pathways for conductance that are not blocked by insulation as ordinarily installed. Some methods of construction provide easy thermal "bridges" to the outdoors (for example, in the form of masonry or cement blocks) or thermal bypasses from basement heating plant areas to largely unoccupied attic space.

Air infiltration—which can be limited by double-glazed storm windows, weatherstripping and caulking, and dampers in flues—may be the least understood loss. It cannot be estimated for a given house without detailed examination or testing. The heat loss (or gain in summer) associated with air infiltration is compounded when there is a need for additional humidification.

Near- and long-term improvements.   Again, it is useful to focus separately on (1) reduction in lossiness and (2) improvements in combustion equipment and heating systems generally. (This chapter will not deal in any detail with such a fuel-saving technology as residential solar heating units; for a discussion of this and other decentralized energy technologies, see chapter 11.)

Conductance through windows can be reduced significantly by nighttime and seasonal use of movable shutters or drapes; in addition windows with special coatings to inhibit radiative transfer should be on the market soon. Heat loss caused by an infiltration can also be reduced by improving windows, doors, and flues, and by using a plastic vapor barrier in the outer wall and roof. If the reduction is effective enough, the separate question of adequate air exchange could arise; but some Swedish housing already solves that potential problem by combining the system to introduce fresh air in a controlled way with a heat exchanger to recover heat from the ejected air.

What prospective improvements exist for heating systems, appliance integration, and controls? At least six developments show definite promise:

1. Zoned temperature control—already being used to a small extent—allows different rooms to be held at different temperatures and on different schedules.

2. Electric heat pumps are now being introduced that improve on conventional heat pumps by 50 to 100 percent in heat delivery per unit of primary energy consumption (that is, consumption at the power plant). Further refinements of heat pumps involve (a) the extraction of warmth from water (if available) rather than air, thus allowing greater use on colder days than is possible with existing units because water temperature declines less than ambient air; and (b) the use of combustible fuel rather than electricity as an energy source, thereby reducing conversion losses and allowing waste heat utilization.

3. Cogeneration (on-site production of electricity and heat) can save as much as 30 percent of the "base" fuel energy use. The heat

provided by a cogeneration system can be thought of as the waste from the electricity generation process. Problems with cogeneration include (a) the necessity for the correct balance of heat and electricity demands—a situation requiring import and export of electricity from the site; and (b) scaling down cogeneration units, which are currently designed for very large buildings or facilities, to the level of single-family residential needs.

4. Solar heating, although widely publicized, is a technology still undergoing rapid change. Systems involving flat collectors with short-term storage are not widely economical (see chapter 11). Nevertheless there is potential economic attractiveness in combining (a) dependable sunlight, (b) seasonal storage capability, and (c) performance of more than one function (for example, solar cogeneration of heat and electricity).

5. Passive solar heating can be a very economic technology. It combines large (roughly south-facing) windows with massive walls and floors (to suppress daily thermal variation) and adjustable shading to control overheating.

6. Integrated appliance use to serve multiple functions—for example, internal venting of a clothes dryer for winter heat—is a major area for innovation.

An important reservation about all these technical opportunities is that skill and ingenuity may be required to design and develop applications of new ideas—and even to implement existing technology effectively.

Performance and Economic Analysis

We might begin with a word of caution about performance and economic analysis. Evaluation of a given energy-saving practice should differentiate between independent and interactive cost effectiveness. Energy-conserving steps that are separately cost effective need not be so when taken collectively.

For example, substantial improvements are possible in both the shell and the heating equipment of new structures. With heating system improvements *alone,* their annualized cost today may amount to about $2 for each million Btu decrease in annual energy consumption. However, if heating system improvements were to be made after the shell had already been improved (so that the equipment had to handle perhaps only one-fourth the original load), the cost of "saved energy" associated with the heating system improvements might double. As a general rule, extensive heating system improvements are less attractive once extensive improvements have been made to the shell and vice versa.

Economic evaluations have been made of the most standardized types of retrofits. Unfortunately, the variety of actual buildings and the performance of retrofits in practice—as contrasted with simple calculation—make such evaluations suspect as accurate guides to the economic performance of retrofits across the nation. Some obvious conclusions can be drawn, however: retrofit investments promise a greater return if the house initially has low thermal integrity; and recent energy price increases provide a very high return to investment in retrofit of such housing. Yet even if a house is already well insulated and has low air infiltration, ingenious nonstandard retrofit techniques (such as plugging the thermal bypasses mentioned above) may yield an economically attractive return on investment.

On the basis of limited economic evaluations of retrofit investments for several regions and single-family housing types, figure 5-1 proposes an estimate of retrofit cost per unit of saved fuel versus total fuel savings over one heating season. This curve will be the basis for projecting retrofit fuel savings later on; but it is worth noting here that large energy savings relative to the estimated average household consumption of heating fuel of 122 million Btu per year appear possible at a cost substantially below what consumers pay for fuel. A rough weighted figure for current fuel costs may be in the vicinity of $2.50 per million Btu if electricity is evaluated in terms of primary fuel inputs rather than electrical energy. Modifications in new construction are likely to mean even greater cost effectiveness, although—since new housing starts constitute a small percentage of the nation's housing stock—such savings would represent relatively little dampening in overall national energy consumption for some years. Once again, it is difficult to generalize with any precision; but a given level of energy savings in new houses could typically be achieved at a cost substantially below that indicated for retrofit housing in figure 5-1.

Barriers to Implementation

It would be nice if investments in energy-conserving technology for home heating would be made at least to the degree justified by economics, but

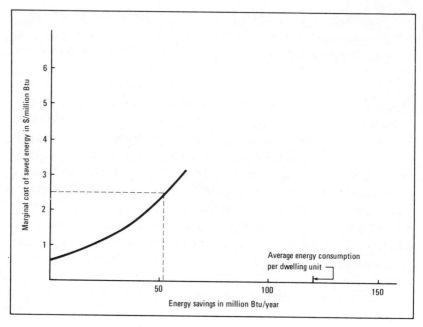

Figure 5-1. Unit cost of energy saved by improvement to shell versus total amount of energy saved, retrofit, single-family housing. Author's estimate of annual cost of retrofit per unit of annual fuel savings at the margin versus total fuel savings over one heating season per single family dwelling unit. A nominal capital charge rate of 10 percent per annum is used to annualize retrofit capital costs. At this capital charge rate and a price of energy of $2.50 per million Btu, the dashed lines show that retrofits resulting in some 55 million Btu annual reduction in fuel use could be economically justified.

there are many barriers to such extensive investment across the population of dwelling owners. Here are some of the principal ones, not necessarily in order of importance:

1. The building industry finds innovation difficult because of building code specifications, industry fragmentation and stratification, a craft-based work force, and low capitalization.
2. Feedback to residents is long delayed and hard to interpret. Monthly-to-annual meter reading does not permit easy experimentation with blinds, thermostat, and furnace adjustment, and closing off rooms.
3. The occupant of a dwelling unit often does not pay the utility bills directly.
4. The builder lacks incentive. He is sensitive to first cost, and the energy performance his building will have is not obvious.

5. Because of variety in buildings, many retrofits are hard to standardize. Some buildings are in very poor condition. Skill is needed to rectify some design flaws.

6. Conservation costs are typically compared to average energy costs, which are lower than marginal costs and well below the level dictated by true social costs, figured on a long-term replacement basis.

Although many of these barriers arise from economic factors—distorted incentives which hamper operation of the market—they also involve lack of information about the technically complex nature of residential heating and a resulting hesitancy to put the putative benefits of conservation investments to the market test.

Accurate, credible, and easily accessible information—of a type that has begun to reshape attitudes in other sectors of the economy—could greatly alter the perceptions of customer, designer, builder, financial institutions, and regulator concerned with residential heating. It could make each one aware of the present efficiencies and inefficiencies in a given heating system, the energy costs associated with them, and the practicalities of improving the situation. Such "information technology" seems simple and obvious, yet it is not now generally available. The information needed falls into three general categories:

1. Performance indexes. The energy performance index par excellence is the comparative miles-per-gallon EPA ratings for automobiles. Evaluating building performance in a similarly straightforward fashion (given the variation in design, construction, and climate) is, for the moment, problematical. For example, at a considerable expense—currently absorbable only in the case of large buildings—one can compute what a building's performance will be on the basis of building design. It is not known how accurate or costly such a survey would be for housing in general. Infrared sensing to reveal thermal radiation from buildings is another example of a promising monitoring approach. Modest R&D support might yield greater certainty that such possibilities will mature.

2. Feedback to user. The feasibility and cost of providing households with conveniently placed readouts showing energy use or cost for a recent lapsed interval is another worthwhile development topic.

3. The "house doctor." Skilled specialists in the whole field of residential energy conservation could be produced through a relatively

inexpensive program of research and training involving regional housing stock. Such persons could be a source of comprehensible on-site technical and financial advice to individual homeowners.

Development of information technology for housing is currently a wide-open field, both for technologists and policymakers. Successful development of such technology *might* help make people as sensitive to residential fuel conservation as they apparently are becoming to automotive performance.

Public Policy Options to Foster Implementation

Some policy issues are implicit in what has already been said. A pervasive issue, of course, is that of energy pricing; and it will be treated in some detail in chapter 17. Energy prices are held down at present by a variety of government interventionist policies. If prices rose to the extent justified by market-clearing criteria—that is, using a replacement-cost basis, but also allowing for external costs—this would simultaneously strengthen the momentum for energy conservation. The higher the energy price, the more attractive is an investment in equipment with improved energy performance.

Other public policy initiatives are of a more programmatic character; and a number of these have been undertaken already by state and federal governments, at least at a low level. Such initiatives include investment incentives for energy-conservation technology; research, development, and demonstration (RD&D) in conservation technology; direct government procurement of conservation technology; RD&D (and some subsidization) of information technology; formulation of performance-based thermal standards for new construction; and encouragement of utility involvement in conservation investments.

Finally, policies aimed at the mortgage market that would overcome some of the legitimate homeowner concern with first costs of a building (to the neglect of lifetime cost considerations), may be well worth considering. One idea is to continue to base the required down payment percentage in home financing partly on the projected burden of such operating costs as repayment of principal, interest, taxes, and insurance, but with an explicit allowance (namely, a reduction) for savings in operating costs which might reasonably be anticipated from an initial investment in conservation.

Projection of Energy Consumption and Conservation Potential

The amount of energy that will be used for residential space heating in the year 2000 can be thought of as the product of:

number of dwelling units $\times$ energy use per dwelling unit

Thus, a projection can be made rather simply if those two values can be estimated. Our calculation will distinguish between structures already existing in 1975 and those built after 1975—the reason being the variation in how much energy-saving potential can be counted on from technological improvements within new homes as opposed to retrofits, especially in terms of building-shell improvements.

Number and types of dwelling units. The U.S. housing stock is projected to grow from roughly 70 million to 114 million between 1975 and 2000. The projection (shown in table 5-1) is based on the study by Hirst-Carney cited earlier.[7] The demographic and economic assumptions governing their projections conform closely to those characterizing the mid-range population and GNP estimates in chapter 4. In line with an existing trend, the projected total of 114 million units corresponds to a drop in occupancy per dwelling unit from 3.0 to 2.3 persons and a drop in adult occupancy (20 years and over) from 2.0 to 1.6. The new housing is also assumed to have more floor space per dwelling unit than existing housing, as has been the trend in recent construction practice.

Space heating energy consumption per unit. Projections of average consumption depend heavily on judgments as to what we can expect on the basis of economics and technology from improved performance in heating system efficiency and from improvements in the building shell. For this reason, a range of three consumption projections might be considered:

1. *A mid-range, present-program projection* that assumes the future price trajectory described earlier (see footnote 5 to this chapter) (including marginal cost pricing for electricity), use of a rapid pay-back period, and the implications of existing legislation and policies.

[7] Hirst and Carney, *Residential Energy Use.*

Table 5-1. Projected Distribution of Dwelling Units in the Year 2000
(rounded to nearest million)

Dwelling units	Housing in 1975	Housing in the year 2000		
		Existing in 1975	New since 1975	Total
Single family	47	36	32	69
Multiple unit	21	15	23	38
Mobile home	3	0	7	7
Total	71	52	62	114

Source: Eric Hirst and Janet Carney, *Residential Energy Use to the Year 2000: Conservation and Economics* (Oak Ridge, Tenn., Oak Ridge National Laboratory, September 1977) (Report ORNL/CON-13).

2. *A low, or conservation-oriented projection* that assumes a more rapid rate of price increase, more aggressive conservation policies, and acceptance of a more modest pay-back period.

3. *A high projection* that accepts the unadjusted ORNL price assumptions, makes conservative assumptions on the diffusion of conservation practices, and contemplates a more energy-intensive housing mix.

In the case of building shell improvements, a distinction is made between retrofits and new structures. The heating system improvement factors are assumed to be the same for the three projections, irrespective of whether the residences are new structures or retrofits. They are based on the simple modifications of gas furnace systems discussed earlier. The average fuel reduction achieved is taken to be 20 percent. From the conservation standpoint, this is pessimistic for new structures using gas or oil as heating fuel. Where electric heating is used in new structures, heat pumps would account for about the same fuel use as the improved gas furnace system in the same building shell. The low and mid-range projections assume that resistive heating would be installed only in smaller units, in units with better than average construction, or in those located in warmer climates.

The basis for projecting single-family energy demand by using marginal cost curves is illustrated in figure 5-2. The "present-program" projection involves presently expected energy prices and the assumption that virtually all improvements justified by a five-year payback are made. A weighted average price of about $3.60 per million Btu in the year 2000 is implied (see footnote 5 to this chapter). By following the dotted line from $3.60 on the right-hand vertical scale of figure 5-2 to the points of inter-

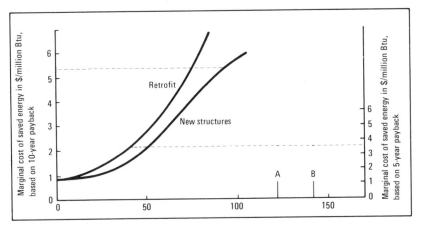

Figure 5-2. Unit cost of energy saved by improvements to shell and heating system versus total amount of energy saved, for retrofits and for new single-family housing, respectively. Shows cost of shell and heating-system improvements per unit of savings for a range of total fuel savings over one heating season per single-family dwelling unit. Two alternative payback and capital-charge assumptions are depicted on the vertical axes at left and right. Point A on the horizontal scale represents average household space heating energy use in existing single-family housing; point B is the average total for new, larger housing units. The ten-year payback on the left-hand axis involves a capital charge rate of 13 percent (including repayment of principal), while the five-year payback on the right-hand scales involves a capital charge rate of 23 percent. An interest rate of 12 percent was used for retrofits (home improvement loans), and 9 percent was considered for new construction. Allowance was also made for inflation and tax effects.

section with the two curves, one can obtain a rough estimate of potential energy savings in existing and new single-family housing. In its policy aspects, this is considered a reasonable projection of the eventual impact of present legislation but allows as well for the effect of public persuasion, regulation, and government procurement.

The conservation-oriented projection assumes that prices will rise 50 percent beyond those considered in the present-program projection and also that most improvements will be made if they are justified by a ten-year rather than five-year payback. The projected weighted price is about $5.40 per million Btu. The dashed line drawn from this point on the left-hand axis of figure 5-2 thus intersects the curves at points spelling substantially greater savings (in fact, about twice as great). This conservation-oriented projection is assumed to be a reasonable outcome if further national difficulties with energy supply during the next decade should lead to additional energy price increases, to the development and adoption of information technology, and to strengthened conservation regulations and incentives.

Comparative projections. The combined effects of heating system improvements (previously estimated at 20 percent) and improvements in the shell for the present-program and conservation-oriented projections are shown in table 5-2, which also projects total U.S. energy consumption for space heating on the basis of the increase in number of units postulated above. In addition, table 5-2 shows: a "high projection" based on the assumption that certain parts of the present program might fail to achieve expected results. It also shows the improvement factors for fuel use in space heating from two other studies. Two principal reasons for the differences between the present-program projection of fuel performance in this report and that of Hirst and Carney are: (1) the difference in the marginal cost curve for retrofits, implying somewhat greater energy savings with higher investment; and (2) the higher relative price for electricity assumed in this report, which suggests that electrical resistive heating will not dominate in new structures. There was no deviation from the Hirst-Carney assumption that retrofits would take place in almost all (96 percent) of the existing single-family homes where the move was economically justifiable.

It is assumed in this analysis that energy price changes do not significantly affect behavior—that is, do not demand life-style adaptation —except with respect to selection and use of new equipment and a willingness to make cost-effective decisions. Otherwise day-to-day behavior of 1975 was taken as the norm, without impinging on amenities. At most, such practices as installing thermostat setback devices (which *does* assume a willingness to sleep in lower temperature surroundings) have been assumed.

It is interesting that the present-program projection leads to energy consumption in the year 2000 near (and even a bit below) the present level. Thus, the net impact of a more than 50-percent increase in the number of dwelling units would be more than compensated for by technically feasible and economically justified improvements in equipment and structures. Furthermore, even the capital cost projection seems relatively low; we estimate that such a program involves an investment of roughly $500 per dwelling unit (in 1975 dollars).

The projected near-zero rate of change in energy use for residential heating purposes would be a radical departure from the postwar growth

Table 5-2. Projected Energy Consumption for Space Heating in the Year 2000 Based on Economically Justifiable Technological Improvements in Heating Systems and Building Shells

	Energy consumption per dwelling unit compared with 1970		Total U.S. space heating energy consumption	
	Retrofits	*New structures*	*10^{15} Btu*	*Percentage of 1975*
This report:				
Present-program[a] (5-year payback)	0.61	0.52	8.0	93.0
Conservation-program[a] (10-year payback)	0.36	0.23	4.5	52.0
High projection[b] (assuming relative failure in conservation goals)	N.A.	N.A.	11.1	129.0
Hirst-Carney[c]	0.72	0.61	9.4	110.0
Energy Research and Development Administration[d]	0.75	0.50	N.A.	N.A.

Note: This table shows the combined effects of heating system improvements (about a 20-percent saving) and thermal integrity improvements (see figure 5-2) on fuel use for space heating for the average dwelling unit, and on total fuel consumption for residential space heating for the year 2000. N.A. = Not applicable.

[a] The fuel reduction factors shown apply specifically to single-family housing and are governed by figure 5-2. For total energy consumption, multiple-unit and mobile home fuel reduction factors for the present program were taken as the Hirst-Carney thermal integrity improvement factors. For the conservation-oriented program, they were estimated to be 70 percent of the Hirst-Carney factors. (According to ratios supplied by Hirst, fuel use per dwelling unit in 1970 was 151, 62, and 92 million Btu for single-family, multiple family and mobile home, respectively.) Improvements were assumed by Hirst to take place in only 38 percent of multifamily housing, but the opportunity for greater individual improvement in the thermal integrity of such structures was also taken into account.

[b] See the text for assumption behind this result.

[c] Weighted mean of single-family, multiple-unit, and mobile home improvements with expected federal programs in place. New single-family dwellings are assumed to be electrically heated, and no heating system improvement is included. This example was selected from among the several developed. (Eric Hirst and Janet Carney, *Residential Energy Use to the Year 2000: Conservation and Economics* (Oak Ridge, Tenn., Oak Ridge National Laboratory, September 1977) (Report ORNL/CON-13). This publication presents results for total residential energy use. Underlying detail on the space heating component was provided by Hirst.

[d] George R. Murray and J. Michael Power, "End-Use Technology—The Next Twenty-Five Years" (Washington, D.C., Energy Research and Development Administration, Office of Conservation Planning, March 1977). This projection for fuel use for all residential purposes has a comparison year of 1975.

rate of 2 to 3 percent per year. The present-program reduction in fuel use per existing dwelling unit of 39 percent attributed to retrofit improvements can be given some perspective by comparing it with the *actual* conservation response to the fuel price increases and shortages that began in 1973. The American Gas Association has found that use of gas per dwelling unit for residential space heating fell 9 to 13 percent in the winters of 1973 to 1976 compared with the previous norm (with the greatest reduction during the cold winter of 1976). *These reductions are corrected for climate variation* (that is, they are for fuel use per degree day); and they combine the effects of lowered thermostats, closed-off rooms, conscientious use of equipment such as storm windows, the beginnings of investment in insulation, and so forth. It almost goes without saying that the potential reduction in unit consumption offered by a conservation-oriented program (namely, 64 percent) goes far beyond the nation's initial response to energy-conscious exhortations.

The projection based on more vigorous encouragement for conservation indicates that nationwide fuel use for residential space heating might drop to only about half its 1975 amount. This radical change reflects the capability of technology at a level justified by substantial, but perhaps acceptable, energy price increases and other conservation policies. The improvements would involve an incremental investment of roughly $2,000 per dwelling unit (in 1975 dollars) built under prevailing construction practices.

Finally, it is of interest to probe the factors that might credibly lead to greater energy use than in the present-program projection. It seems quite unreasonable to suppose that day-to-day behavior would become *more* wasteful (for example, that thermostat settings would be higher, or windows left open more often). It also seems quite likely that improvements in new structures that have been mandated or called for by existing legislation (requiring, say, up to $500 investment per dwelling unit) will be made. Furthermore, although more fuel use in new structures could result from larger housing units, a dramatic increase in floor space per person has already been assumed.

A very important cause of increased fuel use probably more important would be a massive shift to electrical-resistance heating, with its overall heating system efficiency of approximately 0.3 instead of the 0.69 assumed in the present-program projection. Suppose also that the cost of electricity does not rise to its present long-run marginal cost as in the present-program projection, but follows the Department of Energy projection used by Hirst-Carney, with a price in the year 2000 that is 30 percent lower than our estimate. This cost differential—although still implying a considerably higher price for electric, compared to nonelectric, heating—would have an effect. Assume, therefore, that an additional 50 percent of new housing is electrical-resistance heated. (The fuel use factor for new housing would then be 0.86 instead of 0.52.) Assume further that federal programs for retrofits are ineffective and that only 33 percent of single-family housing is improved rather than 96 percent. (The improved fuel-use factor for existing housing then drops only to 0.87 instead of 0.61.)

The final consideration is the number of units as given earlier (table 5-1). Although the total number of units seems unlikely to exceed the projected level, one can contemplate a shift of, say, 3 million new structures from the multifamily to the single-family category. This would contribute to higher consumption as energy use in a single-family unit is much greater.

National fuel consumption, for residential space heating in 2000 with this high projection is 11.1 quads, or 129 percent of 1975 consumption, corresponding to a growth rate of less than 1.0 percent per annum. Thus, even with the high projection, it must be concluded that the past energy growth rate will not continue because of changes already at hand in demography, energy prices, and policies.

Automotive Transport

Our study of the potential for energy conservation through technological developments in automotive transport leads to several general conclusions: (1) The personal motor vehicle is likely to continue dominating passenger transportation into the indefinite future. (2) The 1985 automobile fuel economy standards can be met without significant reduction in the interior size of automobiles; indeed, only moderate weight reduction of the automobile fleet as a whole is involved. Thus fuel economy standards well beyond the 1985 standards could certainly be achieved by down-sizing. (3) Considering the fuel economy improvements that now appear clearly achievable with little incremental cost, it is feasible that rising petroleum prices could reach a level where synthetic fuels from virtually inexhaustible resources become dominant in the automotive field.

The Present Situation

Energy used in transportation—almost entirely oil—has accounted for about one-fourth of the nation's energy consumption in recent years.[8]

---

[8] Factual material underlying this discussion is largely from *Transportation Energy Conservation Data Book*, 2d. ed. (Oak Ridge, Tenn., Oak Ridge National Laboratory, October 1977) (Report ORNL-5320); and the transportation chapter

Table 5-3. Selected Data on Passenger Vehicles, 1975

Item	Automobiles	Light trucks used as passenger vehicles
Energy use (quads)	9.1	1.1
Passenger miles per capita	10,500	720
Travel time per capita/day (minutes)	53	4
Load factor (occupants/vehicle)	2.0[a]	1.4
Vehicles (millions)	100[a]	11
Vehicle miles (billions)	1.03	0.10
Energy performance (mpg)	14	12

Sources: Derived principally from Demand–Conservation Panel, Committee on Nuclear and Alternative Energy Systems (CONAES), *Alternative Energy Demand Futures* (Washington, D.C., National Academy of Sciences, forthcoming 1979); Oak Ridge National Laboratory, *Transportation Energy Conservation Data Book* 4th ed., (Oak Ridge, Tenn., October 1977) (Report ORNL-5320).

[a] Different sources give somewhat different estimates. The load-factor range is from 1.9 to 2.2; the range for vehicles from 98 to 110 million.

Within transportation, in turn, private passenger vehicles are the dominant component. They contribute roughly half of the transport sector's energy demand and over 85 percent of the energy devoted to passenger travel overall. Similarly, private passenger vehicles are the overwhelming source of the passenger mileage recorded by U.S. travelers. Some key data on passenger vehicles appear in table 5-3. (In our usage, private passenger vehicles consist of both automobiles and light trucks used as passenger vehicles; but the following discussion will usually differentiate explicitly between these two transport modes.)

Although costs associated with the automobile exact a significant proportion (about 12 percent) of the household budget, the fuel portion of those outlays is not the dominant annual cost of operating an automobile. The total annual budget for automotive fuel is about $400 per automobile, or about one-quarter of the total personal auto budget. If this critical economic fact is not entirely responsible for the policy strategy of outright regulation which is now being used to reduce gasoline consumption, it is at least consistent with it.

The price of fuel has not increased much with respect to other costs, as was noted in chapter 3. Indeed, the real price of gasoline declined gradually through 1973, when the sharp price hike restored the price to about its 1957 level. Since then, until very recently, the real price has un-

of the Report of the Demand–Conservation Panel, Committee on Nuclear and Alternative Energy Systems (CONAES), *Alternative Energy Demand Futures* (Washington, D.C., National Academy of Sciences, forthcoming 1979).

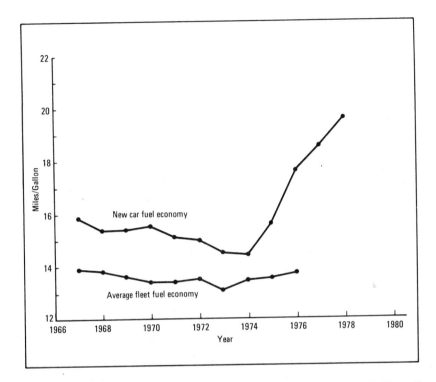

Figure 5-3. Average fuel economy for the automobile fleet, 1967–78, and new cars, 1967–1976. New car fuel economy based on 1975 Federal Test Procedure (FTP) city/highway weighted. For the 1975–78 model years the new car fuel economy is sales weighted by manufacturers' sales forecast data. For earlier model years production data were utilized. Average fleet fuel economy calculated by the Federal Highway Administration. From A. B. Rose, *Energy Intensity and Related Parameters of Selected Transportation Modes: Passenger Movements* (Oak Ridge, Tenn., Oak Ridge National Laboratory, January 1979) (Report ORNL-5066).

dergone another drift downward. Given this history of fuel prices, the history of automotive fuel economy has no surprises to an economist. The fuel economy of automobiles in miles per gallon (mpg) was steadily deteriorating through the 1975 model. Then it began to improve, as is clear from figure 5-3.

The deterioration in fuel economy during the 1960s and early 1970s was significant. Although the rapid improvement since then may have been stimulated in part by consumer concern with the price of fuel and possible shortages in fuel supply, the major thrust for improvement has been federally mandated fuel economy improvements.

The Energy Policy and Conservation Act of 1975 (EPCA) required that for 1978 model year automobiles the production-weighted average for each manufacturer be a fuel economy of at least 18 mpg (combined fuel economy measured by EPA). Thereafter, the standard rises to 19 mpg in 1979, 20 mpg in 1980, and ultimately to 27.5 mpg in 1985. Because of the automobile mix, it takes several years before new car fuel economy improvements significantly affect the average fuel economy for the total domestic automobile fleet.

Figure 5-3 shows that U.S. manufacturers evidently have the flexibility to shift toward the fuel-efficient automobile that European and Japanese companies successfully began marketing years earlier. Moreover, the American producers made this shift without disrupting the overall stability of the automobile industry.

Technology

Available technology. The overall energy performance of an automobile depends on (a) the efficiency with which fuel is converted and delivered as mechanical energy to rotate the wheels, and (b) the effectiveness with which that rotational energy accomplishes the task of propulsion. Although about 88 percent of the fuel consumed is lost en route to the drive wheels, that loss may not be the principal target for improvement in automobiles. Rather, it often centers on the combination of air resistance, brake losses, and tire losses involved in operation of the auto. Because all these losses are roughly proportional to the weight of the vehicle (other factors being equal), it is not surprising that *the energy performance of an automobile turns out to be approximately proportional to its weight.* For example, among the family of 1977 models, moving from a 5,000 to a 2,500 pound automobile typically means an increase in fuel economy (EPA combined rating) from 14 to 28 miles per gallon.[9] Coincidentally, the first figure corresponds to the fuel performance of the average auto in use in 1977 (all vintages) while the second figure conforms to the mandated 1985 standard.

However, the sizable improvement in fuel economy that occurred between 1975 and 1977, as depicted in figure 5-3, was achieved almost entirely without the benefit of weight reduction. Instead, improvements *at a given weight* were brought about by using radial tires as well as improved engine and transmission efficiency. For example, a major efficiency

---

[9] The weights discussed here are inertial weight, or curb weight plus 300 lb.

improvement stems from a reduction in engine power, so that losses associated with engine operation at part load are reduced. More recently (in 1977–79 models), sizable weight reductions are being achieved without loss of interior space.

Near-term improvements. In addition to weight reduction without loss of interior space, further improvements in tires, aerodynamics, and transmissions (such as those that produce a more smoothly varying ratio of engine speed to wheel speed) are among the modifications now being made by manufacturers to enhance fuel performance. The growing market penetration of diesel engines should reinforce this trend. An advanced version of the Volkswagen Rabbit diesel (inertial weight of about 2,400 pounds) is believed capable of a fuel economy of nearly 60 miles per gallon, compared to the present Rabbit diesel's (combined EPA) rating of 44 miles per gallon. Compared with a typical automobile, the advanced version's higher price would most probably be offset by savings through reduced fuel consumption.

Long-term improvements. Two diverse possibilities may be mentioned for the long term: (1) electric vehicles, and (2) substitution of communications for travel.

In spite of the government's commitment to a major development program, the electric vehicle illustrates the technical difficulties in greatly improving the kind of private cars now available or under advanced development. It is true that special-purpose commercial vehicles powered by storage batteries are already in use, but the future of a general-purpose vehicle is cloudy at best. Batteries are a heavy, bulky, and extremely costly substitute for stored chemical fuel. The weight and high cost of storage severely restrict the driving range of an electric vehicle. Even if batteries using lighter materials could reduce the weight penalty of lead-acid cells, the weight of batteries and structures to support them implies a substantially greater weight for electric cars than for gasoline engine cars of even roughly comparable capabilities.

On balance, economics and performance do not favor extensive substitution of electric vehicles for fuel-driven vehicles, but environmental considerations and fuel type might favor the electric car. The environmental consideration would have to weigh reduced urban air pollution from automobile engines against increased impacts from the production of electricity. If conventional oil-fired generators were used at central station plants to produce the energy that charges an electric car's batteries, it turns out that electric vehicles projected for the year 2010 would still be providing the equivalent of only about 20 miles per gallon—hardly a conservation bonanza—although there *might* be some logic in coupling electric automobiles with generating systems based on fuels that are more plentiful than oil. In the projections of automotive energy demand that follow, electric vehicles are not considered.

A future based on electronics and intensive telecommunications could dramatically alter transportation patterns, but the change could be either upward or downward. Undoubtedly telecommunications might substitute for some considerable portion of existing transport activity, especially that which is business related. On the other hand, some travel could actually be increased by telecommunications as people are exposed to the attractions of expanded travel opportunities. All things considered, a net reduction in physical transport activity seems a fair presumption.

One can, for example, visualize: business acceptance of telecommunications as a way to stagger work weeks and schedules; a growing service sector based on telecommunications and electronic newspapers and mail. Even now, the electronics revolution (of which telecommunications is a part) is proceeding with relatively little notice of its potentially profound implications for business and personal relations. One ironic twist is that the potentially "benign" features of a less transport-oriented society might give way to alarm over the "dehumanization" of an electronically molded life-style.

The Demand–Conservation Panel of the Committee on Nuclear and Alternative Energy Systems (CONAES) concludes its analysis of the substitution of communications for travel with a hypothetical estimate of passenger travel demand: the maximum impact of communications is estimated to be a reduction in projected travel by about one-quarter by the year 2010. Such a possibility, perhaps more credible as one contemplates a still longer time-horizon, suggests that telecommunications as a substitute for travel appears to merit serious investigation as a means of reducing future transportation energy demand.

Economics

The dominant position of the private automobile. The liquid-fuel-powered private vehicle is the prevailing mode and technology for short- and medium-haul passenger transportation in the United States, and this situation is likely to continue for the indefinite future because of (1) relative cost (both in fixed costs and in fuel and nonfuel operating costs), (2) benefits (convenience, travel time, style), and (3) the apparent solubility of what may be considered the major problems posed by present-day private vehicle usage (fuel availability, pollution, safety, congestion). Several factors favoring the private automobile are almost overwhelming in themselves. One is the extraordinary potential for fuel economy improvement at a relatively low addition to fixed costs. Indeed, potential improvements in automobile fuel economy are so great that drivers should always find themselves able to pay enough per unit of fuel to guarantee a supply of fuel. To put it another way, fluid chemical fuel will probably continue to be available indefinitely at a price. As discussed below, given feasible improvements in fuel economy, the price of fuel can rise substantially without inhibiting the use of automobiles.

Substantial fuel economy improvements can be achieved without substantial changes in interior automobile size and in style, but further sizable improvements might also stem from down-sizing vehicles. There is every reason to believe that consumers in almost all localities would prefer a *smaller* private car to a *substitute* for that automobile. Sociological speculation about the symbolic meaning of a large showy automobile is far less relevant than the fact that a private automobile provides something significantly useful in almost all localities—access to fast and inexpensive transportation on demand.

Whether using a small or a large automobile, a person in Ann Arbor, Michigan can travel at will from anywhere in Ann Arbor to, say, downtown Detroit in less than one hour. The distance is about 40 miles, and the incremental cost is roughly 6¢ per mile. This remarkable service cannot even be approached in the foreseeable future by any means other than a vehicle under private control, even though the example chosen—radial travel to an urban center—is not one in which the automobile has a particular advantage. This whole argument does not necessarily apply in areas with a very high density of population or in high population corridors at certain hours. Under these conditions there may be more convenient alternatives. But the predominant share of passenger travel in the United States occurs in lower population density situations.

U.S. housing and locational patterns have evolved with automobile transportation in mind for over fifty years. Although changes can occur in these arrangements in the next decade or so, it would take much longer than that to alter such patterns on a large enough scale to make alternatives to traveling by private automobile more convenient and less costly for most trips.

Congestion and air pollution, the most unfavorable aspects of the car, will be limited by two developments. First, as shown in the projections below, the number of vehicle miles driven per year appears to be approaching saturation. Second, smaller automobiles take up less space and tend to emit fewer pollutants. These developments may not in themselves solve existing problems, but they should ease the solution of old problems and limit the extent of new ones.

Improved automotive performance versus fuel cost. It is of some interest to consider the question of cost and availability of fuel for automotive use. How problematic would it be to raise the price of fuel to the point where fuel could be provided (for example, via alcohol derived from biomass or hydrogen via nuclear) indefinitely? The recent wholesale price of gasoline, excluding taxes, has been about 40¢ per gallon, retailing margins and taxes about 25¢ per gallon, and the fuel economy of the U.S. automobile fleet about 14 miles per gallon. Consider the following exercise: fix the average cost per mile of fuel at its present level and imagine that the U.S. automobile fleet has achieved a fuel economy of 42 miles per gallon. This could, in principle, be accomplished in two or three decades, since there are cars on sale today that meet this standard. The price of gasoline could thus rise in constant dollars to $1.70 per gallon plus the same 25¢ for markups and taxes. The wholesale price of $1.70 per gallon corresponds to about $70 per barrel, or between $13 and $14 per million Btus. At this price, is it not reasonable to suppose that fuel or power can always be produced in adequate quantities?

Another important question is how the cost of creating cars with improved fuel economy compares with the value of fuel savings. The investment program of U.S. automobile manufacturers in making fuel economy improvements has been estimated to have a *cumulative seven-year* cost of roughly $35 billion.[10] The fuel cost savings is estimated at $25 billion, but it is to be realized *annually*. It is clear that the economics are overwhelmingly favorable.

The potential role of mass transit. Some people see improved and expanded mass transit as a means of making cities more livable and reducing energy use in transportation by diminishing the use of private

[10] For example, the incremental investment in the period between 1978 and 1985 associated with meeting *all* regulatory requirements is estimated to be $35 billion in the Harbridge House study, "Corporate Strategies of the Automotive Manufacturers" for the National Highway Traffic Safety Administration, 1979.

vehicles. On the second point analysis suggests that their expectations are exaggerated.

Mass transit (short-haul buses, trolleys, trains, and new types of conveyances) now accounts for 5 to 6 percent of total passenger miles in the United States. Even in industrialized Western European countries, mass transit accounts for less than 20 percent of all passenger miles. The critical fact about mass transit is that it does not function well in the absence of high-density areas and high-density corridors. In moderate suburban density areas, there are far too few passengers outside of rush hours to justify equipment needs. Offpeak vehicles run essentially empty. This is true for whatever variations one may think of, including that which involves banning the use of cars.

Furthermore, even where there are enough rush-hour passengers in suburban areas to fill buses and trains, the cost is surprising. Typically, time does not permit vehicles to make more than one rush-hour run. Until time for the return trip in the afternoon, the vehicle is idle or runs with minimal loads. These vehicles must generally be very heavy duty, and their cost is extremely high. Labor costs, assuming full-time employment is required, are also extremely high; a full-time driver will typically make only one well-loaded trip in an 8-hour day, or two such trips in a 12-hour day. Energy use by heavy buses is also high. A full bus uses only slightly less fuel per passenger mile than a 40 to 50-mile-per-gallon car carrying a driver and one passenger; and the extra costs implied by the low-duty factor are enormous. Typical bus or dial-a-ride trips in a small city cost the transportation agencies about $2 per rider. Deficits of public transportation systems have been rising at a staggering rate. It is therefore most unlikely that the modest rejuvenation of the nation's buses, commuter trains, and other mass transit systems in recent years can become a significantly growing trend.

Gradual redistribution of the nation's population from the dispersed, suburban configuration adapted to the personal automobile to more concentrated centers of population seems like an attractive long-term possibility, although European experience suggests that such a shift would have less effect on the relative importance of the automobile than it would on bringing about a reduction in total demand for short-haul transportation. Per capita travel in the larger, highly industrialized European countries is roughly half that of the United States, with much of the reduction probably in short distance travel.[11] Europeans tend to live in close-in

[11] Joel Darmstadter, Joy Dunkerley, Jack Alterman, *How Industrial Societies Use Energy: A Comparative Analysis* (Baltimore, Md., Johns Hopkins University Press for Resources for the Future, 1977) especially chapter 5.

urban and suburban centers that provide relatively complete services and are much smaller than corresponding centers in the United States. The notion of reducing transportation needs through urban and economic redesign merits extensive study.

A different, more promising, and practicable transportation system to supplement the private automobile is jitney service: the use of automobiles or vans that are designed to meet local commuter needs.[12] If any new type of short-haul public transportation is to become nationally important in the next few decades, this may be it. Company automobiles or vans, vans owned by other organizations, or personal automobiles can be used to transport small numbers of people from home to work. The driver can do this job on a part-time basis, or the driving can be shared. Such jitney service reduces the need for second cars, reduces street congestion and parking problems, and reduces fuel use. It could be encouraged by assignment of expressway lanes, special parking privileges, information services to put prospective riders in touch with a driver, and special insurance provisions. Legislation would be required to permit and encourage common carriage.

In one way or another, U.S. personal transportation will continue to be dominated by automobiles.

Barriers to Improving Automotive Fuel Performance

There are various barriers to attaining feasible goals in automotive fuel performance. The principal ones to be considered here are: the low cost of fuel, the "light truck loophole," tradeoffs between fuel economy and the environment, and the problem of small car safety.

The low cost of fuel. The cost of gasoline, which in 1978 was about 4¢ per mile, or $400 per year for the average vehicle, may not be high enough to make most consumers sensitive to either (a) their volume of driving or (b) the fuel economy of the cars they buy. There is little dispute about point (a). As for point (b), examination of car sales by weight indicates that only a small minority may find the high fuel economy of the smallest cars important enough to overcome other considerations.

---

[12] See Frank W. Davis, Jr. and Larry F. Cunningham, "Will the Reaction of the Auto Transportation System to the Energy Crisis be Technological or Institutional?" *Transportation Engineering,* February 1978, pp. 26–31.

European experience suggests that it may take gasoline prices three times the U.S. level to influence buyers toward acquiring fuel-efficient automobiles.

Perhaps because of the presumed insensitivity of American motorists to fuel price increases, or—more likely—because it was politically simpler, the decision was made to improve automotive fuel economy by regulation. Will regulation be effective in the long run without being reinforced by economic pressure? Probably—but we cannot be sure. Certainly, fuel economy "imposed" by regulation deviates for a variety of reasons from the fuel economy of actual driving. No doubt, the energy savings resulting from fuel economy improvements would be more secure if fuel prices were also increasing sharply.

The light truck loophole. Light-weight trucks, weighing up to 5 tons, comprise three-fourths of all trucks. These vehicles—mainly pickups with significant numbers of panel trucks and vans—are now used primarily for personal transportation. In a 1972 survey, 53 percent of light truck use was for personal transportation (including recreation). The proportion of this type of use has been rapidly increasing and is now about 80 percent.

Trucks of under 3 tons now come under strict emissions control and gasoline mileage standards, as is the case with passenger automobiles. Indeed, the sales-weighted average for fuel economy of these vehicles is believed to be slightly better than that for passenger automobiles. In 1977, it was 19.0 miles per gallon as compared with 18.6 miles per gallon for automobiles.

The loophole involves the heavier light trucks. The emissions and fuel economy of trucks weighing between 3 and 5 tons have not been regulated in the past. Sales of these trucks are increasing very rapidly—a boom evident to the casual observer of the American scene. With a market developing for a passenger vehicle that escapes standards, much of the benefit from the fuel economy standards for passenger automobiles could be effectively negated by a continued surge in the sale of these vehicles. The fuel economy of these vehicles is not known, but is certainly well below that of passenger automobiles. Considering their relatively heavy weight, an estimate of 10 miles per gallon is probably not far off.

Attention is now being given to imposing fuel economy standards on these vehicles. The executive branch has recently set standards for 3- to 4.25-ton trucks for 1980 and 1981. The performance that will be required of 1985-model light trucks is yet to be specified at this writing. Consumer interest in trucklike passenger vehicles could be served by vehicles under 3 tons with average fuel economy as good as that for regular passenger automobiles. Time will tell whether the government will succeed in modifying the plans of the manufacturers so as to close the light truck loophole.

Fuel economy–environmental tradeoffs.   As in some other areas of energy supply and utilization, increasing the energy efficiency of transportation vehicles involves tradeoffs in environmental emissions, control costs, or both. Petroleum-based engines emit hydrocarbons, carbon monoxide, nitrogen oxides, and other pollutants. New automobile emissions which affect air quality have been under federal control since 1968. The Clean Air Act of 1970, and subsequent amendments, serves as the current regulatory basis for these emissions controls. The Environmental Protection Agency (in coordination with the Department of Transportation) administers the environmental standards and controls for transportation.

There has been, and will probably continue to be, major controversy about the levels of emissions controls for new cars. To date, controversy has revolved around (a) delays granted in implementation of various standards specified in the Clean Air Act of 1970, (b) the fuel penalty inherent in tighter emissions controls, and (c) the specification of ultimate new-car emissions controls.[13] Emissions standards may have an important effect on the propulsion technologies available for automobiles and light duty vehicles. For example, future nitrogen oxides standards mandated by present law might limit diesel engines as an option; and even more stringent emissions standards might require electric propulsion or a new engine type.

Automobile emissions standards are also controversial because their health implications are unclear. The National Academy of Sciences, in evaluating the 90-percent reduction standard, concluded several years ago that "the existing studies that provide a rationale for the present federal motor vehicle emission standards are believed to be inadequate."[14]

Table 5-4 shows the emissions levels of automobiles in three cases: precontrol, present (1977) standards, and the goals of the Clean Air Act

---

[13] The fuel economy of 1977 cars sold in California is approximately 15 percent less than their forty-nine state counterparts because of emissions standards in California, which are more stringent than any other state standards.

[14] National Academy of Sciences, National Academy of Engineering Coordinating Committee on Air Quality, *Air Quality and Automobile Emission Control,* Committee Print, Serial no. 93-24, Senate Committee on Public Works, 93 Cong. 2 sess. (1974) vol. 3, p. 8.

Table 5-4. Auto Emissions Levels
(grams per mile)

Cases	Hydrocarbons	Carbon monoxide	Oxides of nitrogen
1968 auto fleet (uncontrolled)	8.7	87	3.5
1977 new car standards	1.5	15	2.0
Clean Air Act statutory goals	0.41	3.4	0.4

Source: Demand–Conservation Panel, Committee on Nuclear and Alternative Energy Systems (CONAES), *Alternative Energy Demand Futures* (Washington, D.C., National Academy of Sciences, forthcoming 1979).

of 1970. An eventual growth of vehicle miles to between two and two-and-one-half times the 1968 levels shows that 1977 standards imply a drop of more than 50 percent in total hydrocarbon and carbon monoxide emissions but an absolute rise in emissions of nitrogen oxides. Moving to standards originally set out by the original Clean Air Act would imply drastically lower emissions than those in 1968. While the goals originally set out by the Clean Air Act are difficult to achieve and perhaps not fully justified, a substantial shift to lighter vehicles would make it substantially easier to approach those goals.

Safety and the small automobile. Could safety considerations inhibit a substantial move to smaller vehicles? For many people, small automobiles have a poor reputation for withstanding crashes. However, they *can* be designed (with some weight penalty) to withstand crashes as well as a large automobile—for example, in terms of impact to the passenger on striking a fixed barrier at a given speed. In this connection, design efforts are being supported by the Department of Transportation's National Highway Traffic Safety Administration. In principle, crash-avoidance characteristics of the small automobile should, in addition, be better than for a large automobile. Thus, with appropriate attention to design, the important safety issue that remains for small automobiles is their disadvantage in two-vehicle collisions. This issue has not yet been carefully investigated.

If a major move to small passenger vehicles becomes necessary in order to achieve fuel economies *beyond* the 1985 standard, major design efforts would undoubtedly continue to improve the crashworthiness of small automobiles. It is also conceivable that trucks and buses, as well as those large private passenger vehicles that remain, could be isolated from small passenger cars to some extent on major high-speed highways.

Public Policies to Enhance Fuel Saving

Public policy here encompasses four major tools: (1) pricing, (2) regulation and standards, (3) public information and persuasion, and (4) government R&D activities. A number of such public-policy options have been discussed.

The most important appears to be the miles-per-gallon standard. Major issues involve (a) its effective coverage of the heavier light trucks used primarily for passenger transportation and (b) further improvement beyond 1985. The best models in 1977 (weighing less than about 3,300 pounds) exceeded the 1985 fleet standard of 27.5 miles per gallon. We discussed the particular example of the Volkswagen Rabbit diesel and its prospective descendants. The CONAES Demand–Conservation Panel estimated 37 miles per gallon to be the technological limit for automobile fleet fuel economy; but the rapid progress to date and the great potential for simply reducing size and weight suggest that even this figure may be conservative in the long term. For the fleet average in the year 2000, 37 miles per gallon is perhaps a reasonable maximum goal for a regulatory policy—if there is a policy need for substantial improvement beyond 1985.

Because there is so much room for improvement by size and weight reduction, a tax disincentive on gas-guzzling automobiles remains an attractive adjunct or alternative to more stringent regulation of fuel economy. Similarly, an increased fuel tax could complement mildly tougher regulation. As discussed earlier, fuel prices could be too low to provide much incentive for purchasing automobiles with better fuel economy, so that a very large tax would be required to have much effect. A tax of $1 a gallon[15] might not even be large enough in itself to have a significant effect, although it would bring enormous revenues. These revenues could very reasonably be used to subsidize such public transport facilities as continue to serve an important social objective, with particular attention to the transportation of those who cannot conveniently use a private automobile.

As for publicly supported activities, dissemination of facts about fuel economy and automotive R&D activity are advancing at a pace which suggests that no bold new policy initiatives are required.

---

[15] In the past, combined state and federal taxes on gasoline have often made up about one-third of the pump price, so the imposition of an excise tax amounting to roughly one-half of the retail cost per gallon does not seem inconceivable.

Projections of Energy Consumption

Future fuel use in private motor vehicles (dominated by automobiles and light trucks devoted to passenger transportation) will be proportional to

$$\text{fuel intensity} \times \text{vehicle miles}$$

where the fuel intensity is fuel consumption per average mile.

A variety of projections of vehicle miles has been made. Several of the high projections, however, do not take into account the effects of saturation. The total number of vehicle miles (VM) can be expressed in a variety of ways to bring out the effect of saturation, and two will be considered here. In the first:

$$VM = (\text{speed} \times \text{time/load factor}) \times \text{population}$$

where speed is the average speed of travel for all automobiles, time is the time spent in cars per capita, and load factor is the average number of people per vehicle. At present, speed = 32.6 mph, time = 57 minutes per day, and load factor = 2.2 are thought to be good estimates. There are no powerful reasons to expect any substantial changes in speed and load factor. Time will certainly not willingly be increased very much. That is an effect of saturation.

The second way to bring out the effect of saturation is:

$$VM = \text{adult population} \times \text{vehicle ratio} \times (VM/V)$$

where the adult population is taken to be all people sixteen through seventy-nine years of age; the vehicle ratio is the number of passenger motor vehicles per such person; and VM/V is the number of vehicle miles traveled per vehicle per year. In 1976, the adult population of driving age was 153.5 million, the vehicle ratio 71 percent, and the miles per vehicle roughly 11,000. The vehicle ratio is effectively bounded at 100 percent and cannot become much larger than 71 percent because there are young, infirm, and very elderly people, as well as people living in urban centers who will remain without cars, and there are one-car households which will remain that way. That, again, is an effect of saturation. The number of miles per vehicle has apparently reached saturation: a time-series plot spanning the last twenty-five years would show very little upward trend.

A satisfactory projection of total vehicle miles to the year 2000 can perhaps be obtained using the second expression—assuming, as we have been doing, the Census Bureau's Series II projection for population

Table 5-5. Projections of Automotive Energy Consumption for the Year 2000

Conservation level	Fuel economy of auto fleet (mpg)	Vehicle miles (ratio to 1976)	Fuel consumption	
			(10^{15} Btu)	(Percent of 1976)
No improvement beyond 1985 models	27.5	1.38	7.0	69
Continued improvement beyond 1985 models	37.0	1.38	5.3	52

Note: Includes light trucks used for passenger transport. See accompanying text for discussion of a substantially higher projection of fuel consumption.

(which signifies an increase in those aged sixteen to seventy-nine from 153.5 to 188.5 million), an increase in the vehicle ratio from 71 percent to 80 percent (largely because of an increased participation by women and partly because of increased income), and an unchanging 11,000 miles per vehicle. With this threefold set of assumptions the number of vehicle miles in 2000 would be 38 percent greater than that in 1976; and the average per capita time in private motor vehicles would rise to 65 minutes per day. The stock of vehicles would rise from a 1976 level of about 109 million to approximately 151 million in 2000.

Table 5-5 shows two projections of fuel use for the year 2000 based on this projection of vehicle miles. The two fuel economy projections are 27.5 miles per gallon and 37 miles per gallon (as mentioned in the public policy discussion above). The 27.5 miles per gallon projection is based on the test standard mandated for 1985 cars. (Some improvements beyond that standard are assumed so that the *total* existing fleet performance meets the new-car goal.) Projected energy consumption for automotive transport in the year 2000 is seen to vary from 31 to 48 percent *below* levels prevailing in 1976.

Are there any conditions under which the projected consumption level for motor fuel might substantially exceed these figures? Reverting to our light truck discussion, we could assume, for example, that in the 1990s the passenger-car fleet in use (including under-3-ton trucks) provided an average of only 25 miles per gallon—and, further, that light trucks of 3 to 5 tons used for passenger transportation accounted for 20 percent of the vehicle fleet and performed at only 16 miles per gallon. Under those bleak conditions, the effective fuel economy of the whole automotive fleet would rise to only 22.5 miles per gallon. Even based on this fuel economy—and also assuming one-third more vehicle miles than assumed for the other projections—fuel consumption in 2000 would still be just 11.5 quads, or 108 percent of 1976.

Under any conditions that now seem likely, it appears that forces already set in motion will probably end the trend since World War II of sharply increasing energy consumption by automotive vehicles in this country; and there is good reason to expect a sizable decline in such consumption.

Industrial Process Steam— With Particular Emphasis on Cogeneration

The Basics of Cogeneration

Energy is basically consumed either as thermal energy (which manifests itself as heat) or as nonthermal energy (which manifests itself as work), or both. Each form can be converted into the other, and many of our applications of energy depend on such conversions. When thermal is converted into nonthermal energy, however, some residual thermal energy invaribly results as an end product or by-product. This has often been characterized as "waste heat."

Conventional heating systems (for example, furnaces) convert fuel into heat, a very inefficient process from the second-law standpoint when the heat required is of very "low quality," that is, at a temperature near the ambient temperature. Meanwhile, when central power stations convert fuel into heat, they operate turbines to generate electricity, but some heat is also "rejected" as unusable. Ultimately, this heat is released by the cooling system to the environment without performing any function. Cogeneration is based on the idea that at least some heat of this type can be usefully employed, displacing conventional heating systems. Instead of designing a generation system that converts a thermal input into a single useful work output, one may design a *co*generation system that converts the thermal input into *two* outputs—one consisting of usable heat and one consisting of usable mechanical energy.

Conventional electric-generating equipment ejects heat at low temperatures (roughly 100°F) so as to maximize the amount of electricity produced. Cogeneration equipment, on the other hand, is designed to maximize the *combined* values of the two products—electricity *and* heat. Because heat of high temperature is much more valuable than heat of low temperature, it can be profitable to reduce the output of electricity somewhat in order to keep the by-product heat at a higher temperature.

Overall, fuel inputs needed for a given amount of useful output may be reduced as much as 30 percent by employing a cogeneration approach, and this fuel saving is cogeneration's major advantage. Other potential advantages include: (1) a total investment of less capital in generating equipment; (2) the possible reduction of distribution and transmission costs for industrial and commercial users of cogenerated electricity; (3) reduced cooling water requirements; and (4) shorter planning and construction times for incremental generating capacity, permitting greater flexibility in adjusting to electricity demand patterns as they evolve.

The two major potential applications for cogeneration are "district heating" of residential and commercial buildings and heat for industrial processes. (Cogeneration was also mentioned briefly earlier as a potential future source of small-scale residential heat and power.) Here, we restrict our attention to cogeneration in the production of industrial process steam[16]—an end use which we cited earlier as accounting for roughly 10 percent of all U.S. energy consumption.

Joint production of industrial process steam and electricity can be carried out either at central power stations or at industrial plants, but the cogeneration potential at central power plants is probably very limited. First, the generating technology now in use offers little scope for significant fuel savings; and very substantial modifications would be required to adapt the equipment for effective use. Second, it is uneconomic to transport process steam over long distances. Third, the long lifetimes of central power plants would require long-term commitments on the part of industrial users, which would limit the users' locational and planning flexibility. We will therefore emphasize cogeneration at industrial plants.

Cogeneration is not a new phenomenon. In 1922, 22 percent of all U.S. electricity was generated by industry rather than by utility enter-

---

[16] This discussion depends heavily on R. H. Williams, "Industrial Cogeneration," in *Annual Review of Energy* vol. 3 (Palo Alto, Calif., Annual Reviews, Inc. 1978). The following three studies were also consulted extensively: (1) Dow Chemical Company, Midland, Mich., Environmental Research Institute of Michigan, Ann Arbor, Mich., Townsend-Greenspan and Company, New York, N.Y., and Cravath, Swaine and Moore, New York, N.Y., *Energy Industrial Center Study*, Report to the National Science Foundation (Midland, Mich., Dow Chemical Co., 1975); (2) S. E. Nydick, J. P. Davis, J. Dunlay, S. Fam, and R. Sakhuja, *A Study of In-Plant Electric Power Generation in the Chemical, Petroleum Refining, and Paper and Pulp Industries*, Report to the Federal Energy Administration (Waltham, Mass., Thermo Electron Corporation, 1976); (3) P. Bos and coauthors, *The Potential for Cogeneration Development in Six Major Industries by 1985*, Report to the Federal Energy Administration (Cambridge, Mass., Resource Planning Associates, Inc., 1977). These studies will be referred to as the Dow Report, the Thermo Electron Report, and the R.P.A. Report, respectively.

prises, and a considerable fraction of that may have been—loosely speaking—cogenerated. By 1975, the industrially generated share of electricity had declined to less than 5 percent; but in today's terms that smaller percentage corresponds to about one full quad of fuel input for electrical generation, and a certain amount of industrial electricity is definitely cogenerated.[17] An additional measure is the amount of process steam produced by cogeneration.

About 15 percent of the process steam used in 1975 by six major industries (food, textiles, pulp and paper, chemicals, petroleum refining, and steel) was cogenerated.[18] If these six industries are representative of all process steam users (estimated at 10.1 quads in terms of fuel input), this would indicate that roughly 1.5 quads of fuel went into cogeneration systems throughout the country for steam production. The fuel input to electricity and the fuel input for steam must be added together to gauge the total size of cogeneration facilities, but in this case the correct sum will be *less* than the combined parts taken separately—because cogeneration offers some fuel saving over the separate generation of the two products. Thus, with a considerable amount of caution, we might estimate that the total fuel input to cogeneration systems in recent years has been *less* than 2.5 quads—but probably something in the order of 2 quads.

Economic and institutional forces have fostered the trend to central power generation. The cost of electric generation declined constantly, and demand growth was much higher for electricity than for process steam. Utilities actively resisted the concept of industrial cogeneration by charging very high rates for delivering backup power and offering very low rates in purchasing industrial power generated in excess of on-site needs. Future prospects for cogeneration are somewhat brighter, however. Electricity costs show a reversal from a downward to an upward trend, so that cogeneration at competitive costs will be easier. Moreover, the emphasis in energy policy on enhancing efficiency may succeed in removing institutional and legal barriers.

[17] Electricity consumption in 1975 was about 20 quads in terms of fuel equivalent required to generate it. About 5 percent is generated at the plant site, although—as the text points out—not all of this is cogenerated. (U.S. Department of the Interior, *Energy Perspectives 2* [Washington, D.C., GPO, 1976]).

[18] Estimates of industrial process steam use vary from as low as 5.7 quads to as high as 13.1 quads for the mid-1970s. (High figure from R.P.A. Report; low figure derived on basis of data from Energy and Environmental Analysis, Inc., *End Use Energy Consumption Data Base: Series I Tables,* prepared for U.S. Department of Energy (June 1978) (NTIS, PB 281-817). Since the cogeneration projection (below) is based on the better known use of large boilers, it is more reliable than suggested by the uncertainty in total steam production. The 15-percent figure is based on the ratio of cogenerated to total steam in six major industries (R.P.A. Report).

Technical Aspects

Cogeneration technologies that are commercially available today consist of steam turbine systems, gas turbine systems, and diesel engines. Figure 5-4 illustrates flow in the first two types, comparing them with the separate production of process steam and electricity.

In the steam turbine cogeneration system, fuel is burned to raise steam in a high pressure boiler. The high pressure steam drives a turbine, producing electricity. Low pressure steam is exhausted from the turbine at the appropriate temperature for direct use in industrial processes. This system is the same as conventional electric generation except that the steam is exhausted from the turbine at much higher temperatures than would be normal in generating electricity alone.

In the gas turbine cogeneration system, the very hot combustion gases from the fuel (1,500°F and higher) drive a turbine that generates electricity. The hot exhaust gases from the turbine (still at 600° to 1,000°F) are used to raise steam in a waste heat boiler at temperatures appropriate for industrial use. Combustion turbines are used now to some extent in central-station generation of electricity although they tend to be less fuel efficient than steam turbines for that purpose alone. In cogeneration systems, however, we shall see that they have a number of advantages.

A third cogeneration possibility, the diesel engine, differs from the two depicted in figure 5-4 because it is based on an internal combustion engine; but its flow is more like that of the gas turbine system. The electric generator is driven directly by the diesel-cycle engine, whose hot exhaust gases (600° to 800°F) raise steam in a waste-heat boiler for use in industrial processes. The diesel engine and gas turbine now operate on natural gas or on petroleum derivatives, while the steam turbine can operate on a variety of fuels. One limitation in the application of diesel generators is the relatively small capacity of individual units—which would be quite costly to install and maintain in sufficient numbers to provide more than a few megawatts output at one site.

The most important characteristics of sample cogeneration systems are listed in table 5-6. Some types produce a relatively large proportion of steam as an end product, while others produce a relatively large ratio of electricity to steam. The diesel engine generates about eight times as much electricity per unit of useful steam as the steam turbine does, while the gas turbine occupies an intermediate position. Another way of expressing the differences in performance characteristics is to state the fraction of fuel converted to electricity. Again, this is highest for the diesel

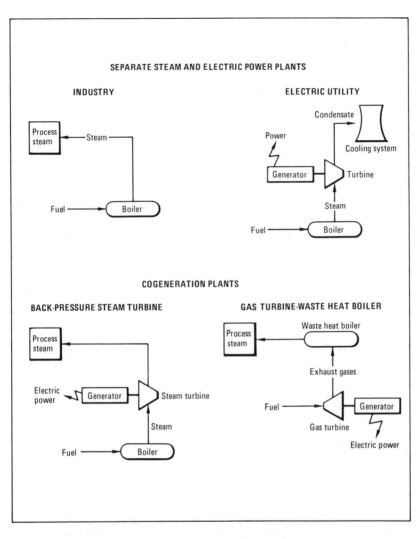

Figure 5-4. Flow diagrams of separate electricity-process steam systems and two types of cogeneration systems. From P. Bos and coauthors, *The Potential for Cogeneration Development in Six Major Industries by 1985* (Cambridge, Mass., Resource Planning Associates, Inc., 1977).

Table 5-6. Sample Technical Performance Characteristics for Cogeneration Systems

	Steam turbine	Gas turbine	Diesel
Electricity/steam ratio			
(kWh/million Btu of steam)	50	200	405
(Btu electrical/Btu of steam)	0.17	0.68	1.38
Fuel fraction converted to electricity	0.13	0.30	0.35
Net fuel consumption for electricity			
(Btu fuel/kWh)[a]	4,550	5,700	6,950
Net fuel consumption for process steam			
(Btu fuel/Btu produced)[b]	0.87	0.28	−0.10
Fuel savings overall			
(Btu fuel saved/Btu of fuel input)[a,b]	0.16	0.27	0.24
Fuel savings ratio[a,b]			
(Btu fuel saved/Btu of process steam	0.27	0.86	1.24
Second-law efficiency[c]	0.42	0.50	0.48
	(0.35)	(0.36)	(0.37)

Note: Process steam pressure for all systems is 150 psig at saturation. See accompanying text for discussion of this table.

Source: R. H. Williams, "Industrial Cogeneration," in *Annual Review of Energy* vol. 3 (Palo Alto, Calif., Annual Reviews, Inc., 1978).

[a] Assuming a boiler efficiency of 88 percent for process steam production in a separate facility.

[b] Assuming heat rate of 10,000 Btu/kWh for central station power.

[c] The second-law efficiency for separate central station electricity and process steam generation is shown in parentheses. Second-law efficiencies were calculated by Williams in cited reference.

and lowest for the steam turbine. The two methods of measurement do not yield proportional results, however, because of differences in electric-generating efficiency.

It is probably worthwhile to point out that "fuel fraction converted to electricity" is the number we usually associate with the conversion efficiency of a single-purpose electrical generator. The low rating of the steam turbine cogenerator in this respect (0.13) indicates how much of a penalty can be involved in raising the normal exhaust temperature.

The overall efficiency of a cogeneration system is sometimes expressed in terms of *net* fuel consumption per unit of electricity (or steam) produced. This figure is obtained by computing the amount of energy required to produce each unit of electricity (or steam) after subtracting the energy input that would have been required to produce the by-product steam (or electricity) separately.

For a steam turbine operating on a cogeneration basis (fourth row of numbers in the table), the net fuel consumption per kWh of electricity is less than half that required for conventional central power plant generation (typically more than 10,000 Btu/kWh). And for the diesel engine, the net fuel consumption per Btu of steam (row 5) is *negative,* implying that the cogeneration system can deliver a certain amount of process steam in addition to the electricity it generates while using less fuel than a conventional power plant would use to generate the electricity alone.

Another measure of technical efficiency is total fuel savings per Btu of fuel input, which refers to fuel savings through cogeneration compared with a system in which the same amount of electricity and steam are produced separately. The gas turbine is the most successful of the three technologies in saving fuel.

Perhaps the best criterion for measuring performance, however, is fuel savings per Btu of steam produced—because process steam production is considered to be the primary function of the cogeneration system in this study. Here the diesel engine again ranks first, with a figure exceeding 1.0. For the steam and gas turbine, the figures are 0.27 and 0.86, respectively.

Finally, one may consider the second-law efficiency of each system— the ratio of fuel required by the best possible system performing a given task to the fuel used in the system being considered. It appears that cogeneration systems operate in the range from 0.42 to 0.50, while systems with separate generation facilities range from 0.35 to 0.37. Note that gas turbines and diesel engines, which are considerably more efficient than steam turbines, both have a relatively high electricity-to-steam ratio.

Figure 5-5 graphically summarizes table 5-6 by showing the amount of fuel input needed by the various systems, with their respective mixes of steam and electricity, to produce a given amount of steam. Their total fuel savings (compared with separate conventional production of electricity and steam) are also indicated. For comparative purposes, the conventional systems for generating electricity and steam are also shown graphically.

Because gas turbines and diesel engines are now fueled by natural gas or petroleum derivatives (both of which face relative scarcity and rising prices), there is some urgency in adapting these generating systems to burn coal—our most abundant mineral-fuel resource. The most interesting option for burning coal in connection with gas turbines is fluidized bed combustion, discussed in chapter 9. The coupling of fluidized bed combustion technology to cogeneration systems is an attractive prospect for enhanced efficiency in industrial energy use.

Longer term possibilities include development of a coal-fired diesel engine or the development of coal-fired engines based on the Sterling or Ericsson cycles. The latter two possibilities are particularly interesting candidate technologies because they are externally fired and thus offer

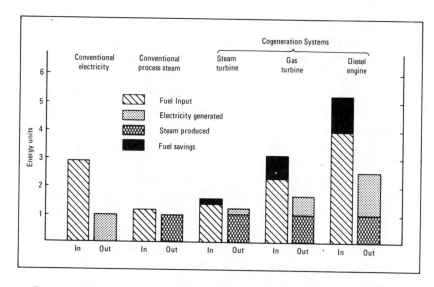

Figure 5-5. Energy inputs and outputs for sample cogeneration technologies. The fuel savings (solid areas) represent the difference between fuel consumption by each cogeneration system and the fuel which would be required if separate equipment were used to produce the steam and electricity which results when a given amount of steam is cogenerated by that particular system. From R. H. Williams, "Industrial Cogeneration" in *Annual Review of Energy* vol. 3 (Palo Alto, Calif., Annual Reviews, Inc., 1978).

the advantage of fuel flexibility. They are characterized by high electricity-to-steam ratios, and their best hope for utilization lies in decentralized applications because they offer no economies of scale.

Economic Aspects

Two issues are critical in evaluating the economic prospects for cogeneration. The first concerns the fact that the potential for fuel savings happens to be much greater for technologies with a high electricity-to-steam ratio, as indicated in table 5-6 and figure 5-5. High electricity-to-steam technologies are economic even at sites with small steam loads. This consideration is important for the market penetration of cogeneration. If only the low electricity-to-steam technologies are considered, the economic potential for cogeneration is estimated at 20 to 61 gigawatts by 1985. But if high electricity-to-steam technologies are also considered, the total market potential for cogeneration expands; it has been estimated at 85 to 257 gigawatts by 1985.[19] For many practical reasons, cogeneration could not be introduced this rapidly, but it is useful to begin an economic analysis by recognizing some reasonable upper limit such as this.

The second critical issue concerns the appropriate costs of electricity to be used for comparative evaluation. Utility pricing, being based on average—rather than marginal—cost concepts, insulates customers from the high cost of new electricity facilities. If, as is widely held by economists, social welfare is enhanced by using marginal cost pricing, the latter should govern comparative analysis of future facility expansion. The following discussion emphasizes facilities with *high* electricity-to-steam ratios and economic comparisons with the *marginal,* or replacement, costs of electricity rather than *low* electricity-to-steam facilities and comparison with *average* costs of electricity.

The technical performance criteria summarized above cannot be used as sole guides for economic decisionmaking. Whatever a particular system may save in fuel costs, it is clear that no economic advantage results if the capital costs to build the system are proportionally higher.

Table 5-7 presents unit capital costs for alternative cogeneration systems. It is important to note that, although cogeneration unit capacity may be only a small percentage of the 1,000-megawatt (Mw) capacity typical of modern central power plants, unit capacity costs can be comparable to—and even less than—unit capacity costs for such central power plants.

It is likely that the minimum size of facility to be adopted will not depend only on capital costs, but also on servicing and staffing costs. A facility of 5 to 10 megawatts of electrical capacity, considered the minimum size for anything but completely automated cogeneration facilities, would justify two full-time-equivalent employees. On the other hand, it would take a substantially larger facility to support continuous dedicated staffing. A capacity of 5 to 10 megawatts corresponds to roughly 50,000 to 100,000 pounds per hour of steam, or 50 to 100 million Btu per hour of thermal energy—the equivalent of a thermal output rating of just under 15 to 30 megawatts.

Industrial facilities with process steam loads over 100,000 pounds per hour account for 67 percent of all process steam.[20] In the six major steam-using industries mentioned above, 83 percent of all process steam

---

[19] See the Dow, Thermo Electron, and R.P.A. Reports. The figure quoted is the central station generating capacity which could be displaced by cogeneration facilities if all economically defensible installations took place.

[20] Dow Report.

Table 5-7. Capital Costs of Alternative Power Generation Units
(1976 dollars/kW)

Central station power	Cogeneration systems[a]			
	Gas turbine		Steam turbine	
1,000 Mw	10 Mw[c]	80 Mw[d]	5 Mw[e]	30 Mw[f]
650–800[b]	340	200	760	440
	(470)	(290)	(1,475)	(860)

Source: R. H. Williams, "Industrial Cogeneration," in *Annual Review of Energy* vol. 3 (Palo Alto, Calif., Annual Reviews, Inc., 1978).

[a] The cogeneration capital cost estimates given here are those prepared for the Thermo Electron study. The cogeneration cost figures in the first line apply to cases where capital costs of steam-producing equipment can be shared between electricity generation and steam generation. Figures in parentheses apply to situations where existing steam-producing equipment is not ready for retirement, so that the total cost of cogeneration equipment must be assigned to electric power production.
[b] Typical values for coal and nuclear plants ordered in 1976.
[c] For a process steam flow of 50,000 pounds of steam per hour.
[d] For a process steam flow of 400,000 pounds of steam per hour.
[e] For a process steam flow (at 150 psig) of 100,000 pounds of steam per hour.
[f] For a process steam flow (at 150 psig) of 600,000 pounds of steam per hour.

is produced at locations with loads over 100,000 pounds per hour and 94 percent at locations with loads over 50,000 pounds per hour.[21] However, production at one location does not necessarily mean production by one boiler. In one estimate, only about 38 percent of all steam is produced by boilers producing more than about 80,000 pounds of steam per hour.

The capital cost data in table 5-7 can be used to calculate the cost of delivered electricity from new facilities (table 5-8). Capital charge rates applicable to industrial cogeneration are generally higher than for utilities, because utilities require lower rates of return than industrial enterprises; but table 5-8 assumes utility ownership of the cogeneration facilities (see discussion below). The table presents the cost of electricity delivered by four cogeneration systems and, for comparative purposes, by central station power. The major conclusion is that although the cost of cogenerated electricity is greater than the present (national) average price of electricity from existing central power plants (except for the case of the larger steam turbine plant), in all cases it is less than the projected cost of electricity from new facilities.

A similar conclusion can be reached by calculating an internal gross rate of return. It appears that for gas turbine systems, gross rates of return

[21] R.P.A. Report.

Table 5-8. Delivered Electricity Costs, Central Station Versus Cogenerated Power (mills/kWh in 1976 prices)

	Central station power	Cogenerated power			
	Cost of elec. from a new nuclear plant	Gas turbine (oil-fired)		Steam turbine (coal-fired)	
Costs		10 Mw	80 Mw	5 Mw	30 Mw
Capital[a]	14.00	5.43–7.51	3.20–4.64	12.12–23.56	7.03–13.74
Fuel	5.22	15.39[b]	15.39[b]	4.32.[c]	4.32[c]
Operation and maintenance	2.30	4.60	4.60	3.00	3.00
Busbar costs	22.40	25.42–27.50	23.19–24.63	19.46–30.88	14.35–21.06
Transmission and distribution	8.90	N.A.	N.A.	N.A.	N.A.
Cost of delivered elec.	31.3[d]	26.0–27.9[e]	24.0–25.3[e]	23.7–34.0[e]	18.6–24.7[e]

Note: N.A. = not applicable.
Source: R. H. Williams, "Industrial Cogeneration," in Annual Review of Energy vol. 3 (Palo Alto, Calif., Annual Reviews, Inc., 1978). Somewhat different assumptions and statistical techniques account for variations between this cost computation for nuclear generated electricity and the carefully generalized one used for comparison with coal-fueled plants in chapter 9; but in both cases the tables are internally consistent. Their purpose in each instance is to provide an economic basis for choice among competitive systems.

[a] The capital charges shown here are based on the capital costs given in table 5-7, and utility ownership of cogeneration systems is assumed. The carrying charge rates for central station plants and industrially sited cogeneration systems, respectively, are 10.6 percent and 11.2 percent per year, while corresponding capacity factors are assumed to be 65 percent and 80 percent. For cogeneration systems, the lower capital charge values are based on the first line of table 5-7; the higher values refer to the parenthetical figures in the second line of that table.

[b] Levelized price of oil of $2.75/million Btu.

[c] Levelized price of delivered coal of $0.95 in mills/Btu.

[d] The average cost to large customers of utility-generated electricity in 1976 was 21 mills.

[e] For the gas turbine system, which exports more electricity than is consumed on-site, there need be no allowance for standby charges on backup power from a utility. However, for the steam turbine system there are standby charges which typically double the price of supplementary electricity purchased from a utility. In the gas turbine case, the (slight) excess of delivered cost over busbar cost arises from the cost of back-up power; back-up power is assumed to be 10 percent of the total and to cost 31.3 mills/kWh.

are in the 20 to 40 percent range, if the price at which excess electricity is sold equals the cost of electricity from new facilities. However, in case only the average cost of central plant generation is paid for excess electricity, conventional cogeneration systems (oil-fired turbines) are uneconomic, and—in fact—only the hypothetical coal-fired gas turbine will be economic.

Public Policy and Implementation

The ability of cogeneration to conserve energy resources is clear. Furthermore, the economics of cogeneration are potentially favorable—in the sense that electricity may be typically cheaper to produce and deliver by means of a new cogeneration facility than by means of a new central power station, if a favorable market for excess electricity is available. However, several major barriers to implementation exist:[22] (1) Most utilities have resisted wide implementation of cogeneration. (2) Many industrial managers do not relish the notion of engaging in production of electricity. (3) Present utility regulatory practice discriminates against cogeneration. (4) Generation technology with a high electricity-to-steam ratio is not yet ready to use coal as its fuel.

Some of these barriers would be less formidable if ownership and management of the cogeneration facilities were vested in the utility rather than the industrial firm involved. One possible reason for reluctance on the part of utilities to undertake cogeneration, however, may be possible overcapacity in electric-generating facilities. The utilities may have, and may be building, more generating capacity than is likely to be needed. Average capacity factors have dropped sharply in the last decade: from producing about 54 percent of their full-time, full-rated output in the late 1960s, plants cut back to producing only about 45 percent in the mid-1970s. At the same time, average gross peak margins have increased sharply; the percentage by which total capacity exceeds peak demand climbed from 18 percent in the late 1960s to more than 33 percent in the mid-1970s.[23] Even though recent cancellations and postponements in construction might again cause reserve capacity to dwindle—especially

[22] Norman L. Dean, "Institutional Obstacles to Industrial Cogeneration," unpublished working paper prepared for a Ford Foundation energy study group at Resources for the Future (Washington, D.C., August 1978).

[23] Capacity factors and margins are derived from data shown in Edison Electric Institute, *Statistical Year Book of the Electric Utility Industry for 1977* (New York, N.Y., EEI, October 1978).

on a regional basis—the present low capacity factors and high peak margins may persist well into the 1980s. Much of the capacity expansion undertaken through the early 1970s was planned with the expectation of a growth in electricity demand of 6 to 7 percent per year. Given the electric price trend reversal, a figure of 4 percent for the growth of electric demand may be more faithful to the current situation. To the extent utilities preserve a fixed rate of return, overcapacity may result in higher prices—further suppressing demand growth. It is also possible that both technological and regulatory improvements in load management might smooth out demand peaks to a point where less total capacity is really needed.

The fact that cogeneration with high electricity-to-steam ratios is economically the most attractive aggravates the problem, for it implies that most industries must find a way to sell electricity. Utilities already confronted with overcapacity problems may clearly be hesitant in cooperating to promote cogeneration.

A major objective of present national energy policy is to encourage industry to shift from oil and natural gas to coal. Although this move in principle is favorable to introducing cogeneration equipment because it encourages the early retirement or simple replacement of existing boilers, rapid conversion could actually affect the prospects of cogeneration adversely. First, utilities are being pressed now to convert their own facilities, so their resistance to further change may be greater than ever during the next decade or so. A second reason is that coal cogeneration technology—for example, coal-fired gas turbines—is not yet fully developed. If primarily steam turbines—with their low electricity-to-steam ratio—were to be installed, there would be only modest scope for fuel savings.

Besides the major barriers to implementation, there are a number of less important problems. The environmental, safety, and health aspects of cogeneration have not yet received sufficient attention, although they are not likely to have any major effect when compared to conventional (separate) generation. In addition, since cogeneration (by definition) ties electric generation to steam generation, some industries will be unwilling to accept the degree of inflexibility such a system is perceived to imply.

Two types of public policy measures are available to reduce the barriers to implementation of this particular conservation technology. First, one could stimulate the development of the necessary new coal technology. Second, one could change the regulation of utilities. This latter option involves three major possibilities: (a) stimulus toward ownership of cogeneration facilities by utilities, (b) incentives for development by industry or third parties (perhaps under a leasing arrangement by firms that manufacture or market cogeneration equipment), or (c) deregulation of the generation of electricity.

Utilities might be attracted to cogeneration ownership by public policy whenever a power company was formulating expansion plans. As soon as a decision was made to increase capacity, a comparison might be made between the building of a new central power station and the building of a sequence of utility-owned cogeneration units. Since a regulated monopoly requires lower rates of return than the average industry, utility ownership could spur the penetration of cogeneration. And because a utility can easily export excess electricity into its own grid, the high electricity-to-steam ratios of the most promising systems would be acceptable. Going even beyond this, some regulatory groups might decide to mandate cogeneration in certain cases—or at least encourage its implementation via rate structure reform.

In the case of industry or third party ownership, public regulators could specify that the owners be allowed to sell excess electricity to utilities at rates appropriate to the cost of electricity from new facilities that it might be presumed to be replacing. Such rates would have to depend, of course, on the timing and reliability of the power.

The economics of cogeneration facilities owned by industry or third parties will also be greatly influenced by the standby charges that utilities levy to cover the costs of the extra capacity they must maintain in order to deliver services when needed and the extra transmission and distribution equipment required. As a matter of fact, widespread use of cogeneration should minimize the costs associated with maintaining extra capacity, because many industries can (to a considerable extent) share a common capacity reserve. Moreover, electricity sold to the utility would utilize the same transmission and distribution systems—operating, as it were, as a "two-way street." Both of these factors should permit lower standby charges.

These situations, however, involve only minor changes in regulatory practice. A more sweeping possibility is also suggested by cogeneration: serious reexamination of utilities as "natural monopolies."

Two beliefs underlie the historical assumption that the provision of electric power is a natural monopoly: (1) the larger the facilities, the lower will be the costs; (2) competition would require an unusually burdensome duplication of facilities. Technological developments have modified both premises, however. The electric utility industry can be divided into three parts: generation, transmission, and local distribution.

Transmission and distribution may well be natural monopolies; but generation—which involves more than half the costs—no longer requires the same status. Consider these technical and economic developments: feasibility of long-distance transmission; infeasibility of ever-larger central power plants; and prospective competitiveness of small cogeneration units. The first development means that generation facilities over a wide area could supply any particular demand. The second and third developments mean that the economies of scale for generation may have already been exceeded.

A reasonable proposal for study is then: the separation of generation, transmission, and distribution businesses; the deregulation of generation; and the requirement that transmission companies provide service at appropriate rates to all customers.[24] If generation of electricity became a competitive business, one result that could almost surely be counted on is that the opportunities offered by cogeneration would be fully exploited.

Deregulation could create problems—such as the difficulties of assuring system reliability when common ownership is absent. There are remedial measures for such problems, but discussion of those issues is beyond the scope of this book.

A final matter of policy interest concerns the move toward industrial conversion to coal. Although the long-term benefits of that policy seem clear, the nation probably should not neglect the resource-conserving advantages of oil-based cogeneration in the short-to-medium term. Oil-based cogeneration might serve well in a demonstration phase, during which the institutional and regulatory problems mentioned above could be worked out. Although oil-based cogeneration may not be as attractive economically as coal-based cogeneration, it still is more attractive from the standpoint of saving energy than many other applications of oil. Finally, cogeneration fuel need not compete directly with the demand for such products as home heating oil and motor fuel. Residual oil can be used for cogeneration with gas turbines or diesel engines.

Projections of Industrial Process Steam Use and Associated Cogeneration

If fuel use for process steam is assumed to grow proportionally with industrial output, such fuel use might equal about 22.7 quads in the year

---

[24] See either Almarin Phillips, ed., *Promoting Competition in Regulated Markets* (Washington, D.C., The Brookings Institution, 1975); or William H. Shaker, ed., Wilbert Steffy, co-ed, *Electric Power Reform: The Alternatives for Michigan* (Ann Arbor, Mich., University of Michigan Institute of Science and Technology, 1976).

Table 5-9. Selected Projections of Fuel Requirements for Process Steam in the Year 2000

Projections	Fuel use (quads)	Growth rate[a] per year
High projection		
No conservation[b]	22.7	3.2%
Mid-range projection		
With conservation—Exxon[c]	17.9	2.2
With conservation—Exxon[c]—and adding cogeneration savings based on present policies	16.6	1.9
Low projection		
With additional conservation envisioned in this report	13.6	1.2
With additional conservation and 45-percent penetration of market by cogeneration	10.1	0.0

[a] Fuel use for process steam is estimated by this study to have been 10.1 quads in 1974. See footnote 18 in this chapter.

[b] Estimated on the basis of the projected GNP (see chapter 4) and by considering the past relationship between overall GNP, industrial gross product, and process steam demand.

[c] M. H. Farmer, E. M. Magee, and F. M. Spooner, "Application of Fluidized-Bed Technology to Industrial Boilers," Report to the Federal Energy Administration (Linden, N.J., Exxon Research and Engineering Co., July 1976).

2000. That is 225 percent of the 1974 level—representing annual growth of about 3 percent (see table 5-9). However, this may not be a reasonable projection, because a persistent trend in the industrial sector points to continuing substantial reductions in the use of fuel per unit of industrial product. Unfortunately, any projection made at this time will be very crude indeed; not enough quantitative information about industrial energy use is available.

To assess the basis for substantially lower growth in fuel demand for industrial process steam, we begin by considering the present policies and presently anticipated fuel price increases. Under these conditions, an Exxon study has projected a reduction of fuel use for process steam per unit of production of approximately 1 percent annually, resulting in the aggregate projection of 17.9 quads in 2000 shown in table 5-9. This projection can be combined with a projection of cogeneration based on present policies and presently projected fuel prices.[25] Under these conditions, cogeneration will be mainly restricted to large coal-fired steam turbine engines, with nationwide generating capacity in the likely range of

[25] If the future price of oil has been seriously underestimated here in relation to the escalating marginal cost of central station electricity, the shares of industrial cogeneration allotted to gas turbines and diesels would have to be revised downward.

30 to 50 gigawatts by the year 2000. Fuel savings associated with cogeneration would be 1.0 to 1.5 quads annually compared with 0.5 quads at
present. The combined projection of fuel use associated with process
steam is 16.6 quads, or 164 percent of present fuel use. (From table 5-9:
17.9 less savings of, say, 1.3 = 16.6 quads.)

A lower projection results, however, if one considers the adoption of
further policies to support conservation. The most interesting case involves a changed regulatory setting to accommodate utility involvement
in cogeneration, either through ownership of cogeneration facilities or
through extensive buying of excess electricity. This implies implementation of high electricity-to-steam cogeneration systems with marginal, that
is, replacement, cost pricing for electricity. Such aggressive conservation
measures would probably be accompanied by strong measures in support
of reducing the demand for conventionally produced process steam, and
also measures in support of improved efficiency for conventional process
steam production. For example, improving control and maintenance techniques, boilers, and the types of processes used, as well as redesigning the
final products, will help to limit the expansion of fuel demand for process
steam.

Suppose one assumes—as seems to us quite reasonable—a 2 percent
annual decrease in fuel use for process steam per unit of production. This
projection has a twofold rationale: examination of the actual short-term
response of industry, and modeling of certain investment decisions relating to conservation. For industrial energy uses of all kinds, the short-term
response of industry has been a striking 15-percent reduction of fuel use
per unit of product in the period from 1972 to 1976 (that is, 4 percent
per year). There are strong reasons to believe that prevailing trends and
changes in maintenance and operations that may be largely responsible
for this improvement will continue for an extended period.

For longer term prospects, an effort of particular interest here is directed toward modeling improvements in industrial boilers and in waste
heat recovery schemes. A reduction of over 20 percent in fuel use per unit
of production has been projected in connection with these types of
changes.[26]

A projected 2 percent per year reduction in unit energy requirements
for process steam implies fuel use of 13.6 quads in the year 2000 (table

[26] The analysis in question is contained in the government's so-called MOPPS
study: U.S. Department of Energy, "Market Oriented Program Planning Study,"
Final Report, vol. 1 (Integrated Summary) (Washington, D.C., December 1977
Review Draft).

Table 5-10. Projection of Possible Total Cogeneration Capacity for the Year 2000

Method	Central station equivalent capacity[a] (gigawatts)	Fuel savings (quads/year)
Steam turbine[b]	21	0.6
Diesel[c]	43	0.8
Gas or gas/steam turbines		
Coal-firing with fluidized-bed combustion[d]	49	1.6
Oil-firing[e]	21	0.5
Total	134	3.5

Note: Projection is based on 45-percent penetration of process steam market.

[a] This is central station capacity that would be displaced by installed cogeneration capacity. For the comparison system of separate electrical and steam generation, the central station capacity factor is 65 percent, and boiler efficiency is 88 percent.

[b] For 20 percent of the steam load and electricity-to-process steam production of 50 kWh per million Btu. To permit replicating figures in these two columns, the following description explains the six steps involved for the steam turbine. (Data for the other three configurations can be similarly derived.) *Step 1:* 20 percent of 13.6 quads (primary energy equivalent projected in table 5-9), process steam = 2.72 quads. *Step 2:* 2.72 quads times boiler efficiency of 0.88 = 2.39 quads of delivered process steam. *Step 3:* At the ratio of 50 kWh per million Btu of delivered steam, 2.39 quads signifies 119.7 billion kWh. *Step 4:* A capacity factor of 0.65 signifies 5,694 hours per year. *Step 5:* 119.7 billion kWh divided by 5,694 hours results in the 21 gigawatts of central station equivalent capacity shown in the first column. *Step 6:* To calculate corresponding fuel savings shown in the second column, we refer back to the next-to-last line, first column, of table 5-6, where we find a fuel savings ratio (that is, Btu fuel savings per Btu of process steam) of 0.27. Multiplying the 2.39 quads of delivered process steam by 0.27 gives estimated fuel savings of 0.6 quads.

[c] For 5 percent of the steam load and 400 kWh per million Btu.

[d] For 15 percent of the steam load and 150 kWh per million Btu.

[e] For 5 percent of the steam load and 200 kWh per million Btu.

5-9). This can be combined with a projection of cogeneration—more sanguine than the 1.3 quad savings considered a moment ago—based on the economics of utility ownership and on development of coal-fired gas turbine technology. Under those conditions we assume that about 45 percent of steam production (of 13.6 quads) is cogenerated. The fuel savings are projected to be 3.5 quads, with details given in table 5-10.

Thus, with reasonably optimistic assumptions about public policy support and success in technical development, it appears that cogeneration *could* help maintain total fuel use for process steam by the end of the century at only 10.1 quads per year—or almost exactly what it was in 1974.

6   *What Can We Say About Future Energy Consumption?*

This chapter concerns prospective energy-demand paths for the United States over the next twenty-five years or so. Its purpose is to develop a set of projections that are credible in terms of their possibility of occurrence, constructed in an analytically sound manner, and faithful to the underlying economic, technological, and policy assumptions upon which they depend. We will begin with a brief reference to several other energy-demand studies and consider their orientation and principal findings. For the purpose of fashioning a long-term projection of U.S. energy demand, we will adopt the results of the detailed inquiry (contained in chapter 5) into three important components of energy use—home heating, automotive transport, and industrial process steam. These results will then be combined with an analysis of other key end-use, energy-consuming categories in order that we may project overall U.S. energy consumption. In the final portion of the chapter we will speculate on other aspects of future energy-demand growth and consider factors that strengthen or weaken one's confidence in the projections that have been made.

It is useful to bear in mind two elements in the growth of energy demand. First, we must remind ourselves that energy is needed not as a good in itself but as the wherewithal to provide goods and services that are desirable: for example, mobility, warmth, and a source of power for efficient operation of machinery. An energy-demand projection must therefore contend itself not only with the aggregate growth of the economy but also with the way in which parts of the economy and society change over time. (These matters were elaborated conceptually and historically in chapter 3.) Clearly, major subsectors of the economy do not all change in the same proportion; for example, there are now signs that, as compared with the past, the extent of automobile ownership relative to income is slowing down. Food consumption has for some time lagged behind income growth. Changing tastes, relative price developments, locational characteristics, and other phenomena interact with income growth so as to generate at least some momentum toward a restructuring of economic activity. The energy-demand analyst must be sensitive to the more noticeable of these forces, for disparate trends toward relative expansion or contraction can signify disparate trends in energy demand. Expansion of multifamily housing at the expense of single-family, detached housing, for example, means dampened energy growth. While expanded demand for certain personal services might likewise contribute to slower energy growth, other types of consumption—for example, accelerated growth in the volume of airline traffic—could help swell energy demand.

Second, along with the nature and consequence of such compositional changes, we must be alert to the prospects for changing energy requirements per unit of activity in given tasks—for example, how much energy we will need to heat a given amount of residential floor area, to accommodate so many vehicle miles of traffic, or to satisfy a specified volume of manufacturing output. The technological and economic ease or difficulty of substituting nonenergy resources—insulating materials, here; capital equipment, there; labor, in perhaps other instances—for energy are an important aspect of this issue.

It is impossible to do complete justice to this twofold dimension of future energy-demand growth within the confines of the present study. One would need to immerse oneself deeply in household budget studies and input–output schema in order to thoroughly probe the emerging pattern of final demand in the economy and the associated energy implications. However, neither of these analytical tools, in their present state of development, are easily adaptable to analysis of future energy demand. Nevertheless, even keeping the issue in mind *as a matter of conceptual importance* is useful, for it will be possible to reflect these two elements of energy consumption, at least crudely, as we work out our projections.

A Brief Review of Some Recent Energy Projections

A number of major efforts to explore or chart future U.S. energy consumption have been undertaken in recent years. Here, we will briefly note the highlights of some of these studies. Our principal purpose is to convey a sense of the diversity of approaches and results, thereby providing a firmer basis for the judgments expressed in this book. A more detailed review appears in the appendix to this chapter.

Table 6-1 identifies and summarizes the overall results of five such major efforts. (In the following discussion, we cite the shorthand designation used in the table.) Note that four out of the five studies reviewed come up with projected levels of energy demand in the year 2000, ranging from 111 to 114 quads. (In 1975 the average figure was 71 quads; in 1977, 76 quads.) The figures cited are baseline or mid-range numbers surrounded, within each of the studies, by both higher and lower projections. The demographic and macroeconomic assumptions accompanying the five projections tend to be reasonably uniform among themselves and quite similar to the mid-range assumptions noted in chapter 4. That is, the long-term rate of population growth proceeds at a pace of about 0.8 percent per year or slightly lower, and the GNP within the range of 3 to 3.5 percent per year. The three projections showing consumption of 114 quads in the year 2000 signify energy growth somewhat under 2 percent yearly and, consequently, an energy–GNP elasticity coefficient of approximately 0.6. In the Electric Power Research Institute (EPRI) projection, the coefficient is virtually 1.0.

Although four out of the five projections show comparable levels of energy use in the year 2000, and even though the studies are governed by similar macroeconomic assumptions, they are in other respects characterized by certain important differences.

First, in two of the cases the matter of future energy demand was subsidiary to the central topic addressed by the study. The Market Oriented Program Planning Study (MOPPS) effort was more concerned with prospects for commercial penetration of energy supply and delivery systems than with demand and conservation questions. The Resources for the Future–National Institutes of Health (RFF–NIH) study set out to probe the long-term consequences for the environment and resources in general—not just energy—of alternative assumptions regarding demographic and economic growth.

Second, only in the Institute for Energy Analysis (IEA) study was there any attempt to determine whether the GNP which constitutes the driving force for estimating energy demands might *itself* be jeopardized as a consequence of rising relative energy prices and problems concerning substitutability of energy by other resources. (The IEA investigators concluded that the initially stipulated GNP growth averaging a bit over 3 percent could be resilient even to real energy price increases of 4 percent per annum; but even this IEA "test" was conducted in a fairly aggregative and abstract framework.)

Table 6-1. Projected Energy-Consumption Levels in the Year 2000: Comparison of Five Recent Studies

Source	Energy consumption (in quads)	Comments
Institute for Energy Analysis (IEA)	114	IEA projected low (101.4) and high (125.9) figures, of which 114 is the midpoint.
CONAES Demand–Conservation Panel	111	Study projected four principal cases to the year 2010. The 111-quad figure, a subsidiary version of case "B" conforms most closely to our mid-range economic and demographic projections (see chap. 4) and assumes a real energy price rise of 2 percent yearly. The figure is interpolated from a 1975–2010 time path.
MOPPS	114	Figure is described as the "base case" projection.
EPRI—Demand 1977	159	Figure is described as baseline, falling between a "conservation" case (146) and a "high" case (196).
RFF–NIH Study	114	Baseline case. Study featured wide variety of additional cases.

Sources: IEA: Institute for Energy Analysis, Oak Ridge Associated Universities, *U.S. Energy and Economic Growth, 1975–2010* (Oak Ridge, Tenn., IEA, September 1976).

CONAES: National Academy of Sciences, Committee on Nuclear and Alternative Energy Systems (CONAES) "Outlook for Energy Demand and Conservation," Report of the Panel on Demand and Conservation (in preparation). The acronym CONAES denoting the parent committee is used here as it has been elsewhere. For a summary discussion of the panel's findings, particularly with respect to low energy futures, see "U.S. Energy Demand: Some Low Energy Futures," *Science* (14 April 1978) pp. 142–152.

MOPPS: U.S. Department of Energy, "Market Oriented Program Planning Study (MOPPS)," Final Report, vol. 1, "Integrated Summary." (Our reference applies to the December 1977 Review Draft version of this document.)

EPRI: Larry J. Williams, James W. Boyd, and Robert T. Crow, *Demand 77: EPRI Annual Energy Forecasts and Consumption Model*, EPRI EA-621-SR, vol. 1 (Palo Alto, Calif., Electric Power Research Institute, March 1978). A summary account appears in Robert T. Crow, "Demand 77," *EPRI Journal* (December 1977) pp. 20–23.

RFF–NIH: See Ronald G. Ridker and William D. Watson, Jr., chap. 5, "Energy," in "To Choose a Future: Resource and Environmental Problems of the U.S., A Long-term Global Outlook," an RFF study sponsored by the National Institutes of Health (in preparation). A compressed account appears in Ronald G. Ridker, William D. Watson, Jr., and Adele Shapanka, "Economic, Energy, and Environemental Consequences of Alternative Energy Regimes, An Application of the RFF/SEAS Modeling System," in Charles J. Hitch, ed., *Modeling Energy and Economic Interactions: Five Approaches* (Washington, D.C., Resources for the Future, 1977). However, this latter discussion, while a lucid description of the approach followed in the RFF–NIH project, introduces and tests the effect of somewhat different underlying assumptions so as to conform to identical assumptions governing other contributions to the Hitch volume.

Third, the methodology varied. EPRI employed an econometric model. RFF–NIH depended on use of a number of interlinked models (including input–output). The remaining studies were methodologically eclectic. Generally speaking, within the overall economic-demographic framework of the respective study, a set of specific variables—each closely related to energy use—was projected. These would include, for example, the projected stock and use of automobiles, commercial floor space, residential housing units, steel production, and selected other components of industrial activity. (The interrelatedness of these activities—for example, as between the steel and automotive sectors—tended to be ignored.) For each indicator, the associated energy demand is typically projected on the basis of analysis regarding future changes in energy intensity—in turn, influenced by judgments regarding price changes and technological innovations.

Fourth, the role assigned to price ranges from explicit to implicit or from substantial to modest, or both. (But no study assumes zero change.) Thus, IEA specifies real energy price increases of from 4 to 5 percent per year (a very large rise) but conducts its analysis essentially independent of the price factor. The Committee on Nuclear and Alternative Energy Systems (CONAES) projections, given in table 7-1, assume a 2 percent energy price increase annually. MOPPS assumes the much more modest price increases implicit in the administration's proposed 1977 National Energy Plan (NEP). The considerable degree of energy conservation nonetheless reflected in MOPPS stems from the lagged effect of price increases that have already occurred or from implementation of conservation practices whose previous lack of adoption was due to factors other than price.

What Emerges from These and Other Studies?

The handful of energy-demand projections selected for inclusion in this summary review could easily have been augmented by numerous others. Public agencies, academic institutions, the corporate sector, and public interest groups have all been active in this field. But the ones cited probably serve adequately to typify the kind of assumptions, approaches, and judgments entering into recent energy forecasting. One of the striking conclusions to which one cannot help being drawn is the progressively scaled-down expectation regarding future energy-demand growth that has occurred in recent years. True, a precise comparison of the current crop of projections with those of, say, five years ago, would have to take note of which changing perceptions have given rise to these changing expectations. Higher projections governed by the pre-1973 world oil price regime may have entertained wrong assumptions but need not have been analytically "wrong." On the other hand, there may formerly have been an underappreciation of the conservation potentials to be realized—as is the case with automotive fuel economy—even apart from price changes.

Prior to the last several years, which span the period of the studies reviewed here, among other prominent efforts, only the 1974 report of the Ford Foundation Energy Policy Project countenanced a decisive deceleration in the energy growth rate. Its so-called technical fix scenario, which fell within a range bounded by a high "historical growth" trend and a low "zero energy growth" projection, envisaged energy demand growth of 2.3 percent yearly, signifying a level of 124 quads in 2000. (The GNP was projected at 3.3 percent per year.) In contrast, other studies, more or less contemporaneous with the Ford Energy Policy Project, continued to emphasize substantially higher growth paths. For example, a major 1975 Interior Department report projected a year 2000 consumption level of 163 quads, or a future growth rate of 3.4 percent per year.[1]

There is no need to belabor the point: energy-demand sights are being lowered, of which no more dramatic illustration exists than the recent releases from oil companies, institutions which in the past tended to be skeptical that historic energy growth rates could be deflected downward without serious repercussions. Exxon's energy-demand projection for the period 1977–90 falls a bit below 2.3 percent per year. A sharp slowdown in demand, emanating from the transportation sector, figures significantly in this assumed deceleration. Shell's outlook over the same period foresees energy growth of around 2.6 percent accompanying the GNP's assumed growth of over 3.2 percent.[2]

---

[1] The publications referred to were Energy Policy Project of the Ford Foundation, *A Time to Choose* (Cambridge, Mass., Ballinger, 1974); and U.S. Department of the Interior, *Energy Through the Year 2000* (Washington, D.C., GPO, 1975).

[2] See remarks by W. T. Slick, Jr., senior vice president, Exxon Company, USA, "The U.S. Energy Outlook," at a meeting of the National Association of Fleet Administrators, Houston, Texas, April 3, 1978; and Shell Oil Company, "National Energy Outlook in 1980–1990: An Interim Report" (February 1978). The Shell report projects a GNP growth of 3.2 percent per year during the 1980–90 decade, implying probably somewhat faster growth when measured from 1977.

Guided both by our earlier review of five specific projection studies as well as a skimming of additional recent efforts, we would point to the following four major findings:

1. Recognizing that different results flow from alternative cases or scenarios, "base case" (or a synonymous designation) economic growth (GNP) is commonly judged to range from 3 to 3.5 percent per year. The projection of GNP is generally an *input* to the energy models, not an *output*.

2. Although the energy-demand projections cited included ones spanning a wider range of possibilities, a distinct clustering in the range of 115 to 130 quads for the year 2000 emerges. A number of studies envisage a future energy–GNP elasticity coefficient of between 0.5 and 0.6.

3. Virtually all studies surveyed assume real energy price increases, with gas prices expected to rise fastest and coal and electricity prices the least rapidly. An overall energy price factor is something of an abstraction, but an average annual rise of something like 2 percent pervades (implicitly) a number of the studies. But in spite of the widespread presumption of the influential role of price, it is really not possible to say (a) that its effect on future demand has usually been explicitly dealt with, or (b) that close agreement on future price trends signifies close agreement on future energy-demand trends, or vice versa. In other words, price elasticity of demand frequently occupies an obscure role. Analysis of technologically induced conservation impulses is more clearcut and, one is almost tempted to say, determining.

4. With some exception, the feedback effect on the GNP from low, or severely constrained, energy futures is only lightly touched upon. Since some of the studies contemplate the possibility of surprisingly low energy-demand levels in the year 2000 without any evident negative impact on the level of economic activity, the important issue of energy–GNP linkages has not been disposed of.

Notwithstanding the final point, let us take these observations just a bit further. Without pretense at either refinement or sophistication, we can use these emerging findings to illustrate the four-pronged interrelationship that exists among energy growth, GNP growth, energy prices, and price elasticity of demand for energy. Suppose the consensual GNP growth rate of 3.3 percent gave rise to energy growth of 2.7 percent, under conservative, historically based assumptions of an energy–GNP elasticity coefficient of 0.8. This implies the use of about 136 quads in the year 2000. But the projections cluster nearer to 120 quads, a level about 12 percent lower that reflects about a 2 percent growth rate. A real energy price rise averaging 2 percent yearly signifies an "average" energy price level in the year 2000 that is some 64 percent above that for 1975. The derived elasticity of approximately -0.2, if it were independently imposed, could not really be viewed as being injudiciously high. In fact, it seems quite low. On the basis of this crude, preliminary calculation, the integrity of the interrelationships survives, and an energy growth projection in the vicinity of 120 quads has to be regarded, tentatively, as a sensible one. Indeed, it could be argued that anticipating only minimal responses to changing energy realities could justify such an outcome.

Long-Term Outlook for Aggregate Energy Use

Recapitulation

We have now had occasion to consider future energy-demand paths from two perspectives: first, earlier in this chapter, we reviewed a number of prominent energy-demand projections, which tend roughly to bunch at a projected level of under 120 quads in the year 2000. This compares with our recent annual consumption of approximately 75 quads. (Accompanying assumptions regarding GNP growth, price developments, and conservation considerations seem to support a figure of around 120 quads as, tentatively, a reasonable one.) Second, in chapter 5, we presented a set of specific analytical explorations into the economic, technological, and institutional factors governing energy performance in residential space heating, industrial process steam, and automotive transport. The latter analysis suggests that future energy demand for these three significant components of energy use might materialize at levels only modestly above —or perhaps even absolutely below—recently prevailing quantities.

This finding needs to be firmly kept in view as we consider components of energy consumption not covered by the detailed analysis and the outlook for energy demand overall. In table 6-2, we see that the three categories represented around 40 percent of national energy consumption in recent years. The highest projection represents a growth rate of approximately 1.8 percent yearly for the three components taken together, the middle projection being about 0.3 percent. The low projection envisages an absolute decline. Our task in what follows will be to look at the projections for the other 60 percent of energy consumption. The objective

Table 6-2. Recapitulation of Projections for Residential Space Heating, Industrial Process Heat, and Automotive Transport, 1976 and 2000

(in quads)

	1976 actual	2000 projected
Residential space heating	8.8	
Low		4.5
Medium		8.0
High		11.1
Industrial process steam	10.2	
"Conservation plus co-generation"		10.1
"No conservation"		22.7
Automotive transport	10.2	
Low		5.3
Medium		7.0
High		11.5
All of the above	29.2	
Low		19.9
Medium		31.4
High		45.3
All other components	45.1	?
Total energy consumption	74.3	?

Sources: The three detailed components—historical and projected—come from chap. 5. (However, the figures for process steam and space heating were recalculated for 1976 from 1974 and 1975 base year estimates, respectively. The recalculation was done very roughly.) The total 1976 figure comes from U.S. Department of Energy, *Monthly Energy Review* (March 1978).

Note: In the projections, this table uses the terms *low*, *medium*, and *high* although the earlier discussion did not. Also, in depicting the projected range for all three categories taken together, we have implicitly assigned to industry a midpoint figure of 16.4 quads.

is to draw upon a sufficiently representative and exhaustive selection of energy uses so as to be able to say something useful about the nation's *aggregate* energy-demand outlook. We will do this in a less fastidious way than the treatment accorded the three categories in chapter 5. We hope, however, to be able to apply at least some useful lessons to the "uncovered" functions on the basis of what we have already considered.

Commercial Sector

Commercial energy use grew half again as fast as national energy use during the period 1950–75.[3] Heating currently accounts for about 45

---

[3] Information relating to commercial energy use comes from Jerry R. Jackson, Steve Cohn, Jane Cope, and William S. Johnson, *The Commercial Demand for Energy: A Disaggregated Approach,* Report ORNL/CON-15 (Oak Ridge, Tenn., Oak Ridge National Laboratory, April 1978).

percent of end-use functions in this sector; the addition of cooling and lighting brings identified uses to nearly 90 percent. Electricity (figured on a primary input basis) is the leading energy form employed; it made up half the total for 1975. A variety of users—not all commercial in the strict sense—generate this demand. Prominent among these are retail and wholesale trade establishments (24 percent of commercial energy use in 1975); educational facilities (19 percent); finance and other office buildings (16 percent); health facilities (12 percent); and hotels and motels (6 percent). These add up to 77 percent of commercial energy use.

The rising share of the GNP spent on services (see chapter 4) is one important reason for the growth of commercial energy use. Different phenomena are at work. Rising female labor-force participation has shifted some household responsibilities to outside the house, for example, from the kitchen to fast-food emporiums. Growth in income has also contributed to the trend, for example; witness a growing relative demand for recreational, medical, educational, and lodging services. The betting is that such a dynamic is not about to spend itself. The question then arises as to its implications for energy.

The Oak Ridge National Laboratory (ORNL) study contains two projections of growth in the commercial sector up to the year 2000, which take such factors into account.[4] A baseline estimate is constructed on the basis of assumptions regarding growth in income, relative prices, population, school enrollment, and the stock and associated floor-space characteristics of different building types. (Census Series II serves as the population projection, as it does in our mid-range estimate in chapter 4. The GNP growth implied by the ORNL disposable income projection conforms closely to our 3.2 percent midpoint projection.) Assumed long-term trends in real energy prices range from a 1 percent annual increase in electricity to 3.5 percent in gas, with a weighted average of around 1.6 percent for all energy forms.

The resulting baseline projection shows commercial energy use growing from 9.45 quads in 1975 to 23.40 quads in the year 2000. Sizable cost-effective conservation opportunities (both retrofit and new) are assumed to be exploited in this projection, though not up to the level of new building standards recommended in ASHRAE 90-75.[5] The assumed

[4] Ibid.

[5] American Society of Heating, Refrigeration, and Air-Conditioning Engineers (ASHRAE), *Energy Conservation in New Building Design,* ASHRAE 90-75 (New York, ASHRAE, 1975).

incorporation of these standards forms the basis of ORNL's alternative projection, showing commercial energy use rising from 9.45 to 20.26 quads. Three-quarters of the "savings" represented by the lower projection are assumed to stem from efficiency improvements in space heating. In both projections, electricity expands its share of the commercial energy market substantially, going from 53 percent in 1975 to over 70 percent in the year 2000.

Although the ORNL study is skillfully done, one wonders whether conservation potentials are not unduly inhibited. The detailed analysis (in chapter 5) of residential heating, with numerous characteristics similar to those of commercial facilities, suggests energy-saving possibilities comparatively far greater than those contemplated in ORNL's commercial sector analysis. On the other hand, ORNL may be more cautious in translating cost-effective criteria into actual behavior by energy users.

Freight and Airline Transport

A detailed and insightful account of alternative trends in transport activity and the associated energy requirement is contained within the CONAES Demand–Conservation Panel Report. Passenger cars, of course, dominate energy use in the transport sector (accounting for two-thirds of the sectoral aggregate in 1975), and their future has already been discussed in chapter 5.

Freight accounts for one-fourth of energy use in transport; of that, three-fourths originates in trucking. The CONAES analysis anticipates little long-term truck-to-rail shift. Thus, the prospects in trucking dominate the freight energy outlook. There are promising conservation potentials, for example, a greater degree of dieselization, more efficient engines, and drag reduction. Freight energy is expected to continue growing less rapidly than the GNP. Total energy consumption for freight modes is projected to rise from 3.8 quads in 1975 to 5.3 quads in 2000.

Airline energy consumption (at 1.2 quads) represented only around 7 percent of transport energy use in 1975, but its annual growth has been rapid. In contrast to automobile travel, air travel may grow at a relatively high rate over the next twenty to thirty years, given the dual phenomena of income growth and substantial untapped markets. As a result airline energy use may increase significantly. Between 1975 and 2000, this demand is projected to rise from 1.2 to 3.3 quads. The energy-use implications, while substantial, may be cushioned by introduction of more efficient planes, higher load factors, and better operating procedures.

Industry

The industrial sector accounts for somewhat under 40 percent of national energy use. Its consumption in 1976 was around 28 quads. It is dominated by manufacturing activity (which makes up approximately 90 percent of the industrial energy total) but includes also certain mining, agricultural, and construction activities. The process steam used by manufacturing industries has been analyed in detail (see chapter 5). It amounted to around 10 quads in 1975 (35 percent of industrial energy consumption), leaving the 18 quads represented by other uses (65 percent of the industrial total) still to be dealt with. What can we say about this 18-quad segment for the future?

Valuable research into manufacturing energy use—past and future—has been performed and is reported in two studies (1974 and 1978) by the Conference Board.[6] Both studies found unmistakable evidence of a significant conservation momentum by the manufacturing sector, both in the pre-1973 period of stable or declining prices and (at an accelerated pace) since 1973. Declining energy intensity resulted from installation of energy-replacing capital as well as from some intramanufacturing shift away from energy-intensive industries.

In our industrial energy-use projections, we have assumed that (1) growth in industrial output will continue to exceed growth in the GNP, but by a diminishing margin, keeping disproportionately fast growth of service activities in mind. Specifically, we assume that industrial growth will outpace GNP growth by a factor of 1.2, so that a long-term rate of around 3.8 percent accompanies our mid-range 3.2 GNP projections to the year 2000. And (2), we assume that the industrial energy–output ratio will continue to decline, but (viewing the matter conservatively) only at approximately its preembargo pace. For the period 1976–2000, this signifies a growth in energy consumption from 18 to about 31 quads.

[6] See the Conference Board in cooperation with the National Science Foundation, *Energy Consumption in Manufacturing,* A Report to the Energy Policy Project of the Ford Foundation (Cambridge, Mass., Ballinger, 1974). An updated analysis is contained in John G. Myers and Leonard Nakamura, *Saving Energy in Manufacturing: The Post-Embargo Record,* a project jointly sponsored by the Conference Board, the Alliance to Save Energy, and the Ford Foundation (Cambridge, Mass., Ballinger, 1978).

Residential Sector

Residential energy use in 1975 totaled 16.2 quads.[7] Of this amount, 8.6 quads, or 53 percent, went to space heating, already analyzed in chapter 5. The remaining 7.6 quads comprised the following functions: water heating (2.28); refrigerators (0.92); freezers (0.38); cooking (0.76); air conditioning (1.08); lighting (0.90); all other (1.31). Electricity is by far the preponderant energy form in these seven categories, accounting for some 75 percent of the total.

The Hirst-Carney ORNL study presents projections of residential energy use under a variety of alternative assumptions.[8] A baseline case (implicitly) shows a growth in the nonheating portion of residential energy use from 7.6 quads in 1975 to 13.6 quads in the year 2000, an annual rate of 2.4 percent. The demographic and economic growth assumptions accompanying this baseline case are nearly identical to our mid-range estimates (see chapter 4). The baseline price assumptions are a real annual increase of 1.2 percent for oil, 2.3 percent for gas, and 0.9 percent for electricity. A rough weighted average comes to around 1.5 percent per year. In contrast to the baseline case, a high-demand case, in which constant energy prices are assumed, projects nonheating demand to be 15.7 quads in the year 2000, nearly a 3 percent annual rate of increase.

Both of these cases incorporate conservation impulses—in the high case, because of the sharp energy price increases of the early 1970s; in the baseline case, for that reason, as well as because of assumed future increases. However, the conservation actions are assumed to be limited to those voluntarily triggered, such as the substantial insulation retrofit activity witnessed in the last few years.

An additional case considers the dampening effect on energy-demand growth of a number of federal residential conservation programs enacted by the Ninety-Fourth Congress and expanded upon in the President's 1977 proposals. In the nonheating area, these programs include mandatory efficiency standards and labeling for appliances. The study finds that implementation of such practices over the course of the next twenty-five years is technically feasible and yields (in present value terms) net economic benefits—that is, circumstances where fuel savings exceed

---

[7] Much in this section is drawn from Eric Hirst and Janet Carney, *Residential Energy Use to the Year 2000: Conservation and Economics*, ORNL/CON-13 (Oak Ridge, Tenn., Oak Ridge National Laboratory, September 1977).

[8] Ibid.

equipment or improvement costs, or both. The ORNL study details quantitatively significant, cost-effective energy-saving improvements in such appliances as water heaters, refrigerators, air conditioners, and freezers.[9] It seems reasonable to conclude that in this "intensified conservation" case, the baseline projection of 13.6 quads in the year 2000 might easily drop to below 13 quads. All three cases, it should be noted, allow for further diffusion of appliance ownership.

For purposes of the present study, what emerges as a sensible mid-range projection? Perhaps the Department of Energy price-increase assumptions adopted by ORNL are too modest, as may be ORNL's appreciation of technical conservation possibilities.[10] For both reasons, the ORNL baseline estimate may be high. Certainly, the housing discussion in chapter 5 points to greater payoff possibilities than are countenanced in the ORNL analysis. On the other hand, there is uncertainty concerning the surfacing of new and unanticipated energy uses. (Some argue that electronic and semiconductor-based technology, which is not energy-intensive, cushions against that eventuality.) We must also allow for market imperfections, the persistence of first-cost bias and behavioral inertia generally, and a sluggishness in equipment turnover that might retard the realization of energy savings. As a judgmental reflection of such considerations, let us adopt a 2000 mid-range figure for nonheating, residential energy use of 14 quads.

An Aggregate Projection for the Year 2000

We can now merge the results of the three detailed case studies of chapter 5 with the more discoursive four-part review just concluded. Table 6-3 and figure 6-1 provide a convenient summary of a mid-range national energy-demand projection. Between 1976 and 2000, energy consumption is projected to rise from 74 to around 115 quads, implying an average annual growth rate of 1.8 percent. At a GNP growth rate of 3.2 percent, this signifies an elasticity factor of 0.56 and an annual reduction in the level of the energy–GNP ratio of 1.5 percent. It is interesting to note that a discrete examination of energy consumption by end-use functions produces an aggregate estimate that is compatible both with the thrust

[9] For example, a 15 percent energy saving in electric water heaters through improved jacket and distribution-line insulation is estimated to add $42 in cost but save $36 in electricity (at 1976 utility rates), that is, repayment in just a year or so.
[10] See chap. 5, p. 127, note 5.

Table 6-3. A Mid-Range Energy Projection to the Year 2000
(in quads)

Energy uses	Actual 1976	Projected 2000
1. Residential space heating	8.80	8.00
2. Industrial process steam	10.20	16.40
3. Automotive transport	10.20	7.00
4. Subtotal	29.20	31.40
5. Commercial sector	9.80	21.83
6. Freight transport	4.00	5.30
7. Passenger air transport	1.30	3.30
8. Industry (excluding process steam)	18.00	31.00
9. Residential (excluding space heating)	7.63	14.00
10. Subtotal	40.73	75.43
11. All other	4.37	7.90
12. Total energy consumption	74.30	114.73

For 1976, lines 1 through 3 and line 12 appear in table 6-2; line 11 is calculated as a residual. Sources for lines 5 through 9 are given in the text. However, where a text estimate for 1975 needed to be changed to 1976 (for purposes of the present table), that adjustment was made on a rough basis, using 1975–76 changes for the sectoral totals shown in U.S. Department of Energy, *Monthly Energy Review* (March 1978). For the year 2000, lines 1 through 3 come from the medium figures (or average of the range shown) in table 6-2. The basis for lines 5 through 9 is described in the text. Line 11 was arbitrarily moved proportionately to line 10.

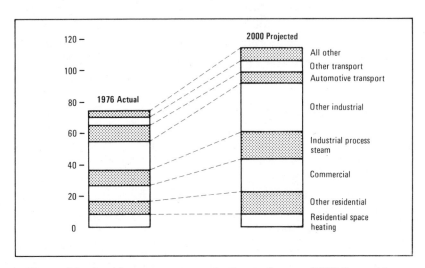

Figure 6-1. A mid-range energy projection to the year 2000 (in quads).

of most of the other studies surveyed at the beginning of this chapter and with the more sweeping and simple macroeconomic estimating effort following that survey.

The reader may be struck by the extent to which the three detailed case studies lead to considerably more restrained future energy demands than the components accorded more general treatment. But here, it is important to bear in mind that the case studies were themselves selected as reflecting those energy uses which, presumptively, seemed to promise important energy-conservation payoffs (augmented, in the case of automobiles, by the probability of a noticeable saturation effect). Recall also (from chapters 2 and 3) that, in the case of home heating and autos, we are talking about important components of the *final demand sector* of energy use. That is, in contrast to its role in industry, constrained use of automotive and home heating-energy—whatever else its ramifications—need not seriously hamper the production capability of the economy.[11] The significance of this distinction is captured by the fact that industrial unit energy consumption is—conservatively, we believe—not being projected at a faster rate of decline than was achieved under declining or stable real prices. Finally, automobiles and, prospectively, thermal standards in construction, happen to be two areas where governmental standards may have an important effect in restraining energy use. Thus, the fact that residential space heating and automotive transport may actually represent sources of declining levels of energy demand, in contrast to other components which expand, need not appear to be quite so disconcerting a phenomenon as, at first blush, it may seem to be.

Alternative Levels of Projected Energy Use

The 115-quad projection for the year 2000 is governed by a number of mid-range demographic, economic, technological, and policy assumptions. While this projection has received our primary emphasis, it is also important to speculate about circumstances under which future energy demand might reach higher or lower levels. Of course, extreme assumptions about economic variables, technology, or behavioral characteristics can produce wide-ranging levels of future energy demand. Where esti-

---

[11] Of course, one should not push the economically "inconsequential" nature of final-demand energy use too far. Workers requiring private automobiles to commute to their jobs would not take that view.

mates involving radical discontinuity (as in a CONAES 56-quad case for the year 2010) lack rigorous analytical backup, it is easier to be intrigued than persuaded by the projections.

What sort of credible range can one specify around our 115-quad figure, while retaining the 3.2 percent GNP growth rate? Reviewing the alternative projections for various end uses (those detailed in chapter 5, along with those dealt with more generally in the present chapter) suggests a lower bound of around 97 quads and an upper limit of about 140 quads (see figure 6-2). These imply, respectively, annual growth rates in energy demand of 1.0 and 2.7 percent and energy–GNP elasticity coefficients of 0.32 and 0.84.[12]

The low figure (97 quads), in particular, deserves a word of comment. The case-study exposition in chaper 5 disclosed substantially greater breadth of possibilities for restrained energy use than, for example, did the more conservatively framed ORNL analysis. If one applied to the "uncovered" 60 percent of energy use the same detailed analysis of technology, policy, and economics which governed the case studies, it is quite likely that one could contemplate a still lower bounded level of energy consumption amid otherwise stable economic growth.[13]

Consumption of Different Energy Forms

In today's economy energy forms are to a large extent substitutable in major uses: oil, gas, and electricity continue to compete, and, in the past, competed actively, in residential and commercial space and hot-water heating. All fossil fuels are able to energize a variety of industrial processes. Nonsubstitutable, captive markets comprise principally lighting,

---

[12] Specifically, for the three end uses covered in detail in chap. 5, we reverted to the range of alternatives given in table 6-2. For commercial and residential nonspace heating uses, we adopted figures from Jackson and coauthors, *The Commercial Demand for Energy;* and from Hirst and Carney, *Residential Energy Use to the Year 2000.* For the industrial sector, we assumed that—relative to the mid-range assumption of a 1.5 percent annual reduction in unit energy consumption—a high-demand level for the year 2000 might ensue from a 1 percent decline, while the low-demand project accompanies a 1.8 percent annual drop. To comprehend the nation's overall energy consumption, we arbitrarily applied the percentage variability for the summed foregoing components to the residual components. In the sources used, high or low projections were, in some cases, not merely a function of price assumptions but of policy, technological, and behavioral factors as well. Thus, no quantitatively tidy specification of "driving forces" is possible.

[13] Other factors given, greater or lesser GNP growth than our 3.2 percent mid-range estimate would, of course, widen the range of energy-consumption prospects.

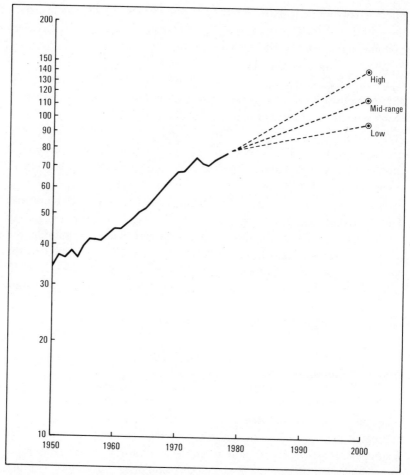

Figure 6-2. U.S. energy consumption, historical, and alternative projections, 1950–2000 (in quads).

mechanical drive and certain electroprocess industries (for example, aluminum reduction) for electricity; and liquids within the overwhelming portion of the transport sector. (The electricity market, capable of being served today by all fossil fuels, nuclear, and hydro power, and in the future, perhaps by direct solar is not our concern in this chapter.)

In the future, as in the past, relative price will be an important determinant of fuel choice, though policies preempting "premium" fuels to select uses (for example, feedstocks), environmental regulations, economic tradeoffs between the cost of different fuels and their associated

Table 6-4. Percentage Distribution of Energy Consumption by Form of Energy Used, for 1976, and Various Projections for 2000

Energy source	1976	*Implicit in present study*	*IEA*	*CONAES*[a]	*RFF–NIH*	*MOPPS*	*EIA*[b]
				Year 2000			
Coal	5.5	10	10	10	6	14	6
Gas	23.2	17	12	15	13	15	17
Liquids	42.6	33	28	39	42	27	41
Electricity	28.7	40	50	36	38	40	35
Total	100.0	100	100	100	100	100	100

Sources: Data for 1976 come from U.S. Department of Energy, *Monthly Energy Review* (March 1978). The basis for projected 2000 data is given in the text. The columnar abbreviations refer to the studies surveyed earlier in this chapter, except for "EIA" which refers to Energy Information Administration, *Annual Report to Congress*, vol. II, 1977 (Washington, D.C., GPO, 1978). Included in the total (4 percent in the MOPPS projection and 1 percent in the RFF–NIH study) but not shown separately are solar, biomass and other presently negligible categories. Note that the four energy forms apply only to deliveries in end-use activity (though expressed in primary input equivalents). Thus, the specific energy sources used in electric generation or in synthetic gas or liquids production cannot be identified in this table.

[a] Refers to the year 2010.
[b] Refers to the year 1990.

equipment, and perceptions about future supply stringency will figure in the determination as well. In the future, also, innovative energy forms are likely to appear (for example, solar) or, with improvements in their conversion or utilization technology, reappear (for example, coal used in fluidized-bed combustion).

Our own analysis did not permit a comprehensive treatment of the changing mix of energy forms in future energy-using functions. Some information and analysis were contained in the sources and background material which formed the basis of the projections assembled in table 6-3; and from these references we can construct an approximate, "implicit" future distribution of energy forms, as shown in the second column of table 6-4. The other projections shown in table 6-4 reflect the way in which others perceive the changing composition, by form, of future energy demand. For the most part, these other projections refer to studies surveyed early in the chapter.

The distribution shown in table 6-4 applies to energy forms confronting *end-use applications* only (expressed on a primary input basis, however). That is, the distribution does not reflect the changing composition of energy sources going either into electric generation or into that portion of liquids or gases based on coal or biomass. Indeed, the high oil

shares in several of the projections evidently suggest optimism regarding
the outlook for such conversion technology.

Two sets of conclusions emerge from table 6-4. First, the shares of
electricity and coal (the latter primarily because of assumed increases in
its industrial use) are to varying degrees projected to rise markedly. Our
own judgment is that the electric share may rise from 29 percent in 1976
to approximately 40 percent in the year 2000. This rising proportion reflects a projected growth in power consumption of around 3.5 percent per
year—a significant reduction from past electricity growth rates.

Whether an electricity share approaching the 50 percent indicated in
the IEA analysis is, in fact, a realistic prospect, is a question requiring
more intensive research and analysis. Substantial shifts away from the
present mix pattern toward more electricity may pose greater substitution
problems than past experience dictates. For example, some electric applications may simply be precluded by high cost or unyielding technological
difficulties connected with electric-power storage, or both. And electricity
cannot displace significant amounts of liquids and gases that may be
needed as feedstocks.

The second point that appears to emerge from table 6-4 is that solar
and other "frontier" energy forms are not expected to figure prominently
by the year 2000. That impression is justified in part, but not entirely.
True, the economic analysis governing the space-heating discussion in
the preceding chapter and ORNL residential and commercial examination cited earlier both see higher energy prices promoting large-scale
conservation efforts without, however, being driven to replace conventional with solar energy inputs. A solar presence is, of course, implied
even in table 6-4, for at least part of the conservation practices just mentioned imply displacement of conventional sources by means of "passive"
solar design technology. We did not attempt to quantify the magnitude of
this displacement, but it *is* implicitly embodied in our projection of dampened residential energy consumption. Then, too, solar—in the broad
definition now frequently favored by writers on the subject—is reflected
in the hydroelectricity (both "high-head" and "low-head") component
of electric-power consumption. These things apart, there seems little
doubt that some additional solar contribution—not reflected in table 6-4
—*will* enter the nation's energy balance even without passing the market
test and even if burdened with continuing technological uncertainties.
There will be governmentally sponsored demonstration programs; some
homeowners are bound to go the solar route because of personal preferences; and there will no doubt be policy stimulus through subsidies or

regulatory means. But we made no effort to chart solar energy trends arising from these factors to the year 2000. As one looks beyond 2000, one
would almost certainly have to assign rising weight and much more explicit quantitative recognition to solar's presence in U.S. energy consumption.

Total Energy Demand Beyond the Year 2000

Aside from the temptation to dramatize the completed millennium, the
emphasis here on the year 2000 was governed by a number of reasons
(including the practical one that numerous studies with a similar time
horizon facilitated our comparisons.) The year is far enough away to
probe the energy implications of changes that have a chance to unfold in
the interim: energy-associated capital stock has a chance to turn over;
market penetration of commercially viable technologies has a chance to
advance; sustained price increases—actual and anticipated—can produce
stable, long-run adjustments in demand; a conservation philosophy has a
chance to take hold; and a role for new policies and institutions has a
chance to be weighed, thoughtfully instead of convulsively. At the same
time, the end of the century is close enough to instigate early R&D decisions on long lead-time items—such as advanced nuclear reactors, high-
cost solar technologies, or energy-storage systems—which could have
significant consequences for both energy demand and supply. And while
there are conflicting views about the prospects for an oil and gas "crunch"
in the 1980s, there is far more unanimity regarding the probability of
supply tightening in the 1990–2000 decade.

But there are good reasons for also thinking about the post-2000
period. As resource stringency in conventional oil and gas resources
develops, some promising, near-term technologies looked on as replacements may not yield to efforts to render them environmentally and
economically acceptable, so that insurance programs with more distant
prospects of success need to be pursued, for example, fusion and more
sophisticated solar variants. Then, too, environmental burdens which are
now creeping may become rampant by the next century, and managing
these problems may require a lead time that extends beyond the year
2000.

While post-year 2000 projections serve a valuable purpose, therefore,
it is obviously more difficult to express respectable judgments about the
likely evolution of U.S. energy consumption the longer the time period

under consideration. Still, one can spin out some hypothetical notions. Recall that the implicit energy–GNP elasticity coefficient between 1976 and 2000 worked out to 0.56. Consider the factors tending, with time, to depress that coefficient further. There will be scope, after the year 2000, for continued replacement of capital stocks associated with inefficient energy use. (Many of today's buildings will survive the turn of the century.) Saturation for some energy-intensive products and a shift in the product mix that is, on balance, less energy intensive than the previous mix, may have proceeded further. Any acceleration in the pace of real energy price increases would, of course, reinforce such forces. As against these possibilities, there is our vast uncertainty regarding new goods and services on the market—some of which may serve to increase energy demand (for example, more widespread development of inside climate control)—and the unpredictability of long-term expenditure patterns. There is also the difficulty of dealing with the introduction of innovative energy forms, such as solar, both in estimating their pace of penetration and in handling their role conceptually.

Perhaps a reasonable compromise in this dilemma would be to assume that something not much above the *lower-bound* elasticity to the year 2000 applies to the extension of the *mid-range* figure beyond that time. Applying an elasticity of, say, 0.4 to the 2000–2025 mid-range GNP growth rate of 2.2 percent yields an energy growth rate of 0.9 percent per year or an energy-demand level in 2025 of nearly 143 quads. Those, in whose judgment even greater deceleration in energy growth looms, may appreciate that some erring on the high side may be defensible where one important reason for the projection is to test the capability of the energy *supply* system to match that level of demand.

Energy and the Changing Structure of Final Demand

In our projections, the compositional shifts in national expenditures are largely embodied implicitly. For a number of specific components of economic activity examined, we took particular account of their evolving relationship to rising levels of income (for example, housing) or dealt with prospective degrees of saturation (for example, automotive transport). But we cannot be certain as to how much inconsistency there might be between a total energy-demand estimate built up on the basis of an exhaustive accounting of changes in the projected pattern of national expenditures, on the one hand, and the more selective process used to derive the energy-demand projections in this book on the other. In our own work, we clearly cannot pretend to have thoroughly explored the energy implications of whatever important shifts may occur in the spending patterns for household consumption, business investment, and government.

It is hard to say how seriously this deficiency imperils the reliability of our projections; certainly, an intensive analysis of the overall energy implications of a changing final demand mix should be an area of priority research. One internal cross-check on the tenability of our findings, however, is already present: the summed result of our detailed case studies and other sectoral perspectives seems to accord very reasonably with what one would come up with, dealing on a macroeconomic level of aggregation, in terms of assumed overall price trajectories, along with income and price elasticities of demand. (See the discussion on pages 183–184.)

The implications for energy that one might draw—in further support of the aggregate results—from inferred compositional changes in the economy are harder to pin down. There appears to be agreement, for example, that some considerable rise in the investment share of national expenditures (over recent levels) is in order if the rate of productivity advance is to be stabilized and the economic growth rate postulated over the next several decades achieved. But how would a rising investment share be offset? While the estimated energy content (direct and indirect) of the average final demand dollar spent on investment is about 30 percent below that spent on *overall* personal consumption, when the comparison is with personal consumption excluding direct energy purchases (such as household utilities and motor fuels), the investment energy content is actually 46 percent higher.[14] Since we have already allowed for substantial energy savings in home heating and automotive fuel, a relative expenditure shift toward investment, and away from this non-direct energy component of consumer spending, may spell some intensified, rather than lessened, energy demand.

On the other hand, a steady, if modest, growth in the share of services within consumer budgets might work in the opposite direction—that is, toward a dampening of energy demand. Table 6-5 indicates that a number of service-related categories embody a below-average energy content.

[14] These estimates (for 1967) come from Robert A. Herendeen, Barr Z. Segal, and Donna L. Amado, *Energy and Labor Impact of Final Demand Expenditures, 1963 and 1967,* Technical Memorandum No. 62 (Urbana, Ill., Center for Advanced Computation, October 1975).

Table 6-5. Selected Consumer Energy Intensities

Consumer goods	Thousand Btus / $
Appliances	59
Automobiles (excluding operation)	56
Furniture (approximate)	45
Food	41
Restaurant visits	32
Religious and welfare activities	28
Hospital care	26
Communications	19
Physician care	11
All personal consumption[a]	70

Source: Bruce Hannon, "Energy Conservation and the Consumer," *Science* vol. 189 (July 1975) pp. 95–102.

[a] The high-consumption figure of 70,000 Btu per dollar arises from the influence of direct energy expenditures, with an obviously very high energy intensity, for such things as utility purchases and motor fuels not shown separately.

Implications of the much discussed trend toward a service and leisure-oriented society prompts a reminder, however, that not all such shifts spell lessened energy intensity. Some activities give rise to closely linked energy-intensive purchases; for example, longer vacations may justify acquisition of recreational vehicles and, under any circumstances, result in substantial demand for transport fuels. Still, it seems reasonable to believe that if the services sector expands its relative role faster than it has done historically, that phenomenon, on balance, should mean more subdued energy-demand growth as well.

It is sometimes feared that the very realization of energy savings through the adoption of conservation practices, may actually leave the ultimate consequence for energy consumption uncertain, depending on what happens to the monetary proceeds of the saved energy. There is strong reason to doubt that such energy savings would be cancelled out by offsetting new demands.

First, major energy savings almost certainly lead, on the average, to expenditures on items that are inevitably far lower in their energy content as compared with the use of fuel and power they have replaced. The "composite" bundle of household purchases on which a consumer may spend saved heating-fuel dollars typically embodies substantially less energy. Second, it is quite unlikely that the real income equivalent of such energy savings will be disposed of by an offsetting expansion of the activity in question: there is no evidence that halving the fuel requirements of a vehicle-mile will be neutralized by a doubling of driving. There may be *some* offsetting fuel consumption but surely far less than would be necessary to entirely wash out realized fuel savings; in fact, the evidence points to saturation effects in driving.

Will Energy Constraints Dampen Economic Growth?

Nothing contributed by this study can answer that question conclusively. Nor, indeed, has the puzzle yielded to inquiry by preeminent scholars. Our study, like almost all others, relies almost exclusively upon a specified future level and growth rate of the GNP to drive energy demand. The extent to which the resulting level of projected energy demand may, in itself, be such as to undercut attainment of the very size of the GNP employed in its estimation is a topic often found in the literature. But such discussion takes the form, principally, of a clarification of the conceptual issues involved (a topic broached briefly in chapter 3); or it signals to the reader a series of provisos about the confidence one can have in the projections.

Perhaps the most concise statement of the "reverse energy GNP feedback" issue is to be found in an effort conducted not long ago as part of the National Academy of Sciences' CONAES study.[15] To the question as to whether a price induced reduction in energy demand will depress the GNP below what it would otherwise have been, the study notes that "virtually everyone will agree that such a reverse effect exists. . . . the real question is how large or small it is, in various circumstances."[16]

Among the factors bearing on the extent of such an impact, there is, first of all, the precipitousness with which higher energy costs (and the associated constraint on use) are inflicted upon the economy. The disruption in economic activity brought about by the 1973–74 embargo and price escalation or by the natural gas deficiency in the winter of 1976–77 are inapplicable where price increases and supply constraints are gradual and can be allowed for in one's planning perspective. Two important points connected with the timing issue are (1) the existence of an accommodating government economic policy to blunt negative effects on

[15] National Academy of Sciences, Committee on Nuclear and Alternative Energy Systems (CONAES), *Energy Modeling for an Uncertain Future,* Supporting Paper 2, Report of the Modeling Resource Group of the Synthesis Panel (Washington, D.C., National Academy of Sciences, 1978). Another valuable source is William W. Hogan and Alan S. Manne, "Energy-Economy Interactions: The Fable of the Elephant and the Rabbit," in Charles J. Hitch, ed., *Modeling Energy–Economy Interactions: Five Approaches* (Washington, D.C., Resources for the Future, 1977).
[16] National Academy of Sciences, *Energy Modeling.*

employment and economic activity induced by reduced energy use; and (2) the condition that substitution of energy with nonenergy resources coincides reasonably with phasing of the investment cycle for new capital assets: important improvements in the efficiency of energy use—for example, industrial cogeneration—may involve investment in new equipment, and this creates a dilemma for producers whose existing assets are far from the end of their planned period of service. A too idealized energy future shares the problems of a vision of the New Jerusalem: a road map to remind us of detours along the way is a handy thing to have.

Aside from problems connected with the time path along which changes in energy use, ranging from the smooth to the precipitous, may occur, there remains the all-important question of whether, on a nationwide basis, the process of reducing the intensity of energy use by substituting other resources exacts a negligible or major economic penalty. In introducing this topic in chapter 3, we noted that the critical parameters determining the extent of any reverse feedback of energy upon the GNP are the elasticity of substitution or the price elasticity of demand for energy. The CONAES Modeling Resource Group, reporting on a number of other studies and models, finds that for a price elasticity not smaller than −0.5, the long-run effect on the GNP, caused by gradual cuts in energy use until a level substantially below a baseline scenario is reached,[17] would be very small indeed. Although the report appears to be relatively comfortable with the plausibility of an elasticity of this approximate magnitude, it emphatically acknowledges the weakness of the data base underlying this figure and recognizes the importance of strengthened empirical research in order to advance our understanding of, and confidence in, these relationships.

The present study is unable, in any conclusive sense, to affirm either the value of an aggregate long-run price elasticity of demand for energy or the consequences for economic growth of reduced energy use if a given elasticity prevails. A degree of reassurance emerges, however, from two considerations. One, our study is least "bold" in hypothesizing large-volume energy savings in industry, that is, in the sector where the effect of constrained energy upon output is potentially greatest. Significant savings, by contrast, are concentrated in the personal component of final demand where, though our calculations of potential savings may be im-

---

[17] The baseline characteristics were GNP growth of 3.2 percent, energy growth ranging from 1.7 to 2.9 percent, and energy price increases ranging from 0.5 to 1.0 percent.

perfect, such savings are unlikely to seriously jeopardize economic activity. Second, in a range of energy-using activities which has been considered, the engineering or technological basis for achieving energy savings was validated by cost-effectiveness criteria; this at least represents an improvement upon approaches where savings are hypothesized purely in terms of technical principles or feasibility, but where the implicit economics may be unrewarding and much more seriously in conflict with a stipulated level of GNP. Nevertheless, one should be clear that (1) some of our components of energy demand were treated far less thoroughly than others, and this affects the reliability of the conclusions; and (2) even where both technical and economic criteria support the attainability of specified energy savings in any given area, the combined, nationwide effort to effect the resource substitutions necessary for the realization of these savings may strain the capacity of the overall economy, thus lowering the GNP to below its stipulated level.

Concluding Remarks

Compared with its historical trend, the future rate of growth in U.S. energy demand seems almost certain to be decisively lower. This chapter concurs, in this finding, with a wide and growing body of opinion. This deceleration stems both from the expectation of dampened population and economic growth; and, even more important, from a reduction in the energy intensity associated with a variety of energy-using activities. This reduction, triggered largely by the assumption of a fairly steady upward course for real energy prices but also as a result of assumed policy changes, seems to us defensible in terms of the prospects for adoption of cost-effective technologies, some innovative, others more conventional ones which up to now have been held back by an unattractive economic or policy milieu, or both.

Compared with a level of energy consumption of 74 quads in 1976, the projected level of demand in the year 2000 is 115 quads, with an upper bound of 140 quads and a lower one that could fall measurably below 100. But even the low end of the range presupposes a fair amount of absolute addition to the annual level of consumption.

We are not oblivious to, nor do we attempt to refute, studies which contemplate zero energy growth, even at the assumed 3.2 percent economic growth rate. There is no reason to question whether such a scenario is possible or whether it is analytically sound. In such a scenario, however, the question of the impact of major discontinuities in energy use upon the GNP assumes critical importance. Our state of knowledge regarding this reverse feedback of energy upon the economy is too primitive to permit confident judgments even at more moderate departures from traditional energy-growth paths, much less under the conditions of a zero energy-growth path.

Appendix: A Review of Selected Recent Energy Projections

A number of major efforts to explore or chart future U.S. energy consumption have taken place in recent years. This appendix reviews the highlights of some of these studies. Our major purpose is to illustrate the diversity of approaches and results and thus to help provide a firmer basis for the range of judgments that are expressed in the present book. In each case, we describe the general character of the study, indicate the approach employed, summarize major findings, and add a few evaluative sentences.

Institute for Energy Analysis (IEA)

This 1976 study by the IEA contains projections of U.S. primary energy consumption in two variants (low, high) to the year 2010.[18] Estimates are presented of demand by energy form (coal, oil, gas, electricity, and heat produced via solar and geothermal systems and through cogeneration); by major end-use sector (residential, commercial, industrial, transport); and by selected functions or components within each of these end-use sectors (for example, heating–cooling, cars, steel industry). Although the analysis is conducted in terms of demand at end-use stages, energy quantities are expressed in terms of primary fuel-input equivalents.

Methodologically, the IEA study specifies low and high levels of the future GNP on the basis of analysis and assumptions regarding key factors underlying economic growth: that is, population, labor force, and productivity. Within this economic–demographic framework, a set of more

---

[18] Institute for Energy Analysis, Oak Ridge Associated Universities, *U.S. Energy and Economic Growth, 1975–2010* (Oak Ridge, Tenn., September 1976).

specific variables—each closely related to energy use—is projected. This set of estimates includes, for example, the projected stock of automobiles, commercial floor space, residential housing units, steel production, and selected other components of industrial activity. For each indicator, the associated energy demand is projected on the basis of analysis and assumptions regarding future changes in energy intensity. The latter step is, of course, crucial to the entire analysis. It involves consideration of prospective technology, saturation, and life expectancy of different durable assets, and—to a degree—the effect of policy measures. Energy price change is introduced only *implicitly* at this stage of the analysis. Prices enter more directly at a final sequence in the projections process, where the calculated energy demands, relative energy prices, substitution possibilities between energy and nonenergy resources are incorporated, along with other factors of production (capital, labor), in a simple macroeconomic growth model. This model seeks to test whether the initially stipulated level of the future GNP is compatible with the approach wherein the GNP is derived as a result of assumptions concerning energy supply and price along with the various factors of production just mentioned.

Since the IEA report has received a fair amount of attention, the summary of its major findings—presented in table A-1—may be of interest. Primary energy consumption in the year 2000 is projected to range between 101 and 126 quads—implying (in either case) a substantial deceleration of historic growth rates. The deceleration is less a consequence of an assumed slowing down of overall economic growth than it is of a marked decline—both at the aggregate level and in specific energy-using activities—in energy intensity. Thus, the energy–GNP "elasticity" falls from 0.9 during the past quarter century to a range of 0.45 to 0.72. This declining trend in the overall projected energy–GNP trend follows from a number of underlying assumptions concerning the realization of conservation potentials in different sectors of the economy. For example, substantial improvements in energy efficiency are foreseen in automotive transport and commercial structures. Residential space conditioning and industrial processes are also expected to experience enhanced efficiency, though to a somewhat less marked extent.

These projected conservation practices did not involve explicit introduction of prices. As the report stated, "We have given independent estimates of energy prices, based generally on extrapolation and judgment. . . . Implicit in our projections are price elasticities, and it is necessary to determine whether these elasticities are plausible. . . . We find these

Table A-1. Summary of Energy-Demand Projections by the Institute for Energy Analysis (IEA)

| | Comparison of 1950–75 period with projected 1975–2000 period | | |
| | | 1975–2000 | |
	1950–75	Low	High
Average annual rate of change			
Population	1.4	0.6%	0.7%
GNP	3.3	3.1	3.2
Energy consumption	3.0	1.4	2.3
GNP per capita	1.9	2.5	2.5
Energy per capita	1.6	0.9	1.6
Energy–GNP ratio	−0.3	−1.6	−0.9
Energy growth rate ÷ GNP growth rate	0.91	0.45	0.72

| | Comparison of 1975 and 2000 | | |
| | | 2000 | |
	1975	Low	High
Energy consumption (quads)	71.1	101.4	125.9
Percentage distribution			
By end-use sector			
Households	22.2	17.8	19.3
Commercial	13.1	10.7	12.2
Transport	26.2	21.9	22.3
Industry	38.5	49.6	46.1
By end-use energy form			
Electricity	28.3	46.6	50.8
Coal	6.5	10.5	8.9
Oil	41.4	27.5	27.9
Gas	23.9	13.4	10.8
Heat	—	2.0	1.6
Selected energy intensity changes (1975 = 1.0)			
Residential heating/cooling (energy per housing unit)	1.0	0.71	1.02
Commercial heating/cooling (energy per ft²)[a]	1.0	0.77	0.72
Automobiles (energy per vehicle mile)	1.0	0.52	0.52
Industry (energy per unit of output)	1.0	0.86	0.88

Source: Projections and 1975 data from Institute for Energy Analysis, Oak Ridge Associated Universities, *U.S. Energy and Economic Growth, 1975–2010* (Oak Ridge, Tenn., IEA, September 1976); 1950–75 growth rates from U.S. Department of the Interior, *Energy Perspectives 2* (Washington, D.C., GPO, June 1976); and from Executive Office of the President, *Economic Report of the President* (Washington, D.C., GPO, January 1978).

[a] Intensity is lower in the "high" projection because of the larger number of new (hence, more energy-conserving) buildings.

elasticities to be well within the range of elasticities obtained in other studies."[19]

Of the projected distributional shifts within total energy consumption, two stand out. Electricity's share goes way up—from 28 percent to the 45 to 50 percent range. And the proportion accounted for by transport falls noticeably. Indeed, motor fuel consumption by automobiles, even in the high case, declines absolutely between 1975 and 2000.

The IEA results summarized thus far describe the energy implications of a postulated GNP growth and other specified assumptions. To test the reasonableness of these results, the authors of the IEA report constructed a simple macroeconomic growth model in which they sought to determine the impact on the GNP itself as a consequence of rising relative energy prices and judgments about substitutability of energy by other resources. They conclude that, if price increases for energy (all forms taken together) do not exceed about 4 percent yearly and if such increases are smooth, the GNP need not be materially affected. Thus, the initial stipulations of per annum GNP growth averaging a bit over 3 percent in the period to the year 2000 and an energy-demand range of 101 to 126 quads in that year is regarded as standing up well.

Several evaluative observations may be made concerning the IEA study. First, projected amenities and product demands serviced by energy (housing, office space, vehicle miles, steel, and so on) are projected relative to the aggregate GNP rather than within the context of the evolving mix of goods and services that comprise national output. Moreover, these projected energy "service" functions are nowhere viewed in terms of their long-term historical evolution. To this extent, the projections rest on a tentative, rather than firmly established, foundation. Second, the potential contribution of solar energy is minimal. It is not clear whether this is an explicit result stemming from analysis. Third, energy-conserving potentials in different sectors and functions are not explicitly judged for cost-effectiveness, though implicit assumptions to that effect may not be unreasonable. Fourth, the driving forces accounting for the low and high cases involve, principally, differences in assumptions about conservation technology rather than the consequences of high or low energy prices. (Only one basic set of energy prices is projected.) This is in contrast to some other projection studies, where price variants are a principal or, at least, an additional major driving force.

---

[19] Ibid., p. 3. The assumed annual rates of real-energy price increases (for both the low and the high case) referred to are gas, 9.6 percent; oil, 3.6 percent; and coal and electricity, 2.0 percent.

*Report of the Committee on Nuclear and Alternative Energy
Systems (CONAES) Demand–Conservation Panel*

This study comprised part of a larger effort undertaken by the National
Academy of Sciences–National Research Council on behalf of ERDA and
its successor functions and organization within the Department of Energy.[20] The panel was assigned the task of depicting a variety of long-term
(to the year 2010) energy-demand futures, whose plausibility was to be
grounded in detailed attention to economic and technological characteristics of specific key constituents of total energy consumption. The resulting
demand projections were designed to be useful to other segments of the
broader CONAES study—for example, by delineating the bounds of
future supply requirements—as well as, in their own right, to illuminate
policy issues surrounding energy-demand growth and conservation.

The study's principal effort was directed at charting four alternative
energy-demand paths encompassing a range judged to be within the
bounds of possibility. Of course, anything is hypothetically possible. The
CONAES demand alternatives were viewed (collectively, by a majority
of the panel, if not individually by each panelist) as having enough claim
to reasonableness and plausibility as to merit the attentions of the policymakers and public at large, for whose benefit the entire National Academy
project was undertaken. The four alternatives rested on a common population and economic growth assumption: population increase was governed by Census Series II (as described in chapter 4 and approximately
binding, as well, in the IEA study)—that is, projected growth of about
0.7 percent yearly over the long run; the GNP was assumed to rise, on
the average by 2 percent yearly to 2010—exceeding that rate in the near
term and falling below it toward the end of the period. The driving force
giving rise to the four different projections were four assumptions regarding energy price trends, accompanied by schedules for the introduction of
feasible and cost-effective energy-saving technology. Compositional
changes in the national product were introduced insofar as they involved
discernible evolving trends—for example, proportionate declines in food
and clothing and proportionate increases in consumer durables and services—but were not injected in the light of assumed energy constraints or
desired energy outcomes.

[20] National Academy of Sciences, Committee on Nuclear and Alternative Energy
Systems (CONAES), "Outlook for Energy Demand and Conservation," Report of
the Panel on Demand and Conservation (1979). For a summary discussion of the
panel's findings—particularly with respect to low energy futures—see "U.S. Energy
Demand: Some Low Energy Futures," *Science* (14 April 1978) pp. 142–152.

Table A-2. Summary of CONAES Demand–Conservation Panel Findings

Scenario	*Average annual percentage rate of change (1975–2010) in*			*Energy consumption in 2010 (quads)*[a]
	GNP	*Energy price*	*Energy consumption*	
Major cases studied				
A	2	4	0.0	73
B	2	2	0.8	94
C	2	0	1.9	136
D	2	−2	2.3	159
Subsidiary cases				
Higher GNP[b]	3	2	1.8	133
Very low energy[c]	2	4	−0.7	56

Source: National Academy of Sciences, Committee on Nuclear and Alternative Energy Systems (CONAES), "Outlook for Energy Demand and Conservation," Report of the Panel on Demand and Conservation (1979).

[a] Compared with 71 quads in 1975.
[b] Variant of scenario B.
[c] Variant of scenario A.

Two subsidiary exercises were coupled to the main analysis. The next-to-lowest of the four cases was varied to test the consequences of a 3 percent, rather than 2 percent, GNP growth rate. And an extremely low demand situation, that *did* involve purposeful, energy-minimizing life-style changes, was explored.

The heart of the CONAES panel's work involved detailed working group analyses—both economic and technological—of three major components of national energy consumption: residential and nonresidential buildings and their equipment and appliances; transportation; and industrial processes. The overall panel findings were decisively shaped by the sectoral results. However, a macroeconomic test of the reasonableness of those "bottom-up" projections was performed. This involved the construction of a projected national market basket (a "final-demand bill of goods," in input–output terminology) and the application to each expenditure category of energy-output coefficients (direct and indirect, thus permitting derivation of a set of nationwide energy demand aggregates).

A summary of the panel's key numerical findings appears in tables A-2 and A-3. The principal cases studied yielded a range of demand levels in the year 2010 from 73 (that is, essentially unchanged from recent levels) to 159. The higher GNP variant (3 percent per year)—which accords more nearly with the IEA economic growth assumption and the mid-range assumptions cited in chapter 4—leads to energy consumption of 133 quads in the year 2010, or an interpolated figure of roughly 111 quads

Table A-3. Some Characteristics of Scenarios B and C, CONAES Demand–Conservation Panel

	1975	2010 Scenario B	Scenario C
Energy consumption (quads)	71	94	136
Percentage distribution by form in end-uses			
Liquids	42	40	36
Gas	24	11	19
Coal	6	14	7
Electricity	28	33	36
Active solar	—	2	1
Percentage distribution by end-use sector			
Buildings	23	14	15
Industry	30	35	29
Transport	24	21	19
Conversion losses	24	30	38
Selected energy intensities (1975 = 1.00)[a]			
Residential heating	1.00	0.63	0.76
Automobiles (mpg)	14	27	20
Light trucks/vans (mpg)	12	21	16
Passenger air travel	1.00	0.45	0.50
Truck freight	1.00	0.80	0.90
Iron–steel	1.00	0.76	0.83
Aluminum	1.00	0.63	0.79

Source: National Academy of Sciences, Committee on Nuclear and Alternative Energy Systems (CONAES), "Outlook for Energy Demand and Conservation," Report of the Panel on Demand and Conservation (1979).

[a] Except for autos and trucks, which are shown in miles per gallon.

in the year 2000. The latter figure, about midway within the IEA range, implies an energy–GNP elasticity factor of between 0.5 and 0.6.

The panel's results are heavily dependent on the adoption of technologies driving down the unit energy requirements in a variety of end-use functions (see table A-3). The technologies assumed in all analyses either exist today or are close to engineering practice. Although no major breakthroughs are presumed and the postulated efficiency improvements are judged cost-effective in terms of assumed energy prices, they are not expected to be achieved in the absence of supportive policies—for example, mandated standards to overcome the inertia arising from a lingering "first-cost bias." No heroic assumptions are made about large-scale reliance on a number of popularly regarded energy-using systems: for example, mass transit (especially rail) and electric cars are discounted. Dampened growth in transportation occurs via the harnessing of significant efficiency improvements for given modes and a sharp deceleration in growth of automotive vehicle miles. Uncertainty surrounds passenger air travel, which has the potential for exceeding the trend-line extrapolations laid down.

The greatest strengths of the CONAES Demand–Conservation Panel report can confidently be said to reside in the detail accorded technological potentials within the various end-use sectors. But there are also some critical issues left hanging. First, the two low-demand scenarios that were charted (cases A and B) invite questions about possible feedbacks upon the GNP. No reassurance about the absence of such feedbacks emerged from either the Demand–Conservation Panel nor from other groups within CONAES, although members of a Modeling Resource Group tackled the conceptual and analytical nature of the problem in great depth. Second, the still lower subsidiary energy scenario (56 quads in the year 2010)—implying very large per capita energy declines—was handled with far less analytical rigor than the other cases studied, even though its persuasiveness and feasibility require perhaps more, rather than less, attention. Third, and relatedly, it is perhaps somewhat misleading to say that "no scenario is presumed to be more probable than the others."[21] The converse logic of that statement is that each scenario has an equal probability of occurrence. Surely, those cases signifying large-scale discontinuity with the past must be judged as being less probable.

U.S. Department of Energy Market Oriented Program Planning Study (MOPPS)

Numerous federal government studies have been devoted to, or contained, long-term energy projections. The MOPPS was basically concerned with an analysis of conditions under which new energy technologies would enter the commercial marketplace over the next thirty to thirty-five years.[22] The conditions in question concerned cost, speed of commercial penetration, and competitive circumstances. The study was more heavily preoccupied with prospects for energy supply and delivery systems than with demand and conservation questions, although even the more subordinate treatment of the latter topics—coming within a voluminous report— meant that they received significant attention. Hence the inclusion in this review.

[21] "U.S. Energy Demand," *Science,* p. 146.

[22] U.S. Department of Energy, "Market Oriented Program Planning Study (MOPPS)," Final Report, vol. 1, "Integrated Summary." (Our discussion applies to the December 1977 Review Draft version of this document.)

The predominant attention in the MOPPS demand analysis is directed to a base-case projection, and this is the case discussed here. As a springboard for derivation of the base case, there is also a reference case, representing a kind of "business-as-usual" estimate. And a number of sensitivity analyses depict the results of varying some of the principal base-case assumptions and parameters.

The broad demographic–economic assumptions underlying the base-case projection are not too dissimilar from the other studies thus far reviewed. Population growth during 1975–2000 is set at 0.8 percent per year—slightly above the Census Series-II projection discussed in chapter 4. GNP, likewise, is somewhat above our mid-range value: the MOPPS figure works out to 3.4 percent yearly to the year 2000. These aggregates served as a framework within which the more specific end-use demands for energy-associated activities could be projected. These demands comprised the housing stock and commercial floor space in the residential and commercial sectors; transport volume for the various passenger and freight modes; and major industrial processes. To project the energy demands arising from these detailed activities, the MOPPS analysts closely examined the prospective penetration of conservation potentials, given the status of the technology, present and expected costs, market imperfections, and, of course, energy prices. For example, base-case energy demands for the residential sector in the year 2000 incorporate a host of efficiency improvements in insulation and heating–cooling systems that capture energy "savings" of about 33 percent, as compared with the reference case referred to above. A noteworthy aspect of the MOPPS demand analysis is that prices, which are assumed to be a major driving force in some of the other projections reviewed, are assumed to rise only modestly —especially in the years after 1985. This assumption is in large part explained by the fact that MOPPS operationally (and perhaps arbitrarily) adopted the assumption that future price increases reflect those contained in the Carter administration's 1977 Energy Act proposals. Thus, the considerable degree of energy conservation that is, nonetheless, reflected in the base-case projections stems from the lagged effect of price increases that have already occurred or from the implementation of conservation practices whose previous lack of adoption was due to factors other than price. The study emphasizes also that its concern is with the potentials for more productive energy use rather than speculations on the possibility of major life-style changes and their energy consequences.

More efficient energy utilization results in large reductions in energy demand by the year 2000—from the 140 to 150 quads associated with the nominal, reference-case projection down to 114 quads in the base case, implying an average annual energy growth rate of 1.8 percent from 1975. It is interesting to observe that the MOPPS economic and energy projections point to an energy–GNP elasticity coefficient of 0.58 for 1975–85 and 0.47 for 1985–2000—figures spelling significant reductions from historical experience.

Table A-4 summarizes the MOPPS demand projections. We quote below some of the remarks in the MOPPS report bearing on the indicated large potential reduction in demand through conservation:[23]

... Major new technologies account for much of the liquid fuels savings in the Transportation Sector. The potential impact of alternative ... engines is very large and therefore potentially a key element in liquids problem solution. ... Electric vehicles are projected to penetrate intra-city auto use significantly by 2000. The effect, however, is fuel switching rather than reduced total fuels (measured at primary).

In the Residential/Commercial Sector, projected savings are based on both existing (insulation, double glazing, etc.) and new techniques and technologies. Institutional research is needed to overcome barriers to the adoption of conservation measures.

Most savings in the Industrial Sector result from implementing new advanced technologies. Overall industrial savings are important enough to justify a modest, carefully targeted, federal role.

Integrated energy systems offer major conservation potential in all sectors. Cogeneration and cascading approaches offer potential fuel utilization improvements of up to 100% in overall efficiency depending on the specific processes. For example, a dedicated electrical generation plant converted to the cogeneration approach may improve overall efficiency from 33% to 70% or even higher. Furthermore, with proper community design and energy system integration, transportation requirements also may be reduced in the longer run.

The MOPPS report provides a comprehensive identification of conservation technologies and a useful discussion of market penetration potentials. However, since—as noted above—only modest price increases are assumed, the operation of nonprice stimuli toward realization of these potentials is not always clearcut. On economy-energy connections, the consistency between overall economic growth rates and the substantial capital turnover that—implicitly—makes possible introduction of energy-conserving processes and facilities is neglected. So is the issue of whether

[23] Ibid., pp. 16–17.

Table A-4. Primary Energy Demands by Sector, MOPPS Study
(in quads)

	Delivered fuel forms	1975[a]	1985	2000
Residential–commercial sector	Liquids[b]	4.74	5.00	3.78
	Gas	7.59	8.20	7.78
	Coal	0.25	0.25	0.46
	Electricity	12.24	16.81	22.72
	Solar	—	0.18	0.80
	Geothermal	—	0.02	0.27
	Biomass	—	0.05	0.22
	Subtotal	24.82	30.51	36.03
Transportation sector	Liquids[b]	17.75	18.99	17.99
	Gas	0.60	0.77	0.54
	Electricity	0.05	1.47	2.32
	Subtotal	18.40	21.23	20.85
Industrial sector	Liquids[b]	7.02	7.34	8.79
	Gas	8.55	7.86	8.25
	Coal	3.81	8.30	15.84
	Electricity	7.95	15.01	20.47
	Industrial waste	1.57	2.04	2.92
	Solar	—	0.01	0.05
	Geothermal	—	0.09	0.49
	Biomass	—	—	0.06
	Subtotal	28.90	40.57	56.87
All sectors	Liquids	29.51	31.33	30.56
	Gas	16.74	16.83	16.57
	Coal	4.06	8.55	16.30
	Electricity[c]	20.24	33.29	45.51
	Industrial waste	1.57	2.04	2.92
	Solar	—	0.19	0.85
	Geothermal	—	0.11	0.76
	Biomass	—	0.05	0.28
	Total demand	72.12	92.39	113.75

Source: U.S. Department of Energy, "Market Oriented Program Planning Study (MOPPS)," Final Report, vol. 1, "Integrated Summary" (Washington, D.C., December 1977, Review Draft), p. 6.

[a] Principal source for the 1975 figures is the Bureau of Mines news release, March 14, 1977, modified by MOPPS to conform to its accounting conventions.

[b] All lubes, waxes, asphalt, and road oil are included in the industrial rather than transportation or residential–commercial liquids total. The quantities are 1.40 quads in 1975, 1.90 quads in 1985, and 2.46 quads in 2000.

[c] Electricity demands stated here are in terms of primary quads and as such include losses in generating and delivering the electricity to the users.

stipulated GNP growth holds up in the light of the significant deceleration of energy-demand growth projected by the study.

Electric Power Research Institute (EPRI)—Demand 77

This report, one of a series of annually updated long-term projections, contains estimates of energy consumption forward to the year 2000.[24] The projections were developed through the use of an econometric model featuring equations applicable to the different energy-using sectors and end-use forms (coal, petroleum, gas, and electricity). The model calculates energy demand through time in one-year increments.

The model assumes a GNP growth of 3.4 percent yearly. This economic growth forecast is coupled to three scenarios concerning energy prices and conservation policy. The scenarios, in brief, comprised a baseline case, which assumed a most likely increase in real energy prices (averaging out, over the next twenty-five years, to 2.5 percent per year for oil, 5 percent for gas, 1 percent for coal, and 3 percent for electric power) and adoption of no significant new conservation policies; a high case, characterized by high electricity consumption, accompanied by low oil prices and minimal obstacles to the use of coal and nuclear power in electric plants; and an energy conservation scenario, embodying the proposals in the Carter administration's 1977 National Energy Plan.

Compared with a 1975 level of energy consumption of about 70 quads, the EPRI analysis leads to the following projected estimates for 2000 (figures in parentheses indicate the share supplied by electricity): baseline, 159 quads (48 percent); high, 196 quads (49 percent); and conservation, 146 quads (47 percent).

In all three cases, these are high results, at least when judged by the other studies reviewed. The baseline scenario reflects an average annual energy growth rate of 3.3 percent, implying an energy–GDP elasticity factor virtually equal to unity. The EPRI authors acknowledge the high demand level in their high scenario and hint at its unreasonableness: "We regard this scenario as approaching the upper limit of plausibility." They go on to observe that, with respect to the conservation scenario, "Although

[24] Larry J. Williams, James W. Boyd, and Robert T. Crow, *Demand 77: EPRI Annual Energy Forecasts and Consumption Model,* EPRI EA-621-SR, vol. 1 (Palo Alto, Calif., Electric Power Research Institute, March 1978). A summary account appears in Robert T. Crow, "Demand 77," *EPRI Journal* (December 1977) pp. 20–23.

most observers of energy analysis and policy would not regard this as being as much an 'outside' representation of conservation as the high electricity consumption scenario is of high consumption, it is of interest to real decisions now being made."[25] But one must point out that the upper limits of demand in several other studies reviewed here (for example, the IEA and MOPPS) barely reach, if they do not fall significantly below, the EPRI conservation case.

Resources for the Future–National Institutes of Health (RFF–NIH) Study

With support from the NIH, a team at RFF set out to probe the long-term environmental and resource consequences of alternative assumptions regarding demographic and economic growth.[26] Energy is accorded special emphasis. The rather intricate modeling approach followed can only be briefly touched on here. (In any case, the more complex features of the model were more specifically designed to address problems of environmental impacts.) The project revolved around the use of a number of interlinked models—most prominently the one known as Strategic Environmental Assessment System (SEAS)—whose original development occurred within the U.S. Environmental Protection Agency; and a detailed, dynamic input–output model of the U.S. economy, developed at the University of Maryland.

The RFF–NIH study hypothesized a wide variety of future scenarios, two of which related to the possibility of a complete phaseout of nuclear facilities and a significant reduction in the real world oil price. Here, we will only cite the results of the so-called baseline case, though it is worth noting that all the RFF–NIH scenarios are characterized by declining rates of growth in energy over time—partly because of declining rates of

---

[25] Both quoted statements appear in Williams and coauthors, *Demand 77,* p. xii.

[26] See Ronald G. Ridker and William D. Watson, Jr., chap. 5, "Energy," in "To Choose a Future: Resource and Environmental Problems of the U.S., A Long-Term Global Outlook," an RFF study sponsored by the National Institutes of Health (in preparation). A compressed account appears in Ronald G. Ridker, William D. Watson, Jr., and Adele Shapanka, "Economic, Energy, and Environmental Consequences of Alternative Energy Regimes, An Application of the RFF/SEAS Modeling System," in Hitch, *Modeling Energy–Economy Interactions.* However, this latter discussion—while a lucid description of the approach followed in the RFF–NIH project, introduces and tests the effect of somewhat different underlying assumptions so as to conform to identical assumptions governing other contributions to the Hitch volume.

growth of population and the GNP, even in the high-energy-growth scenarios, partly because of compositional, technological, and other changes making for a declining energy–GDP ratio.

In the baseline scenario, energy demand—reaching a level of 114 quads in the year 2000 and averaging an annual growth rate of 1.7 percent—accompanies a projected GNP growing at 3.2 percent per year. Projected relative energy prices (delivered basis) work out to the following average annual rates of increase for the period 1975–85: liquids (0.4 percent), gas (9.8 percent), coal (2.3 percent), electricity (1.9 percent). For the years 1985–2000, it is assumed that prices will stabilize (that is, that in nominal terms, they will follow overall inflation), though an upward trend is assumed to resume at the turn of the century.

Price elasticities of demand are given full play in the industrial sector, where an elasticity of 0.7 is assumed to work itself out over a fifteen-year time span. The comparable elasticity for commercial activities is assumed to be 0.4 with a twenty-year lag. For the residential and transport sectors, the approach is more eclectic; it takes into account saturation effects, legislated energy efficiencies, and related influences. In raw material and feedstock uses, zero elasticity is assumed.

While realization of energy conservation potentials is assumed for all sectors of the economy up to a point, the main source of aggregate dampened energy demand growth comes from efficiency improvements in residential buildings. In the industrial sector, a continuation of rapid growth foreseen in the use of energy as raw materials (for example, plastics, fertilizer, drugs—where more economic use of energy is not easy to bring about) will offset efficiency gains achievable elsewhere in industry. And while the authors accept the likelihood of impressive efficiency gains and saturation in the automotive segment of transportation, they postulate significant growth in passenger airline traffic.

As noted earlier, the RFF–NIH project has features that we could not touch on here. The technical attributes of the model structure alone deserve extended discussion, as do the alternative energy, resource, and environmental scenarios depicted in the model.

Part III

Energy Supply

7 *Mineral Fuel Resources*

Future energy supplies from mineral fuels depend ultimately on the quantities of coal, oil, gas, uranium, and other mineral fuels within the earth—and on the costs of extracting these supplies and delivering them to the consumer in useful form. Beyond the traditional categories of mineral fuels there are other energy sources, such as solar energy, geothermal energy, and nuclear fusion. The technologies for their application, which is the decisive factor in their potential usefulness, will be considered in later chapters.

The analysis of mineral resource availability starts with estimates of the earth's natural stock of such materials; but our knowledge of these stocks varies considerably from one fuel to another. Coal is at one extreme. Its origin and formation are fairly well understood. Furthermore, coal beds tend to be continuous over a fairly broad area, making it possible to project them for some distance from their outcrop and to categorize them in terms of bed thickness, depth of overburden, and other characteristics that affect availability and cost. Petroleum, on the other hand, is quite different; we do not fully understand the origins of fluid hydrocarbons, the transformation of organic matter in rocks, and the maturation and migration of petroleum. Even less is known about uranium. In the United States, uranium seems to occur most commonly in sedimentary rocks, but major finds outside the United States have been made in metamorphic and igneous rocks. This diversity of geological environments makes it quite difficult to extrapolate what we know about uranium ores generally.

Apart from underlying differences in what is "knowable" about natural stocks of the various mineral fuels, the statistics pertaining to them vary according to who gathered the data and what they were trying to measure. Thus, the most widely used statistics for oil and gas in this country have been reserve estimates developed by the industries themselves, through the American Petroleum Institute (API) and the American Gas Association (AGA). These statistics refer to "proved reserves"—defined as discovered resources which can be recovered by methods currently being used, and at costs which make economic sense at present-day prices. For U.S. coal, on the other hand, the most widely cited estimates have come from the U.S. Geological Survey (USGS). They are based on detailed reports from individual states, and they go a long way toward providing a measure of the *total* resource endowment as circumscribed by specifically defined physical limits of overburden depth and seam thickness. The proved reserves estimates for oil and gas have a primarily commercial purpose; the USGS figures on coal resources go beyond present commercial limits to approximate how much of the mineral fuel exists in the earth—whether we are likely to be able to use it in the foreseeable future or not.

Numerous efforts have been made in recent years to compile resource estimates for the various mineral fuels which would permit us to compare them meaningfully with each other, and also to derive a grand total for all of them. We will present such tabulations in this chapter, although wide disparities in the underlying data base make such efforts less than totally successful. Because of the confusing variety of measures that pervade estimates of mineral reserves and resources, we will begin by attempting to clarify terminologies and underlying concepts.

Terminology and Concepts

For all practical purposes, the total amount of natural resources of any particular mineral fuel can be considered fixed; but the fact that resources exist does not imply that we know how extensive they are or where they are—much less that we have the technical and economic means to recover them. The total natural stock may be called the "resource base." That portion of it which has been estimated with at least a small degree of certainty and which might be recovered some time in the future is termed "resources." That portion of resources which has been located with considerable certainty and that can be recovered with present technical and economic means, may be termed "reserves." Thus, data and estimates about minerals are classified along the spectrum from resource base through resources to reserves by two criteria: geological assurance of their existence and economic feasibility of their recovery.

The broad distinction between resources and reserves is of basic importance in our analysis. Reserve data are meant to satisfy quite different objectives than are resource data. Companies investing capital in a well or a mine want to be sure that their investment has a good chance of paying off. They require a high degree of certainty about the quality and quantity of available deposits before starting operation. Of course, commercial operators are interested in deposits that may exist in addition to actual reserves, but they have a much less pressing need to know about them. Exploration is expensive, and its costs to an individual company soon exceed the benefits of having detailed information about deposits that will not be exploited until much later.

On the other hand, strategic energy decisions require knowledge of total resource availability and general cost ranges rather than detailed information about specific deposits and specific costs. Such broad knowledge can serve to shape public policies on an international, national, or regional level.

Thus, in general, reserve data tell society about the quantity and costs of fuel supplies that can be produced in the short run, while resource data provide insights about the long-range prospects for fuel supplies.

The methods of estimating reserves and resources are basically different. While reserve data rely upon the physical evidence provided by drilling, resource estimates are based on analytical models which involve both geology and economics.

Three types of methods of resource estimation can be distinguished: (1) behavioristic methods; (2) volumetric methods; and (3) geostatistical methods.

Behavioristic methods use historical data on production and discovery as their basic input. Mining industries pass through definite stages in the course of time; and relatively simple mathematical models can approximate the normal paths of discovery and the production variables. Past experience allows one to estimate at least the range of how much is likely to be discovered or produced in the future. This procedure is illustrated in part A of figure 7-1.

Volumetric methods use a basic input of geological data on deposit formation and the host environments of minerals discovered thus far. This approach assumes that mineral deposits are characterized by distinct formation processes, which have occurred only in certain types of geological settings. By drawing analogies between known producing areas and potentially producing areas, one may estimate deposits that have not

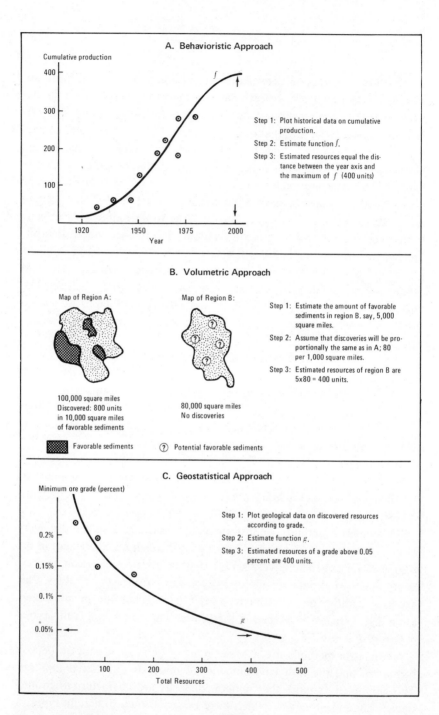

Figure 7-1. Methods of resource estimation.

yet been discovered. Part B of figure 7-1 illustrates one such procedure.

Geostatistical methods use detailed geological data on the size, grade, and depth of known deposits and host materials as their basic input. By extrapolating these data according to derived statistical functions, the size, grade, and depth of unknown deposits can be predicted; and this permits calculation of total deposits surmised to exist (including lower-grade ores which have not been exploited). An example of this type of procedure is illustrated in figure 7-1, part C.

These different methods can yield widely varying results, and none of them is universally accepted. Consequently, the results are surrounded by controversy as to their validity and usefulness.

U.S. Reserves and Resources

An effort to place the statistics for reserves and resources of coal, oil, gas, and uranium on a common basis is presented in table 7-1. As our subsequent discussion of the separate fuels will show, this still falls far short of full comparability, but the statistics do reveal a great deal about the comparative abundance of different energy sources.

Coal

The coal estimates in table 7-1 were compiled by the USGS. The underlying reports covering different coal fields were aggregated, setting limits on minimum allowable seam thickness and maximum allowable depth of occurrence. "Inferred" and "hypothetical" resources are mainly estimated continuations of known deposits: the inferred resources are at relatively shorter distances from known deposits and occur primarily at depths less than 1,000 feet; hypothetical resources are at relatively long distances from known deposits and occur primarily at depths between 1,000 to 6,000 feet. Clearly, the economics of recovery will differ enormously between coal reserves and the additional inferred or hypothetical resources.

The numbers indicate that vast quantities of coal resources (on the order of 1.8 trillion recoverable tons, or 36,000 quads) are available. These resources are by far the largest among the various fuels, except for uranium if breeder reactors are employed. Of course, we do not know the cost schedule of making various quantities of these resources available over time.

Table 7-1. U.S. Recoverable Reserves and Resources of Conventional Mineral Fuels

Fuel	Identified[a] Reserves[b]	Identified[a] Inferred resources	Undiscovered[a] hypo- thetical resources	Total	Quads of Btu equivalent[c]
Coal (billion short tons)[d]	260	648[e]	895	1,803	37,863
Oil (billion barrels)	34	23	82	139	806
Natural gas liquids (billion barrels)	6	6	16	28	115
Gas (trillion cubic feet)	209	202	484	895	917
Uranium (thousand short tons)[f]	890	1,395	1,515	3,800	1,140 (LWR) 68,400 (FBR)
Total (quadrillion Btu)	6,163	14,391	20,287		40,841 (LWR) 108,101 (FBR)

Note: The adjective "recoverable" indicates that the estimates refer to how much material may possibly be recovered and not to how much material is in place. However, the intention is to go beyond what could be recovered with today's technological and economic means. The coal estimates include thin beds, which cannot be recovered economically at the present time; and the uranium estimates include materials recoverable only at costs above present market prices. Although the hydrocarbon estimates refer to quantities that could be recovered economically today, improved conditions are unlikely to affect them substantially. LWR = Light Water Reactor; FBR = Fast Breeder Reactor.

The adjective "conventional" indicates that the estimates refer to fuels which are presently produced commercially in significant quantities. For oil shales, natural gas from geopressured zones, uranium from low-grade shales, and the like, see tables 7-4 and 7-5.

Sources: Coal—Paul Averitt, *Coal Resources of the United States, January 1, 1974*, U.S. Geological Survey Bulletin 1412 (Washington, D.C., GPO, 1974).

Oil and gas—Betty Miller and coauthors, *Geological Estimates of Undiscovered Recoverable Oil and Gas Resources in the United States*, U.S. Geological Survey Circular 725 (Reston, Va., USGS, 1975); *Oil and Gas Journal* vol. 76, no. 16 (17 April 1978) p. 53.

Uranium—U.S. Department of Energy, *Statistical Data of the Uranium Industry, January 1, 1978*, GJO-100(78) (Grand Junction, Colo., DOE, 1978).

[a] There are many systems of classifying resources which are presumed to exist in addition to known reserves. All serve to indicate the degree of confidence one may have in the geological existence of the resource. For our purpose two classes suffice: inferred and hypothetical resources. The term "inferred resources" applies to materials contained in relatively unexplored extensions of known reserves. Although they are identified one can be less confident about their accuracy than is the case for reserves. The term "hypothetical resources" applies to undiscovered materials assumed to exist in known producing regions and under known geological conditions as well as extensions of identified resources. Since all of these estimates exclude so-called "speculative resources" (which may exist outside known producing regions or under unknown geological conditions), they can be considered on the conservative side.

[b] Reserve data are as of January 1, 1978. In the case of coal, the statistics for resources date back four years; and the resource data for oil, gas, and NGL are three years old. No attempt has been made to update them, because such a procedure would be highly arbitrary and, in any case, it would not change the figures substantially.

[c] One quad is 10^{15} Btu. Heat equivalents used here are: coal, 21 million Btu per short ton; oil, 5.8 million Btu per barrel; NGL, 4.1 million Btu per barrel; gas, 1,025 Btu per cubic foot; uranium, 300 billion Btu per short ton (if used in LWRs) or 18 trillion Btu per short ton (if used in fast breeders). See appendix to this chapter for a discussion of the heat contents used for uranium.

Coal reserves as measured by in-place quantities are further specified by area, rank, mining method, and sulfur content in table 7-2. All anthracite and a large percentage of the bituminous coal (85 percent) is found east of the Mississippi. All of the subbituminous coal and almost all lignite (97 percent) is found west of the Mississippi. This means that, in terms of heating value per ton, eastern coal is much more valuable than western coal. While total quantities of coal in the East are roughly equal to those in the West, 80 percent of eastern coal requires underground mining versus only 60 percent of western coal. Finally, the western coal is primarily low sulfur (77 percent has less than 1 percent sulfur), while the eastern coal is primarily high sulfur (80 percent with more than 1 percent sulfur).

The data permit a few inferences about the future potential of coal. First, most coal of low heating value is in deposits far from the major energy consuming regions, thus presenting transportation problems. Second, surface mining methods are indicated in the arid, ecologically vulnerable West, presenting environmental problems. Third, much coal of high sulfur content is located in the East, where ambient air quality is often deficient.

Coal production in 1975 was slightly over 650 million tons; and for a variety of reasons it was still almost exactly the same in 1978. Obviously, reserves are ample to support a very large expansion in production. In addition, the average mine-mouth price of coal was about $20 per ton in 1975, or $1.00 per million Btu; that is, less than half the world price of oil. Nevertheless, rapid expansion of production will pose problems. Comparative resource availability points to increasing amounts of coal production from the West. In addition, the fact that most eastern coal is higher in sulfur content may increase the demand for western coal. However, the expansion of western coal production faces environmental, manpower, and infrastructural problems that will not be easily solved in the

---

d Recovery factors are included in the background sources for the hydrocarbon and uranium estimates, but not for the coal estimates. For coal, we assumed recovery factors of 60 percent for reserves, 50 percent for inferred resources, and 40 percent for hypothetical resources. This implies that all beds will be economically recoverable, but that it is technically more difficult to mine the thinner and deeper beds in the inferred and hypothetical classes. The rate of 60 percent for reserves is well accepted. The other two percentages may be more uncertain.

e Includes all identified resources in thin beds and from 1,000 to 3,000 feet deep in addition to resources inferred by extension.

f All estimates concern resources producible below $50 forward costs (see table 7-5, note a). The figures for inferred resources correspond with those for "probable potential resources" in the source publication, and the figures for hypothetical resources correspond with those for "possible potential resources" in the same document.

Table 7-2. U.S. Coal Reserve Base by Area, Type, Mining Method, and Sulfur Content (billion short tons)

Type	East of the Mississippi			West of the Mississippi			Total		
	Sur-face	Under-ground	Total	Sur-face	Under-ground	Total	Sur-face	Under-ground	Total
Anthracite	—	7	7	—	—	—	—	7	7
Bituminous	39	155	195	8	27	34	47	182	229
Subbituminous	—	—	—	61	108	168	61	108	168
Lignite	1	—	1	33	—	33	34	—	34
All types	41	162	203	101	135	235	141	297	438
Percentage of low sulfur coal[a]	19	20	20	69	83	77	55	49	51

Note: Figures may not add to totals due to rounding. The U.S. Bureau of Mines terminology defines *reserves* as recoverable reserves and *reserve base* as in-place reserves. Thus, the figures presented in this table refer to in-place quantities.

Sources: U.S. Bureau of Mines, "Demonstrated Coal Reserve Base of the United States on January 1, 1976," in *Mineral Industry Surveys* (Washington, U.S. Bureau of Mines, August 1977); U.S. Bureau of Mines, *The Reserve Base of U.S. Coals by Sulfur Content*, U.S. Bureau of Mines Information Circulars 8680 and 8693 (Washington, GPO, 1975).

[a] Represents all coal with a sulfur content by weight of less than 1 percent as a percentage of all coal for which sulfur content is known. Sulfur content is known for at least 84 percent of all coal in each category presented.

short run. (Some of the problems associated with the expansion of coal production are discussed in chapter 18.)

Conventional Oil and Gas

Conventional oil and gas resources are substantially less plentiful than those of coal, as table 7-1 shows clearly. Table 7-3 examines these oil and gas estimates in somewhat greater detail.

We will focus on the undiscovered resources category, because it bears heavily on long-run prospects. The range of estimates given corresponds to different probabilities of actual occurrence. Total undiscovered resources of oil are estimated along a range between 50 billion and 127 billion barrels, with a mean value of 82. Adding these to reserves and inferred resources (34 billion and 23 billion barrels, respectively) gives a total of between 107 billion and 182 billion barrels of recoverable crude oil resources, with a mean value of 139. Undiscovered natural gas resources are estimated in the same manner at 484 trillion cubic feet, with a range of 322 trillion to 655 trillion cubic feet. Adding reserves and

Table 7-3. U.S. Recoverable Reserves and Resources of Crude Oil, Natural Gas, and Natural Gas Liquids

Location	Identified resources Re-serves	Identified resources Inferred	Undiscovered resources[a] Range	Undiscovered resources[a] Mean	Total resources[b] Range	Total resources[b] Mean
Crude oil (billion barrels)						
Onshore						
Lower 48 states	20	14	29–64	44		
Alaska	10	6	6–19	12		
Offshore						
Lower 48 states	3	3	5–18	11		
Alaska	—	—	3–31	15		
Total crude oil	34	23	50–127	82	107–182	139
Natural gas (trillion cubic feet)						
Onshore						
Lower 48 states	146[c]	119	246–453	345		
Alaska	32	15	16–57	32		
Offshore						
Lower 48 states	31[c]	67	26–111	63		
Alaska	—	—	8–80	44		
Total natural gas	209	202	322–655	484	733–1,066	895
Natural gas liquids (billion barrels)	6	6	11–22	16	23–34	28

Note: Reserve data are as of January 1, 1978. Data for inferred and undiscovered resources are as of January 1, 1975. No attempt has been made to update the latter data, because this would involve a highly arbitrary procedure, which would not change the figures significantly. Figures may not add because of rounding.

Sources: Reserves—*Oil and Gas Journal* vol. 76, no. 16 (17 April 1978) p. 55. Inferred and undiscovered resources—Betty Miller and coauthors, *Geological Estimates of Undiscovered Recoverable Oil and Gas Resources in the United States,* U.S. Geological Survey Circular 725 (Reston, Va., USGS, 1975).

[a] There is a probability of more than 95 percent that at least the lowest figure is actually available, while there is only a 5 percent chance that the quantity actually available exceeds the high figure. The third figure is the statistical mean of a lognormal probability distribution function. Ranges cannot be summed arithmetically and means are not midpoint estimates of the range.

[b] We assume that reserves are known with certainty and equal to the values presented. Thus the interpretation of the range and mean for total resources depends entirely on the interpretation of the range and mean for undiscovered resources.

[c] The latest American Gas Association data on reserves from the *Oil and Gas Journal* were not specified according to onshore and offshore occurrence. We assume that since 1974, for which the USGS Circular 725 specifies onshore and offshore reserves, production and additions to reserves occurred in proportion to 1974 onshore and offshore shares.

inferred resources yields a total for recoverable resources ranging from 733 trillion to 1,066 trillion cubic feet, with a mean value of 895.[1] (For an explanation of the range and mean, see table 7-3, footnote a.)

In addition to crude oil, natural gas liquids contribute to the supply of liquid hydrocarbons. Natural gas liquids are found in association with natural gas, and are usually estimated as proportional to natural gas resources. The mean of total recoverable liquid hydrocarbon resources thus amounts to 167 billion barrels.

Besides the aggregate quantity of recoverable resources, their geographical distribution is important. The prominence of Alaskan and offshore sources, particularly for oil, is remarkable. Alaskan oil accounts for 33 percent of undiscovered resources, offshore oil (including Alaskan) for 32 percent.[2]

It is important to recognize that the USGS figures are based on a set of economic conditions that predates the sharp price increases of recent years, so they are somewhat biased toward the conservative side. Today there is greater economic potential for extraction in remote and hostile environments and for secondary recovery. Estimates that take the higher prices into account indicate natural gas resources of around 1,000 trillion cubic feet and crude oil resources of up to 200 billion barrels.[3]

Nevertheless, even the most dramatic price increases in the future are expected to affect available domestic conventional oil and gas resources only slightly. But unconventional resources will become increasingly attractive at higher prices, and substantial amounts of such sources are available.

Unconventional Oil and Gas

The quite limited conventional resources of oil and gas, which even the most optimistic current assumptions suggest exist within the United

[1] For oil, this range conveniently brackets most of the available estimates of U.S. recoverable crude oil resources published in recent years. For gas, the range of estimates from other sources is somewhat wider than that of the USGS, pointing to somewhat greater uncertainty than for oil.

[2] Although there seems to be some agreement on the aggregate level of oil and gas resources to be discovered in the United States, there is substantial disagreement about where it is to be found. In an estimate by Mobil Oil, for example, onshore gas in the lower 48 states accounts for only 15 percent of total undiscovered resources, while the equivalent number for the USGS estimate is 85 percent. See John D. Moody and Robert E. Geiger, "Petroleum Resources: How Much Oil and Where?" *Technology Review* vol. 77, no. 4 (March–April 1975) p. 40.

[3] Stanford Research Institute, *Fuel and Energy Price Forecasts,* Final Report EPRI EA-433 (Palo Alto, Calif., Electric Power Research Institute, February 1977) pp. 4-37 and 4-59.

Table 7-4. U.S. Unconventional Oil and Gas Resources

Resource types	In-place quantities	Recovery factor (percent)[a]	Quantity recovered	Quads of Btu equivalent[b]
		Recoverable quantities		
Oil (billion barrels)				
1. Oil shales	330	60	198	1,148
2. Heavy crude oils	150	20	30	174
Total	480		228	1,322
Gas (trillion cubic feet)				
3. Tight sands	793	25	198	203
4. Black shales	284	25	71	73
5. Coal seams	850	10	85	87
6. Geopressured zones	3,000	10	300	308
Total	4,927		654	671

Sources: Line 1—National Petroleum Council, *U.S. Energy Outlook, An Initial Appraisal by the Oil Shale Task Group, 1971–1985* (Washington, D.C., NPC, 1972).

Line 2—U.S. Department of the Interior, *Heavy Crude Reservoirs in the United States: A Survey*, Bureau of Mines Information Circular 8263 (Washington, D.C., GPO, 1965).

Lines 3–5—U.S. Department of Energy, *National Gas Survey*, Report on Nonconventional Natural Gas Resources to the Federal Energy Regulatory Commission (Washington, D.C., GPO, June 1978).

Line 6—B. R. Hise, "Natural Gas from Geopressured Aquifers," in National Academy of Sciences, *Natural Gas from Unconventional Geological Sources* (Washington, D.C., NAS, 1976).

[a] Sources usually specify in-place quantities. Assumptions about recovery are our own.

[b] Heat contents: Oil shale and heavy crudes, 5.8 million Btu per barrel; and unconventional natural gas, 1,025 Btu per cubic foot.

States, are augmented substantially by taking unconventional resources of oil and gas into account. Table 7-4 shows estimates of such unconventional resources.

For oil, the major potential for unconventional domestic resources rests in oil shale deposits found mainly in Colorado and also in Utah and Wyoming. The total amounts in place are estimated at the staggeringly high figure of almost 170 trillion barrels.[4] Focusing only on resources having a near-term commercial potential (that is, shale containing over 30 gallons of oil per ton) almost 200 billion barrels are available for recovery. If the limit is dropped to 15 gallons per ton, the potential total recoverable content rises above 1 trillion barrels. The former figure is equivalent to the total estimated recoverable conventional oil resources

[4] D. C. Duncan and V. E. Swanson, *Organic Rich Shale of the United States and World Land Areas,* U.S. Geological Survey Information Circular 523 (Washington, D.C., GPO, 1965).

in this country, while the latter is five times that amount. Quite clearly, shale oil would substantially enhance the domestic oil outlook if technical and economic feasibility could be achieved at acceptable environmental costs. These questions will be explored later in this book. In addition to oil shales, a modest quantity of heavy crude oils is available. Of a total volume of 150 billion barrels in place, perhaps 30 to 45 billion barrels may be recovered eventually.

Many unconventional sources of natural gas are also known to exist: tight sands, black shales, geopressured zones, and coal seams (see table 7-4). Again, the critical questions concern economic and technical feasibility and environmental impacts.

Extraction from tight sands (found primarily in Colorado, Utah, and Wyoming) and black shales (found in the Devonian shale complexes of the Appalachian Basin) involves massive fracturing techniques that are costly and not yet perfected. Even without new technology, there has been some production for decades from eastern Devonian shales; but the low porosity of the formations keeps production rates extremely low. If we assume that 25 percent of the gas contained in tight sands and in black shales will be recovered, these sources would ultimately produce 198 trillion and 71 trillion cubic feet, respectively. By comparison, recovery rates of up to 90 percent are now obtained for conventional gas.

Geopressured zones, which occur both on- and offshore in the Gulf Coast Basin, pose an entirely different set of technical and economic problems. Some are related to deep drilling, others with the environmental consequences of fluid withdrawal (subsidence) and disposal (thermal pollution). Vast estimates of in-place amounts range from 3,000 trillion to 49,000 trillion cubic feet.[5] Even using the low estimate and a recovery factor of only 10 percent yields an ultimate production of 300 trillion cubic feet, but the potential might be substantially higher. The technology of production from geopressured zones is far less developed than for tight sands and black shales, however. The geopressured zones could become much more promising economically if a total energy system were developed in which—in addition to natural gas production—the pressurized hot water at the wellhead could be used first for hydraulic generation of electricity and then for process heat. This possibility, however, is merely speculative at present, although the state conservation laws

---

[5] Paul H. Jones, "Gas in Geopressured Zones," in R. F. Meyer, ed., *The Future Supply of Nature-Made Petroleum and Gas* (New York, Pergamon Press, 1977) p. 905.

of Texas and Louisiana are both written to encourage the multiple use of the resources.

Coal seams are another potential source of methane. Based on estimates of the degree to which coal and gas are associated, our total national coal resources (identified plus hypothetical) might contain 850 trillion cubic feet. At a 10 percent recovery factor, that would yield 85 trillion cubic feet.

In summary, the total amount of gas which we estimate unconventional resources may yield almost matches conventional gas resources. Of course, the margins of uncertainty are large. There are more uncertainties about in-place quantities, and the hypothetical recovery factors could easily be far off the mark because they are not based on actual experience. The estimates of recoverable quantities, therefore should only be used with extreme caution.

Oil and Gas Reserves and Production in Recent Years

Our discussion of oil and gas resources has focused so far on the more distant future, but many of the nation's most serious energy difficulties arise from the fact that domestic reserves and production of both fuels have been declining in the recent past.

Figure 7-2 shows the trend in U.S. proved reserves of crude oil (that is, those that support current output) from 1945 to 1976. Proved reserves increased steadily from 1945 to about 1959, remained nearly constant from 1959 to 1967, started to decline in 1967, and have declined sharply every year since then except for 1970 (the year that Alaskan oil reserves were first reported).

In U.S. production practice, the ratio of reserves to production (R/P) runs between 8 and 12; the exact relationship varies with geologic conditions in the reservoir. Thus, as reserves decline, the rate of production declines with it. Between 1970 and 1975 proved oil reserves declined by 23 percent, and production declined 16 percent.

The relationship between yearly additions to reserves and yearly levels of production is shown in figure 7-3. Both have been declining in recent years after a long history of relatively constant additions to reserves and a steady increase in production. Since 1970, annual production has outstripped additions to reserves.

A summary of the recent history of domestic natural gas reserves is shown in figure 7-4. It shows a declining trend of natural gas reserves similar to that for crude oil reserves. At the end of 1976, proved reserves

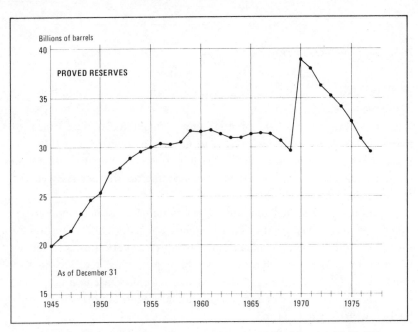

Figure 7-2. Proved reserves of crude oil in the United States, 1945–77.

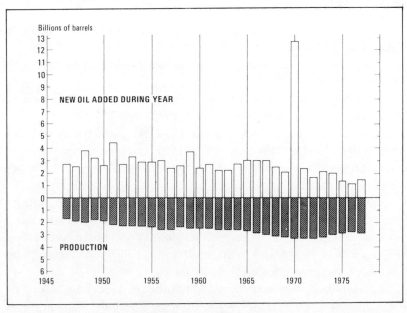

Figure 7-3. Crude oil production and additions to reserves, 1945–77.
Both from American Gas Association, American Petroleum Institute, Canadian Petroleum Association, *Reserves of Crude Oil, Natural Gas Liquids, and Natural Gas in the United States and Canada as of December 31, 1977* vol. 32 (Washington, D.C., American Petroleum Institute, June 1978) p. 84.

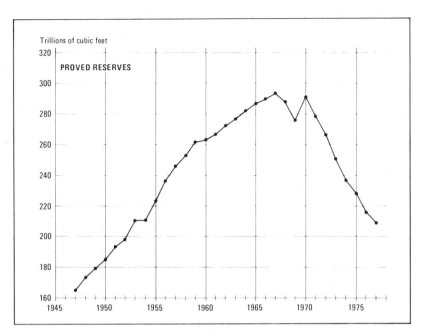

Figure 7-4. Proved reserves of natural gas in the United States, 1947–77.

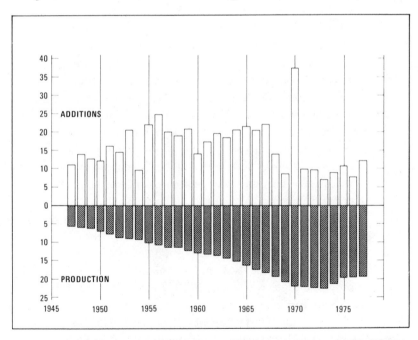

Figure 7-5. Natural gas production and additions to reserves, 1947–77.
Both from American Gas Association, American Petroleum Institute, Canadian Petroleum Association, *Reserves of Crude Oil, Natural Gas Liquids, and Natural Gas in the United States and Canada as of December 31, 1977* vol. 32 (Washington, D.C., American Petroleum Institute, June 1978) p. 111.

of natural gas stood at 210 trillion cubic feet, compared with nearly 290 trillion cubic feet only six years earlier (when hydrocarbons on the North Slope of Alaska were discovered).

As seen in figure 7-5, production of natural gas increased each year from 1947 to 1970, then stayed relatively constant until 1973. Since then it has declined yearly. Yearly additions to reserves were in the range of 10 to 15 trillion cubic feet per year until about 1954, after which they hovered about 20 trillion cubic feet per year until 1967. Except for the inclusion of Alaskan gas in 1970, the yearly additions since 1967 have been in the range of 10 trillion cubic feet per year—or about one-half of yearly production. As a result, the reserves-to-production ratio fell from 20 in 1960 to only 11 in 1976. This is about the lowest level considered to be satisfactory for normal production.

Uranium

Nuclear power is a comparatively new industry in the energy sector, so not nearly as much knowledge can be drawn from experience about nuclear fuel reserves and resources as is the case with fossil fuels. Furthermore, our knowledge about uranium mainly reflects exploration activities within presently producing regions, while exploration for oil, gas, and coal has taken place widely—both within and outside presently producing regions. As a result, the uranium data base is far more limited than for fossil fuels. Even geological analogy, one of the techniques used in estimating oil and gas resources beyond the limits of the data base, has limited value here because of uncertainty in geological knowledge about the formation of uranium deposits.

The official source of information for domestic reserves and resources of uranium is the Grand Junction, Colorado, office of the U.S. Department of Energy (DOE). Their latest estimates, shown in table 7-5, have been made under the National Uranium Resources Evaluation (NURE) program, which was started in 1974 in an effort to resolve major uncertainties about uranium resources. The four classes of reserves and resources are subdivided into categories of ore cost. The "forward cost" concept used by DOE is explained in footnote a of table 7-5.

The logic for estimating reserves over such a wide spectrum of ore costs lies in the fact that the economics of nuclear power generation are dominated by capital cost (see chapter 9). An increase in the cost of uranium of $1.00 per pound raises the cost of generating electricity in today's light

Table 7-5. U.S. Uranium Reserves and Resources
(thousand short tons U_3O_8)

		Potential resources				Quads of Btu equivalent[b]	
	Reserves	Probable	Possible	Speculative	Total[a]	LWR	Breeder
Forward cost[c] (1977 dollars per pound)							
Under $15	370	540	490	165	1,565	470	28,170
$15–$30	320	475	645	250	1,690	507	30,420
$30–$50	200	380	380	150	1,110	333	19,980
Subtotal	890	1,395	1,515	565	4,365	1,310	78,570
Uranium recoverable as a by-product from copper and phosphate through year 2000	—	—	—	—	140	42	2,520
Gassaway member of Chattanooga shales, major counties, 30 percent recovered[d]	—	—	—	—	1,555	467	27,990
TOTAL					6,060	1,819	109,080

Note: Uranium resources are generally measured in terms of uranium oxide (U_3O_8), the product that first enters commerce, rather than uranium.
Sources: U.S. Department of Energy, *Statistical Data of the Uranium Industry, January 1, 1978,* GJO-100(78) (Grand Junction, Colo., DOE, 1978), and U.S. Department of the Interior, *Uranium from the Chattanooga Shale,* Bureau of Mines Information Circular 8700 (Washington, D.C., GPO, 1976).

[a] Includes "speculative reserves," not included in Table 7-1.

[b] Heat rates used are 300 billion Btu per ton for LWR technologies and 18 trillion Btu per ton for breeder technologies (see the appendix to this chapter).

[c] Forward cost, the concept used in the DOE estimates, includes all operating costs and those capital costs not yet incurred, and excludes all exploration and development costs. Such a figure bears an uncertain relationship to market price.

[d] For an explanation of this entry, see p. 239.

water reactors by less than 0.5 percent. Advanced technologies for converting larger and larger amounts of natural uranium into fissionable materials, a process which reaches its limits with the breeder reactor, are even more insensitive to uranium costs.

At a forward cost of less than $50, total recoverable reserves are estimated here at 890 thousand tons, while potential resources are estimated at 3,475 thousand tons—giving a total of well over 4 million tons. These estimates are controversial, however. Two sharply contending viewpoints are represented by the Nuclear Energy Policy Study Group of the Ford Foundation,[6] which considers the estimates unduly low, and the Uranium Resources Study Group of the Committee on Nuclear and Alternative Energy Systems (CONAES) of the National Academy of Sciences,[7] which says they are unduly high. The Ford Foundation group stresses that the commercial uranium mining industry is still in its infancy. It reasons from experience with other minerals that large amounts of additional uranium resources will be added over time by commercial and technical forces, and there will be more knowledge about where uranium occurs. On the other hand, geological uncertainties lay behind the cautious appraisal of the CONAES panel. It was willing to accept only the DOE reserves figures as having a high degree of certainty, and saw only the "probable potential" class of other resources as having a reasonable probability of becoming available in the future.[8]

In addition to the DOE estimates, other students of the subject have made uranium resource estimates; but again the range is wide—largely because different methods are employed. Behavioristic approaches generally yield comparatively low estimates, ranging between 1 million and 4 million tons of remaining resources, but volumetric and geostatistical approaches have yielded estimates running over 10 million tons.[9] Given

[6] Nuclear Energy Policy Study Group, Ford Foundation, *Nuclear Power Issues and Choices* (Cambridge, Mass., Ballinger, 1977). See particularly the conclusion on p. 92.

[7] Committee on Nuclear and Alternative Energy Sources, National Research Council, *Problems of U.S. Uranium Resources and Supply to the Year 2010,* Supporting Paper 1 (Washington, D.C., National Academy of Sciences, 1978).

[8] Both analyses were performed within the context of policy studies related to government RD&D support for the nuclear breeder reactor. The Ford Foundation group's optimism on uranium resources was coupled with a policy view that a decision on breeder technology demonstration could be delayed, while the CONAES panel's pessimistic attitude on resources produced a greater sense of urgency concerning the breeder decision.

[9] M. A. Lieberman, "United States Uranium Resources—An Analysis of Historical Data," *Science* vol. 192, no. 4238 (30 April 1976) pp. 431–437; DeVerle P. Harris, *The Estimation of Uranium Resources by Life-Cycle or Discovery Rate*

the brief history of the commercial uranium mining industry, it is likely that behavioristic methods (which rely on historical data) would err on the low side. On the other hand, there is no solid basis for evaluating the reasonableness of the estimates yielded by the volumetric and geostatistical methods, even though they yield levels which are more in keeping with long-term historical experience with other minerals.

The major unconventional sources of nuclear fuel are thorium and uranium from low-grade shales, granites, and other rocks. Low-grade uranium resources are estimated to include over 40 million tons with a grade higher than 0.001 percent.[10] Of those unconventional resources, the Chattanooga shale has received most attention; and within this formation the so-called Gassaway member is regarded as potentially the most favorable to mine. Perhaps about 1.5 million tons could be recoverable from an estimated 4.2 to 5.1 million tons in place there. The economics and technology of mining such a low-grade shale deposit would obviously differ in a major way from that experienced in mining conventional high-grade sandstone deposits. The CONAES panel study estimates that producing uranium from Chattanooga shale would cost at least $500 per pound. Clearly, shale deposits cannot be considered economic under present conditions or those expected in the near future.

The DOE estimates also include 140,000 tons of uranium to be recovered as a by-product from the copper and phosphate industries up to the year 2000. This source of uranium is presently negligible, but it could gain in importance as prices rise.

In certain nuclear reactor technologies, thorium can also be used (like U238) to produce additional nuclear fuel (see chapter 9). Identified domestic thorium resources are 294,000 tons, of which 46,000 tons are recoverable (primarily as a by-product). Of the remaining 248,000 tons, only 106,000 tons are of a grade above 0.01 percent.[11] Most important among the latter are the vein deposits in the Lemhi district of Idaho and Montana, estimated at 100,000 tons. This information about thorium is

---

Models—A Critique GJO-112(76) (Grand Junction, Colo., U.S. Energy Research and Development Administration, October 1976); Milton Searl, *Uranium Resources to Meet Long Term Uranium Requirements,* Special Report EPRI SR-5 (Palo Alto, Calif., Electric Power Research Institute, November 1974); S. M. Stoller Corporation, *Uranium Data,* Final Report EPRI EA-400 (Palo Alto, Calif., Electric Power Research Institute, June 1977).

[10] Battelle Pacific Northwest Laboratories, *Assessment of Uranium and Thorium Resources in the United States and the Effect of Policy Alternatives* (Richland, Wash., Battelle, December 1974) p. 5-19.

[11] M. H. Staatz and J. C. Olsen, "Thorium," in *U.S. Mineral Resources,* U.S. Geological Survey Professional Paper 820 (Washington, D.C., GPO, 1973) p. 474.

not comparable to the DOE uranium estimates either in purpose or in terms of accuracy; the figures cited here are extremely rough and very dated, and they do not address economic recoverability. Therefore, not too much can be said about the potential of thorium as a source of extra nuclear fuel. If thorium is to be considered as an important potential energy source, major exploration and development programs would have to be initiated.

Even more than with fossil fuels, the size of nuclear fuel resources cannot be separated from questions of the technology for employing them. In particular, the efficiency which alternative technologies achieve in converting natural uranium and thorium into fissionable materials will determine how much useful energy the natural supply will yield. Breeder technologies, at the most efficient extreme, can utilize material about 60 times more effectively than the currently utilized light water reactor (see the appendix to this chapter). Enhanced conversion efficiency would make our natural uranium and thorium resources last longer, whatever their ultimate size; but in addition to that it would make the mining of lower-grade materials economical because the raw material itself would become more valuable in terms of the energy it could provide.

World Reserves and Resources

In considering world energy reserves and resources, it is important to bear in mind that the amount of effort that has gone into exploration varies widely around the world, depending on the economic incentives which have driven the search. Statistics of reserves and resources such as those shown in table 7-6 may reflect the relative play of economic forces in different countries as much as (or more than) they reflect the comparative richness of these countries' natural resource endowments.

To illustrate the possible role of economic incentives: the United States (occupying 7 percent of the world's land mass) shows up here with roughly 20 percent of world fuel resources, while Africa (with roughly 20 percent of the world's land mass) accounts for roughly 1 percent of global fuel resources. Thus, the United States appears to contain sixty times as much in the way of energy resources per unit of surface area as Africa. This disparity may be explained, at least in part, by the fact that the search for resources has been far more intensive in the United States.[12]

[12] Bernardo F. Grossling has often made this point in a more sophisticated way. For example, with regard to oil, he showed that the developing nations possess 50

With this word of caution, we turn to a consideration of the different fuel resources. The possible importance of new discoveries around the world will be considered as we discuss the significance of the estimated amounts.

Coal

The most obvious characteristic of world coal resources is their truly impressive size: over 5 trillion (10^9) metric tons, or more than 140 quintillion (10^{18}) Btu in heat value. This represents roughly 15 times the energy contained in either world oil or world gas resources. With world energy consumption at a constant 275 quadrillion (10^{15}) Btu (approximately the present level), coal resources would last more than 500 years.

Three other facts characterize world coal resources: (1) the strong geographical concentration—with almost 90 percent of total resources in China, the Soviet Union, and the United States; (2) a high resources–reserves ratio of 8; and (3) a high reserves–production ratio of almost 200. By comparison, the world ratio between oil resources and reserves is only 3; the worldwide reserves–production ratio for oil is 30. Admittedly, this comparison may be somewhat misleading, because oil reserves are mostly developed while coal reserves are not. In other words, the high reserves–production ratio for coal does not imply a high potential for additional production immediately. Nevertheless, these facts clearly indicate that the demand for coal has been the main constraint on its production, and that coal holds great potential as a world energy supplier.

The United States is richly endowed with coal, so this country does not have to look beyond its borders for potential supplies in the future. Quite the reverse. As for coal-deficient parts of the world, however, the sizable overall resource potential dwindles when possibilities in other countries are evaluated realistically. Under present economic and technological conditions, transportation costs often remain prohibitively high for the use of coal in electricity generation; and environmental and infrastructural problems loom large. Moreover, domestic demand throughout the

---

percent of the world's prospective petroleum areas, although only 4 percent of the world's exploratory drilling has taken place there. See his "The Petroleum Exploration Challenge With Respect to Developing Nations," in R. F. Meyer, ed., *The Future Supply of Nature-Made Petroleum and Gas* (New York, Pergamon Press, 1977).

Table 7-6. World Recoverable Reserves and Resources of Conventional Mineral Fuels

Region or nation	Coal (billion metric tons coal equivalent)		Oil (billion barrels)		Gas (trillion cubic feet)		Uranium (thousand metric tons U)	
	Reserves	Resources	Reserves	Resources	Reserves	Resources	Reserves	Resources
United States[a]	178	1,285	29	110–185	205	730–1,070	643	1,696
Canada	9	57	6	25–40	59	230–380	182	838
Mexico	1	3	16	145–215	32	350–480	5	7
South and Central America	10	14	26	80–120	81	800–900	60	74
Western Europe	91	215	24	50–70	143	500	87	487
Africa	34	87	58	100–150	186	1,000	572	772
Middle East	—	—	370	710–1,000	731	1,750	—	—
Asia and Pacific	40	41	18	90–140	89	[b]	45	69
Australia	27	132	2	[c]	31	500	296	345
Soviet Union	110	2,430	71	140–200	910	2,850	n.a.	n.a.
China	99	719	20	[b]	25	[b]	n.a.	n.a.
Other Communist areas	37	80	3		10		n.a.	n.a.
Total	636	5,063	642	1,450–2,120	2,502	8,710–9,430	1,894	4,288
Quintillion (10^{18}) Btu[d]	17.7	140.6	3.7	8.4–12.3	2.6	8.9–9.7	7.4 (LWR) 443.2 (FBR)	16.7 (LWR) 1,003.4 (FBR)

Note: All resource figures are cumulative. They include reserves. The figures for international coal reserves and resources in this table are given in metric tons of fixed heat content rather than actual metric tons, while the domestic coal reserves and resources (table 7-1) are given in actual tons with an *average* heat content of 21 million Btu per ton. Similarly, 300 million Btu per short ton U_3O_8 (table 7-1) corresponds to 390 million Btu per metric ton U in this table.

Sources: Coal—World Energy Conference, *Coal Resources* (Guildford, England, IPC Science and Technology Press, 1978). A recoverability factor of 50 percent is assumed for resources.

Oil and gas—Reserves: *Oil and Gas Journal* vol. 76, no. 52 (25 December 1978) pp. 102–103; U.S. resources: U.S. Geological Survey estimates as reported in table 7-3; Canadian resources: Department of Energy, Mines, and Resources as reported in *International Petroleum Encyclopedia 1978* (Tulsa, Okla., Petroleum Publishing Co., 1978) p. 39; Mexican resources: PEMEX data as reported in *Mexico's Oil and Gas Policy: An Analysis,* Committee Print, Joint Economic Committee, 95 Cong. 2 sess. (Washington, D.C., December 1978) p. 13. An uncertainty margin of 20 percent for possible resources is introduced; other oil resources, Richard Nehring, *Giant Oilfields and World Oil Resources,* Report R-2284-CIA (Santa Monica, Calif., Rand Corporation, 1978) p. 88; other gas resources, Joseph D. Parent and Henry R. Linden, *A Survey of U.S. and Total World Production, Proved Reserves, and Remaining Recoverable Resources of Fossil Fuel and Uranium* (Chicago, Ill., Institute of Gas Technology, January 1977) p. 15.

Uranium—International Atomic Energy Agency/OECD Nuclear Energy Agency, *Uranium: Resources, Production and Demand* (Paris, Organisation for Economic Co-operation and Development, 1978) pp. 20–21. The 300,000 metric tons of Swedish uranium have been excluded from the reserves.

[a] There are several differences between the U.S. estimates in table 7-1 and those in table 7-6. Coal data are given here in metric tons of coal equivalent (at 27.78 million Btu per metric ton) instead of short tons of coal (at 21 million Btu per ton). A smaller recoverability factor (40 percent instead of 50 percent) is used for part of the coal resources in table 7-1. Oil and gas reserve estimates are somewhat lower here because the *Oil and Gas Journal* definition of reserves is less comprehensive than the one used in table 7-1. Oil and gas resource figures are the same. Uranium data are given here in metric tons of short tons of U_3O_8 (for 1 January 1977 instead of 1 January 1978). We have chosen to maintain the units of measurement of the source publications and we have not corrected the other small differences in order to maintain comparability within each table.

[b] Included in Soviet Union.

[c] Included in Asia and Pacific.

[d] Heat contents: coal, 27.78 million Btu per metric ton; oil, 5.8 million Btu per barrel; gas, 1,025 Btu per cubic foot; uranium, 390 billion Btu per metric ton U (without breeder) or 23.4 trillion Btu per metric ton U (with breeder).

world has shifted away from solid fuels toward more convenient forms (see chapter 16).

In the long run, coal liquefaction and gasification technology and economics might improve to the point where coal-derived liquids and gases instead of unprocessed coal would be traded internationally. This would also allow the continued use of the enormous capital investments in the terminals and the transportation and distribution equipment designed for conventional oil and gas. Of course, this is only a speculative possibility; it relates to developments that might not unfold until well into the twenty-first century.

Oil and Gas

The outlook for world oil reserves and resources is of great importance to the United States, because almost 50 percent of U.S. oil consumption (20 percent of U.S. total primary energy demand) is imported. Whether such a level of imports can be maintained or even expanded in the coming decades has become a major energy policy issue. Estimates of world oil reserves and resources are an important input for discussion of this issue. A multitude of estimates of resources has appeared over the years;[13] since the mid-1960s these estimates have hovered around 2 trillion barrels of ultimately recoverable resources, including past production. A recent study by the RAND Corporation, based on a detailed analysis of the world's giant oil fields for 1975, gives a range of 1,700 billion to 2,300 billion barrels. That includes 335 billion barrels of past production and known reserves of 675 billion barrels.

A mid-range estimate of the recoverable resources that remain, taking into account the recent Mexican developments, comes to about 1,800 billion barrels (see table 7-6). On this basis, present world annual consumption of roughly 22 billion barrels could be maintained for over seventy years—into the second half of the next century. But suppose, instead, a growth rate in world oil demand of 4 percent; that would be low compared with the historical 7.5 percent, but high compared with the postembargo 2.5 percent. In that case, production still might not peak until the beginning of the next century, because the aggregate reserves–production ratio in the year 2000 could still be above 15. This simplified

---

[13] For a comprehensive list see Workshop on Alternative Energy Strategies, *Energy: Global Prospects 1985–2000* (New York, McGraw–Hill, 1977) p. 115.

calculation assumes that discoveries would be made early enough to allow a smooth production path, and that production would only be restrained by the amount of reserves available (regardless of their geographic distribution).

However, much of the argument about the relative adequacy of oil resources through the end of the century turns on this very matter of the geographic distribution of recoverable resources. It is clear from table 7-6 that about 50 percent of these resources occur in the Middle East (while, as will be seen in chapter 16, demand for oil is concentrated mainly in the industrialized countries of Europe, North America, and Japan). Those who argue that international oil supplies might become inadequate during the late 1980s or 1990s make the case by showing that the burden of exporting to meet world demands will fall increasingly on just one or two Middle Eastern countries with high reserves (such as Saudi Arabia) and that they may choose not to expand production in sufficient amounts because of physical or economic constraints that will arise.

On the other hand, there are those who argue that resource estimates similar to those shown in table 7-6 are not only too low, but that they also exaggerate the relative importance of Middle East resources. They cite the recurrent history of concern about the near-term exhaustion of resources and argue that more resources will be found in the future as they have been in the past, particularly outside the Middle East. The recent emergence of Mexico as a major potential source of supply is cited as an indication of what may well happen elsewhere. In Mexico, estimates of potential oil and gas resources have risen during the past several years from about 20 billion to perhaps 200 billion barrels oil equivalent, and even these estimates are judged to be low by some experts.[14]

We do not take a stand on the validity of these new, high estimates for Mexico. But they do illustrate the volatility of resource estimation. Add to this volatility the potential of such areas as the heavy oil belt of Venezuela, where enormous resources are known to exist (up to 3 trillion barrels in place),[15] although they are beyond the realm of current economic recovery, and it is obvious that the true oil resource base *might* greatly exceed current estimates. Moreover, the geographical distribution of such an expanded resource base would probably be less concentrated, thus avoiding the problems of ultimate reliance on one or a few Middle

[14] *Energy Daily* (14 December 1978).
[15] *World Oil* (15 August 1977) p. 100.

Eastern nations. The implications of these possibilities for U.S. import policy are considered in chapter 16.

The recoverable resources of natural gas in the world are similar in magnitude to world oil resources in terms of energy content. However, the volume of natural gas traded internationally is minor compared with oil, essentially because of high transportation costs. Environmental and safety problems associated with liquefied natural gas tankers and terminal sites further cloud the prospects for natural gas contributions from overseas. Regulatory action designed to address these problems is likely to cause delays and raise costs even further.

The regional distribution of gas resources differs considerably from that of oil resources. The share of the OPEC nations is less, while the share of the United States, the Soviet Union, and Western Europe is higher. However, in view of the large domestic requirements in the latter group of countries, the OPEC countries must still be regarded as the major potential exporters for the future. Concerns about energy independence will thus affect gas imports in much the same way they affect oil imports.

Many of the same considerations that affect oil, in respect to potential new discoveries, apply also to natural gas; and policy aspects of U.S. gas imports are also presented in chapter 16.

Uranium

Uranium is very attractive, in principle, as a commodity for international trade. It can be produced in uniform quality and transported at a very low cost per unit of energy. The threat from trade embargoes and price escalation is also comparatively small, because the uranium present in reactor cores constitutes a large stock and additional stockpiling is relatively cheap. Nevertheless, the geographical concentration of uranium resources and enrichment facilities and the dangers of nuclear proliferation and theft (see chapter 14) have inhibited the development of a smoothly functioning market. Nuclear fuel assurance problems may very well turn the international uranium market into a rigid network of bilateral contracts, motivated by considerations other than the criteria of economic efficiency.

The most comprehensive publication on world uranium supplies and requirements is a joint report of the OECD Nuclear Energy Agency and the International Atomic Energy Agency (IAEA), which is revised every two or three years. Table 7-6 presents their latest set of data. (As with other fuel resources, data are obtained from national sources and this raises questions as to comparability.) Two categories of resources are distinguished: "reasonably assured resources," which are comparable to the DOE "reserves" category; and "estimated additional resources," which are comparable to the DOE "probable potential resources" category (see table 7-5).

The size of world uranium resources compared with other mineral resources depends crucially on the technology utilized. If only nonbreeding reactors are used, the energy content of world uranium resources is about the same as the energy content of world oil and world gas combined. With full utilization of breeder reactors, world uranium resources would account for over 1 million quads (10^{21} Btu). At a constant world consumption level of 275 quads, this would last at least 4,000 years—more than 100 times as long as world oil.

One notices immediately that the majority of reserves and resources of uranium outside the communist areas are located in only four nations: Australia, Canada, South Africa, and the United States. They account for 77 percent of all resources and 79 percent of all reserves. Australia, Canada, and South Africa all have reserves clearly in excess of foreseeable domestic requirements, so they could become important sources of exports.

The OECD–IAEA report also compares world uranium reserves and resources with projected requirements; and it reaches three significant conclusions. First, world reserves will be sufficient to support a modest nuclear growth program from the present level of roughly 100 gigawatts installed to a level of 1,000 gigawatts installed in the year 2000. An accelerated nuclear growth program, however, would require substantial additions to reserves from estimated additional resources. A determined effort to introduce breeder technology would not be sufficiently influential by the year 2000 to change this conclusion in a major way. Second, world reserves and resources will not be sufficient to support continued nuclear growth far past the year 2000 unless heavy reliance is placed on breeder technology. Even in the case of rapidly expanding breeder utilization past the year 2000, substantial additions must be made to estimated reserves and resources. Third, world reserves will not even be sufficient to support a modest nuclear growth program to the year 2000 without substantial additions to those reserves, if requirements are calculated on the basis of the fuel commitments needed for the lifetime of installed capacity. This is actually a more realistic method of calculation than considering only the annual use per reactor, given the emphasis on nuclear fuel assurance which would normally accompany heavy capital investment in a long-lived generating plant. In addition, breeder technology would have to be introduced earlier and more rapidly according to these calculations in order to sustain continued modest growth rates of nuclear power past the year 2000.

Of course, one must keep in mind, in evaluating these conclusions, that the resource estimation problems regarding domestic uranium sources (see page 238) are magnified on a world scale. In other words, the OECD estimates may be considered basically conservative. If one wishes to adopt a more optimistic perspective, the validity of these conclusions becomes more debatable.

Appendix: Measuring the Heat Content of Uranium— Some Simplified Calculations

The heat content of fossil fuels is determined rather easily by burning the fuel and measuring the heat released. Heat content is usually measured in British thermal units (Btu). One British thermal unit is the heat it takes to raise the temperature of 1 pound of water 1 °F at its maximum density.

The problem is more complicated for nuclear fuels, because they are not burned in the conventional sense. Nuclear fuels produce heat through nuclear fission reactions; and this heat is used in the typical U.S. nuclear power plant for raising steam to generate electricity. The first problem of determining heat content for uranium is thus: Should the heat content be calculated as the heat value originally released, or as the heat value of the generated electricity—exclusive of the waste heat? The convention is to use the first value, which generally is about three times the second value. The rationale is that a nuclear power plant today is considered as an alternative for a fossil fuel power plant rather than as an alternative for direct use of fossil fuels in residences, cars, factories, or elsewhere. If nuclear electricity should start to replace fossil fuels in what are now nonelectric uses (for example, in propelling automobiles) this convention would need to be reconsidered.

A second and more pervasive problem in evaluating the heat content of uranium is that the amount of electricity produced per short ton of uranium depends crucially on the technology utilized. Today's light water reactors utilize in principle only the 0.7 percent of fissile uranium 235 which is contained in natural uranium, but breeder reactors may be employed in the future to utilize all uranium isotopes eventually. Thus, in principle, LWR reactors use $(100/0.7) = 140$ times as much uranium as breeder reactors. Unfortunately, however, this is also an oversimplification.

Fissile plutonium 239 is produced within light water reactors from the uranium 238 which makes up 99.3 percent of natural uranium. Some of the plutonium joins in the LWR reactions increasing the heat output. On the other hand, LWR fuel is usually removed before all the uranium 235 has fissioned. To further complicate matters, breeder reactors are unable to utilize all natural uranium, since the repeated reprocessing of nuclear fuels necessary to operate the breeder cycle entails substantial cumulative losses. Finally, both LWR and breeder technologies consume a small percentage of fissile material nonproductively, through nuclear reactions that release little energy.

Taking these considerations into account, we have assumed that light water reactors of optimal design and under optimal operational conditions utilize 1 percent of all natural uranium effectively. We assume that future breeder reactors of optimal design and under optimal operational conditions will utilize 60 percent of all natural uranium effectively.

Besides today's light water reactors, which are based on a uranium-plutonium fuel cycle, an alternative converter reactor based on a thorium-uranium fuel cycle is possible (see chapter 9). The ratio of 60 to 1 proposed for a comparison between breeder and LWR technologies could be reduced considerably by using such advanced converter reactors.

Sufficient data are available from the operation of light water reactors to calculate the heat content of a short ton of uranium utilized in those reactors. A 1,000-MW LWR reactor with a burnup of 30,000-megawatt-days per metric ton of uranium fuel, a capacity factor of 65 percent, and a busbar efficiency of 32 percent needs $(1,000 \times 365 \times 0.65)/(30,000 \times 0.32) = 24.7$ tons of enriched uranium (U) each year. At 0.2 percent tails, 3 percent enrichment, and 15 percent conversion and fabrication losses, 202 short tons of natural uranium (U_3O_8) are required to produce this annual core replacement. Thus, evaluating electric energy at the equivalent thermal input of 10,665 Btu per kilowatt hour, 1 short ton uranium (U_3O_8) equals $(1,000 \times 365 \times 24 \times 0.65 \times 10,665 \times 1,000)/202 = 300$ billion Btu. Using a comparative ratio of 60 to 1, breeder reactor technology would result in a heat content of 18 trillion Btu per short ton uranium (U_3O_8).

Finally, we must stress strongly that the heat contents derived here are based on long-run equilibrium operation. To start up a large breeder program requires much more uranium than suggested by simply considering operational conditions over the long run. Depending on the speed of introduction and the type of reactor utilized to produce initial feedstocks, initial requirements may actually be a multiple of the number suggested by the figures presented here.

8 Synthetic Liquid and Gaseous Fuels

The Range of Choices

A great deal of oil, or hydrocarbon material closely related to oil, exists in forms and locations that are not customarily utilized by oil producers. One source of oil is the substance kerogen, contained in the rock formations called oil shales.

Two additional possible oil sources deserve passing mention, but they will not be covered in detail in this book. One is the so-called tar sands, geological formations containing suitable hydrocarbons that are not amenable to the usual oil-drilling and recovery methods. These deposits appear to be somewhat limited in the United States. The other source is even more exotic and largely speculative at present. The sap of certain plants of the family Euphorbiaceae—allied to the rubber plant—contain quantities of hydrocarbons. In this case, however, no broad developmental effort has yet taken place.

A variety of gaseous and liquid fuels can be produced from coal or from animal–vegetable matter (biomass). Some of these technologies will be described here briefly and their estimated costs will be compared.

Technology for Utilizing Oil Shale

A promising source of natural hydrocarbons is oil shale. For a long time oil shale extraction has been carried out on a small scale in Europe and elsewhere; however, present systems for mining and retorting the shale to "extract" the oil (that is, to convert the kerogen to readily usable hydrocarbon fuels) are not yet economically feasible for modern commercial operation, nor do these older processes take into account

our current environmental concerns. These concerns arise partly because surface mining of oil shale involves essentially the same activities
as surface mining of coal. Indeed, oil shale zones can be much thicker
than coal seams, and some proposed surface oil shale mines would be
deeper and larger than typical surface coal mines. Less environmentally
disruptive underground mines, probably utilizing the well established
room-and-pillar approach that is common in coal mining, could be used
when oil shale deposits suitable for underground mining are thin or
deep.

After mining, the oil shale is crushed, and then retorted to extract the
oil. All current retorting processes heat the shale to pyrolytic temperatures (that is, from 800°F to 1,000°F), which produce an oil fraction,
gases containing hydrocarbons of lighter molecular weight, and solid–
carbonaceous residues which remain in the shale. As is the case with
crude oil, shale oil must be upgraded by refining. This involves the
distillation of the heavy oil as well as other refinery operations in order
to improve the product quality.

The processed shale and overburden (when strip mining is used) can
present a severe solid waste problem. The main area for disposal will
probably be the mined-out areas themselves. However, the volume of
material to be disposed of is larger than the original undisturbed
volume, and additional disposal areas must usually be utilized (see
chapter 13 for environmental effects).

Instead of mining the shale, it has also been proposed to drill into
the shale deposits, extracting the oil by in situ methods—that is, by
heating the shale in place in order to pyrolize the hydrocarbons directly
within the rock. A basic problem with this method is that some type of
hydraulic, explosive, or other method of breaking up the deep rock
strata must be used in order to increase the permeability of the shale so
that it can be retorted economically. Ground subsidence can also occur
as the kerogen is removed from the subterranean rubble. Certain modified in situ methods have also been particularly favored in recent proposals. For example, part of the shale might be mined underground and
the entire column of rock above the mined-out section can then be
broken up by explosives. When the top of the column is ignited, the
hot gases and oil can be recovered. Unlike the pure in situ method, this
technique would require that the mined portion of the shale would still
have to be retorted at the surface by conventional means if it were to be
utilized—meaning that the waste-disposal problem would be reduced

but not eliminated. However, the shale removed in order to apply the modified in situ method could be simply treated as spoil and discarded.

For purposes of energy resource conservation, the choice of methods for producing shale oil will make some difference. For a 100,000 barrel-a-day plant, underground mining requires the greatest amount of ore commitment (about 900,000 tons per day) because pillars of ore must be left underground. The more efficient conventional surface mining need extract only some 500,000 tons. Neither the standard in situ process nor its modified version can extract all the kerogen from the shale, and both would probably utilize intermediate amounts of shale.[1]

Not only can oil be made from oil shale, but methane can also be produced by controlled heating of oil shale in a hydrogen atmosphere. Since there was no demand in the past for gas corresponding to the need for lamp oil that sparked older shale oil operations, production of gas from shale has not been undertaken anywhere, although the results of recent research appear promising.

Resources

Like many other resources, the total amount of oil shale available—at various ore grades and extraction costs—is very large. It has been estimated that, for the United States, shale containing 10 to 65 percent organic matter represents over 300,000 quads of energy, while shale containing 5 to 10 percent organic matter would comprise over 1.5 million quads. What part of those deposits it will actually be feasible to extract economically, however, is controversial.[2] One might infer that such economic reserves of oil shale in the United States are really negligible, based on the observation that no firms have actually carried out successful commercial operations, despite the long-standing and well-known feasibility of the processes on a small-scale basis. Even if we reject such a pessimistic outlook, estimates still vary greatly, since they depend on the quality of the shale, the geologic setting, and the

[1] Harry Perry, "Production of Liquids and Gases from Other Resources," draft prepared for the National Energy Strategies Project (Washington, D.C., Resources for the Future, 8 June 1978). Available from RFF's Center for Energy Policy Research.

[2] D. C. Duncan and V. E. Swanson, *Organic-Rich Shale of the United States and World Land Areas*, U.S. Geological Survey Circular 523 (Washington, D.C., GPO, 1965).

rate of technological development. Different sources have speculated that from 200 to 1,600 quads of energy could be obtained from deposits of varying thicknesses containing 10 to 14 percent organic matter—25 to 35 gallons of oil or more per ton of shale.[3]

Economics

Oil shale economics under modern conditions is not well established for commercial plants. Studies made before the full impact of the oil crisis occurred showed prices ranging from about $3.50 to $5.50 (in 1975 dollars) per barrel for conventional mining and surface retorting, and from $6.50 to $10.50 per barrel for in situ processes.[4] If such estimates were correct, however, it is evident that at recent world prices of some $13 (1975 U.S. dollars) per barrel of oil, one would expect that oil shale technology would be considerably more advanced than it now is. However, these earlier estimates do not reflect recent escalations in capital and operating items that would be applicable to shale, nor do they take into account greatly increased costs for environmental protection.

Newer estimates for a particular geologic setting (a depth of 1,125 feet) and quality of shale (25 gallons of oil per ton) range from $23 to $37 per barrel for the usual mining techniques, while standard in situ extraction would cost almost $50 per barrel, with modified column or tunnel in situ processes having intermediate values.[5]

As is the case for all new energy sources, it must be noted that all these cost estimates must be regarded as tentative. As with many of the technologies considered below, evidence of commercial interest may be the most important indicator of cost feasibility.

[3] Ibid. Also see A. E. Lewis, "The Outlook for Oil Shale" (Berkeley, Calif., Lawrence Livermore Laboratory, 1974) p. 4; National Petroleum Council, Committee on U.S. Energy Outlook, *U.S. Energy Outlook* (Washington, D.C., National Petroleum Council, 1972); Stephen Rattien and David Eaton, "Oil Shale: The Prospects and Problems of an Emerging Energy Industry," in Jack M. Hollander, ed., *Annual Review of Energy*, vol. 1 (Palo Alto, Calif., Annual Reviews, Inc., 1976) p. 173.

[4] S. H. Chiang, J. T. Cobb, Jr., and G. E. Klinzing, "Alternative Technologies for Producing Liquids and Gases (1985–2000 and Beyond)," second draft report prepared for Resources for the Future (Pittsburgh, Pa., University of Pittsburgh, January 1978) chap. IX, tab. 2.

[5] These figures are for utility financing; private financing could be expected to cost $5 to $14 more in June 1975 dollars. See Perry, "Production of Liquids and Gases," p. 17-111. One barrel is equal to 5.8 million BTUs.

We estimate that government expenditures on R&D for oil shale total $60 million a year, while experimental private efforts are perhaps costing $50 million to $100 million a year. However, serious commercial ventures are still not under way.

Evaluation

With all the technical, economic, and environmental uncertainties surrounding the development of these resources, projections of future production are speculative. Estimates from one earlier study range from under 200,000 barrels per day to over 800,000 for 1985 production.[6] At present, even the lower estimate seems optimistic. However, before the environmental issues relating to oil shale assumed their present importance, estimates of the maximum size of an oil shale industry ranged from 1 to 5 million barrels per day. The later, smaller estimates were influenced by the availability of water, the need to prevent increased salinity in local rivers, and a general belief that large waste-disposal and socioeconomic problems might be unmanageable in the limited geographic area where the high-quality oil shale deposits are found. In particular, the wide range of all estimates reflects differing assumptions with respect to how much water would be available to an oil shale industry, the type of technology that would be utilized, and the increase in capital costs that might be necessary to reduce water consumption.

With the public's increased concern over environmental issues, a shift in emphasis has occurred in the type of technology that is being investigated. In place of conventional mining and above-ground retorting, increasing efforts are being directed toward the development of in situ or modified in situ methods for producing shale oil. Should these new processes appear promising, environmental limitations should be less restrictive, and an industry as large as 5 million barrels per day may well be possible—although this figure might still be an upper bound unless still further improvements in the technology occur. On the other hand, if tests of both the in situ and modified in situ processes are unsuccessful and the means to overcome the environmental barriers

---

[6] See U.S. Department of the Interior, Interagency Task Force on Oil Shale, *Project Independence: Potential Future Role of Oil Shale—Prospects and Constraints* (Washington, D.C., GPO, November 1974).

associated with other technology are not found, it may be very difficult to start an oil shale industry of any appreciable size.

Sources of Synthetic Oil and Gas

Oil and natural gas are valuable because they represent particular combinations, or compounds, of carbon and hydrogen that can be burned to produce a relatively large amount of heat—that is, large in terms of their weight and volume. They are easily handled and can be transported at low cost. Furthermore, their pollutant aspects are less than for some other sources, coal in particular. Carbon and hydrogen, however, exist in many other forms. Therefore, it is plausible that modern technology can be used to convert other fossil and presently existing compounds of carbon and hydrogen into synthetic oil and gas. This means that a compact form of carbon and hydrogen (like coal) is especially suitable; but all kinds of biomass, including trees and other types of plants, can also be used. It follows that wood products such as building materials wastes and the animal and vegetable wastes ordinarily found in municipal refuse are also eligible candidates as a feedstock to produce liquid and gaseous fuels.

One very common method for making carbon-rich materials that are inconveniently bulky, or otherwise difficult to handle and convert to energy, into more amenable oillike liquids and gases is by heating them in the absence of air, thereby converting them into their constituent compounds by so-called pyrolytic processes. Pyrolysis in general produces a combination of coke-type solids, liquidlike oil, and gases, which may or may not be a convenient mix of end products. For conversion of coal into useful gaseous or liquid hydrocarbons, other possible processes involve direct hydrogenation—that is, combining hydrogen, or hydrogen in the form of water, with coal in an oxygen-poor environment.[7] Certain solvents can also transform coal into cleaner solids or liquids.

So it is evident that many processes will produce either gases or oil-type liquids from coal, wood, and other biological matter; furthermore,

---

[7] It is possible to treat any organic material directly with hydrogen at high temperatures and pressures to get methane. An experimental process for coal, developed by the Institute of Gas Technology, has operated on municipal wastes at temperatures of 1,025° F and pressures of 1,300 psig, producing a gas of methane quality.

gas-producing processes can be adapted to produce liquids by further chemical reactions. In addition, another useful liquid fuel—wood alcohol or methanol‸—can be obtained, for example, by combining carbon with hydrogen and oxygen in catalytic reactions using an H_2-CO gas feed. For biological material, the well-known wine-making process of fermentation can convert whatever sugars are present in the waste to another useful fuel—grain alcohol or ethanol.

Technologies

Coal gasification. Much attention has recently focused on the production of so-called low-Btu gas, which is made by combining coal with air and steam to produce a gas containing the burnable fuels carbon monoxide and hydrogen.[9] The difficulty with such a gas is that its comparatively low heating value per unit of volume makes it uneconomical to transport through pipelines for more than very short distances. Its heating value ranges from 150 to 250 Btu per cubic foot, as compared with 1,000 Btu per cubic foot for natural gas. However, it is hoped that the comparative simplicity of the process will make it economical enough for use by large industries located at or very near to a gasifier. In particular, a gasifier can be part of a coal-fired power plant operating on a combined cycle—utilizing a gas turbine and using its exhaust gases to operate a boiler for an ordinary steam turbine.

If oxygen is substituted for air in the gasification process, the inclusion of nitrogen, which dilutes the heating value, in the gas is avoided, and the so-called medium-Btu gas (300 to 400 Btu per cubic foot) that results can probably be economically piped for 25 to 50 miles. These distances would be practical for many large industrial operations, which could be served by a central gasification plant if costs of gasification, the oxygen, and related equipment are reasonable.

The highest-quality synthetic gas, similar to natural gas, is made by converting the carbon monoxide and hydrogen from a medium-Btu gas into methane in the presence of a catalyst (that is, $2H_2 + 2CO = CH_4 + CO_2$).[10] This process thus makes gas useful for pipeline transport, but involves sometimes considerably higher costs than the other gas types.

---

[8] Alcohols contain a small portion of oxygen; that is, instead of the C_xH_y formulas for hydrocarbons, alcohols have C_xH_yO.

[9] Perry, "Production of Liquids and Gases," p. 17-4.

[10] See Perry, "Production of Liquids and Gases," pp. 17-6, 17-9, and 17-10.

In other countries, existing plants for converting coal into low- or medium-Btu gases have often been based on the established Lurgi gasification process; in the past, this process has been suitable only for types of coal that do not agglomerate (for example, coke or noncoking coals), but newer technology may extend its applicability. Other existing processes, such as the Koppers-Totzek, can utilize all types of coal but require more oxygen and higher temperatures; the Winkler process is a fluidized-bed process and has intermediate oxygen requirements.[11] A number of other new processes are now under development as well,[12] but none has been used in commercial plants.

Efficiencies of energy conversion—an important consideration for both costs and environmental impact analysis—vary for the different processes; and ambiguities in definition of efficiency make comparison of different reported processes difficult. For the main categories of low-, medium-, and high-Btu gases derived from coal, gasification efficiencies of 70 to 80 percent, 65 to 75 percent, 56 to 68 percent, respectively, have been estimated in a study for this project.[13]

Coal liquefaction. Liquids can be obtained directly from coal by pyrolysis, the distillation of coal in the absence of air. In this process, a combination of solids, gases, and liquids is typically produced, and the fractional amount of liquids obtained from the natural volatile elements in coal is usually relatively small; however, the gases are also valuable and the solid char can be later gasified by other methods, or used to provide heat for the reaction.

Other methods are available for adding hydrogen to the carbon in the coal, in amounts that will produce a liquid rather than a gas. This can be carried out in several ways. One is by solvent extraction, that is, by using a material that will dissolve the coal and, at the same time, act as a hydrogen donor to the carbon fraction. Other methods call for the addition of hydrogen to the coal by putting it into direct or indirect contact with a catalyst. Aspects of both of these features are combined in some methods. Alternately, low- or medium-Btu gas can be formed from coal and, by using a catalyst, one can indirectly induce the hydrogenation reaction that produces liquids.

[11] It uses a liquidlike mixture of coal dust and air; see chapter 12.
[12] These processes include Hygas, an oil slurry process; Synthane, a fluidized-bed process; Cogas, which needs no oxygen input; and the two-stage Bigas process (see Perry, "Production of Liquids and Gases," pp. 17-9 and 17-10).
[13] Ibid., p. 17-13.

A traditional indirect hydrogenation method is the Fischer-Tropsch process, used in some German plants during World War II and in today's Sasol plant in South Africa.[14] This type of plant reacts a synthetic gas at high temperatures and moderate pressures over a catalyst in order to produce both a low-octane gasoline and a medium-Btu gas. However, in indirect liquefaction, one can get various mixes of gasoline-type hydrocarbons, boiler fuel oils, or other fractions, depending on the process conditions used.

In seeking replacement fuels for oil and gas in existing utility boilers, the SRC-II process (employing a single reactor and no catalyst) may provide a way to a commercial technology. However, the H-Coal catalytic process and the EDS process, which involve a donor solvent, also appear to have promise.[15]

In addition to hydrocarbons, methanol (methyl alcohol) can also be made from coal. In particular, methanol is now made commercially by reacting natural gas,[16] after reforming, over a catalyst, and this same type of process could be carried out with a gas synthesized from coal.

Again, from the point of view of providing new supplies of energy, differences in liquefaction efficiency can be significant, not only for direct costs but also for local constraints on air quality, water, and land use. It has been estimated that direct hydrogenation can be carried out with an energy efficiency of 60 to 70 percent, while the Fischer-Tropsch process has an efficiency rate of 40 to 45 percent. Methanol-generating processes have been estimated at 50 to 65 percent energy-conversion efficiency.[17]

Biogas. As mentioned above, gas from organic components of municipal wastes and other kinds of biomass can be generated in ways similar to the coal-conversion methods, plus a few others.[18] One of the specific methods produces a methane–carbon dioxide mixture of 500 to 700 Btu per cubic foot from biomass by anaerobic digestion—that is, using naturally occurring bacteria. This process produces gas in an

[14] Ibid., pp. 17-52 and 17-53.

[15] "Scaling Up Coal Liquids," *EPRI Journal* vol. 3, no. 7 (September 1978) pp. 6–13.

[16] Methanol can be used as a clean boiler fuel, or it can be mixed with gasoline for use in engines; however, a tendency for methanol to absorb water and its other combustion and storage characteristics require attention in internal combustion use.

[17] See Perry, "Production of Liquids and Gases," p. 17-56.

[18] Note that economic plant sizes could be smaller than for coal, because of transport problems for less "energy-dense" biomass inputs.

oxygen-poor environment. This method has been widely used on animal wastes and also on agricultural residues in less-developed countries. The "gobar (dung) gas" plants of India have pioneered in small-scale applications in this field.[19, 20] For large-scale applications, gasification efficiency can be increased, both by controlling temperatures at optimal levels and by introducing an additional stage of preparation—so-called enzymatic solubilization—that facilitates the subsequent formation of alcohols and esters by one population of bacteria and then the conversion of those products to methane and carbon dioxide by another.[21] Yields for some types of these anaerobic or bacterial processes have been estimated at 9,000 to 13,000 cubic feet of gas per ton of input material. The gas yielded has an energy content of some 500 to 700 Btu per cubic foot, or net energy yields of probably 30 to 60 percent of energy inputs. Biogas processes also yield a nitrogen-rich slurry residue that is valuable as a fertilizer and in some cases may save on waste-disposal costs.

Biomass liquids. Biomass feedstocks can also be used to produce liquids. In particular, methanol can be obtained from a synthetic gas derived from biomass just as well as from coal. Pyrolytic techniques can be used on wood wastes and other biomass materials to distill usable liquids, plus gas and solids. Cellulosic materials can be converted catalytically to oil or methane-rich gases in the presence of carbon monoxide and water, a process called carboxylolysis.[22] Finally, ethanol or grain alcohol can be produced from the fermentation of sugars; where sugar-rich biomass is not available, enzymes or sulfuric or hydrochloric acids can be used to turn the cellulose in biomass to sugar.[23]

Resources

Coal resources are very large (see chapter 7). Naturally, supplies of coal for gasification must contend with demand and supply pressures

[19]Elizabeth Cecelski, Joy Dunkerley, and William Ramsay, with Emmanuel Mbi, *Household Energy and the Poor in the Third World,* Research Paper R-15 (Washington, D.C., Resources for the Future, 1978) sect. III.

[20] Chiang and coauthors, "Production of Gas from Biomass," in "Alternative Technologies," chap. XIV.

[21] Ibid.

[22] S. Friedman, H. H. Ginsberg, I. Wender, and P. M. Yavorsky, "Continuous Processing of Urban Refuse to Oil Using Carbon Monoxide," *Third Mineral Waste Utilization Symposium* (Chicago, Ill., International Telephone and Telegraph Research Institute, March 1976).

[23] Chiang and coauthors, "Alternative Technologies," chap. XIV.

imposed by other coal users. But competition with other coal users is likely to be a less crucial factor than environmental and institutional problems.

Organic wastes that could presumably be used for production of gases or energy liquids are available in significant quantities; however, estimates are somewhat speculative because of incomplete records. One estimate puts them at over 1 billion tons a year, of which the major proportion is made up of agricultural and food wastes (almost 40 percent), while another 25 percent each come from animal wastes and from municipal refuse.[24] If all these wastes were to provide an energy input of approximately 10 million Btu per ton,[25] and if they could be used to produce gas liquids at 50 percent efficiency, or result in an output of about 5 million Btu per ton, then, theoretically, 5 quads per year could be produced from this source. However, in practice the wastes are scattered widely, and collection costs may be high, so that only part of the total waste resource can be used as fuel. The amount we use will depend on the price of competing fuels and on how much credit can be assigned to the resource for avoiding its disposal by other means.

For potential biomass from crops of trees or other plants that could be grown on presently idle land, it has been estimated that over 20 quads could be produced by biomass from idle U.S. acreage, for example, on the 5 percent or so of the country which is now idle farmland.[26] This rough estimate of the potential biomass includes, however, about equal parts of cropland not presently in crops, permanent pastureland, and rangeland. Water needs and competition with food uses for crops and pasture would affect the economics of such utilization. On the other hand, there are about 400 million acres of forestlands not now being utilized and, subject to difficulties in harvesting, storage, and transportation, productivity of 5 to 13 tons per acre per year might be obtained from a good fraction of that acreage,[27] an amount on the order of 7 quads of yearly energy.[28] Without further investigation of the detailed economics

[24] L. L. Anderson, *Energy Potential from Organic Wastes,* U.S. Bureau of Mines Information Circular 8549 (Washington, D.C., GPO, 1972) 1980 figures.

[25] Cecelski and coauthors, *Household Energy.*

[26] This is based on 15 tons per acre and a 5 million Btu net energy output per ton, for, say, 300 million acres. J. M. Fowler, "Fuel from Wastes-Bioconversion," in *Fact Sheet* (Oak Ridge, Tenn., U.S. Energy Research and Development Administration, 1977); and D. L. Klass, "A Long Range Approach to the Natural Gas Shortage Utilizing Non-Fossil Renewable Carbon," *Energy Sources* vol. 3 (1977) p. 177.

[27] R. E. Inman, *Silvicultural Biomass Farms,* Technical Report 7347 (McLean, Va., MITRE Corporation, May 1977).

[28] Assuming 10 tons of production from one-tenth of this acreage at 16.5 million Btu per ton.

of cultivation, collection, transport, and conversion, and a knowledge of how much land will be devoted to agricultural use in the future, it is impossible to say how much of this potential could be tapped.

Economics

Costs for gasification from coal are uncertain. For example, three new Lurgi high-Btu gasification-methanation plants, with an output of about 250 million cubic feet per day, have been proposed for the early 1980s, one at a capital cost of $1.6 billion and two at a cost of $1 billion. Costs for the less complex medium- and low-Btu gas demonstration plants should be less.[29]

Unit costs are even more speculative, but table 8-1 compares estimates for coal and biomass conversion products and shale oil. As shown in table 8-1, a study done for this project has estimated that low- or medium-Btu gas might cost anywhere from $1.60 to $4.60 (1975 dollars) per million Btu, with the more probable values in the middle range.[30] If newer processes for high-Btu gas work out, the range of estimates is similar ($1.80 to $5.10); however, it is estimated that gas from the better established Lurgi technology for high-Btu gas will cost at least $3 per million Btu. Costs at the lower end of those scales would be competitive with other sources, but the achievement of such low costs would depend on apparently optimistic assumptions about technical success as well as on stable real prices for coal: a complication is that many operations integrate coal extraction with other processes, thus making it difficult to assign an unambiguous price to the coal feed. At any rate, some believe that even the gasification prices shown here could eventually be reduced by 50 percent if gasification were to follow the learning curves associated with other industries. For example, unit cost reductions in gasoline refining of 60 percent were reportedly achieved in the years 1939–68 and cost reductions of 20 percent for each doubling of output have been reported in the machine tool industry.[31] On the other hand, for a plant in operation by the early 1980s, the American Natural Resource Company's estimate

---

[29] General Accounting Office, *Status and Obstacles to Commercialization of Coal Liquefaction and Gasification,* report prepared for the National Fuel and Policy Study, Senate Committee on Interior and Insular Affairs (Washington, D.C., GPO, 1976) p. 27, tab. 5; and telephone conversations with L. Wahrhaftig of the Bureau of Natural Gas, Federal Power Commission (1977).

[30] Perry, "Production of Liquids and Gases," p. 17-42.

[31] Chiang and coauthors, "Alternative Technologies," chap. III, p. 46.

Table 8-1. Typical Ranges of Estimates for Unit Costs of Gases and Liquids from New Sources

	Dollars per million Btu	
Source	*(1975$)*	*(June 1977$)*
Coal (by product)		
Low- or medium-Btu gas	1.6–4.6	1.8–5.1
High-Btu gas	1.8–5.1	2.0–5.8
Liquids	2.5–3.3	2.8–3.8
Biomass (by sources and product)		
Municipal refuse		
Gas (medium-Btu or biogas)[a,b]	0.4–3.6	0.5–4.0
"Fuel oil"	6.7	7.4
Methanol	9	10
Ethanol	18	20
Wood and agricultural wastes		
Gas, anaerobic (biogas)[b]	0.7–1.6	0.7–1.8
Gas, pyrolytic (medium-Btu)	2.0–3.1	2.2–3.5
Liquids, pyrolytic	4.5–8.1	5.0–9.1
Ethanol, fermentation[c]	9–14	10–16
Shale oil		
Conventional	4.0–6.4	4.4–7.1
In situ	8.5	9.4

[a] The original publications are not clear to what extent the lower estimates include credits taken for waste disposal, and total costs are sensitive to this factor. For pyrolytic projects, costing is further complicated by the typical product mix of solid, liquid, and gas.

[b] Note that the original publications are not clear as to the extent that biomass transport costs are included, and total costs may therefore be typically much higher.

[c] The lower estimate represents future goals.

for a synthetic gas made from coal indicated a cost of over $7 per million Btu in future current dollars,[32] or perhaps $4.50 in 1975 dollars; hence this late estimate (still based largely on theoretical calculations) does not anticipate large cost decreases.

Costs for coal liquids also could benefit from learning curves, but, even without such an assumption, it is conceivable that the price for liquids could range, as shown, between $2.50 and $3.30 per million Btu.[33] The cost estimate is complicated, not only by the great uncertainty, but also by the fact that many of the processes produce solids as well as liquids; some of these combination-product processes have estimated costs ranging from $2 per million Btu up to $3.30, depending on the process used. Again, costs will depend on coal prices, explicit or implicit. However, one study predicts a variation in product prices of

---

[32] For utility financing; private financing would be some 25 percent more expensive (see Perry, "Production of Liquids and Gases," pp. 17-64, 17-66, and 17-68).

[33] Ibid., p. 17-184.

±15 percent for coal price variations of ±30 percent, with an average base price of $1 per million Btu.[34] Prices for final useful products will also depend on refining costs, which may vary greatly with the technology involved.

The cost estimates for gas or burnable liquids and solids from municipal wastes are subject to a set of conditions and options that differ from those for coal. The capital costs for gasification and pyrolysis plants, on the basis of very skimpy experience and probably optimistic estimates, run in the neighborhood of $30 million for a 1,000-ton-per-day plant,[35] while the costs of an anaerobic plant have been estimated at somewhere between $10 million and $15 million. However, the central financial complication is the cost of the source material. The waste material can either be considered (1) free; (2) collectable at a cost; or (3) representing a bonus, that is, one could assume some financial credit for getting rid of rubbish that would have to be disposed of in another manner. Costs therefore for either process could range (as is shown in table 8-1) from as low as 40 cents per million Btu, if credit is given for rubbish disposal, up to $3 or $4, or even more, per million Btu if sizable costs of collection must be assumed.[36] For liquids, the problem is essentially the same—if collection costs at $20 per ton of material are assumed, output costs are quite high: for example, $6.70 for fuel oil, $9 for methanol, and $18 for ethanol.[37]

A disadvantage of waste usage, which could affect costs, is the fact that limited amounts are available at given locations; hence, either high fuel-transport costs must be incurred or economies of scale in plant size may have to be forgone. The same tradeoff holds, in general, for the use of all material relatively low in energy density, such as biomass from crops and forests. A related problem is with the mere handling of large amounts of material, and with the processing of unhomogeneous material such as municipal wastes. Indeed, the higher costs quoted for waste—compared with those for coal—reflect to some extent the difficulties in scaling up from pilot projects because of handling and sorting problems.

[34] Chiang and coauthors, "Alternative Technologies," chap. X, fig. 6, assuming 22.5 MMBtu per ton of coal.
[35] G. Kramon and M. Sanders III, *Garbage Power 82: An Integrated Plan for the Conversion of Solid Waste to Energy in Santa Clara County*, NP-20892 (Stanford, Calif., Institute for Energy Studies, Stanford University, November 1975).
[36] Perry, "Production of Liquids and Gases," p. 17-195.
[37] D. L. Klass, "A Perpetual Methane Economy—Is it Possible?" *Chemical Technology* vol. 4 (1974) p. 161.

While there are some plants here and abroad that utilize municipal wastes, the more general use of agricultural or forest biomass in industrialized countries is less well established. However, estimates ranging from 70 cents to $1.60 per million Btu have been made for anaerobic gasification processes.[38] These estimated costs correspond roughly to the range of costs for the somewhat smaller biogas plants found in developing areas.[39] However, one must be careful to include the correct costs of the biomass inputs. The low estimates given here may typically not include the all-important cost of biomass transport.

On the other hand, if wood is converted into medium-Btu gas through such process as the Purox method,[40] costs would be much higher,[41] ranging from $2.00 to $3.10 per million Btu, depending on the price of an oven-dried ton of wood.[42] Correspondingly, hydrocarbon liquids from similar plants at similar wood prices can be calculated to cost from $4.50 to $8.10 per million Btu, while methanol produced by the Purox process from wood-derived gas could be expected to run from $5.00 to $7.00 per million Btu.[43] These costs are high, and other processes may lower them; but the inherent difficulties of handling relatively large volumes of low-energy-density material may keep biomass costs higher than those for coal.

For the production of ethanol from similar sources, using acid hydrolysis plus an ordinary fermentation process, the prices of the product ethanol are estimated to be very high, $14 or $16 per million Btu.[44] On the other hand, it must be noted that in Brazilian experience, ethanol derived from sugarcane is priced (on a subsidized basis) at about $1 per gallon;[45] current prices in the United States for ethanol for fuel have been reported at $1.10 per gallon, but prices of 70 or 75 cents a gallon are envisaged by some,[46] amounting to about $9 per million Btu.[47] It must be noted, however, that ethanol is a substitute for

[38] Perry, "Production of Liquids and Gases," pp. 17-68 and 17-69.

[39] Cecelski and coauthors, *Household Energy*, sect. III.

[40] The Purox process is a proprietary gasification method, using pure oxygen as a component in a modified pyrolysis setup.

[41] Inman, *Silvicultural Biomass Farms*.

[42] The price ranges from $15 to $30, both for a 3,400-oven-dried-ton-per-day plant.

[43] Inman, *Silvicultural Biomass Farms*.

[44] Ibid.

[45] "Alcohol: A Brazilian Answer to the Energy Crisis," *Science* vol. 195, no. 4278 (11 February 1977) p. 565.

[46] Anthony J. Parisi, "Gasoline-Alcohol Mixture Ignites Dispute," *The New York Times* (3 May 1978) sect. M, p. 53.

[47] At 6.6 pounds per gallon and 11,600 Btu per pound.

higher-priced gasoline rather than for crude oil. A recent refiners' price of about 40 cents per gallon of gas corresponds to about $3 per million Btu. Additionally, combustion efficiencies for alcohol are better than those for gasoline, so that fewer Btus are needed to perform equivalent end uses. However, certain operational problems must be addressed, such as the need for preventing water contamination that can cause phase separation of the gasoline–alcohol mixture. Experience in the use of grain alcohol in Brazil may eventually help to clarify these questions.[48] Nevertheless, the fact that sugar from either sugar crops or starches or cellulose tends to be expensive may mean that the ethanol will remain a somewhat expensive energy source. On the other hand, the fact that alcohol production is an established commercial process means that it could conceivably be an important energy option for fallback supplies of transport fuel, despite high prices.

Evaluation

In general, in the production of synthetic fluid fuels, more attention has been paid to gases than to liquids, even though the differences in the lowest and highest price, as estimated above, are relatively small in comparison with the uncertainty in the estimates. Institutional reasons are the primary cause: gas can be sold under regulated conditions, using utility-financing cost factors, and the price of new expensive gas can often be rolled into the price to the consumer.[49] Also, gasification is at a more technically advanced stage than liquefaction, based on a considerable number of operating Lurgi medium-Btu plants now in existence; however, the key methanation step to produce high-Btu gas has been tested only in pilot projects. Despite these advantages, the present economics for producing gas from coal cannot compete with natural gas, so that the high-Btu technology has not yet been used commercially.

Comparing coal with municipal refuse and other biomass, coal and waste processes are both more technically advanced than large-scale nonwaste biomass conversion (neglecting present high-price grain alcohol processes). Plants using pyrolytic or gasification methods applied to municipal refuse are now being planned, already in construc-

---

[48] "Energy: Brazil Seeks a Strategy Among Many Options, *Science* vol. 195, no. 4278 (11 February 1977) pp. 566–568.
[49] Perry, "Production of Liquids and Gases," p. 17-71.

tion, or finished; however, these plants are generally relatively small scale, as compared with the proposed coal-conversion facilities. Although the production of gas or liquids from other biomass sources, such as grain, wood, or straw, is in some sense at an earlier stage of development, in terms of producing fuels designed for a competitive market, the option is of special interest because of the existence of a long-established, if rather expensive, technology and large sources of supply—that again may be expensive relative to prices for other feedstocks. Coal has the advantage of having assured sources of supply; the key advantage of utilizing waste is that it helps to solve a disposal problem while also solving an energy problem. Comparing these two sources overall, the coal-conversion option is of somewhat more interest because feasible coal supplies at low prices appear to be much larger than supplies of municipal waste, and coal handling and preparation problems are much less.

The degree to which the coal-conversion option will penetrate the U.S. energy market is difficult to predict.[50] If subsidies or other new encouragements are minimal, a study done for this project estimates less than 1 quad of energy from coal-conversion plants by the year 2000.[51] On the other hand, coal-gasification technology is already relatively advanced; and if new developments enabled its product to compete with natural gas in price,[52] the figure might expand to 2 to 3 quads.[53] A fairly large amount of government assistance and encouragement could press annual output even higher by the end of the century—beyond 6 quads; and an effort and conditions simulating a wartime emergency might even produce as much as 10 quads. Without important government incentives to establish a coal-gasification industry, however, an industry is likely to develop very slowly. The technology is very capital-intensive, and the large investments would have to be made at a high risk. Furthermore, there are other potential sources of natural gas (possibly at significantly lower costs than gas obtained from coal) as well as for other fuels discussed in this chapter that might be able to compete with gas.

[50] Ibid., pp. 17-71–17-78.

[51] Ibid.

[52] The average price of natural gas delivered to residential consumers in the United States during 1977 was about $2.25 per 1,000 cubic feet, which is equivalent to $2.20 per 1,000 Btu. Marginal replacement cost, of course, is considerably higher —with wellhead prices for "new gas" now nearly $2.00 per 1,000 cubic feet, compared with an average wellhead price in 1977 of $0.79 per 1,000 cubic feet.

[53] Perry, "Production of Liquids and Gases," pp. 17-28 and 17-69.

The other potentially large source of fuel supply—that of biomass from wood, agricultural residues, or special crops—is at too early a stage of development to predict its feasibility. Important technical choices may still have to be explored. For example, the relative advantages of pyrolysis—its less expensive initial costs and its ability to use automatic controls on a continuous process line—must be balanced against the advantages of anaerobic processes, which have greater energy efficiency and a lesser environmental impact.

The potential of all these new sources of gas and liquids for energy strategies depends also on health and environmental effects (see chapters 12, 13, and 14) on the costs of electricity (chapters 9 and 10) and solar energy (chapter 11).

9 Central-Station Electricity from Coal and Nuclear Fuels

Significance of the Coal–Nuclear Comparison

The special usefulness of electricity as an energy form has grown rather than diminished in recent years. The electric motor, modern lighting, radio and television, and now the developing importance of computers of all sizes and uses have made sources of electric current indispensable to an industrialized civilization. Opinions differ on how many new electrical plants will actually be needed within the next decades; but there is no controversy over the fact that new sources of supply will best serve society by being as economical as is consistent with health, environmental, and other essential social concerns.

Leaving discussion of the health, environmental, and social concerns over electrical power sources to chapters 12, 13, and 14, what can we say about the basic technical and financial aspects? One big question mark involves the economic costs of coal versus nuclear power—the predominant choices available at present for large new generating facilities. In the past such a question was usually left entirely to utility planners, but today it is a matter for public debate among environmentalists, consumer activists, utility managers, government regulators, and other special groups.

Since growing health and environmental concerns appear to dictate that coal must be burned more cleanly, an essential subsidiary question involves the cost of new, cleaner, and perhaps more efficient ways of using coal. In regard to nuclear power, the increasing proliferation of nuclear weapons and questions concerning the adequacy of uranium resources make it necessary to evaluate alternative nuclear technologies as well as the currently widely used light water reactors.

This chapter offers background and costs on generating electricity from fossil fuel and nuclear technologies as preparation for discussing

269

such questions. Because the concept of costs may need some interpretation, the accompanying "Note on Comparing Generating Costs" explains the procedures followed here.

This chapter deals with the comparative costs of producing equivalent amounts of constant (or "baseload") electricity at central nuclear or fossil fuel generating stations.[1]

Despite current interest in smaller scale technologies (see chapter 11), large-scale plants will be considered here. Although there is a good deal of variation in plant size, a 1-gigawatt (million kilowatt) plant is chosen here for comparative purposes. Chapter 10 will deal with renewable sources of such large-scale electrical energy, and chapter 11 will treat some decentralized energy sources that might be substituted in part for electricity in some end uses.

Another question has to do with the costs of electricity that are neither generating costs, nor properly the health or environmental costs that are considered in other chapters. These include transmission and distribution, as well as hidden costs involved in lack of reliability of service and possible vulnerability of electricity supply systems to catastrophic events. This subject is treated very briefly in the appendix to this chapter to facilitate later comparisons between different energy sources in chapter 11.

Overall System Descriptions

If this were a discussion of the basic commercial technologies of today, the roles of oil, gas, and hydroelectric power would be exceedingly important. However, for obvious reasons related to future oil supply uncertainties, future expansion of oil-fired capacity seems unlikely except in special cases. Since supplies of natural gas appear to be limited, it has become a matter of national policy not to expand the use of that

---

[1] Because of seasonal and even hourly fluctuations in the demand for electricity, electric utility systems are compelled by overall economics to develop a generating "mix" that includes cyclical and peak-load units that may not match either the cost per kilowatt-hour or the fuel-conservation potential of baseload operations. The supply of baseload energy, however, is the crucial question for future energy strategies. Therefore, a treatment of such nonbaseload units—or of the load management techniques and R&D in energy storage that might alter the traditional generating "mix"—is not given in this volume. Relevant factors are treated in an underlying study [Center for Energy Studies, The University of Texas, "Future Central Station Electric Power Generating Alternatives," prepared for Resources for the Future (Austin, Texas, 1978) pp. 2.21ff].

resource for generating electricity. It might be possible to expand some hydroelectric power plants at existing sites, but such a policy would run into environmental opposition because of effects on stream ecology and local land use. Also, most of the best sites for hydroelectric plants have already been used. Therefore, coal and nuclear power appear to be the obvious major choices of available commercial technologies over the course of the next decade.

Obvious as these choices may be, the utilization of these technologies, even putting to one side health and environmental considerations, involves many difficulties that increasingly affect their nature and cost.

Coal

The generating of electricity from coal involves certain key costs. First, it requires a relatively large amount of coal to produce each kilowatt hour of electricity: millions of tons will be needed every year for the 1-gigawatt (GW) plant considered as a standard here. This large amount of fuel constitutes a major—sometimes dominant—factor in the cost of the electricity generated. Second, there are environmental drawbacks (for details, see chap. 12). It suffices here to point out that coal contains sulfur and a great number of other compounds, mostly in the ash, that are potential environmental pollutants. Indeed, most of the reasons for wanting to develop new methods of generating electricity from coal involve its basic environmental drawbacks.

Technology. All commercial coal-fired power plants now operating work on the familiar principle of direct combustion: the carbon and hydrogen in coal are combined with the oxygen in the air to release heat.[2] This heat is used to make steam in a boiler; the steam then drives a turbine that drives an alternator that generates the electric current.

In practice, there are variations on these basic principles. In the most common types of boiler systems, the air used in combustion is preheated, and powdered coal and preheated air are introduced into a chamberlike furnace. The luminous flame from the combustion radiates heat to water-filled tubes that are placed vertically around the inside walls of the chamber, and the steam is formed and carried by these tubes out of the chamber and eventually to the turbine.

[2] Coal is not made up entirely of carbon and hydrogen but also contains moisture and other elements—mostly minerals. Some of these minerals form ash.

A NOTE ON COMPARING GENERATING COSTS

Technologies are being compared here in terms of unit costs—that is, the average cost for each kilowatt hour (kWh) of electricity produced. Generally, this cost consists of three main parts: (1) amortized capital charges, (2) fuel costs, and (3) operation and maintenance costs. For the most part, the capital charges are the cost of the power plant and other capital items that represent annual wear and tear (that is, depreciation) and also the "opportunity cost," which is the cost of holding the investment in the power plant rather than turning it to other uses.[3]

The annual capital charge is usually taken as a fixed percentage of the total capital investment. Because any method of determining opportunity costs is open to dispute, we employ two alternative capital charge rates here: 10 and 15 percent.[4] These correspond to returns on investment (in *deflated* dollars) of about 6 percent and 12 percent, respectively.[5] The lower figure reflects estimates of actual returns to equity in the late 1960s, although recent deflated returns have been even lower. The higher figure represents the possibility of higher opportunity costs. Returns to utilities in earlier years were indeed somewhat higher. To obtain a unit cost, the sum of plant fuel costs, operation and maintenance costs, and capital charges for a year is divided by the net total of electricity actually generated in that year.[6] This cost is expressed here in mills (0.1 cent) per kilowatt hour.

All calculations are done in real (constant) 1975 dollars, including estimates of rates of return to fixed amounts of capital. High interest rates paid in ever-depreciating dollars must be reduced to lower interest rates if the return is to be considered as being paid in dollars of constant value.[7] Many other studies use current dollars or mixed dollars (for example, one can use high interest charges reflecting inflationary pressures but expressed formally in dollars of one year); and the results here would have to be multiplied by appropriate inflation factors to be compared with the apparently higher values in these other studies.

This procedure is used consistently for all technologies in the remainder of the book, ensuring that costs in terms of actual resources expended are "levelized" (that is, do not change from year to year because of inflation).

---

[3] Certain taxes and insurance premiums are also usually included in these charges.

[4] See William Ramsay, "Electricity from Conventional Coal and Nuclear Central Stations," draft prepared for the National Energy Strategies Project (Washington, D.C., Resources for the Future, 1978) app. 14-A. Available from RFF's Center for Energy Policy Research. The difference between two capital charge rates such as 10 and 15 percent can make a large difference in the cost of energy; however, the difference between types of electricity generating schemes considered for either charge rate are usually less sensitive to the choice, depending on the capital–fuel cost ratio.

There are two currently popular systems for actually introducing coal into a furnace. Traveling grate stokers use a louvered conveyor belt to transport the fuel; combustion takes place continuously in the furnace as the belt moves the coal through. A slightly newer form of coal combustion utilized especially in larger boilers uses highly pulverized coal; the fuel is fed into the furnace essentially like a gas, in the form of a powder carried along in a stream of air.

An important technical point to be noted about normal coal combustion is that the minerals contained in the coal must be disposed of in some way. Some elements contained in the coal (such as sulfur and many small particles of ash) are usually emitted into the flue gases—either as gaseous compounds or as suspended particulates, leading to concerns about air pollution. Heavier ash particles must be disposed of as solid waste.

One of the problems in evaluating the economics of coal power plants is knowing what and how much pollution control is to be applied to the flue gases. It will be assumed here that coal-fired plants meet current and proposed future EPA regulations for removing most of the sulfur and particulates from the flue gases by scrubber systems before release into the

[5] See ibid., app. 14-A, where it is argued that rates of return to utilities over the past fifteen years or so fall from a high of 8 percent in 1961 to negative returns in 1974. A 6 percent (deflated) rate of return, corresponding to returns to capital in the year 1967, is adopted here for the lower capital charge rate as corresponding to returns needed by a viable utility industry. It must be emphasized that this calculation takes into account the inflationary impact of general price level rises on interest rates by deflating rates of return. This figure must be added to costs of depreciation and nonincome taxes to get the items that are customarily included in capital charges. The straight-line depreciation rate for thirty years is 3.3 percent; however, a correctly levelized treatment—giving uniform charges every year—requires calculation on a sinking fund basis.

The corresponding sinking fund for depreciation rate is only 1.2 percent for a 6 percent (deflated) opportunity cost of money over thirty years. Including nonincome taxes of between 2 and 3 percent, a figure of approximately 10 percent can be derived for the low estimate of the total capital charge rate.

Since numerical values of opportunity costs, treatment of tax credits, depreciation schemes, and methods for deflating returns are controversial, possibilities for an alternative higher real rate of return of 12 percent have also been considered: at this higher percentage the charges to a sinking fund for depreciation require only a very small additional percentage charge. Therefore, with taxes, one calculates a capital charge rate of approximately 15 percent for the high alternative estimate.

[6] For average future plants, this amount is calculated by multiplying the capacity of the plant times the number of hours in a year (8,760) and a "capacity factor" or fraction of time the plant produces at its rated capacity.

[7] See the reference in the previous footnotes and Stephen A. McGuire and Jose G. Martín, "A Monetary Correction Model of Economic Analysis Applied to Nuclear Power Costs," *Nuclear Technology* vol. 18 (June 1973) pp. 257–266.

air, and costs of these systems will be considered as normal costs in these calculations.

Economics.   As indicated earlier, the cost of coal is one of the major factors in coal-plant economics because the fuel costs in such plants can be upwards of one-third of the total generating cost. With the current emphasis on coal as a source of energy for electricity and for industrial process heat, it is difficult to predict future coal prices with any confidence; but some of the facts and factors relating to coal resources and supply prospects were discussed in chapter 7 and others will be treated in chapter 17. However, to give a gauge for comparison, a study done for this project estimated that in 1985 the average cost of coal delivered to generating plants might vary, by geographic region, from about 5 mills per kilowatt hour to 13 mills per kilowatt hour (see table 9-1).[8] The study assumed efficiencies characteristic of a 1-GW (1,000 megawatt, or million-kilowatt) plant, which is the standard unit considered here.

One should by rights expect to be able to accurately estimate average labor costs and other day-to-day operation and maintenance costs of typical coal plants. Unfortunately, the introduction of scrubbers for flue gas desulfurization and other pollution control systems have complicated the question, and it is no longer certain what average costs of this kind will be. However, they should still be relatively small compared with other components. Table 9-1 shows operation and maintenance (O&M) at 2.1 mills per kilowatt hour, thus allowing for more than a doubling of operation and maintenance costs for plants as a result of adding the new scrubber systems.

Finally, there is the most controversial cost component of all: the capital costs of the plant itself. In the first place, there is a good deal of uncertainty as to what the costs of new plants will be, especially those with the scrubber systems that satisfy Best Available Control Technology (BACT) standards set by the Environmental Protection Agency. But in addition the cost of plant construction has in recent years escalated at rates higher than the general inflation rate. The cost estimate taken here, however, reflects an analysis done in a study for this project that allows $77 million for new pollution control systems and predicts only 1 percent net long-term escalation in constant dollars, positing that

[8] Center for Energy Studies, "Future Electric Alternatives." Table 9-1 also shows another type of fuel cost, the "fuel inventory cost," which is the cost associated with keeping a supply of coal on hand at the plant.

Table 9-1. Generating Costs for 1985 by Region for Pulverized Coal-Fired 1,000-MWe Steam Plants with Flue Gas Desulfurization
(in mills per kilowatt hour, 1975 dollars)

Reliability Council region[a]	*Capital charges*[b]	*Inventory*	*Fuel*	*Operation and mainte- nance*	*Total*[b]
Northeast Power Coordinating Council (NPCC)	8.6–13.0	0.1	13.1	2.1	23.9–28.3
Mid-Atlantic Area Council (MAAC)	8.6–13.0	0.1	9.8	2.1	20.6–25.0
East Central Area Reliability Coordinator Agreement (ECAR)					
(Eastern)	8.1–12.1	0.1	9.8	2.1	20.1–24.1
(Western)	8.1–12.1	0.1	8.7	2.1	19.0–23.0
Southeastern Electric Reliability Council (SERC)					
(Coast	7.3–10.9	0.1	10.2	2.1	19.7–23.3
(Interior)	7.3–10.9	0.1	8.7	2.1	18.2–21.9
Mid-Continent Area Reliability Coordination Agreement (MARCA)	7.8–11.6	0.1	7.7	2.1	17.7–21.5
Southwest Power Pool (SPP)	7.8–11.6	0.1	7.5	2.1	17.5–21.3
Electric Reliability Council of Texas (ERCOT)	7.2–10.8	0.1	7.5	2.1	16.9–20.5
Western Systems Coordinating Council (WSCC)					
(Mountain)	8.1–12.1	0.1	4.8	2.1	15.1–19.1
(Coast)	8.1–12.1	0.1	10.4	2.1	20.7–24.7
National average (= Mid- America Interpool Network, MAIN)	7.9–11.9	0.1	8.7	2.1	18.8–22.8

Source: Center for Energy Studies, "Future Central Station Electric Power Generating Alternatives" (Austin, Tex., The University of Texas for Resources for the Future, 1978) table 4.3-16 and table 4.3-20. Also see text.
[a] For region definitions, see figure 9-2.
[b] The calculations are made for two alternative capital charge rates (10 percent and 15 percent), an assumed capacity factor of 67.5 percent, and uniformly deflated costs (see "A Note on Comparing Generating Costs").

recent escalation trends in construction in relation to general price movements will tend toward this value in the long run.[9]

Under these assumptions, an average 1-GW coal-fired plant in the United States completed in 1985 but valued in terms of 1975 dollars, would be estimated to cost $446.3 million, or about $450 million. Table 9-2 shows the engineering details of this estimate of "overnight" construction costs—neglecting for the moment construction delays, but assuming a net escalation of construction costs over general price levels of 1 percent annually.

[9] Ibid., app. 4-C.

Table 9-2. Overnight Construction Costs for a 1,000-MWe Pulverized Coal-Fired Steam Plant, Delivered in 1985
(thousand 1975 dollars)

Category	With flue gas desulfurization	Without flue gas desulfurization
1. Improvement to site	2,000	2,000
2. Earthwork and pilings	4,100	4,100
3. Circulating water system (wet mechanical draft)	21,000	18,000
4. Concrete	9,600	9,000
5. Structural steel, lifting equipment, stacks	28,600	26,000
6. Buildings (indoor construction)	12,100	11,600
7. Turbine generator	29,600	29,600
8. Boiler, fuel handling, and pollution control	147,700	95,000
9. Other mechanical equipment	14,700	14,700
10. Piping	17,300	16,000
11. Insulation and lagging	10,900	10,900
12. Instrumentation	2,700	2,500
13. Electrical equipment	25,400	24,000
14. Painting and finishing	1,800	1,700
15. Land (excluding cooling system)	600	600
Total direct	328,100	265,700
16. Indirect construction	28,600	27,000
17. Architect-engineer fees	41,800	38,000
Total direct and indirect	398,500	330,700
18. Contingencies	47,800	39,600
Total estimate	446,300	370,300

Note: "Overnight" means costs incurred because construction takes time to complete are not included.

Source: Center for Energy Studies, "Future Central Station Electric Power Generating Alternatives" (Austin, Tex., The University of Texas for Resources for the Future, 1978) table 4.3-15.

The $450 million estimate does not include two important factors. It does not include the fact that constructing a power plant takes a great deal of time and therefore the delay costs—or opportunity costs of the capital tied up in the project—can be significant (see the time profile for construction expenditures in figure 9-1). It also does not take into account the fact that construction costs can vary by region; this variation is estimated in table 9-3. The final range of total capital costs, taking both of these factors into account, for a standard 1-GW station including expected delay costs, then ranges between approximately $430 and $510 million for different (electric reliability) regions.[10] The na-

[10] See fig. 9-2.

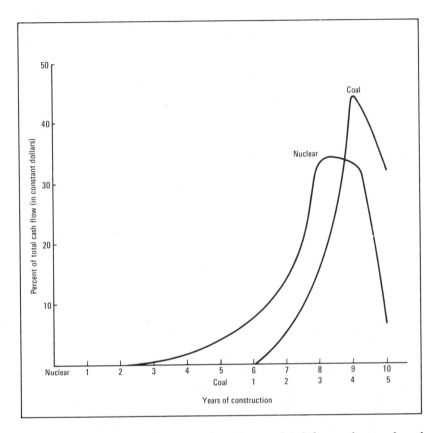

Figure 9-1. Yearly percentage of work completed for nuclear and coal plants under construction. From the "1973 Power Planning Study for the Generation Task Force of the NEPOOL Planning Committee" (West Springfield, Mass., 1973), quoted in Center for Energy Studies, "Future Central Station Electric Power Generating Alternatives" (Austin, Tex., The University of Texas for Resources for the Future, 1978).

tional average is about $470 million, reflecting a typical surcharge for construction delays of about 5 percent, or a net delay cost of $20 million.

The final capital cost question that must be settled is the amount of electricity that is produced every year, so that the capital charge rate times the capital cost itself can be apportioned to give a unit capital cost for each kilowatt hour during the plant's nominal thirty-year life. A range of capacity factors of 60 to 75 percent or an average of 67.5 percent has been chosen here: that range roughly corresponds to the spread between the pessimistic and optimistic estimates commonly made in this

Table 9-3. Regional Capital Cost Variations from Base Plant Costs

Reliability Council	*Percentage*
Northeast Power Coordinating Council (NPCC)	+9.0
Mid-Atlantic Area Council (MAAC)	+0.0
East Central Area Reliability Coordination Agreement (ECAR)	+2.0
Mid-America Interpool Network (MAIN)	0.0
Southeastern Electric Reliability Council (SERC)	−8.0
Mid-Continent Area Reliability Coordination Agreement (MARCA)	−2.0
Southwest Power Pool (SPP)	−2.0
Electric Reliability Council of Texas (ERCOT)	−9.0
Western Systems Coordinating Council (WSCC)	+2.0

Note: The variations shown are due to labor wage rates and average materials costs at site. See figure 9-2 for regions shown.

Source: Center for Energy Studies, "Future Central Station Electric Power Generating Alternatives (Austin, Tex., The University of Texas for Resources for the Future, 1978) table 4.0-8, p. 4.28.

controversial area.[11] Some power plants, of course, are operated intermittently because of changes in the electric load and will thus tend to have lower capacity factors. However, the plants considered here are assumed to provide "baseload" (quasi-continuous operation) capacity.

Putting all these factors together, we obtain the unit capital costs shown in table 9-1, giving costs of between about 7 and 9 mills/kWh for various regions for a (deflated) capital charge rate of 10 percent. The capital costs are 50 percent higher if the (deflated) capital charge rate is taken to be 15 percent. (See "A Note on Comparing Generating Costs" and footnotes.)

This unit capital cost is then added to unit fuel and operation and maintenance costs. The final result is that, from table 9-1, the national average cost is about 19 mills/kWh. The total costs vary widely over regions, from about 15 to 24 mills/kWh for a capital charge rate of 10 percent, and a range of 19 to 28 mills, with an average of 23 mills, for a 15 percent rate.

These figures show that (1) the regional variation is quite significant, and (2) as seen in the third column in table 9-1, the result is fairly sensitive to the future price of coal.

Nuclear

For nuclear power, this fuel price situation is rather the opposite of that for coal. The price of electricity, as will be seen later, is much less

[11] Center for Energy Studies, "Future Electric Alternatives," p. 4.222, tab. 4.3-18.

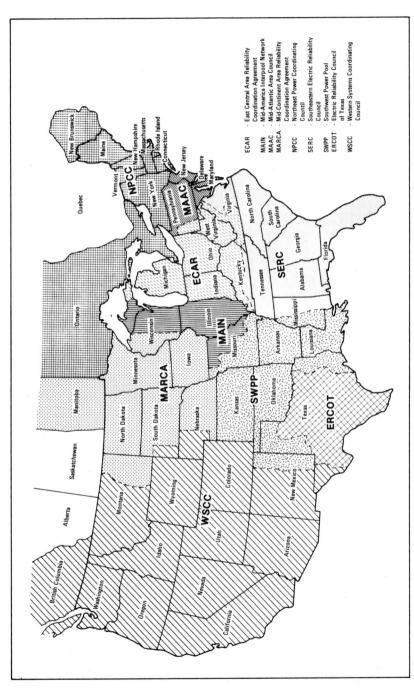

Figure 9-2. The nine reliability council regions. From the Federal Power Commission, *Factors Affecting the Electric Power Supply 1980–85*, A Special Study by the Bureau of Power (Washington, D.C., FPC, 1 December 1976, p. 228).

dependent on the cost of uranium at the mine. Uranium has much more energy per unit weight and volume than coal in the first place, and most of the nuclear fuel costs are in any case a result of enrichment and other processing costs. On the other hand, nuclear energy has the potential disadvantage of being very capital intensive. Therefore, escalation in the price of materials or labor, safety and environmental regulation difficulties that cause delays, and other capital-related factors can be a more serious affair in dollar terms than for coal. Furthermore, if capacity factors—the measurement of the reliability of a baseload plant—turn out to be low, relatively expensive systems would be left idle for long periods of time, causing a large cost increase to the consumer. On the other hand, having high costs embedded in an existing nuclear plant could be a retrospective advantage in an inflationary period. The question of cost is exacerbated by the relative newness and complexity of the technology— as we shall see below—and consequently a lack of knowledge about reliability and long-term economics. Note that the nature of the technology is also discussed later in relation to health and safety and other problems such as nuclear weapons proliferation in chapters 12 and 14.

Technology. The source of energy in a nuclear power plant is the binding energy of certain atomic nuclei. When neutrons (neutral nuclear particles) cause the fission of those nuclei, heat is ultimately released. The remainder of the process for generating nuclear electricity is approximately the same as for fossil-fired generation: the collection of heat to boil water, produce steam, and operate a turbine-alternator that generates electricity. However, while the collection of heat by water in the pressure tubes in a coal boiler has relatively little effect on the nature of the process itself, the efficiency of the nuclear reaction process is quite sensitive to water or other matter adjacent to it. This means in practice that the design of a nuclear power plant is usually restricted in choice of structural materials and heat-collecting fluids.

Virtually all of the nuclear power plants now operating on a commercial basis in the United States are light water reactors. One of the properties of light water (that is, ordinary water[12]) is that it slows down neutrons, and this results in a greater efficiency in the fission process. The fuel for this type of reactor is contained in individual rods arranged inside a large water-filled pressure vessel.[13]

---

[12] Water has other, more exotic forms: see the discussion of "heavy water" in the CANDU reactor section.

[13] Incidentally, since the outer tubing or cladding of the rod that holds the uranium oxide powder fuel must also not impede the reaction by absorbing too many

The nuclear reaction can thus be viewed as merely a special kind of boiler. This is a particularly close analogy for one main class of light water reactors, the boiling water reactor. In another kind of reactor, the water is heated under pressure but maintained in liquid form, and the pressurized hot water is passed through a heat exchanger to generate steam for the turbine. In either case, the main segments of the system that contains the fissioning fuel are filled with water and the water is radioactive. Special safety systems are needed to provide an emergency water supply to reduce the risk of overheating in the event that the normal flow of water is interrupted,[14] because a meltdown of fuel or similar accidents could release a significant amount of radioactivity inside the plant and eventually to the outside environment. Special containment barriers are also often used to slow down or prevent the release of this radioactivity.

The nuclear reaction is efficient in terms of the amount of energy produced per ton of fuel weight (over 1 trillion Btu), and a commercial power reactor needs to be refueled only in intervals of a year or so by replacing each time one-fourth to one-third of the approximately hundred tons of uranium fuel used in a 1-GW plant. However, since the fuel rods are all contained together inside the reactor vessel, and many of the rods not removed must be relocated, the reactor must be shut down for a number of days or indeed weeks to carry out refueling. Also, after the spent fuel is removed, it remains significantly radioactive because of elements created during the fission process which have not had time to decay; spent fuel removal is thus the beginning point of the well-known nuclear waste problem.

The nuclear reactors also incidentally produce a certain amount of a fissionable material, plutonium, during the course of normal operation. Some of the plutonium fissions in place, adding to the heat output of the reactor, but some remains in the spent fuel when it is withdrawn. This fact and its consequences will be emphasized later in the discussion of chapter 14 on catastrophic threats.

Economics. The problem of uranium resources has been discussed in chapter 7, where some of the same basic uncertainties involved with

---

neutrons, it is generally made of a special alloy of zirconium. The nuclear reaction is restricted by the temperatures of the melting points of the cladding and of the fuel itself, so the thermal efficiency of light water reactor generating systems is usually restricted to levels somewhat below that of coal plants.

[14] Because of continuing nuclear decay, reactors continue to build up heat after a shutdown.

A NOTE ON THE NUCLEAR FUEL CYCLE

The production of nuclear power depends on a fairly complex fuel cycle. The salient features of this fuel cycle are:

1. Mining. Uranium-bearing ores are mined in surface pit mines or in underground mining operations.

2. Milling. The ore is crushed and chemically processed to extract the uranium oxides; the latter are often yellow and the product is always called yellowcake. The radioactive residues of the milling process are deposited in tailings ponds.

3. Conversion. The uranium oxides are converted into uranium hexafluoride, a substance that is a gas at modest temperatures and thus is suitable for enrichment purposes.

4. Enrichment. The gasified uranium compound is passed through a network of filters, separating the fissile uranium-235 atoms from the more numerous nonfissile uranium-238 atoms, in a process called gaseous diffusion. (Other enrichment processes have been planned or proposed.)

5. Fuel fabrication. The enriched uranium gas is turned into an enriched uranium oxide powder and this is heat compacted into ceramic pellets which fit into the fuel rods of reactors.

6. Power production. The fuel in the fuel rods undergoes fission inside the reactor vessel, releasing energy that heats water to produce steam for electric generators.

7. Waste management. Spent fuel, which remains highly radioactive, is stored in pools of water at the reactors. The question of whether it should be processed at central locations to separate reusable materials (including both uranium and plutonium) from waste residues has been postponed indefinitely by current U.S. policy. Plans for further disposal of nuclear waste, for example in salt deposits underground, are now being discussed.

Table 9-4. 1985 Generating Costs for a 1-GW Nuclear Reactor
(1975 dollars)

Sample region[a]	Capital[b]	Fuel inventory	Fuel	Operation and maintenance	Total[b]
NPCC	10.5–15.7	0.7	4.8	1.5	17.5–22.7
WSCC[c]	10.8–16.1	0.7	4.8	1.5	17.8–23.1
SERC[d]	8.8–13.2	0.7	4.8	1.5	15.8–20.2
National average (also MAIN)	9.6–14.4	0.7	4.8	1.5	16.6–21.4

Source: Center for Energy Studies, "Future Central Station Electric Generating Alternatives" (Austin, Tex., University of Texas for Resources for the Future, 1978) tables 4.1-8 and 4.1-9.

[a] See figure 9-2 for definition of regions; the regions not shown have values intermediate to those displayed here.

[b] Alternate deflated capital charge rates of 10 percent and 15 percent are utilized.

[c] Highest cost region (includes seismic surcharge).

[d] Lowest cost region.

coal also appear in the uranium case; that is, the future cost of uranium fuel (and so the future cost of nuclear electricity) will depend not only on the uranium resource base, but also on the current costs of ore production. In addition, to manufacture the fuel used in ordinary light water reactors, the uranium must be converted into a gaseous form and then enriched to increase the ratio of a fissile isotope of uranium (uranium 235) in relation to the nonfissile uranium 238, which is more abundant in ordinary uranium. The cost of these processes is a major component in fuel costs (see "A Note on the Nuclear Fuel Cycle"), amounting to twice as large a share as the cost of the raw uranium "yellowcake"[15] for the 1985 timeframe in calculations made for this study.[16] The total cost of the nuclear fuel (estimated as an average for uranium fuel to be used in generating electricity in 1985) contributes 4.8 mills/kWh to the overall cost of generating electricity (see table 9-4).[17]

For nuclear power, estimates for average operation and maintenance costs are uncertain because experience has been relatively limited: an average of 1.5 mills/kWh has been estimated here for a 1-GW plant.

[15] This is true despite the fact that over 5 pounds of yellowcake are needed for each pound of fuel.

[16] Center for Energy Studies, " Future Electric Alternatives," p. 3.63, tab. 3.1-14.

[17] The uranium fuel will be "stockpiled," that is, contained for a number of years in the reactor before it is entirely utilized. Therefore, there must be a relatively significant fuel capital charge—compared with coal stockpiles—associated with the operation of a typical plant. This charge is taken as 0.7 mills/kWh here.

The problem of the capital costs—the cost of the plant itself—is even more difficult to treat than in the case of coal-fired plants. The costs of nuclear power plants have tended to grow as manufacturers have revised earlier estimates in the light of experience, as new safety systems have been required by government regulators, and as safety and environmental reviews have often become lengthy. Even considering new problems that could arise as a result of analysis of the Three Mile Island accident, many of these factors have presumably stabilized.[18] Nevertheless, predicting a future rate of real cost escalation—that is, over and above general price inflation—is difficult. However, according to the study by the Center for Energy Studies, past trends in recent years indicate that rates of between 1 and 2 percent might be applicable. This study has therefore assumed that real construction prices will rise by 1 percent annually and has estimated, as shown in detail and referenced in table 9-5, the resulting costs for 1985 operation (in 1975 dollars) at about $530 million for a standard 1-GW plant.

Regional differences are relatively unimportant in the cost of uranium fuel as contrasted with coal because the fuel is high in energy per unit weight and so can be transported at a relatively low cost. However, regional factors can be significant in construction costs. The percentages adopted here for nuclear are the same as shown in table 9-3 for coal with one exception: a surcharge of 10 percent is added for extra engineering costs to guard against earthquake damage in the generally seismically active Western Systems Coordinating Council region.

The question of costs of construction delay is particularly irksome. Many nuclear power plants have been plagued by delays. Whether they are primarily due to direct intervention by environmentalists and others, to lengthy safety and environmental reviews by government agencies, or to labor or financial problems is controversial. Periods of delay have indeed often been long; however, the major part of the delay costs— that is, the opportunity costs of capital involved in the project—is still usually associated with the last few years of construction, as shown in figure 9-1. The costs of delay for an average real plant over that of a hypothetical overnight construction time is thus taken here at 7 percent, or somewhat above the coal delay factor. Total adjusted capital costs

---

[18] See Doan L. Phung, *Cost Comparison Between Base-Load Coal-Fired and Nuclear Plants in the Midterm Future (1985–2015)*, ORAU/IEA(M) 76-3 (Oak Ridge, Tenn., Institute for Energy Analysis, Oak Ridge Associated Universities, September 1976) pp. 8–9 for a similar view.

Table 9-5. Overnight Capital Cost of a 1,000-MWe Light Water Reactor (1975 dollars)

Category	Cost (*thousand dollars*)
1. Improvement to site	1,700
2. Earthwork and pilings	10,200
3. Circulating water system (cooling pond)	23,000
4. Concrete	44,900
5. Structural steel, lifting equipment	43,600
6. Buildings (indoor construction)	16,600
7. Turbine generator (1,800 rpm)	41,600
8. Boiler, fuel handling, environmental protection	72,300
9. Other mechanical equipment	20,900
10. Piping	45,900
11. Insulation and lagging	3,700
12. Instrumentation	2,900
13. Electrical equipment	43,200
14. Painting and finishing	2,100
15. Land (excluding cooling system)	400
Total direct	373,000
16. Indirect construction	38,300
17. Architect-engineer fees	62,600
Total direct and indirect	473,900
18. Contingencies (12 percent)	56,900
Total estimate	530,800

Note: Assuming a hypothetical instantaneous construction.
Source: Center for Energy Studies, "Future Central Station Electric Power Generating Alternatives" (Austin, Tex., The University of Texas for Resources for the Future, 1977) vol. 1, sect. 4.0.2.

vary among regions from about $520 million to about $640 million for a new 1-GW reactor.[19]

As far as the costs of capital to be associated with each year of operation are concerned, the question is just the same as that for coal discussed above: the capital charge rates to be chosen are a function of utility industry accounting and tax structures and are almost identical for coal and nuclear power plants. The (deflated) rates considered here therefore are, as before, either 10 or 15 percent.

In order to determine how much of that capital charge rate is to be associated with each unit of electricity, the average rate of use of the power station must be determined. Unfortunately, experience has been

[19] Center for Energy Studies, "Future Electric Alternatives," tab. 4.1-7.

very spotty. Many reactors have good operating records; however, some others have been plagued by troubles, and a whole literature has grown up around the alleged failure of nuclear capacity factors to improve with experience and with the increasing size of reactor scale. Still, it has been argued elsewhere[20] that one can expect nuclear factors to improve. Nuclear technology is relatively new, and it seems intuitively reasonable that with further operating experience, equipment will improve in reliability. Furthermore, to the extent that new safety system requirements for plants are no longer added—in contrast to what has often happened within the past decade—problems with untried components or systems in the newer nuclear plants should become fewer. While the Three Mile Island experience could eventually lead to some new safety systems and new reliability problems, such effects, if any, are impossible to trace at this time. At any rate, a capacity factor of 67.5 percent is adopted here, as for coal (see above).[21]

For a national average figure,[22] capital charges are thus 9.6 mills/ kWh for a 10 percent (deflated) rate and 14.4 mills/kWh for 15 percent.

Taking all these estimates, one can make a calculation of the total amount of yearly plant cost to be associated with each kilowatt hour of electricity generated by nuclear power plants. Adding all the cost categories, the unit cost of nuclear electricity, as shown in table 9-4, is 16.6 mills/kWh (10 percent capital charge rate) or 21.4 mills/kWh (15 percent capital charge rate). These are national averages: sample regional variations show total unit costs as much as 5 or 6 percent lower in the South; other regions show intermediate variations.

Coal–Nuclear Comparisons

The costs of coal and nuclear power as recapitulated in table 9-6 are fairly similar, with nuclear power showing a slight edge in some regions.[23] Specifically, tables 9-1 and 9-4 show that in New England and

[20] Ibid., sect. 4.1.

[21] Note that Phung, *Cost Comparison Between Coal and Nuclear* (p. 10) chooses 65 percent for nuclear and coal plants with scrubbers.

[22] The national average is represented by the MAIN Reliability Council region in the midwest.

[23] Note that Phung, *Cost Comparison Between Coal and Nuclear* (as clarified by a private communication) shows coal costs in mills per kilowatt hour as 19 to 28, with an average of 22, and nuclear costs of 18 to 22, with an average of 19. This investigation compares a wide range of cost estimates from different sources. Phung

the coastal areas of the western states coal is relatively expensive compared with nuclear power. Even though the nuclear edge is small in most regions—5 to 15 percent—the cost differences are large in absolute terms and would be noticeably reflected in monthly utility bills. Differences in coal and nuclear costs stand out in areas of capital and fuel costs. Furthermore, the rate of utilization of the plant could be an important cost factor.

It must be emphasized that these costs are expressed in constant dollars, including deflation of capital returns and interest rates (see "A Note on Comparing Generation Costs") and will appear lower than costs expressed in depreciating dollars—or in "constant dollars" but with inflated rates of return on capital.

Capital costs are significantly higher for nuclear power plants, about 20 percent greater, as shown in table 9-6.[24] Therefore the validity of the estimates for these costs is a crucial factor in the analysis. In this regard, the question of escalation of nuclear power plant costs above the level of general inflation has been a matter of great controversy. Some studies have extrapolated from very high increases of costs within the past decade and have predicted very large rates of escalation over and above increases in the general price level.[25] A study prepared for this report[26] estimates, however, that costs will stabilize; and its analysis assigned only 1 percent escalation to anticipate costs of new safety and environmental regulations. Specific predictions about whether construction

---

suspects that the different estimates, if converted into the "base-year constant dollars" (see R. Michael Harnett and Doan L. Phung, *Three Modes of Energy Cost Analysis —Then-Current Dollars, Base-Year Dollars, and Perpetual-Constant Dollars,* ORAU/IEA-78-10(M) (Oak Ridge, Tenn., Institute for Energy Analysis, Oak Ridge Associated Universities, June 1978) used here, would be similar to the values obtained in the present study.

[24] Note that this is the same ratio suggested in State of New York, Public Service Commission, "Recommended Decision by Administrative Law Judge Robert D. Reed," Case No. 26974. Proceeding on Motion of the Commission as to the Comparative Economics of Nuclear and Fossil Fueled Generating Facilities (Albany, New York, December 18, 1978) p. 47 as the result of a review of expert testimony.

[25] See, for example, "Statement of Charles Komanoff, Komanoff Energy Associates" in *Nuclear Power Costs (Part 2),* Hearings before the House Committee on Government Operations, 95 Cong. 1 sess (Washington, D.C., GPO, 1977) pp. 1181–1204 and 1691–1729; Irvin C. Bupp, Jean-Claude Derian, Marie-Paule Donsimoni, Robert Treitel, *Trends in Light Water Reactor Capital Costs in the United States: Causes and Consequences,* CPA 74-8 (Cambridge, Mass., Center for Policy Alternatives, Massachusetts Institute of Technology, December 18, 1974); and William E. Mooz, *Cost Analysis of Light Water Reactor Power Plants,* R-2304-DOE, prepared for the U.S. Department of Energy (Santa Monica, Calif., Rand Corporation, June 1978).

[26] Center for Energy Studies, "Future Electric Alternatives," sect. 4.

Table 9-6. Recapitulation of Coal and Nuclear Power Costs, Showing Regional Spread and Average National Figures, in 1975 mills/kWh for 1985 Operation

| | Capital costs[a] | | Fuel inventory | Fuel | Operation and maintenance | Total[a] | |
	10 percent	15 percent				10 percent	15 percent
Coal							
Regional spread	7.2–8.6	10.8–13.0	0.1	7.5–13.1	2.1	16.9–23.9	20.5–28.3
National average	7.9	11.9	0.1	8.7	2.1	18.8	22.8
Nuclear							
Regional spread	8.8–10.8	13.2–16.1	0.7	4.8	1.5	15.8–17.8	20.2–23.1
National average	9.6	14.4	0.7	4.8	1.5	16.6	21.4

Sources: Tables 9-1 and 9-4.
[a] At the alternative capital charge rates shown (see page 272).

cost escalation will thus stabilize—compared of course with other costs in the economy—are difficult to justify. Nevertheless, for purposes of the coal/nuclear comparison, escalation is of primary concern only if prices for nuclear construction were to rise much faster than for coal. Even though there are uncertainties about new safety systems for nuclear plants and new pollution control systems for coal plants, the point of view is adopted here that a vast difference between changes in capital cost trends for the two is unlikely.

Should escalation occur at higher rates than posited here, however, what would be the consequences? The very high rates of escalation found by some persons for both coal and nuclear plants—but more markedly for nuclear plants[27]—would of course change the conclusions drawn here. More modest variations, however, would probably not upset them very much. For example, the result of one analysis, which supposed on the basis of a review of the literature a nuclear plant escalation rate of 9 percent (in current dollars), can be examined for its effect on our conclusions.[28] If coal escalation is kept at 1 percent as before, then the results of applying this nuclear escalation rate to our calculations show that a total capital cost of a nuclear plant should be increased by 36 percent—giving an increase of total nuclear costs of 21 percent (10 percent capital charge rate) at a final cost of 21 mills/kWh. This would raise the nuclear costs to 7 percent over the cost of coal-fired electricity.[29] Such a change would then make the coal option more favorable on the average than nuclear, but would not disturb the rough equivalence of the cost of the two technologies.

A related factor that may produce large differences between cost estimates is the cost of delay in the construction of nuclear power plants. One might anticipate that delays caused by regulation should decrease. The past decade has seen planned plants or those currently being built delayed because the original designs no longer fitted into more stringent safety rules, or because new health and environmental issues were brought up in regulatory or judicial proceedings; however, one might

---

[27] Mooz, *Cost Analysis of Light Water Reactor,* pp. 43–44.

[28] See Jim Harding, Memorandum (1 October 1977) to staff of Resources Agency of California, in House Government Operations Committee Hearings, *Nuclear Power Costs (Part 2)* p. 1785. Compare also Phung, *Cost Comparison Between Coal and Nuclear* p. 10.

[29] Using a 5.5 percent inflation rate to give a net real rate of 3.5 percent, less the 1 percent already assumed, gives finally an added rate of 2.5 percent. An interest and equity charge rate in real terms of 4 percent was assumed and the construction time schedule in figure 9-1 was utilized to assign cash flows to future years.

expect these questions would have a lesser effect in future years as safety questions and environmental concerns are resolved. Again, delay costs will affect the comparison to a large extent only if delays for nuclear plants are far greater than those for coal, or vice versa; nevertheless, delays of nuclear plants have happened in the past and could recur. One can indeed test the effect of underestimating delay costs. If, for example, the calculation here were modified to take account of a possible three-year delay—assumed in this case to take place after the plant is completed—the total increase for a deflated rate of interest of 4 percent[30] is 12 percent in the total capital cost of the nuclear plant. This would produce a nuclear unit cost of electricity (for a 10 percent capital charge) of 17.8 mills/kWh, 7 percent higher than the previous nuclear costs, but still smaller than the average cost of electricity from a coal-fired plant.

Uncertainties in fuel costs can also exist. If fuel costs escalate because of energy supply pressures or because of monopolistic practices or other means, the comparison could be affected. If coal prices were to rise sharply, while uranium costs and costs of construction for both technologies did not rise in real constant dollar terms, the coal/nuclear comparison could be affected to the detriment of coal. However, the effects of fuel cost rises should be minor otherwise; and indeed, if construction and fuel costs all rise in concert with general price inflation, the framework of the comparison will still be intact.

Health and environmental effects have, of course, not been considered; such impacts will be discussed in chapters 12, 13, and 14. However, in the aftermath of the Three Mile Island accident, it should be noted in the present context that public concern about nuclear health and safety could result in demands for more reactor safety systems that would raise nuclear costs. In addition, problems of liability insurance and of allocating the cleanup costs of accidents could lead to increases in the cost of nuclear-generated electricity.

Advanced Coal and Nuclear Technologies

Coal or other fossil fuels and such nuclear fuels as uranium or thorium could generate electricity by techniques differing from those utilized in conventional fossil-fired plants and light water reactors. Changes can

---

[30] A real interest and equity charge rate of 4 percent was assumed.

be made either in the way the fuel is burned or in the character of the fuel itself. Or the intermediate steps of transferring heat from the boiler to the electric alternator can be modified. Finally, experimental processes exist that would do away with the conventional electric alternator entirely.

Modifications in established technologies can be considered as answers to both economic and environmental questions. Coal technologists have been particularly hard pressed to devise methods of generating electricity while producing less air pollution. In the nuclear industry, there has been interest in producing more efficient reactors; however, a more important drive has been toward developing reactors that can utilize more of the energy inherent in natural uranium, rather than merely the rather small fraction available in directly fissionable uranium 235. "Breeder" reactors therefore constitute an especially important nuclear alternative.

Some cost estimates are given for future unit costs of electricity using these advanced technologies. However, it must be noted that such estimates often represent *targets* rather than estimates. In other words, most estimates originate with proponents of the new technologies; as interested parties, they will naturally anticipate having to drive costs of new systems down to levels that will be competitive with present coal and nuclear power generation.

This caveat may also apply even in the cases below where independent estimates have been prepared in studies for this project, since data must of necessity be gathered from groups actively working on such technologies. However, for costs estimated independently here—as noted below—efforts have been made to cost out subsystems and components separately and to review critically other existing cost estimates.

New Coal-Based Processes

If the sulfur in coal can be removed from the coal before it is burned, pollution problems can be lessened. As described in chapter 8, various methods have been proposed for separating the coal into clean solids and liquids by the use of special solvents. We have estimated that such methods could turn out to cost as little as 1 or 2 mills extra per kilowatt hour.[31] However, the important question may not be the cost, but

[31] See William Ramsay, "Electricity from Advanced Fossil and Nuclear Technologies," draft prepared for the National Energy Strategies Project (Washington,

the efficiency of cleanup: some pilot systems do not extract sufficient sulfur to meet anticipated government antipollution regulations.

Gasification of coal into a low-Btu form was also discussed in chapter 8. The level of the extra costs of gasification for generating electricity would of course depend on the very uncertain cost of the gasification process itself. However, from the minimum estimates of gasification costs in chapter 8, a net surcharge of approximately 10 mills/kWh might be expected. This surcharge estimate makes some effort to take into account costs that would be saved by higher efficiencies in gas combustion and the capital and maintenance costs of scrubbers[32] that would be saved. However, other estimates of gasification used with a combined cycle (see below) predict a more favorable outlook.[33]

The coal can also be purified during combustion by burning it in the form of a powder that is suspended in a stream of compressed air— the so-called fluidized-bed combustion method. Flame temperatures can be lower, thus reducing the amount of pollutant nitrogen oxides; and if limestone is also added, the sulfur in the coal is expected to be efficiently removed during combustion. Heavier ash will be naturally removed by gravity, but particulate removal systems for lighter ash may still be required. One special advantage of this proposed system is that it possibly could be even cheaper to operate than an ordinary coal plant with scrubbers, that is, proponents argue that costs could be as low as 18 to 21 mills/kWh.[34]

There is another possibility for improving the efficiency and therefore reducing the cost of electricity from coal generation. If the hot

---

D.C., Resources for the Future, 1978) pp. 15–21. Based on claims to be able to make 30 to 40 percent of U.S. coal environmentally acceptable at a cost of $2.50 to $5 per ton [see "New Desulfurization Ways Could Triple Amount of Eastern Coal Meeting Standards," *Energy Resources Report* vol. 5, no. 13 (1 April 1977) p. 129] and assuming 24 million Btu per ton of coal, and a thermal efficiency of 36 percent, a 1-GW plant operating at a 67.5 percent plant factor will consume 68 trillion Btu per year. Therefore the extra cost per ton will be $6.8 million to $14 million extra per plant year, or 1 or 2 mills for each of the 5.91 billion kilowatt hours generated.

[32] At about $1.00 per million Btu for coal, 20.2 trillion Btu (5.913 billion kilowatt hours) electrical output, and 36 percent efficiency, fuel costs are $56 million. For $3.00 per million Btu gas and 43 percent efficiency, fuel costs are $140 million, for a difference of $84 million or 14 mills per kilowatt hour; comparing the two columns in Center for Energy Studies, "Future Electric Alternatives," tables 4.3-18 and 4.3-19 and noting that operation and maintenance cost savings would be 1.2 mills, the net scrubber savings would be 2.7 mills (at 10 percent capital charge rate), or a net gas surcharge of 11 mills. This estimate does not include the effect of differences in basic capital costs for gas versus coal.

[33] Dwain Spencer and Oliver Gildersleeve, "Market Potential for New Coal Technologies," *EPRI Journal* vol. 3, no. 4 (May 1978) pp. 19–26.

[34] Center for Energy Studies, "Future Electric Alternatives," p. 4.229.

gases, instead of merely heating a boiler, can first be used to drive a gas turbine and then to heat a conventional boiler, much more electric energy can be extracted per unit of energy input. If the coal is gasified or otherwise improved so that tiny fly ash particulates do not erode turbine surfaces, such systems could be used with coal. In any case, however, they can be and are being used with oil plants: in those cases where oil systems must be used—perhaps because of insuperable local pollution problems—such combined cycle systems might be able to reduce unit costs or provide economical nonbaseload capacity.

Another possibility for improving the intermediate stages between combustion and actual generation of the electricity is based on better working fluids—that is, substitutes for the water and steam of the usual power cycle. If, for example, liquid metals were used instead of water, one could achieve higher (and therefore more efficient) temperatures without raising pressures beyond the strength of the types of materials ordinarily used for piping and heat exchangers.[35] Such systems have often been proposed in a combined cycle or "binary" form, with the liquid metal or similar working fluid first operating a turbine generator of its own and then being used to boil steam in order to drive ordinary steam turbines. Research on modern coal-fired binary cycles is as yet in too preliminary a stage to speculate usefully on costs or practicality.

Finally, there may be no absolute necessity for using an ordinary alternator (or generator) to generate electricity from coal. In magneto-hydrodynamic (MHD) generation, the hot gases themselves can in theory be utilized as an electric current: highly heated gases contain a large number of electrons and ions (atoms deficient in electrons). A magnetic field can be used to move the positive ions and the negative electrons in different directions, so that with the proper kind of hot gas—in this case, coal burning in a very high temperature range—the hot gases themselves can be tapped for an electric current. This concept, however, faces many practical difficulties. The actual amount of ionization that occurs is small, unless the combustion gas is seeded with an expensive "catalyst" which can be corrosive and which must be recovered at the end of the cycle. Very high temperatures are needed for the ionization (5,500°F), meaning that key items such as electrodes may have very short lifetimes and incidentally that a combined cycle operation is an economic necessity.[36] Furthermore, a relatively large amount of nitrogen

---

[35] Incidentally, the heat transfer aspect of this system is used in the liquid metal fast breeder nuclear reactor described below.

[36] Center for Energy Studies, "Future Electric Alternatives," pp. 4.229 and 4.231.

oxide pollutants is produced. Finally, there is the added inconvenience and expense occasioned by the fact that MHD produces direct current instead of alternating current. Despite these formidable difficulties, some have estimated that electricity can be produced by this method—twenty-five years from now—at competitive rates.[37]

Fuel cells are perhaps an even more interesting alternative to the standard use of the mechanical motion of magnets in an alternator to generate electricity. A fuel cell functions essentially like an ordinary electric battery. One "pole" (electrode) of the "battery" (fuel cell) is supplied with air or oxygen or some other oxidizer, and the other with a gaseous hydrogen-rich fuel. The resulting chemical reaction will sustain a flow of current, as electrons move to one electrode and positive ions to the other.

This method is particularly elegant because the chemical binding energy contained in the fuel is converted more or less directly into the motions of the ions and electrons in the electrolyte, so that theoretically very large efficiencies are possible; in practice, efficiencies of 50 percent or more have been realized from pure hydrogen–oxygen combinations. A further practical engineering advantage is that there are almost no moving parts, at least in the fuel cell itself. However, there are drawbacks in that so far fuel cells have generally required expensive catalysts that can easily be poisoned by fuel impurities such as sulfur; therefore, special fuel conditioning may be needed. For use in utility networks, one must also take into account the fact that the fuel cells produce only direct current. Finally, lifetimes of existing fuel cells are short, perhaps as little as 10,000 hours of operation;[38] and research now underway to lengthen lifetimes to 40,000 hours might be of critical importance.

One estimate for the cost of electricity from a dispersed system of fuel cells was 37 to 40 mills/kWh. However, such estimates are quite sensitive to the fuel costs assumed; in this case, for a gas derived from coal, these were taken to be 28 mills.[39] Furthermore, lower costs have

[37] See Ramsay, "Electricity from Advanced Fossil and Nuclear," p. 15-25.

[38] See ibid., pp. 15-17 and 15-18.

[39] Arthur D. Little, Inc., *Assessment of Fuels for Power Generation by Electric Utility Fuel Cells*, EPRI 318, Final Report (Palo Alto, Calif., Electric Power Research Institute, October 1975) table 4. Taking a 10–15 percent capital charge on a capital cost of $376 per kilowatt, and an operating year of 5,500 hours, or 6.8 to 10.3 mills per kilowatt hour, and adding 2 mills for operation and maintenance costs and a fuel cost of $3.73 per million Btu at a heat rate of 7,500 Btu per kilowatt hour, or 28 mills per kilowatt hour, gives 37 to 40 mills per kilowatt hour.

been estimated for fuel cells operating in conventional central station modes.[40]

Finally, there are few economies of scale, if any, in fuel cell power plant operation; small plants may be as economically attractive as large. This means that even if fuel cells were unsuitable for very large base-load operation they might be used for decentralized production of electricity, thus saving on electricity transmission and distribution costs and perhaps other diseconomies of large scale.[41]

New Nuclear Technologies

New types of nuclear technologies come in two forms: various types of converter reactors—which, like LWRs, merely burn (mainly)[42] uranium 235 to make energy—and breeder reactors—which in addition to burning uranium 235 also convert some of the more common isotope uranium 238 into fissionable plutonium.

Finally, the ultimate nuclear method, nuclear fusion, is a hope for the distant future.

Converter reactors.   Other types of commercial reactors have been developed and built in such other countries as Canada, the Soviet Union, and Great Britain. Also, other advanced reactors exist and one has been operated commercially.

The CANDU.   The only existing foreign reactor that has so far been able to compete in the world market against the American light water reactor is the Canadian CANDU reactor. Its obvious advantage is that it operates on natural uranium, which does not need costly enrichment. It can do this because it fissions more efficiently by using water incorporating a heavy isotope of hydrogen. This deuterium oxide or "heavy water" slows down or moderates the fission-causing neutrons while absorbing fewer of them than ordinary water would. Obviously, the production and use of heavy water entails added cost. But, since the CANDU reactor design uses individual pressurized water tubes instead of one large pressure vessel, it can be refueled without shutting

[40] Ibid., table 4-17.
[41] See Amory B. Lovins, "Soft Energy Technologies," in *Annual Review of Energy 1978* (Palo Alto, Calif., Annual Reviews, Inc., 1978) vol. 3, pp. 477–517, especially pp. 483–489, for one point of view on this question of scale.
[42] All reactors do some breeding and so burn some plutonium as they go along.

down—as is necessary for light water reactors. This means better plant utilization.

While official cost figures for the CANDU are not available, a study done for this report estimates that capital charges for the relatively complex steam and moderator systems involved in the CANDU reactors tend to be somewhat larger than for light water reactors; however, the total generating costs have been estimated at 18 mills/kWh at a 10 percent capital charge rate (24 mills at a 15 percent rate).[43]

The HTGR. Another existing advanced converter reactor in the United States itself could be of interest. The use of water for heat transfer and of uranium oxide contained in metal-clad tubes limits the possible light water reactor operating temperatures the high temperatures of the high temperature gas-cooled reactor (HTGR) are obtained by using helium to transfer the heat and graphite as the agent to moderate (slow down) the neutrons for the fission reaction. Besides the higher generating efficiencies thus obtained compared to LWRs, other novel features exist, at least in the one example of a commercial HTGR now in operation at Fort Saint Vrain, Colorado. This reactor is designed to run on a cycle that, based on a fissioning core of highly enriched uranium, breeds new fuel from the otherwise not very valuable element thorium. Some of the fission neutrons, produced when the uranium 235 atoms in the enriched core split, interact with thorium atoms to yield another fissionable isotope of uranium, uranium 233. Its widespread use would necessitate the development of new types of nuclear reprocessing plants as well as new fuel-fabrication facilities with special features for worker safety and resistance against diversion. Less fuel is made than is burned; nevertheless, the total supply of useful nuclear fuel could in theory be extended by using HTGRs. However, the amount of thorium economically available in the United States or in the world requires further investigation.

Breeder reactors. Since there is a good deal more uranium 238 in natural uranium than there is uranium 235 (about 140 times as much), the possibility of breeding new fissionable fuel from U238 is intriguing.[44]

---

[43] Center for Energy Studies, "Future Electric Alternatives," sect. 4.0.2.

[44] A difficulty with breeders, however, is that the plutonium must be recovered from the fuel by reprocessing and then the plutonium must be taken to a fabrication plant and made into new fuel elements. Since plutonium is a suitable material for making nuclear weapons, the possible creation of a wide trade in plutonium has been a drawback to acceptance of the breeder idea. Indeed, the ongoing major U.S. project in breeder reactors, the liquid metal fast breeder reactor plant at Clinch

The LMFBR. The liquid metal fast breeder reactor uses fuel assemblies similar in form to those employed in the LWR, but which contain a mixture of natural uranium (or even "depleted" uranium[45]) and a considerable amount of fissile plutonium.[46] Excess neutrons from the fission reaction interact with the uranium 238 contained in an extra blanket of fuel assemblies surrounding the central fuel core; some of these neutrons convert U238 atoms into plutonium. Liquid metal (sodium) is used in these reactors because it is a good heat transfer agent and—while fission is most efficient with slow neutrons—breeding can be carried out efficiently with fast neutrons; water can slow down to an undesirable extent the neutrons needed for the breeding reaction. The sodium loop that picks up the heat energy and some radioactivity from the reactor then transfers the energy to a second sodium loop. This second, less radioactive loop transfers the energy finally to a heat exchanger where water is boiled to run the turbines. Capital costs for the first few LMFBRs to be built have been projected by the French (who are among the leaders in the technology) to run about 30 to 39 percent higher than for LWRs, although this capital cost penalty might drop to about 16 percent as design reached a mature level.[47] In a study done for this project, it was estimated that the costs of electricity from the first generation of hypothetical "commercial" LMFBRs in the United States would be (at 10 and 15 percent capital charges, respectively) 19 and 26 mills; however, a more mature technology might produce electricity at 17 to 23 mills in a plant size approximating that taken as a standard in this volume.[48] These costs are, of course, only estimates before the fact.

Other breeders. Another kind of breeder design being considered is the gas-cooled fast breeder reactor (GCFBR), which is still in the R&D stage. It promises a higher rate of reaction of neutrons with uranium to produce plutonium (a higher breeding ratio) than the LMFBR, and therefore a faster production rate of new fuel. Also under development in the United States is a light water breeder reactor (LWBR); like the HTGR described above, it would breed new fuel by

River, Tennessee, has during the past few years been the subject of great political controversy—not all related to proliferation, to be sure. (See chapter 14.)

[45] "Depleted" uranium contains an even smaller percentage of uranium 235 than does the uranium found in nature. It is available as a residue of the enrichment process.

[46] Center for Energy Studies, "Future Electric Alternatives," pp. 3.66 and 3.67.

[47] Ibid., p. 4.94.

[48] Ibid., p. 4.96.

transforming thorium into fissile uranium 233.[49] One question about the LWBR concept which remains to be answered by a developmental demonstration still underway at the Shippingport (Pennsylvania) power plant is whether clever design can overcome the inherently lower breeding capability of reactors that use water as a coolant; but a major advantage to the design is that it might make it possible to convert existing light water reactors to breeders or near breeders—if the technology proves out at reasonable cost. Economic considerations are relatively complex, for several reasons. For instance, the installation of a thorium blanket within the reactor pressure vessel of an existing nuclear power plant would presumably reduce the size of the fuel core (as it has at Shippingport[50])—thus simultaneously cutting the electric generating capacity and raising generation costs per kilowatt hour.

Finally, the proliferation threat—the possibility of nuclear weapons spreading throughout the world as the result of promoting breeders—has prompted the design of breeders that are "proliferation resistant" (see chapter 14). More work will probably be done on these within the near future. However, one large experimental reactor that has operated in the United States, the molten salt breeder reactor (MSBR), would reduce the exposure of fissile material in outside commerce by using a liquid fuel that is reprocessed continuously. (The MSBR is generally associated with the thorium cycle.) A recent proposal is being studied—the so-called Civex system—to adapt the in-plant reprocessing idea by maintaining a constant high level of deadly radioactivity in the reactor system and so making diversion even more difficult. However, one must note that both the commercial feasibility and the antiproliferation potential of such systems remain to be demonstrated.

Fusion power. The ultimate nuclear technology now envisaged is nuclear fusion. Without many of the safety problems of fission— although it has some of its own—fusion also promises a virtually unlimited supply of fuel from elements which are (relatively) common in the oceans of the world. Typical fusion fuels are deuterium and tritium, both isotopes of hydrogen. Deuterium oxide, or heavy water, is found naturally in water and is indeed routinely extracted for use in natural uranium reactors in Canada and India (see the CANDU

[49] Ibid., pp. 3.71–3.73.
[50] *Light Water Breeder Reactor (LWBR),* a descriptive booklet published by the Department of Energy's Division of Naval Reactors (which is conducting the demonstration at Shippingport), indicates that use of the LWBR core cut electrical power output from 100 MWe to about 60.

reactor, above). Lithium is also used as a fuel in some designs: Total reserves of lithium are not accurately known,[51] but easily accessible surface sources presently identified represent thousands of years of supply, even if fusion plants were to supply all U.S. energy needs. Tritium is not naturally available as a practical resource. However, reactors can be designed so that the neutrons from the reaction will breed enough tritium to supply all future fuel needs.

Fusion is the opposite of fission; the former involves bringing smaller nuclei together to form larger ones instead of splitting large nuclei into fragments. Just as for atoms in chemistry, combining nuclei may either yield energy or require it, depending on the individual characteristics of the nuclei involved. In fact, the energy in a fusion reaction is derived from binding the nuclei of certain light atoms together in a manner quite analogous to binding the carbon in coal with atmospheric oxygen to produce power in coal-fired power plants. Since the nuclei are positively charged, however, they tend to repel each other; and it is necessary to accelerate them to high velocities to accomplish the binding. Therefore, very high temperatures—of the order of hundreds of millions of degrees—are required. Because such high temperatures must be maintained, ordinary enclosures cannot be used for the process. Some proposed systems for exploiting fusion power use magnetic fields, since charged particles like those in a "plasma" containing fusionable nuclei can be channeled by magnetic forces. Others utilize inertial confinement, in which temperatures are raised by imploding small pellets of fusionable nuclei with converging laser beams to induce the fusion reaction.

A recent review has characterized the particular magnetic confinement scheme using a doughnut-shaped vessel as the most promising current direction for research;[52] however, the possibility that laser fusion may be achievable in relatively small units may give that method some relative advantage in future commercial applications.

None of the fusion schemes has yet achieved the combination of confinement time, temperature, and plasma density necessary to deliver more energy than is put in. There are still problems in designing confinements for larger and larger energies in magnetic methods, as well as in dealing with impurities and methods for supplemental heating of the plasma.

[51] R. G. Mills, ed., *A Fusion Power Plant,* MATT-1050 (Princeton, N.J., Plasma Physics Laboratory, Princeton University, August 1974) p. 20.
[52] Atomic Industrial Forum, Committee on Fusion Report No. 1, *Fusion Power Development and Commercial Prospects* vol. 3, no. 6 (15 May 1976).

Assuming the scientific problems can be conquered, there are problems of an engineering nature that must be considered in designing a practical fusion reactor: these involve the development of large superconducting magnets and therefore very large low-temperature systems, and the maintenance of outsized vacuum chambers to contain the plasma. Materials problems arise, too, from the fact that the neutrons passing through the walls of the vacuum chamber are of very high energy and therefore may make the walls brittle. Also, as presently envisaged, power generation would not be continuous. Therefore, to maintain a continuous electric output to the utility system, a storage system (such as a liquid sodium thermal reservoir) might be required.

Since even scientific feasibility has not yet been demonstrated for fusion power, it is somewhat premature to discuss detailed reactor economics. Capital estimates are uncertain because existing studies of reactor design have been based on sparse data. Estimates of operation and maintenance costs are especially speculative: in particular, the possible necessity for frequent replacement of the vacuum chamber wall due to neutron embrittlement could pose serious economic problems. Nevertheless, designers of one prototype reactor estimated capital costs of $1,000 to $3,000 per kilowatt. For other designs, total generating cost was estimated between 40 and 60 mills per kilowatt hour;[53] however, if costs were to prove out this high, fusion would become economical only after uranium, coal, and other fuel materials became considerably more expensive.

Effects of Advanced Systems on Comparisons of Fossil and Nuclear-Based Systems

The new combustion methods, such as fluidized-bed combustion, are being designed with the goal of achieving the required cleanup job on coal at modest cost savings over conventional coal plants with scrubbers. Projected cost savings, of course, could be more significant if actual scrubber costs turn out to be larger than expected because of reliability problems with scrubber systems. Comparing a proposed 750-MW atmospheric[54] fluidized-bed system with a standard coal-fired plant of the same size, it is hoped that perhaps 1 or 2 mills/kWh could be

---

[53] Robert W. Conn and Gerald L. Kulcinski, "Fusion Reactor Design Studies," Letters section, *Science* vol. 193 (20 August 1976) pp. 630–633.
[54] Or its sister system, the pressurized FBC system.

saved over present costs, and that then the average price of coal-generated electricity would be about 18 mills (at a 10 percent capital charge rate), similar to that of a 750-MW LWR.[55] This optimism, of course, depends on the still-uncertain success of current R&D efforts.

Fuel modification processes also hold some promise. In principle, the solvent-refined coal process could be a relatively inexpensive method of solving the pollution problem; the effectiveness of the desulfurization, however, remains an important open question. If it does succeed, it might offer an attractive and cost-effective method of generating coal-fired electricity without the expense of scrubbing equipment.

For gasification, the cost can be relatively large—about 10 mills extra per kilowatt hour for the final electricity produced, as noted above; but the penalty might be reduced substantially by efficient combined cycle operation. Whatever the final cost, pollutants associated with health hazards may be significantly reduced over those involved in conventional coal combustion (see chapter 12).

Finally, the really unconventional methods of coal conversion present varying prospects. The magnetohydrodynamic option is theoretically capable of high efficiency, but many engineering problems—connected with the nature of coal and with new and difficult thermodynamic conditions at high temperatures—could cause serious difficulties. Fuel cells, when used together with coal gasification, would share any cost disadvantages of that conversion technology. However, in return, the fuel cell operation is quite clean. Fuel cells can also be used to help decentralize the electricity supply network and hence reduce transmission and some kinds of reliability costs (see the appendix to this chapter).

Therefore, new types of coal technology may meet existing standards for air pollution at less cost (fluidized bed combustion) or at least provide a means of paying more (low-Btu gasification) to get still cleaner air. The relative tradeoff with nuclear options will depend then on the attitude toward health and environmental costs.

As far as the nuclear options are concerned, it is difficult to see, within the next few decades, a convincing cost-reducing economic argument for a relatively rapid introduction of any of the types of breeder reactors mentioned, including the light water breeder reactor, the gas-cooled fast breeder, or the liquid metal fast breeder reactor. At foreseeable fuel prices over the next decades, total costs for initial versions

---

[55] Center for Energy Studies, "Future Electric Alternatives," pp. 4.81, 4.229, and 4.231.

of these systems should be somewhat higher than for LWRs, especially for use in the United States. The argument for the breeder depends essentially on its ability to increase the availability of nuclear fuel resources and thus hold down future fuel prices by converting U238 or thorium 232 to fissile materials. For this reason a U.S. breeder economy can of course be promoted as a necessary part of a world breeder economy, attuned to the more desperate energy situations of other industrialized nations and developing countries. However, medium-term policy decisions must consider that breeding is a fairly slow process,[56] and the first few generations of breeder reactors would only achieve a fraction of the theoretically possible savings in uranium supply. Furthermore, there are cogent national and international security reasons against early introduction or perhaps even the development of breeder technologies (see chapter 14).

Some of the same considerations about present costs and future resources apply to the high temperature gas-cooled reactor, which, while not a self-sustaining breeder, does make possible the use of thorium reserves to generate power—thus extending the life of world uranium supplies. Among other converter reactors, the CANDU reactor competes on a global basis with the light water reactor (although government subsidies obscure the comparison) and is an established, viable technology. A major disadvantage of this technology for the United States is that costs may be high, partly because enrichment facilities are already established here and represent sunk costs to the U.S. economy.

It therefore appears that in the medium run—measured in decades— there is somewhat more scope for exerting downward pressure on the price of coal-generated electricity through the introduction of improved technology than there is for nuclear electricity. By some later time, in the twenty-first century, it would, however, not be unexpected that some types of breeder technologies would become cheaper than either the light water reactor or conventional coal plants—the exact comparison

---

[56] Perhaps the most meaningful statistic in regard to a specific breeder design's ability to extend fuel resources is its "doubling time." This is defined as the length of time required to accumulate a mass of additional fissile material equal to that with which the core started—in other words, the time needed to produce a fresh fuel loading for another reactor. [See Raymond I. Murray, *Nuclear Energy: An Introduction to the Concepts, Systems, and Applications of Nuclear Processes* (New York, Pergamon Press, 1975) p. 142.] Even advanced research by the U.S. Department of Energy only envisions fuel-doubling times of "less than 15 years," and early designs may be expected to take much longer to "breed" additional fuel. [See *Fission Energy Program of the U.S. Department of Energy FY 1979*, DOE/ET-0048(78) (June 1978) p. 71.]

probably being highly dependent on the long-term price of uranium and coal. By that time, furthermore, fusion power may have become an engineering reality and a strong contributor to energy supplies.

These considerations must of course be modified by the health and environmental aspects considered in chapters 12, 13, and 14. Furthermore, in interfuel comparisons, other electricity costs must be considered: transmission and distribution costs, reliability, and vulnerability to war and terrorist acts. These last problems are briefly reviewed in the appendix to this chapter.

Appendix: Other Electricity Cost Factors

Besides the technological factors and costs considered in chapter 9 and the health and environmental and social costs considered in later chapters, other costs must be considered for electrical systems: transmission and distribution, reliability, and the implicit costs of vulnerability to war and terrorism.

These costs, having to do with the quality of the product provided (electricity) and the cost of getting it from the generating plant to the customer, do not affect comparisons between types of generating plants. Therefore they are not relevant to comparisons between coal and nuclear power, or between nuclear power and biomass or solar central electric stations. Nevertheless, they can be relevant for comparisons between types of delivered energy, such as contrasting electricity with synthetic gas, or synthetic gas with home solar heating.

Transmission and Distribution Costs

Transmission and distribution costs must be added into the usual busbar costs (that is, costs at the generating plant) of electricity if one is to compare alternative systems of supplying energy end uses. The average cost of transmission and distribution is taken here—based on modified values from a standard reference[57]—as 14 mills per kilowatt hour averaged over all customers; for residential customers, the average cost is closer to 19 mills. To this should be added the cost related to the

[57] Martin Baughman and Drew J. Battaro, "Electric Power Transmission and Distribution Systems: Costs and Their Allocations" *IEEE Transactions on Power Apparatus and Systems* vol. PAS-95, no. 3 (June 1976) pp. 782–790.

average loss during transmission and distribution of a quantity of electrical energy equal to about 10 percent of the busbar generation total, that is, an approximate 10 percent surcharge to busbar costs.

Reliability

Although the American utility industry has a good record as far as reliability is concerned—a figure of 99.98 percent for meeting electric demand has been cited, translating into a loss of less than 2 hours per year per customer[58]—large blackouts can nevertheless inflict heavy social costs. In particular, there have been two severe blackouts, one affecting New York City and the other the entire Northeast, within the past decade or so, together with other less serious blackouts in Florida, the Midwest, and elsewhere.

Estimates have been made of the value of kilowatt hours lost during a blackout, to take into account not only the physical damage to such obviously sensitive products as frozen foods and to certain interrupted industrial processes, but also psychological impacts and loss of production and consumption functions: one such speculation was 60 cents for each kilowatt hour lost.[59] However, the presence of complex social costs (such as the failure of airport and hospital lighting—both of which have happened during recent episodes—plus the occurrence of widespread looting during the New York blackout) could make this kilowatt hour cost an underestimate for large losses occurring over an extended period of time. For example, if 50 million kilowatt hours were assumed lost in the most recent New York City blackout, the total cost of the blackout at, say, $1 per kilowatt hour would be assessed at $50 million. However, such an estimate might seem relatively modest for physical damages plus indirect effects on society.

Service Interruption from Terrorism or War

Large centralized systems are in principle vulnerable to attacks from hostile sources during wartime or as a result of terrorist or guerrilla

---

[58] Michael L. Telson, "The Economics of Alternative Levels of Reliability for Electric Power Generation Systems," *The Bell Journal of Economics* vol. 6, no. 2 (Autumn 1975) p. 691.

[59] Ibid., pp. 629–697.

activity. However, studies of the vulnerability of the American electrical grid to possible nuclear attack show a surprising resiliency. One study predicted that utilities could still serve 90 percent of the electrical load —the load itself would of course be reduced by the effects of the attack—during a period of 15 days after the attack; subsequently, utilities could indeed be expected to improve on that percentage.[60]

A special problem, however, comes from an "electromagnetic pulse" (EMP) emitted during the hypothetical wartime nuclear attack. This pulse might bypass standard lightning avoidance systems, causing trouble in transmission and distribution systems. In particular, it could cause difficulties with the computer circuits that control electrical generation and distribution.

[60] U.S. Department of the Interior, Defense Electric Power Administration, *Vulnerability of Electric Power Systems to Nuclear Weapons* (Washington, D.C., GPO, 1964) p. 5.

10 Central-Station Electricity from Renewable Sources

The modern technologies currently being considered for some "renewable" energy sources (including direct and indirect solar energy, as well as tidal and geothermal sources) are still mostly in exploratory stages. Some of the renewables represent old technologies that are being revived in newer and larger scale contexts. Others are technologically established but not yet proven out commercially. Consequently, cost estimates for many of them rely heavily on theoretical studies prepared by proponents, and tend to be optimistic.

In a way, the uncertainties of project costs for these technologies are similar to those for the advanced coal and nuclear technologies discussed in chapter 9. However, cost estimates for some renewables are very speculative indeed. Despite this, a study performed by a University of Texas group for this report has estimated the costs of individual subsystems, providing an independent view on the possibilities for solar thermal, solar photovoltaic, wind, and geothermal energy.[1] The relative validity of the cost estimates will be discussed further below and especially in the Comparisons section. As in chapter 9, the power plants may be assumed to be constructed as of 1985; dollar amounts, however, are given in 1975 dollars and (deflated) capital charge rates of 10 percent and 15 percent are considered.

The emphasis in this chapter is on power plants to supply energy for standard networks of electrical grids and on large central generating stations (since many technologies experience economies of scale). Uses of smaller electrical generating units for decentralized applications will be discussed in chapter 11.

---

[1] Center for Energy Studies, The University of Texas, "Future Central Station Electric Power Generating Alternatives," prepared for Resources for the Future (Austin, Texas, The University of Texas, 1978).

Direct Solar

A relatively conventional way of using solar energy to produce electricity is to collect and concentrate the heat of the sun by using lenses or mirrors and then generate electricity in the usual way through a steam turbine. High temperatures from a concentrated source allow standard proven power plant turbines to be used, and their relatively high efficiency minimizes the amount of collector surface needed for a given power output.[2]

Mirror collectors vary from fixed systems to parabolic troughs that rotate from east to west during the day and track the sun's movement. Other systems rely on lenses instead of mirrors. The most prominent current solar electric project is the so-called "power tower," which uses banks of ground-level mirrors that track the sun individually and focus the rays onto an absorber atop a tall central tower.

The key problem with almost all kinds of solar energy, of course, is loss of power at night and its reduction during periods of cloudy weather. For that reason, the choice is either to feed the intermittent power from the sun into a more complex utility grid that contains other sources, or to utilize storage systems. For the current power tower project, a system of storing the sun's heat in melted salt at higher temperatures and in oil at lower temperatures has been suggested. With such a storage system, fairly long periods of continuous power might be obtained.

In one sense, the resource base for such projects is no problem. There is no doubt that the amount of direct solar energy available is large. Indeed, the amount of energy received on each unit of the surface directly facing the sun would be about 1.4 gigawatt (GW) for every square kilometer if there were no atmosphere. The atmosphere absorbs, reflects, or otherwise renders unavailable a good percentage of this, although the differences in energy received based on latitude alone are not as great as one might expect if the collector is tilted at a suitable angle.[3] Cloud cover is of course a problem, and continually cloudy areas are not suitable for most common types of collecting systems.

---

[2] However, standard concentrators do have the disadvantage—compared with ordinary flat plate (greenhouse-type) collectors—that they generally collect only the direct beam radiation from the sun and the diffuse solar radiation that provides significant amounts of energy on cloudy days is not collected.

[3] H. J. Killian, G. L. Dugger, and J. Grey, eds., *Solar Energy for Earth,* an *AIAA Assessment* (New York, American Institute of Aeronautics and Astronautics, 1975).

The cost of such a solar thermal system depends on the average amount of available sunlight, as well as the cost of the collector surfaces. Even at what seems right now to be a fairly optimistic estimate for power tower collector costs—$100 per square meter—a 150-MWe plant would cost approximately $280 million. Such a cost turns out to be high in terms of kilowatt hours delivered: even in a favorable (90 percent daytime sunlight) region of Texas, the cost of its electricity is estimated to be 60 mills/kWh at a capital charge rate of 10 percent,[4] or 90 mills/kWh at a 15 percent rate.

A more elegant way of generating electricity from the sun is the photovoltaic method. Photons—or light rays—can deliver enough energy to detach electrons from atoms when they are absorbed. By using "one-way" materials such as semiconductors, these disassociated electrons can be channeled in one direction and utilized as an electric current.

Photovoltaic systems have been used for decades in space flight applications. Since their engineering is rather uncomplicated, there are hopes that they may be especially useful for low maintenance applications on earth.[5]

Solar cells can be made from a variety of materials. One common type is made of crystals of silicon, which have moderately high efficiencies—up to 15 percent—and fairly good long-term outlook for stability.[6] Gallium arsenide cells are relatively more expensive, but are good absorbers and may be able to attain high efficiencies—20 percent or more. Other materials and indeed other possibilities exist, such as using simpler cells made from glassy rather than crystalline material.

Photovoltaics also have some special disadvantages, however. It is difficult to design photovoltaic cells that will absorb all the different wavelengths radiated by the sun: 25 percent of available energy may turn out to be close to a practical maximum, unless special multiple-collector systems are used. And the usual problems with direct current systems arise, exacerbated by the fluctuating nature of the output.[7]

---

[4] William Ramsay, "Electricity from New Technologies," draft prepared for the National Energy Strategies Project (Washington, D.C., Resources for the Future, 27 June 1978) p. 16-17. Available from RFF's Center for Energy Policy Research.

[5] Elizabeth Cecelski, Joy Dunkerley, and William Ramsay, *Household Energy and the Poor in the Third World*, RFF Research Paper R-15 (Washington, D.C., Resources for the Future, 1978) section III.

[6] Center for Energy Studies, "Future Electric Alternatives," p. 4.299.

[7] However, the direct current could conceivably be used to operate a direct current pump in conjunction with a pumped storage system or other type of storage facility. The energy extracted from the storage systems could actuate an alternating current generator.

The cost for large photovoltaic systems has not yet been established. However, a detailed but still speculative calculation of possible future costs for power plants was carried out for arbitrary but plausible future prices of cells: for future cell costs of $1.50 per (peak) watt and 50 cents per peak watt, capital costs of about $3,000 and $1,800 per kilowatt, respectively, were estimated.[8] For a 10 MWe plant, the regionally adjusted unit costs are fairly expensive, even for the lower cell prices quoted. The lowest rate calculated for a region in Texas with a favorable capacity factor ranges from about 70 to 100 mills/kWh, depending on whether a 10 or 15 percent capital charge is chosen.[9]

Because of the simple engineering of the photovoltaic scheme, the question arises as to whether this technology could become economical if photovoltaic cell costs fell far enough. Indeed, the goals of promoters of photovoltaic power are apparently to reduce the total costs of the array—that is, the photovoltaic cells and necessary framework—to fit a figure of 50 cents per peak watt. Given differences in assumed cell efficiencies, this goal could correspond to as low as 25 cents per peak watt for the cells themselves in the present calculation. There is no means of knowing whether such a goal is achievable or not. But even achieving this goal would reduce the costs shown here by only 15 percent. It seems difficult to make major reductions in the costs of the structural supports and framework assumed here ($50 per square meter, or about $5 per square foot) even by using very inexpensive structural materials. The basic dilemma of using diffuse sources is clear: to make them economical, very large collector areas require very cheap materials for structural purposes as well as for active elements such as collector cells. The same would not necessarily be true, of course, for small-scale photovoltaic installations placed on existing structures (see chapter 11).

Satellite Solar

The best-established use of photovoltaic cells is in outer space flights where solar fluxes are high. The solar resource base in outer space is considerably larger than on earth: net solar radiation would be relatively high, and shadowing by the earth of an orbiting satellite (see below) would result in a loss of probably only 1 percent of the total

---

[8] See Ramsay, "Electricity from New Technologies," chap. 4.

[9] Ibid., p. 16-22; the average efficiency, taking into account the presence of some dust and the usual type of reliability factors, is taken as 12½ percent.

solar energy available over the year.[10] Photovoltaic cells (or even solar thermal engines) could thus be operated efficiently outside the earth's atmosphere, and in theory the power generated could be transferred back to earth for use in electric power systems.

One scheme that has been suggested for such a conversion of energy is to put a 24,000-ton satellite into a geosynchronous orbit 22,300 miles above the earth: the symmetrically arranged solar cell arrays on the satellite would convert sunlight to electricity which in turn would be fed to a microwave generator for transmission to the earth. The microwave transmissions would be collected by a large receiving antenna system covering over 30 square miles. After conversion of the microwave energy to ordinary alternating or direct current, the net output from one such satellite would be expected to be 5 GW.[11] Instead of photovoltaics, solar thermal engines with large parabolic mirrors could be used to concentrate sunlight in a "solar cavity" and heat helium gas. This gas could then operate a gas turbine, generating electricity, which in turn would generate microwaves for transmission to earth.

For either system, one of the biggest problems is the expense and technical uncertainties associated with delivering and maintaining the station outside the earth's atmosphere.

Capital costs of approximately $1,700 per kilowatt for photovoltaics and $1,300 per kilowatt for thermal electric plants have been estimated in theoretical studies[12]—in both cases for large (5 or 10 GW) plants. The programs to develop better cells, heavy lift rockets, and other equipment would also be expensive, at least in absolute terms: costs from $40 billion to $60 billion have been estimated.[13] Only if hundreds of satellites took advantage of this research and development could the total attribution of R&D costs to each be reduced to a reasonable range of mills per kilowatt hour. Proponents of photovoltaic systems have estimated unit costs of electricity of 20–35 mills/kWh (10 or 15 percent capital charge rates), or 15 to 23 mills/kWh for the thermal electric systems; but the extremely speculative nature of such estimates must be emphasized.[14]

---

[10] Peter E. Glaser, "Solar Power from Satellites," *Physics Today* vol. 30, no. 2 (February 1977) p. 34.

[11] Ibid., p. 32.

[12] See D. L. Gregory and G. R. Woodcock, "Derivation of a Total Satellite Energy System," presented at AISS/AAS Solar Energy for Earth Conference, AIAA paper 75-640 (New York, American Institute of Aeronautics and Astronautics, 1975), and Glaser, "Solar Power from Satellites," p. 16-34.

[13] Glaser, "Solar Power from Satellites," p. 16-34.

[14] Ibid.

Wind Energy

With wind energy, one is not dealing with exotic new techniques. Wind-mills have been used for centuries for pumping water and other pur-poses, and within the past century they have been widely used in rural areas to generate electricity. Small-scale wind generators, despite their possibilities for certain end uses (see chapter 11) tend to be a fairly ex-pensive source of electricity for standard grids. With modern improve-ments in technology and corresponding efficiencies of scale, there is some prospect that they could become suitable for large-scale electricity gen-eration. However, large wind-powered generators, with blades extending many tens of meters in length, have yet to be proved out in test operations. Indeed, some recent test systems have experienced materials failures in operation (see "A Note on Problems with New Technology").

As with all methods relying on intermittent sources of energy, flat-tening the electrical output curve can pose a problem.[15] If wind power is used to supplement other sources of electrical power, a more even supply could be obtained through synchronous generators. Alternatively, storage systems could be used; 10-hour storage systems involving pumped hydro—the storing of water behind an impoundment for later hydroelectric generation—have been proposed.

Potential wind resources are large. The total amount of kinetic en-ergy generated by the sun in atmospheric pressure systems amounts to the equivalent of perhaps 15,000 GW over the contiguous United States, compared with existing electric generation in the range of 500 GW.[16] A recent, perhaps optimistic study concludes that the amount of energy that could actually be extracted from wind by erecting some 54,000 generators would be 1 trillion kilowatt hours of electricity annually.[17] However, proper estimates of the wind power resource base would re-quire large amounts of detailed geographic and climatic data.

The capital costs for a modern wind energy generator have been variously estimated from as low as $250 to as high as $1,400 per kilo-

[15] This problem is compounded in wind generators, because the generators oper-ate at different efficiencies with different wind velocities. Incidentally, some com-promises have to be made in design between optimization for average wind velocities and for higher and lower velocities within the annual range.

[16] See Bent Sørensen, "Dependability of Wind Energy Generators with Short-Term Energy Storage," *Science* vol. 194, no. 4268 (26 November 1976) pp. 935–937, and "Wind Energy," *Bulletin of the Atomic Scientists* vol. 32, no. 7 (Septem-ber 1976) pp. 38–45.

[17] Electric Power Research Institute, "Unconventional Energy Resources," paper prepared for The Conservation Commission, World Energy Conference (Palo Alto, Calif., EPRI, 1977) p. 43.

A NOTE ON PROBLEMS WITH NEW TECHNOLOGY—
THE CASE OF LARGE-SCALE WIND GENERATION

While technical problems arise with any technology, the sometimes small but important engineering difficulties typically associated with new technologies must be taken into account in assessing future costs. Some examples from recent experimentation with wind illustrate this point:

Mod O, the first large wind machine built in the United States, developed problems in 1976 at the National Aeronautics and Space Administration Plum Brook field station. The 100-kW machine experienced severe oscillations and unexpected impulse loads on the propeller, limiting the total operational time to 57 hours during the first eight months of operation.[18]

The 200-kW machine built by the Lockheed Corporation for NASA and the U.S. Department of Energy at Clayton, New Mexico, revealed three 1- to 2-inch cracks on the leading edge of the 125-foot diameter blades after 1,000 hours of operation.[19] Over-machining of the blades was the apparent cause, and replacements have been installed.

A relatively small (15 kWe) installation by the New England Telephone Company on Block Island has experienced severe difficulties. There was a failure in the mechanism which shifts the blades to protect them from high gusting winds, and the blades blew off. Subsequent to repairs for this incident, a burned-out bearing required the ordering of a new housing. Upon installation of the housing, it was discovered that the shaft had been bent and wires damaged during a blizzard.[20]

These events, one must hasten to add, are not necessarily to be taken as a discouraging comment on the future possibilities of wind energy generation. In particular, smaller scale wind machines, although perhaps not well suited to central station electricity generation, may be useful in other contexts (see chapter 11) and have been adequately proved out in practical operation. The problems illustrated here could occur with any technology that is new or with the extension of proven technologies to new scales of operation or new uses.

---

[18] "Wind Energy, Large and Small Systems Competing," *Science* vol. 197 (2 September 1977) p. 971.

[19] "NASA Discovers Cracks in Clayton Mill," *Solar Energy Intelligence Report* vol. 4, no. 27 (3 July 1976) p. 198.

[20] "Block Island Windmill May be Scrapped, Out of Order Since October 1977," *Solar Energy Intelligence Report* vol. 4, no. 6 (17 April 1978) p. 113.

watt.[21] However, a study done for this project[22] predicts within the next decade a capital cost of $930 per kilowatt on the basis of independent estimates of subsystem costs, and that figure has been used to project total costs. Capacity factors will depend on the average wind speed and plant design,[23] and one can estimate costs for wind speeds of 12, 15, and 18 miles per hour and designs appropriate to them.[24] Assuming an operations and maintenance cost of 3 mills, the cost is 29 or 40 mills/kWh for winds of 12 miles per hour, depending on the choice of a 10 or 15 percent capital charge, 23 or 32 mills/kWh for 15 miles per hour; and 21 or 30 mills/kWh for 18 miles per hour. According to these estimates, wind generation could be economic in some locations if reliability problems can be solved for systems now being tested.

Waves

Ocean waves are generated by the wind and may therefore be considered still another aspect of solar energy which might be tapped. Various devices have been proposed for extracting this energy: (1) using the vertical rise and fall of successive waves to run a turbine; (2) using movable vanes to transfer energy in the rolling motion of waves to turbines; and (3) concentrating waves in converging channels to form a kind of hydroelectric head of water, as in a dam. Wave-activated turbine generators have been used successfully to generate very small amounts of energy for more than ten years, particularly in Japan. Research is continuing on other concepts in Japan and in the United Kingdom.

The total amount of energy available is difficult to estimate, but one study put the potential capacity of a wave device in the waters near the United Kingdom at roughly 50 MWe for each linear mile of wave conversion device.[25] This wave power potential varies with the weather, although some locations have fairly constant waves—or at least wave

[21] David R. Inglis, "The Potential Must be Stressed to Get the Bureaucracy Moving," *Bulletin of the Atomic Scientists* vol. 32, no. 3 (March 1976) p. 60; Sørensen, "Wind Energy," pp. 38–45; and Center for Energy Studies, "Future Electric Alternatives," pp. 4.317–4.345.

[22] Center for Energy Studies, "Future Electric Alternatives," p. 4.336.

[23] It is true that in some cases site deficiencies can be compensated for by increasing the height of the windmill structure tower.

[24] Center for Energy Studies, "Future Electric Alternatives," p. 4.338.

[25] "R&D Programme for Wave Power," *Atom* (U.K.) vol. 236 (June 1976) pp. 174–178.

action that happens to vary seasonally with projected changes on electric loads.

The economics of ocean wave energy is not yet established. Transmission is an obvious problem area. However, capital costs for several projects have been estimated at from $1,000 to $2,000 or even less. Proponents of one floating buoy system in Japan have estimated production of electricity at a cost of 20 mills/kWh;[26] Norwegian estimates of 13 to 30 mills/kWh have also been noted.[27] However, a recent English study reportedly estimated costs at 400 mills/kWh![28] These estimates have not been reviewed in detail here, and their validity is not clear.

Ocean Thermal Energy Conversion (OTEC)

Energy can also be extracted from the temperature differences maintained between different layers of sea water as a result of the absorption of solar heat. In engineering terms, the warm surface water would be used as a heat source, while the cooler water underneath would be used like the cooling water for a condensing system in a conventional power plant. However, such a plant's turbines would be driven either by a low-pressure water vapor obtained by evaporating ("flashing") the warm sea water in a vacuum, or by a substance with a low boiling point such as the freon used in refrigerators—which would be heated and vaporized by contact with the warm sea water in heat exchangers.

Work on such systems is still experimental. Since the temperature differences are small, most components must be relatively large to generate conventional amounts of electricity; but the operation of large cold water intake pipes in an oceanic environment has not yet been tested. Quite large heat exchangers would also be required. Furthermore, facilities might be subject to corrosion, scaling, and fouling by sea-water organisms.

Although the ocean temperature layers are remarkably constant sources of stored solar energy, it might be a problem to obtain reliable underwater transmission of large amounts of power for long distances without incurring unacceptable power dissipation through heat losses.

[26] See Ramsay, "Electricity from New Technologies," p. 16-53.
[27] E. Mehlum and J. Stamnes, "Bølgekraftverk basert på fokusering av havdønninger" (Oslo, Norway, Sentralinstitutt for Industriell Forskning, 3 April 1978) quoted by Amory Lovins in a private communication.
[28] *Energy Daily* vol. 7 (4 January 1979) p. 4.

The amount of total energy stored has been estimated to be very large, in amounts equivalent to hundreds of thousands of gigawatts of power contained within a band of 10 degrees latitude on either side of the equator.[29] In practical terms, the amounts which might be recovered may depend not only on feasible locations for power plants, but also on the extent of OTEC-produced temperature changes in the surface waters which would be considered environmentally permissible. Nevertheless, one estimate for the Gulf Stream predicted a potential U.S. capacity of 200 gigawatts from that source alone, assuming certain environmental constraints were satisfied.[30]

Estimates of capital costs for OTEC systems vary widely;[31] some put costs between $1,500 and $2,000 per kilowatt capacity. As to unit costs, one estimate for OTEC (1990 operation) costs—at unspecified capital charge rates—ranges between 28 and 42 mills per kilowatt hour.[32] It can hardly be overstressed, however, that such estimates pertain to subsystems that often have little or no existing operating experience and to systems that are still in the experimental stages.

Small-Scale Hydroelectric Power

Hydroelectric power is a well-established technology, and in fact small hydroelectric installations have been regularly used in the United States for years. In small hydroelectric plants, as with large ones, water is dammed to make an impoundment and intake structures are built so that a flow of water can be run through a turbine generator. Although standard types of hydroelectric turbines used in large installations can be used for smaller dams, experience in France has suggested that for low heads axial-flow propellor ("bulb") turbines can improve performance.[33]

If water supplies are regular enough, small hydropower facilities can be run for base loads—that is, for continuous generation of electricity— and water levels in the impoundment can be kept fairly constant. If stream flow is intermittent, or if the power is used for meeting peak elec-

[29] Center for Energy Studies, "Future Electric Alternatives," p. 4.151.
[30] Ibid., p. 4.152.
[31] Ibid., p. 4.157.
[32] W. H. Avery, letter to *Science* on "Solar Energy: The Prospects for OTEC," *Science* vol. 198, no. 4321 (9 December 1977) pp. 990, 992.
[33] Ramsay, "Electricity from New Technologies," p. 16–77. "Head" is the height of the water held by the dam.

tric loads, the resulting drawdown of water could produce unfavorable environmental impacts. This problem arises especially if units are built at existing small dams but must meet new water demands without inflicting greater reservoir drawdown. Such adaptations for local circumstances may mean that capacity factors (which could be quite high for hydropower in general) might be restricted to an average of say, 30 percent for such modifications at existing dams.

One study estimates that developable capacity at existing small dams —roughly those that would produce 5 MW or less in capacity—is about 27 GW.[34] Such potential is spread fairly evenly throughout the humid regions of the United States. This does not count an additional 28 GW that could possibly be utilized by rehabilitating or expanding existing hydropower dams or installing hydropower at existing non-hydropower dams of larger size.

The costs of small-scale hydrosystems will vary with site, but the range of $700 to $1,200 installed costs per kilowatt seems plausible.[35] Costs could possibly be reduced if turbines and dam components were standardized and mass produced. One U.S. Department of Energy estimate for the unit cost of electricity for a typical small-scale hydroelectric plant—but without impoundment costs—is 20 mills/kWh.[36] On the basis of these predictions, it seems probable that "mini-hydro" can be operated economically at some locations, especially if existing impoundment structures can be utilized.

Biomass Technology

The burning of biomass to generate electricity represents a principle that is far from new. Not only is the combustion of wood or organic wastes as boiler fuel a reasonably straightforward matter, but existing coal-fired facilities can often be used for burning wood or wastes by merely adding a new furnace door. Furthermore, storage is not normally a major problem for biomass, the fuel being similar to coal in many respects when compacted. However, efficiencies of boiler systems for biomass fuel may be somewhat lower than those for coal.

[34] U.S. Army Corps of Engineers, Institute for Water Resources, "Estimate of National Hydroelectric Power Potential at Existing Dams" (Alexandria, Va., 20 July 1977, rev. 2).

[35] Personal communication from Ron Corso, Federal Energy Regulatory Commission (1978).

[36] *Business Week* (20 March 1978) p. 146-L.

The unique aspect of burning biomass for electricity, in the context of modern energy needs, is in collection and preparation. These processes are somewhat different in nature for the major biomass categories of interest: (1) municipal refuse, (2) wood, and (3) crops and crop residues.

With municipal refuse, one is dealing with something that is normally collected already. The problem, then, is not with collection, but with preparation, since the burnable materials are varied and are mixed with nonburnable substances. Demonstration plants use shredders to reduce the size of large particles, sorters to recover glass and metals, and compressed air devices to separate heavy from light materials.

Whole-tree chippers are used to process wood for fuel. These can convert all parts of the tree quickly to materials suitable for burning. Residues of lumber mills can also be used for boiler fuel. For crops and crop residues, special harvesting equipment that blows crop material into a hydraulic compressor can compact the organic matter and make it more economical for transport.

As already mentioned in chapter 8, this resource base is large—at some price. For municipal wastes, the dry weight in tons of organic wastes for the year 1980 has been estimated at well over 200 million tons[37] or, at 10 million Btu per ton, about 2 quads. Possible sources of wood biomass include the 400 million acres of forest land in the United States not now being commercially utilized.

Other noncommercial uses of forest land must of course be considered in making energy resource assessments. Nevertheless such lands could provide, with proper management, perhaps 7 quads of energy per year (see chapter 8). Furthermore, even wooded land that is now being utilized could undoubtedly supply more energy in terms of presently unused waste organic matter. For field crops, the present wastes from agriculture have been estimated at 400 million tons per year, or potentially about 4 quads.[38]

If special crops were to be grown for energy purposes, of course, the yields per acre would be much larger. The question then narrows down to the relative availability of land and the economics of alternative uses. Apart from land use economics, however, production of between 10 to 20 tons of biomass per acre per year (or perhaps 100 million to 200

[37] L. L. Anderson, *Energy Potential from Organic Wastes: A Review of the Quantities and Sources,* U.S. Bureau of Mines Information Circular 8549 (Washington, D.C., GPO, 1972).
[38] Ibid.

million Btu per acre per year) would not be technically impossible.[39] This amounts to a requirement of about 5 million to 10 million acres per yearly quad of energy from special crops.

Power plants which operated on compacted wood would not be very different from coal plants, and their economics could be reasonable. We have estimated $500 per kilowatt for capital charges.[40] Operating costs could be somewhat higher than for coal, but for assumed fuel costs of from $1 to $3 per million Btu, costs of electricity have been estimated at from 23 to 43 mills/kWh—for a 10 percent capital charge rate— and from 32 to 52 mills/kWh for 15 percent. These costs would probably also be typical for energy crops.[41] The key question is the price of the fuel, which depends heavily on location and transportation. While the power plant itself would feature economies of scale, except for the compacting equipment, it would be cheaper to process the fuel on a decentralized basis to lessen transport costs. Therefore, the usefulness of biomass from forest and field crops and crop wastes may depend on the development of economical small-scale fuel preparation facilities or combined fuel preparation and electricity generating stations.

The situation is somewhat different for municipal refuse, as is discussed in chapter 8. Economic assessments depend in large part on whether or not one can take credit for the landfill costs that are avoided, and if the cost of separating suitable organic wastes from other material proves reasonable after shakedown of systems presently being tested. Municipal waste could contribute a not insignificant amount of electricity at reasonable cost.

Tidal Power

Tidal power, the harnessing of gravitational forces exerted by the sun and the moon on the oceans, can be utilized by constructing systems of dams and sluice gates across suitable ocean bays and estuaries. The incoming tide fills up the enclosed basin, at the same time passing through hydraulic turbine generators. After the high tide flows, the gates and turbines are shut down; then, as the tide recedes, the head of water is allowed to pass back through the hydraulic turbines. One

---

[39] John A. Alrich and R. E. Inman, "Energy from Agriculture," in *Clean Fuel* symposium papers of the Institute of Gas Technology, Orlando, Florida, January 1976 (Chicago, Ill., Institute of Gas Technology, 1976) pp. 287–310.
[40] Ramsay, "Electricity from New Technologies," p. 16-68.
[41] Ibid.

existing example of a tidal power plant, at Rance in northwestern France, consists of a 2,500-foot dike impounding 5,400 acres of sea water. "Bulb" turbines are used to generate electricity in both directions.

The periodic nature of the tidal flow can cause variations in electric output. On the other hand, the impoundments could be used to store energy from other generating facilities at off-peak hours as a kind of pumped hydroelectric facility.

One estimate puts the total yearly potential output of practical U.S. tidal power sites at 350 billion kWh, corresponding to an approximate peak capacity of 120 GW.[42] Apparently, however, only a few potential large-scale U.S. (and Canadian) tidal power sites have been considered: Cook Inlet, Alaska, Puget Sound, Washington, and Passamaquoddy Bay and the Bay of Fundy on the Maine coast.

An estimate for the Rance facility gives a cost of approximately $740 per peak kilowatt at a 32 percent capacity factor.[43] Estimates of Canadian studies for possible sites in the Bay of Fundy, however, yield a range of $900 to $1,500 per peak kilowatt. If other operation and maintenance costs are about 1 mill/kWh, and assuming all capacity factors are 32 percent, this gives a range of costs of from 27 to 55 mills for a 10 percent capital charge rate, and from 49 to 80 mills for 15 percent. These costs seem somewhat high, compared with established costs for more conventional generating systems, but both the capital costs and capacity factors will depend greatly on site-specific factors.

Geothermal Technology

The use of geothermal systems is characterized by a certain elegant simplicity. Nature provides free steam or hot water which can be used to power facilities similar to conventional power plants. Indeed, such a plant, operating on hot dry steam, was installed in Italy in the early 1900s and one operating commercial plant exists in California today.

The resource question for geothermal is complex. The total geothermal resource is very large. The source of the geothermal energy stored in water, steam, and dry rock is believed to be the continuing natural decay of long-lived radioactive matter and thus is virtually inexhaustible. However, particular sources may or may not be renewable,

---

[42] K. R. Vernon, "Hydro Energy," *Philosophical Transactions of The Royal Society of London,* Series A (London, 1974).

[43] Center for Energy Studies, "Future Electric Alternatives," pp. 4.166 to 4.180.

and the limits of current drilling technology necessarily restrict the available volume that can be tapped. Nevertheless, it has been estimated that more than 1 billion quads of energy are stored in the perhaps 25,000-foot-thick layer that can plausibly be regarded as available to present technology.[44]

The situation in present practice is quite different, however. Geothermal resources are useful right now only if located at relatively shallow depths and if either naturally occurring steam or hot water—preferably steam—can be brought to the surface. Such areas are fairly restricted: for example, the only known dry steam resource in the United States, outside of national parks, is the already partially developed Geysers field in California. Furthermore, the effective lifetime of such resources in a given area is largely unknown.

Three or four other forms of geothermal energy have been mentioned as potential energy sources. One possibility is "normal gradient" resources, which consist of the almost limitless supply of moderately warm waters that are widely available in many locations. Another source is the masses of hot dry rock that are believed to exist below the surface in much of the western United States. The key problem with this latter resource is of course extracting the heat, just as the key difficulty with normal gradient resources is that the heat is of such low quality. Actual liquid magma intrusions of very high temperature also exist in the United States, but the drilling problems for such exceedingly hot sources may be severe. Finally, an unusual sort of double-threat energy source exists: moderate-temperature waters at high pressure that are also saturated with natural gas. These "geopressured" sources could be attractive and now are being actively investigated.

Geothermal technology options vary and must be matched to resource characteristics. In principle, the dry steam (vapor-dominated) geothermal resources are the easiest to use. Nevertheless, the resource is not without problems: the steam is usually contaminated with potentially corrosive substances, and systems of separators and strainers must be used to clean the steam before it is used. Even so, turbines for geothermal steam will in general require metal surfaces that are more resistant than normal to attacks of corrosive materials. Despite these problems, costs of vapor-dominated geothermal generating plants are presumed to be competitive with other current methods of electrical

[44] D. F. White and D. L. Williams, eds., *Assessment of Geothermal Resources of the United States—1975*, U.S. Geological Survey Circular 726 (Washington, D.C., GPO, 1975).

generation. However, because of the apparent small number of sites where such resources can be tapped, interest is currently centered on liquid-dominated resources. These plants, which use a hot brine found underground under pressure, allow this liquid to flash (boil by reducing the pressure) at the surface. The resulting steam is either used directly or is passed through a heat exchanger to produce a cleaner steam for power generation.

The costs of liquid-dominated geothermal plants are not yet established, but an independent detailed estimate of costs has been done for this project.[45] For one type of "two-stage flashing" plant, capital costs for the plant itself range from about $500 to $600 per kilowatt, depending on the location and the temperature of the water (brine), which affects the size of the cooling system needed.

The other critical geothermal cost category involves the network of wells and pipes to gather steam. The calculation of these costs is complicated by the quality (or temperature) of the brine, as well as the depth of well required to tap the resource, plus possible needs to reinject the brine to satisfy environmental constraints (see chapter 13). In the usual power plant terms, these "fuel costs" would also constitute "capital costs" because they will depend on the capital charges chosen. For a 10 percent capital charge and a 5,000-foot well, these costs can run from 1 to 5 mills/kWh over a moderate range of brine temperatures. Operation and maintenance costs are also associated with both the generating plant itself and with the "fuel" supply system.

At any rate, taking all such costs into consideration, total costs of generation, for a 100-MWe plant at 10 percent capital charge, run from 15 to 30 mills/kWh depending on brine temperature, region, and well depth.[46] These figures are competitive with costs of conventional sources, but only in localities where brine is sufficiently available and inexpensive to reach and collect.

Comparisons

For reasons cited above, the potential economics of renewable energy sources are difficult to examine in the same terms as those for established central station generating technologies. Costs for those renewable systems which have been specifically analyzed in the study carried out

---

[45] Center for Energy Studies, "Future Electric Alternatives," pp. 4.262 and 4.263.
[46] Ibid., tab. 4.4-7.

for this project are used here primarily as a guide in comparing the systems with each other—and as a means of highlighting the cost sensitivities of factors which remain uncertain and/or highly variable.

The total amount of energy that would be available from respective renewable sources is likewise difficult to pin down, because the economic feasibility of varying qualities of resources in different geographical areas is still poorly understood. For that reason, we discuss the technologies successively in a geographical framework, in terms of (a) those that are ubiquitous, or nearly so—such as solar and biomass; (b) those that appear to occur at feasible resource levels at far fewer places—such as wind and geothermal; and (c) the other technologies that usually occur in special locations and could involve transmission problems, along with other difficulties.

Solar energy is affected by latitude and climate, but is reasonably available in many locations. However, large-scale direct solar sources of electricity seem unpromising for the United States within the next couple of decades, even assuming improvements in costs of thermal collectors of photovoltaic cells. Electricity costs for concentrating thermal collector systems will tend to remain high because of their complexity—60 mills/kWh or more was estimated in the text—while the low temperatures characteristic of flat plate collector systems mean low efficiency and therefore more costly hardware per kilowatt. Photovoltaic costs could fall significantly if cell technology greatly improves, yet—because of the diffuse nature of the source—structural costs for arrays may still remain large and costs near 70 mills/kWh can be expected. Thus, barring dramatic improvements in cell efficiencies, the use of photovoltaics might well be restricted to decentralized applications as opposed to central power stations.

Biomass is not universally available, but presumably could be tapped in many different regions. Its similarity to coal as a generating fuel (particularly in compacted form) means that for the power conversion steps itself costs ought to be reasonable. Collection, processing, and transportation costs require further technical experimentation and economic study. Nevertheless, some biomass schemes appear to offer attractive options on a cost basis. The use of municipal refuse seems to take care of two problems at once—assuming that ongoing tests of sorting plants work out. The practicality of using agricultural residues and forest products is more questionable, although there are indeed vast amounts of forest which are not being fully utilized at present. In general, by making some sort of compromise in designing plant size and location to take into account both transportation costs and economies of scale in plant size, significant contributions to electrical power in the United States might be realized from biomass conversion within the next few decades. Ultimately, however, the key decisions probably revolve around land use questions (see chapter 13).

Wind and geothermal systems may or may not be suited for widespread usage for electricity generation. This depends, for example, on technologies for utilizing low-speed winds and on making use of relatively low temperature geothermal fluids. However, at costs of from 21 to 28 mills/kWh (depending on wind speeds), it should be practical to use wind generators in some locations. Wind power could therefore make a useful contribution to central station electricity energy needs if the large systems now being tested work out. Problems of intermittent supply, however, could be as bad or worse than for direct solar— necessitating efficient storage systems or coordination with existing generating grids.

Predicted costs of 15 to 30 mills—depending on the "fuel costs"— for hot geothermal liquids appear attractive.[47] Furthermore, geothermal vapor-dominated resources will certainly be used by utilities where available, provided environmental constraints permit (see chapters 12 and 13). Testing is being carried out for other types of geothermal resources, and if all goes well, they could make significant contributions within appropriate geological areas.

For the last group of new energy options, power will generally be producible only in special locations. However, these proposed sources of power vary from relatively familiar and probably cost-effective schemes to very tenuous plans for extraterrestrial collection of energy.

Small-scale hydroelectric facilities should logically be added to the supply picture, as representing established technologies associated with rather reasonable economics. The main question might be the size of the resource available: that assessment may well hinge on esthetic and environmental considerations connected with new impoundments.

Tidal power can perhaps be viewed as a kind of unconventional hydroelectric source, which may be appropriate to local needs where suitable sites are available.

Satellite power systems, while appealing in the amounts and constancy of the solar power available, represent great expenditures of capital for a necessarily uncertain developmental program.

Possibilities for wave power and OTEC appear as yet to be rather speculative.

[47] Center for Energy Studies, "Future Electric Alternatives," pp. 4.274 to 4.277.

11 Solar Heating and Other Decentralized Energy Technologies

The history of energy conversion in the modern world has generally been one of increasing scale because larger facilities can usually produce less expensive energy for the consumer. But the rationale for this historical trend has been called into question in our times. One reason is that the economy-of-scale phenomenon has ignored some important areas of increasing concern, such as health and environmental impacts. While it can't be assumed that these impacts are disproportionately worse for a large plant than for a small plant, they are at the very least more publicly visible. Another reason to question the value of centralization concerns the economic calculation itself: centralized production of electricity at remote sites, which often characterizes large facilities, presupposes growing transmission networks. As a result, despite cost savings through higher voltage lines, the contribution of transmission and distribution costs to total electricity costs tends to become increasingly larger.[1]

Doubts about the overall desirability of centralization have become markedly more prominent in recent years as the hunt for new energy sources intensifies. Centralization can make eminent sense when one is dealing with oil or nuclear power, where scale economies in generation exist and the fuel can be transported easily over long distances at relatively small cost. However, where fuel transport costs are very high, or scale economies are weak or nonexistent, decentralization may be

[1] Some believe that large plants are themselves becoming less economic. Their key contention is that new large plants are experiencing pervasive reliability problems. The evidence for this, however, is necessarily based on somewhat limited experience and could be misleading. See Amory B. Lovins, "Soft Energy Technologies," in *Annual Review of Energy 1978* (Palo Alto, Calif., Annual Reviews, Inc., 1978) vol. 3, pp. 477–517, especially p. 485, for one such opinion.

more desirable (as mentioned in chapters 9 and 10). For example, if the direct rays of the sun are the fuel, the possible economic advantage of collecting and using that energy domestically for home heating, as opposed to collecting it for later distribution in a centralized electrical network, becomes a calculation of great interest for energy planning. Indeed, there has been a good deal of recent speculation about possible roles for small-scale and medium-scale energy sources—which are typified by direct solar energy, but also include other sources, such as wind, biomass, geothermal, and even some nonrenewable options.

Changes in the scale of energy supply-and-demand patterns could conceivably change society in fundamental ways through changes in employment, local control of social decisions, and other effects of technological choices.[2] This problem is complex and will be treated elsewhere.[3] Furthermore, small-scale energy systems may have significant health and environmental effects; some of these are discussed in chapters 12 and 13. In this chapter we will discuss the technical and cost features connected with the use of small-scale and medium-scale energy sources.

Passive Solar Heating

In energy discussions, concepts of supply, demand, and conservation cannot be divorced from one another. This blurring occurs particularly in many applications of solar energy. If a house is built so that most of its window area faces south, it can depend on gathering more solar energy for heating. Going one step further, the south windows can be made unusually large, or areas of the south walls can be painted black and covered with glass. Such a design will decrease the need for external energy, at least in the right circumstances. Whether such actions should be seen as increasing supply or reducing demand through energy conservation is unimportant; the key fact is that such passive solar gains in energy—for new housing at least—can sometimes be achieved at little or no cost.

Of course, since solar is an intermittent source, it is very desirable to store incoming energy for later use. Fairly large steps can be taken to

[2] Amory B. Lovins, *Soft Energy Paths: Toward a Durable Peace* (Cambridge, Mass., Ballinger for Friends of the Earth, 1978) chaps. 9 and 10.
[3] Elizabeth Cecelski and William Ramsay, "Scale, Energy and Society" (submitted to *Journal of Energy and Development*, 1979).

modify requirements for conventional energy if storage mechanisms are included during the original construction. Some such changes can be made inexpensively; and some promising ideas have been suggested that may turn out to be economic in many applications. For instance, attached greenhouses or a so-called Trombe wall design can passively collect and store solar heat and transmit it later into living spaces. Similarly, roof ponds can collect heat and hold it for later distribution into the house.

Many other possible means exist for making more use of ambient solar energy. Window shades can be designed to reduce glare and reflect sunlight onto ceiling panels that are designed both to prevent propagation of air temperatures greater than 23°C during daylight hours and to store excess heat for use at night. Perhaps the ultimate method for using solar energy passively is underground housing, which takes advantage of the smaller seasonal temperature differences below ground levels. A compromise with total undergrounding could be made by earth berming, that is, utilizing banks of soil for insulation. The building and operating costs of such totally or partially underground houses would reflect needs that differ from conventional dwellings—such as needs for dehumidification and structural changes. It is difficult to generalize about cost premiums or savings, but exact cost comparisons are probably less important than the willingness of homeowners to live in such dwellings.

The costs of passive solar measures are difficult to characterize. As indicated above, some may involve only an energy-conscious design for new dwellings at little or no extra cost. However, other passive ideas (for example, extra windows and shutters, and heat-retaining ceilings) could significantly increase housing costs. One recent study examined a set of passive designs, including greenhouses, Trombe walls or a direct-gain (extra window) scheme, that cost $3,300–$3,600; these designs produced units of additional heat at a cost of about $8 per million Btu.[4]

Active Solar Heating

From the passive measures described above it is only a relatively small conceptual step to actively collecting the sun's heat and applying it to

---

[4] Larry Sherwood, "Passive Solar Systems: The Economic Advantages" (unpublished document, New Mexico Solar Energy Association, Santa Fe, New Mexico, 1978).

heat water or air for space heating, for hot water heating, or even for air conditioning. However, some special characteristics of solar energy present problems for such purposes.

First, solar energy is diffuse compared with the concentrated energy stored in fossil fuels. This means that the physical system of collecting the energy is apt to be large and, other things being equal, expensive. Furthermore, solar energy is not received at equal rates over the earth's entire surface; it varies by latitude and weather conditions. It also, of course, varies by time of day and by season of the year. This means that the solar energy must be stored during sunny periods for later use, or that backup systems using fossil or other energy sources must be utilized. Under either option, extra costs must be added to the total system to have a dependable energy supply. In addition to being costly, energy storage alternatives tend to be bulky.

The collector is therefore the key part of the solar energy system. In principle, collectors for home solar heating could use concentrating lenses and mirrors, such as those discussed in chapter 10 for large-scale solar electricity generation. However, only relatively low temperatures are required for solar space heating, so nonconcentrating collectors are probably more cost effective in most applications. Flat plate collectors, which consist of pieces of glass that cover a system of tubing for heating either water or air, have been a popular design. The solar-heated water or air can be transferred to living spaces by a network of piping or ducts. If water is selected as the heat-carrying fluid, it can also be used directly for domestic hot water supplies. To supply air conditioning, the heat gathered from the sun can be used in the same way as the flame in a gas refrigerator.[5]

It is evident that these collector systems are made up of simple materials. But even such ordinary materials as glass and common metals may cost several dollars per square foot; and, because of the diffuseness of solar energy, it might require 300 square feet of collector surface to supply only 50 percent of the space heating for a typical residence as far south as Arkansas.[6] When the costs of fabrication, construction, and labor are added, it appears unlikely that standard collector costs could be reduced much by better engineering or industrial improvements. Indeed, current developmental efforts to reduce solar costs now center on ways to use cheaper materials, such as plastics, in collector design.

[5] In this case, however, it might be more economical to use concentrating collectors, which produce higher temperatures. See text below.

[6] *The Economics of Solar Home Heating,* Joint Committee Print, Joint Economic Committee, 95 Cong. 1 sess. (Washington, D.C., GPO, 13 March 1977) p. 44.

There are similar complexities in considering the storage problem. If collectors were large enough to supply peak heating needs in winter, when the sun is low and the days are short, their cost would be astronomical. Therefore, the only practical storage system for a completely solar-heated residence is one that stores energy in the summer when the sunlight is more intense, and delivers it in winter when heating loads are high. Such a system tends to be rather expensive for standard types of houses, even with some energy conserving features added.

Another option involves a hybrid solar system which requires backup from an alternative energy source, most commonly electricity or natural gas. This option has been the one most commonly adopted thus far for standard buildings. With such a backup system, a relatively cheap daily storage system can be utilized, instead of the disproportionately more expensive systems used for seasonal storage. Of course, the capital cost of a conventional home heating system must then be added into the total cost of the hybrid solar system.

Although the capital costs of solar heating are high, relative to conventional heating, they are not uniformly so for all applications. The cost problem is least bothersome for hot-water heating because hot-water-heating systems already have a built-in storage facility—the hot-water tank itself[7]—and demand for hot water remains relatively steady on a year-round basis. But for space heating the system is used only part of the year, with the equipment standing idle the rest of the time.[8] Furthermore, most energy is collected during that part of the year—the summer—when it is needed least. Although air conditioning matches solar heat in its supply-to-demand patterns, the development of effective air conditioners from solar energy presents problems of a different and perhaps more serious kind. Cooling systems have to be designed to run on the relatively low-temperature heat characteristics of simple solar collectors, or else, as noted above, more expensive, sophisticated collectors must be used to raise working temperatures to higher levels.

The costs of a solar heating system may depend to a critical extent on the cost of the collectors. Nevertheless, the costs of backup, pumps and controls, and storage are by no means negligible. In one analytical study, the total cost of a typical one-family residential system was estimated to be $9,600.[9] Of this total, collector costs were about 60 percent

---

[7] Usually an extra storage tank is also used, however.

[8] Some solar space heating systems also require a water-to-air heat exchanger, which is more expensive than the usual kind of water-to-water heat exchanger.

[9] Office of Technology Assessment, *Application of Solar Technology to Today's Energy Needs,* U.S. Congress (Washington, D.C., GPO, 1978) vol. II, p. 269.

and backup system costs about 20 percent, while the rest of the costs were fairly evenly divided among a thermal storage unit, pumps and controls, ducting, and piping. Therefore, efforts to lower costs of conventional solar systems must also deal with the difficulty of reducing the costs of these standard ancillary components. Another major study shows total costs to be about double the amount above.[10]

The two detailed cost estimates referred to are fairly high, and lower costs have been reported in various locations in the country. Therefore, the results of these studies are not taken as representative of costs in the near future. Rather, on the basis of a selection of total systems costs reported from several sources, without specification of subsystems details, a total range of $5,000 to $9,000 is estimated as typical for the cost of a solar space and water heating system over the next decades.[11] To facilitate comparisons, half of the capital, operation, and maintenance costs of a backup system is also assumed to be included in these estimates.[12] The solar heating system is assumed to supply 50 percent of the total space and water heating needs (taken here to be 90 million Btu per year) of an average new, detached dwelling in an average U.S. location.[13]

These assumed costs are adapted from costs of present systems, and could drop somewhat with future improvements. In particular, the results would be expected to be sensitive to any energy-conserving design features in a residence. Costs projections for using solar energy in houses that are energy efficient to begin with tend to be lower. Furthermore, cost comparisons for solar in regions with more sun, higher prices of competing energy, or lower energy needs could be more favorable than the rough average treated here. On the other hand, the systems

[10] MITRE Corporation, "Systems Descriptions and Engineering Costs for Solar-Related Technologies," in *Solar Heating and Cooling of Buildings,* MTR-7485 (McLean, Va., MITRE Corporation, April 1977 draft) vol. II, p. 75.

[11] See, for example, California Energy Resources Conservation and Development Commission, Solar Implementation Committee, *Solar Energy in California: Residential Thermal Applications* (Sacramento, Calif., draft report February 1978) tab. I-6; *Solar Engineering Magazine* vol. 1, no. 8 (October 1976); and Acorn Structures, Inc., "A Status Report on Solar Heating at Acorn," *Technical Bulletin* no. 3 (September 1975).

[12] This makes marginal costs of backup fossil energy equal to marginal costs of pure fossil systems. In this way, the cost of the backup unit (for example, gas) energy is the same as that of the same technology operated as an independent source. The average cost of a hybrid solar system will then in this formulation be the average of the solar and the gas costs. The cost differences between this and other solar–fossil cost allocation methods are negligible for the accuracies involved.

[13] See, for example, Joint Economic Committee, *The Economics of Solar Home Heating,* pp. 42–43, assuming 5,000 heating degree days, from map 1 on p. 43. This would correspond to average heating degree days for cities in Missouri (5,046), New York (4,871), or West Virginia (5,211). From table 3 on p. 44, the required collector area for the Missouri location would be 390 square feet.

Table 11-1. Costs of Typical Solar Hot-Water and Space Heating Systems

Capital costs	Capital charge rate (%)	Repair and maintenance rate (%)	Yearly solar heating costs	Solar energy produced (million Btu)	Cost per million Btu solar
$5,000 (low estimate)	10	1	$ 550	45	$12
	15	1	800	45	18
$9,000 (high estimate)	10	1	990	45	22
	15	1	1,440	45	32

Source: Derived from text.

costs reported, on which this estimated range is based, were weighted toward Sun Belt locations; they probably would not supply 50 percent of the average heating load in most U.S. dwellings. Furthermore, repair and maintenance costs could well be greater than assumed here.

Table 11-1 shows that the unit costs for the solar heat energy supplied by such systems would be between $12 and $22 per million Btu at a 10 percent capital charge rate, and between $18 and $32 per million Btu for a 15 percent rate.[14] As shown later in this chapter, these costs are high compared with a variety of alternatives.

Systems with backup are, nevertheless, not the most expensive solar options. Independent solar space heating systems—even under very optimistic assumptions about storage costs in the future—appear to be more expensive than solar with backup for an average location, and, of course, still higher in cost than alternative fossil energy systems.[15] It should be pointed out, however, that interesting experimentation with independent solar systems in the context of highly energy-conserving housing, containing also passive solar features, has been taking place;[16] the results of further tests on such schemes should be of interest for future energy strategies.

For hot water heating alone, the corresponding costs are considerably smaller. If a system supplying half of the hot water needs is assumed to cost about $1,300 in a new building,[17] costs for the 7.5 million Btu of

[14] Capital charge rates of less than 10 percent could be chosen, because loan costs to homeowners might be lower than utility capital costs. It is assumed here, however, that, for social accounting, opportunity costs of resources in either case should be equal, and that indeed the solar option would, in general, involve shifts of capital away from utilities.

[15] See Andrew McLennan and William Ramsay, "Decentralized Energy Systems," draft prepared for National Energy Strategies Project (Washington, D.C., Resources for the Future, 2 June 1978) app. 18-A. Available from RFF's Center for Energy Policy Research.

[16] Amory B. Lovins, Memorandum on Saskatchewan conservation house, 2 December 1978.

[17] California Energy Resources Conservation Commission, *Solar Energy in California: Residential,* app. I-A.

hot-water-heating energy supplied to a typical household would be about $8 per million Btu. While hot-water heating is usually a less-important source of energy demand, nevertheless such a cost figure could make this solar application of interest in some localities (see the appendix to this chapter).

Decentralized Photovoltaics

Photovoltaic cells, which convert light rays into electric current, were described in chapter 10 as a possible source of central station electricity. These cells could also be used in individual home installations to provide a direct domestic source of electricity. Indeed, because arrays of PV cells may show little or no scale economies, small- or medium-scale installations could well be a more intelligent use of this technology. Although costs are still high, the outlook for future cost reductions as a result of either scientific or engineering progress is fairly favorable (see chapter 10). A critical expense item is the photovoltaic cell itself, which is made from crystals of a semiconducting substance. Cheaper crystals might become available, new materials for crystals could be found, or glass-like cell arrays could be used instead of the more expensive crystalline setups. If the current, seemingly ambitious U.S. Department of Energy goals of 50 cents a peak watt for photovoltaic cells is eventually reached—and if the cells can be incorporated directly into existing roofs to avoid incurring large structural support costs—one study estimates that a future photovoltaic system (with a gas-fired generator backup, providing household electricity independently of external grids) could become competitive with all-electric houses for household electricity costs of 25 mills per kilowatt hour or about $7 per million Btu delivered heat energy.[18] However, this cost comparison depends strongly on the assumed cheapness of the backup system and on the low capital charge rate chosen in the Office of Technology Assessment (OTA) study. Other types of systems combinations considered in that study were not judged to be competitive.[19]

[18] Office of Technology Assessment, *Application of Solar Technology* vol. I, pp. 33 and 44. The backup system is variously described as either gas or diesel—see vol. II, p. 330.
[19] The definition of competitive involves various assumptions about fossil fuel costs and solar subsidies. For the precise comparisons, see ibid., vol. II, pp. 18–19, where it appears the real capital charge rate is 5.5 percent. See also note 14 above. For the model costs for utility-type financing, see vol. II, p. 30, and the costs given in parentheses in table C.

Other Sources

Considerable experimentation has taken place with new versions of the ancient and well-established technology of wind power, applying it to various modern domestic needs. Wind can supply electricity on a small-scale, decentralized basis; it can also produce heat directly, pump water, or operate heat pumps. Government research and development goals of $750 per kilowatt have been set for a household 8-kilowatt system; but various private projects here and in other countries already report installed costs at or below this figure.[20] On the other hand, household wind energy converters costing $2,500 per kilowatt have been reported to generate electricity at 62 mills per kilowatt hour,[21] and even such fairly substantial unit costs would be much higher without the system's two-way interconnection with an existing utility network.

Fossil and biomass conversion (in the form of burning coal and wood, respectively) can conceivably be used as individual domestic heat sources just as they have for centuries—but using new technological ideas to help solve old problems with their use. Woodburning stoves, typically costing from $200 to $800 or more,[22] have made some progress in regaining former markets under the pressures of the search for new energy sources. Reported urban prices of $70 to $80 per cord of wood, however, correspond to unit input energy costs of about $2.50 per million Btu. This may or may not be cheaper than some fossil fuel alternatives, depending on efficiencies of combustion (see the appendix). Naturally, rural prices can be much lower or even involve no cash outlays. Small fluidized-bed combustors have been proposed as a possible way of reintroducing coal heating for individual dwellings in a cleaner, more modern way.[23]

The need for at least some stoking, as well as the air pollution and solid waste aspects of both coal and wood in home energy-conversion schemes could also constitute disadvantages. Therefore, such systems might be expected to have a restricted usefulness, unless the prices of coal or biomass (wood or possibly burnable wastes) are locally depressed compared with the cost of other energy sources or are essentially free goods.

[20] Amory B. Lovins, "Soft Energy Technologies," p. 496.
[21] William Diem, "NASA Has Trouble with Its Big Windmill," *The New York Times* (27 June 1976) sect. F, p. 3.
[22] Robert N. Christensen, EN–R–GY SAVER, Inc., Holliston, Mass., personal communication (19 April 1978).
[23] Lovins, *Soft Energy Paths*, pp. 46–48.

Neighborhood and Industrial Applications

Sometimes medium-scale energy supply and distribution systems can be more economical than either large-scale or individual units. If housing densities are appropriate, for example, economical district heating systems can be set up for an area smaller than that served by a typical utility. Such systems would pipe steam or hot water from a central heater through a network to individual housing units. Heating systems of this type have existed for many years both in the United States and in other countries. District heating is relatively commonplace for large academic campuses or medical complexes. It was also once a dominant form of heating in Sweden, before growing suburbanization decreased the economic attractiveness of networks using conventional pipes.[24] There are now efforts underway to reintroduce district heating in Swedish communities making use of newer, less-expensive piping materials.[25] District heating is especially suitable for energy sources such as nuclear power that are not easily reducible to household scale. It may also be economically combined with the cogeneration of electricity (an option noted in chapter 5).

There may be distinct advantages in neighborhood or district use of solar energy—at least compared with single-dwelling use. Storage facilities are generally characterized by economies of scale, because surface-to-volume ratios become smaller at higher storage capacities. One study, however, has calculated that, under present and projected energy prices, a solar heating and hot-water system (with seasonal thermal storage) would not compete with solar systems using conventional backup for high-rise apartment complexes without government subsidies to apartment owners installing solar units.[26]

Schemes have been proposed to supply energy for space and water heating to 100 households in the northeastern United States by storage of solar energy in a pond that has a capacity of approximately 100,000 cubic meters. The bottom and interior sides of the pond would be covered by a black plastic vinyl film. Plastic would also be used in the construction of a combined daytime solar collector and nighttime insulator covering the pond surface. The warm water from such a pond could

[24] Måns Lönnroth, "Swedish Energy Policy: Technology in the Political Process," in Leon N. Lindberg, *The Energy Syndrome* (Lexington, Mass., D.C. Heath, 1977) p. 277.

[25] Lovins, *Soft Energy Paths*, p. 119, footnote 8.

[26] Office of Technology Assessment, *Application of Solar Technology*, vol. I, p. 47.

be used for space heating directly, or to operate a freon engine that generates electricity, or both. The feasibility of such schemes depends in part on the development of long-lasting plastic materials. The proposed use of inexpensive material like plastics, at the cheap price of 10 cents to $1 per square foot of collector area,[27] at least provides hope in these solar pond schemes for avoiding the basic materials costs problem of standard solar collectors. However, the precise life-cycle economics of the heat engine generators remains to be determined, although the OTA staff reports that the capital costs for pond applications should be $500 to $1,000 per kilowatt. The social feasibility of districtwide total-energy schemes in this country also remains to be established.

Industry and agriculture put heat to a wide number of uses aside from space or water heating—drying, textile processing, metal finishing, and others. Active solar heating can be used for many such processes. The amount and temperature of water or steam used in these processes varies greatly. At the lower temperature end, solar ponds might be able to supply water at reasonable costs. These costs were estimated in one study at less than $4 per million Btu.[28] Other applications of low energy heat using conventional solar reflectors to supply heat at less than 100°C have been estimated at costs from $3 to $5 per million Btu.[29] For temperatures above 100°C, concentrating collectors are commonly used and costs may be higher. One study estimates costs for such applications at $10 per million Btu.[30] However, other studies show wide cost ranges, depending on the application, the use of cogenerating steam, and so on—so that costs could be between $3 and $8 per million Btu for higher temperatures.[31] These estimates are consistent with costs quoted elsewhere for a solar system delivering 300°C process heat at $7.3 per million Btu.[32] Because of the wide ranges of temperatures and forms of heat used, it is difficult to assess the significance of these costs without a detailed examination of industrial and agricultural end uses. For many end uses in industry, it may be relatively more difficult to

[27] Theodore B. Taylor, "A Preliminary Assessment of Prospects for Worldwide Use of Solar Energy," draft prepared for the Rockefeller Foundation (10 February 1977) p. VI-29.

[28] MITRE Corporation, "Systems Descriptions and Engineering Costs," p. 50.

[29] Ibid., pp. 53, 55, and 58.

[30] Battelle Columbus Laboratories, *Survey of the Applications of Solar Thermal Energy Systems to Industrial Process Heat,* vol. 1: *Summary,* TID-27348/1 (Columbus, Ohio, Battelle, January 1977) p. vii.

[31] MITRE Corporation, "Systems Descriptions and Engineering Costs," pp. 61, 63, and 65.

[32] Lovins, "Soft Energy Technologies," p. 502.

compete with conventional fuels because of low rates, reflecting distribution and billing costs, and regularity of industrial loads. Cogeneration with conventional fuels and energy conservation in the processes themselves might compete, furthermore, as fuel costs rise in the future.[33]

Wind power can be applied to district or industrial schemes in a manner similar to that for domestic usage. As for all intermittent sources, however, the backup or storage problem is critical. Unless utility grids can be tapped for backup, storage or independent backup equipment costs will raise windpower prices considerably. One study calculated that electricity from an independent wind generating system operating at a capacity of 60 to 145 kilowatts would cost 270 mills per kilowatt hour or more.[34] At the other extreme, costs of 36 to 59 mills per kilowatt hour have been reported for wind-generated electricity.[35]

Other solar-related systems can be utilized for district heating. Municipal rubbish, which has already been discussed for gasification (chapter 8) and for generation of electricity (chapter 10)—is used in Europe and in some U.S. locations to produce steam for district heating or industrial purposes. Once again, this option is often tied to cogeneration (see chapter 5).

Geothermal power has been used in district heating in many countries—Iceland, in particular, but also in the Soviet Union, Japan, Hungary, New Zealand, and France, as well as in the United States. Even though little development has taken place here during the recent era of cheap energy, a geothermal district heating system has been operating in Boise, Idaho, since the 1890s, supplying well over 200 houses and business firms. The energy resource picture is of particular interest in this context: low-temperature geothermal fluids that might not be suitable for the efficient generation of electricity might still be adequate for the low-grade temperatures of district heating, or agriculture and industrial uses such as greenhouses, fish growing, and crop drying.

Costs per million Btu for district geothermal schemes have been characterized as quite low—in the neighborhood of $1.[36] The ultimate

[33] Office of Technology Assessment, *Application of Solar Technology,* vol. I, pp. 51, 55. See also chap. 5 in this volume.

[34] Raymond Tison and Nicholas P. Diederman, "A Farm Energy System Employing Hydrogen Storage," paper presented at First World Hydrogen Energy meeting (Miami Beach, Fla., 1–3 March 1976) p. 9.

[35] Lovins, "Soft Energy Technologies," p. 502.

[36] J. H. Howard, ed., *Present Status and Future Prospects for Nonelectrical Uses of Geothermal Resources,* UCRL-51926 (Berkeley, Calif., Lawrence Livermore Laboratory for ERDA, 15 October 1975) NTIS UCRL-51926, p. 82.

extent of such relatively inexpensive geothermal resources remains questionable, however. It has been estimated that such low-grade temperature resources are fairly extensive in North America—with water of temperatures between 100° and 150°C constituting a resource of a million quads.[37] Further investigation of location and extraction costs is necessary.

Even nuclear reactors have been proposed for district heating schemes, particularly in earlier studies in Sweden and in more recently announced Russian plans. However, it is not clear that very small-scale reactors would be competitive in the first place or that in the present climate of U.S. public opinion such nuclear applications would be practical in a political sense.

Comparisons

Can solar energy become economical for single-unit and multiunit dwellings? Some types of passive solar systems undoubtedly are so now. But comparing the active solar costs reviewed above to the costs of the alternatives shown in table A-1, active solar energy using conventional collectors in standard housing would apparently not be economic in the average U.S. home until oil prices reached the equivalent of about $30 per barrel (1975 dollars) or $5.2 per million Btu at producer prices. These prices are much higher than the costs of heating fuel to the householder (see table A-1) at present producer prices of $2 per million Btu for oil and less than that for gas. But solar costs would also be greater than home-delivered costs of synthetic gases and probably also more than costs of liquid synthetics and shale oil, which have basic production costs of $4 or $5 per million Btu, or even less (see chapter 8). On the other hand, solar could conceivably compete with electric resistance heating. Electric heat pumps could in theory be considerably cheaper than solar; but less economical performance in practice has been reported in colder sections of the country,[38] and solar might be able to compete with less-efficient heat pump systems.

[37] Electric Power Research Institute (EPRI), *Unconventional Energy Resources* prepared for Conservation Commission, World Energy Conference (Palo Alto, Calif., EPRI, August 1977), p. 71; and McLennan and Ramsay, "Decentralized Energy Systems," p. 18-39a.

[38] Electric Power Research Institute (EPRI), *Load and Use Characteristics of Electric Heat Pumps in Single-Family Residences,* EPRI EA-793, Final Report (Palo Alto, Calif., EPRI, June 1978) vol. 1, p. S-3.

Consequently, in order for home solar heating to be competitive, some economic premium for solar use might have to be paid by the consumer. From the appendix to this chapter, a suitable cost premium to replace coal-derived gas as a fuel could be $3 or more per million Btu. These conclusions could be changed by further reductions in the cost of solar heating, but the comparison made here is with the lower end of the range of present solar heating costs reported. They could turn out to be overoptimistic as projections for practical, reliable systems called upon to supply, as assumed, half of the space heating energy to a typical U.S. household. It should also be noted that the costs assumed for synthetic fossil fuels are somewhat toward the high end of the estimates given in chapter 8, and lower costs there could increase the premium differential required for solar.

This comparison of course does not take into account possibilities for using much cheaper materials, such as plastics, for individual solar installations. It also does not encompass possible combinations of energy conservation and passive solar design, with minimal contributions from active solar elements. Nor does it take into account the possibilities of reducing cash-basis labor costs by do-it-yourself installation or maintenance. The effects of regional differences in solar costs and in the costs of competing fuels must also be taken into account. Sun Belt regions should be more amenable to solar energy. Hot water heating, in particular, might turn out to be a good option in particular regions. On the other hand, less favorable areas for solar might require even larger solar premiums than those shown by table A-1 to induce households to use solar units for space heating.

The use of district heating as a substitute for either fossil-fired domestic systems or for highly centralized electricity plants is an option of interest. Costs could be acceptable if population densities are sufficiently high, because of economies of scale in furnaces, but installing and maintaining large underground networks of pipes can produce institutional difficulties. The problem then enters the realm of urban planning, and it becomes difficult to analyze in any straightforward way that can be expressed in terms of marginal costs of household energy use.

Because of both scale economies and intermittency problems, wind energy electrical generators do not appear to be especially suited to small- and medium-scale uses unless storage costs drop drastically. Low-temperature geothermal resources, on the other hand, seem potentially well-adapted to such neighborhood or industrial applications, although the extent of such resources available for inexpensive recovery remains an open question.

Table A-1. Model Costs of Energy per Million Btu for Space Heating Systems in Individual Residences

Fuel	Fuel production cost ($ per million Btu)	Fuel distribution and other costs ($ per million Btu)	Approximate efficiency of end use	Net cost of fuel energy delivered to end use ($ per million Btu)	Annual capital operation and maintenance costs ($)	Capital and operation and maintenance costs per energy unit supplied ($ per million Btu)	Total energy cost per million Btu delivered ($ per million Btu)[a]
Solar[b] (low and high estimates)	0	0	1.	0	460–820[c]	12–22	12–22
Gas	1.0	1.4	0.7	3.4	110	1.5	4.9
Synthetic gas	4.0	1.4	0.7	7.7	110	1.5	9.2
Oil	2.0	1.5	0.7	5.0	180	2.4	7.4
Synthetic oil	5.0	1.5	0.7	9.3	180	2.4	11.7
Electricity							
Resistance heating	5.5	6.1	1.	12.0	90	1.2	13.2
Heat pumps	5.5	6.1	1.5	7.7	240	3.2	10.9

Source: Derived from appendix text.

a. Totals may not add, due to rounding.

b. For solar, 37.5 million Btu have been assumed supplied; for others, 75 million Btu. Results have been rounded.

c. Seventeen percent of the $550 (or $990) total solar capital and operational and maintenance costs are charged to hot-water heating (not shown here, but included in table 11-1).

Appendix: Cost of Units of Energy Delivered to Home Space Heating Uses by Gas, Oil, Solar, and Electric Sources

To put the estimated costs of solar space heating for homes in some context, rough estimates are made below of the delivered cost of conventional heat energy to typical homes.

The solar systems are assumed to be those now available or those available within a few years, using conventional collectors and delivering energy at the costs described in the text.

Field market prices of natural gas are currently in flux, but $1 per million Btu has been chosen here as a typical average price for the near future. Distribution to residential users is costed at 89 cents per million Btu and transmission costs at 48 cents[39]—giving a total transmission and distribution cost of $1.37.

Oil costs are taken at 1978 world prices of crude oil, plus a unit mark-up of $1.50 for refining and distribution.[40]

Electricity-generating costs are taken as 18.8 mills per kilowatt hour for coal-fired plants, from the 10 percent capital-charge national average costs in table 9-1; transmission and distribution losses and costs are taken from the appendix to chapter 9.

Costs of synthetics are taken to be consistent with the range of figures given in chapter 8 for high-Btu gas and shale oil. Coal liquids could cost less.

A 10 percent capital charge is assumed for the heating system used for each technology. Capital costs for solar heating systems are taken from the text, and 1 percent annual charge for repair and maintenance is assumed.

Capital costs for the fossil and electric technologies are taken as $1,100 for gas, $1,500 for oil, $900 for electric resistance heating, and $1,900 for electric heat pumps.[41] Operation and maintenance (O&M)

---

[39] U.S. Department of Energy, Energy Information Administration, *Monthly Energy Review*, DOE/EIA-0035/4 (Washington, D.C., GPO, April 1978) p. 78.

[40] Based on average production price of oil in the United States of $1.40 to $1.60 per million Btu and observed delivered prices in the Washington area of 45 cents per gallon (1975 dollars) or about $3.10.

[41] Office of Technology Assessment, *Application of Solar Technology*, vol. II, where averages for Albuquerque and Boston are taken (including ducting) converted to 1975 dollars and rounded; see pp. 148, 155, 168, 191, 201, 211, 218, and 234.

costs are taken from the same study as $0 for gas, $30 for oil, $0 for resistance heating, and $50 for heat pumps.

Efficiencies of combustion are taken to be those readily obtainable in new furnaces designed with higher energy costs in mind.[42] A net average coefficient of performance of 1.5 for heat pumps is assumed.[43]

On the basis of the estimates adopted here, the costs of foreseeable conventional solar home heating systems will be significantly greater than that for present fossil systems, but could be competitive with electric resistance heating for the low end of the solar estimates. Competition with electric heat pumps appears a more marginal matter.

For synthetic fossil fuels, costs of synthetic oil almost overlap the low end of the solar range, while costs for synthetic gas are some $3 below the solar costs. This could be interpreted as indicating that solar systems would require a premium of $3 or more to compete with the lowest cost fossil alternative.

The solar unit is assumed to supply 37.5 million Btu to space and hot-water heating; the other units 75 million Btu, corresponding to the average demands assumed in the text. To facilitate marginal comparisons, the solar unit costs are assumed to include one-half the cost of the backup units.

[42] Ibid., vol. I, pp. 514–517.
[43] Electric Power Research Institute, *Load and Use Characteristics of Electric Heat Pumps*, p. S-3, where somewhat over 5,000 degree days is assumed.

Part IV

Health, Safety, and Environmental Impacts

12 Health Impacts of Energy Technologies

Energy technologies present risks to human health; these risks can vary from predictable small increases in the usual illness rates among the general public to well-documented accidents to coal miners. In any case, they constitute an important cost of electricity and other energy technologies that is not usually included in any societal balance sheet. Unfortunately, it is hard to compare the number of fatalities, illnesses, and injuries with dollar costs of energy production. In fact, it is difficult, if not impossible, to express all health risks themselves in the same type of units. Nevertheless, these important impacts must be considered; here both fatalities and illnesses, but especially fatalities, are utilized as a measure of the impacts from various technologies.

We will begin with a subject of prime concern—the nature of the impact on the general public of coal-induced air pollution. We will then consider the threat of health risks from nuclear radiation that is normally released from nuclear power plants plus the possible effects of nuclear wastes and the role of nuclear power plant accidents. Other health effects may be less dramatic but still important, such as accidents to those repairing solar home energy systems or involved in automobile collisions with coal trains. Workers in energy industries are also subject to a number of health risks from different types of occupational accidents and illnesses.

The standard unit of comparison for health impacts from centrally generated electricity is the energy derived from a standard 1-gigawatt (1-GW) power plant. For the nonelectric technologies, the same amount of energy is used as a unit of comparison. Specifically, the amount of energy delivered to home-heating use by such a plant— 19.6 trillion Btus—is used as the "effective plant-year equivalent."[1]

[1] This assumes that the output of the electric plant is at a capacity factor of 75 percent, producing 6.75 billion kilowatt hours (kWh), or in caloric terms, 22.4 trillion Btus. (Note that the plant-year output given in chapter 10 is exactly 10 percent

Air Pollution

Coal-Fired Power Plants

The burning of coal in power plants produces significant amounts of air pollutants.[2] Sulfur dioxide and other sulfates, similar to those resulting from the combustion of the small amounts of sulfur contained in coal, are known to have deleterious effects on the entire body, particularly the lungs, at high concentrations. The much lower concentrations usually present in polluted airsheds have also been associated with an increased number of respiratory and cardiac illnesses, as well as an increase in the mortality rate. Some nitrogen oxides, formed from nitrogen in fossil fuels and from the heating of the nitrogen in the air during most types of combustion processes—not just in power plants—are also respiratory irritants. In addition, nitrogen oxide compounds can interact with sunlight and along with a third pollutant—unburned traces of coal, oil, or natural gas hydrocarbons—can produce the oxidizing irritants contained in Los Angeles-type smog. Trace elements contained in fossil fuels, such as mercury, lead, cadmium, selenium, nickel, arsenic, and such organic compounds as benzo(a)pyrene (BaP), can be poisonous or carcinogenic. Small quantities of the radioactive gas radon is also a common effluent. Finally, carbon oxides can be a problem; for example, carbon monoxide, from fossil fuels, has been associated with the aggravation of cardiac illnesses. Carbon dioxide, while not toxic at the levels under discussion, may also have an important effect on climate (see chapter 14).

---

smaller than this value; for virtually all comparisons, this discrepancy is far smaller than data uncertainties.) At an 87.5 percent net efficiency of transmission, distribution, and conversion to electric resistance heating uses, 19.6 trillion Btus in useful end-use energy results.

Since the efficiencies of various coal-conversion processes differ, the amounts of either input or plant-output energies corresponding to this effective plant-year equivalent will vary according to the technology used (see Eli J. Salmon, "Health and Environmental Implications of Various Energy Systems," draft prepared for the National Energy Strategies Project (Washington, D.C., Resources for the Future, May 1978) p. V-2. Available from RFF's Center for Energy Policy Research.

This unit will, of course, be less suited for policy decisions that are directed toward uses other than domestic space heating. However, with the use of the efficiencies quoted in the tables for this chapter, the impacts may be converted to equivalent plant outputs, inputs, or other measures for other analytic purposes.

[2] For references to these effects, see William Ramsay, *Unpaid Costs of Electrical Energy: Health and Environmental Impacts from Coal and Nuclear Power* (Baltimore, Md., Johns Hopkins University Press for Resources for the Future, 1978) pp. 14–15 and 20–22.

It is far easier to list the number of air pollutants than to specify how they affect human health and the environment. For example, one pollutant from burning coal that has received a great deal of attention is sulfur dioxide. This compound is known to be a respiratory irritant.[3] However, the sulfur dioxide is often transformed in the smokestack, or in the outside atmosphere, into other compounds of sulfur, some of which are even more hazardous to the lungs. Furthermore, these compounds can form or be condensed on microscopic bits of fly ash, and these so-called particulates can have negative effects on the respiratory system. However, their presence in the air at the power plant does not permit one to predict at what time or place they will be present to cause impacts on human beings. Their ultimate nature, quantity, and location depend on winds, intervening chemical processes, and population distributions. Finally, when the sulfur compounds and particulates are inhaled, their precise health impact is not known. This complex set of impacts, with all the uncertainties involved, has been reviewed extensively elsewhere.[4] Here one can merely note that the estimates of numerical ranges of probable health impacts are necessarily very wide

[3] Ramsay, *Unpaid Costs*, pp. 14–15.

[4] See reviews in William Ramsay, "Coal and Nuclear: Health and Environmental Costs," draft prepared for National Energy Strategies Project (Washington, D.C., Resources for the Future, August 1978) pp. 1-6–1-9 (available from RFF's Center for Energy Policy Research); and in U.S. Congress, Senate, Committee on Public Works, *Air Quality and Stationary Source Emission Control,* Report prepared by the Commission on Natural Resources of the National Academy of Sciences/National Academy of Engineering/National Research Council, 94 Cong. 1 sess., ser. no. 94-4 (March 1975) pp. 138ff. Also see Lester B. Lave and Warren E. Weber, "A Benefit–Cost Analysis of Auto Safety Features," *Applied Economics* vol. 2 (1970) pp. 265–275; Lester B. Lave and Eugene P. Seskin, "Air Pollution and Human Health," *Science* vol. 169 (21 August 1970) pp. 723–733; Lester B. Lave, "Air Pollution Damage: Some Difficulties in Estimating the Value of Abatement," in Allen V. Kneese and Blair T. Bower, eds., *Environmental Quality Analysis, Theory and Method in the Social Sciences* (Baltimore, Md., Johns Hopkins University Press for Resources for the Future, 1972) pp. 213–242; L. D. Hamilton, ed., *The Health and Environmental Effects of Electricity Generation: A Preliminary Report,* BNL 20582 (Upton, N.Y., Brookhaven National Laboratory, 30 July 1974); and David P. Rall, *A Review of the Health Effects of Sulfur Oxides* (Bethesda, Md., National Institutes of Health, National Institute of Environmental Health Science, 9 October 1973) p. 13. See also W. A. Buehring, W. K. Foell, and R. L. Keeney, *Energy/Environment Management: Application of Decision Analysis,* Research Report RR-76-14 (Laxenburg, Austria, International Institute for Applied Systems Analysis, May 1976); Brookhaven National Laboratory, Biomedical and Environmental Assessment Group, "The Effect of Air Pollution from Coal and Oil Power Plants on Public Health," BEAG-HE 11/74 (Upton, N.Y., Brookhaven National Laboratory, 17 May 1974); and L. D. Hamilton, *Health Effects of Air Pollution,* BNL 20743, U.S. Energy Research and Development Administration (Upton, N.Y., Biomedical and Environmental Assessment Group of Brookhaven National Laboratory, July 1974), as reviewed in Ramsay, "Coal and Nuclear," pp. 1-17–1-21.

Table 12-1. Health Effects of a Coal-Fired Power Plant from Air Pollution Measured by Sulfur Emissions, Per 19.6-Trillion-Btu Effective Plant-Year Equivalent

Health effect	No.
Fatalities[a]	0–8
Illnesses[b]	
Chronic respiratory-tract illnesses in adults, no. of cases	60–6,000
Lower respiratory-tract illnesses in children, no. of cases	10–1,000
Aggravation of heart-lung symptoms in the elderly, no. of person-days	600–60,000
Asthma, no. of excess attacks	100–10,000

Note: Output to home heating of a 1-GW plant at a 75 percent capacity factor, emitting 10.8 million pounds of sulfur annually.

Source: William Ramsay, *Unpaid Costs of Electrical Energy: Health and Environmental Impacts from Coal and Nuclear Power* (Baltimore, Md., Johns Hopkins University Press for Resources for the Future, 1978) fig. 2-1, p. 18; and in the same source, app. A to chap. 2 (pp. 28–30) discusses the evaluation problems. The upper bounds for these estimates represent the highest estimates in major studies, corrected for varying levels of sulfur control technology assumed. Recent critiques have stressed the great uncertainties in predicting lower bounds, especially for fatalities; comparing the estimates from existing studies with observed incidences of particular diseases from all causes sometimes also shows values that appear too large. These considerations suggest adopting radically lower limits at the bottom of the range of estimates. Therefore, the lower limits are estimated here as two orders of magnitude lower than the high-end estimates.

[a] Evaluations of existing studies (see text and notes to text) of fatalities suggest that values of zero are possible, given the great uncertainties in the data.

[b] Estimates of diseases due to air pollution are very controversial. Recent reviews (see text and notes to text) have emphasized the deficiencies in the earlier studies supporting high estimates. On the basis of such criticisms raising the question of whether statistically valid relationships do in fact exist, it may be that the lower part of this range is more credible than the higher.

because of great uncertainties in the available physical and medical data.

Because existing studies have stressed measurements of the sulfur level, table 12-1 uses the level of sulfur dioxide emissions as a surrogate (indicator) measure for all pollutant-caused fatalities. It shows that as few as zero to as many as eight fatalities can be attributed to the yearly emissions from each 1-GW coal-fired plant with scrubbers.[5] The incidence of illnesses is also highly uncertain, and the high and low estimates for illnesses given here differ by two orders of magnitude. It must be remembered that these estimates are based on studies of a very controversial and inconclusive nature and that sulfur levels have been used here as indicators for all pollution impacts.

---

[5] See Ramsay, "Coal and Nuclear," pp. 1-31 and 1-32, where corrections have been made here for scrubber operation.

Even less is known about the ambient levels and the possible health effects of nitrogen oxides and of trace elements, and, for this reason, we will not assign them specific separate values. However, a special concern—more so for coal-conversion than for coal-fired power plants —has been voiced recently about the presence of toxic carcinogenic elements in coal, some of which could affect the general public through its use of coal. However, it has been estimated, for example, that present BaP emissions from coal-fired power plants have amounted to less than 1 percent of the total U.S. emissions from coking ovens and other such sources.[6] The health significance of the low doses to be expected from such emissions has not been established.

Newer Coal-Using Technologies for the Generation of Electricity

As mentioned in chapter 9, modified methods of coal combustion, such as fluidized-bed combustion, cyclone furnaces, and ultrafine pulverization, are designed so that they can at least meet and often improve upon the emissions levels for sulfur, and usually those for particulates, without using scrubbers. The situation is somewhat different, however, for some of the more radical new technologies such as magnetohydrodynamics and fuel cells.

The high temperatures related with magnetohydrodynamics (MHD) produce large amounts of nitrogen oxides.[7] However, the essential part of this technology will be efficient gas cleanup—not as an antipollution measure, but in order to recover the expensive "seed" elements that are used as catalysts. If such a cleanup of the hot gas can be achieved, the simultaneous removal of nitrogen oxides, sulfur compounds, particulates, and other pollutants also should be feasible.

For fuel cells, the outlook is even more favorable. The fuel cell utilizes a clean, hydrogen-rich gas, producing mostly water as a byproduct: elements such as sulfur must be removed with high efficiency beforehand, as in the case of MHD, in order for the cell to function

---

[6] Eli J. Salmon, "Environmental, Health, and Safety Impacts of Different Technologies," draft prepared for National Energy Strategies Project (Washington, Resources for the Future, August 1978) p. 13/14-69. Available from RFF's Center for Energy Policy Research.

[7] Center for Energy Studies, "Future Central Station Electric Generation Technologies" (Austin, Center for Energy Studies, the University of Texas for Resources for Energy Policy Research) pp. 4-149ff.

properly. Nitrogen oxides will probably be generated only in small quantities.[8] However, the impacts from the production of the gas fed into the fuel cell must also be considered; however, the most likely choices of fuels have not yet become evident.

Therefore, for these new technologies, some pollutant levels could be very low; however, it is too soon to predict relative impacts for practical commercial systems. Indeed, whether any of these new technologies will make the grade from a technical or competitive cost standpoint is as yet another question (see chapter 9).

Coal-conversion plants for electricity generation. One of the primary motivations for developing coal-conversion processes, in addition to securing a more conveniently usable fuel and a substitute for what is expected to be a dwindling supply of natural gas and petroleum, is to reduce pollution from sulfur and other compounds. From this point of view, these conversion processes are a substitute for the scrubbers and precipitators or bag houses that remove sulfur compounds and fly-ash particulates from the flue gases of ordinary coal-fired power plants. Most of these processes are capable of removing 90 percent or more of such pollutants and will most certainly be redesigned to correspond to or to exceed standards similar to those for scrubbers.

In converting coal, some of the coal supplies heat for the rest of the reaction. This burned coal produces emissions that are treated by standard techniques; however, the coal that is converted to gas can be treated somewhat differently. The raw gas from the reactor contains the usual particles of carbon, fly ash, and sulfur compounds. But it is planned that the sulfur, usually in the form of hydrogen sulfide and other organic sulfur compounds, will be efficiently removed from the final gas product. If this low-Btu gas is fed into a combined-cycle power plant that produces the same amount of electricity as a standard coal plant with flue gas desulfurization, a study made for this project estimates that the relative amount of sulfur emitted will be only 10 percent of the standard plant emissions.[9] Emissions of other pollutants may not follow this same pattern: for instance, an integrated low-Btu-gas plant can be expected to produce almost half the amount of nitrogen oxide as an ordinary coal-fired power plant with scrubbers. However, assuming that the sulfur emissions give a better measure of the total impact, the

[8] Center for Energy Studies, "Future Central Station," vol. 2, p. 4-193, originally in Westinghouse Corp., *Energy Conservation Alternatives Study (ECAS)*, Phase I Final Report, vol. 13, *Fuel Cells* (Westinghouse Corp., Pittsburgh, Pa., 1976).

[9] Salmon, "Health and Environmental Implications" (May 1978) tab. V-1.

Table 12-2. Estimated Fatalities Among the General Public from Air Pollution, Per Effective Plant-Year Equivalent

(1)	*(2)*	*(3)*	*(4)*	*(5)* = [*(2)* + *(3)*]/*(4)*
Energy technology	*Fatalities from plant emissions*[a]	*Fatalities from emissions during home heating*[a]	*Relative efficiency factor*[a]	*Efficiency-adjusted total per effective plant-year equivalent*[b]
Standard coal-fired power plant[c]	0–8	Not applicable	1	0–8
Low-Btu combined-cycle	0–0.8	Not applicable	1	0–0.8
High-Btu gas from coal	0–0.5	Negligible	0.83	0–0.6
Coal liquids	0–0.3	0–0.8	0.71	0–1
Shale oil (surface retorting)	0–0.1	0–0.8	0.71	0–1

Source: See text, p. 350.

Note: See notes to table 12-1 for a discussion of uncertainties in air pollution impacts; these uncertainties are as great or greater for the newer technologies considered here.

[a] The fatalities shown in columns 2 and 3 are given in terms of emissions corresponding to an output of 22.4 trillion Btus at the generating plant or the conversion plant. For electric-resistance heating only this corresponds to 19.6 trillion Btus delivered to the home. The relative efficiency factor in column 4 corrects this to take into account that more energy is lost from plant output to home end use for some technologies because of greater energy distribution or home combustion losses, or both. It is defined as the *ratios* of the fractional energy delivered from an electric plant to the home-heating end use (taken here as 0.874) to the fractional energy delivered from coal conversion or shale oil plants to home-heating uses (taken as 0.73 for high-Btu and 0.62 for the liquids). They are derived from the ratios of output energies in Eli J. Salmon, "Health and Environmental Implications of Various Technologies." This draft, prepared for the National Energy Strategies Project (Washington, D.C., Resources for the Future, August 1978), is available from RFF's Center for Energy Policy Research.

[b] This figure shows the number of fatalities expected for each technology for each 19.6 trillion Btus delivered to home heating. Rounding of figures applied column by column may affect results in last column.

[c] A 1-GW plant with scrubbers, taken as emitting 10.8 million pounds of sulfur a year.

reduced air pollution impact on fatalities from power plants fired by low-Btu gas is shown in table 12-2. Illnesses are not shown in table 12-2, but under the assumptions used here, they would be proportionally reduced from those shown in table 12-1.

Coal conversion for nonelectric uses. Similar comparisons can also be made for medium- or high-Btu gasification and for coal liquefaction. However, for these processes, emissions during combustion in home-heating plants may also be significant. Furthermore, the problem of a unit of comparison can arise. Energy is lost in converting coal to gases and liquids, and these fuels generally have different end uses, or at least employ distribution networks and appliances which are different in nature from those in the electric case. Therefore, the calculation is divided into four steps:

1. The relative amount of sulfur emitted from a plant fired by high-Btu gas is estimated in terms of the net energy output at the plant, or at about 6 percent of the total for a coal-fired power plant.[10] For coal liquefaction, the amount of sulfur dioxide generated at the conversion plant is much less,[11] about 4 percent. These percentages have been applied to the standard coal plant (see table 12-1), and the resulting air pollution fatalities are given in column 2 of table 12-2 for each plant-year (equivalent). These large differences from the standard coal-fired plant case arise partly from the superior efficiency of the conversion plants in producing output energy, but mostly from the estimated superiority of the pollution-control devices in these plants.

2. Column 3 in table 12-2 shows the extra emissions from home-heating combustion for the gases and liquids.

3. Column 4 shows the relative efficiency factor—that is, a measure of the losses from burning high-Btu gas and liquids in the home relative to the smaller losses in electric resistance heating (the reference system).

4. Column 5 shows the efficiency-adjusted total emissions from all sources, adding the plant emissions from column 2 to the home emissions from column 3, and dividing the sum by the efficiency factor. It can be seen that, at the level of accuracy available here, the last factor makes little difference in the end result.

The table shows zero to 8 fatalities per effective plant-year equivalent for the standard coal plant, with zero to 0.8 for the low-Btu-coal combined-cycle electric plant. For nonelectric technologies, high-Btu gas shows zero to 0.6 fatality, and coal liquids zero to 1 fatality for sulfur-related air pollution impacts.

It must be emphasized that difficulties in assessing air pollution impacts are especially formidable for relatively new and untried processes. Emissions of certain other pollutants, in particular certain polynuclear

[10] Salmon, "Health and Environmental Implications" (May 1978) tab. V-4, p. V-18, corrected for the efficiency factors described in tab. 12-2 in this chapter. Derived from Energy Research and Development Administration, Market Oriented Program Planning Study (MOPPS), *Assessment of Environmental, Health, and Safety Constraints on Selected Energy Technologies* (Washington, D.C., GPO, final draft, September 1977).

[11] Ibid.

aromatic hydrocarbons, are expected to be larger for coal-conversion processes than for coal-fired power plants.[12] Still, the contributions to the total national loading will probably be small. At any rate, the size of the risks from the national ambient level of these compounds and other poisonous and carcinogenic elements is undetermined.

Shale Oil

Shale oil is retorted, either in a surface retort or in situ underground, in order to extract the oil from the rock. In this process, some of the sulfur contained in the oil may be released. However, according to Salmon,[13] the amount of sulfur released by surface or underground retorting and other oil processing amounts to 2 or 1 percent, respectively, of the coal plant standard for equivalent amounts of output energy delivered by the plant. On the other hand, oil shale can produce up to 45 percent of the particulates associated with, for example, a coal-fired power plant.[14] If sulfur is again taken as the most important pollutant, and if comparisons are made as was done above for the coal technologies in order to derive equivalent energy delivered to home end use (19.6 trillion Btus), the figures given in column 5 of table 12-2 show that air pollution from the use of oil shale is expected to contribute less than one excess fatality among the general public and perhaps none at all.[15]

Other Sources

Air pollution from biomass is difficult to categorize because there are so many different kinds of fuel based on living matter. One analysis of spruce bark, for example,[16] shows only about 0.1 percent sulfur. This

---

[12] Salmon, "Environmental, Health, and Safety Impacts" (August 1978) p. 13/14-69.

[13] Salmon, "Health and Environmental Implications" (May 1978) p. V-18.

[14] Ibid.

[15] This discussion does not consider the role of hydrocarbons and their interaction with sunlight and nitrogen oxides to produce Los Angeles-type smog, partly because the dominant emissions of this kind come from automobiles and natural vegetation. But one can note that emissions of hydrocarbons from oil shale operations—in particular—can be larger than those for coal (see Salmon, "Health and Environmental Implications" (May 1978) tab. V-1).

[16] William H. Beardsley, "Forests as a Source of Electric Power," in *Clean Fuels* (Chicago, Ill., Institute of Gas Technology, 1976) p. 357.

would make sulfur emissions very low. In one pilot plant, indeed, the use of fuel derived from municipal wastes in combination with coal in one boiler led to a marked decrease in sulfur dioxide emissions.[17] Particulate emissions, however, can pose a pollution problem, and particulate-removing equipment such as electrostatic precipitators or bag houses will undoubtedly be necessary for biomass conversion for boiler fuel.

For other renewable sources, geothermal energy is the only one with apparent possibly significant air pollution consequences, and abatement measures may be necessary. The pollutants are from impurities within the geothermal fluid and naturally vary a good deal from place to place. Indeed, many wells emit the radioactive gas radon (see the section on Long-Lived Radioactive Elements). However, a principal noticeable pollutant is hydrogen sulfide, which is both disagreeable to smell and toxic to human beings at high concentrations. Concentrations in the steam discharged from the wells at one plant in New Zealand were 30 parts per million, a value well above the established threshold for irritation to the eyes and lungs.[18]

Comparative Air Pollution Effects

From table 12-2, one can see that low-Btu-coal gasification promises a sizable decrease in air pollution fatalities—and inferentially in illness as defined in table 12-1—from electric generation compared to the direct burning of coal to generate electricity. The difference shown here is a 90 percent reduction.

If the standard coal-fired power plant with scrubbers is compared with a home furnace fired by high-Btu gas, the difference shown in table 12-2 is again a more than 90 percent reduction—from zero to 8 the range decreases to zero to 0.6, even though gas is less efficiently distributed and used in the home. For coal liquids and shale oil, the emissions at the plant are quite low, only a few percentage points of the standard coal plants; however, the home emissions add in a sizable total, and

[17] Variance of the sulfur content of different batches of coal were taken into account in this calculation. See James D. Kilgroe, Larry J. Shannon, and Paul Gorman, "Environmental Studies on the St. Louis Union Electric Refuse Firing Demonstration," in *Clean Fuels* (Chicago, Ill., Institute of Gas Technology, 1976) p. 423.

[18] Robert C. Axtmann, "Environmental Impact of a Geothermal Power Plant," *Science* vol. 187, no. 4179 (7 March 1975) p. 797.

the results—including relative efficiencies of end use—show that coal liquids and shale oil users will emit somewhat more than 10 percent of the sulfur pollution by a standard coal plant.

Radiation Risks

The operation of nuclear power plants leads inevitably to the creation of certain risks from radioactivity emitted during their operation.

Routine Radiation

Radioactive atoms are routinely released into the environment during the operation of a nuclear power plant. It is known that rays from the decay of these atoms can impinge on the human body directly or can enter the body through the ingestion of food or water or by breathing contaminated air. Radiation impacts can cause a wide variety of damage to the cells of human beings and other organisms, specifically, radiation sickness, cancer, and genetic defects.

However, radiation escaping during the normal operation of power plants occurs at too low a level to cause the radiation sickness that results from the use of nuclear weapons. Indeed, it is impossible to tell by measurements whether such small amounts of radiation actually do cause cancer or genetic defects; the tumors and mutations involved would be a very small addition to, and indistinguishable in nature from those normally occurring. But there are cogent reasons for believing that even extremely low levels of radiation are carcinogenic.[19] Therefore, it is usually assumed for official safety calculations that these low doses to large populations from nuclear power plants do cause cancer in numbers precisely proportional to those that are induced by high doses to small populations—such as doses from nuclear bombs or from extensive radiation treatments for acute medical problems.[20]

Even so, the level of radiation reaching the general public as a result of normal operation of nuclear power plants is lower than that from the natural background radiation that is emitted from naturally occurring radioactive minerals and gases or from medical X rays. This conclusion

[19] See Ramsay, *Unpaid Costs*, pp. 45–46.
[20] This is called the linearity hypothesis. There is some controversy as to whether this is an overestimate or underestimate. See Ramsay, *Unpaid Costs*, chap. 3, app. B.

Table 12-3. Estimated Fatalities Among the General Public from Nuclear Power, Per Effective Plant-Year Equivalent

Source	No. of fatalities
Routine radiation from short-lived isotopes	0.001–0.005
Long-lived isotopes in waste gases, discounted at 5 percent[a]	0.07–0.3
Reactor accidents[b]	0.0002–2
Total	0.07–2

Note: Catastrophic impacts such as effects of nuclear proliferation or diversion are not included here. Totals may not add because of rounding.

Source: William Ramsey, "Coal and Nuclear Health and Environmental Costs," draft prepared for National Energy Strategies Project (Washington, D.C., Resources for the Future, August 1978) tab. 2-2 and app. J. Available from RFF's Center for Energy Policy Research. Also, William Ramsay, *Unpaid Costs of Electrical Energy: Health and Environmental Impacts from Coal and Nuclear Power* (Baltimore, Md., Johns Hopkins University Press for Resources for the Future, 1978) fig. 10-2. Original reactor accident estimates modified as described here in the text.

[a] See text for explanation. Undiscounted total would be very large—100 to 800.

[b] Based on theoretical models of accidents (see text).

is also generally true for other parts of the uranium fuel cycle.[21] Indeed, the total contribution to fatalities from most types of normal nuclear radiation is noticeably smaller than other nuclear risks (see table 12-3). Related illnesses, such as benign growths on the thyroid gland, are also of relatively minor significance.

Long-Lived Radioactive Elements

An important but peculiar exception exists to the low levels of doses characteristic of routine nuclear operations. Much of the radiation from a nuclear power plant or other nuclear facility comes from short-lived isotopes that decay away rather quickly; however, there are also a number of very long-lived isotopes emitted in gaseous form that will continue emitting radiation for many years into the future.

Current and projected radiation levels from these long-lived radioactive elements are also very low compared with those from other common sources of radiation.[22] But their persistence in the environment changes the nature of the health risk involved. Elements such as the tritium and carbon 14 emitted from reactors will persist in the environ-

[21] Ibid., fig. 3-1, p. 35.

[22] Ramsay, "Coal and Nuclear." Table 2-2 shows these as 0.005 to 0.02 fatality for one plant *for the first year* (p. 2-34).

ment for decades or more. The radioactive gaseous element radon will continue to be produced in uranium mill tailings and uranium mines for tens of thousands of years, unless abated by new policies now being discussed for the deep burial of tailings, and will apparently inflict small but continuous health risks on future generations. If all of the predicted deaths over all future years were to be added up, the totals would be very large, 100 to 800 per plant.[23] Some analysts propose discounting these effects to yield their present-day equivalents,[24] just as future incomes are discounted to represent the smaller value of future events in present-day calculations. If these effects are discounted at reasonable rates, such as 5 percent, contributions for each plant-year would be between 0.07 and 0.3 fatality (see table 12-3). Such a treatment of the problem is necessarily controversial; however, this expedient is adopted here as a reasonable compromise solution.

Radon and carbon 14 constitute gaseous nuclear wastes. Other long-lived elements, such as plutonium, form part of a different and more publicized aspect of the nuclear waste problem.

Nuclear Wastes

The radioactive elements in spent fuel from nuclear reactors are the subject of intense debate and public concern. This nuclear waste problem does not deal with a health impact that has happened or that need happen at all, but only with a problem that might happen in the future. The public concern is of course justified in the sense that the dangerous radioactive elements in the fuel wastes are very long-lived, many having half-lives of up to hundreds of thousands of years, and it is impossible to assume that human control will be exercised continuously over the wastes for such a long period of time.

There are severe technical problems that must be overcome in order to keep the nuclear fuel wastes isolated in places where they will not be brought into the human environment in the future, either by accident or by design. Burial is complicated by two facts: (1) the fission products remain physically hot for many hundreds of years; and (2) more important, the waste must be isolated or protected from water if

---

[23] William Ramsay and Milton Russell, "Time-Adjusted Health Impacts from Electricity Generation," *Public Policy* vol. 26, no. 3 (Summer 1978) pp. 387–403, especially pp. 396–397.

[24] Ibid., p. 391.

one is to prevent its later leakage into the local water table. Nevertheless, the total volume of waste is fairly small; in fact, all U.S. power reactor wastes produced up to the year 2000 would take up a volume of less than 100 acre-feet.[25] And if current schemes for burying the waste in salt deposits or in certain rock formations prove to be practical, there appears to be no compelling reason to believe that the substances would not remain isolated from the human environment for indefinitely long periods. Nevertheless, failure to develop a feasible waste-disposal plan is one of the major failures of current U.S. nuclear policy.

Low-level wastes from contaminated clothing and other equipment that have been used in the processing of nuclear fuels or other nuclear materials must also be safely disposed of. Since these materials do not emit much heat, it would seem they could be isolated from the human environment with relative ease. Nevertheless, careless disposal practices in the past have been responsible for radioactivity in the area of the burial site. Although no clear danger to the public health has been established,[26] improved burial techniques are evidently desirable.

A problem that is not yet of immediate concern is how to dispose of old reactors. When reactors become obsolete, the reactor equipment and building remain significantly radioactive. Mothballing or isolating these reactors is feasible but can be costly, and even with a complete and relatively expensive dismantlement, future uses of the site must be restricted. One estimate of prorated dismantlement costs runs to over $500,000 a year per reactor,[27] a tidy if not overwhelming addition to the average total operating costs of $100 million or so for each plant (see chapter 9).

Nuclear Reactor Accidents

One technical disadvantage of the nuclear reactor is that the core continues to generate heat even after the reactor is turned off. Should operating problems occur, the main nuclear reaction in the fuel can be stopped quickly, but the heat from waste products remains at a high level for long periods of time. This means that the nuclear fuel must

[25] Ramsay, *Unpaid Costs,* chap. 5.
[26] Ibid., p. 65.
[27] Ibid.

be cooled continuously or else the metal-encased fuel rod will melt, releasing radioactive gases and clouds of particulates.

Despite the presence of numerous safety systems that provide emergency supplies of water in case of such an event, the possibility of an accident does remain, as emphasized by the recent accident at the Three Mile Island plant in Pennsylvania. This accident, which for the first time emitted a significant amount of radioactivity and inflicted small but measurable radiation doses on the general public, occurred at a time when the question of nuclear safety prediction was already in a state of flux. According to a major study done earlier on this problem (see "A Note on the Rasmussen Report"), the chances of accidents were said to be very small; the expected number of fatalities from a given nuclear reactor, caused by severe nuclear accidents, was estimated to range from 0.003 to 0.06, prorated over each year of operation.[28] Illnesses related to such an accident were estimated to range from 0.007 to 0.6 per plant-year. However, critical reviews of this report had stressed necessary uncertainties in data and deficiencies in the methodology of the study; a review officially sponsored by the Nuclear Regulatory Commission, the Lewis report, emphasized that the error limits on the Rasmussen calculation should be greatly increased, by some unspecified amount.[29]

These theoretical criticisms were reinforced by the fire in Alabama's Browns Ferry plant in 1975, when a threat to the integrity of the reactor core occurred owing to a sequence of events that was not included in the original Rasmussen calculations.[30] The full-fledged, but not cata-

---

[28] Ibid., fig. 4-1, p. 49.

[29] See Henry W. Kendall, "Nuclear Power Risks," A Review of the Report of the American Physical Society's Study Group on Light Water Reactor Safety (Cambridge, Mass., Union of Concerned Scientists, 18 June 1975); American Physical Society, "Report to the APS by the Study Group on Light-Water Reactor Safety," *Reviews of Modern Physics* vol. 47 (Summer 1975) suppl. 1; Ford Foundation, *Nuclear Power Issues and Choices,* report of the Nuclear Energy Policy Study Group, administered by MITRE Corporation (Cambridge, Mass., Ballinger, 1977); H.-P. Balfanz and P. Kakfa, *Kritischer Bericht zur Reaktorischerheitssudie WASH-1400* (Critical Report on the Reactor Safety Study), IRS-I-87, MRR-I-65 (Cologne, Institut für Reaktorsicherheit der TÜV E.V., Laboratorium für Reaktorregelung und Anlagensicherung, April 1976); Christoph Hohenemser, Roger Kasperson, and Robert Kates, "The Distrust of Nuclear Power," *Science* vol. 196, no. 4285 (1 April 1977) pp. 25–34; and H. W. Lewis, chairman, Ad Hoc Risk Assessment Review Group, *Risk Assessment Review Group Report to the U.S. Nuclear Regulatory Commission,* NUREG/CR-0400 (Springfield, Va., National Technical Information Service, September 1978).

[30] The probabilities for fire-related events were calculated for the final Rasmussen Report, but it was estimated that they would not change the results significantly.

A NOTE ON THE RASMUSSEN REPORT—
A THEORY OF NUCLEAR ACCIDENTS

The Reactor Safety Study calculated the probability that (1) a nuclear reactor accident would occur with a significant release of radioactivity, and
(2) the radioactivity would be carried to locations where it could expose a
population to possible health risks.

All possible components in the plant that might break down so as to eventually lead to such an accident were examined. For example, one possible way
for an accident to occur would be for a large pipe to break, then for both the
emergency core cooling system and the containment spray system to fail, and
then for the containment itself to be breached, releasing radioactivity into
the atmosphere. One must calculate the probability for this total sequence of
events, and for all the different possible events—including human errors—
that could lead to a core meltdown or other serious accident, such as the
bursting of the reactor vessel.

This type of probability calculation was carried out for two typical existing
reactors. Normal uncertainties in the design and the failure rates of components were also taken into account in order to reflect differing conditions
in one hundred typical reactors.

If the radioactive material gets outside the reactor, then its destructiveness
depends on whether the wind is blowing in the direction where people live,
whether there is rain, and how many people live in the affected area. The
chance of ninety different kinds of weather conditions occurring at each of six
representative sites was then calculated, taking into account local populations.

For example, the probabilities for a worst-case accident could be calculated
as follows: (1) The probability of an accident occurring in each reactor in
which a substantial amount of radioactivity would be released was 5 in 1
million; (2) the probability of the weather being unfavorable and exposing a
large population to the radioactivity was 1 in 1,000; (3) the chance of a
worst-case accident happening was then 5 out of 1 billion for each reactor-
year; and (4) the number of latent cancers inflicted on such a large population from such an amount of radiation would be 48,000; (5) this can be
interpreted to mean that we "expect" only 0.0002 fatalities per reactor-year
from this worst-case accident.[31]

---

[31] Ramsay, *Unpaid Costs,* p. 50.

strophic accident at Three Mile Island may have involved events that have some implications for the completeness or assessment of probabilities in the Rasmussen formulation.[32] Furthermore, while one accident, of whatever size, throws little light on long-term minimum or maximum risks, it must underline the reality of at least some level of risk.

For these reasons, we adopt here a rather wide range of maximum and minimum values for expected accident fatalities from reactor accidents; in table 12-3 these are shown as two orders of magnitude above and below the Rasmussen value, that is, 2×10^{-4} to 2 fatalities per plant year.[33] This choice should provide elbow room for future unanticipated accident sequences and deficiencies in other relevant probabilities; the result at the upper limit is also of the same order of magnitude as that proposed on somewhat different grounds in another recent study.[34]

The reactor accident problem has another aspect that complicates our evaluation of it. What is society's attitude toward catastrophic nuclear accidents? Although the average annual number of fatalities expected could turn out to be small, the worst-case accident could cause, according to the Rasmussen calculations, 3,000 relatively quick deaths from radiation sickness plus 45,000 later deaths from radiation-induced cancers. The apparently remote chance of such an accident happening could well be viewed by the public as qualitatively different from routine risks (see chapter 14).

The Breeder Reactor

Breeder reactors generally involve the fabrication, shipment, and use of plutonium fuels, and plutonium is a known carcinogen. Nevertheless, the Energy Research and Development Administration's (ERDA) environmental impact statements for the breeder assert that with careful handling, the chance of plutonium escaping into the environment in dangerous quantities is small.[35] However, the commercial transport and

[32] As of this writing, an analysis of the Three Mile Island accident is not generally available. However, from newspaper reports, the accident appeared to involve human error in operating the reactor without auxiliary pumps in commission, a failure of valves to close, a failure of instrumentation and a related questionable judgment to turn off an emergency cooling system, and, apparently, the unforeseen development of a hydrogen gas bubble in the reactor as a result of fuel damage.

[33] Lewis, in *Risk Assessment Review* (p. 12), suggests that the Rasmussen limits of a factor of 5 or so are definitely too small; the choice of outside limits here is then about twenty times greater than those bounds.

[34] See Ford Foundation, *Nuclear Power Issues*, pp. 229–230.

[35] See U.S. Atomic Energy Commission, *Draft Environmental Statement: Liquid Metal Fast Breeder Reactor Program*, WASH-1535 (Washington, GPO, March

storage of plutonium fuels and their possible effect on nuclear diversion and proliferation is also of great concern (see chapter 14).

The liquid metal fast breeder reactor (LMFBR) has been the subject of intensive research in the United States. It has a different type of cooling system and a different kind of reactor core from the standard light water reactor (LWR), and the probability of reactor accidents could differ from that for LWRs (see chapter 9). The cooling system itself, while involving a very active substance, liquid sodium, is not pressurized; that aspect should tend to make it safer than an LWR system. On the other hand, the energy structure of the core in the breeder is somewhat more dangerous than that in LWR cores. It is possible that the breeder core could come apart violently, leading to a spread of radioactivity into the plant environs. Exact comparisons are not yet feasible, but on balance, safety problems for the breeders seem to be different from those for the LWRs but not necessarily better or worse.

Comparative Radiation Impacts

The total fatalities projected for the general public from a nuclear power plant and its ancillary nuclear fuel cycle range from 0.07 to 2 per plant-year equivalent. Routine radiation from short-lived isotopes has the least impact on the fatality rate. The radiation from long-lived isotopes, mainly radon from uranium mills and mine wastes, has a greater impact, but under our discounting assumptions, the greatest number of fatalities stems from the theoretical maximum averaged-out fatalities from nuclear power plant accidents. The calculated contribution from the long-lived isotopes depends on how future events are viewed, and the total could be considered much larger (or smaller) than that adopted here.

Other Safety Impacts on the General Public

There are safety problems associated with energy technologies that may impinge on the general public. One of the least publicized but largest of known safety hazards is the danger to the general public from motor

---

1974) p. 4.1–5; U.S. Energy Research and Development Administration, *Liquid Metal Fast Breeder Reactor Program*, ERDA-1535, Final Environmental Statement (Washington, GPO, December 1975) 3 vols.

vehicle accidents associated with the transport of energy, specifically, grade-crossing accidents of automobiles with trains carrying coal. This source has been estimated to cause between 0.5 and 1.5 fatalities per plant-year, hardly a negligible contribution.[36] A low-Btu combined-cycle electric plant uses 95 percent as much coal as a standard coal-fired plant, and therefore has a proportional safety impact. Coal-conversion gas and liquids, when used to produce the same amount of useful end-use energy for home heating, require about 70 percent as much coal for gases and 76 percent as much for liquids; the relative safety impact from these technologies is proportional to these percentages. Certain dangers are also involved in the distribution of either electricity or of gaseous and liquid fuels after their production (for example, accidents with high-voltage lines and natural gas explosions). Natural gas is subject to safety hazards at normal pressures, in transmission and during utilization. It has been estimated that pipeline distribution failures could cause about 0.1 death and 1 injury for every 1-GW plant supplied by natural gas.[37] Impacts could be of the same order of magnitude for synthetic gas from coal, but no estimate is adopted here because it is uncertain how far synthetic gas will be transmitted and in what locations and functions it will be utilized.

Renewable energy sources can also cause fatal injuries to the public. It is too early to try to estimate the corresponding fatality rate for a plant using biomass as a boiler fuel: transportation distances may well differ because of the larger bulk that has to be carried, and transportation modes might be different. However, one might not be surprised to discover a significant problem in this area.

Definite solar-related risks also exist; in particular, the known, fairly dangerous nature of roofing work indicates that repair accidents can be associated with the safety of the general public to the extent that solar repairs are done on an amateur basis. The rate for amateur repair might be somewhat speculatively set at 0.1 to 1 fatality per plant-year equivalent.[38] This would imply that solar and coal technologies could have equivalent impacts in this miscellaneous accident category.

[36] Ramsay, *Unpaid Costs*, pp. 106–107.

[37] Derived from U.S. Environmental Protection Agency, *Accidents and Unscheduled Events Associated with Non-Nuclear Energy Resources and Technology,* EPA-600/7-77-016 (Washington, D.C., GPO, February 1977).

[38] See William Ramsay, "Small-Scale Energy Technologies," draft prepared for the National Energy Strategies Project (Washington, D.C., Resources for the Future, June 1978) p. 18-92, where existing incidences of roofing accidents and estimated solar repair times are used in the calculation. Available from RFF's Center for Energy Policy Research.

Occupational Illnesses and Accidents

Occupational illnesses and accidents form a demonstrably significant part of the total health impacts expected from conventional coal and nuclear power. Such occupational risks are present also in many of the proposed substitute technologies. Table 12-4 shows the pattern of occupational fatalities for some of the better documented energy sources.

Standard Technologies

For coal, one of the potentially largest health impacts is from occupational illnesses. In particular, one type of black lung disease, coal workers' pneumoconiosis (CWP), has been convincingly associated in the past with a large number of disabilities and deaths. It should also be noted that as many as fifty cases of CWP per plant-year may occur. However, there are great uncertainties about these figures (see table 12-4); these uncertainties are more closely examined in "A Note on Uncertainty in Occupational Risks."

The other major impact from coal is the coal-mining accident. These mining accidents, as well as those in processing, plant construction, and other fuel-cycle activities, give a sizable and—compared with CWP—a much better defined contribution to the occupational total; for fatalities, including both accidents and illnesses, 50 to 130 cases per coal-fired plant-year are estimated.

For nuclear energy, the key occupational disease has traditionally been believed to be pulmonary malignancies among uranium miners and millworkers, arising from the inhalation of radon gas or of uranium dust. From observed fatality rates at higher doses, it may be inferred under the assumptions of linearity (see footnote 20 and related text) that between 0.04 and 0.2 fatality per year could be attributed to such radiation exposures.

Mining accidents occur among nuclear workers, just as they do for coal workers. However, uranium mining—per energy unit—tends to be much safer, since less rock or sand tends to be moved per million Btus of fuel extracted because of the higher energy content of uranium as fuel in comparison with coal.

When construction fatalities and injuries for reactors are also considered, the accident fatalities total is estimated at 0.06 to 0.2 per plant-

Table 12-4. Estimated Occupational Fatalities, Per Effective Plant-Year Equivalent

	Illnesses	*Accidents*	*Combined total*
Electricity generation			
From standard coal-fired power plant	0–4	0.3–1	0.3–5
From combined-cycle, low-Btu-gas-fired plant	0–4	0.4–1	0.4–5
From nuclear-fired plant	0.04–0.2	0.06–0.2	0.1–0.4
Other energy[a]			
High-Btu gas (from coal)	0–3	0.3–0.9	0.3–4
Coal liquids	0–3	0.3–0.9	0.3–4
Shale oil	—	2–6(?)	2–6(?)
Solar home heating[b]	—	0.02–0.1(?)	0.02–0.1(?)

Note: Totals may not add because of rounding.

Sources: The occupational impacts for coal and nuclear are taken from William Ramsay, *Unpaid Costs of Electrical Energy: Health and Environmental Impacts from Coal and Nuclear Power* (Baltimore, Md., Johns Hopkins University Press for Resources for the Future, 1978); the accident figures are taken from the appendix to chap. 9, "Accidents to Workers." The figures for disease are taken from pp. 109 and 111, where the figures per USW (2 trillion kilowatt hours) translate into 0 to 3.5 fatalities for coal diseases and 0.04 to 0.2 fatality for nuclear diseases. The figures for the other technologies (except solar, see separate footnote) are derived for mining and processing by considering that the low-Btu gas to make electricity uses 95 percent as much coal, the high-Btu gas 70 percent as much, and liquefaction plants 76 percent as much (see energy input ratios in table V-1 of Eli J. Salmon, "Health and Environmental Implications of Various Energy Systems." This draft, prepared for the National Energy Strategies Project (Washington, D.C., Resources for the Future, May 1978), is available from RFF's Center for Energy Policy Research. Impacts for construction of facilities are taken from Ramsay, *Unpaid Costs,* as modified by the ratios indicated in Eli J. Salmon and Harry Perry, "Environmental Health and Safety Implications of Increased Coal Utilization," draft prepared for the National Academy of Sciences (Washington, D.C., Resources for the Future, September 1978) tab. 15. For the newer technologies, conversion plant fatalities are adapted from tab. 15, where an arbitrary error band of 50 percent has been assumed. Conversion plant diseases (cancers) take the number of fatalities in tab. 15 as the upper limit and zero as the lower limit.

[a] Given in terms of an equivalent energy of 19.6 trillion Btus delivered to home-heating uses.

[b] A rough estimate of fatalities to professional repairmen (see text).

year. For nonfatal nuclear occupational injuries—illnesses are of minor significance—the total is 10 to 20 per nuclear plant-year.

Newer Technologies

Occupational risks could be qualitatively different for the complex processes of deriving gases and liquids from coal. In particular, it is conceivable that carcinogens arising from the gasification or liquefaction processes could cause significant numbers of occupational fatalities.

A NOTE ON UNCERTAINTY IN OCCUPATIONAL RISKS

A paradox in occupational health analysis is the presence of marked uncertainty in the estimates. At first glance, there appears to be little grounds for uncertainty. Such things as mining deaths and injuries are well documented, and it is known, for example, that some 140 miners are killed in U.S. mines every year.[39] What is not known, however, is whether past trends will continue into the future. Two issues in particular are unclear. Will a recent trend—perhaps the result of changes in mining safety legislation—toward fewer mining accidents per worker-hour and per ton of mined coal continue into the future? Will strip mining for coal, which is much safer for the worker than underground mining, become the predominant method of extraction? These questions make the estimates for coal-mining accidents necessarily uncertain.

For fatalities from CWP, the situation is even more difficult to ascertain. Mining legislation within the past decade has set stringent new standards for ventilation in mines. In the British experience, this type of legislation has practically eliminated the more severe forms of CWP.[40] Will this also happen in the United States, where mining conditions differ from those in Great Britain? Since CWP apparently has a long latency period, it may be some time before this question can be answered; hence uncertainties arise about total mining-related illnesses, and these uncertainties are reflected in estimates for all the coal and coal-conversion technologies.

For nuclear technology, one must note that the mining industry has been changing rather rapidly during the past decade in response to the growth of nuclear power. Hence patterns of nuclear mining accidents are not yet fixed, making it difficult to project future accident rates. For the mining- and milling-related illnesses, radiation doses are either measured or at least carefully estimated, but the effects of the low-level radiation on health are not well known. The predicted fatalities from radiation shown cannot be distinguished even statistically from the background of normally occurring cancer deaths at the low levels of radiation experienced, and estimates are therefore necessarily uncertain.

For shale oil, it is exceedingly difficult to estimate occupational accidents for a relatively untried technology. The estimates given in table 12-4 rely on inferences comparing shale oil to coal. Shale oil should be somewhat safer to extract than coal, because there is less danger of roof and wall collapses during the mining process. However, since the energy content of shale by weight and volume is disproportionately low as compared with that of coal, one can estimate that, on balance, the dangers from shale extraction could be some five times greater than that of coal per energy unit.[41]

Uncertainties for the new solar home-heating industry arise from our lack of related experience. Even though it is known that the roofing industry is a fairly dangerous occupation, key factors such as the frequency of repair and maintenance for rooftop solar units are not yet known.

[39] U.S. Department of the Interior, Mining Enforcement and Safety Administration, "MESA Safety Reviews: Coal-Mine Fatalities in December 1976" (Washington, D.C., February 1977).

Such a pessimistic prognosis may or may not be correct; although it can be estimated from comparisons with coking industries that such carcinogenic risks are small and correspond to less than 0.09 fatality per plant-year,[42] a much smaller risk than that for coal mining-derived illnesses. Furthermore, the in-plant industrial accident rates are projected to be higher for gasification and liquefaction plants than for standard coal-fired power plants.

The major difference between coal conversion and standard coal combustion in boilers, however, hinges on the amount of coal needed for the various processes, since many of the coal-derived illnesses and accidents are associated with mining in direct proportion to the amount of coal utilized. In terms of the effective plant-year equivalent of 19.6 million Btus for home-heating purposes, the low-Btu combined-cycle plant is calculated to use almost 95 percent as much coal as the standard coal-fired power plant, but the plant fired by high-Btu gas uses only 70 percent as much, and the coal-liquefaction plant uses 76 percent as much. Using these modifying factors, accidents and illnesses induced from coal conversion can be readily inferred (see table 12-4).[43]

The situation may be markedly different for occupational fatalities associated with shale oil. Again, fatalities during the surface retorting of ore have been estimated to occur at a rate of between 2 and 6 fatalities per plant-year (see "A Note on Uncertainty in Occupational Risks"). In situ retorting ought to be much safer, at about 0.5 fatality. Nonfatal injuries for shale oil operations are quite likely large also, ranging from perhaps 90 to 300 for surface retorting.[44] But all these last estimates are quite uncertain.

For solar energy, roof repairs are important causes of homeowner injuries. A number of additional direct fatalities could be expected among professional repairmen—very roughly 0.02 to 0.1 (and 10 to 20 lost-time injuries per year) for solar home systems that supply an output energy equivalent to one equivalent plant-year.[45]

---

[40] Argonne National Laboratory, "Health and Ecological Effects of Coal Utilization," draft report, U.S. Nuclear Regulatory Commission (December 1976) sect. 7.312.

[41] Salmon, "Environmental, Health, and Safety Impacts" (August 1978) p. 13/14-54.

[42] Salmon, "Health and Environmental Implications" (May 1978) p. VI-39.

[43] Ibid. (May 1978) tab. X-1.

[44] Salmon, "Environmental, Health, and Safety Impacts" (August 1978) p. 13/14-53.

[45] Ramsay, "Small-Scale Energy Technologies," pp. 18-90 and 18-91.

Comparative Occupational Impacts

Comparing the technologies, table 12-4 shows that standard electricity generation by coal has a higher rate of total occupational fatalities than does nuclear power. Rates for nonfatal diseases and accidents are also generally lower for nuclear.

Table 12-4 also shows that rates for standard coal generation and low-Btu gas combined-cycle coal generation are virtually identical.

For coal conversion to gasification and liquefaction, occupational fatalities may be somewhat smaller than for standard coal-fired plants; however, the ranges are very similar, and the difference is apparently insignificant at the level of accuracy of the data.

Shale oil could present the worst occupational hazard of all, on the basis of the very rough estimates given here.

Solar home heating—again on the basis of the very rough estimates shown in table 12-4—could be the safest technology for workers of all those shown in the table; however, in addition to uncertainties in data, the role of greater occupational accidents and illnesses in industries supplying solar equipment may deserve consideration. That is, a capital intensive—and currently expensive—technology like solar could be assigned its fair share of the occupational accidents and illnesses associated with materials such as glass, steel, and copper, and the manufacturing processes that take place in producing solar collectors, for example. However, such a total risk analysis is necessarily complex and prone to error, and may indeed be inconsequential for technologies delivering energy at equivalent prices.[46]

Overall Health Comparisons

By combining all the impacts on the general public plus the occupational impacts discussed above, table 12-5 compares the three main electricity technologies.

---

[46] This total risk analysis concept has been suggested most prominently in Herbert Inhaber, *Risk of Energy Production,* AECB-1119/Rev-2 (Ottawa, Canada, Atomic Energy Control Board, Nov. 1978), which, however, does not provide a consistent new evaluation or reevaluation of previous work on various technologies.

Since the evaluation is so complex—involving so many types of equipment and systems having different (and often questionable) accident and illness rates, it may be that it is preferable in practice to use an "equilibrium risk" model. That is, for products of the same cost, assume the same level of risk to start out with, and then identify specific high-risk (or low-risk) areas to modify the calculation accordingly. In fact, such a procedure might produce results very similar to those in the text obtained from the usual type of partial risk analysis.

Table 12-5. Estimated Total Fatalities for Workers and the General Public from Electricity-Generating Technologies, Per Effective Plant-Year

Standard coal-fired power plant	
Air pollution[a]	0–8
General safety	0.5–1[b]
Occupational safety	0.3–5
Total	0.8–14
Combined-cycle, low-Btu-gas-fired plant	
Air pollution	0–0.8
General safety	0.5–1
Occupational safety	0.4–5
Total[c]	0.9–7
Nuclear	
Routine radiation	0.001–0.005
Gaseous wastes[d]	0.07–0.3
Reactor accidents[e]	0.0002–2
Occupational	0.1–0.4
Total[f]	0.2–3

Source: Tables 12-2, 12-3, 12-4, and text.

[a] See notes to tab. 12-1 for qualifications about uncertainties.

[b] Rounded down here to 1 from 1.5 to emphasize its essential equality with the coal low-Btu result. (The total is derived from two-place estimates and is not affected by this choice.)

[c] Catastrophic effects like climate modification are not evaluated in this total (see chap. 14).

[d] Assuming future fatalities are discounted at 5 percent. Assuming no discounting, or rates much below 1 percent, would make totals markedly larger.

[e] Based on theoretical models of accidents.

[f] Hypothetical effects of nuclear power on nuclear terrorism or proliferation are not included (see chap. 14).

For the comparison between nuclear and standard coal technology it appears that the general range of nuclear estimates overlaps significantly that for coal. Fatalities from reactor accidents, air pollution-induced illnesses and coal mining-induced illnesses are highly uncertain (see "A Note on Uncertainty in Occupational Risks"). If the impacts from coal illness are indeed very large, the values toward the upper end of the coal range should be applicable, and some discrepancy between nuclear and coal should arise to favor nuclear. The advantage for nuclear would be greatly heightened if, as the result of further experience or improved safety analyses, the nuclear safety risks turned out to fall near the lower, rather than the upper end of the estimates.

On the other hand, even the very wide range of estimated impacts from reactor accidents are still based on projections and not on actual events (see "A Note on the Rasmussen Report"), and even the upper limit could be questioned. Future fatalities from radon emissions can be calculated only by means of controversial techniques. A reevaluation of either of

Table 12-6. Estimated Total Fatalities for Workers and the General Public from Several Nonelectric Technologies, Per Effective Plant-Year Equivalent

Technology	Air pollution fatalities[a]	General safety (accident fatalities)	Occupational fatalities (disease and accident)	Total
High-Btu gas (from coal)	0–0.6	0.4–1	0.3–4	0.7–6
Coal liquids	0–1	0.4–1	0.3–4	0.7–6
Shale oil (surface retorting)	0–1	—	2–6 (?)	2–7 (?)
Solar home heating	—	0.2–1 (?)[b]	0.02–0.1 (?)	0.2–1 (?)

Source: Tables 12-2, 12-4, and text.
Note: Catastrophic effects like climate modification are not included in these totals.
[a] See notes to tab. 12-1 for uncertainties.
[b] Fatalities occurring during homeowner repairs.

these effects could change the coal-nuclear picture to favor coal. In addition, no impacts from nuclear terrorism or nuclear proliferation are shown, for one reason because no such impacts have yet occurred. If these impacts are large, they could affect the comparison; however, because of their special nature, they are considered in chapter 14.

As one might expect, a key question in comparing electricity from a standard coal plant to that from a low-Btu-gas combined-cycle plant hinges on air pollution. We see clearly that the combined-cycle plant has a definite advantage if the high end of the range for air pollution impacts is correct. If not, the standard coal plant might be as good, or even better, than the new type of facility.

Table 12-6 shows the same breakdown of fatalities for both workers and the general public for the nonelectric technologies.

The key comparison to be made here is between coal-fired electric plants (see table 12-5) and high-Btu gas derived from coal (see table 12-6). The fatalities for the former range from 0.8 to 14, while those from the latter range from 0.7 to 6. Again, the only significant difference is in air pollution; however, if air pollution impacts are large, high-Btu gas should produce more than a 50 percent saving in fatalities. The same conclusion, incidentally, holds for coal liquids.

Another comparison—of subsidiary but not negligible interest—can be made between coal liquids and shale oil. The uncertain roles of two impacts that dominate the total impact calculations are crucial here: black lung in fatalities for coal liquids; the estimated mining accident deaths for shale oil. How important each of these problems really is will probably determine the net tradeoff between these two means of getting liquids.

The newer, renewable sources are a much more indefinite affair. Very tentative totals for solar home heating are shown; however, these questionable values, 0.2 to 1, only serve to demonstrate that the range of estimates for solar home heating could overlap that of the more conventional coal technologies. For biomass and geothermal energy and many of the other renewables, no estimates are given here; the key problems are probably occupational accidents for biomass and air pollution for geothermal sources.

13 Environmental Impacts of Energy Technologies

Energy systems, like any other result of human activity, have impacts on the natural environment. These impacts vary in strength and nature, and their significance to human beings is generally a matter of controversy.

Some of the chief environmental impacts on land, water, and air related to the various energy technologies will be discussed here. A limited number of environmental problems with possibly catastrophic consequences—carbon dioxide buildup in particular and climate modification in general, as well as acid rain—will be discussed separately in chapter 14.

Impacts on Land Use

The term *land use* includes direct impacts on land—that is, the temporary or permanent occupation of land for energy extraction, conversion, and delivery, or for the disposal of energy wastes—and indirect land impacts, such as noise, esthetic insult, or other factors more difficult to analyze quantitatively.

Use of Land for Energy Production and Waste Disposal

The direct uses of land for various types of energy-related facilities and waste disposal are shown in table 13-1.[1]

---

[1] Here, as elsewhere in this chapter, selection of the technologies for the table entries may reflect the adequacy of the data available.

Table 13-1. Land Areas Converted to Energy Use Per Effective Plant-Year Equivalent

Form of energy	Acres
Electricity	
Coal	
Mines	300–600
Power plants[a]	
Station site	3
Cooling lakes (optional)	40
Scrubber wastes	20–30
Nuclear	
Mines	60
Power plants[a]	
Station site	1–7
Total site (including exclusion areas)	7–70
Cooling lakes (optional)	70
Mill tailings	8
Solar electric[a]	70–300
Biomass	10,000
Other energy	
Oil shale (conventional)	
Mining	2,000–3,000
Additional shale-disposal areas[b]	10–25
Oil shale (in situ)[a]	7

Note: Based on 19.6 trillion Btu delivered to home heating end uses, taken for the electricity technologies as equivalent to 1-GW plant-year of 6.57 billion kWh.

Source: William Ramsay, *Unpaid Costs of Electrical Energy: Health and Environmental Impacts from Coal and Nuclear Power* (Baltimore, Johns Hopkins University Press for Resources for the Future, 1978) chap. 8 (for electricity technologies); Harry Perry, "Production of Liquids and Gases from Other Resources," draft prepared for the National Energy Strategies Project (Washington, D.C., Resources for the Future, 1978) pp. 17-100, 17-105, and 17-106 (for oil shale); William Ramsay, "Electricity from New Technologies," draft prepared for the National Energy Strategies Project (Washington, D.C., Resources for the Future, 1978) pp. 16-26 and 16-61 (for solar and biomass). The last two reports are available from RFF's Center for Energy Policy Research.

[a] Land use for sites occupying a fixed number of acres for a long period are normalized to a thirty-year lifetime and then prorated annually; that is, a typical cooling lake for a coal-fired plant will take up an actual area of 40 × 30 = 1,200 acres.

[b] See text for explanation.

Considering the standard electricity technologies, coal and nuclear power, the most dramatic use of land for energy production is that utilized in surface mining of fuel resources. Coal mining has been especially responsible for the disturbance of enormous land areas. In fact, a recent survey of all surface and underground mines shows an average land use of between 300 and 600 acres per plant-year,[2] and this should

[2] Thomas W. Hunter, *Effects of Air Quality Requirements on Coal Supply,* U.S. Department of the Interior, Bureau of Mines, supplement to *Bituminous Coal and Lignite Distribution Reports* (Washington, D.C., U.S. Bureau of Mines, May

be relatively insensitive to small changes in future mining practices. Nuclear energy, in the form of light water reactors (LWRs), utilizes 60 acres per plant-year for mining. Although this is an official estimate based on experience with typical existing mines,[3] it is probably subject to change. In particular, as grades of uranium ore will undoubtedly decrease over future years, more ore will have to be moved to get equivalent amounts of uranium. Therefore, the amount of land used by such mines may increase considerably. Naturally, breeder reactors would use much less uranium and therefore would produce many fewer land impacts from uranium mining operations than do nonbreeders.

The significance of the impacts from both these technologies hinges on how well the land can be reclaimed. Reclamation after coal mining has been mandated under federal laws which direct the approximate restoration of original land contours and reestablishment of vegetation. Nuclear mining areas must usually be reclaimed under state laws or under federal nuclear energy regulation of mine-mill complexes. However, such reclamation may be unsuccessful, especially in arid areas, and standard reclamation techniques for the recreation of the landscape may not yield "satisfactory" results, at least in the judgment of the public.

In addition to the purely esthetic effects of reclamation, there are other considerations as well. Effects on local groundwater could be significant, and, indeed, new laws restrict mining in alluvial valley areas. Plant life in formerly mined areas may be permanently changed. If new types of vegetation are purposely introduced, as has been done in Montana, the change may be beneficial at least to some forms of animal life, by the creation of improved grazing land.[4] However, effects on native fauna can be quite complex; for example, the reduction of native vegetation and changes in land forms may decrease the effective habitat for native species, thus contributing to pressures on survival.[5]

1976). Hunter gives values for tons per acre and cites coal usage by region. The result is about 350 to 580 acres per plant-year, where the uncertainty is in regional contributions.

[3] See U.S. Nuclear Regulatory Commission (NRC), *Final Generic Environmental Statement on the Use of Recycled Plutonium in Mixed Oxide Fuel in Light Water Cooled Reactors: Health, Safety and Environment,* NUREG-0002 (Washington, D.C., NRC, August 1976) pp. IV F-16 and IV F-22.

[4] Edward J. DePuit, "Plant Response and Forage Quality for Controlled Grazing on Coal Mine Spoils Pasture," Research Report No. 115 (Bozeman, Montana State University, Reclamation Research Unit, Montana Agricultural Experimental Station, August 1977) pp. VIII-56 and VIII-57.

[5] William Ramsay, "Priorities in Species Preservation," *Environmental Affairs* vol. 4, no. 4 (1976) pp. 595–616.

The impact from power plants differs entirely from that of surface mining. The area needed for a coal-fired station site itself is small, especially when it is prorated over the thirty-year plant-life, at 3 acres annually. However, for nuclear plants, the problem of decommissioned reactors arises, since part or all of the 1 to 7 acres (encompassing from 30 to 200 acres over the plant's lifetime) may have to be severely restricted from other land uses for hundreds of years. In line with the discussion in chapter 12, the future usefulness of abandoned reactor sites depends to some extent on how much money is spent on the decommissioning process—and on whether established sites are used for future generations of reactors.

In addition to the station area itself, large amounts of land, an average of 1,000 acres, are customarily set aside at each nuclear site as an exclusion zone, for safety reasons or for the location of the cooling system.[6] Indeed, the largest land use effect associated directly with power plants may, in fact, arise from cooling ponds or lakes that serve as one way to carry out closed-cycle cooling. These cooling ponds can be very large for coal or nuclear plants, averaging 2,000 acres or so for the standard nuclear plant or, on the basis of a thirty-year lifetime, some 70 acres or more per plant-year.[7] The conversion of such a large area to impoundment can be a fairly major land use change for the locality; however, many lakes can be used for other purposes, and there seems to be little reason why the land cannot be reconverted into other uses after the plant has been decommissioned.[8]

The problem of noxious residues from the conversion process is heightened for those technologies where waste disposal is already of concern. Coal ash ponds are one such example, but probably more serious for coal-fired power plants during the next decades will be the question of how to dispose of scrubber wastes. If limestone scrubbing methods continue to be used in the future, scrubbers could produce volumes of waste that are large in quantity as well as being difficult to solidify. These wastes might be produced at a rate of some 600 acre-feet per plant-year, with the amount of land used depending on the depth of the landfill for these wastes. Assuming a depth of from 20 to

[6] U.S. Atomic Energy Commission, *Nuclear Power Facility Performance Characteristics for Making Environmental Impact Assessments*, WASH-1355 (Washington, D.C., GPO, December 1974) p. 4-15.

[7] Ibid., p. 4-97.

[8] William Ramsay and Phillip R. Reed, *Land Use and Nuclear Power Plants*, WASH-1319, U.S. Atomic Energy Commission (Washington, D.C., GPO, October 1974) p. 20.

30 feet, these landfill areas would require some 20 to 30 acres per plant-year.

For nuclear plants, high- and low-level wastes can cause localized problems. However, if prorated for total plant-years, the affected land areas are relatively small. Unfortunately, this is not necessarily true for the land affected by mill tailings. The fact that these wastes emit gases such as radon that may affect the general population has been mentioned in chapter 12. Furthermore, radium and other radioactive elements found in the mill tailings must be prevented from leaking in significant quantities into local aquifers. The extent of this problem will depend on the state of the nuclear industry and would be reduced considerably in a breeder economy; but, whatever the exact numbers of acres involved, the use of reclaimed mill tailings for other human purposes must be severely restricted for an indefinite time. Thus, unless new disposal methods now being proposed are adopted, this represents a quasi-permanent land use.

Oil shale extraction produces a direct impact on 2,000 to 3,000 acres for each plant-year equivalent. Additional land is required for the restoring process and for the disposal of wastes. The disposal area, however, requires fewer acres, beginning with 25 acres per plant-year, and eventually dropping to 10 acres as more waste shale is disposed of by returning it to the mine.[9] However, all acres are not equal: the reclaiming of the shale disposal area could become a greater problem than the mined area itself. In situ mining involves a much smaller commitment of land, about 7 acres per plant-year.

Table 13-1 shows that solar electricity central stations require the dedication of a considerable amount of land, probably a total thirty-year commitment of some 2,000 to 10,000 acres. This land must be defoliated and then covered with arrays of solar collectors; however, after decommissioning such a plant, the land could be returned to productive uses with less damage than that expected for surface-mined land, for example. Satellite solar systems require large areas for their receiving antennas, and because of the microwave radiation involved, some land uses such as industry, housing, or even agriculture might have to be excluded.

For tidal power and for small-scale hydroelectric plants, types of land use impacts occur that are similar to those associated with other

---

[9] University of Oklahoma, The Science and Public Policy Program, *Energy Alternatives: A Comparative Analysis,* prepared for CEQ, ERDA, EPA, FEA, FPC, DOI, and NSF (Washington, D.C., GPO, May 1975) p. 2-38.

impoundments, such as cooling lakes. The construction of a tidal impoundment, for example, has a fairly major effect on some ecological niches in the local aquatic community. Similarly, if hydro projects are associated with new dams, the system impacts for aquatic species can be severe. If, on the other hand, only existing impoundments are used, and drawdowns are not excessive, little effect need be feared.

The key land uses for biomass power plants would be devoted to fuel production, as is the case for coal and nuclear plants. However, important differences do exist. Much more land is involved in the harvesting of established trees or crop wastes and for the growth of special trees or other crops for energy purposes. On the basis of some 3 million tons of fuel needed each year for the standard plant, and perhaps 10 tons an acre produced yearly on a sustaining basis, a single standard generating plant using forests or crops dedicated to its fuel production could require a total of some 300,000 acres, or 10,000 acres per plant-year. If this number were examined uncritically, it would appear that the net land use impact is enormous. However, one must deal with the fact that forests and, indeed, cropland are often considered by the public to possess positive scenic values. The harvesting itself—lumbering in particular—may introduce negative landscape features; but assessing such familiar impacts may involve the subtle matter of public tastes in environmental values. Biomass production from forest or crop residues would of course require little or no new land use changes.

Indirect Land Use Effects

Mines, power plants, and other energy facilities can have important effects on neighboring lands. Surface mining of coal, uranium, or oil shale can inflict a higher social cost through its impact on the scenic values of the surrounding landscape than the mined acreage itself would do. The contrast is even more marked in the case of transmission lines, where the impact on farming or dwellings in the transmission corridor may be relatively minor as compared with the scenic impact on the whole countryside. A similar conclusion may hold for solar electric plants and solar heating installations in homes, where the sheer size of of the collector area and the possibility of glare from the installations—plus possible conflicts over tree removals and the general questions of sun rights—can be the most important consequence for neighboring areas. The same phenomenon may arise in the case of windmills: as far as one can tell from most existing designs of large, modern wind-powered generator systems, individual machines may have to be linearly separated by more than a mile because of air-stream requirements. For large arrays, the total esthetic effect on the neighborhood therefore could be significant.

A more serious problem in regard to general land use and safety is that of land subsidence over old mine galleries. This has caused difficulties for communities situated over abandoned coal mines in the past, but it is hoped that improved regulations will diminish this danger for new coal and, presumably, for oil shale mines.

Certain types of nuisance effects also occur. For example, the plumes from mechanical draft cooling towers on power plants can cause fog or icing in nearby areas. Plumes from natural draft towers can cause shadowing of nearby land, and their moisture emissions can produce local snowfalls. When used with brackish or salt water, such cooling towers also require special precautions to avoid damaging salt deposits. Mechanical draft cooling towers constitute a local noise nuisance, as do the hammer mills that are associated with the use of municipal refuse as a biomass resource. The public has also on occasion objected on esthetic grounds to the setting up of new waste-collection points for municipal refuse.

What effect have power plants on nearby land use? In particular, population projections for the neighborhoods of nuclear power plants are set at certain limits in order to lessen the impact of a possible severe reactor accident. However, after the licensing takes place, in practice no further restriction applies; future residents of the area may incur an extra safety risk that is not taken into account in any energy option analysis—at least until a new operating license is sought, forty years later.

Impacts on Water

Significant impacts can be made on water resources, both in quantity and quality, as a result of the operation of power plants, mines, and other energy facilities.

Water Quality

Water quality problems are exceedingly difficult to evaluate; in addition to uncertainties about water pollutant data, the effect of pollutants on drinking water and on the local ecosystem is quite controversial. Public interest in these problems often has been intense; a popular concern in recent years has been "thermal pollution" from power plants. Since a typical nuclear power plant using once-through cooling can deposit 1,600 cubic feet per second of warm water into local water bodies, the effects on local aquatic life could be severe, depending on local topography, the size of the water body, the temperature of the discharge, and the nature and timing of the life cycles of the species present. The problem also exists for coal plants; but significantly (about 40 percent) less water is discharged because of higher efficiencies and because heat loss from coal plants also occurs in the stack gases. However, this type of water pollution has been closely regulated under laws passed within the last decade, and the Environmental Protection Agency (EPA) has issued stringent rules that can be expected to alleviate this impact greatly, mainly by requiring closed-cycle cooling. New legislation to adapt these rules to ocean environments might be needed, incidentally, if newer sources, such as ocean thermal energy conversion (OTEC), become practical. In fact, its proponents usually anticipate some restrictions on the temperature of OTEC discharges under future environmental guidelines.

Chemical pollution of water from all power plants is currently regulated by the EPA. There is also great concern about sedimentation and other pollution from mining operations. This is especially true for acid mine drainage, which is the contamination of neighboring watersheds with acidic effluents from abandoned mines. Under current EPA rules, however, the ongoing water control procedures in the new mines should greatly decrease the impact of acid drainage in future years.

Chemical pollution of water from coal-conversion plants is of special concern for the coal-gasification and liquefaction processes. In addition to the usual sulfides, nitrates, and chlorides present in ash runoffs, quantities of such substances as phenols, tars, oils, and various polynuclear aromatic hydrocarbons and other trace elements are often present.[10] Water quality standards have only recently been proposed for many of these potentially hazardous substances, and the costs and effectiveness of control measures are not yet clear. For oil shale, the discharge of waste water could be a major difficulty. Many projects have proposed a zero-discharge policy (that is, the cleaning and complete

[10] See Harry Perry, "Production of Liquids and Gases from Other Resources," draft prepared for National Energy Strategies Project (Washington, D.C., Resources for the Future, 1978) p. 17-27. Available from RFF's Center for Energy Policy Research.

recycling of waste-water discharges[11]), but the cost feasibility of this proposal has not been established.

Among the newer sources, such as wave power or OTEC systems, mechanical or chemical damage to aquatic organisms could take place; this is a traditional problem for all power plants, but is now often closely regulated for onshore facilities. Geothermal energy systems also have been known to discharge such toxic elements as arsenic and mercury into the local watersheds. Although these substances will be closely regulated, the cost implications of such regulations are unclear. As a result of growing special forest or crops for a biomass conversion plant, greater potential impacts can be expected from increased erosion, and fertilizer and pesticide runoff. Impacts of such operations have not yet been analyzed fully.

Water Consumption

In contrast to water quality problems, which are difficult to quantify, many water quantity needs are subject to somewhat more precise study. Table 13-2 estimates the amount of water consumption by power plants and some other energy facilities. Despite uncertainties in many of these estimates, the largest contributions certainly come from a relatively well documented impact, that is, the cooling water typically evaporated by power plants. For our purposes here, we have assumed the presence of cooling towers.[12] If once-through cooling or cooling ponds are utilized instead, the water consumption is usually estimated to be less. But much heat loss occurs by evaporation in any system. Once-through cooling generally means that more water is evaporated downstream rather than at the plant site, even though over one-half the heat is indeed lost by radiation or conduction. Cooling ponds, while responsible for somewhat less direct evaporation for cooling than cooling towers, often contribute a "natural" evaporation loss of some significance.[13] While the estimates for mining, especially those for the newer technologies, are

---

[11] Ibid., p. 17-9.

[12] U.S. Atomic Energy Commission, Directorate of Regulatory Standards, *Nuclear Power Facility Performance Characteristics for Making Environmental Impact Assessments*, WASH-1355 (Washington, D.C., GPO, December 1974) p. 4-72.

[13] Robert T. Jaske, "Is There a Future for Once-Through Cooling?" Paper presented at the 79th National Meeting of the American Institute of Chemical Engineers, Houston, Texas, March 18 (Richland, Wash., Battelle Pacific Northwest Laboratories, 1975) p. 14.

Table 13-2. Water Consumption Rate Per Effective Plant Equivalent
(in cubic feet per second)

Energy		Water consumption
Electricity		
Nuclear		
Cooling (using cooling tower)	30[a]	
Mining (including reclamation)	1	30
Coal		
Cooling (using cooling tower)	20[a]	
Mining (including reclamation)	0.2–3	20
Other energy		
High-Btu gas		
Mining	0.1–2	
Processing	2–5	2–7
Coal liquids (crude oil type)		
Mining	0.2–2	
Processing	2–5	2–7
Shale oil		2–6

Note: Rate of water usage of a plant delivering 19.6 trillion Btus to home-heating uses each year; for plant-year totals, results may be multiplied by the factor 3.15×10^7 seconds per year (or multiplied by 725 to get acre-feet per year). All totals are rounded to one significant digit.

Source: William Ramsay, *Unpaid Costs of Electrical Energy: Health and Environmental Impacts from Coal and Nuclear Power* (Baltimore, Md., Johns Hopkins University Press for Resources for the Future, 1978) chap. 8 (for electricity); Harry Perry, "Production of Liquids and Gases from Other Resources." (Washington, D.C., Resources for the Future, 1978) p. 17-59 (coal conversion), and p. 17-101 (shale oil). This draft, prepared for the National Energy Strategies Project, is available from RFF's Center for Energy Policy Research.

[a] Yearly maximum values; values averaged over seasons could be some 25 percent less.

quite uncertain, it therefore seems clear that power-plant cooling systems will usually require more water than other parts of the energy sector. The amount of water used by a low-Btu combined-cycle plant should be roughly equivalent to the amount used by the typical coal-fired plant, with the former extra water uses being balanced by greater plant efficiency.

What is the significance of such impacts? A U.S. Nuclear Regulatory Commission study estimated a carrying capacity for energy use of approximately 85,000 cubic feet per second for all regions of the United States.[14] This carrying capacity, calculated as a small percentage of total available runoff, would support a maximum nuclear capacity of from

[14] U.S. Nuclear Regulatory Commission (NRC), Office of Special Studies, *Nuclear Energy Center Site Survey—1975,* NUREG-001 (Washington, D.C., GPO, January 1976) part V, pp. 3-24 ff., and p. 3-29.

3,000 to 7,000 GW. This compares with the 1,400-GW capacity predicted for all electrical generation in the entire United States in the year 2000.[15] Particular regions—for example, that comprising Colorado, Kansas, and Nebraska—were judged capable of supporting only a 25-GW capacity at most, but to be sure, energy needs in this region could remain low. Allocating water among different water users within specific regions presents a major problem for policymakers. The potential for the country as a whole for possible electricity use is apparently large. But that means only that true availability depends on the growth rate for competing uses of water, especially for western agriculture. Indeed, in some cases, the use of more expensive dry cooling towers may be necessary in order to construct power plants in arid environments.

At any rate, it is evident from table 13-2 that coal-based systems have some total advantage over nuclear-based systems. Of course, the greater need for water in reclamation of coal surface-mining sites must be taken into account in regional evaluations. In addition, the newer gas and liquids technologies, if our uncertain estimates are correct, do not involve as high a demand for water as electricity technologies, although local and regional demands could still be significantly high. This holds true especially for shale oil, where relatively low water requirements nevertheless present some difficulty because of the aridity of regions in which the present resources are located.

Impacts on Air

Air pollution impacts were discussed in chapter 12 in terms of their health effects. We turn now to those consequences of air pollution that are more strictly environmental. Some of these can be expressed in actual dollar costs, but there are others that are more difficult to quantify, even though they are of obvious importance. The sulfur and nitrogen particles released into the air can form acids and other compounds that can be injurious to materials and to plants; zinc and other metals can be particularly affected. In assessing this effect for energy-production facilities, it is difficult to specify which damage is caused by air pollution because other air pollutants—notably oxidants produced by motor vehicle emissions—may also cause damage. However, from

[15] William Ramsay, *Unpaid Costs of Electrical Energy: Health and Environmental Impacts from Coal and Nuclear Power* (Baltimore, Md., Johns Hopkins University Press for Resources for the Future, 1978) fig. 11-5, p. 142.

existing surveys of materials deterioration rates, it can be estimated that damages to property in general may range from $200,000 to $2 million per coal plant-year. In addition, it is estimated that $60,000 to $600,000 worth of crop damage will occur.[16] The polluting acids also have a general effect on plants and animals, particularly aquatic fauna. It is at least conceivable that such an effect on a large scale could produce a kind of ecological catastrophe (acid rain is discussed more fully in chapter 14).

Air pollution has an effect on visibility and the landscape. Particulates and sometimes the brown gas nitrogen dioxide help to obscure the atmosphere and degrade the visual landscape. This esthetic impact is difficult to measure in monetary terms. Studies in changes in property values could provide some information on this topic. For example, Ridker's earlier study measured correlations between sulfate levels in Saint Louis and decreases of property values of single-family units.[17] However, presently all that can be reasonably said is that the esthetic impact is an obvious, if unquantified social disbenefit, and is undoubtedly reflected indirectly in some kinds of dollar costs.

Comparative Impacts on Land, Water, and Air

The different environmental concerns are not strictly commensurable. However, within the categories of land, water, and air, certain patterns emerge.

For coal and nuclear power, the land use impact in terms of disturbed acreage is much larger for the former. Indeed, even if grades of uranium become much lower so that much more land has to be disturbed for each ton of ore, the coal-mining impact should remain larger because of the greater tonnage involved per energy unit. However, the special nature of some of the land uses that involve a seemingly permanent dedication to nuclear power, such as uranium mill tailings and the sites of old reactors, must be taken as countervailing nuclear disadvantages.

[16] William Ramsay, "Health and Environmental Impacts of Coal and Nuclear Electricity" (Washington, D.C., Resources for the Future, draft 1978) chap. 5, modified for stricter emissions standards: 10.8 million pounds of sulfur annually. Available from RFF's Center for Energy Policy Research.

[17] Ronald G. Ridker, *Economic Costs of Air Pollution: Studies in Measurement* (New York, Praeger, 1970) pp. 115–140.

The same considerations hold for the low-Btu-coal combined-cycle option: its land uses, which have not been analyzed explicitly here, will be slightly less than that for the standard coal option, because the coal amounts to only 95 percent of the needs of the coal-fired boiler plant. Coal liquids and gases will continue to be dominated by coal-mining impacts, with the land area totals being somewhat less than for the standard coal power plant.

Land impacts are large for some of the newer technologies, especially for oil shale, at 2,000 to 3,000 acres per plant-year equivalent of output energy. Solar electric is estimated to involve an averaged-out use of 70 to 300 acres per plant-year for a typical 2,000- to 10,000-acre plant; however, it should be noted that these acres may be subjected only to temporary defoliation rather than to severe soil disturbance. Finally, biomass has a very large land use impact in the sense that hundreds of thousands of acres of forest are devoted to supporting a single power plant, an average rate of 10,000 acres per plant-year. Social attitudes, however, are very important here. New lumbering operations to gather wood for biomass conversion in established forests could be considered as environmental degradation. But new biomass-fuel forests and farms could be considered a relatively benign impact on the local landscape or could even constitute a positive scenic good, as far as public attitudes are concerned.

Water problems are of great regional importance, but it is difficult to generalize about resource utilization, consumption, and pollutant patterns.

In recent years the focus of chemical and thermal pollution problems has shifted from the difficulties of environmental assessment toward those of compliance with clean water regulations. The only probable exception is biomass conversion. Biomass cropping could have important erosion, chemical runoff, and sedimentation effects. These effects would not be covered by present water pollution standards for point sources; however, the amounts of the impacts would depend closely on cultivation management procedures and on what alternative land uses the bioenergy crops replaced.

Water supply problems can be somewhat more clearly defined. The amount of water used to cool condensers in coal-fired plants, because of greater efficiencies and loss of heat through flue gases, is less than that used in nuclear plants. Indeed, this difference has been considered by policymakers when deciding what sort of plant is to be built in some arid areas. The alternative of using low-Btu gas should not affect this comparison greatly.

Table 13-2 also shows that the water requirements for the gas and liquid technologies are considerably lower than those for the electrical alternatives.

Some general conclusions can be drawn, based on the all-important role of cooling water. Biomass efficiencies being similar to those of coal, biomass conversion should fall into the same general impact category. Efficiencies for solar and geothermal power should be lower, and therefore their water impacts should be the largest among the electricity technologies.

Comparisons of property and crop damage from air pollution are entirely proportional to those for fatalities from air pollution-related diseases, since the sulfur emissions are taken here as a surrogate measure for all effects. Therefore, from the air pollution figures shown in chapter 12 (table 12-2) for electricity technologies, low-Btu-gas-fired power plants should be viewed ten times more favorably than standard coal plants, at least in terms of reduced property damage and crop impacts. For the nonelectricity technologies, the high-Btu gas is the most desirable in that category. However, for interfuel comparisons, coal liquids and shale oil will show effects that are as small as those from low-Btu-gas-fired power plants.

The final environmental assessment depends to a great degree on the relative values to be placed on avoiding impacts on air, water, and land. Of the three fuel sources, coal has the greatest impact on air quality, is second to shale oil in its impact on land, and second to nuclear power in water use. If an equal weight were given to all three media, standard coal-fired plants would likely be the least desirable from the point of view of environmental impacts (that is, of course, if we neglect the environmental catastrophes discussed in chapter 14). The ranking of the other technologies would be more ambiguous on this assumption of assigning equal weights to land, water, and air impacts.

Some environmental media may be perceived as either having more general societal importance or as suffering from generally graver impacts from energy use. Land use, for example, appears to be an especially critical area. If land use impacts were assigned somewhat more weight than those for water and air, coal-fired boilers would still be the least recommended option, while shale oil would be assigned the second least desirable technology, followed by coal-conversion processes and nuclear power. The rating of the renewables in this land use-oriented evaluation would be somewhat ambiguous, as has been discussed, because of the qualitatively different nature of some of the key impacts involved.

14 Catastrophic Threats Associated with Energy Technologies

Apart from the health and environmental impacts that are apt to occur routinely, year in and year out, there are also the threats of some infrequent (perhaps very highly improbable) events that could produce catastrophic effects. Generally such events have not yet occurred, and perhaps they never will; but there is a fear that they might, and they deserve separate treatment here for that reason. If an energy catastrophe actually took place, the public might consider any technology closely identified with it unacceptable for further use. In fact, because some aspects of coal, nuclear, and other energy technologies can be associated with *hypothetical* catastrophes, the public may choose to place a special value on minimizing even the remote possibilities of their occurrence.

For our purposes here, the word *catastrophe* is taken to mean a highly uncertain or at least low-probability event having possibly severe impacts on a large number of people. Energy-related events of a catastrophic nature might include grave environmental consequences of routine technological operations, such as possible worldwide climatological changes over time caused by cumulative carbon dioxide emissions from the burning of all fossil fuels. The interaction of politics with technology could also cause *social* catastrophes, and it is possible that—by broadening the availability of nuclear fuels and technology—the use of nuclear power could indirectly increase the probability of catastrophic nuclear warfare.

Similarly, widespread damage to the environment could also come from the effects of air pollution residuals on the acidity of surface waters. And as an example of an instantaneous occurrence leading to a catastrophe, gross technical failures in nuclear reactors could lead to accidents releasing large amounts of radioactivity.

Climate Modification

The burning of coal, oil, natural gas, and biomass produce carbon dioxide as a combustion product. Carbon dioxide is a nontoxic compound at any concentrations that could be expected in the atmosphere. Indeed, its presence is necessary to sustain plant life. During the past few millennia the amount of carbon dioxide in the atmosphere appears to have been maintained normally at relatively low levels by complex physical and chemical equilibrium processes. However, there is evidence that since 1958 the carbon dioxide concentration has risen by about 25 percent. If the carbon dioxide inventory is artificially increased (for example, by burning fossil fuels), the gas—which tends to retain within the atmosphere —heat reradiated from the earth's surface—will increase the average temperatures of the atmosphere. Depending on the size of this temperature change, it could affect the warmth of ocean waters and, therefore, the distribution of marine life, as well as the growth and melting cycles of polar ice caps. Perhaps more important, sufficiently high temperature rises could change the normal wind circulation patterns and hence rainfall distribution and world agricultural patterns.

To be sure, the effects of such a heating would be uncertain. In some areas climate modification might even be desirable: for example, the favorable climate existing tens of thousands of years ago in such present-day arid areas as Iraq suggests that modification toward higher temperatures might be worthwhile. Such an artificial warming might be especially beneficial if the present near-term trend persists toward worldwide cooling as the result of a variety of poorly understood causes.

In addition, the physical facts are not clear; the carbon dioxide balance is so complex that it is difficult to predict the course and magnitude of the increased heating effect. The net amount of carbon dioxide emitted into the atmosphere does not necessarily remain there; in the past the excess has been absorbed by the deep layers of the ocean. The future rate of absorption remains an important scientific unknown. It is also possible that greater inputs of carbon dioxide could stimulate plant life—which absorbs the gas and thus lowers atmospheric levels. Furthermore, fossil fuels also emit particulates, which could either act to raise or lower temperatures.

Nevertheless, it is a fact that significant increases in the average atmospheric content of carbon dioxide have been measured over the past decades. Presumably these increases are caused by the burning of fossil fuels and by the destruction of forests. Furthermore, such increases can reasonably be expected to influence global temperatures in an upward direction. And, finally, such temperature changes could be exceedingly destructive for agriculture and other human activities. The phenomenon is then real enough and involves enough risks for the future of civilization that it must be seriously considered in assessing energy strategies involving fossil fuels.

The extent and timing of the problem is controversial. It has been estimated, by bold extrapolations of existing crude models, that additional cumulative emissions of perhaps 1.2 trillion metric tons of carbon dioxide are necessary to raise the temperature of the earth as much as 1°C, a change of magnitude that could be significant.[1] The amount of carbon dioxide emitted by a typical 1-gigawatt (1-GW) coal plant per year is only a tiny percentage of this, about 5.5 million metric tons. Oil and gas would emit smaller amounts for the same efficiencies, respectively about 80 percent and somewhat less than 60 percent of the tonnage from coal.[2] However, it can be assumed that the effect is cumulative, so that these small contributions go on adding up year by year. It has been estimated that coal-fired power plants in the United States operating between 1977 and the year 2000, will emit a total of 39 billion metric tons of carbon dioxide into the atmosphere.[3] When smaller contributions from oil and gas generation are included, some 45 billion tons of carbon dioxide will be emitted, and a net global temperature increase of almost 0.05°C from electricity generated in the United States alone seems possible. From now to the end of the century, the cumulative total from all U.S. energy uses could contribute as much as 0.1°C change in the global temperature,[4] and these U.S. emissions would only be a small part of the world total. Nevertheless, levels of emissions corresponding to several degrees Celsius would probably not be reached before the middle of the twenty-first century, although observed changes might be detectable shortly after A.D. 2000.[5] Note that these estimates are based on very crude

[1] See William Ramsay, *Unpaid Costs of Electrical Energy: Health and Environmental Impacts from Coal and Nuclear Power* (Baltimore, Johns Hopkins University Press for Resources for the Future, 1978) chap. 7, for much of the discussion that follows and for references on climate.

[2] The National Research Council, *Energy and Climate* (Washington, D.C., National Academy of Sciences, 1977) p. 61.

[3] Ramsay, *Unpaid Costs,* p. 147.

[4] Assuming electricity will average roughly one-third of U.S. energy use, and that most fuels used are fossil fuels.

[5] Ralph M. Rotty, "Uncertainties Associated with Global Effects of Atmospheric CO_2," (mimeo, Oak Ridge, Tenn., Institute for Energy Analysis, Oak Ridge Associated Universities, 1978) p. 21.

mathematical models of how temperatures change with respect to carbon dioxide, and the predicted temperature increases could be significantly lower—or higher.

Any contribution to the carbon dioxide problem from biomass conversion would depend upon the exact nature of the source. For equivalent energy inputs, carbon dioxide contributions during the combustion of a quantity of biomass should be very similar to those for fossil fuels; however, the biomass would at any rate have been converted to carbon dioxide eventually through decay or other metabolic processes. In fact, in equilibrium, new plant growth should, on the average, absorb a virtually identical amount of carbon dioxide, leaving little net additional input to the atmosphere or none. On the other hand, biomass sources will emit particulates, and these emissions could also affect the global temperature balance in uncertain ways.

Nuclear energy and satellite solar energy, too, could have their own particular climatologic effects. The radioactive gas krypton 85 has been thought to cause changes in the ionization level of the atmosphere surrounding the earth.[6] This gas is emitted in such small quantities from present-day reactors that it is of little concern; however, if fuel is reprocessed for recycle in light water reactors (LWRs) or for breeder reactors, it will be emitted in much larger quantities—unless emissions are controlled. The exact effects of changing the ionization level of the atmosphere are not known; however, it is supposed that the nature of thunderstorms would be changed, and that therefore one of the important mechanisms of heat transfer between the tropics and temperate regions would be modified, with unknown but possibly dangerous consequences.[7] Indeed, because of the uncertainties involved for both climatologic impacts and radiation doses, it might be desirable to recover krypton-85 emissions at reprocessing plants by established techniques. Microwave radiation, used to transfer energy from a solar satellite to the earth, could conceivably affect the ionosphere and, consequently, the amount of higher energy radiation hitting the earth's surface.

In addition to substances emitted from energy-conversion sources, the energy itself—for example, the low-grade energy in the form of waste heat that is rejected from a power steam cycle—together with the moisture emitted from cooling facilities can cause changes in weather

[6] William L. Boeck, "The Meteorological Consequences of Atmospheric Krypton 85," *Science* vol. 193 (July 16, 1976) pp. 195–198.
[7] See William Kellogg, quoted in *Energy Daily* (January 3, 1977) p. 4.

and climate. These changes are demonstrable on a microscale level at power plants, especially in the formation of plumes or clouds of moisture. Heat and moisture also contribute to the urban heat island effect. However, the global problem of large-scale climatologic changes caused by such heat emissions appears to be of much less urgency than the carbon dioxide emissions, primarily because the overall temperature change predicted for direct heat pollution should remain relatively small over the next century.

Acid Precipitation

Large increases in the amounts of acid rainfall have been found in the northeastern United States, even in locations well removed from concentrations of fossil fuel-combustion sources. The exact source of the acids is not clear, but one naturally suspects that sulfuric and nitric acids may be produced from the sulfur dioxide and nitrogen oxides present in polluted air and often transported far from their points of origin.

The consequences of the increased acidity of precipitation are difficult to judge. But even fairly low levels of acid could be expected to leach nutrients out of the soil, injure leaf surfaces, and otherwise endanger the health of plant and animal communities. Effects on fish and other aquatic life in rivers and lakes are especially important: for example, newly hatched salmon are unable to survive very long when acidity rises above moderate levels.[8]

However, the problem is not well understood. It is indeed possible that in many circumstances acid rain may only increase incrementally the normal acid levels of the soil and surface waters;[9] but this problem is properly considered here because its consequences could conceivably be great. If the acid levels become high and the problem widespread, environmental disasters involving a widespread degradation of ecosystems are not out of the question. This could mean a widespread danger to the viability of many communities of plants and lower animals as well as affecting the entire food chain. At our present stage of knowledge, however, it is difficult to predict what probability there is that

[8] See Ramsay, *Unpaid Costs,* p. 23, for references.
[9] F. Fraser Ross, U.K. Central Electricity Generating Board, "A 1977 Approach to Sulfur Oxide Emissions." Paper prepared for ASME/IEEE Meeting, Los Angeles, September 1977, p. 13.

continued burning of fossil fuels—mostly from coal and other fossil-fuel power plants, but also potentially from coal liquids and gases and shale oil—could contribute to such events.

War and Terrorism

There is a fear that the use of nuclear fuels for a civilian power industry could lead to the proliferation of nuclear weapons capabilities and, hence, increase the risk of nuclear warfare among nations. A companion concern is that terrorists might be able to acquire nuclear fuel materials and use them to make bombs.[10]

The proliferation problem—the possibility of the spread of nuclear weapons capabilities to other nations—is a complex one, mixing elements of civilian nuclear power with international political and strategic matters and the arms race. Special international institutions, including the Nuclear Nonproliferation Treaty (NPT) and the International Atomic Energy Agency (IAEA), have been designed to prevent new nations from acquiring nuclear materials for weapons use. In concrete terms, international inspection of nuclear power plants has become an established technique that is designed to prevent civilian power from being used for warlike purposes. In addition, the United States in particular and major nuclear supplier countries in general have acted to limit the spread of knowledge about uranium enrichment and reprocessing. Even though the technical options can be fairly complex, the two key points are that (1) the fissile uranium-235 atoms used in ordinary LWR fuel can, if further concentrated by enrichment, be used in weapons; and (2) all types of reactors regularly produce the fissile element plutonium by transmutation of uranium-238 atoms. This plutonium would have to be recovered through reprocessing. Indeed, the introduction of breeder reactors (which use plutonium as basic fuel) or the recovery of plutonium for reuse in LWRs has been opposed by some because the material would then be exposed to potential misuse through widespread international trade.

The connection between nuclear power technology and proliferation, however, is complicated. Even if the United States and other nuclear supplier nations were to refuse to supply technology, facilities, and fuel

---

[10] See Ramsay, *Unpaid Costs,* chap. 6, for much of the discussion that follows and for references.

A NOTE ON NUCLEAR PROLIFERATION AND TECHNOLOGIES

Some of the technical areas related to proliferation are described below.[11]

Reprocessing. Reprocessing is the act of separating out the uranium and plutonium from spent fuels by chemical processes that are relatively simple in principle. Reprocessing is optional, and little has been carried out for LWRs, but it is a necessity for breeders.

Enrichment. Enrichment is a process of sifting out the "filler" uranium-238 atoms from the fissile uranium-235 atoms in normal uranium so that the mixture is rich enough to start a nuclear reaction. Enrichment can produce fuels solely for reactors, or fuel for reactors and for weapons. Up until now most enrichment has been done by a very elaborate (and traditionally secret) process called gaseous diffusion. A simpler, but still formidable process, utilizing a centrifuge, will probably become more popular in the future. Even easier processes, using nozzles that spray uranium against a circular wall instead of using a centrifuge and lasers (which are sensitive to the miniscule chemical difference between uranium 238 and uranium 235), have not yet been proved, but they could make enrichment (regrettably?) easy to carry out.

Fuels. Ordinary LWRs use a low-enriched fuel (about 3 percent uranium 235 and 97 percent uranium 238) which is useless for bombs, at least without further enrichment.

Breeder fuel uses about 20 percent plutonium (instead of uranium 235) in 80 percent uranium 238. The use of this fuel for a bomb is marginal, but still conceivable. But the plutonium could be extracted from the mixture chemically for better weapons-building. Shipments of the plutonium portion by itself would be much more worrisome, both for proliferation and for terrorist diversion.

---

[11] Ramsay, *Unpaid Costs*, p. 70.

for nuclear development in new nations the results would not be certain. Although recent nuclear deals between European suppliers and developing nations tend to suggest that some of the nations of the "south" view the direct supply of ready-made and fully tested fuel and facilities as very desirable, new nations could conceivably build their own enrichment and reprocessing facilities without help. A further complication is that diverting fuel from nuclear power plants or other fuel cycle facilities is not the only way to acquire material for nuclear weapons. In fact, all nations now known to have nuclear weapons have either built them through special weapons programs or have done so clandestinely in research reactors. Furthermore, uranium can be enriched even in small quantities with laboratory-style equipment, and weapons can be stolen or purchased from other nations.

However, it is also true that having civilian nuclear power is the only way to build up an inventory of plutonium in a casual, indeed, unplanned way, without any special prior intentions of building nuclear weapons. This question of planning and forethought is relevant, because the presence of such an inventory would make it possible for a nation to reach a quick decision to build nuclear weapons in response to newly perceived strategic objectives or to a change in national leadership.

The situation, of course, involves more than just a weapons capability problem. It is not absolutely clear that proliferation of weapons capability will lead to more likelihood of weapons use. Some would even argue that, if nuclear weapons are widely available, the chances of a catastrophic war will become less, rather than greater, because of the very destructiveness of the nuclear option. However, past long-term experience with the escalation of other weapons systems used in warfare gives little encouraging evidence for this point of view.

Another question involves the fact that this present study focuses specifically on U.S. energy strategy options and, therefore, on U.S. decision making. What difference does it make for world proliferation whether the United States has LWRs or even breeder reactors? Other nations may not follow the U.S. lead in nuclear matters. Even if they did, the United States in principle could probably act to discourage proliferation abroad, while going full speed ahead with breeder reactors at home.

In practice, however, demonstration effects tend to be important, and the United States would probably have to put restrictions on its nuclear industry—as indeed the present administration has sought to do for the breeder reactor—to make a nonproliferation-oriented foreign policy work. Furthermore, the mere existence of an American interest in civilian nuclear power acts as a powerful support to the American nuclear fuel and facility vendors, who have traditionally supplied a very large segment of the worldwide nuclear supply market. Therefore, U.S. domestic energy policy certainly has some effect on foreign nuclear policy. If energy policy were in addition tied to other U.S. foreign policy initiatives, U.S. energy strategies could exert an important, even key impact worldwide.

Although our discussion of the connections between U.S. energy decisions and international nuclear proliferation suggests that the connection is tenuous in extreme, it is nevertheless true that possible impacts of making the wrong decisions can be very great. The specific probability of civilian nuclear power contributing to such wars could well be small, but the consequences—indeed, the *expected* consequences —might still be much larger than the usual coal and nuclear health impacts.

Mitigation possibilities exist for this problem; in particular, the strengthening of the IAEA has been proposed, and investigations of multinational approaches to the organization of the nuclear fuel cycle are currently being made. Perhaps more promising is the possibility that liquid-fuel reactors, such as the molten-salt breeder reactor, and the recently proposed Civex fuel cycle might discourage proliferation through schemes for relatively inaccessible in-plant reprocessing.

Another problem is the spread of nuclear weapons, not among nations, but to small groups of criminals, terrorists, or other subnational groups. The growth of terrorism is one of the more interesting and disturbing new social phenomena of the past decade or so. The growth of jet travel and of television appear to have contributed to the development of this problem, and it may well be that modern society has become peculiarly vulnerable to terrorists.

Up to now terrorists have not used nuclear weapons, perhaps because of the difficulties in getting nuclear material or the dangers associated with utilizing it, or from what they see as its other shortcomings. Homemade nuclear bombs may not be such a promising idea: even though it is technically possible for a small group of persons to reprocess nuclear material or to assemble stolen nuclear material into some kind of weapon, the use of crude homemade nuclear weapons instead of sophisticated conventional bombs is probably awkward and relatively ineffective from a purely mechanical point of view. Nor have other types of conceivable nuclear threats (such as plutonium-toxicity weapons and sabotage of nuclear facilities) been used successfully. Indeed, although plutonium is carcinogenic, as a poison administered to the public at large it is probably much less effective than many other possible substances. And while nuclear facilities have been the site of some bombings, the sabotage of an operating reactor to release radioactivity to the environment has not been attempted and, indeed, might be rather difficult to carry out successfully, given the many redundant nuclear safety systems involved.

Despite these shortcomings, the theatrical element is important in terrorism and even in criminal blackmail attempts, and the precise risk that a society using nuclear power will be subject to effective nuclear terrorist threats is difficult to evaluate. Therefore, the degree of vulnerability of the nuclear fuel cycle to diversion is an important consideration.

Vulnerability is of course relative. Nuclear facilities are protected against theft or embezzlement of dangerous nuclear material by guards, fences, and by tamper-proof safes, and by established materials accounting systems. None of these devices is perfect; in particular, accounting for very small quantities of material can be difficult. However, it is likely that most bomb-grade nuclear material would be difficult to steal by overt means without using a fairly large force of men or rather sophisticated weapons, such as rockets and tanks.

Vulnerability also depends on the precise technology used. If there is no breeder economy, the danger from terrorist diversion of bomb-grade nuclear material is very low indeed for LWRs (see "A Note on Nuclear Proliferation and Technologies"). But the situation worsens if plutonium becomes an object of worldwide trade as part of the breeder reactor economy. It may be that schemes for the internationalization of nuclear fuel cycle facilities could help reduce this problem, even in a breeder economy. However, such centralization of sensitive nuclear facilities would still require the close protection of shipments to other centers where the production of power would take place. And, in fact, the addition of more and more guards and more sophisticated communications equipment may show a decreasing marginal return in the amount of security provided. Furthermore, some critics have expressed concern, justified or not, that the spreading of more security measures for nuclear plants and other facilities would be a dangerous step because of its implications for civil liberties. Whether this last is true, the addition of even more security measures may, overall, be of questionable help in solving the problem.

All in all, the strong irrational element in many terrorist activities, and the fact that these activities often appeal to real, if sometimes exaggerated, public fears, makes terrorism a real concern, and one that should be considered in assessing nuclear energy options—especially the breeder strategy.

Reactor Accidents

In chapter 12, the possibility of reactor accidents was considered. Rough estimates were made of the maximum number of likely casualties from such reactor accidents per plant-year. Such accidents, however, would not occur regularly, but presumably over many years, with the casualties averaged out over the intervening years between hypothetical accidents. However, even though very severe accidents—producing perhaps on the order of 50,000 fatalities—may be very improbable, they are large enough to be regarded as catastrophic if they were to occur. So even if the average risks of an accident are considered to be small, the possibility of disastrous consequences makes the nuclear reactor accident a legitimate source of public concern. This concern could in itself become a complicating factor if public reactions to a single large nuclear accident were to result in mass shutdowns of nuclear stations.

The Special Status of Catastrophes

The health and environmental impacts examined in chapters 12 and 13 include, at least in principle, all impacts, no matter how uncertain, and therefore they properly should include the expected casualties from future nuclear wars—if such a figure were available—and the probable loss of life and health in hypothetical nuclear reactor accidents. However, catastrophes are considered separately in this chapter because it is not certain that the public views small averaged-out impacts of very improbable catastrophes in the same way that it does other small impacts. If only the averaged-out effects of large gains and losses mattered, there would presumably be no reason for such institutions as property insurance and state lotteries where the customer can expect to lose—on the average. Therefore, it is useful to consider catastrophes as a special category of impact.

To do this does not answer the question of whether society generally chooses to take special care to avoid catastrophes, or on the other hand, whether it neglects very improbable events. There appears to be no firm answer to this question, and public attitudes toward low-probability events remain to be definitely investigated.[12] However, it is possible to discern alternatives. If catastrophes are to be viewed by the public predominantly as small risks that could well be taken without great concern, then, even though one would still have to consider them, the effects viewed in this chapter would have less importance than the routine health and environmental effects considered in chapters 12 and 13. If, on the other hand, the public wishes to view catastrophes as of special importance, then this analysis becomes crucial. At any rate, in the discussion that follows we will compare the relative importance of the various types of catastrophes.

Comparisons Between Energy Technologies

Among today's technologies, nuclear energy is especially associated in the public mind with catastrophes. The dangers of nuclear diversion and proliferation are exceedingly complex and difficult to analyze, especially in the restricted context of the role of a breeder economy or even of a LWR economy in the United States alone. However, the possible consequences of such diversion or proliferation are great. Furthermore, the risk is immediate, in the sense that new nations could acquire nuclear capabilities at any time, possibly from the use of materials from nuclear power plants, or terrorists could conceivably explode small weapons at any time in the near future. On a somewhat more modest scale in this global context, nuclear power plant accidents could pro-

---

[12] The avoidance of catastrophes could be motivated by a fear of huge events that threaten the individual, or even by horror at scenes of great violence, whether a potential threat exists to an individual member of society or not.

More generally, societal risk decisions may partake of the same ambiguity as individual "risk-avoidance" and "risk-taking" decisions. Attitudes may vary according to circumstance. There is the evidence of the popularity of insurance: many persons will pay larger amounts than actuarially required in order to be sure of receiving large amounts of compensation for undergoing particularly harmful, low-probability events. On the other hand, it can be argued that little effort is expended in avoiding improbable disasters like being struck by lightning, for example. However, in the latter case, it might be that one would seek to avoid the catastrophe except that the steps to be taken to avoid it are too troublesome and therefore involve excessive personal costs in money, time, or worry.

duce local health disasters. The probability of such an accident occurring in the near future will become greater as more reactors become operative, but the risk, such as it is, is always immediate.

In contrast, the primary catastrophic effect from coal (and oil and other fossil fuels) is the possibility of a drastic change resulting from the emission into the atmosphere of carbon dioxide and, perhaps, particulates. Many questions of scientific fact and theory on the climate-modification problem remain unresolved. Although the problem may not be amenable to last-minute solutions, there seems to be general agreement that—without denying that energy strategies planning must deal with this problem on a timely basis—great temperature changes will not occur for many decades yet. Furthermore, schemes for collecting carbon dioxide through biomass conversion, or through its direct collection and disposal, require further investigation.[13]

The possibility of acid rain caused by sulfates and nitrogen oxides emitted during the burning of fossil fuels could produce an ecological crisis in the near term. However, threats to plant and animal communities would probably be detected initially on a relatively small scale. Furthermore, such active chemicals would normally be cleansed out of the environment by ongoing atmospheric and biological processes, meaning that recovery of ecosystems should often be possible—if the damage has not exceeded the limits of species viability.

For the newer technologies, the coal-conversion methods and shale oil share the characteristic of burning large amounts of fossil carbon, adding to the carbon dioxide emitted. However, standard coal combustion is slightly penalized versus coal-conversion technologies because more coal per unit of delivered energy is used and, therefore, somewhat higher carbon dioxide emissions. Since sulfur emissions for the newer technologies would be lower, the acid rain impact should be considerably less.

As emphasized above, attitudes toward energy-related catastrophes depend on whether one places a special value on catastrophes, treats them neutrally, or, indeed, ignores them. Furthermore, a direct comparison cannot be made of the different types of catastrophes discussed here. Nuclear war and long-term climatologic changes have no obvious

---

[13] See Freeman J. Dyson, "Can We Control the Carbon Dioxide in the Atmosphere?" *Energy—The International Journal* vol. 2 (1977) pp. 287–291; and Cesare Marchetti, "On Geoengineering and the CO_2 Problem," Rm-76-17 (Laxenburg, Austria, International Institute for Applied Systems Analysis, March 1976), where a cost penalty of 20 percent of fuel costs is estimated for a 90 percent efficiency in carbon dioxide removal.

common denominator; each would be catastrophic in its own way. There is, however, a scale on which they can be compared, and that is time proximity. To the extent that nuclear power technologies enhance the probabilities of nuclear warfare, that risk has an element of immediacy. Climate modification, on the other hand, is a threat, if at all, for the more distant future. The nearer-term threat, other things being equal, is more to be feared, even neglecting preferences for putting off disagreeable events until tomorrow: the longer a threat is delayed, the greater the possibility to cope with it through innovations that can be achieved over time.

Part V

The Process of Making Energy Choices

15 *Conflicting Perceptions of Energy's Future Role*

Views on the future of energy are strongly affected by more general attitudes about the conditions which the world will face and the direction human society should take. In simplified terms, two diametrically opposed world views have tended to influence broad energy policy choices. The inability of the adherents of these views to agree has stymied progress toward solving energy-related problems, and the conflicts that have occurred have nearly poisoned the prospects for compromise in the future. For the sake of comparison and contrast, we might list some of their respective tenets:

"Expansionist" view	*"Limited" view*
• The expanded production of goods and services and the increases in per capita consumption that have characterized western economies since the industrial revolution are good, and they have yet to run their course.	• Expansion has already overshot the ability of the earth to sustain it, and its benefits have been overestimated.
• The benefits of economic growth have yet to be spread as widely as they might be.	• Redirection of output, restructuring of production, and redistribution of wealth are urgently required if disaster of various types is to be avoided.
• While some redirection of effort may be necessary to accommodate such growing problems as environmental degradation and population expansion, no fundamental change is required now.	• Changes in value systems and life-styles are required and can be achieved; these changes demand that new institutions gain ascendance.

There are other ways of characterizing these extreme views. Moreover, many persons might find that their own positions contain some of the elements ascribed here to the two sharply opposing camps; views about energy and society can no more be neatly packaged or defined than views about economics or politics. Nevertheless, this categorization provides a framework from which some of the major differences about policy can be discerned.

The Expansionist View

A consumption-oriented, expansionist, problem-solving, optimistic attitude has dominated public policy and private thought in the United States throughout most of its history. Whether it was manifested in the expansion of the western frontier in the 1800s or the "New Frontier" of the Kennedy years, and whether it was shaped by the industrial revolution, the eighteenth century enlightenment, or the science-based explosion of knowledge, the American outlook has been characterized by improvement, expanded control over nature, and widening horizons. There have been transitory periods of uncertainty and pessimism, of course, and there has always been a minority undercurrent of dissatisfaction. Nonetheless, the essence of the "American" approach has been "growth." And, in the public mind and in government policy, that growth has been associated to a remarkable degree with increased reliance on inanimate energy.

In the United States the industrial revolution of the late eighteenth and early nineteenth centuries was premised upon using inanimate energy (from falling water and steam) to do work previously performed by man. The expansion of trade had as a precondition more efficient ship design, which allowed better use of wind. Public works emphasized the infrastructure—ports, roads, canals, and later railroads—through which transportation of goods and people could be accomplished more efficiently via greater concentrations of energy. And the post-Civil War agricultural revolution depended upon development of animal and steam-powered machinery which made large areas economically cultivatable. "Scientific" management, electrification, and the assembly line, which were broadly applied after the beginning of the twentieth century, were essentially innovations which substituted more effective use of machinery and energy for strong backs and nimble hands.

The Great Depression interrupted a long period of economic growth in the United States, but it had little effect on the long-term increasing importance of inanimate energy in the economy; nor did it shake the perception that greater use of energy was a means of making life better for all. The successful conduct of World War II not only gave America back its confidence, but also suggested that almost anything—domestically or internationally—could be accomplished. Astounding production miracles had been associated with getting, using, and deploying energy. The later development of nuclear power for civilian use seemed to open the final door. It promised unlimited energy and even the transmutation of materials. The postwar era was expected to be one of unprecedented progress.

Progress, to most Americans, has meant the widening of access to the "good things of life." Those good things have included mobility, enhanced access to health care and education, reduced drudgery, more leisure, and more "stuff." For virtually everyone—the farmer, the housewife, the laborer, and the businessman—energy use has helped overcome the obstacles of space and time. Ultimately, an industrial system fueled by abundant energy was expected to overcome want by spreading the blessings enjoyed by the American middle and upper classes to all.

Over the past century, predominant dependence on renewable and natural energy sources—animals, wood, wind, and water—has shifted to primary reliance upon exhaustible fossil fuels: first coal, and then petroleum and natural gas. Periodic concern about the long-term availability and cost of these fuels proved groundless as new reserves or new energy sources became available. The U.S. petroleum industry increased output during the Great Depression and World War II and, with the end of the war, gave every indication that it could and would expand production still further. The knowledge that reserves of oil were ultimately finite seemed irrelevant as long as the size of the known domestic reserve was growing, when the outer continental shelf had scarcely been touched, and when deposits abroad—firmly under the control of mostly U.S. interests—were being discovered with unprecedented ease. Moreover, natural gas—which had been the unsought stepchild of petroleum for decades—was newly available to distant markets because large-scale, high pressure natural gas pipelines could be built economically. Potential energy supply was multiplied when this extremely clean, efficient, and cheap fuel became available. Consequently, some functions that were inexpensive to serve with oil became even more cheaply served by natural gas. Finally, nuclear power was on the horizon, lessening uncertainties about the long-term accessibility of energy. In reserve were enormous quantities of coal, which could be used to generate electricity or—if necessary, be converted into liquid and gaseous fuels.

Energy policy decisions have flowed from three main tenets of this expansionist perception:

1. The use of energy is good, and the more of it the better. Hence policy should be directed toward making energy as cheap and plentiful as possible and available to everyone.
2. The energy future lies with development of new sources which will replace depleting reserves at an appropriate time. There is a faith that scientific research will reveal such sources and that technology will be able to exploit them. Hence, policies have facilitated technological and other developments that support continuation of an energy-absorbing industrial system to meet the expanding wants of a growing economy, taking due notice of evolutionary changes required in response to the changing relative costs of different resources, including the environment.
3. Secure supplies of energy are essential to avoid sudden shocks to the economy.

This "expansionist" viewpoint sees the primary energy policy objective as facilitating the process of making supplies available to meet consumer desires. It recognizes that changing conditions lead to shifts in the source of energy and to alterations in the way it is used, but it does not seek to impose any constraints on energy acquisition and use beyond those that flow from the objective conditions of energy supply and demand. From what is seen of these conditions, they make growth appear feasible, and the products of growth make it appear desirable. Energy production is favored so long as the market price covers its costs. The prescription for a better tomorrow that results from this viewpoint is to increase energy availability from new sources rather than to save existing energy supplies for use later. Given this view, the proper public debate over energy centers on questions of method and of dividing the spoils; it does not involve questions about the desirability of "more."

The "Limited World" View

Support for "expansion" as the self-evident end of policy was never unanimous, but it became increasingly fragmented after the mid-1960s. To some observers, the "realities" on which it was based began to appear shaky. Technological improvement came more slowly than anticipated, happiness did not track the GNP, and the efforts against poverty—both domestic and foreign—did not make it vanish. Further, the real cost of energy (especially the heightened estimates of the environmental amenities lost in its acquisition and use) began to rise instead of fall. New conditions and revised values had made a naive "growth" viewpoint vulnerable even before the 1973–74 jump in the cost of energy made it infeasible.

A view of the world fundamentally different from the expansionist vision gained impetus from disillusionment with the growth prescription, but it exhibits positive attributes as well. Essentially, it suggests that the natural world is "limited" so long as man seeks satisfactions in exploiting and dominating it, but that continuity and indeed happiness can come with a restructuring of human behavior into "natural" flows.

Again, three tenets underlie this position:

1. Resource constraints make it impossible to sustain the current path of energy supply growth.
2. Attempts to continue on this path will disrupt human values and lead to unaccceptable risks.
3. Ever-growing energy use by an affluent minority represents an unfair diversion of world resources to a few, so that a limitation of energy demands is required in the interests of the broad community —including future generations.

Several factors contributed to the formulation of these tenets. Resource constraints were newly found to be binding. They led to pessimism about potential energy supply from exhaustible resources and "hard" technologies, as well as about the ability of existing political and economic systems to meet the changed energy supply and use patterns required for the future. Congestion lowered amenities, and made many persons aware of the disutilities associated with population growth—even population growth outpaced by output of goods. The ability of the natural environment to absorb additional residues from production and consumption was being strained, and a growing portion of gross output was being used up in seeking to offset the environmental deterioration created by production and consumption activities. Indeed, the belief grew that "more" often meant "less" when full costs were accounted for. Finally, extrapolation of the physical requirements of U.S. life-styles (either into the future or over most of mankind) seemed to indicate that the goals of the expansionist perception were literally not feasible.

Changing perceptions of the large and small physical risks associated with energy (explored in chapters 12 through 14) have added support to the "limited world" rejection of economic growth. First, there has been an accretion of knowledge that indicates that some biological systems are more fragile than once thought, and that activities once commonplace and accepted may indeed prove harmful. Second, and of more concern to people, the interrelations of biological, political, and social systems have become closer and more visible. Further, as material goods have increased in availability, the importance of nonmarket amenities has come to be ranked higher than before. There is less willingness to gamble such amenities against the additional capacity to produce traditional goods and services. The overall result is that fewer risks are acceptable than formerly in acquiring and using energy. This shift is revealed in hostility toward technological change, and specifically in suspicion of nuclear power and in willingness to forgo its possible benefits.

Enhanced concern for communal values is the final tenet of the move away from the expansionist vision. It takes many forms—including a broadened definition of community to include nonhuman values, and a changing perception of the requirements for equity, which has come to cover the whole of mankind and to stretch across generations.

An identifying element here is the treatment accorded "nature." Both the expansionist and the limited world viewpoints have a place for the protection of nature, but each starts from a very different premise. The expansionist approach is man-centered: natural amenities are defined by the value accorded to them by people who are alive at this moment—including *their* preference for leaving something of value to those who come later. These goals are achieved through rules adopted by members of society to guide each others' conduct. The limited world value system includes the desire to preserve or enhance "nature" *for itself,* and this is an entirely different matter. For example, wilderness areas have been set aside on the ground that it is important to preserve such areas—not necessarily as a means of achieving specific goals for human beings, but for the sake of wilderness itself. The view here is that "man" is part of nature, not the lord over it, and in preservation lies a duty beyond enlightened self-interest. "Wild rivers" are to be preserved intact, not harnessed, even at the sacrifice of man's own narrow "best interests," however they might be projected or discounted. While the defense of endangered species is often justified on the basis of unspecified unknown future benefits *for* mankind, there seems to be beneath that man-centered rhetoric a fundamental belief that other species deserve to be protected *from* man—just for themselves.

Another factor in the enlarged view of community is a revision in the concept of the tradeoff among generations. In the "limited" view of possibilities for the future, the conclusion is that the future might be better served if we consumed less now. This contrasts with the expansionist view that prospects for the future are enhanced if we bequeath future generations a larger stock of goods and a larger productive capacity.

The implications of this difference are striking. The expansionist view may present areas of intergenerational rivalry, but within a general scheme of intergenerational harmony. In the other case, however, the conflict is unrelieved; additional production and consumption today carries a presumption that it will make future generations worse off. This "limited world" perception is of a "storehouse" world, which—when emptied—will no longer support life. The expansionist alternative sees a "factory" world, in which the use of a barrel of oil now can help to find new sources of energy for the future.

Another difference in values has to do with concerns about interpersonal, interregional, and international equity. Society and its instruments have long signaled that the distribution of income and wealth is of more than individual interest, but the criteria for social intervention and its goals depend heavily on one's starting point. In the case of an optimistic view of unlimited opportunities for expansion, the focus tends to be on equality of opportunity, so the accepted starting point is that returns to individuals should be based on contributions to output. In the other view, goods should be distributed among members of society as a matter of right; production—or lack of it—is a less powerful source of legitimizing variations from the average level of well-being.

Tied to the increased importance placed on collective values is the contention that (in the interests of equity) the community should have some influence over which "wants" people "should" be able to satisfy. Productive capacity is perceived to be limited, and output belongs to the broader community as a whole. Thus the behavior of any individual (or nation) who takes more than his share of goods "out" (notwithstanding how many he or it puts "in") is seen as unfair.

To put this in energy-related terms: When desire for a fairly even distribution of benefits is combined with a pessimistic view of prospects for additional energy supply, an energy-intensive life-style appears antisocial. Reducing energy consumption becomes a goal in itself.

The thesis that the world's resources are limited leads to acceptance of a different set of energy policy options than those which would appeal to the expansionist viewpoint. Because prospects for enhancing energy supply are seen as poor, and because of the high overall costs and risks that the quest for such increases is thought to bring, the emphasis is placed on reducing energy wants. This view includes the perception that the existing energy-economic system is not in long-run equilibrium, particularly because of dependence on nonrenewable and depleting resources (including the environment). Thus, it assumes that the existing decision system—predicated on the primacy of individual wants—will not lead to timely adjustments. It seeks a change in institutions in order to move the system off its self-destructive path.

The Weight of Evidence

The historical analysis, examination of available resources, and projection of future trends in the earlier parts of this book give some support to each side in the dichotomy of views we have outlined here. There are certainly limits of all sorts in regard to our continued use of energy; they are pressed upon us by the economist, the geologist, the public health specialist, the politician, the diplomat, and a host of others. On the other hand, there are just as surely indications that continuing economic growth in the traditional sense continues to be possible. Technology and wise direction offer hope of overcoming the ever-present threat of environmental degradation; and new energy sources suggest that our depletable stores are not about to run out—or at least that they can be augmented and supplemented by new approaches.

The next four chapters endeavor to examine the policy setting and policy options which seem to emerge from our study of the facts about America's energy status and outlook. There is little reason to believe, however, that what we intend as even-handed discussion will necessarily be accepted as such by those who hold either an extreme "expansionist" view or an absolute conviction about the "limited world" philosophy we have described. The best hope for achieving a workable national energy policy, in fact, lies in the strong likelihood that a large number of U.S. citizens fall in the broad spectrum *between* those opposing attitudes. Therein rests our optimism about achieving a nationwide consensus on energy policy—a prospect we shall return to in the final chapter.

16 The World Energy Setting and U.S. Policy

U.S. energy policy has an international dimension. The world is a single energy-using and energy-producing entity, and actions in one part of the globe affect conditions elsewhere through effects on prices, income flows, resource use, and environmental transfers. The nature and magnitude of these worldwide effects undoubtedly make them of critical significance in the formulation of any policy affecting the level of U.S. energy imports.[1]

Considering the facts of world energy consumption, production, and trade—especially in light of the relative position of the United States in world energy matters—petroleum holds a special role. It is largely through the petroleum trade that actions in one country affect the price and availability of energy in others. As reported in chapter 7, the global resource base can permit that trade to continue for some time—and indeed grow for at least a decade or two. Whether it will do so, however, depends on political and economic developments—and on choices made by sovereign governments, including ours.

Were it not for the uncertainties of supply, imported petroleum would clearly be the most attractive source of additional liquid fuels at present. Its importation and use present fewer environmental problems and, on balance, its cost is lower than that of any alternative. But high U.S. oil imports affect some other nations adversely, and reliance on imported oil presents dangers to the continued stability of our own economy. These disadvantages must be reckoned as part of the cost of petroleum (a cost not reflected in the market price) when comparing imported petroleum to other ways of meeting energy needs. In this chapter, we explore the nature

[1] In a different context, energy production and use release pollutants to the air and water which can travel throughout the world. They affect the global environment, including perhaps the climate, in complex and as yet not well-understood ways. While these and other external effects also make energy a subject for international concern, those matters are not treated separately here.

of these costs, and suggest means of lowering them in case this country does not wish to forgo all the benefits which a prudent continuation of oil (and natural gas) imports can still bring.

Energy Consumption, Production, and Trade

Energy Consumption by World Sector

World energy consumption is difficult to measure at any one time and is impossible to compare precisely over time or by geographical area because of problems with definition and coverage.[2] Clearly, though, energy consumption has been rising. This growth has not been steady; it has been affected by the level of economic activity and by the relative price of energy, as well as by technological innovation. And the overall growth in world consumption masks several shifts, the most important of which is the change in the relative shares of commercial energy consumption by major country groupings (figure 16-1). While the United States remains the premier energy consumer in the world, its share of the total dropped a third (from almost 45 percent to 30 percent) between 1950 and 1976. Over the same period, the share consumed by the developed market countries as a whole (including the United States) fell from three-fourths of the total to less than three-fifths. The share used by the centrally planned economies increased 50 percent, and consumption by the USSR went from 11.5 percent to 16.2 percent of the world total. Developing countries, including those in the Organization of Petroleum Exporting Countries (OPEC), saw their share of consumption nearly double, but on a per capita basis they still lagged far behind the rest of the world.[3]

---

[2] Energy flows through commercial channels can be traced with some precision and do provide an indication of the trends in energy use. But when total energy use is considered, there are insurmountable problems in measuring certain important sources, such as firewood in households, animal power devoted to agricultural and industrial pursuits, and local exploitation of fossil fuel deposits, wind, and water power. Energy from such sources probably provides a smaller percentage of the total now than it did in earlier years, although it provides a larger share in less developed economies than in more industrialized ones. Hence, various biases exist in data which only cover commercial energy use. Nevertheless, better data are not available, and—unless otherwise noted—data presented in this chapter refer exclusively to commercial energy flows. See, for example, Elizabeth Cecelski, Joy Dunkerley, and William Ramsay, with Emmanuel Mbi, *Household Energy and the Poor in the Third World*, Research Paper No. R-15 (Washington, D.C., Resources for the Future, 1979) for a discussion of the noncommercial fuel data problem.

[3] Comparisons based on these data are somewhat misleading, however, because developing countries have relied to a greater extent on the use of noncommercial energy. Commercial energy may be replacing subsistence energy more rapidly in some country groupings than in others.

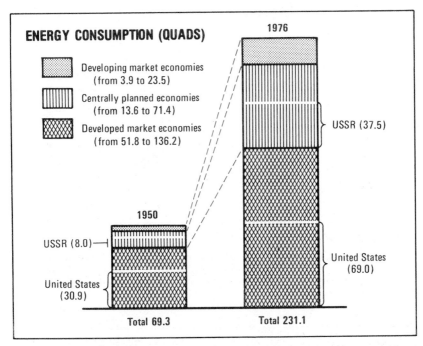

Figure 16-1. Overall growth and regional shifts in world consumption of commercial energy (quadrillion Btus). Note that quantities are converted at 27.78 million Btus per metric ton coal equivalent. The amount shown for U.S. consumption differs from that given in earlier chapters because of the conversion factors used by the United Nations Statistical Office. (Based on data from United Nations, *World Energy Supplies, 1950–1974,* Series J, no. 19 (New York, UN, 1976), tables 1 and 2; and *1972–1976,* Series J, no. 21 (1978), tables 1 and 2.)

A more remarkable change occurred in the distribution of energy use by fuel forms, with petroleum replacing coal as the dominant fuel (figure 16-2). Comparing 1950 with 1976, the coal share of world energy consumption declined from 62 percent to 32 percent, while the share of liquid fuel rose from 27 percent to 45 percent. Coal use in absolute terms rose by three-quarters during this period, but petroleum consumption overshadowed it by growing five and one-half times. For the market economies, coal use fell from 56 percent of the total to 23 percent, while oil use rose from 20 percent to 53 percent. In the United States the shift was less spectacular during this period: petroleum use went up from 39 percent to 45 percent, and coal use fell from 40 percent to 22 percent; natural gas was the big gainer. The change was most dramatic for Japan, where petroleum use rose from 4 percent to 74 percent of a much larger total, while coal use dropped from 85 percent to 19 percent.

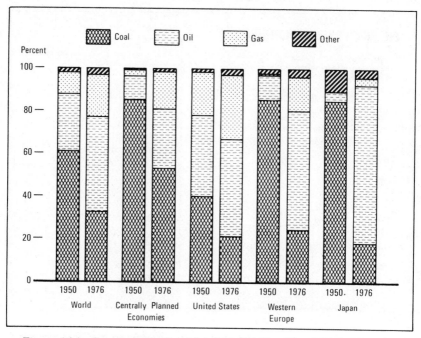

Figure 16-2. Commercial energy consumption by fuel type and by country groupings. (Based on data from United Nations, *World Energy Supplies, 1950–1974,* Series J, no. 19 (New York, UN, 1976), tables 1 and 2; and *1972–1976,* Series J, no. 21 (1978), tables 1 and 2.)

Energy Production by World Sector

Energy production, like energy consumption, is unevenly distributed around the world. In 1976 the United States, the world's leading energy consumer, was also the leading producer. It produced almost one-fourth of the world total (figure 16-3). (It also was the largest net energy importer as we shall see below.) The nonmarket economies, led by the Soviet Union, also were major producers and consumers of energy; but, unlike the developed market economies, they were net exporters. The developed market economies other than the United States contributed 13 percent to the world production total. The OPEC countries were the major exporters of energy; together they produced about 26 percent of the total in 1976 while using only 2 percent. Non-OPEC developing countries were not very important in either production or consumption of commercial energy, but the trends foreshadow increasing importance for this group in the future.

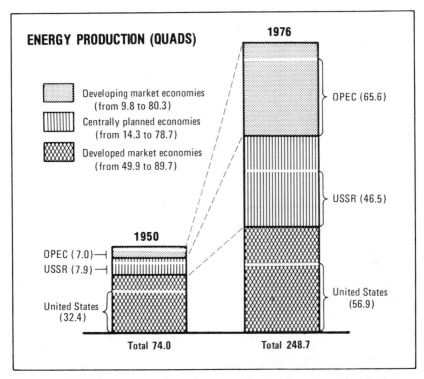

ENERGY PRODUCTION (QUADS)

Developing market economies
(from 9.8 to 80.3)

Centrally planned economies
(from 14.3 to 78.7)

Developed market economies
(from 49.9 to 89.7)

1976

OPEC (65.6)

USSR (46.5)

United States
(56.9)

1950

OPEC (7.0)

USSR (7.9)

United States
(32.4)

Total 74.0

Total 248.7

Figure 16-3. Increases and shifts in world production of commercial energy (quadrillion Btus). Note that quantities are converted at 27.78 million Btus per metric ton coal equivalent. The amount shown for U.S. production differs from that given in earlier chapters because of the conversion factors used by the United Nations Statistical Office. (Based on data from United Nations, *World Energy Supplies, 1950–1974,* Series J, no. 19 (New York, UN, 1976), tables 1 and 2; and *1972–1976,* Series J, no. 21 (1978), tables 1 and 2.)

Energy Trade

Immense quantities of energy move across national borders. Table 16-1 lists the top six net energy importers and top nine exporters in rank order in 1976. It also shows the size and direction of the net trade of each in solids, liquids, and gases. The United States was the leading energy importer in 1976, replacing Japan (which had led in 1975). Together, the United States and Japan imported in 1976 roughly as much energy as did the next seven largest importers combined. On the export side, Saudi Arabia and Iran play an analogous role.[4] Together they export more en-

---

[4] At the time of this writing the prospects for resumption of Iranian exports after the 1978–79 disturbance are uncertain.

Table 16-1. Net Energy Trade of Selected Countries, 1976

Country	Total net energy trade	Solid fuels	Petroleum	Natural gas	Total net energy trade as a percentage of OPEC net petroleum exports
	Million metric tons oil equivalent[a]				
Leading net importers:					
United States	347	−36	361	22	24.4
Japan	289	41	241	7	20.3
Federal Republic of Germany	149	−7	133	23	10.5
France	146	14	119	13	10.2
Italy	117	8	99	10	8.3
United Kingdom	81	1	79	1	5.7
Leading net exporters:					
Saudi Arabia	−409	0	−409	0	28.7
Iran	−275	0	−267	−8	19.4
USSR	−162	−14	−137	−11	11.4
Venezuela	−110	[b]	−110	0	7.7
Iraq	−104	[b]	−104	0	7.3
Kuwait	−103	0	−103	0	7.3
Nigeria	−100	[b]	−100	0	7.0
United Arab Emirates	−94	0	−94	0	6.6
Libya	−92	0	−89	−3	6.5

Source: Compiled from United Nations, *World Energy Supplies, 1972–1976*, Series J. no. 21 (New York, UN, 1978) tables 3, 6, 10, 15, and 21.

[a] Minus sign denotes net exports.

[b] Less than 0.5 million metric tons oil equivalent.

ergy than the United States and Japan import, and these exports are about the same magnitude as are those of the next six exporters combined. The USSR exports all forms of energy, but except for it and Iran (with exports of natural gas) other exporter countries in 1976 were primarily sellers of petroleum. The last column of table 16-1, which shows the ratio between net energy trade and OPEC exports of petroleum, is presented simply to provide perspective.

The value of energy trade, especially when related to the size of the economies involved and the size of their overall trade, helps to explain the role energy plays as an international issue. Table 16-2 presents 1976 data for six major importers and nine exporters. For importers, such energy trade is small in comparison with their gross domestic product, but for net exporters it is large by this yardstick. When the comparison is made with the size of all trade, however, energy trade assumes substantial importance to importers as well. For major exporters, changes in the value of energy trade are critical to income levels; for some, national income is almost identical with energy exports. For importers, on the other hand, energy

Table 16-2. Relative Magnitude of Energy Trade in Selected Economies, 1976

Country	Net petroleum trade as a percentage of GDP	Net energy trade as a percentage of GDP	Net petroleum trade as a percentage of merchandise (imports/exports)	Net energy trade as a percentage of merchandise (imports/exports)
Importers:[a]				
United States[b]	1.8	1.7	25.3	24.4
Japan	4.2	5.1	36.0	43.7
Federal Republic of				
Germany	2.9	2.9	14.7	14.7
France	3.2	3.7	17.5	19.9
Italy	4.7	5.2	18.8	20.9
United Kingdom	3.5	3.6	14.0	14.1
Exporters:[a]				
Saudi Arabia	76	77	98	99
Iran[c]	36	36	98	98
USSR[c]	2	2	26	31
Venezuela	28	28	94	94
Iraq	53	53	99	99
Kuwait	74	74	93	93
Nigeria	38	38	91	91
United Arab Emirates	73	73	94	94
Libya	55	56	97	99

Note: Net energy trade includes coal, coke, briquettes, crude petroleum, petroleum products, natural and manufactured gas, and electrical energy. Imports are on a c.i.f. valuation basis except for the United States and USSR which have f.o.b. valuations. All exports are f.o.b. port of exit.

Sources: United Nations, *Yearbook of International Trade Statistics 1977* (New York, UN, 1978), vol. I; *World Energy Supplies 1972–1976*, Series J, no. 21 (New York, UN, 1978); *Yearbook of National Account Statistics 1977* (New York, UN, 1978), vol. 2, table 1A; International Monetary Fund, *International Financial Statistics* (Washington, D.C., IMF, January 1979).

[a] Listed by rank order of quantity of net energy trade in 1976.

[b] United States, including Puerto Rico.

[c] 1976 value of energy trade estimated from quantity data.

prices and volumes exert a major influence through less direct channels. For example, changes in energy trade can seriously perturb international financial relations, and energy price changes can affect both employment levels and output.

Petroleum Imports— The International Energy Connection

The energy-producing and -using sectors of the world's economies are linked through the international petroleum trade, and domestic energy decisions affect this global linkage. An action to substitute alcohol for petroleum in Brazil's motor fuel is relevant to the United States because of its influence on world oil demand. Substitution of nuclear power for fuel oil to produce electricity in Korea may affect the availability and price of oil to Germany. Energy conservation practices adopted in the United States affect the prospective prosperity of oil-exporting Indonesia, as does Mexico's attitude toward accepting foreign investment to expand its petroleum export industry.

The premise that petroleum serves to interrelate all energy demand and the supply of energy from all sources follows from a set of facts and relationships, including these:

1. The potential supply of natural petroleum, though unknown in magnitude, is limited.
2. In some major uses, no close substitutes for natural petroleum are available at near comparable costs.
3. Petroleum can and does perform the functions also served by other energy sources.
4. The petroleum that moves on the world market is produced by a small number of countries, most of whose price and production policies are loosely coordinated by OPEC.

Oil production and distribution facilities and institutions work on a world scale to direct additional supplies quickly to any consuming sector. In contrast, a lengthy planning period and substantial capital investment are required to expand use of most other types of energy. Hence, increases in energy consumption translate generally into use of additional petroleum. Conversely, reductions in energy use and additional production of energy from other sources largely result in lower petroleum consumption. Changes in petroleum consumption affect sales by oil exporters, and the effects of those sales changes are felt in time by all importing countries.

Import Demand and World Oil Prices

Individually and as a group, petroleum exporters have some discretion over the terms under which they make oil available to satisfy world demand, but their discretion is limited by factors such as these: (1) their own desires for imports (which dictate that some oil will be put on the market); (2) the effect of oil prices on the prosperity and stability of the economies in which their surplus funds are invested; and (3) the costs of current production (including the surrender of future sales at potentially higher prices as world resources decline). In finally determining the actual level of production and price of oil, the economic and political goals of the exporters (as well as other influences) may also come into play.

To oversimplify a complex relationship which is sometimes overlooked, an increase in oil consumption raises the cost of producing oil in the present. It does so in part because more rapid depletion of reserves increases the value of the oil in the ground, representing the cost at the margin of future sales forgone. Current unit production costs may also rise as more is produced in the same period. Heightened world demand weakens the threat of conflict for markets among oil exporters. And, since importers are willing to buy more, it signals an increase in the relative value of oil as compared with the goods imported by the oil producers. Because oil markets are not purely competitive, an increase in the demand for oil imports does not in any mechanistic way dictate an increase in the price of oil (much less the amount of the increase), but it does raise both the lower and the upper limits of the range within which oil exporters exercise discretion over the price. Conversely, a reduction in the demand for oil imports lowers that range.

Levels of Imports—
Why Do They Matter?

Changes in import demand can alter the distribution of income and wealth among countries, affect the stability of the international economic system, and influence prospects for peace. If an increase in imports brings an increase in price, all oil is affected. The world oil bill goes up by the value of the added imports *plus* the change in price *multiplied* by previous world oil production. Conversely, reducing imports by even a small amount can have large effects on the receipts of oil exporters, if it leads to a price drop. To the extent that other energy prices are determined by oil prices, the effect on the total cost of energy to consumers is multiplied again. Thus the effects of changes in oil import demand are highly leveraged; they can alter the distribution of income between oil-importing and oil-exporting nations by an amount out of proportion to their direct effects—*if* prices change.

The level of oil import demand also affects the flow of trade and capital among countries. The bulk of any increase in the world's oil bill will flow to payments-surplus countries (because they are the ones with excess oil productive capacity), and this more than proportionately increases the quantity of funds which they must recycle into productive use to avoid deflationary effects worldwide. Part of the increase also flows to payments-deficit exporters, but in that case most of it serves to increase the demand for goods produced by a small subset of (industrialized) oil importers. In both situations, stresses are placed on the institutions and processes by which trade and financial flows are directed around the world. Conversely, a decline in import demand lowers the balance of payments surplus of oil exporters, lessens the amount of adjustment required of currency values, and lowers the level of the compensating capital flows which must be accommodated.

U.S. oil imports have an amplified effect on international monetary values. An energy policy within the United States that is expected to lead to growing oil imports jeopardizes confidence in the stability of the U.S. economy and leads to speculative sales of the dollar. Moreover, since oil is such a large component of U.S. imports, small percentage changes can have a substantial effect on the overall terms of trade experienced by the U.S. economy. Both of these matters are serious. Domestically, depreciation of the dollar can lower the real income of U.S. workers and investors. Internationally, depreciation of the dollar is destabilizing to the oil-exporting countries because much of their foreign asset holdings is in dollar-denominated instruments. As those holdings decline in value, the incentive of surplus countries to produce more oil falls, and the price demanded for that which is sold rises. Other countries are also affected if monetary developments reduce the United States market for their goods.

International political stability can also be affected by levels of oil imports. The prospect of "wars" for energy may be small, but the lower the need for imports, the less likely it is that tensions and temptations will arise. The prospects for disruption of world oil markets through extraneous events (political turmoil, production accidents, and the like) or deliberate manipulation by oil exporters are lower if surplus productive capacity exists. Further, action to reduce oil imports (and hence to lower energy prices) may be a less costly and less disruptive way to fulfill humanitarian impulses toward lesser-developed nations than would be the alternatives—including direct transfers of income.

Import Demand—The International Dimension

National policies of conservation, fuel substitution, and domestic supply enhancement which reduce oil imports have effects beyond the borders of the country which acts. They tend to lower oil prices, lessen stresses on the international financial system, and improve the prospects for political and economic stability. In doing so, they make both the country that reduces imports and all other oil importers better off. To the extent that such policies are only carried far enough to offset distortions (subsidies, monopoly power, and the like) elsewhere in the energy sector, they allow consumers and producers to react efficiently to the prices and terms of access to imported oil.[5] While the economic gains to importers are partially offset by losses to exporters, potential world output is enhanced because resources are generally allocated more efficiently.

The situation changes when actions are taken to lower imports below the level where the result is solely to eliminate the effects of distortions. Here the gains to importers from price reductions are found solely in a redistribution of income away from exporters; indeed, potential world economic output would fall because resources would be used less efficiently.[6] The costs of reducing imports would be borne by the country which incurred them, but their benefits (economic and other) would be shared among all oil importers. For each importing country, then, the incentive to reduce oil imports is lessened because it does not fully capture the benefits from its actions that flow to others. And the more narrowly the importer conceives the community for which it is concerned, the less beneficial programs of import reduction will seem to be. The "collective good" character of import reduction has meant that internal policies which affect oil imports gain international attention and invite external interference. For example, scarcely hidden acrimony has typified the reactions of other oil consumers to the failure of the United States to adopt an energy program which would further restrict oil imports.

Motivations to reduce oil imports would be enhanced if importers could be induced to act jointly. Then costs would be shared as well as

[5] Interpretation of these prices and terms of access is important, however; and "efficient reactions" does not imply a laissez-faire policy toward oil imports reckoned at private sector costs. For example, the insecurity of foreign oil supplies raises their implicit cost, and perhaps justifies a fee to cover costs of programs to lessen insecurity risks. A fee would lower imports by restricting energy use and encouraging domestic output. The effect of oil imports on the terms of trade and the balance of payments may make a tariff beneficial. Support of conservation R&D, of efforts toward fuel substitution, and so forth may follow from market failures or from the prospects for future external political manipulation of the access to imported oil. These issues are discussed in the sections that follow.

[6] Importing countries would incur costs in reducing oil imports (doing without oil, or substituting more expensive energy sources) which are greater than the costs avoided by the exporters in reducing their oil production. But the important matter from each importer's point of view is what happens to the size of *its* income. If the sum of the reductions in its particular oil-import bill is greater than the other costs involved for it, any one importing country may decide that it benefits.

benefits. The International Energy Agency (IEA) was founded to bring about such cooperation among energy importers. Activities of that organization include reviewing the energy conservation program of each member and noting where each succeeds or fails in carrying its share of the import reduction burden. The Agency also has sought to promote research and development cooperation in increasing domestic energy supplies.

Another aspect of the IEA program is to facilitate the sharing of oil supplies in the event of a major disruption in oil flows. Such sharing, by spreading the cost of lower supplies among all nations, lessens the prospective loss sustained by each and hence reduces the temptation to compete for more than one's share of the limited oil flow. A loss of 7 percent of the supplies of a member nation triggers the sharing arrangement. In concert with this emergency provision, the Agency monitors the levels of oil inventories around the world and imposes storage targets for each nation. Enforcement of IEA recommendations is limited; it comes mostly through the tenuous controls imposed on sovereign nations by diplomacy and by linkage with other negotiations.

Policy Responses to the Global Situation

The United States is the largest importer of oil, a major force in developing and using energy sources which may substitute for petroleum, and the leading financial center. From this position it can influence energy outcomes to its own advantage and to the advantage (or disadvantage) of others. It can do so by altering its level of oil imports and, through actions which affect the level of oil imports demanded by others, the quantity of energy produced around the world and the operation of the international economy.

In choosing an optimal level of oil imports, the United States must consider the contribution such imports make to domestic wealth and income, to the timely development of alternative energy sources, to the world price of oil, to its terms of trade, and to the prospects for avoiding disruptive energy price changes in the future. To the extent these impacts affect others (and they do, in important ways), it must also consider feedbacks upon the U.S. economy.

On balance, these factors suggest that it would be preferable for U.S. oil imports to be somewhat lower than the level that would follow from private decisions regarding oil use, even if market failures were removed.[7] But the uncertainty of the effect of import levels on world oil prices, and the cost of doing without cheap oil if that effect is small, suggest caution in adopting any policy that would substantially reduce imports below the level dictated by the actual and anticipated cost (including external costs) of petroleum. Low-cost and low-risk policies seem appropriate, but costly efforts to cut oil imports substantially and quickly do not. We abstract here from policies to lessen the risks from imports (which may also affect their level) which are discussed below (page 430).

It is also in the interest of the United States to induce other countries to reduce their purchases of oil abroad; and several goals would be served if U.S. actions could increase the ability and willingness of all energy producers, especially those who are not now major producers, to expand their respective energy supplies. Therefore, we turn next to policies to achieve such import reduction and world supply expansion—and to their potential effects on oil trade.

Reducing Energy Consumption

Since imported oil is the source of energy not met by domestic production, any change in energy consumption has a proportionally greater effect on imports. For example, a 5 percent reduction in the 1977 U.S. energy consumption of about 38 million barrels per day oil equivalent could have reduced U.S. oil imports by about 23 percent, and could have lowered the market for OPEC oil by 7 percent. Such a reduction would have been equal to the total petroleum produced by the smallest three OPEC members in 1977.

Earlier chapters of this book evaluated the prospects for reducing energy consumption and explored the impact such reductions might have on economic growth and on satisfying other social wants. We concluded that continued prosperity and an acceptable standard of living were consistent with lower levels of energy use than would occur through continuation of current policies. And the analysis above of the effects of additional oil

---

[7] By market failure we mean conditions in which economic actors—consumers, producers, investors, and resource owners—are not induced to act in a way to maximize the discounted present value of the society's income stream. Conditions leading to market failure include monopoly power and external effects. By the latter, we mean benefits or costs from an action which affect parties other than those directly involved in the transaction. In the presence of market failure, the free choice of individual economic actors may not lead to an optimal outcome. It is then feasible for government interference to increase overall well-being.

imports suggests that lower levels of energy use can be economically desirable. It is of critical importance, however, how that lower level of consumption is achieved. Though some opportunities for efficient intervention with the market mechanism have been identified, we conclude in general that price reform (discussed in chapter 17) is the critical first step in achieving lower energy use. Decontrol of oil and gas prices and marginal-cost pricing of utility services are the basic policy changes required. In addition, it may be necessary to subsidize conservation research and development, to improve access to capital for energy-saving technologies, and to provide information on which consumers can depend in making energy- and money-saving decisions.

These actions do not, however, address one issue; namely, even at the world price, energy consumption may be too large. That is, the full cost of additional imports—taking into account effects on oil prices and on economic and political stability—is probably somewhat higher than the price that is charged. While uncertainties exist, the evidence points to distortions that are not large; hence Draconian import-reducing measures are not called for. Perhaps all that is required is that decisions about potential energy conservation programs be weighted toward doing more rather than doing less than what otherwise would be appropriate in rectifying market failure. The administrative problems and opportunities for inefficient application of most mandatory conservation programs probably suggest that they should be avoided since their potential benefits seem low and their costs may be substantial.

If the evidence becomes clear that some special conservation program is required, an ad valorem tariff to raise the price of imported oil above the world level would be an effective instrument, and one less susceptible to abuse than most. A tariff would be most beneficial if its imposition is coordinated with other oil importing countries. However, caution should be exercised in introducing such a tariff because it is difficult to determine what the "correct" level of the tariff should be. Specifically, it should start at a low level and then escalate so as to allow time for efficient adjustment by consumers and domestic energy producers. Its effects should be reassessed periodically so that its ultimate level could be determined on the basis of better information.

Enhancing Energy Production

Domestic petroleum resources remain large. The United States ranks fifth in the world in proved and probable reserves, and it is the third largest oil producer. Some expansion of petroleum output could be induced through higher prices and by making available promising exploration targets on public lands (and offshore). But truly significant increases in domestic energy production could only come from the nation's vast deposits of coal and oil shale and from its large uranium and (possibly) natural gas resources.

Oil import demand could be reduced by restructuring demand to fit the nonliquid energy forms available domestically and by implementing fuel conversion processes to turn oil shale deposits, coal, and biomass into the liquid and (perhaps) gaseous fuels that are required. Reforming natural gas pricing could increase output of this resource, and institutional changes could facilitate faster nuclear and solar power development. At present, however, imported oil appears to be less costly than some of these alternatives, and most actions (beyond price and institutional reform) to bring about substantial demand shifts or large-scale synthetic liquids or gas production would require subsidies or increased prices through measures such as a tariff on imported oil. Some such support may be desirable for reasons discussed above.

A policy that tilts toward domestic energy production seems clearly indicated, but the case for a crash program to substitute domestic for foreign energy is far from obvious. Research and development support for domestic energy production is discussed in chapter 17, and measures to promote synthetic liquid and gas production, solar energy use, coal production, and nuclear power output are examined in chapters 18 and 19.

Technology developed within the United States can also be exported to increase energy production and reduce energy use abroad. Oil shale or coal conversion processes may have potential elsewhere, and applications of solar energy could be adopted widely. Multinational development of resource base information and joint support of basic research may also be in order, along with research and development directed toward better utilization of noncommercial energy sources.

The supply of oil itself could also be increased. Technology can be made freely available to all oil producers. Whatever other factors are involved, it is in the best interest of the United States, where energy is concerned, to support the oil industries of communist countries such as the USSR and China. Also, U.S. petroleum firms could be encouraged to expand their efforts abroad, with special concentration on exploration and development in promising energy-deficient regions. Some of these supportive roles can best be carried through by international bodies such as the International Bank for Reconstruction and Development (World Bank). Such international bodies are free of some of the suspicion that handicaps

U.S. government effectiveness and they can reassure host countries and foreign firms alike that the agreements made are fair and will be consummated. United States diplomatic initiatives may be required, and greater flexibility on financial guarantees may be necessary. Quiet assurances to the firms of support in controversies abroad might be helpful in getting U.S. companies involved in such countries as China and in Southeast Asia, including Vietnam. Efforts there could hasten oil production from those regions and introduce new exporters to the world market.

Special assistance to oil development in countries such as Mexico would help diversify oil sources and expand oil supplies; both effects would be favorable to U.S. interests. Improvement in overall relations with Mexico—including policies relating to trade, immigrants, illegal aliens, and drug programs—may serve as the basis for greater collaboration on touchy energy issues. These include natural gas trade and foreign technical assistance in developing Mexico's apparently huge hydrocarbon deposits. In a slightly different context, nonconventional oil supplies in Venezuela are immense; some can be exploited at costs lower than synthetic fuels can be produced in this country. As a major foreign market for Venezuela's output, the United States is the logical leader in supplying special inducements to Venezuela to press exploitation of those reserves. For example, encouraging development of refining capacity to handle the heavy crudes that Venezuela can produce would tend to induce investment in production by assuring that markets would exist when the crude was available.

Finally, the rate at which oil exporters are willing to supply oil depends importantly on their degree of integration into the world economic system and upon their expectations as to its stability. In assessing the benefits from producing oil rather than saving it for the more distant future, they will consider whether current financial surpluses can be invested at home or abroad to support employment and consumption when depletion forces lower oil production and when needs have risen. The United States can contribute to expanded oil output by reassuring those nations of its dedication to economic development and diversification abroad, to free flows of capital, to maintaining the value of the dollar, and to making the ultimate transition to other energy sources both smooth and timely.

Prospects for Energy Trade

A major consideration driving energy policy for the intermediate term—through, say, the end of this century—is the uncertain availability and price of petroleum in world markets. While any number of developments could combine to restrict the availability of oil on world markets below the level needed to maintain satisfactory levels of world economic growth, it also appears that sufficient oil *could* be available.

There are two ways of thinking about resource constraints to the future availability of oil. The first is in real price terms, and the second is in terms of the peaking of production. For the moment let us ignore the possibility of political misadventure, civil disturbance, accident, or behavior by oil-exporting countries that rejects conventional economic goals. If we do so, our analysis presented in chapter 7 suggests that the petroleum and natural gas reserve base is adequate to support growing world oil and gas consumption for at least a decade or so at cost levels in real terms not much above current prices. Beyond conventional oil and gas lie higher-cost resources such as the heavy oil belt of Venezuela. While exploitation of those resources would require costs above the *average* costs of conventional oil, these costs could be below or slightly above the prices for oil now being charged by OPEC. As to the peaking of production, this depends on the shifting relationship between output and addition of reserves, both of which are affected by price and many other factors. Given the substitution possibilities among fuels, moreover, other energy sources may share the pressures of demand, so that increases in oil output may be dampened by relatively small price increases for energy, if adjustments are allowed.

These conclusions about the resource base and about technical possibilities are widely shared. Even studies evidencing concern about prospective energy availability suggest constraints arising more from what probably *will* be done than from what *could* be done. Furthermore, most assessments of resource constraints ignore the cumulative effect of numerous minor adjustments in both supply and demand that would be encouraged by far less than another doubling of the oil price. Assuming then that oil may be available and cheaper than alternatives, it is prudent to consider the basis on which to develop policies if the United States should choose to depend on oil imports for a significant proportion of future energy needs.

Defensive measures are necessary because various events could spoil the somewhat sanguine assumptions about possible energy availability and price underlying the passage above. First, the development of oil resources, of alternative energy supplies, and of energy-conserving processes and behavior may not take place as smoothly as postulated above. The period of relative abundance may include interludes of supply stringency. Second, there is always the possibility of economically irrational behavior on the part of oil exporters, political disruption, or natural catastrophe.

The reductions in oil exports due to the political troubles which started in Iran in 1978 is illustrative. Again, supply shortfalls accomplished by disruptive price increases could occur.

What, then, are prudent assumptions about the prospects for oil price and availability from which a U.S. policy toward oil imports may be derived? Three elements are important:

1. Based on technology and on what we know about the natural endowment, oil and natural gas can be available for at least a decade or so at something near current real prices, and in significant and probably growing quantities. It may be that no "crunch" (either in price or availability) will occur. If it does, however—and it might— we could expect serious consequences. Therefore, U.S. policy should not be based on the certainty that oil and gas imports *can* continue and grow, but instead on the possibility that they *may not*.

2. While the petroleum and natural gas era is not over, the contribution of these fossil fuels to world energy requirements will probably pass its peak within the lifetime of most persons now living. Real energy prices will almost certainly rise before that peak is reached. These changes will demand many adjustments.

3. For the next decade or so at least, the major issues regarding oil and gas trade will arise from political and social considerations of importing and exporting nations. These issues include: (a) preferences of oil exporter governments for current (as opposed to future) revenues; (b) the ability of oil-exporting governments to satisfy the demands of their citizens and thus avoid internal upheavals; (c) the degree of risk from disruption of oil supplies countries are willing to bear, and thus the cost they are willing to pay to lower imports— and those risks; and (d) the avoidance of open international conflict that disrupts oil supplies.

Policies to Lessen the Risk of Energy Imports

Risks to national security or to economic prosperity posed by energy imports may be interpreted as added social costs—analogous to environmental and other costs which can be internalized. These additional costs lower the net benefits from importing energy. Since the costs are imposed on the economy as a whole rather than on energy importers as such, however, they do not customarily affect private decisions as to how much to import. Nor do they induce corrective measures on the part of private parties to limit their impact. Thus, government measures may be required.

It is important from the first to understand that the risks posed by oil imports must be weighed against the benefits from allowing imports to continue. Those benefits flow from using cheaper foreign oil and gas in place of more expensive domestic alternatives or of doing without energy. If oil and gas imports lower the cost of the energy input to consumption and production, then more goods and services can be produced and enjoyed. On the other hand, the risk that these benefits may be cut off by a disruption of the import pattern lowers the expected net value of a free import policy.

Given these facts, what do we do? To forbid oil imports leads to extraordinary costs to the economy. Yet it appears similarly unwise to allow oil to enter freely without taking any defensive measures. We can envision some policies which may reduce risks while still allowing most of the benefits from importing oil to flow through to consumers. In discussing these policies, we will focus on oil imports, although many of the considerations here relate to natural gas as well. However, some special factors affecting the dangers of interruption to gas imports (and specialized counterpolicies) are considered in a separate section at the end of the chapter.

Assessing the Risks

There are two ways in which importing energy gives rise to uncompensated risks not otherwise covered in private transactions.[8] The first derives from the risk that imported oil prices (availability) may fluctuate rapidly through variations of future supply by oil sellers. The possibility of increased supply from abroad (and lower import prices) would discourage conservation investment and domestic supply, but the major concern is about supply *decreases*—even transitory ones. They could be seriously disruptive, whether their effects were transmitted through rising prices or through some form of physical rationing. The second risk is that oil supplies could be unexpectedly and permanently diminished or cut off, leaving the United States with extraordinary energy costs because efforts to replace those imports had not been taken earlier. Such cutoffs could occur through international conflict, because of internal disruptions within

---

[8] We assume here that environmental and other externalities have already been internalized, and that policies have already been adjusted to neutralize the economic disadvantages of importing more rather than less oil.

oil-exporting countries, or through decisions by one or more major suppliers that oil simply would not be sold in the quantities anticipated.[9]

Some of the damage from rapid and unexpected energy supply restrictions and subsequent (perhaps transitory) price increases would follow because an abrupt change was imposed on the economy. Besides losses due to the spurt of inflation that would probably occur, there would also probably be losses due to the transitory unemployment or underemployment of resources.[10] Productivity of the employed stock of capital and of the labor force would decline because of a mismatch between requirements under the new price regime and the mix of equipment and labor skills developed under the old.

Some of these dislocation costs would be imposed on the economy whether or not the United States had been a major importer of oil. For example, trade patterns with foreign nations would be upset, and U.S. nonenergy exports would diminish, as the ability of oil importers to buy declined and offsetting purchases by oil exporters did not rise as rapidly. But it is important to note that a more nearly energy self-sufficient economy is better able to determine its rate of adjustment to world price changes. By adjusting more gradually, it can soften the dislocation impact it would suffer if energy prices shot upward.[11]

In contrast to the dislocation costs of a transitory shortage or price increase, the harm from an unexpected permanent reduction in world energy supply comes from the failure to undertake energy supply-enhancing or demand-reducing activities soon enough to bring them on smoothly at the time they are needed. Energy prices thus overshoot their long-run level, excessive disturbances occur, and new energy supplies and conservation measures are more costly to develop than they would otherwise have been.

Our dependence on imports imposes certain noneconomic costs whether or not interruptions or permanent restrictions of supplies actually occur. The primary costs lie in a diminution of the international position

---

[9] It could be argued that our importing energy might exacerbate the magnitude of the costs imposed on others but these costs are sufficiently speculative that we choose to ignore them in this discussion of risks to the United States from its oil imports.

[10] This unemployment would arise from macroeconomic causes as demand for exports declined and as domestic activity slowed due to uncertainty and indecision. Even with perfect demand management, moreover, there would still be microeconomic causes; unemployment would rise until resources were fully deployed in producing new patterns of output, using the new optimal input mix, both occasioned by the change in relative prices.

[11] This does not mean, of course, that self-sufficiency is desirable at *any* price. A nation gives up the benefits of being able to import cheaply what it otherwise would produce itself expensively. An optimal level of imports balances those costs and benefits.

of the United States and in restraints on its foreign policy choices. These restraints arise mostly from the ability of foreigners to impose economic penalties on the United States. Because of import vulnerability, the United States must expand its military forces to guard supply lanes and take an active (and sometimes expensive) role in supporting regimes which control oil supplies. U.S. involvement in the Middle East and along the Horn of Africa is dominated by considerations of oil supply, and revision of U.S. policy toward illegal immigrants from Mexico took on new urgency with the announcement of sizable new hydrocarbon discoveries in that country. The United States' energy vulnerability also makes it a less fearsome foe or trustworthy friend. The difficult-to-define but nonetheless real factor of national prestige depends to some extent on relative impregnability.

The social costs imposed by all these risks cannot be quantified very satisfactorily, much less related to the size of U.S. imports or the ratio between them and total energy supply. Nevertheless, there are some general considerations that affect any policy judgment about the extent of the protective program that is necessary:

First, supply reductions and price increases may not occur. It is uncertain whether any economic costs (as distinguished from the noneconomic costs associated with the very fact of imports) will ever be imposed.

Second, any loss imposed from such events will be borne in the future (although possibly very soon). Future costs are less painful than current ones.

Third, a loss imposed on the economy depends on the size of the price increase (or severity of rationing) created by a supply reduction. The loss could be small or large, but it would rise more than proportionately with the size of the price increase. The price increase itself may not move directly with the size of the interruption, however; and the relationship between the size of the interruption and the price increase could change over time.

There is clearly no linear relationship between the size of U.S. oil imports and the amount of losses that reductions in oil supply abroad threaten.[12] Moreover, as long as imported oil is the incremental source of fuel, price changes will be imposed on the economy no matter how small imports are (though the redistribution of income to foreigners would be

---

[12] It is even plausible that U.S. reliance on imports may lend stability to energy supplies because of the incentive of exporters not to offend a major world power. Thus the probability of an interruption may be lowered if the United States imports more oil—leaving the net impact (probability times effect) unclear at best.

smaller if the import level is lower). Further, even if the U.S. energy supply were insulated from foreign imports, an interruption of supply to others would have an effect on the United States. Thus the size of the risk we run cannot be predicted by the amount of our imports, and a reduction in the level of imports may not have much effect on the size of the risk.

Policy Options

The prospective cost of disruption in imports may be lessened by insulating the economy from external changes in energy price and availability. The impact of permanently reduced imports can be moderated by shortening the time lag before introducing additional domestic energy supply and conservation capacity. Both approaches enhance the resilience of the economy in the face of energy shocks. The size and probability of harmful supply and price changes can also be reduced. The following policies would contribute to these goals:

Strategic storage. The economy can be insulated against some of the more harmful effects of transitory price increases through strategic oil storage. Such storage can be held privately or by government, as long as it represents a stock of fuel which can be drawn upon if oil imports should be interrupted. Such a stockpile would provide an interval during which diplomacy could work, foreign oil shipments could be reinstituted, domestic energy consumption dampened in an orderly way and alternative foreign and domestic supplies brought on stream. With regard to the latter, time would be gained for taking various limited but helpful steps: coal-based electricity generation could be enhanced as coal supplies were increased to fuel (perhaps obsolescent) electric generating facilities; additional connections and pumping equipment could be installed to produce domestic oil and gas more rapidly than before; and adjustments could be undertaken in refinery operations.

The difficulties in establishing a strategic reserve should not be minimized, as frustrating experience with the effort to date attests. Further, no stockpile could be large enough, or be used wisely enough, to prevent damage from a large or long-term interruption; but the shock and effects of such an event could be dampened. A small or temporary supply interruption could be weathered without forcing the economy to make and then unmake expensive adjustments. By removing some of the urgency from action, a stockpile could also lessen the danger of armed conflict over oil. It would certainly improve the national sense of security and reduce the risk of surrendering vital foreign policy objectives in the face of oil blackmail.

Strategic storage might even reduce the temptation of oil exporters to make demands, because they would know that an interruption would need to go on for a long time (at high cost to them) before it really harmed the United States. Further, the availability of the stockpile would reduce the impacts on other oil-importing countries; and its very existence would improve our leverage in inducing others to build up similar stockpiles.

The size chosen for a strategic stockpile depends on how much risk the nation wants to eliminate and how much it is willing to pay for additional security. For example, if a year's protection from significant economic disruption were the policy goal, a stockpile equal to about 120 days' imports would be required. This assumes that about one-half of normal imports would continue to arrive, that domestic energy production could be increased about 5 percent within the year while energy consumption was being reduced at the same rate, and that normal commercial stocks (not considered part of strategic storage) could shrink by 20 percent. At 1978 import levels, 120 days' imports amount to about 1 billion barrels. The early experience with the Strategic Petroleum Reserve suggests that the full annual cost of storing a barrel of oil (including opportunity costs) would be about \$2 to \$2.50 per barrel.[13] If 120 days storage were required, the cost per barrel of *imports* would be about \$0.75.

Rules for use of the stockpile need to be formulated. They would, perhaps, be keyed to previously determined triggering price increases and scaled to exhaust the reserve (more rapidly at first) over the course of a year. The danger is that government will be either too timid or too aggressive in using the stockpile. Since the stockpile is a defense against economic disruption, allocations from it should be determined by their potential contribution to production, employment, and consumption. This can best be achieved through market instruments, but some form of rationing with free exchange of rights (a white market) may be required to meet equity goals.

---

[13] The total annualized SPR cost consists of the opportunity cost of the investment in oil, the capital and depreciation cost of the storage facilities, and annual operating costs. The largest component of costs is the investment in the stored crude oil. Its value may appreciate; to the extent it does, there will be an offset against the SPR costs. The rough estimates presented here were based on a 10 percent discount rate, Department of Energy estimates of the costs of building storage presented to the U.S. House Subcommittee on Energy and Power of the Committee on Interstate and Foreign Commerce (Washington, D.C., December 18, 1978), 1978 costs of oil, and recent estimates of storage operating costs.

Developing alternatives to imports. In the event of a large, apparently permanent shift in the costs of imported oil, a number of adjustments would start taking place in the economy. Long lead times are ordinarily required to reduce energy consumption and to bring energy supply alternatives into production, however, and the disruption can be very great until such adjustments are made. Programs to shorten lead times include planning and even installing (but not necessarily using) certain devices and processes which produce or conserve energy at total costs greater than those from using imported oil at its predisruption price. They also include moving more rapidly than might otherwise be justified on research and development for technologies that are not expected to be economic until the more distant future. For cases in which lead times amount to a decade or more, a few years' saving by such means is possible and could prove very valuable.

Specifically:

- Oil- and gas-burning installations could be built with the capacity for conversion to other fuel forms. While this capacity might have some benefits even during a transitory disruption, its major contribution would be to speed long-run adjustments if they proved necessary.
- Some energy-absorbing environmental protection devices can be turned off with acceptable effects on health; if such devices were identified in advance, energy could be saved in the least harmful way when shortages forced a change in the tradeoff between energy and the environment.
- Conservation technologies which would not be economically competitive at expected prices might be developed with the intention of implementing them fully only if shortages drove prices up.
- Uneconomic mass transit equipment (including rights-of-way) can be mothballed rather than scrapped, so that it can be used again if the energy cost of the private automobile skyrockets.
- Transmission lines could be enlarged at critical points to facilitate the emergency interchange of power from nuclear and coal-fired electricity generating plants to systems now dependent on oil and gas, permitting diversion of those fuels to other more pressing uses.
- The knowledge and industrial base could be developed from which the output of synthetic liquids and gases could be expanded rapidly if necessary (see chapter 19).

Uncertainties as to future oil price and availability will motivate the private sector to invest in some of these programs on its own. Investment would be further encouraged if the government made it clear that prices would be allowed to rise in the event of an oil shock, with the result that those who had prepared need not share their gains with others. In some cases, the governmental policy might impose the costs of preparation on energy users (through requiring dual firing capacity, for example). In other cases, budget expenditures might be appropriate to identify expendable environmental controls and in connection with the synthetic liquids program.

Formulating a response to shortfalls. Any disruption of oil imports will require adjustments in fuel-using and fuel-producing sectors. Since the nature and extent of disruptions may vary, specific actions cannot be identified and programmed ahead of time. It is possible, however, to formulate the principles on which such actions will be based and to forge agreement on the general courses of action to be taken and on the order in which they will be pursued as the size of a prospective problem mounts. To delay such efforts until a serious problem exists risks unwise actions taken in the frenzy of crisis. Proper contingency planning could avoid the kind of policy paralysis that can greatly compound the effects of relatively minor disruptions in domestic fuel markets. The events of early 1979 are an instructive example. Such policy inertia leads to what may be the worst of all worlds: a failure either to allow prices to rise until markets clear or to adopt a formal rationing system. In that circumstance hoarding develops, black markets arise, the unscrupulous benefit, faith in social institutions is frayed, and time, money, and fuel are wasted. Just as important, failing to take decisions before the need to implement them arises makes it impossible for firms and individuals to adjust their own behavior to take proper account of what may occur.

Another important benefit of planning for future possible shortfalls and subjecting alternatives to thorough debate is that it exposes the public to the real choices available outside a context where the temptation is to seek out scapegoats. It can be made clear, for example, that a rationing scheme makes income distribution choices explicit, but imposes administrative costs and leads to an allocation of fuel that, in practice, generally fails to maximize economic output. Similarly, the point can be made that allocation by price, which is efficient, may yield results which are offensive on income distribution grounds, and thus if such a policy is adopted, attention may well be paid to rectifying at least some of its more serious distributional impacts. And the brutal fact that in a shortfall everyone *cannot* be protected from harm can be driven home.

It is beyond the scope of this chapter to outline the substance of a policy response to shortfalls. Still, some principles on which it could be formulated can be identified:

- Maximum use should be made of price signals to allocate fuel so that flexibility can be assured and efficient adjustment to change can be achieved. If rationing is imposed, for example, coupons should be freely marketable.
- Mechanisms which preserve equity are critical. Equity is not only important in itself; it is an essential ingredient for sustaining social cohesion in a time of national trauma. A commitment to equity in the plans will foster the political support needed to assure that the system selected will be implemented and maintained.
- A capacity for a graduated response should be built into the system. It is important to avoid a program that is limited to major escalations of intervention because the strain of deciding when to make them places burdens on the decision-making process when it is already under stress. Moreover, the uncertainty involved imposes unnecessary costs on (and sometimes causes contradictory behavior by) the private sector, which must try to anticipate if and when a new measure will be imposed.
- Careful attention must be paid to the conditions under which various measures will be taken. No rigid "triggering points" can be defined because circumstances will vary, but the principles to be followed can be debated and decided on.

Lowering the probability of disruption.   Some policies which have already been mentioned can reduce the likelihood that oil supplies will be disrupted. These include diversifying sources of oil supplies, reducing the size of world oil import demands, supporting the political and economic stability of oil-exporting countries and supplying incentives for them to continue producing oil, and increasing the effectiveness of the international monetary and trade system.

Oil production almost certainly will remain concentrated in what are now the major exporting countries, but if opportunities to encourage output elsewhere are used, substantial diversification can result. The risk of disruption would be lessened because declines in oil supply are likely to exhibit a regional or national character. Events that disrupt output in Iran may not affect Arab production, and closing of the Persian Gulf would only indirectly affect production in Nigeria. However, the policy of diversifying a single country's supply sources would not be particularly useful to that individual oil importer in case of a supply disruption. Oil flowing in world markets effectively forms a single pool from which all importers draw, and the critical question is how much of the world supply is at risk. Each country will get whatever portion of that supply it seeks to buy, but at a higher price.

Paying for Lower Risks—A Political Question

The costs of such policies as a strategic oil storage program, early development of energy production and conservation alternatives, and a series of international initiatives will not be small, even though they should be less than the costs of forgoing imports or accepting their risks without protection. The purpose of these expenditures is to permit imports to continue during normal times—with the lower energy prices to consumers that importing oil implies. Since energy users benefit from imports, they may reasonably be expected to pay the cost of programs to make them safer; and an instrument by which these costs could most easily be imposed on energy consumers is an import fee on oil (distinct from the tariff mentioned above, but collected in the same fashion).

The effect of a "security fee" on imports is to raise the price of energy relative to other goods and services. Imported oil is the incremental source of energy, and when its cost rises, domestic substitutes previously priced out of the market can be produced and sold. More expensive domestic oil and natural gas (from deeper or smaller pools, for instance) can profitably be produced, and installation of solar space and water heating is encouraged. Higher-cost substitutes are brought closer to economic production. Higher prices for energy also make it worthwhile to undertake conservation efforts that were not economically justified before. Thus, by lowering overall energy demand, by lessening the proportion of that demand met by oil, and by increasing domestic energy supply, the effect of an import fee itself is to reduce imports. The fee, then, tends to reinforce the effects of the risk-reducing instruments for which its application pays.

A security fee may have other advantages as well. By reducing total demand for the products of oil-exporting countries, a fee could encourage stabilization or reduction of the world oil price. From another point of view, the reduction in demand would diminish the disruptive power of those countries within the oil cartel which bear the major burden of restraining current production in order to keep prices above competitive levels. In any cutback, an exporter surrenders part of its old market share to those who insist on maintaining (or even increasing) normal production; but in a market diminished by the security fee, exporters who may be tempted to reduce sales for international political purposes are closer to the lower limit of production they can tolerate economically. As that limit is approached, each additional reduction in output becomes more harmful to an exporter's economic interest. As it is made more costly to exporters, use of the "oil weapon" may become less likely.

Implementing a security-motivated oil import fee is relatively straightforward. It can be accomplished either by executive order or through legislation. It could be administered through the same structure that now assesses and collects the small fee already imposed.[14] While it is important for the public to see the link between the prospective revenues from a higher fee and the costs of protecting against disruption, a formal "trust fund" need not be established.

Determining the proper level for such an oil import levy is a very difficult matter.[15] This security fee would be imposed *in addition* to any program adopted to reconcile the private cost of oil with the extra social costs associated with importing more rather than less, as discussed in a previous section (p. 422). The issue of oil import risks discussed here is conceptually separate from the question of whether riskless oil imports impose costs, even though the instruments for dealing with each problem may overlap and be mutually reinforcing.

[14] This fee was instituted in 1973 as a replacement for the quota imposed under the Mandatory Oil Import Program. Because of its heritage, some imports are exempt from fee. Refined petroleum products are charged a larger fee to protect refineries from foreign imports. These and other special provisions would not necessarily be appropriate for a fee designed to meet very different import risks than those envisioned in 1973. President Carter in April, 1979, announced that he was suspending this fee temporarily in order to offset somewhat the increase in consumer prices resulting from the OPEC price increase. ("Imports of Petroleum and Petroleum Products, Proclamation 4655, April 6, 1979," *Weekly Compilation of Presidential Documents,* April 16, 1979, vol. 15, no. 15, pp. 621–668.)

[15] The size of the import fee required would depend on the cost of the strategic storage reserve, the actions to promote alternatives, and programs to lessen the chance of disruption. We have not attempted to estimate these costs with any precision, but the level of effort we have in mind might lead to an annual cost of $5 to $7 billion, and to an import fee of about $2 per barrel at 1978–79 import levels.

This approach is not very satisfactory conceptually. Analytically, the proper approach would be to compare costs at the margin for lessening disruption with the present value (discounted) of the expected reduction in disruption that those expenditures would buy. Unfortunately, beyond providing a framework for asking the right questions, this approach does not get one very far in determining such issues as what size stockpile is appropriate or whether $100 million or $150 million should be added to the coal liquefaction program. Thus we have not undertaken a formal analysis here.

Natural Gas Imports—Special Considerations

Natural gas is imported by ship in liquefied form and by pipeline from Canada. Pipeline imports from Mexico are in prospect.

Natural gas importation differs from international flows of other commodities in that trading partners are tightly linked by transportation facilities with little alternative use. Facilities such as pipelines and gas liquefaction and transportation installations are capital-intensive and integrated. They are usually developed as a package—from gas production to the point where the gas enters the importer's pipeline system for delivery to final consumers. Thus, excess capacity elsewhere cannot substitute readily for supplies from the prime gas source, if those should be restricted. Since demand is highly inelastic in the short run, reliance on a foreign supplier who can unilaterally abrogate a contract gives great leverage to the seller. It also means that any interruption of supply can have disruptive consequences even if the interruption is localized and relatively minor in terms of world output.

The bargaining power of suppliers vis-à-vis importers can best be neutralized by a policy which places responsibilities on the exporting agent demanding a continuous flow of funds. For any gas imported into the United States, for example, the seller could be required to bear the investment risk for all facilities dedicated to this trade, at least up to the point on U.S. soil where title to the gas passed to U.S. parties and control over its availability to the U.S. government. In such an arrangement the exporter not only would risk opportunity losses from delaying production of his gas, but also would bear the uncompensated out-of-pocket investment costs of idle facilities. In the liquefied natural gas case, for example, this policy implies that the producing country would own liquefaction facilities and tankers, and would finance them through borrowings other than from U.S. parties or government entities such as the Export–Import Bank. This exchange of "economic hostages" in the natural gas trade would lower the risk of unilateral moves by the seller.

Risks from a gas supply interruption can also be mitigated through a storage program. Storage to meet seasonal needs is an integral part of gas industry operations; but an increase in storage could be ordered, specifically to provide relief in adjusting to an interruption of foreign supplies.

A second policy for limiting risks is to require interconnection between importing firms and other gas transmission companies. Some capacity exists among consumers on any pipeline system to reduce use at relatively low cost. Thus the impact of an interruption is more than proportional as the affected percentage of supply rises. An interconnected system is more resilient to any single interruptive event than the individual firms that make it up—even if each imports gas—so long as all gas is not cut off at once; and the factors which might lead to an interruption in supply from one source are unlikely to be replicated in other producing regions. Interconnection requires that physical facilities be in place to move gas, and, even more important, that institutional arrangements be worked out so that the costs of insecurity are placed on those importing gas and reflected in the charges that their customers bear.

In implementing the storage and interconnection requirements the government can use an instrument already available. Because they are regulated utilities, gas pipeline companies are required to obtain certificates of convenience and necessity to build facilities, including those required for importing gas. Using this requirement, gas imports from any one source could be limited to an amount which, if interrupted, can be made up (at some policy-determined level of cost) through fuel switching or use reduction. The decision to allow additional imports would balance the costs of insecurity in imported gas against its price attractiveness to final consumers. Thus, a certification procedure could be used to constrain price demands by prospective purveyors of gas.

With policies like these in place (and if imported natural gas proves as economically attractive as imported petroleum is now), it can be counted as an important but limited component of future energy supply for a long time to come.

17 Formulating Energy Policy—The Complexities and Uncertainties

Energy choices are not easy, and much controversy about them remains. Better information about the technical possibilities that exist and about the relative attractiveness and risks associated with alternative courses of action can narrow the areas of disagreement over what different policies would achieve. Earlier parts of this book have tried to summarize and highlight such information. Even with this information, however, the nation's ability to make energy choices effectively and efficiently is limited by policy and institutional constraints.

Policy and institutional difficulties are associated mainly with six aspects of the processes by which decisions regarding energy are made: (1) pricing energy services; (2) determining the magnitude and type of expenditures to preserve environmental quality; (3) achieving fairness to all parties in energy-related matters; (4) defining intergovernmental relations; (5) dealing with uncertainties about the effects of policies; and (6) the whole class of other issues that economists lump together as "market failure," embracing the inability of an unsupervised market to reflect or respond promptly to social costs and needs. This chapter will identify some major generic problems which hinder effective operation of the energy system, and it will present some common approaches which can help surmount those obstacles.

Energy Pricing

The Need for Pricing Reform

Effective energy policy requires a pricing system which correctly signals producers and importers as to what energy is worth to consumers and which lets consumers realize what energy is costing the society.

Consumers as a group are better off, of course, when energy costs are low. Then they can have more energy and more of other things as well. When energy costs to the U.S. economy rise, as they did with the OPEC actions of 1973–74 and early 1979, the loss to consumers would be minimized—though it could still remain large—if everyone responded to energy prices which correctly reflected the drain on the economy from using more of each form of energy, and the contribution to the economy from additional supplies. This can only occur with energy prices that reflect the marginal cost of the energy supplied.

If energy is priced below that cost (because of price controls, for example), then consumers as a group use too much of it. As a result, they unconsciously give up benefits (in doing without other commodities and services) that are worth more than the satisfactions they get from the last units of energy consumed. Conversely, when energy is priced above its marginal cost, too little is used. Consumers as a whole would be better off if they could trade some of the other things they consume for additional units of energy. In the simplest terms, the amount of goods and services an economy can provide is maximized when the price of each commodity or service is equal to the marginal cost of acquiring it. Government controls keeping it below that level make energy a poor bargain, because its apparently low monetary price is accompanied by hidden rises in living costs from lower productivity in the rest of the economy, by deterioration in the international terms of trade, and by added vulnerability to future energy shocks.

As noted earlier, the incremental source of energy in the world market is imported crude oil. Hence its cost to U.S. consumers is the basis for the marginal cost of all energy used. Imported oil does not carry a competitive market price; but so long as the United States depends on imported crude, that price represents what must be surrendered in economic value (in the form of exports or debts to foreigners) for the incremental barrel imported. Importing oil also imposes additional social costs. These arise from the insecurity of imports (because of which, costly countermeasures must be initiated or risks borne) and from the net costs to us of the higher prices all other consuming countries must pay for oil because of our incremental drawdown of world supplies. While they are impossible to ascertain precisely, these extra costs are probably greater than the nominal tariffs now imposed on imported oil. Hence, the true marginal cost of oil to the U.S. economy under the present tariff structure probably lies above the private market price of imported crude oil. Furthermore, this is likely to remain true no matter how much of a "profit margin" oil exporting countries choose to add to their production costs for such oil.

The marginal cost of imported oil determines the value to society of domestic energy (although not necessarily its price). This is because domestic fuels contribute to well-being by displacing imported crude oil (at its full marginal cost). At the raw material stage, that contribution is measured by subtracting from the full cost of the imported oil the cost of processing, using, and transporting the substitute fuel so that it performs the same functions as the imported oil.[1] Consumers, of course, respond to prices at the end-use point. For prices at that point to lead to efficient allocation of resources, they should reflect the marginal costs of all the commodities and services which are needed to make the energy available.

The present U.S. energy system fails to meet the fundamental test for rational energy decisions because price signals fail in major ways to reflect marginal costs. For instance, the price of imported oil does not now cover the cost of supply insecurity. As another example, some domestic crude oil is controlled at below world prices. Electricity services are priced at average *historic* costs rather than at current *marginal* costs, which are higher. Gas consumers are making consumption decisions based on average costs of gas in their local markets, while the marginal gas supplied may cost three times as much. Because of regulation rather than cost variations, different producers and consumers receive or pay greatly different prices for the same commodity. Despite efforts to avoid imposing environmental impacts, such impacts do exist; and unpaid environmental costs from energy production and use remain. As compared with a regime of marginal cost pricing, more energy is being consumed, less energy is being produced domestically, more energy (mainly oil) is being imported, and there are inefficient patterns of energy production and consumption by form and location. The existing energy pricing system

---

[1] This conclusion is limited to cases where full substitution among fuels is possible. In the short run such substitution cannot take place, and in that case the price of some domestic fuels—coal, for example—is held below the equivalent price of oil by market forces. The principle holds in the long run, however, because additional effort to substitute coal is justified and new uses for coal can develop. The proper way of looking at the substitution process is to consider the cost of the fuel *and* of the ancillary expense of using it. Hence, with higher oil prices the price of coal may not rise (because of supply conditions) but the costs willingly borne to *use* coal (through conversion to electricity and the substitution of electricity for oil, for example) will rise to the point where, at the margin, the full costs of meeting the requirement with oil or with coal are the same.

has thus lowered the potential output of the economy and lessened the total quantity of goods and services available to consumers.

Besides increasing the potential output of the economy, adjusting energy prices to full marginal cost would make a number of energy choices easier. It would provide a great deal of information on supply and demand responses which would otherwise be either unavailable or very costly to acquire. For example, a free market for natural gas would reduce uncertainty about whether or not a market would exist for synthetic gaseous fuel at the prospective cost of the new product. Proper pricing of energy would also reduce the size and complexity of the policy issues that government must address, because individual choice would automatically replace many of the uncertain decision-models, questionable data, and imperfect knowledge on which government bases its decisions. Society might still wish for some reason to interfere with private choice, but such intervention would rest on the explicit decision to replace private preferences with ones imposed by government.

Energy pricing reforms are not without problems. They would not be easy to implement, and they would not cause difficult energy choices to go away. Moreover, pricing reform cannot undo the damage to the level of well-being wrought by the oil price increases of 1973–74 and 1979. In a deep sense, all oil-importing nations became poorer; nothing they can do will change that basic fact. But pricing reform is fundamental to minimizing losses for all involved. Without reform, the scope for conflict over energy issues will be greater and wise choices will be less likely.

The Substance of Energy Pricing Reform

Energy pricing reform aimed at achieving these benefits for the whole society would involve three elements: First, energy prices would be decontrolled; second, the external costs of energy importation, production, and consumption would be included in energy prices; and third, specific energy prices to consumers would have to reflect full marginal costs at the consumption point. As we shall see, achievement of each of these objectives poses practical difficulties. In the short run, in fact, those who wish to block rational pricing have little difficulty in dramatizing only the adverse effects that each policy component might cause.

Removal of price controls.   Domestic oil prices are now controlled through a complex set of regulations which limit the price at the wellhead.

Different pricing categories exist, so that domestic crude oil may range from about one-third the imported oil price to the full price. Although the earliest possible removal of price controls might be best from the standpoint of acquiring and using energy efficiently, other important goals might make it more desirable to increase the prices gradually.

President Carter proposed, in his 1977 energy plan, to raise the price of petroleum products to consumers (but not the price of crude oil received by producers) by imposing a tax at the wellhead, which would rise in three annual stages. His proposal also would have allowed (after three years) certain oil discovered after April 1977 to be sold at the 1977 world price, but not to rise with further world price movements. Carter's proposal would have moved toward yielding the benefits associated with using energy based on its replacement cost, but would not have yielded the efficiency gains from having domestic oil production based also on world prices. However, even this limited effort toward reforming petroleum pricing was defeated by Congress.

At the mid-1978 Bonn Summit meeting of the major industrial countries, the president committed his administration to adopting policies which would move oil prices for U.S. consumers to world levels by the end of 1980. The commitment could be met in a number of ways: (1) through deregulation; (2) through imposition of taxes, as Carter had proposed before; or (3) through implementation of an import fee or quota which would bring the *average* price of oil in the United States to the world price even though some domestic oil was held below that price level. The second and third alternatives would sacrifice some oil output for other goals, the most central of which are to avoid redistributing income to domestic oil producers and to make revenues available to government without raising other taxes.

President Carter decided in early 1979 to allow prices to rise gradually to world levels and to recommend to Congress what amounted to a special excise tax to absorb a portion of the resulting revenues from previously regulated oil. The fate of this proposal was not yet clear at the time of this writing. Similarly uncertain was whether a tax on future increases in unregulated domestic oil prices caused by world market conditions, which the president also proposed, would be enacted.

Natural gas prices at the wellhead have been held below free market prices for over a decade.[2] Legislation passed in 1978 expands controls

---

[2] Natural gas sales for resale in interstate commerce have been subject to regulation since 1954, but controls did not actually start holding prices down until some time in the early-to-mid-1960s.

to cover gas not previously regulated (mostly gas used within the state in which it is produced); but it raises the allowed price on much of what is controlled and promises deregulation of most gas by 1985–87. In doing so, it sets up different classifications of gas which will receive different prices as they are produced, and it requires that prices for different classes of gas consumers vary according to rules imposed by Congress. Thus, while the overall price of gas rises closer to its replacement cost under this legislation, the new set of price signals still does not meet the criteria for rational decision making. What is required is a dismantling of all price controls at the production stage. Doing so immediately would result in faster price increases than under the 1978 act. As in the case of crude oil, therefore, goals other than efficiency may weigh in favor of gradualism in removing controls (some of the generic problems in implementing price reform are discussed starting on p. 446).

Cost internalization. Energy importation, production, and consumption impose unpaid costs on the economy which should be reckoned into the decisions of producers and consumers by including them in the price of energy.[3] Two such costs, which this book has already amply discussed, are (1) the supply insecurity and other international costs of importing oil and (2) damages to the environment, human health, and safety. These are costs that remain even after the private sector has installed some excess storage capacity, put certain pollution control equipment in place, and taken other protective measures whose costs *are* already reflected in today's market prices.

Estimating costs that remain unpaid is difficult. Instruments to assess charges to compensate society or to modify behavior are not easy to design or administer. They also impose costs, and perfection is unattainable. The operational test for a policy of further internalizing costs is whether the best program *obtainable* will be better than no program at all.

Clearly, cost internalization should be carried as far as possible in every area where a reasonable relationship can be recognized between damages and remedies. For example, oil consumers (through a charge on imported oil such as the one postulated in chapter 16) would be obligated to pay for storage of oil to lessen the effect of a future supply interruption. Coal users might justifiably bear the full costs of compensating workers for accidents and health effects in mining coal, of reclaiming land, and

---

[3] Unrewarded benefits may also be produced, but these are uncertain in comparison with the costs and, since they appear to be small, are ignored here.

of protecting water bodies. Consumers of synthetic fuel would have to bear the incremental costs associated with providing public services to transitory populations engaged in construction. Automobile users might reasonably pay for costs of congestion and air quality deterioration in cities.

The list goes on, but some effects are individually small enough, or their impacts sufficiently diffused, as to make direct compensation too costly to estimate or collect. If such costs were still judged sufficiently great that energy should be singled out for special treatment, a tax on raw energy at the point of production or importation would probably be the best (albeit imperfect) instrument for shifting the remaining unpaid costs from the society as a whole to energy consumers. The presumption is that such a tax would not *add* to energy costs; it would merely convert existing costs into part of the monetary price borne by those who consume energy.

It is impossible to predict exactly how much the full internalization of costs would increase energy prices. The rises could be significant for some of the more offending sources and uses of energy, although on average they would probably be smaller than the increase in raw energy prices since 1973–74. Nor can we be sure how consumption, production, and technological improvements would respond to these new price changes. Nevertheless, this uncertainty should not be a bar to clearly beneficial action, and adjustments could occur over time.

Marginal cost pricing at point of consumption.   The third major element in getting energy prices right is to assure that each consumer pays the incremental cost of the energy he consumes. If the price of raw petroleum and natural gas has already been decontrolled, as another component of price reform, this issue relates primarily to the regulated gas and electric utilities.

The revenues these suppliers are allowed to earn are based on the accounting costs they incur in producing their services. Thus, consumer charges are based on the average costs of all facilities and purchased products, not on the incremental cost which is actually incurred when added demand requires an expansion of capacity. Because of inflation, the rising relative prices of energy, and the rising cost of capital during the past decade, presently allowable utility revenues are below the true market value of the services they sell.

The regulatory process which determines those allowed revenues is designed to prevent public utilities from exercising to the full the monopoly power that they otherwise would enjoy. Furthermore, regulation aims to require all consumers to share fairly in providing revenues, with "fairly" usually being defined as contributing roughly in proportion to costs incurred in serving their class. From the point of view of economic efficiency and the wise use of energy, however, marginal cost pricing would be preferable. The challenge is to find administratively feasible procedures which reconcile all these goals.

The efficiency goal has two parts: assuring that the fuel component be consumed only when the value it produces is equal to its replacement cost; and assuring that, at the margin, the charge for capital services is fully borne by those who occasion their production. Though no procedures are perfect, a number of approaches could be implemented. The underpricing of fuel can be rectified by imposing excise taxes and using regulatory discrimination in assigning fuel costs to consumers. Capital charges can be brought into line with actual costs via peak load pricing, excise taxation, and changes in the basic rate structure (keeping revenues the same).

Problems in Implementing Energy Pricing Reform

While complex in their effects, the three basic reforms we identify above —price decontrol, internalization of unpaid costs, and marginal cost consumer pricing—could simplify other aspects of energy policy. There would be no further need for much of the maze of statutes, regulations, subsidies, and taxes which have been adopted to buffer the more serious distortions created by past and present policy. Nevertheless, three generic issues associated with energy pricing reform need attention: inflation, transitory economic dislocation, and changes in income distribution (especially those harmful to the poor). Before turning to those issues, however, it will be useful to put them into perspective by summarizing some basic information on the economics of energy.

Energy price and the size of the energy sector.[4]   The price of raw energy jumped in 1973–74 with the OPEC increase, but between then

---

[4] Price data and comparisons supplied below were obtained as follows: Crude oil prices were obtained or estimated from the U.S. Department of Energy, Energy Information Administration, *Monthly Energy Review* (January 1979). Other producer and consumer price data were calculated from the U.S. Department of Labor, Bureau of Labor Statistics, *Wholesale Price Index* and *Consumer Price Index* (computer printouts). All producer prices and indexes were deflated by the WPI "all commodities"; retail price indexes were deflated by the CPI "all items."

and the end of 1978, increases were less rapid. By the end of 1974 imported oil prices (adjusted for inflation) had gone up 136 percent over the preembargo level, but over the next four years the adjusted price dropped 11 percent. The adjusted price of oil produced domestically went up 58 percent by the end of 1974, and it was another 18 percent higher by the end of 1978. Coal prices rose rapidly with the early oil price increases. They were up 65 percent between August 1973 and December 1974, but fell 18 percent between the end of 1974 and the end of 1978. Natural gas prices at the wellhead present a different picture. They were up only 8 percent between August 1973 and the end of 1974, but jumped an additional 139 percent by the end of 1978.

While energy price increases in some cases have been spectacular, they have added only modestly to inflation as measured at the consumer level. Ignoring secondary effects, total consumer prices at the end of 1978 were less than 1 percent above what they would have been had energy prices simply kept pace with the prices of other goods and services after August 1973.

Delivered prices of energy products, especially over a longer time period, offer another perspective. Comparing 1958 with 1978, for example, the price of gasoline in constant dollars actually fell 2 percent. Electricity dropped 7 percent. The price of home heating oil rose 47 percent and natural gas 31 percent during that twenty-year period. The increases in most energy prices dating from the early 1970s are still too recent for full adjustment to the change to have taken place; but those rises clearly reversed a general downward trend.

Energy price changes also have other, more subtle effects on inflation. For one thing, they affect the terms of trade. Moreover, sudden increases in the price of any important commodity tend to trigger wage increases and lead to an upward drift in other prices. But comparisons of overall price increases with and without energy do illustrate that energy is still a relatively small component of the economy in itself. To extend a point made in chapter 2, raw energy of all sorts—oil, gas, coal, and hydro and nuclear electricity—still amounted to only about 5.5 percent of the gross national product (GNP) in 1977. This was nearly double what it had been before 1973;[5] but in terms of primary effects each increase of 1 per-

---

[5] The value of raw energy sources consumed in the United States was calculated as the sum of (1) the value of domestic production of primary fuels and of electricity from water and nuclear power, and (2) the value of net imports of energy commodities. For coal, natural gas, natural gas liquids, and crude petroleum, data on production (valued at the minemouth or wellhead) were obtained from the U.S.

cent in energy prices would still lead to an increase in the GNP price deflator of less than 0.06 percent, even if there were no substitutes for energy. Since some substitution is possible, the effect is smaller.

Consideration of the size of the energy sector in relation to the rest of the economy also provides some insight into the effect of an increase in real energy costs. A *doubling* of the real cost of energy would absorb about 5.5 percent more of the economy's productive capacity even if no substitution took place. This conclusion assumes that the economy is given time to adjust smoothly. It understates, perhaps dramatically, the short-run effect of a sudden price increase under actual conditions.

Inflationary impacts.   If reform leads to the reflection of currently "unpaid costs" in energy prices, the overall measured price level will go up. Cost reductions in such forms as less disease and reduced economic insecurity do not show up in price indexes. Moreover, prices tend to be "sticky" downward—for a series of institutional reasons. These influences tend to negate, at least for a time, the price-reducing effects of productivity improvements from more efficient resource allocation. Hence, higher relative prices for energy will usually not be fully offset by lower prices for other goods. A permanent increase in the overall price level is therefore a likely result of energy pricing reform. Added inflationary pressures must be considered one of the major disadvantages to getting energy prices right. Still, if pricing reform takes place in stages (as it certainly would), the shock effect could be limited, and indeed made smaller than the impact of other price changes (such as many in the food sector) which have been assimilated tolerably in the past.

Inflation due to energy price reform could be lessened, moreover, by appropriately applying the increase in government revenues which pricing reform would also produce. Revenues from the sale of energy resources found on government lands would rise; tax payments from energy producing companies would rise; and the government might receive substantial additional funds via policy instruments mentioned above, such as an insecurity-compensating charge on oil imports, a Btu tax to compensate for external effects, and excise taxes on gas and electricity. Thanks to the

Bureau of Mines, *Energy Data Reports.* The value of mineral fuel imports and exports was reported in U.S. Bureau of the Census. *Statistical Abstract of the United States 1978.* Data on the generation of electric energy by hydropower and nuclear steam and on net imports of electricity were given in Edison Electric Institute, *Statistical Yearbook of the Electric Utility Industry for 1977* (New York, EEI, 1978); quantities were converted to tons of coal equivalent and valued at the estimated cost of steam coal f.o.b. mine.

side benefits of pricing reform, there might be some simultaneous reduction in government expenditures for regulation, for subsidies to energy production and conservation, and for providing social services which would be paid for directly as costs were internalized. All this could make possible some reduction of existing taxes that feed most directly into price levels—offsetting some of the measured inflation induced by energy pricing reform. Appropriate tax targets for this purpose include sales taxes and direct taxes on wages (such as employer social security contributions).

Transitory economic dislocations. Over- and underemployment in some economic sectors or regions and shifts in capital values (and wage rates) would also accompany energy pricing reform; but the effect would differ markedly from that of changes in the price of imported oil. The most important difference is that higher prices paid abroad mean a reduction in total goods and services available to U.S. citizens—a result that does not follow from price reform. Price reform would probably not affect the long-run aggregate operation of the economy, because new equilibria could arise which would leave overall levels of employment and capital utilization essentially unchanged. But it could have noticeable effects in the short run before adjustments took place.

With price reform, patterns of production and consumption will shift. Various individuals will be benefited or harmed, regions will prosper more and less, firms will expand and decline, and economic sectors will wax and wane. Those harmed are likely to see the rise in energy prices as the cause of their distress and will seek to resist the change or to have the government arrange compensation for it. Those benefited, on the other hand, will be more inclined to credit their own endeavor for the gain. Consequently, resistance to price reform will be mobilized unless companion policies can lessen the more obviously harmful effects on certain groups.

General policy instruments such as welfare programs and unemployment compensation can cushion changes, but other actions directed at specific disruptions may also be called for. While most special relief programs cannot be justified on efficiency grounds, they may be required politically if price reform is to be accepted.

Cushioning programs should be designed to disappear along with the transitory problem of dislocation that occasioned them. For example, lump-sum payments to the affected (boomtown) communities to assist in installing certain needed support facilities are preferable to continuing budget contributions. Direct payments to displaced workers or relocation assistance for businesses are better than subsidies to maintain jobs in a declining area. In general, the instrument selected should be self-terminating so that it does not prevent eventual adjustment from taking place.

Income distribution effects. Reforming energy prices also alters income distribution. Wage rates change as some skills become more and others less valuable. Some assets (such as oil in the ground) become more valuable, while others (such as energy-inefficient facilities) are worth less. Some locations, such as those in moderate climates, become relatively less expensive to work and live in. These changes are an integral part of the process through which labor is directed to more valuable occupations, capital is rechanneled to more productive uses, consumption patterns shift to reflect changing price relationships, and the location of economic activity is optimized under the new energy price regime.

As we noted above, paying higher prices for energy sometimes means paying less of the cost in other ways. Greater efficiency in the use of resources leads to greater output, so there are more goods and services to go around. But the benefits from pricing reform need not go to the same people who pay the higher prices. Nor are these benefits usually as tangible as the higher prices themselves. And, finally, the sheer abruptness of a price change can create real hardship.

Effects on the poor pose a special problem—a complex one that is often not well understood. While data on direct purchases of energy as a portion of income show the poor to be disproportionately large consumers of energy, this does not tell the whole story. First, higher-income groups spend a larger percentage of their budgets on indirect purchases of energy (airplane tickets; capital goods). Second, many of the poor are the elderly (or the temporarily unemployed) living in part out of savings. Their consumption is greater than their current income (in contrast to working-age persons who are building up pensions and making investments). Thus, energy purchases as related to *consumption* are not as dissimilar between the poor and the better off as are energy purchases as a portion of *income*. Finally, when looking at the effects of energy price reform, the distribution of countervailing benefits from the resulting greater efficiency of the economy and the improvement in the environment and in international security must be assessed as well. Taking these matters all into account, it is difficult to show that reform of energy prices would *disproportionately* lessen the ability of the poor to consume goods and services.[6] Since the poor have less to begin with, however, they may feel themselves more seriously harmed; and special efforts may be justified in lessening the burden on them.

Changes in energy prices can also lead to sharply higher incomes or capital values for some energy producers and consumers. In the case of petroleum reserves, for example, an import fee on imported petroleum would automatically add to the value of domestic oil under a regime of uncontrolled prices. A long-term contract for natural gas, made at the previous lower price, becomes a more valuable asset to a consumer who can dispose of the gas as he wishes. These increases in wealth—often termed windfalls—pose difficult policy problems. If windfalls are allowed to rest where they fall, some people seem to be enriched at the expense of others. On the other hand, when efforts are made to remove windfalls (through taxation or price controls, for example), wasteful distortions are imposed on the economy. Moreover, the prospect of windfalls attracts investment in activities where returns are uncertain; to remove windfalls after the fact is to signal investors that if outcomes turn out bad, they must bear their own losses, but if they turn out extraordinarily good, their gains will be taken away. Underinvestment is the result, and the economy is the poorer for it.

Policies to buffer all these shifts in income distribution may aid in reducing resistance to energy price changes. Again, the goal for such instruments is to satisfy equity needs, yet to interfere as little as possible in achieving the purposes of pricing reform. No such policies are perfect; a search for perfection leads either to frustration of reform or to a program so complex that inefficiencies waste most of its gains.

Traditionally, income distribution has been adjusted to meet national standards of equity through a politically determined tax and expenditure system. The tax reductions mentioned above (in relation to mitigating inflationary effects) could be centered in the lower-income groups, while expenditures might increase in programs to aid those most harmed, including the poor. On the windfall side, the progressive tax system already in place would dampen the gains of those most advantaged. To do more

[6] For further information on the income distribution effects of higher energy prices see: Robert A. Herendeen and Jerry Tanaka, *Energy Cost of Living,* CAC document 171 (Urbana, Ill., University of Illinois, Center for Advanced Computation, 1975); Dorothy K. Newman and Dawn Day, *The American Energy Consumer* (Cambridge, Mass., Ballinger, 1975) chap. 5; and Nancy McCarthy Snyder, "The Relative Income Distribution Effects of Energy Price Increases" (Ph.D. dissertation, Southern Illinois University, Carbondale, Ill., August 1977).

might have political appeal, but it could have long-run negative effects on the economy.

In general, policy should relieve egregious unfairnesses. For energy pricing reform to succeed, the whole system must be politically as well as economically preferable to the present situation, in which energy prices do not reflect true costs.

Reform of Environmental, Health, and Safety Regulation

Production and consumption of energy sometimes have deleterious effects upon the environment, and such effects are a major concern to this society. Chapters 12, 13, and 14 were designed to clarify the terms of trade between environmental quality and other goods and services, so as to remove some sources of disagreement. But division remains. People have very different attitudes toward environmental risks, toward the present versus the future, and toward the marginal benefits of having more of some services or less of others. Conflicts arising from different perceptions of the public interest can only be resolved through the political process.

There is another side to the issue, however. Are the procedures established to assure environmental quality efficient and effective in producing the mix of environmental quality and everything else that is desired? If processes can be improved, perhaps energy and environmental goals may both be more nearly achieved. In this regard, four major aspects of environmental quality regulation have led to unnecessary reductions in national well-being. The first is a failure to identify properly the goals of regulation, and to be direct about them. Second is the adoption of procedures which lead to costly unnecessary delay and to uncertainty that in itself leads to actions reducing overall well-being. Third is the use of regulatory instruments which are wasteful as well as ineffective. And the fourth is unnecessary administrative complexity and duplication.

Identification of Goals

Goals have sometimes not been made explicit in environmental policy. They should be specified carefully when balancing the benefits of environmental quality improvements against their costs, when comparing the effects of alternative energy production and consumption technologies, and when choosing processes and instruments to ameliorate environmental insults. Moreover, proponents of environmental programs have not always been open in discussing what ends can be achieved and what they would cost. So policies have sometimes been based on approximate objectives which are measurable or popular, rather than on relevant criteria.

As an example, "clean air" has been described as a goal of environmental policy. But is clean air desired for itself or because it is thought to satisfy other wants? The 1970 amendments to the Clean Air Act require that certain portions of the standard-setting process consider only matters of public health in reaching judgments and decisions. The terms of the statute imply that there is documented scientific linkage between polluted air and ill health, suggesting that improvement in the quality of the atmosphere would improve public health. Was health the true goal, therefore, or was the goal clean air? The answer is critical for rational policy making, because there is no substitute for clean air as an end in itself, but there may be many substitutes for cleaner air as a means of achieving better health for the population. Indeed, since the other goods and services sacrificed to get cleaner air may also contribute to improving health, the effort to achieve cleaner air may actually harm health. Yet even "health" is not an unambiguous operational goal. Is community health improved by an energy policy which leads to fewer respiratory illnesses among a large number of persons, but with the tradeoff that a few people develop fatal cancers? We need more specific guidance, in the form of a consensus from an informed public.

On the other hand, if the health rationale was mainly a "respectable" justification for achieving "clean air" as a goal in itself, other problems could arise. For example, if the regulations under the act prove not to benefit health, then those citizens most concerned with health could desert the cause of cleaner air, the regulations could come into disrepute, and the efforts to control pollution could be diminished. Moreover, once the health rationale is articulated, the nature of the regulations may be bent to achieve it—leading, perhaps, to a mix of controls which leave the air dirtier than is necessary. And throughout this process the credibility of the scientific establishment may be harmed.

Similar confusion and policy failures can occur with reference to environmental amenities, including the maintenance of wilderness. The issues are what measure of amenity to adopt and how to compare large benefits (or costs) to a few with small costs (or benefits) to many. Avoiding unsightly or otherwise unpleasant conditions around an energy facility may entail great benefits to its neighbors, but result in marginally higher costs to all consumers, preventing them from increasing the quality of their lives in other ways. The processes by which facilities are sited and approved have often left the interests of those who are affected by higher costs underrepresented. The adversary process demands formally that parties have a substantial standing before they are allowed to participate, and practically that they have a sizable interest to justify the cost of intervening. The tradeoffs should be clarified, and procedures for compensating a few to avoid more costly corrections "in kind" would lessen expenditures on amenities that almost all would consider excessive if the choices were presented clearly.

Reform of Procedure

Procedures for resolving energy–environmental issues often cause unnecessary delay and uncertainty. Delays and prospective delays impose high costs in idle capital, suboptimal investment decisions, and inefficient operations. When unanticipated, they may also impose large losses on energy consumers if they lead to temporary shortages or higher prices. Such costs neither improve environmental quality nor otherwise add to well-being.

Avoiding unnecessary delay.   Unnecessary delay in making decisions arises from regulatory duplication, changes in regulatory criteria, regulatory disagreement among jurisdictions, and from other failures of the administrative process. Duplication is usually undesirable, and it can often be reduced through an effort by the central executive (for example, within the Executive Office of the President) to rationalize approval procedures. Sometimes, though, duplication is inherent in legislation, perhaps because goals were not clearly formulated. When multijurisdictional authority exists, changes sought by one jurisdiction can sometimes upset approvals already granted by others, requiring that the circuit be traversed again.

Occasionally, perverse incentives produce delay. For example, if a regulatory agency sees itself judged by the number of times it loses in court, then it will be extremely cautious in its actions—abstaining from them until every possible consequence is considered. Or again, the intrinsic conservatism of regulatory agencies may cause them to lean heavily in the direction of protecting human health, safety, and the environment, so that delay and continued study is always the safest course unless there are counterbalancing incentives to encourage decision.

Finally, provisions designed to assure due process may be used in an effort to "delay to death" those projects which cannot be killed by direct opposition. The threat of delay can also be used to obtain concessions not obtainable through statute or regulation.[7]

Mediation offers one possible approach to reducing delay. In mediation an "honest broker" seeks to isolate areas of disagreement and then to formulate acceptable compromises which give each party more than it might obtain through conflict. The process is time consuming, but if successful it may still be faster than recourse to long—and more expensive—judicial proceedings and appeals.

No simple and effective remedy to unnecessary delay is at hand. Opportunities for delay represent preferences expressed in the legislation and in the incentive structures built into the regulatory process; they are not a perversion of it. The first step toward removing delay is to get all the parties—as citizens and taxpayers—to understand its costs. They can then make a better comparison of its costs with the benefits it brings. If it is then decided to do so, the political system can change both incentives and processes.

Avoiding unnecessary uncertainty. The effort to enhance environmental quality has also reduced welfare by creating uncertainty about prospective environmental requirements. Such uncertainty delays investment and inspires "safe" rather than optimizing decisions. It has led to making suboptimal choices in facility siting and processes, and to missing opportunities for lower-cost energy. For instance, faced with a choice between a single new coal-fired boiler, which could be used for cogeneration purposes, and a combination of purchased electricity and several oil-fired installations small enough to avoid regulatory attention, an industrial firm will incline toward the latter, if a possible tightening of air quality standards or other requirements suggest a risk that the coal burner could be closed down. The extra cost to the firm of the socially suboptimal energy choice would be less than the prospective catastrophic loss of revenue if the plant should be closed down because of subsequent government actions.

---

[7] One problem is that those who make such threats cannot always assure those threatened that if they respond, the project will be allowed to go through. In the divided and somewhat competitive environmental movement, one group may agree to avoid delay by forgoing further litigation, but another may still sue.

Uncertainty springs from the lack of settled criteria, from the unpredictable nature of interventions by outside groups, and from the changing application of existing regulations. It may also arise, of course, from our imperfect understanding of the health and safety effects of energy processes. The former sources of uncertainty can be lessened by procedural reforms, by processes to resolve conflicts, and by improved management of the decision process, but the latter condition cannot be resolved so easily.

It does not seem to be in society's interest to delay decisions about energy acquisition and use or to avoid using probably benign and otherwise attractive new technologies on the basis of highly unlikely—or even unknown—future environmental problems. At the same time, it is unrealistic to promise that, if good-faith actions are later found harmful, they will be countenanced simply because they conformed to accepted standards when they began. Because of the political pressures that prospective out-of-pocket economic loss may stimulate, however, requirements are not likely to be enforced as strictly on existing installations as on new ones; and this means that some facilities installed in good faith may damage human health and safety even after their danger has been discovered. Thus, the current system probably delays some relatively benign energy systems while maintaining some relatively harmful ones—leading to excessive environmental damage, excessive environmental control costs, and excessive reductions in economic output.

We need a set of policies that will not delay our benefiting from processes which are probably safe, but which will quickly be stopped in the unlikely event that harm is detected. It also seems desirable to spread the economic burden of the uncertain environmental risk over the entire community—for whose benefit the energy choices are made. This would occur automatically in a perfectly functioning market economy where capital markets worked without friction and hedging opportunities were boundless; but in real life the burden of change falls initially on a few who try to protect themselves and use political power to alter behavior in uneconomic ways. Therefore, the theoretical solution of general laissez-faire (along with instructions to regulators to ignore sunk investment) is not feasible.

Taxpayers, consumers, and wage earners together benefit from the greater productivity wrought by using advanced technologies and processes, and more or less the same persons benefit from greater environmental quality. But *individuals* can be seriously hurt if a process or facility is foreclosed or shut down for environmental reasons. One possible way of bringing individual incentives into accord with social benefits is to "hold harmless" (that is, compensate for subsequent loss due to regulatory change) those who in good faith undertake actions which conform with existing environmental requirements. This could give innovators confidence to go ahead, but make it easier to close them down if conditions warranted. Such a policy would promote stricter enforcement of regulations in concert with advancing knowledge, and would increase the efficiency with which resources were used. Both environmental quality and output of goods and services could be enhanced.

The administrative difficulties of a hold-harmless policy are serious, but perhaps not as great as might be imagined. Compensation would be initiated only after explicit actions by regulators are found to have tightened previous standards. Estimation of the damages sustained in closing down an operation is unlikely to be any more difficult than in proceedings which are now settled routinely in administrative and judicial contexts.

Reform of Regulatory Instruments

A third source of unproductive environmental quality expenditures lies in misplaced emphasis on controlling *processes* rather than *results,* and in using instruments which ignore cost differences among alternative means of achieving environmental quality goals.

The most common regulatory pattern is for authorities to place uniform limits on specific emissions from whatever sources, and often to specify the technology by which these emissions are to be controlled. Policy instruments of this type are popular because they appear to be effective, equitable (at least on the surface), and easy to monitor and enforce. Emissions either are or are not within limits; the control technology either is or is not in place and operating. In practice, of course, there are many difficulties with this approach, not the least of which is that the performance of monitoring technology has typically been far behind the requirements placed upon it. Moreover, this approach is intrinsically inefficient. First, it places the same restrictions on emissions which are expensive to control as on those which are cheap. Second, it offers no incentives to polluters to develop innovative control alternatives which could achieve the same goals less expensively.

Environmental quality regulation could just as easily exploit private economic incentives by giving those who produce pollutants a stake in reducing their quantity at the lowest possible cost. For instance, polluters might be charged directly for their emissions. Such a charge would have the twin effects of reducing the quantity of the environmental insult produced and, to the extent pollutants remained, of compensating the community at large for the disamenities and harm they imposed. Even a less satisfactory variant of this approach—the "bubble" concept—would offer marked advantages over the usual standard-setting procedure. Under the bubble approach a firm is given an overall limit of emissions of each type and allowed to choose for itself which sources within its plant are to be limited and to what extent. A further step would be to expand the bubble by allowing neighboring firms to "purchase" emission reduction from each other.

Emission charges would satisfy the cost internalization goal of pricing reform and enable citizens and decision makers to compare the benefits from an improved environment directly with its costs in goods and services forgone. It would lead to the cleanest environment possible for each level of costs, and it would meet common equity standards. Under the emission-charge policy, firms, as firms, would be treated differently, but alike in the sense that the financial sanction imposed depends on the damage to the community that their operations create.

Reform of Regulatory Administration

The burdensome administrative complexity and procedural requirements that have grown up around environmental quality efforts reflect in part the inherent difficulties of the issues involved. Complex procedures also result from the effort to preserve individual rights to equitable resolution of conflicts. Two other factors have added to this burden: multilevel and overlapping regulatory jurisdictions; and the use of procedural technicalities, by those who oppose certain energy activities, to obstruct actions on which conflict over substance cannot be resolved.[8]

Taken individually, none of the reforms which have been suggested appears very promising. For example, the personnel of environmental regulatory agencies are often accused of bias against economic growth or toward extremes in environmental protection; but even if this proved to be the case, there is little likelihood that a proposed switch in personnel would alter results measurably unless statutes and the operations of the courts were changed. Another proposal has been to avoid overlap by con-

---

[8] Jurisdictional conflicts arising from a federal system with discrete political subdivisions are considered in a separate section below.

centrating responsibility in some way—perhaps by source of emission, by type of emission, or by region. However meritorious administratively, this proposal simply puts a new face on the problem without making it go away. The fact is that different substantive interests are represented by each level of government and each regulatory unit; unless these interests can be unified or reconciled, the battle will only be shifted to a different forum. A variant of this proposal, "one-stop licensing," would place a "lead" agency in charge of each proposal and have it bear the responsibility of coordinating all approvals. Unfortunately, until basic conflicts are resolved, this process may only promote additional layering of negotiations; there may be only "one stop," but it may be interminably long.

A related proposal would be to reverse the trend toward separation of promotional and regulatory functions. The argument is that giving an agency a single mission encourages it to promote that mission at any cost. Since other goals are fostered by other agencies, this moves the balancing function to a higher level. Delay is facilitated as decisions are bucked upward, and they are finally resolved at a level where the time and expertise available to consider them is too short for careful consideration of the issues.

In an effort to balance the incentives of regulators, devices such as "inflation impact statements" have been advocated. Unfortunately, agencies have no incentive to take such exercises seriously unless their results are monitored by a body that has the authority to overturn the actions taken. A more promising device might be to assign each agency a "regulatory expenditure budget" which would limit the total expense it could impose on the economy. Such a limit would encourage agencies to balance carefully the costs and benefits of their actions, since to do more in one area would reduce freedom to do as much in another. Interagency regulatory review groups, such as the one introduced in the Carter administration, may also have some beneficial effects.

Efforts to restrict intervention by outside parties as a means of limiting delays are also popular. However, they conflict directly with the settled right of each affected interest to be heard. To label an objection or request for a hearing "obstructionist" (and therefore not protected under law) requires a substantive finding as to its merits—which may take longer, and indeed be more complex, than to face the objection in the first place. Yet, one may want to assign relative weights to issues on which intervention is allowed so as to diminish effort on less important ones.

Along this line, it would be an important advance to establish a clear division between generic issues, such as the safety of nuclear power plants of given design, from site-specific issues, where evidence is required on particular installations. Case law on this matter would be troublesome and difficult to develop; but the expense could be repaid many times over if the principle could be unequivocally established.

In summary, there are no simple ways to eliminate unproductive environmental regulation costs. All of the reforms discussed here would still not solve the problem completely. Perhaps ultimately the most fruitful course is to try to do better what is being done now. Such remedies as tighter managerial control over the bureaucracy, closer identification of responsibility with effective authority, and the creation of incentives for parties to respond quickly and with regard to all costs and burdens are unglamorous, but they do offer prospects for improvements.

Substantial improvements in administering environmental regulations can only come from resolving as many conflicts over substance as possible and from getting people to think about tradeoffs between environmental quality and other things in a new way. In effect, we may need a new "social compact" regarding these issues. Energy "proponents" might have to demonstrate a willingness to go even beyond what are now generally considered to be adequate environmental quality measures. In exchange, their antagonists might have to accept, at least in principle, the necessity for energy development—and be willing to let it proceed with less delay and greater certainty in the future.

The Question of Fairness in Energy Policy

Equity issues permeate discussions of energy policy and have sometimes stymied action. Should prices be controlled to shift incomes and expenditures among persons and regions? Who is to bear the risks of reductions in environmental quality, as compared with who is to pay to avoid them? Should citizens of urban areas suffer greater reductions in air quality in order to keep other regions more pristine? Do beneficiaries from prospective economic growth now living have more claim to the products of technological progress than those who might live in the future?

Such questions are continually being disputed within societies, and not only in regard to energy. Their permanent resolution is impossible; there are no accepted guides to a proper distribution of the benefits which an economy can produce.[9] As a social goal, the substance of acceptable

---

[9] There is not even an accepted means of measuring the sum of human happiness or comparing it with the sum arising from a different distribution of benefits. More-

equity is essentially a matter of preferences; and, since preferences differ, conflicts exist.

It is critical, though, to divorce the conflict over what is equitable from conflicts over energy choices per se. Equity is a broad goal; and it is too restrictive to apply it separately to the price of oil, to the profits of the coal industry, or to levels of air quality in the central city. What matters is the sum of these and all other aspects of life. Equity insists that, taken together, they yield an overall pattern of benefits and costs that the prevailing set of values can consider fair.

As a matter of fact, however, narrower concerns about fairness have interfered with implementing policies which would lead to efficient energy outcomes; and we suggest multiple reasons for this. First, people do not believe that the real cost of energy has risen. They feel cheated when they are forced to pay higher prices. Second, people do not believe that general instruments of social policy will rebalance equities once a change has occurred in the energy sector. Hence, they resist every loss of welfare related to energy, regardless of its positive impact on society as a whole. Finally, the political process responds to *categories* of people—to interest groups or to regions, rather than to individuals. This interferes with compromises that could be accepted as fair by individuals, and leads instead to conflict. In a phrase, there is no "constituency" for overall fairness.

Energy Costs and the Shrinking Pie

The increase in energy's cost to U.S. consumers has come from higher costs of producing it, from an increase in the cost of using energy now rather than in the future, from monopoly exactions by oil exporting countries, and from additional costs now paid by U.S. consumers to overcome environmental, health, and safety costs of energy acquisition and use. Taking the last point first, *some* costs attributable to environmental controls represent what amounts to a change in social accounting; they were paid earlier in lost amenities but are now borne monetarily by energy functions. Additionally, however, environmental insults have grown

---

over, except in cases where the distribution of income and other amenities is dramatically skewed toward either equality or inequality, there seems to be little necessary connection between the degree of equality and levels of production of goods and services.

more than proportionately with energy use as larger quantities of energy have been produced and used and as use has become more concentrated.

It appears that energy resources have been depleting faster than technology has been improving, so that the cost of energy (including the expected value of its use in the future) has gone up recently relative to that of other goods and services.[10] On top of this increase has been added another: monopoly pricing by oil exporting countries. OPEC prices are beyond the effective control of domestic U.S. policy.

The increase in the relative cost of acquiring and using energy means that the nation's (and the world's) capacity to produce goods and services has declined.[11] Getting energy uses up real resources that previously could be used to satisfy other wants. It is not only that energy producers now get more; the world is not as rich as it thought it was. To the extent that this fact is not realized, those who get less will think they are being treated unfairly.

The starting point for muting domestic concerns about fairness is for the public to recognize that the pie everybody must share is smaller than they expected it to be. There may be less anger at relative deprivation based on an inexorable natural process, rather than on depredation by exploiters. But developing such understanding will not be easy. There is ample reason for suspicion: the impetus for price increases came from

[10] This process may have been going on for some time, but a number of factors camouflaged it. First, technological and externality problems with such new technologies as nuclear power and synthetic oil and gas were not fully understood, and their prospective costs were underestimated. Second, some costs were not levied on energy production and consumption itself, but instead on the economy at large. Third, the price of conventional fuels was depressed because of ownership patterns in the prolific oil fields of the Middle East. Output decisions for these fields were made primarily by externally based private firms which had no assurance that they would be able to exploit the fields forever. To them, the value of the oil in the ground was reduced by the probability that their holdings would some day be expropriated. Hence, they were willing to produce more and accept a lower price than would the sovereign nations that succeeded them in making oil output and price decisions. The assumption of full control over oil pricing by the OPEC countries after 1973 meant that the full value of the oil in the ground became one factor affecting output and price decisions, just as did the full cost of environmental quality protection. As these three factors have come together over the past few years, the adjustment of energy costs upward has been very rapid. Of course, technological change is unpredictable, and a new wave of innovation could *lower* energy costs.

[11] The severity of the decline depends on the elasticity of substitution for energy, and it is not yet possible to estimate that relationship with any confidence. The duration of the decline is also unclear, because technological change or new energy discoveries are always possible. In general, though, projected growth of goods and services must be lower now than it was before the 1973 price increase. Income levels are lower than they would have been, or—to put it a different way—it will take more time to reach given income levels at either the U.S. or world level.

exploitative oil exporters; the behavioral record of companies in the energy sector makes charges of collusion believable; and some persons, regions, and economic sectors are indeed benefiting from the increase in the relative price of energy.

Credible information is essential in curing misconceptions, but it is an especially scarce commodity in a field where mistrust is already intense and where information is hard to come by at all. It might help, however, if fuller disclosure of financial information were required. Further, more government effort in data collection and dissemination may be necessary. Industry-developed data on oil and gas reserves may be adequate for decision-making purposes, but a government program may be necessary to dampen suspicions about them that exacerbate equity conflicts. Finally, prompt rebuttals are needed to discourage those who foster misunderstanding about how higher energy costs originate or who suggest that they need not be paid.

Failure of General Equity Instruments

Changes in the energy sector that alter the distribution of income or amenities will be sought or resisted until a system of policies and institutions exists (*and is believed to exist*) through which the net distribution of welfare in all forms among all parties returns to "fairness" after perturbations take place. With respect to energy, it is clear that the public does not believe right now that a special advantage or a special handicap will be offset by general social instruments such as existing tax or welfare programs. Moreover, since energy matters have become politicized, the tendency has been to seek direct action—imposing oil price controls, for example—rather than to rely upon less parochial social processes. There is pressure to make each individual energy change demonstrably "fair." Energy policy has thus been asked to take on an impossible added burden.

The general instruments which society can look toward to achieve its equity goals are such direct devices as a progressive income tax system, unemployment compensation, and income maintenance payments based on the costs of securing an acceptable standard of living. If such instruments automatically and adequately dampened the amplitude of changes in individual welfare, there would be less concern about rises in the cost of energy. Obviously these instruments do not, cannot, and should not counteract every change in relative prices perfectly. Indeed, a system that sensitive would prevent the changes in location, occupation, fuel types, and output mix which is the essence of a dynamic economy's efficient response to a change in relative prices. It might be sufficient that—for the class below the poverty line—an increase in average energy prices would be offset by an increase in welfare payments. Each welfare recipient need not be assured that the increased payment would fully make up for his individual reduction in level of living.

Trying to make energy outcomes themselves fair is wasteful. For example, energy price controls cause consumers to use energy as if its real cost were lower than it is. On the producer side, price controls to eliminate windfall profits lead to less energy being produced domestically. More oil is then imported, at still higher cost. These inefficiencies are joined by inequities. Although special efforts to hold energy prices down benefit rich and poor consumers alike, they may harm persons at all points on the income spectrum. Similarly, special region-based subsidies help businesses which benefit from higher energy prices as well as those harmed, and the amount of the benefit certainly may be unrelated to the income shift produced by higher energy cost. Furthermore, those subsidies are paid for by taxpayers and energy consumers in other regions, some of whom are in the lowest portion of the income scale.

Interest Group Orientation

The political process is geared to responding to interest groups and to thinking about classes and categories of persons. Specific energy outcomes tend to be examined as matters of equity, instead of by asking the question: What new measures are required to assure fairness to individuals qua individuals after energy outcomes change?

Political pressure groups are often motivated by single issues, even though the individuals who make them up have many goals. An "energy industry" pressure group wants mostly to get prices up; it does not concern itself with one member's electricity bills. A "consumer" group may seek to keep prices down, without considering that lower prices for energy may lead to loss of employment for some of its members. An "environmental" group wants to lessen emissions; if local in membership, it may be satisfied if emissions are simply put somewhere else. A "New England" group will try to keep heating oil prices down, ignoring the local insulation salesmen who may benefit from higher prices or those citizens who might be better off if they followed retreating jobs to a warmer climate.

Equity tradeoffs are extremely difficult to achieve when special interests dominate the political process. Each energy decision is evaluated as to its effects on groups rather than on society as a whole and in the context of overall policy. And there is no mechanism for bargaining, as there is when an individual weighs all the benefits and costs from given actions. Pressure group government leads to the conflicts we have examined, to the paralysis of decision making we have seen, and to the inefficiencies and inequities we have noted. Perhaps the only solution lies in broader public recognition of the source of the problem itself and in a vigorous nationwide effort to establish whatever consensus *is* achievable—a matter to be discussed at greater length in the final chapter.

Toward Resolving Equity Issues

The elements of a more desirable equity policy are clear and quite widely shared. They include treatment of people based on their real income levels and not on whether those incomes come from energy production or whether their expenditures include energy purchases. Applied more broadly, such a policy would make it possible for each person to enjoy minimum levels of environmental amenities, but would also offer individuals opportunities for tradeoffs between environment and other things they might want. Policy instruments would allow more pollution in one place in exchange for reductions of emissions elsewhere. Installations would not be treated differently because they were in the energy sector or because they were new or old, but distinctions would be based on the relative expense of controlling effluents. Ideally, such a system could achieve appropriate changes in distribution as the level of total welfare changed and as weights of the components within it shifted.

We are not sanguine about achieving this result. Incremental improvements in policy direction were suggested above, but we see no process in being which will lead to marked shifts in the way energy–equity matters are handled. The constraints on doing things better seem to us a permanent part of the energy scene. But this counsel of despair does not make it any less important to try to improve institutions and to reconcile goals.

Intergovernmental Issues in Energy Choices

Conflicts among different levels of government have often delayed energy supply projects and have hampered efforts to conserve energy. The fundamental problem in intergovernmental relations is similar to that in pressure group government treated above. Governments at different levels respond to different constituencies which sometimes have conflicting goals. Superimposed on this problem are jurisdictional jealousy, the difficult constitutional requirements of a federal system, the wastes of overlapping and duplicative procedures, and additional opportunities for delay by those who seek it.

One important source of interjurisdictional conflict is facility siting. In general, the environmental and social burden of an installation is concentrated on a local population, while most of the benefits of additional energy supply are spread over a large region—or even the nation as a whole. Moreover, the special benefits of the facility which do accrue locally are not distributed equally among the affected population. Take some specific examples: A coal-fired electric generating plant increases the load on transportation facilities, it may preempt local uses of water, and it emits air pollutants that are more concentrated close to the plant. The potential radioactive hazard from nuclear power plants is again heavier in the vicinity of the plants than elsewhere. Synthetic fuel plants of even the cleanest sort are apt to be highly disruptive to the locality within which they are found. In their construction stage, all of these facilities will upset the pattern of community life; a boom–bust cycle is set into motion, and amenities are reduced for most local inhabitants. Some local people may favor a particular project, but those who do not may be able to stop or delay it. If a state or local government acts, it may be able to halt a project that has important net benefits to the nation as a whole.

This class of problems can be minimized when energy pricing truly covers all costs imposed. In principle, local external effects are mitigated, with the abatement expense flowing through to the cost of the energy produced. Compensatory payments are made for those impacts that are not abated. In practice, of course, there are limits in applying this approach. And, even with a majority made indifferent or favorable, a minority could still impose its view and resist a specific development. Overcoming resistance requires a majority actively supporting an action.

National policy can also be *imposed* on states and localities (albeit subject to some constitutional restraints). Coercion may sometimes be the only means of reconciling conflicting goals. For example, preemption of state authority may be required in order to develop a nuclear waste disposal site. But the vitality of the federal system is eroded when the national government preempts the role of units at a lower level and imposes decisions on them. A far more promising path to interjurisdictional harmony is to bring the goals of different governmental levels into accord by giving the subsidiary units a larger stake in the national enterprise. If affected areas are overcompensated for actions of benefit to the nation, the willing cooperation gained may lower overall costs enough (including the costs associated with delay) so as to make all parties better off. To the extent possible, of course, the funds for compensation should be derived from the energy services produced—so that the costs will be internalized. For example, energy impact assistance could be funded through severance taxes, royalties, or other exactions based on producing or using the specific energy source.

Distributing a portion of federal revenues to jurisdictions where fuel reserves are produced is one way of gaining local cooperation. To be effective, however, the affected districts themselves must benefit. For example, sites should be easier to get when payments (or property taxes) on facilities go directly to affected localities rather than to states. Unfortunately, political jurisdictions rarely match the regions of impact exactly, so that precise adjustments cannot be made. While too narrow a distribution of benefits will fail to neutralize all significant opposition, spreading the revenues too widely will reduce their capacity to foster the localized cooperation desired.

For situations in which costs cannot be internalized, general revenue funds may be required. It is not easy to allocate such funds with the proper compromise between efficiency and the competing claim of equity in benefits from the project, and there is no general prescription for the "right" balance.

Any policy to reward the jurisdictions in which energy facilities are bad neighbors has elements of unfairness, because it discriminates against jurisdictions with other sorts of bad neighbors. No better policy suggests itself, however, and this discriminatory treatment may be justified if it is used judiciously. The benefit from going forward with an energy facility may be very large.

A reward system alone, however, is not enough to reconcile national energy goals with local interests. Willingness to coerce is also necessary. Without it, regional extortion may become a popular ploy of state and local politicians. Coercion should be used sparingly, though, because it eliminates the test of voluntary compliance as used to determine whether policies indeed "hold harmless" those affected by energy facilities.

The problem of facility siting is one of the more serious sources of interjurisdictional conflict; but many others are more difficult to handle. Earlier, for instance, we mentioned conflicting goals with regard to environmental quality, as well as differentials in the regional effects of energy price changes. Fuel mix patterns also differ by location, so they give rise to interjurisdictional conflicts. Water use patterns, transportation impacts, and even patterns of urbanization may cause some jurisdictions to favor and others to oppose aspects of national energy policies. Such unavoidable complications are the consequence of the way this nation is organized and decisions are made. Their more serious effects can be mitigated, but not totally neutralized.

Ultimately, then, maintenance of a basically noncoercive federal system—an important social goal in itself—implies some sacrifice of efficiency and even equity in energy acquisition and use. To the extent that regions, states, and localities can be allowed to determine their own contribution to energy development and use, the most serious conflicts can be reduced. But flexibility needs to be stressed and what amounts to a competitive market for facility location should be created.

Price-Cost Uncertainty in Energy Production and Conservation

Energy supply and conservation opportunities are surrounded by uncertainties. The effect has usually been to lessen the speed of energy supply development and to slow the adoption of energy-conserving devices and processes.

We discussed in a previous section a combination of a hold-harmless policy with procedural reform in mitigating uncertainty in environmental regulation, the most important source of nonprice uncertainty in the energy sector. Now we will concentrate on the risks imposed on energy producers and consumers by unforeseen price variations.

As in the case with regulatory uncertainty, the uncertainty about prices and costs contains some components governed by external events and others which are subject to some discretionary control. The externally dictated uncertainties cannot be removed, but their incidence can be shifted. In terms of the others, wise policies can actually reduce the risks to be borne by all. Before considering policies to shift or to reduce uncertainty, its sources and effects can be clarified.

Sources and Effects of Price Uncertainty

Price uncertainty arises primarily from lack of knowledge about underlying world energy supply and demand conditions and from inability to predict OPEC behavior. Further, there is no way to predict what U.S.

government interference may bring in the future. Average prices were held up with oil import controls from the mid-1950s until the early 1970s and held down with price controls afterward. The price uncertainties which are most detrimental from the point of view of energy policy are those which lead to lower domestic energy supply and higher domestic energy demand, and we will concentrate on those uncertainties here.

It bears noting, however, that costs are incurred as well when uncertainty leads to overestimation of the prospective costs and prices of energy. In that case fuel will not be used, even though the benefits that would be derived from its consumption are greater than its actual costs. Investment will be diverted from potentially more productive current uses into energy-saving and energy-producing facilities and processes. The argument that "the facilities will be needed some day, so build them now" ignores the social costs in lost productivity from removing capital from more productive to less productive uses.

The optimal policy is one which brings energy price expectations up to the long-run sustainable price, but not beyond. While deliberate overestimation of future energy costs might be defended in some cases as "insurance" against the serious consequences of being caught short, that insurance does not come free. It is necessary to show that underestimation would be more costly than overestimation to justify such a policy stance on economic welfare grounds.

Shifting Uncertainty: An International Instrument

The United States proposed an international Minimum Safeguard Price (MSP) as one reaction to the embargo and oil price increases of 1973–74.[12] This "floor price" policy represents one general approach to energy price uncertainty, and some variants of this plan (including internationally agreed-upon limitations on imports) are still being discussed and considered. By removing uncertainty on the downside, the MSP approach leads to an upward revision in the *expected* price to which energy consumers and producers in the importing countries respond.

The MSP proposal was for an agreement among major oil-importing nations that they would assure vendors and consumers a minimum price for energy. Downside uncertainty would be shared by all energy con-

[12] This proposal was fully explored in the course of discussions on reactions to the OPEC price increase. A useful summary of the debate can be found in: *The International Monetary Situation and the Administration's Floor Price Proposal,* Hearings before the Subcommittee on International Economics of the Joint Economic Committee, 94 Cong., 1 sess. (March 24 and April 28, 1975).

sumers; it would not be borne solely by those domestic producers who made investments which produced energy at higher costs and then did not have markets, nor solely by those consumers who acted as if energy prices were going to remain high. The benefits would similarly be shared; they would arise from lower prices for energy due to reduced demand for exported oil and from reduced prospects for disruption due to oil supply reductions from abroad.

There are a number of difficulties with an MSP policy. First, violation could be profitable, and there is no mechanism by which an MSP can be enforced on sovereign nations. Second, it may lead to windfall profits to some energy producers, which in the United States might be politically untenable. Third, by interfering with price flexibility it would distort the relative prices of different energy forms and their substitutes— reducing overall economic efficiency. And finally, the MSP would remove the incentive from OPEC to reduce its prices (or to increase them less rapidly) because the oil exporters as a group would know that they could capture no greater share of the total energy market by lowering price. Indeed, the support price would tend to become the price floor for oil exporters as well as for the consuming countries, and oil importers do not serve their own interests by encouraging income transfers to oil producers.

A further issue arises with regard to the credibility of the MSP itself. Pressure from consumers to relax the policy would mount if the world price fell, and a relaxation in any major trading nation would create almost irresistible pressure on others to follow. If producers and consumers do not believe that governments will actually enforce the MSP, they will not alter their behavior to take it into account. Thus its promised benefits may not be realized even if it is enforced and its costs are imposed.

The record of oil prices between 1975 and 1979 illustrates these problems. The world oil price has fluctuated, but has drifted slightly downward in real terms as deflated by the U.S. wholesale price index. Thus, if the MSP had been set at 1974 prices, its use would have been triggered. But, because of differing inflation rates and shifts in currency values, the amount of support would have varied widely among countries. Some would have been required to raise prices one-third or more and others very little. It is difficult to believe that an agreement with such differing costs would have been honored. Thus, despite the greater efficiency of a policy such as an MSP—which affects all energy sources and uses—problems in implementing it may lead to the alternate choice of individual programs, which limit uncertainty in specific circumstances.

Shifting Uncertainty: Some Domestic Instruments

Price uncertainty can be shifted from energy producers and consumers to taxpayers. Uncertainty would continue, but it would be shared in a way that would lessen its distortive effects. For example, a price guarantee to cover production from a synthetic fuel plant would assure investors of a market if the plant were able to perform. (Since such guarantees could be written in the form of contracts to purchase the fuel produced, political risks of reversal by successor governments would also be lessened.) In a similar fashion, the federal government could agree to purchase energy-conserving devices, such as solar installations or new types of engines, at prices associated with the energy cost savings anticipated at the prospective energy price. If energy prices proved lower than anticipated, the production firm would still be able to amortize its investment.

Each potential energy source and energy-conserving technology or process has different characteristics in regard to cost-price uncertainty. For some, uncertainty may not even be much of a disincentive. For example, price uncertainty has relatively less effect when lead times are short, or the capital component is small, or opportunities for change are continuous rather than discrete.

A program of targeted price supports allows the government to select those activities it wants to encourage without offering the same support to all activities. When a competitive bidding system is used as a selection device, the probability is increased that projects are chosen which use the guarantee most effectively. And the amount of government financial exposure can be limited in accordance with the value placed on incremental energy production or conservation.

Reducing Uncertainty: Reforming Government Action

Government energy policies have confused energy producers, consumers, and developers of alternate technologies and processes. As a consequence, private decision makers have had little firm basis on which to plan. Price controls on domestic oil and natural gas have changed, and they may or may not be removed. Special taxes and fees have been suggested; they may or may not be imposed. Some energy producers and consumers have been given subsidies which may be revoked, extended, or increased. And utility price regulations can change with shifts in the political winds. These uncertainties are the product of domestic political choice and of the institutions through which those choices are made. Even though they are not inherent in the energy system, they will not be easy to reform.

Marginal cost pricing, which has already been discussed in relation to its other beneficial effects, is also the starting point in removing unnecessary price uncertainty. Marginal cost pricing could give the energy sector price signals that respond in a systematic way to underlying market conditions. Prices would vary, but they would not be manipulated in unpredictable ways. Unfortunately, however, interference with efficient energy pricing to achieve nonenergy goals has been so prevalent that even if marginal cost pricing were achieved, it might not be trusted at first. Succeeding Congresses or public utility commissions could not be bound, so the public might justifiably anticipate a later reversal of policy. Only substantial experience over a long period of time could allay the uncertainties created by past interferences with efficient pricing. To make any form of consistent pricing credible, however, the best hope would be to begin as soon as possible—and with as much continuity as possible—to avoid government actions which change the prices paid or received for energy away from those anticipated by participants in energy markets.

Market Limitations in Allocating Resources for Energy Research, Development, and Demonstration

Externalities and other forms of market failure (see footnote 7 in chapter 16) are endemic in the energy sector. Virtually all energy production and consumption processes affect persons besides those directly engaged in the activity; as one example, we have described environmental degradation spillovers. Competition does not always exist, and resources are misallocated as a result. Some energy activities involve common property, and it is always difficult to get efficient decisions when property rights are not clearly specified. As a prototype for dealing with all aspects of market failure in energy decisions, we have chosen to round out this chapter with a discussion of the generic question of energy research, development, and demonstration (RD&D). An issue arises because a private market does not supply efficiently the right amount and kind of RD&D to bring new energy production, conversion, and conservation technologies and processes on line at the appropriate time. In the next two chapters we apply our findings to some energy supply alternatives.

"Too much" energy RD&D will lead to resources being consumed in producing energy alternatives that would have greater utility elsewhere. "Too little" energy RD&D would lead to future energy costs being higher than they need to be, with a net social loss. Too much or too little of *any one kind* of RD&D would mean less than maximum output per unit of input. In conceptually defining the "correct" energy RD&D approach we must look to all sectors of the society, not just to energy. We must also consider the future as well as the present, take into account the timing of costs and of benefits, and thus look at the full opportunity costs of greater RD&D expenditures as well as at its social benefits.

This conceptual definition cannot be translated directly into an operational program of RD&D support. It does, however, suggest the principles on which levels of energy RD&D expenditures ought to be determined and the basis on which they should be allocated among alternative options.

The Sources of Market Failure in Energy RD&D

Private markets fail to produce an adequate level of energy RD&D. They would fail to do so even if energy prices were at replacement cost, if environmental impacts were internalized, if international risks were accounted for, and if uncertainties were minimized, with their incidence shifted to those who could best bear them. This failure occurs because those who bear the private cost of energy RD&D cannot gain for themselves all the social benefits those investments may bring. The reasons are many, as some examples illustrate.

First, patent protection for energy production, conversion, and conservation processes is often not complete, nor can it fully cover innovative processes and new ways of achieving energy savings or greater energy production.

Second, much of the RD&D required is basic research, which by its nature has no private market since it promises no directly salable product.

Third, some of the RD&D required is of a scale and gestation period such that private firms do not consider it feasible for them to undertake it.

Fourth, an important aspect of RD&D relates to the interaction between an energy technology and its surroundings. For example, major synthetic fuel facilities will have social and physical effects on the regions in which they are located, which cannot be fully known until they are in operation.

Since one possible outcome from building such a facility may be the conclusion that it cannot be maintained and operated, private parties are loath to go first and bear all the risk. Once the risk is assessed, however, follow-on plants can be built with greater assurance, or else can be modified into acceptable neighbors. Knowledge about these interactions is potentially valuable to any and all who might enter the field later, but they cannot be forced to pay an innovative party for providing it. So no one goes first.

Fifth, given the aspect of depletability, some benefits from increasing energy supply or reducing energy demand accrue in the form of lower prices for consumers who have no direct contact with the product of the RD&D. For example, a new conservation device that leads to lower oil imports into the United States will lower the price of oil to all consumers, domestic and foreign. It will permanently shift to some degree the decline curve for fossil fuels.

Sixth, additional domestic energy supply or reductions in energy consumption due to RD&D may reduce the magnitude of the nation's vulnerability to oil import disruptions, but those benefits are spread over the nation as a whole, instead of being directed to those paying for the RD&D.

Other external effects of energy RD&D could be cited, but the point is clear: the private market does not require "free riders" to compensate those engaged in RD&D for the benefits they receive. As a consequence, without the coercion that can be exercised by government, too little RD&D will take place. Still, two questions remain: What types of RD&D expenditures require public support? And, jointly, how much support would be appropriate and how should it be allocated among various energy supply and conservation options? Again we start with the premise that energy prices are at replacement cost levels as discussed above, and that environmental, international, and other externalities are fully reflected in these prices.

Limits to the Role of the Public Sector

Much energy RD&D yields benefits that are fully capturable in the near term—rendering public support unnecessary. Where the product of the effort leads to patentable devices or processes, for example, no additional incentive for expenditures may be needed. This is also generally true when RD&D produces results which are specific to one firm, industry, or location. Private firms engaged in equipment supply, for example, have clear motivation to perform RD&D for the industry which uses their output. The coal industry, as a case in point, is fragmented and unable to support RD&D into more effective technology and processes efficiently; but mining equipment firms are in a position to benefit from any improvements they make in the products they sell. Hence, RD&D into production aspects of coal technology does not suffer from the same sort of market failure that may afflict efforts to improve mine safety. Petroleum and natural gas exploration, development, and production are supported by large and effective privately financed RD&D efforts. Government support there would either replace private investment or else would lead to "too much" RD&D, in the sense that better use could be made of the resources elsewhere in the economy.

On the conservation side, manufacturers of automobiles, appliances, and other energy end-use devices have at least some motivation to engage in RD&D for energy-saving developments. They obtain benefits from the added value of what they sell. Here the main way to guarantee adequate RD&D is to make sure that consumers have enough information about the full life-cycle costs of alternative devices in order to choose wisely among them. (For a fuller discussion of this point, see chapter 5.) In some cases it may also be necessary to eliminate barriers to consumers who wish to take advantage of energy-conserving developments. For example, such developments often require investment by consumers, and capital markets may not work very well in making funds available unless some public policy intervention takes place. Setting mandatory fuel economy standards has already been effective in inducing technological change and in shifting the product mix toward appliances and automobiles that use less energy, but in a strict sense those standards do not rectify market failure. They actually represent a substitution of political decisions for individual ones.

Nongovernmental institutions can sometimes circumvent market failure, even where adequate private motivations for energy RD&D are not present. For example, the Electric Power Research Institute and the Gas Research Institute, which engage in RD&D in their respective industries, finance their efforts by levies on consumers. In this case private institutions surmount market failure without direct government support. Even without quasi-public status, the National Coal Association engages in limited energy RD&D efforts on behalf of its industry, as do the associations of some major energy-using industries.

There is, perhaps, some additional precedent to be found in the Research Associations of Great Britain, and in the Organization for Applied

Scientific Research (TNO) in the Netherlands. The Research Associations were created between World Wars I and II. Their original aim was to support a program of RD&D by pooling funds from industries in a single industrial sector and combining these with approximately matching funds from the government. Roughly forty Research Associations were created —typically for industrial sectors where individual members were too small to support a meaningful program of RD&D.

With respect to a large segment of the energy production and consumption industry, then, there is no need for RD&D beyond that which would occur as soon as prices reflected replacement costs, and firms and individuals pursued their own private interests accordingly. The costs of such private RD&D are borne by the affected industry, they are built into the price of the energy produced and consumed, and are appropriately charged to those who benefit—the energy consumers. But opportunities remain for government intervention in promoting RD&D.

Principles to Guide Intervention

The appropriate quantity of support for RD&D can best be determined by summing up the specific opportunities available. Where can funds be expended in order to make a net contribution to meeting the goals of the country? The presumption is that those opportunities will arise from market failure, and that the appropriate amount of funds will depend on the gap between prices that fully cover costs and those to which producers and consumers respond. The following principles can assist in selecting RD&D targets, but their application remains a matter for judgment and political decision.

Choose instruments wisely. Energy RD&D requires different instruments from those used successfully in weapons RD&D, where government has had the most experience. In weapons RD&D the government is the customer, and it can define the criteria for success. With energy RD&D the customer is in the private sector, and RD&D will be wasted if a market for the product does not exist. Hence, it is not enough that the device or process simply works; a priority must be placed from the first on whether an activity can and will penetrate the market. Its economics must be attractive, and institutional barriers must be low.

One implication is that government should replicate the incentives and criteria of the private sector when funding energy RD&D. Rather than funding inputs, government should reward output that can find a place in the market. In synthetic fuel RD&D, for example, government could specify the product—synthetic liquids—but not the production process. It could auction off price guarantees to the lowest bidder, letting firms compete on the basis of the economic promise of their ideas instead of on the technical prowess of their approach.

Another implication is that government support should focus on the research and development stage, not on the demonstration or deployment level. It could support the basic and early applied research that lowers component costs, then have the private sector utilize those research findings to move a process or device into the market competitively. In this way, developments would be pursued on the basis of commercial promise; and those who developed them would be ready to use them. There would be no problem in transferring the technology from its originators to its users. As an example, it may be important for government to support research on the reduction of friction (which could have widespread application in saving energy) but not necessary for it to support engineering efforts to improve automobile engine design.

Compare projects properly.   RD&D expenditures on different applications must be evaluated by a common measure. The cost of each effort must be compared to the present discounted value of the stream of benefits over time. Thus, some special yardstick is required to compare a development that enhances supply by a given amount per year, but only for twenty years, with a conservation device which saves energy for, say, forty years, before it is outmoded or irrelevant. Similarly, the expected value of an effort to enhance energy supply with a very great chance of success must be compared with the expected value of those activities with much less certain returns. Placing alternatives on the same footing also means treating their costs properly; the timing and certainty of the prospective costs must be taken into consideration.

Assess alternatives simultaneously.   Evaluation of prospective projects depends on what other efforts are under way or could be preempted. For example, taken separately, two projects to develop new sources of electricity supply might each have a positive net benefit. If both were undertaken, however, neither might be worthwhile. The cost of development of each, spread over only a share of the future market, would more than offset the prospective benefits in the form of cheaper electricity. Similarly, perfection of a device which makes possible some improvement in energy efficiency may preempt justification of further RD&D devoted to an even better technology. The good sometimes is the enemy of the better.

We need some mechanism which will permit us to determine joint priorities and allocations among all potential investments in energy RD&D. Moreover, since they are substitutes, the spectrum of energy supply and energy conservation opportunities should also be examined simultaneously. In addition, periodic if not constant reassessment of RD&D efforts is required. Sudden breakthroughs in one technology may call for abolition of another effort even if it is proceeding well and promises success. Finally, a much broader menu of "starts" than of "finishes" is justified. It may be wise to explore a number of avenues to the same goal through early (and inexpensive) stages, provided that a ruthless pruning of those which appear less promising is possible before *major* expenditures are made. This factor again argues for government to restrict its support to generic problems and to leave commercialization to the private sector. Private firms will automatically take potential market rivals into account before proceeding with an option.

Consider some goals directly. Contradicting the general principle we urged above, some factors affecting energy RD&D choices do not appear in the price system. While they can be defined in price terms, it seems more plausible to deal with them directly. Four examples come to mind: some aspects of international relations and national survival; events which take very long time periods to bring to fruition; events with very small probabilities but large consequences; and consequences with external effects far removed from the energy sector per se.

Oil import levels may have effects on international relations which are difficult to translate into shadow prices. The relative strengths of different power blocs, the prestige of the United States in the eyes of both friends and potential enemies, and the rate of development of lesser developed nations may all be affected by prospective levels of oil imports. Levels of oil imports, in turn, may depend on energy RD&D expenditures. Similarly, energy prices abroad, interregional wealth transfers, and prospects for peace among other nations may be affected by the energy technology developed here. Such international aspects touch the "market failure" rationale for energy RD&D only tangentially, if at all, yet they provide important national incentives to alter energy RD&D programs.

Private markets deal very poorly with events that occupy extremely long time periods. Even a perfectly functioning market may not be a good guide to policy when the time span is measured in generations or centuries instead of years or decades. The research efforts on nuclear waste disposal and on fusion techniques for generating electricity are cases in point. Nuclear waste will remain dangerous for thousands of years. It is unacceptable to adopt a disposal technology that would hand an all but insolvable problem to those living hundreds of years from now, even if that result were consistent with the application of a reasonable discount rate. Nuclear fusion may take a half-century to perfect. There is probably a sequential series of steps to take before it is ready, and these steps probably cannot be compressed. On any normal discounting of costs and benefits, it is unlikely that current research on fusion could be recommended. Yet the thought of requiring those living in the future to suffer several generations of delay in obtaining its possible benefits again is unacceptable.

Some prospective energy technologies may have such low probabilities of success as to preclude any private sector investment in them at all, even though their consequences could be immense. The federal government, with its vast size, can afford to spread the risk of almost certain failure over numerous possibilities. Along the same line, energy RD&D may have externalities beyond those normally considered. Spillovers into other technologies and research may be important. And finally, information about future energy prospects—obtained well before it would be developed by the private sector—may induce adjustments in basic social institutions, in life styles, and in other portions of the economy. Started early, these changes could proceed more smoothly. An early warning system can be very beneficial.

18 Translating New Policies for Energy Sources into Action— Coal and Nuclear Power

A Sampling of Options

A variety of energy supply and conservation alternatives may be developed intensively on an individual basis under future U.S. energy policy, or they may simply evolve as elements of our overall national energy strategies. We have selected four such alternatives as case studies to illustrate the kinds of problems they involve and the nature of the policy instruments that might be adopted to overcome them. The four initiatives considered in this chapter and the next one—increased production of coal, expanded use of nuclear power, production of liquid and gaseous fuels from coal or oil shale, and increased use of solar energy—offer especially useful insights because they so clearly represent real possibilities. Each has its strong proponents and each may well become a critical part of the national energy picture. Many observers (justifiably) also speak of conservation as a "source" of energy—as a means of "finding" additional energy to achieve whatever supply–demand balance we decide to seek. Some key conservation possibilities—including process shifts that lower energy use—have already been discussed extensively in chapter 5. The policy suggestions arising from that discussion will also be reviewed here in distilled form.

The discussion of each initiative begins with the assumption that energy price reform (as outlined in chapter 17) has been achieved. Price reform would make all of these initiatives easier to accomplish, and this basic truth is not repeated in each discussion. By achievement of price reform we mean that price controls have been removed, that a tariff structure sufficient to cover the insecurity costs of imported petroleum and natural gas is in place, that external costs from energy acquisition and use are internalized as far as possible, that other special costs imposed by energy acquisition and use are covered, and that gas and electric rate structures embody marginal cost pricing to the extent practicable. In those cases where pricing reform is central to the initiative under consideration, we will point out the special consequences which its omission would bring— including the need to substitute other policies. Pricing reform itself would be difficult to implement, of course, so each of these initiatives may require an even greater level of political commitment than would otherwise be necessary.

We emphasize that we are not advocating the specific policies described as all or a necessary part of an ideal solution to our energy problems. Rather, we are analyzing ways in which these *possible* policies might be implemented if the nation should resolve to adopt them. Furthermore, the process of analyzing these particular initiatives one by one should not suggest that they are mutually exclusive. Both economic reasoning and the information presented throughout this volume indicate that an effective and efficient energy policy must balance costs and benefits of all prospective energy options at the margin and not treat any one as "the" answer. We believe that the proper approach for the nation is not to foreclose arbitrarily any avenue of energy supply or conservation, but instead to let each option find its role and level of use based on its intrinsic value relative to others.

Coal supply underlies almost any policy to use synthetic liquids and gases, and it is fundamental to using electricity in a major way. The critical issues determining the role of coal lie at the use point—whether it can be burned or converted safely and without major impacts on health or on climate—but those issues have been addressed elsewhere in this study. What concerns us here are the factors that affect the cost of coal and whether government action can reduce that cost. To the extent the supply cost of coal can be reduced, additional expense can be borne at the use point in making its conversion environmentally benign.

The nuclear option involves two aspects which can be distinguished and which should be treated separately. First is the question of what policies might be appropriate to foster continued and expanded use of existing light water reactor (LWR) technology. Controversy surrounds that program, even though LWRs supplied one-eighth of all U.S. electricity during 1978. Even before the accident at Three Mile Island near Harrisburg, Pa., doubts had been expressed as to whether reactors would continue to be built and operated. If that technology is to be important, doubts about its safety must be resolved by appropriate measures, and in ways that will not threaten its economic viability.

Ultimately, LWR fuel constraints will push the cost of this technology upward and limit its expansion potential at some point beyond the year 2000, so a follow-on technology will be necessary if nuclear power is to remain an important element in energy supply. The possible follow-on technology about which most is known is the plutonium breeder. Most R&D work in the United States has been done on the liquid metal fast breeder reactor (LMFBR). Experimental reactors in the United States and French and Soviet results was near-commercial-sized units have shown that this technology works, and no meaningful fuel supply limits are now discernible. Other nuclear possibilities also exist, of course, including other converter fuel cycles, different breeder designs, and possibly nuclear fusion. These possibilities are either remote in time or uncertain, however, and we may not be able to count on them to any effective extent as we enter the twenty-first century. Consequently, the second nuclear technology we will explore here is the LMFBR. The question we ask is what policies would be required to bring it through development and make it ready to deploy in the event its use was both acceptable and economic.

In this chapter, after dealing with coal, we will describe a strategy to make the LWR safer and to facilitate its use, and then describe steps along the critical path which must be traversed if the breeder is to occupy a significant place in energy supply. Chapter 19 will address the questions of implementing policies that relate specifically to conservation, synthetic liquid and gaseous fuels, and solar energy.

Synthetic liquids and gases are potentially important because of the uncertainty of the supply and price of conventional fuels. Liquid-fueled devices dominate transportation, and substantial replacements for them are not even on the horizon. As for gas, there are few requirements for it that cannot be served by electricity or liquids, but an investment of scarcely imaginable scale would be required to replace gas in its residential and commercial uses. If synthetic gas and liquid are not feasible for some reason, we will have to start planning soon if we hope to substitute something else for them or to do without them with minimum disruption.

Solar space and water heating may offer a near-term opportunity to shift from depletable to renewable energy sources. This technology may help to fill energy requirements and also supply a prototype for a series of long-term shifts as the energy sector changes over time. On institutional as well as technical grounds, therefore, the solar space and water heating enterprise has far-reaching implications that give it an important role among energy initiatives.

Expanding Coal Production

Expanded use of coal is a major alternative to further imports of oil and natural gas or to other sources of energy. Coal use, however, has been limited because of the environmental impacts of its combustion and conversion and because it is a bulky fuel and expensive to transport, store, and use. Problems associated with using coal are treated elsewhere in this book; the purpose here is to explore policy and institutional supports at the federal level which would be needed to facilitate the *production* and *transportation* of coal if demand were to increase sharply.

The availability of coal resources lies at the top of any list of *non*-problems with respect to this fuel. However restrictive the definition, chapter 7 pointed out that minable coal resources appear adequate to meet any feasible requirement for generations to come. But coal production has problems, and federal action can reduce coal costs. Those costs, in turn, will affect the quantity of coal used. If coal prices are driven upward by restraints on mining, other fuels will be preferred, less energy will be consumed, and total output of the economy will diminish. To put it another way, the lower the cost of coal at the delivery point, the greater the expense that can be borne in making its use acceptable from the standpoint of safety and health, yet economically competitive with other fuels —including imported oil.

Coal reserves are minable at varying costs, and restrictions on access to some of the least costly deposits in the West could be an important deterrent to lowering prospective coal costs. We will return to this issue later, but first let us consider labor supply, capital availability, and transportation policy as they affect the prospects for expanding coal production.

Labor Supply and Productivity

Rising labor costs drive up coal costs, and it may be difficult to recruit and train enough miners to raise coal production in the future without sacrificing productivity and thus raising labor costs per ton. Two aspects of the problem feed on each other: One reason labor productivity falls is the introduction of new and untrained miners into the industry, but the decline in individual productivity itself is one reason more new miners are needed.

Coal mining is a skilled occupation demanding high levels of training and a motivated, intelligent, and disciplined work force if productivity levels are to be maintained. Rapid expansion dilutes all these factors. And labor recruitment needs in mining are growing because of increases in coal output, the large number of miners reaching retirement age (especially in the case of underground miners), and the growing opportunities for skilled miners to work as technicians in enforcing new federal and state mine safety and reclamation regulations. Industry's ability to train workers in numbers adequate to avoid further deterioration in average skill levels will be strained. Possibly, work force growth has already necessitated dipping lower into the pool of potential workers to meet labor requirements. As time passes, however, necessary training *can* be performed and new entrants *can* be attracted into the regional labor markets from which workers are drawn. Moreover, the recent entry of women into the mining work force will further expand the labor pool over time. Thus, labor deficiencies may be a force pushing up coal cost in the short run, but this condition need not be permanent.

Productivity also suffers with increased labor unrest, especially with wildcat strikes that disrupt production. The past ten years—punctuated by the 1977–78 strike, the longest in United Mine Workers' (UMW) history—has been a period of ferment in labor relations. There is no prospect for a more settled future. The UMW is experiencing internal tension and is not likely soon to regain the stability that characterized it earlier. A growing proportion of coal is coming from nonunion mines, and the effect of this trend on costs in the longer run is uncertain. Again, however, prospects are not bright for soon reversing the downward trend in labor productivity.

Finally, coal mining is dangerous and unhealthy. Major strides have been made in reducing dangers, improving health conditions, and in compensating those harmed. With these changes, more costs once borne by workers and by the community at large have been internalized in the price of the coal itself. Improvements in health and safety have followed from industry–worker negotiations and from changes in the law, and they have been accompanied by declines in productivity. Despite the relative improvements in mining conditions, however, the occupation remains unattractive, which adds to costs (through the higher wage demands it encourages) and hampers recruitment into the mines. These problems are less serious in the case of surface mining, which for some years has been a larger source of domestic coal than underground mines.

The critical issues of labor availability and productivity lie effectively beyond federal reach. There are no quick fixes that lead to more skilled miners, to greater job satisfaction among those who work, or to improved health and safety without cost. There certainly are no federal instruments which can lead to these results, though marginal gains might be recorded with improvements in labor markets, more skilled mediation of disputes, and more care in developing regulations which would protect health and lives at minimum cost. Nonetheless, coal can be mined in increasing quantities even if labor supply and productivity conditions do not improve. It will just cost more.

Financial Limitations

Another issue often raised is whether limitations in raising capital will prevent timely expansion of coal production. Except for the uncertainty introduced into coal operations by unpredictable federal policies, however, capital constraints do not appear to be important.

None of the usual risk considerations that limit access to capital appears to be relevant. The investment required to open even very large coal facilities is not overwhelming to a moderate-sized company; market risks can be minimized through entering into contracts for some portion of output for the life of the mine; and technological risks are relatively small. The key to investment is prospective profitability.

The uncertainty introduced by the prospect of further but unknown governmental actions may pose a problem that cannot be removed by private action. There is no insurance against changes in environmental and health and safety regulations like those that have already altered the basis for operation in some sectors of the coal industry. The prospect of future changes of similar magnitude adds an element of risk that demands a substantial premium for investors. While long-term "cost plus" contracts give some protection against such events, they are not effective against changes in mining laws or other regulatory changes which effectively close down particular operations.

If at a later date concern about such actions seriously depresses investment, a "hold harmless" policy with regard to tightened environmental, health, and safety standards could be instituted. Such a policy would compensate firms for the cost of rectifying compliance failures resulting from a change in standards. It would take effect only with reference to a

facility installed in good faith in full compliance with the regulations
which were operative when it was built. The implications of this basic
approach were assessed in chapter 17.

Transportation

Transportation problems have hampered coal supply sporadically in
some locations, and any substantial increase in output will strain the
ability to move coal. Long lead times are involved in building or upgrading railroad rights-of-way, in increasing the capacity of waterways, and
in building slurry pipelines. Similar periods are required to increase the
production rate for railroad rolling stock, barges, and towboats. While
lags in upgrading transportation capacity may be no longer than those
required to expand coal production and use facilities, this does not mean
a problem may not arise. For example, surplus capacity exists in coal
production, and a policy change affecting environmental restraints might
lead to a sudden increase in coal demand. Some coal transportation
arteries do not seem to have the capacity to meet surges in demand
initiated, for instance, by a new oil embargo. More important, though,
even with what should be enough lead time, financial and institutional
rigidities may interfere with getting the necessary transport facilities
ready. There are problems in acquiring rights-of-way for coal slurry pipelines and in determining who will be responsible for adding rolling stock,
or in knowing what transport rates will be, so that shippers can decide
between rail and river, and carriers can proceed with investment. Thus, a
decision to expand coal use may not be transmitted immediately into
complementary action to increase transportation capacity, and vital lead
time may be lost. Coal transportation constraints do not appear insurmountable, but they deserve early attention in any program to expand
the use of coal and to minimize its cost to consumers.

Railroads. About three-fourths of all U.S. coal leaving the mine
mouth moves by rail. The rail systems of the East which carry the bulk
of Appalachian coal have deteriorated, even though the major coal-hauling railroads have not faced financial problems as severe as those of other
eastern roads. Even apart from age, some trackage has deteriorated because road beds designed for lesser strains are now subjected to heavier
cars. Hopper cars are in short supply on some routes, and there have been
shortages of locomotives. It appears that financial prospects have not
been attractive enough to induce the investment required to maintain and

expand coal-hauling capacity. Another factor has been the uncertain status of coal demand; for example, prospects of tightened environmental standards have limited investment on roads hauling high-sulfur coal.

Some eastern railroads have been further handicapped by a regulatory system which has required them to maintain unprofitable services (balancing them with more lucrative operations) and by work rules which have increased labor costs. They have lost important markets on some of their more promising routes by not being allowed to compete successfully with barge and truck carriers.

The situation is somewhat different for the prospective coal-hauling railroads in the West. Expanded coal production in many cases would require new facilities, and these can be designed to meet modern specifications. Mines are very large compared with the average eastern operation. Many are suited to unit train service in which groups of one hundred cars remain joined with locomotives and shuttle back and forth between locations, thereby maximizing time in operation and lowering the quantity of rolling stock required per ton of coal moved. Most important, perhaps, the western roads have remained financially more secure partly because of their relative freedom from money-losing local services and their insulation from competition in the long-distance, bulk haulage which is their specialty.

Nonetheless, a major expansion of western coal production would strain rail facilities. First of all, main-line trackage does not exist to accommodate it efficiently. Production would be concentrated, as would consumption points, and detours from the direct route between these points sacrifice efficiency. Second, existing trackage may not be designed to handle the volumes that must be moved daily if western coal output multiplies. For example, grade-level crossings abound on western roads. While the interruption of local highway travel for a few trains a day may be acceptable, the near-continuous stream of one hundred-car unit trains that might be focused in some corridors could not be tolerated. Finally, the supply of rolling stock is now inadequate. The needed expansion—depending on its size and rate—might strain manufacturing facilities already occupied in replacing the aging rolling stock that is being retired from service.

Policy support to rectify current and prospective railroad constraints in moving coal is bound up in general regulatory reform in the transport sector. Under the conditions of expanding coal use postulated here, there is no reason why rail transport of coal could not support rates which would compensate railroads for building, maintaining, and equipping an adequate transportation system—for service where rail transport has an advantage over such modes as barges or coal slurry pipelines. The problem is in directing such prospective revenues to the facilities needed to haul coal and in making them available soon enough to have the facilities ready before the coal must be moved. While recent legislation and regulatory changes have begun to address this issue, much remains to be done in such areas as: (1) increasing railroads' authority to abandon non-compensating service; (2) providing flexibility in rate making; (3) enlarging opportunities for profitable investment in rolling stock by non-railroad investors; and (4) facilitating new institutional arrangements, such as long-term contracts for hauling coal, which can provide financial security to both investors and lenders.

Coal slurry pipelines.   Pulverized coal mixed with water—a coal slurry—can be transported by pipelines. While experience with such pipelines is limited, transportation costs seem attractive compared with railroads in some applications. Moreover, since pipelines can be buried, they need not impinge on the environment or esthetics, or on highway traffic in areas through which they pass. Nor do they offer opportunities for accidents, as do railroads.

Two factors have restricted use of slurry pipelines. The first is water. It is scarce in the western coal mining regions, and use for slurry pipelines competes with other uses. In addition, the water from slurries is dirty at the delivery point, and its safe disposal presents a possible environmental problem. Water availability in the western coal mining regions is an emotionally charged issue, and the fact that coal transporters would be willing to purchase water rights on the market and to meet applicable regulations is not sufficient to mollify opposition. Montana forbids outright the exportation of water, and most states have administrative procedures through which transfers of water rights must pass. These are often weighted against industrial use, and in any event they have provided an opportunity for those opposed to energy development to restrict its growth, or at least to impose costly delays.[1]

The second factor restricting slurry pipelines is the difficulty in obtaining rights-of-way to build them. The railroads see slurry pipelines as

---

[1] For a full discussion of water rights and energy development in this area, see Constance M. Boris and John V. Krutilla, *Water Rights and Energy Development in the Northern Great Plains: An Integrated Analysis* (Baltimore, Md., Johns Hopkins University Press for Resources for the Future, forthcoming).

competitors and choose not to allow them to cross railway-owned property. Since any pipeline must cross railway rights-of-way numerous times in the distance between producing areas in Wyoming and consuming regions in Texas, for example, the railroads have an effective veto on any slurry pipeline project.

The water availability issue is not easily susceptible to federal resolution. If adequate financial incentive existed, however, it seems likely that water could be acquired. Indeed, if there were sufficient cost savings in slurry pipelines compared with railway transportation, water could be transferred as needed from regions with water surplus. Again, though, the overriding importance of water in the West (and the fact that water rights in many cases have already been overappropriated) means that water may not be available for pipelines at *reasonable* costs. The federal government probably could act to reduce institutional barriers to water access if the transport savings were deemed sufficiently important. The way would be open for federal preemption of a portion of state authority if building and operating slurry pipelines became a matter of national urgency. Any such federal effort would be strongly resisted, however, and it could evoke a classic states' rights battle that could threaten politically any party (or individuals) pressing it.

The right-of-way issue can be resolved through federal eminent domain legislation, which would give approved pipeline projects the right to condemn property for transit rights upon payment of fair compensation. Some states have already passed such legislation. This measure was defeated in the Ninety-fifth Congress, with opposition to it being led, understandably, by the railroads. Environmental groups also opposed this legislation, but their position appears to have been taken not from opposition to slurry pipelines vis-à-vis railroads, but in part as a means to slow coal mining development in the West. They also were concerned about the transfer of water from water-short regions and about the possible effects of polluted water if it entered the environment at the coal delivery point.

Access to Coal Reserves

The federal government owns approximately 70 percent of western coal resources and can influence the development of another 20 percent that borders on federal lands. Moreover, the regulations under which coal is mined are largely federal or are affected by federal minimum standards.

Policy toward access to western coal reserves and with regard to the conditions under which they may be mined can have an important effect on the costs to be expected with a large increase in coal use. Similarly, policies on coal which are biased toward production in certain regions can affect costs dramatically.

The resource base is large enough so that restrictions on access to certain deposits in the West—or to all federal deposits for that matter—would not prevent coal from being produced in sufficient quantities to meet demand. Thus there is a point to the argument that further coal leasing is, speaking strictly, unnecessary for some time to come. But this view ignores the fact that coal deposits are of unequal value because of mining costs, physical characteristics of the coal, and location. Removing some deposits from potential production leaves a smaller (and hence lower quality) resource base from which to choose. Sooner or later, this leads to higher costs for coal at the delivery point. The policy issue is whether the benefits from restricting access to some reserves justify the extra costs borne in exploiting lower quality reserves.

The government earlier followed a liberal leasing practice, but the de facto policy since 1971 has been to lease no more western coal (though some leases have been granted where contiguous federal properties were required if ongoing mining operations were to continue in an efficient way). Leasing policy is under active review and the stated goal has been to reinstitute leasing under conditions where environmental and socioeconomic values are protected, competitiveness is maintained, and the full value of the resource is captured for U.S. citizens.

Several issues have arisen. One of the most critical has to do with the (broadly conceived) environment–energy tradeoff. What lands will and will not be opened for exploitation? What regulations are required to assure that mining will disrupt the environment to the minimum extent practicable?

Under current legislation, mining is prohibited when it may adversely affect fragile lands with important historic, cultural, scientific, or esthetic values, or harm natural systems. Similarly, mining is not allowed if it would harm renewable resource lands (including alluvial valley floors and prime farmlands), affect natural water systems, or endanger life and property. Interpretation of these statutory requirements is incomplete, regulations in some cases remain to be written, and final resolution of the regulations will require a lengthy testing process in the courts. The more restrictive the limitations on leasing and mining, the higher the direct costs that coal mining operations will bear.

In terms of the prospects for coal costs, an important matter is the question of whether lands now under lease which fail to meet new statutory requirements will be replaced with those that can be mined. If not, lessees could be dispossessed without compensation. Little is known about the volumes of coal on such lands or the amount of money involved. But if leases entered into in good faith are later found to be unminable, and if transfers are not allowed and compensation is not paid, prospective mine operators may demand higher prospective rates of return before making new investments in coal properties.[2]

A revamped leasing policy could promote the formation of logical mining units and thus lower the prospective cost of coal. A "logical mining unit" is an area of coal land which can be developed and mined in an efficient, economical, and orderly manner with due regard to the conservation of coal reserves and other resources. Such a unit requires enough reserves to sustain operations for a long enough period to amortize the extensive capital investment required—customarily forty years. Further, the operation must be on a scale sufficient to satisfy the demand of a large user such as an electric utility if such devices as the unit-train are going to be used to minimize point-to-point transportation costs.

Institutional factors complicate the establishment of logical mining units and other values conflict with it; substantial ingenuity will be needed to achieve even a moderately satisfactory resolution of the dilemmas posed by limitations on access to deposits. One difficulty is that ownership of coal lands is fragmented among the federal and state governments, Indian tribes, railroads, and diverse private parties. Further, the subsurface mineral rights sometimes have been severed from surface rights; typically, the federal government has retained mineral rights on land conveyed to private parties for agricultural uses. Since surface mining destroys (at least for a time) use and occupancy of the surface, conflict between rights is inevitable.

Another complicating factor is that the federal government also wishes to maximize the value received for allowing its coal to be mined. In meeting this goal, competition for leases is necessary, but that competition will not occur if one potential coal producer already controls a portion of the logical mining unit and can restrict access to any other bidder. Another difficulty arises when, as under existing statute, the consent of surface owners is needed to mine the coal. In this case the surface owner can

[2] Part of this higher required rate of return would be shifted onto the federal government through lower future bids for coal properties, but some of the effect would be passed forward because lower supplies would increase prices.

demand compensation up to the full differential value of the coal, effectively reducing the potential return to the federal government to zero.

Specific aspects of a program to make coal lands available in logical mining units are beyond the scope of our consideration here. Clearly, though, future coal costs will be importantly affected by the success of this effort, as well as by the environment-energy tradeoffs implicit in policies for opening western coal lands to exploitation.

Maintaining the Nuclear Enterprise

The light water reactor (LWR) can now fairly be described as conventional technology, and nuclear power based on it can supply a growing proportion of the nation's electricity for some time to come. As the uranium resource is depleted, however, fuel costs for these reactors will tend to rise. Liquid metal fast breeder reactor (LMFBR) technology, which is now being developed both here and abroad, promises a near-inexhaustible supply of electricity without increasing fuel costs. This technology could be in place to take over part of the electricity load from LWRs if and when uranium costs (now a minor part of overall nuclear generating costs) become excessive.

To some extent development of the breeder might conflict with expanded use of LWRs. Some of the opposition to the LWR arises from fear of plutonium, although the presence of that material in a pure (and thus most dangerous) form would only accompany LWR usage if spent fuel reprocessing and recycle occurs. Reprocessing is not essential for LWRs, but is a *sine qua non* of breeder use. Hence opposition to the LWR could be lessened by a firm repudiation of the breeder—adding credence to a decision that reprocessing would not take place either. Thus, one policy choice could be between greater assurance of the LWR contribution for the intermediate term and a lower probability for a near-permanent source of electricity through use of the breeder.

One major purpose of the rest of this chapter is to describe policies which could be used to improve the safety and acceptability of LWR technology if that technology proves attractive on economic and other grounds. The other is to suggest measures which would facilitate development of a breeder technology and make it available for a later decision as to whether it should be deployed commercially. It is *not* our purpose to argue the desirability or undesirability of both or either of these technologies, so our description of supporting policies does not imply that we urge that they be adopted.

Expanding LWR Acceptability

Prospects for expanding nuclear power have deteriorated during the 1970s, even though the costs of oil and natural gas have multiplied and the environmental consequences of using coal appear more serious than before. Estimates of nuclear capacity by the end of this century are one-fourth of what they were in 1972.[3] And the decline in new orders for light water reactors (an average of only three per year since 1975) has reached the point that some observers have questioned whether the reactor manufacturing industry can survive. The potential contribution of nuclear power is sufficiently large that its attainment or nonattainment can make a remarkable difference. For example, the current DOE high estimate for LWR electricity generation in the year 2000 amounts to the rough equivalent of all 1978 oil imports or more than all 1978 coal production.[4]

The reduction in the estimated output from LWRs can be explained partly by declines in projected electricity demand. It also arose from greater uncertainty about future demand levels. The alternatives to nuclear generating capacity have shorter lead times. Given uncertainty, firms have an incentive to delay commitments to new generating capacity, knowing that when demand requirements become clearer they can build combustion turbine plants to bridge the gap until coal units can be brought on-stream.[5] Base-load nuclear plants with long lead times and high capital costs are at a competitive disadvantage in this uncertain demand environment. Another factor depressing the reactor market has been the rising relative cost of nuclear power. Capital costs of nuclear plants have escalated faster than the inflation rate since the 1960s, and while the capital costs of alternatives have also risen, capital is a greater part of the total cost of electricity from nuclear plants than from alternatives. This fact has offset relative increases in the price of nonnuclear fuels to some degree. Nuclear plant delays, due in part but not entirely, to health and safety regulations have been a major cause of capital cost increases.

Beyond these factors, however, we suggest there lies a more fundamental issue: Will nuclear power prove acceptable to the American pub-

[3] Atomic Energy Commission, "Nuclear Power 1973–2000" (WASH-1139). December 1972; Department of Energy Information Administration, "U.S. Submission to the International Nuclear Fuel Cycle Evaluation," April 1978.

[4] Department of Energy, Energy Information Administration, Nuclear Energy Analysis Division, preliminary estimate, April 1979.

[5] This approach is costly to the national interest in at least two ways: (1) off-the-shelf gas turbines are more costly to operate and less fuel efficient than are larger baseload plants; and (2) they are fueled most commonly with oil.

lic in the longer run? After all, an investment in a baseload generating plant must be amortized by operation over thirty years or more, so that a decision in 1979 to add a nuclear power plant (counting the lead time for regulatory approvals and construction) must envision its continuing value past the year 2020. If doubt exists as to whether, or on what terms, operation of such plants will prove acceptable in terms of safety, the electric generation industry will be reluctant to make the commitments needed to get them built. For this reason, in this discussion of maintaining the nuclear enterprise, we give major attention to the safety and acceptability issue, recognizing at the same time that efforts to make the LWR more benign and more acceptable may *add* to costs and hence *lower* the economic attractiveness of this technology. We note, though, that to the extent design and regulatory improvements reduce safety concerns, there may be fewer delays and greater investor certainty, which *lowers* costs.

We can turn now to formulating a strategy for reducing the safety and environmental concerns about nuclear power if it is decided that the LWR enterprise should be maintained. Such a strategy would consist of three elements. The first is to clarify the issues by removing objections that are not relevant to decisions about domestic nuclear operations. The second is to reassure most critics of the nuclear option by a willing commitment to sufficient overdesign of safety precautions so that they can agree that nuclear power is safer and more benign environmentally than its alternatives. We consider this element of the proposed strategy so important that the next section of this chapter is devoted to it exclusively. There will always be some who protest that nuclear energy is "still not safe enough," but they would be restricted in number and greatly limited in influence if an overwhelming majority of the American people firmly believed the statement: "Nuclear power is safer and cheaper than any practical alternative *and* less damaging than doing without energy." The third element of the strategy is to lessen the economic uncertainty resulting from health and safety concerns, which has hindered private investment in nuclear power. This could be done through federal assumption of such economic risks, but in a fashion that requires consumers of nuclear energy to bear the costs of the economic risks accepted in their behalf. This third element will not be dealt with separately because it tends to permeate our treatment of the others. So now we move to the first element—the question of clarifying the relevance of some common "discussion issues."

International issues.   U.S. concerns about the international expansion of commercial nuclear power probably can be reduced to two points:

(1) fear of a link between commercial nuclear power plants and the possible proliferation of states possessing nuclear weapons, and (2) apprehensions about accidental discharges of radioactive materials from foreign nuclear facilities, especially those in countries with a less developed technological base. Actually, however, neither of these dangers would necessarily be increased if the United States expanded its own LWR program.

The major dangers of proliferation are associated with the reprocessing of spent fuel, because weapons-grade plutonium can be produced in that operation. As we have already noted, however, maintaining a domestic LWR industry does not depend on the reprocessing of spent fuel rods. Indeed, the operation of nonbreeder reactors within the United States has no necessary tie to the existence of a plutonium economy abroad: plutonium need not be separated for the LWR cycle, and U.S. commercial reprocessing technology need not be developed, much less exported. But U.S. rejection of a plutonium economy by itself does not prevent foreigners from pursuing that technology. In fact, other nations have built and are operating such facilities. Thus U.S. influence abroad, to be most effective, must rest on policies designed to limit proliferation directly, not merely on rejecting LWRs domestically.

The future of the domestic industry is also largely separable from the possibility of accidental releases of radioactivity abroad. Whether or not we have a large nuclear industry domestically may have little effect on the growth of nuclear generation abroad or on the care with which a power plant elsewhere in the world is operated and maintained and its personnel trained. Because others may follow our example, however, the safety precautions we develop if we maintain a nuclear industry could indeed lessen the probabilities of a malfunction abroad.

The plutonium economy. Without reprocessing, the risks of diverting explosively fissile material from LWRs to terrorist groups is minimized, and a whole category of risks and concerns becomes irrelevant to the decision on whether or not we should press ahead with nuclear power in this country. There is no technical reason why a once-through fuel cycle cannot be followed for LWRs, with spent fuel rods destined irrevocably to permanent and nonretrievable storage. Operationally, though, the prospect for reprocessing rests on the economics of the alternative paths and on the institutions by which decisions about such matters can or cannot be reversed in the future.

The economic reason why we even consider reprocessing spent reactor fuel is that the "unburned" uranium and plutonium which remain in the rods can be reclaimed and used to fuel other reactors.[6] Reclaiming such fuel saves the cost of mining, milling, and enriching new uranium. The economic attractiveness of reprocessing thus rests on the value of the uranium saved (including the enrichment cost) relative to the cost of reprocessing. For a long time it was thought that reprocessing would be very attractive, but rapid escalation of the projected costs of the process and prospective reductions in the costs of enrichment now bring the economics into considerable dispute. Unless uranium prices rise at extraordinary rates, the economic penalty—if any—to a once-through fuel cycle will remain small. Recycling nuclear fuel in LWRs only (without introducing breeders) would also enable us to obtain a bit over 15 percent more energy from any given quantity of uranium ore, but the discussion of our mineral resource base in chapter 7 leads us to believe that this need not be an overriding consideration in any near-term decision about the question of reprocessing. Hence, for a decade or so at least, it appears that the economic drive to reprocess will not be so large as to place great pressure on a decision against doing so. It appears plausible to divorce the reprocessing issue from the basic option of maintaining a large nuclear enterprise.

The economic basis for the breeder reactor rests on a comparison of the fuel costs saved with the extra capital and processing costs of a breeder rather than a converter system. Again, if restricting ourselves to a converter system imposed great penalties in energy costs, the temptation to resort promptly to a breeder technology would be more difficult to resist. As it happens, the projected capital costs of a breeder system in the United States have been escalating more rapidly than have uranium costs. Indeed, the recent decline in demand growth and the latest projections of uranium availability in the United States and abroad suggest that uranium prices could remain relatively stable for some time to come. As a consequence, the decision not to deploy breeder technology has become easier instead of more difficult in the recent past and the pressure in favor of it on the basis of dollar costs now appears less likely to become intense for some time to come. Development and commercialization of breeder technology abroad will apparently proceed no matter what the United States decides about domestic fuel cycles. Hence there is less economic necessity than there otherwise would be to develop and deploy breeders domestically in

---

[6] Some argue that recycling nuclear fuel also lessens the difficulty and cost of waste disposal, by "burning up" the plutonium productively and concentrating the unusable remnants within spent fuel. This argument is noted but not addressed here. For those nations without an indigenous uranium supply, reprocessing of LWR fuel also adds to security of energy supply. The breeder reactor, of course, also serves these purposes.

order to shorten lead times in case breeder economics should turn extremely positive in the future. (For other considerations, however, see the section on commercializing the breeder.)

There is also an institutional aspect to separating the U.S. use of light water reactors from the questions surrounding those using plutonium. It is sometimes argued that technology tends to create its own momentum, so that the capability to achieve some advance is translated more or less directly into the decision to do so. The decisions not to build the supersonic passenger plane in this country or to follow the Apollo space program with more extensive manned moon exploration show that this is an overstatement, but the suggestion has much validity, especially when economic interest is joined with intellectually exciting endeavors. To assure that the LWR will not automatically be succeeded by the breeder, it may be necessary to stop U.S. investigation of breeder technology (but not basic research) *and* to make a formal decision that if a breeder technology is to be deployed here in the future, we will buy it from others. These two acts would prevent our slipping into a plutonium economy. Any future deployment of breeders would require an explicit decision— one which would have to be fully debated in all its particulars—not an incremental step in a long line of similarly marginal decisions.

The military program.   Much of the debate over nuclear power has failed to recognize that some of its problems and risks have already been incurred because of the U.S. military program. For example, a civilian program certainly enlarges the waste disposal problem (although to a fairly minor extent), but that problem would have existed even if no electricity had ever been generated for civilian use and would continue to grow even if commercial nuclear plants all vanished. The need for developing a means to dispose of nuclear facilities which have outlived their usefulness was created by the military program; a civilian program merely requires that such means be adapted and refined. Admittedly, some other problems are related more directly to the magnitude of the nuclear power enterprise—for example, protection against terrorist attacks. But the overall point is nonetheless significant: the economic benefits of the nuclear enterprise increase with the amount of the electrical energy produced, while the overall risks it poses and the costs of mitigating them rise more slowly because they start from the very large base of the military program. Power production is only a part of the total nuclear program, and much of the larger portion of the cost of dealing with nuclear problems should be allocated to the military program, which is now more than thirty years old.

Putting Safety Foremost

The commercial nuclear power enterprise and its regulators in this country have been inclined to think of the dangers from nuclear power in the
same framework with which others consider nonnuclear impacts. The
underlying approach has appeared to be to compare benefits and costs
(including special concern for health and safety risks) and then to reach
decisions which apparently promise optimal results. This decision pattern
and industry practices and the regulations it has spawned have not led to
a level of safety and of public acceptance for the nuclear enterprise that
would make its role secure as a major supplier of energy for the remainder
of this century and beyond. The reasons for this failure probably condense
to two propositions: (1) Safety levels adequate to meet the special requirements placed on nuclear power possibly cannot be assured without
improvements in the process by which safety is induced and monitored,
and (2) the usual processes of decision making may not take adequate account of the seriousness with which society views the large scale of potential impacts, the long time it takes for nuclear materials to lose their
threat, and the fact that large numbers of people could be put at risk
without having any effective choice in the matter.

Putting safety foremost requires changes in institutions to sever the
connection between a direct economic burden and additional safety,
changes in regulatory systems to increase incentives to assure safe operation and avoid unsafe practices, and changes in approach to take account
of the special types of concerns that the public has with regard to nuclear
power. These changes need to be applied in at least three areas: waste
disposal, accidental discharges, and diversion of nuclear materials.[7]

Waste disposal.   The acceptability of nuclear power would be enhanced substantially if the U.S. government made specific arrangements
to take title to and possession of nuclear wastes as they leave reactors or
other commercial facilities. No other policy could give as much assurance
that decisions about its handling would be motivated by safety instead of
narrow economic considerations. Admittedly, the government's record
in managing wastes has not been spotless in the past, but changes in
patterns of responsibility, creation of independent monitoring units, and
heightened public sensitivity to waste hazards all have combined to offer

---

[7] A fourth factor, normal discharges, does not appear now to be a significant
barrier to LWR acceptability. Assuming that tailings are properly disposed of, the
danger from normal operation of the LWR fuel cycle seems to be minimal.

more reassurance for the future. Specifically, with independent monitoring, incentives on the side of maximum safety could be institutionalized. The expected *cost* of handling wastes, of course, should be levied upon the processes which yield them, so the government efforts would be fully compensated by the private nuclear power industry. As an additional safeguard, however, the agency operating the waste disposal effort could be explicitly freed of budget constraints based on the level of fees. Decisions would thus be isolated from economic motivations that might lead to corners being cut.

In implementing the proposal, the immediate requirement would be for the federal government to develop large-scale regional spent fuel depots, where spent fuel assemblies could be gathered from operating reactors after their initial cooling-off period at the respective power plant sites. Prompt creation of such depots will lessen the urgency to implement permanent disposal, which is now based in part on pressure from utilities whose on-site spent fuel storage facilities are nearly full.

A second requirement is to develop and implement a firm government policy for intermediate term (but still retrievable) storage of spent nuclear fuel. Even if reprocessing and the breeder reactor are foreclosed for now, the safety of such processes may be sufficiently established some decades in the future for the question to be reopened. Moreover, the availability of intermediate term facilities would again remove the temptation to proceed with permanent disposal before the selected process was fully understood and tested.

Finally, techniques for safe permanent disposal must be demonstrated. This disposal problem has two parts: First, there is the matter of disposing of obsolete power plants and facilities which have become radioactive during their operation. The principle here could be the same as with spent fuel assemblies: a special agency of the government would take title and possession of such facilities, and—without the temptation to trim costs—see to their dismantlement and disposal. It could use whatever technique offered the greatest assurance of safety. The expected costs of such an operation would be levied upon whatever enterprise generated the wastes, with a trust fund built up over the years of operation and with fees adjusted periodically so that expected full costs would be covered.

Second, there is the matter of the disposal of high level wastes—either intact spent fuel bundles or the residues of military and commercial reprocessing. The most promising method of disposal appears to be burying the wastes in stable geologic formations (for example, salt or rock), where the first line of defense is the relative impermeability of the con-

tainers in which the waste is buried and the second is the time delay
between release from such containers and possible migration of radioactive materials to the surface where they could affect humans and other
biota. But questions remain with regard to this technology. Fortunately,
there is time to refine the techniques so as to lessen uncertainty—especially if spent fuel depots are established and intermediate-term storage
facilities are developed. Again, what is required to get on with the job is
federal responsibility, unhindered by budget constraints, and monitored
by independent bodies.

Accidental discharges.   The possibility that nuclear materials might
be discharged accidentally at any point in the fuel cycle cannot be totally
eliminated, as the Three Mile Island accident reminded us. Nevertheless,
the probability of any substantial discharge can be made exceedingly
small and the adverse effects of an accident can be reduced. What we generally need is reemphasis on ongoing efforts toward careful design to
minimize hazards, "defense in depth" to lessen effects if accidents should
occur, and a set of institutions that separates the diagnosis of potential
hazards from the responsibility to pay for correcting them so as to avoid
conflicts of interest tied to financial incentives. The final provision would
be a new one. It could help to assure performance of the first two, and
lend credibility to the process. The entire subject is highly complex and
technical, but two aspects of possible accidental discharges deserve special
attention here: the siting of nuclear facilities and treatment of possible
loss-of-coolant episodes.

Two criteria should be imposed in siting nuclear facilities: they should
be sited so as to minimize the opportunity for accidents, and sites which
may endanger large population centers should be excluded from consideration. As to the first criterion, vulnerability to accident from geologic
instability, for example, is clearly a matter of degree, but the point would
be to verify that existing regulatory procedures can be depended on to
refuse a tradeoff between a known *special* hazard and economic or other
advantage. Avoidance of some relatively but not maximally safe locations
will obviously impose penalties. For example, it could easily lead to
higher transmission costs (in environmental impact as well as in dollars),
to more frequent siting of plants outside the service areas of the utilities
that operate them, and to problems in obtaining adequate cooling water
(perhaps necessitating a substantial energy penalty in more elaborate
energy-absorbing cooling processes). Those penalties might prove small,
however, compared with the benefits from safer operations, less delay in

obtaining nuclear plant sites, and less uncertainty about the future of nuclear power.

The other nuclear siting criterion relates to the location of reactors near population centers. Once the chance of accident is minimized, the next obvious step is to limit its potential effect. Avoiding sites where accidental radioactive emissions would likely affect many people would raise costs; the amount will depend on the definition of "many" and "affect." With respect to the latter, remote siting may yield relatively little benefit in reducing the number of latent cancers from an accident, but it would restrict the number of early illnesses and deaths, would provide added time for warning so that more preventive measures could be taken before exposure, and would avoid the problem of evacuating a mass of people. The Three Mile Island accident warned us of the need for emergency planning for evacuation, and reminded us that crisis management takes on all-but-impossible complexity if large populations are involved. Some existing plants might violate a stringent interpretation of this population criterion. If so, it might be desirable (on a case-by-case basis and with due regard for the distribution of the costs and adjustments of supply sources) to consider closing them down, partly as a symbol of the renewed dedication to maximum safety in the nuclear enterprise.

More restrictive site criteria will narrow even more the range of locations for nuclear plants, so it would be desirable to set aside prime potential locations as soon as possible in order to prepare for future sitings. The administration has long advocated such early site designation and limited early site reviews are being conducted as part of the effort to streamline the nuclear licensing process. With sites chosen before they are needed, testing could proceed at a more leisurely pace to allow extra care, and government agencies could assist with zoning and other restrictions that would protect sites until they were either approved or rejected. Restrictive easements to limit future changes in population density would probably be required. While the expense of "banking" potential nuclear sites would add to the cost of electricity, the savings from avoiding delay after a decision had been made to build a plant would offset this cost to some degree.

If plant siting has been the most common *general* area of dispute in regard to nuclear power, accidents involving loss of coolant have surely been among the most vigorously debated *specifics*. This was true even before the accident at the Three Mile Island plant. If the coolant that draws usable heat directly from the reactor core ceases to circulate for any reason, temperatures rise; and unless the core is cooled through some emergency means, it will melt within a relatively short time and release radioactive materials. Those materials then may escape from the reactor containment shell and reach the environment. Loss of primary coolant is typically the "maximum" accident considered by the nuclear power industry and a great amount of attention has been devoted to preventing such an accident in any plant or, if it should take place, to providing emergency measures to prevent a meltdown and breach of the containment. Redundant safety design, enhanced training, and careful testing of components and procedures are always required; and new information, such as that provided by the Three Mile Island accident, may suggest that even more stringent controls are required. Even so, such measures can go only so far in lessening the possibility of an accident. Defense against sabotage or terrorist attack can similarly not be absolute. While the resulting level of safety may far exceed the levels demanded in other industries, the public may not be convinced that nuclear power is sufficiently benign that it can willingly accept this source of energy.

What is required is a means of assuring (almost—there can *never* be perfect certainty) that even if a full core meltdown occurs, the danger will be small and the impact restricted. One way to develop such assurance (and the public confidence that depends upon it) might be to put even greater stress than now on "containment strategy." As noted above, the first step would be to locate nuclear plants even farther away from population centers and at sites where air and water movements would be unlikely to transport radioactive materials to those centers. The second step would be to increase the effectiveness of containment—perhaps by making reactors smaller, by adding "core catchers" (additional shielding to dissipate heat in the event of a meltdown), or by placing new plants underground. The announced goal might be that in the worst-case event, fewer lives would likely be lost than in some selected low probability–high consequence event such as the collision of two giant airliners or the sudden collapse of a dam in a populated area.

A credible program to minimize the chance of accidental discharges requires an incentive system that will facilitate recognition of potential hazards and the prompt correction of any that arise. Prompt recognition of hazards is facilitated by independent surveillance of power plant operation and maintenance. Ready correction of potentially dangerous situations involves separating the responsibility to pay for corrections from the responsibility to determine which corrections are needed and when. The most effective strategy to achieve the latter goal is one which has others pay for changes improving safety performance which are found to be desirable after plants have been certified for use.

Obviously, such costs should be included in the price of the electrical service rendered. As in the case of waste disposal, a possible technique would be a surcharge on each unit of electricity, which goes into a trust fund to be used only for safety improvements whose usefulness was perceived after plant design had been approved and operating procedures had been accepted as safe. The federal government would have to provide funds for improvements that exceeded the size of the trust funds and the surcharge could be varied over time to reflect changing expectations as to the amounts that might be required.

Beyond the question of safe power plant design and location lies the question of power plant operation. Safe operation and maintenance require a system which applies effective sanctions against careless operation or willful violation of safe procedures. Fines can be made effective only if they are sufficiently certain and sufficiently large to offset potential gains from unsafe operation. Early reports of safety violations which contributed to the seriousness of the Three Mile Island accident dramatized the low level of possible fines compared with either the revenues produced by the plant while operating or the cost of an accident. Economic risk can also reinforce incentives for safe operation. It may not be feasible for one firm to accept full liability for an accident, but, using the insurance principle, such liability could be shared among all firms operating reactors. Then each member of the nuclear power community would have an added incentive to join in the policing of all others. This prescription implies that federal limits on liability for accidents under the Price–Anderson Act might be raised substantially or removed. Finally, it has been suggested that willful violations of safety regulations might be subject to criminal penalities so that individuals responsible for running power plants would know that jail terms, and not just corporate fines, would be possible if willful violations of important measures were proved (as is now the case in the Coal Mine Health and Safety Act). This and other possible measures with regard to nuclear power safety should be carefully scrutinized in the context of the widespread reevaluation of policy toward liability for and prevention of harmful effects from other industrial processes—such as those that may emit toxic chemicals. Added sanctions and revised incentives, taken together, could strengthen the system for reducing the human error component of nuclear risk. While such measures may increase its cost, and risk making nuclear power unattractive to the electric power industry, they could also make nuclear power more safe—and increase its acceptability by the general public.

Diversion and terrorism. Despite the popularity of this scenario for television programs, conventional nuclear power plants and other major nuclear facilities do not offer particularly attractive targets for saboteurs and terrorists. They are resistive to attack. Other more vulnerable targets exist which can also be used to evoke public response. Furthermore, the nuclear materials produced in a once-through fuel cycle are not suitable for making an explosive device, and are also unsuitable for dispersion as a weapon of terror. Nevertheless, the possibility of such attacks remains, and efforts are required to minimize both the likelihood of success and its possible effects.

To forestall sabotage, for instance, authorities might feasibly provide that no one person could produce a failure of both primary and backup safety systems in case careful screening of employees failed to exclude a potential malefactor. As to frontal attack, vulnerable elements are inside containment structures already resistant to any weapons that terrorist groups are likely to have. What is required is more effective training of guards and more responsive back-up security forces to prevent unauthorized entry in force. Both ends might be achieved, either through tighter federal supervision of security systems or through government takeover of security responsibility, with funding provided by the operator of the facility.

Now that we have explored policy approaches that could make it safer though more expensive to travel along one possible path of nuclear power development in the future (one that emphasizes the LWR), let us retrace our steps and consider what we might need to do now if we decided to follow the other branch of the fork—concentrating on the breeder as an eventual necessity.

Commercializing the Breeder Reactor

The liquid metal fast breeder reactor (LMFBR) is a scientifically proven concept which could extend the nuclear fuel supply into the indefinite future. Since fuel costs would be little affected by normal resource depletion, the cost of power from LMFBRs could have slight tendency to rise beyond prevailing inflation rates. Thus the LMFBR represents a "backstop" electricity supply source for the twenty-first century and beyond—if the technology is established.

Other nuclear technologies could also extend fuel supplies. Reprocessing spent fuel and recycling unburned fissile material into LWRs is one option. Another is to use other reactor designs, either other breeders or those which depend on the thorium fuel cycle or make use of lower enriched uranium. A fusion technology may also be developed some day. All these technologies were considered in chapter 9, but not one combines the near-term availability, the near-permanent fuel supply, and the technical promise of the LMFBR.

Nevertheless, the LMFBR is highly controversial. There are different judgments about its economic viability, for example. If growth of electricity demand is restrained, if coal can be burned cheaply and safely, if enrichment breakthroughs and/or new discoveries of uranium deposits make LWR fuel considerably cheaper, or if alternative electricity supply technologies (solar photovoltaic, for example) become less costly, there may never be a market opportunity for the LMFBR.

Similarly, judgments differ about the safety of the LMFBR fuel cycle. While its proponents believe risks are small and well worth taking, many opponents want to avoid the technology entirely. Opposition is based on concern about accidental discharges (from reactor or reprocessing accidents or waste disposal), about risks of diversion of weapons-grade material to terrorists, and about proliferation—increasing the number of governments which have access to nuclear weapons. The process of making the LMFBR safer, according to some observers, may itself have harmful effects on civil liberties because of the need to introduce police-state features to guard facilities and to prevent plutonium diversion.

The final concern is that further national dependence on nuclear power will lessen the resilience of the energy system to shocks. Highly centralized systems, in this view, are inherently unstable; they cannot easily or quickly be brought back into equilibrium once perturbed. To avoid the dangers of overcentralization, and to gain the social and political benefits of decentralized and more "human" systems, conservation, substitution of other energy sources, and an early scaling-down of electricity demand is advocated. Other analysts argue in contrast that the pressing danger to the longer term stability of the economy is *delay* in making the commitment to breeder technology. Without long-run assurance of electricity at reasonably stable prices, economic growth will wither and the nation will have to depend even more on shrinking supplies of oil and gas and on coal. Oil dependence is a source of international vulnerability and rising cost, while burning coal imposes both short- and long-term environmental problems—even including climate effects of possibly catastrophic consequence. Consequently, a time may come when energy alternatives will be essential if society and the economy are to survive. And if breeder technology is not ready, an important potential source of supply will be lost.

While a breeder economy is not inevitable, it is certainly not unthinkable; in these circumstances the United States must decide what to do about LMFBR research, development, and demonstration. Without prejudging the matter, our purpose here is to sketch out considerations important to policy *if* it is decided that a breeder technology is to play an important role in energy supply early in the next century. Two factors appear to us of central importance: (1) the federal government likely will have to play a far more active role here than it does in other aspects of energy supply, and (2) long lead times must be compressed.

Status of the LMFBR industry.   There are four major components of an LMFBR industry—reactors, fuel fabrication facilities, plutonium reprocessing facilities, and waste disposal. Failure of any one of these parts to reach commercial scale would prevent operation of the whole system, yet none of the four has reached that state as yet. There do not appear to be any unsolvable technical problems, but uncertainty will not be reduced significantly until at least pilot-scale facilities have operated successfully. As experience with LWRs shows, operating costs will not be known with certainty even after prototype commercial scale facilities are in service, though better information will become available as development continues and as experience with breeders is gained abroad.

Each of these component parts of the industry requires construction and operation licenses. The licensing process is long and involved, and it cannot begin until design is complete. Criteria for regulatory approval are not yet settled and, even if they were, approvals could be stymied by intervenor action even if criteria were met. Further, whatever criteria are used, reliability will remain unproven until plants are designed, built, and operated.

Institutional issues regarding such matters as ownership patterns, co-location of different parts of the fuel cycle, regulatory jurisdiction, and financing are still unsettled. More important, perhaps, official government policy has been to go slow on breeder development. While reactor design efforts and basic research continue, the Clinch River breeder reactor project is in limbo. A planned program for reprocessing LWR spent fuel rods to obtain plutonium has been stopped in the United States.

According to an earlier schedule, information necessary for a decision on commercial deployment of the LMFBR was to be available in the mid-1980s, but it is unlikely that this target could be met by continuing the policy in force in early 1979. Though large sums have been expended on the breeder—LMFBR technology has received more research support than any other energy technology—significant deployment of a U.S.-developed breeder remains perhaps two decades away even if a positive decision is made soon and all goes well with the technology. In contrast, using a somewhat different design, the French Phénix reactor (250 MWe) started to operate in early 1974 and the Super Phénix (1,200 MWe) is scheduled for start-up in the early 1980s.

Financing an LMFBR industry. The planning process for a commercial LMFBR industry is complicated by the fact that each component technology demands major financial commitments at different times. No party is eager to make such commitments, however, unless there is reasonable certainty that all components will work and will be approved. So, again assuming a goal of early availability of a domestically produced LMFBR, how might the development program be financed?

Prior planning has assumed that the government will subsidize a progressively smaller proportion of costs as the LMFBR comes closer to commercial scale, with commercial plants being totally the responsibility of the private sector. There are three reasons for this policy. First, if commercial firms are involved from the start, they learn about the processes as they evolve and technology transfer problems are minimized. Second, if commercial firms are involved, commercial criteria can discipline research and development decisions. The result should be that the most commercially practical paths will be pursued, with processes being abandoned promptly if it becomes clear that they will not prove economic or that other ideas are better. Finally, subsidies are lessened because at least some of the costs of development are borne by investors and electricity consumers—so alternative energy sources are less handicapped than they might be otherwise.

The first two reasons are compelling. Those who are going to use the technology—the electric utilities, manufacturers, and architect-engineering firms—must be involved early and substantively if a commercially acceptable industry is to develop. But the last argument—that cost-sharing reduces government subsidies—becomes less tenable if, rather than accept financial responsibility, firms will not cooperate in the enterprise.

If the pattern of sharing LMFBR costs between the federal government and private industry is continued, commercial commitments may not be made when they are needed for speedy development. Administration opposition to the Clinch River breeder reactor, the moratorium on LWR reprocessing that left the Allied General-Nuclear Services Barnwell plant uncompleted, regulatory uncertainties engendered by the Three Mile Island accident, and the uncertain status of waste disposal have compounded the technical and economic uncertainties that existed before. Firms are less ready to invest now than they were only a few years ago. Moreover, since each firm realizes that its success depends on others who have similar reason for delay, there will be a tendency for no firm to act. An integrated process with components that must be produced simultaneously, but by independent firms, may never get started at all.

Consequently, deployment of domestic LMFBRs may be substantially delayed, however economic and safe this technology proves to be, unless the federal government accepts a very large share of the financial risk. The effective institutional arrangement would be one in which the private sector can have a large measure of managerial and operational control, along with responsibility to meet performance goals, but without as much financial risk as only a few years ago it seemed reasonable that it should assume.

Lead times in deploying the LMFBR. Deployment of enough LMFBRs to make a significant contribution to electricity supply will require successful completion of fuel fabrication, plutonium reprocessing, and waste disposal facilities. Assuming that development of each begins at the proper time and proceeds as planned, none of these constituent parts will lie directly on the critical time path. None is far off the critical path either, however, and without careful management any one of them could easily delay the LMFBR system.

The reactor itself is the most time-consuming part of building an LMFBR industry. Even after a near-commercial scale prototype is authorized and built, it takes time to operate it enough to gain experience and build the confidence (as well as know-how) needed for the first-generation commercial plants. Their construction period coincides with a build-up of manufacturing capacity to form the basis for the new industry. Finally comes construction of the large number of follow-on plants which can benefit from any knowledge discovered in building the first-generation machines. At each of these stages, however, there can be technical, economic, or regulatory-safety reasons for delay.

The U.S. experience with the LWR and the French experience with their LMFBR give some insight into the time it might take to bring a domestic LMFBR industry to fruition in this country. The first U.S. reactor, developed for military (submarine) use and modified to produce commercial electric power, began operation in 1957 after a decade of development effort. Follow-on plants were begun before the first reactor began to operate; they produced power in 1960.[8] The first true commercial plants were not operational until around 1970, and it was several years later that LWRs began to supply significant quantities of power. Thus, about fifteen years elapsed between the time a commitment to commercial nuclear power was made and the time commercial-scale operations began. The time lag from initial commitment to large-scale deployment was about twenty years. It took the French seventeen years from early research on the fast breeder reactor to operation of the Phénix, and it will take another eight to ten years before the commercial prototype Super Phénix is producing power. Commercial operation of a French LMFBR is not expected until 1987, and succeeding units may be available by the early 1990s. Both the early U.S. LWR programs and the French LMFBR have been blessed with government support, and there was little effective opposition to cause delay, apart from that required by technical considerations.

Lead times for some aspects of the LMFBR enterprise cannot easily be reduced. The next major stage in the United States is a prototype commercial demonstration plant to follow (or replace) Clinch River. It probably cannot be approved, designed, certified, constructed, and made operational in much less than fifteen years. If this plant is not begun until after smaller test facilities now under way have been proven, and if the first commercial plant is not built until the prototype proves successful, then the cumulative lead time between now and significant commercial deployment could amount to thirty-five years or so, even assuming a firm commitment to proceed. It would be the twenty-first century before we got a good insight into the economic attractiveness of the process, and it would take almost as long before its technical parameters were known.

While the lead time for specific reactor scale-ups may not be very compressible, lead times for the industry as a whole can be reduced. Overlapping development saves time, but with additional risk that some expenditures will turn out to be mostly wasted. In one type of overlap, demonstration, prototype, and first-generation commercial units would be pushed ahead in turn without waiting for full evaluation of the prior

---

[8] Despite the promise of other reactor designs, U.S. LWR technology came to dominate the world nuclear market. This story is interestingly told in Irvin C. Bupp and Jean-Claude Derian, *Light Water* (New York, Basic Books, 1978).

stage. Before large-scale commercial introduction, however, a careful evaluation would be made of experience with the completed plants. An alternative would be to proceed sequentially with the early stages of the development and demonstration process, but then to overlap construction of commercial plants with the last stages of the development process. The first acceleration path might involve a large probability that the commitment could prove premature, but the amount at risk would be relatively small. The second path would involve massive expenditures to construct reactors which then might require substantial modifications as more experience was gained. The risk exposure from the latter course might be magnitudes greater.

If we decide to push the domestic LMFBR far enough to find out whether the nation can count on it, it can be speeded up. Overlapping development and demonstration efforts appear to be preferable to the alternative strategy of sequential development, followed by large-scale commercial commitment to LMFBRs before the technology is mature. The relevant points are these:

1. We cannot be sure when (or if) LMFBRs will become economic.
2. We do not know how long it will take to develop the LMFBR, but the major technical risks are likely to be at the development and demonstration stages (which are also less costly).
3. We are limited by resources of all kinds in the number of technological avenues for the future we can explore fully at the same time. Alternatives to the LMFBR have very long lead times— almost certainly longer than the time it should take to deploy LMFBRs commercially once we reached a decision to do so. Consequently, it would be highly desirable to know whether the LMFBR will be acceptable well before we must decide to start large-scale deployment—in case a major part of the national effort has to be switched to an alternative.
4. If the LMFBR technology is rejected, it is likely to be because of unanticipated safety or environmental problems, or because it cannot compete economically with alternatives. The former problems would probably become apparent at least by the demonstration phase. The earlier they were discovered, the greater the opportunity would be to remedy the defect or to abandon LMFBR technology for a more benign alternative. If some danger is discovered so late that we are forced to choose between deploying LMFBRs anyway and accepting a substantial jump in energy costs (because

there is no time to substitute another technology), there would be enormous pressure to follow the first course. Thus, early development and demonstration actually offers greater opportunity to *abandon* the LMFBR if it should prove hazardous.

The overall conclusions we draw are that the long lead time for safe and economic deployment of domestically developed LMFBR reactors can be compressed somewhat by overlapping the development and demonstration stages, with federal government support being vital and special attention being required for the full nuclear fuel cycle—reprocessing, fuel fabrication, and waste disposal. Such an approach might risk economic waste at various stages, but it might also lessen the expected cost of the whole process, lower the net environmental risk, and permit maximum freedom of choice.

This discussion has proceeded thus far on the assumption that if the United States decides to move to breeders it will develop a breeder reactor domestically. As we noted in the section on expanding LWR acceptability, it might also be possible to purchase technologies developed abroad; the most likely prospect would be reactors of French design. Commercial-sized reactors should be proven by the late 1980s, a decade before domestic designs could be available. The U.S. nuclear industry might demur from such a policy for purely commercial reasons, but business motives assume less importance if the federal government is required to subsidize this program anyway. Cooperation with foreign suppliers would do relatively little to compress either our domestic approval process or the eventual time lag for deployment, but it would certainly speed the time when we know enough about the LMFBR to make a final decision whether we intend to use it or not. Further, international cooperation could reduce some of the economic risks that come from allowing our own development and demonstration stages to overlap, and, by adding financial support to the foreign enterprise, could speed development as well.

Decision process for the LMFBR. A major source of the opposition to LMFBR development and demonstration is the fear that proceeding with this technology will lock the nation and the world into a centralized energy system based on plutonium. If the LMFBR proves economic and safe, and if plutonium trade can be adequately safeguarded, that system probably *will* develop. The important policy matter is to assure that if the LMFBR option proves flawed, it will *not* be adopted.

The startup costs of an **LMFBR** industry are so vast, and the implications so great, that fear of "slipping" into a commitment can be discounted somewhat. Moreover, if (as we suggest) federal investment must dominate the early stages of this process, there will be more opportunities to rethink its wisdom than there would be if it were private from the first. On top of that, the decision to build and use LMFBRs commercially will have to be made by private utilities. Those utilities will not feel compelled to follow through on RD&D decisions that the government has made. Finally, since it is government money at risk and not that of politically powerful private groups, there may be less pressure on succeeding Congresses to subsidize a technology if it begins to indicate it will be uneconomic, or on regulators to approve a technology that threatens to be unsafe.

In short, the LMFBR will have to face a whole series of new decision tests even if development and demonstration are authorized to proceed. Nonetheless, to ease concerns and to lessen the danger of accepting a technology we really would wish to avoid, further attention should be paid to institutional means of making each new stage of the LMFBR development, demonstration, and commercialization process subject to reevaluation—in light of its progress, that of foreign options, and other energy supply and conservation alternatives.

19 Translating New Policies for Energy Sources into Action— Conservation, Synthetics, and Solar Energy

Putting Conservation to Work

To fit the major conservation initiatives discussed earlier into the context of policy implementation, let us summarize them at this point. As noted in chapter 5, the United States has significant potential for energy savings —judged by economic and technological criteria. While some opportunities are available at today's prices, many more conservation practices would come into play if prices rose modestly. The case studies in this book focused on improved residential heating practices, better automotive fuel economy, and the combined production of electricity and process steam in industry. Aside from improvements that can reasonably be foreseen for the near future, there are many other instances in which conservation prospects justify optimism—even considering only present-day technology. For a number of reasons, however, some technologically feasible and cost-effective conservation measures may not be adopted unless policy changes take place.

In certain cases, reductions in energy use beyond that indicated by private decisions have been advocated. Automotive fuel use is a case in point. The view is that although it is possible to obtain the essential transportation services produced by automobiles while using less fuel, manufacturers will continue to produce automobiles that use fuel inefficiently, and many consumers will persist in buying them, even at gasoline prices expected after decontrol, including the oil price increases of 1979. In developing a policy to enhance fuel efficiency, it was concluded in chapter 5 that fuel prices high enough to induce desired efficiency levels could have serious equity effects and, moreover, that adding a tax to achieve such price levels was not feasible politically. A more palatable policy has been to impose fuel-efficiency standards on automobile manufacturers, inducing them to seek more efficient designs. As it has worked out, manufacturers have met existing standards in part through improved designs but partly also by altering the relative prices of the cars they sell. The latter move encourages consumers to purchase more of the smaller cars in their product lines. The discussion in chapter 5 also points out that refinements in the process of mandating design changes could lead to further reductions in fuel use per passenger mile—and, at any rate, that the country has reached a point at which the actual use of automobiles is not likely to continue growing at its recent rate.

In the residential sector, there are some widely recognized barriers to economically rational conservation practices. For example, centrally supplied and unmetered space conditioning and electricity eliminate the incentive of apartment dwellers to conserve fuel. Even more serious is the pervasive "first-cost bias" that prompts consumers to minimize front-end capital costs. Consumers forego the energy-saving attributes of more expensive appliances or equipment even though higher (discounted) costs will be incurred for additional fuel and power than would otherwise be borne over the life of the equipment. Possible policies to counter this bias abound. Precise, easily understood information on the comparative virtues of the two courses of action could help to steer people toward the cost-minimizing choice. The climate for conservation could also be improved by imposing performance standards, for example, minimum insulation requirements for homes. (Extensive regulatory interventions, however, invite bureaucratic complexity and could stultify product innovation.) Lending policies could be made less inhibiting to conservation initiatives: an energy-efficient home or appliance might qualify for more lenient down payment terms without added risk to the lending institution. As we will see in the discussion of solar space and water heating below, the same idea could apply there.

Even if all these policies were adopted, however, the capital cost of energy conservation initiatives would continue to pose a serious problem. In economists' terminology, the discount rates of many consumers (especially in lower income groups) are very high. Equally important, capital markets tend to provide funds far more cheaply to large-scale energy production uses than to small-scale energy conservation functions. The tax system also works in such a way that business investments are favored over those of consumers. Thus, funds are denied to energy conservation initiatives in both the residential and commercial fields while capital is available to support supply efforts whose "costs per Btu" are higher than the price of saving equivalent amounts of energy. Institutional reform to remove this bias seems unlikely if not impractical. Perhaps the next best alternative would be to "lean against the wind" in supporting a multitude of efforts to induce residential and commercial conservation.

In industry, on the other hand, two sorts of problems surround the prospective adoption of energy-conserving practices. One type embraces legal and institutional problems. Cogeneration is a case in point. Joint production of electricity and process steam is virtually proven technologically, and it shows economic promise, but major impediments to its widespread use arise from: (1) questions about appropriate ownership structure (as among industrial enterprises, utilities, or independent parties); (2) the terms and availability of standby central station electricity; and (3) provisions governing the dispatch of excess power from an industrial installation into the grid of a publicly regulated utility. Sorting out these problems may be as formidable a task in stimulating growth of cogeneration as are the remaining problems—the technical ones. The latter include a need to adapt cogeneration systems to coal use and a need to improve the environmental characteristics of smaller scale, on-site cogeneration facilities compared with conventional central power stations.

The second type of problem is the fact that the manner in which corporations normally treat conservation investments exerts a drag on conservation efforts. Investments in energy-conserving equipment and processes must, like other investments, meet certain specified criteria of return-on-investment. But conservation typically is cast into a "discretionary" category, with a much higher return-on-investment requirement than is normally assigned to production investment projects.[1] Under any circumstances, however, a comparison that pits the energy-supply calculus of, say, an electric utility against an attractive energy-conserving system for a manufacturer works to the latter's disadvantage. That is because a public utility can normally prescribe a much lower return on investment than that which must be targeted by a manufacturer with inherently greater risk. To the extent that an overriding national perspective dictates

[1] See G. N. Hatsopoulos, E. P. Gyftopoulos, R. W. Sant, and T. F. Widmer, "Capital Investment to Save Energy," *Harvard Business Review* (March–April 1978) pp. 111–112.

that decisions to expand supply should be no more favored than decisions to reduce demand, it may be in order to develop policies to eliminate cost discrimination against conservation. For instance, an investment tax credit or some corresponding device can be justified for this purpose.

Finally, the role of federal, state, and local governments as energy consumers themselves could be exploited to encourage energy conservation. For example, their acquisition and operation of buildings, motor vehicle fleets, and diverse equipment could emphasize energy conservation, and funds could be budgeted to use these installations in demonstrating to the public that conservation can be cost effective. Government could be a training ground as well as an efficient consumer itself.

Synthetic Liquids and Gases from Coal or Oil Shale

Synthetic petroleum-type liquid fuels and pipeline-quality high-Btu gases from coal or oil shale are not now competitive with natural fuels, even if prices of the latter fully covered all costs. They may become economic, however, with the long-term increase in the price of fuels, and with further development of the technologies involved.

Long-term policy decisions require knowledge about the prospective cost and feasibility of obtaining these synthetic fuels and about the industrial infrastructure they require. If these fuels can be produced in substantial quantities at costs not far above the near-term prices of nature-made fuel (and without serious harm to the environment), the nation could have far more lead time in shifting its energy infrastructure away from the present high degree of reliance on liquid and gaseous fuels. On the other hand, if prospects for synthetic liquids and gases prove chimerical, very early action would be necessary to avoid change at a disruptive rate.

Additionally, the danger of economic disruption from sudden and permanent reduction in our politically uncertain supplies of imported oil and gas could be lessened if lead times in bringing synthetics into production were reduced. A program which yielded an on-the-shelf technology, the rudiments of an industrial base, and a cadre of trained operatives could provide a degree of insurance against the worst effects of a future world energy supply catastrophe. Finally, the prospective availability of synthetic fuel could temper the rate of increase in world oil prices by lowering the prospective price of oil and thus reduce the value of oil in the ground compared with alternative investments.[2] Oil producers would be forced to realize that their oil would not increase in value indefinitely and that higher production now might be in their individual best interest. This realization could put strains on the cohesion of the producer cartel and lead to pricing restraint. This strategy is not without risks: (1) Oil producers may react by adopting an effective joint production limitation program and raise prices even further to take advantage of the inelastic demand for oil until (and even after) synthetic plants come on-stream. (2) Even now price demands may be moderated by the threat that, if oil prices rise too rapidly, synthetic fuels will be produced. Once it is clear that plants will be built in any case, this reason for price restraint is removed. (3) And finally the cost of fuel from synthetic plants may actually prove to be higher than oil producers are now estimating in forming their pricing decisions, causing them to increase their price demands. Whatever these effects, a synthetic fuels program could contribute to long-run energy supplies and hence could help place a limit on the cost of liquid and gaseous fuels. It is important to know with greater certainty what that limit will be, whatever the intermediate-run effect on oil prices. In addition, once a synthetic fuels industry is in operation, it could limit the threat posed by an oil supply cutoff, and, as discussed in chapter 16, relieve U.S. foreign policy of an unwanted constraint and enhance our prestige and authority abroad.

For reasons suggested in chapter 17, timely information on the costs and effects of producing synthetic liquids and gases is unlikely to be obtained by relying solely on the private sector. If earlier information is desired, government support will be needed. And government action can also speed the process of bringing the industry into being. Although liquids and gases may come from many nonconventional sources, it is in coal- and shale-based processes that most of the problems come together. For that reason we will concentrate on investigating the policy support required in connection with those processes.[3]

[2] For a fuller discussion of this point see Douglas R. Bohi and Milton Russell, *U.S. Energy Policy: Alternatives for Security* (Baltimore, Johns Hopkins University Press for Resources for the Future, 1975) pp. 38–45.

[3] The discussion that follows relies on the work reported earlier in this volume and elsewhere, and was influenced by the four-volume *Recommendations for a Synthetic Fuels Commercialization Program,* prepared by the Synfuels Interagency Task Force as a report to the President's Energy Resources Council, November 1975. This discussion is set in a noncrisis policy context in which the synthetic fuels program is viewed as a means to lessen future risks and costs of fuel supply. An emergency context, for example a condition in which world oil exports were thought to be *permanently* reduced by one-third or one-half, would lead to a much different policy—one not addressed here.

Impediments to Commercial Production

Commercial synthetic liquid and gaseous fuels face several production impediments. First, it is not yet certain that some of the technologies will work at commercial scale, and even if they can be made to work, technological uncertainty leads to uncertainty about costs. Second, the expected costs of the product are estimated to be higher than the expected prices of nature-made fuels at the time such plants would go into production. Third, for the shale technology, the required inputs of oil shale and water may not be available—the former because of leasing uncertainties and the latter because most of the water in the shale regions is subject to prior appropriation.

Social policies may also hinder investment in synthetic fuel. The direct environmental insults produced by the plants, even with maximum cleanup, may violate existing or future pollution control requirements. Some plants may not be allowed to operate at all. Even if environmental quality standards ultimately can be met, regulatory approvals may be delayed. Further, the negative social impacts of large installations in sparsely populated regions (the "boomtown" effect) may provoke local opposition. Such opposition may lead to delay, or to siting plants in less economic or less environmentally satisfactory locations. Finally, these installations may be so large that few firms would be of sufficient size to accept the risk of building them. Given the hostile political attitude toward horizontal integration in the energy industries—and the possibly shaky antitrust position of joint ventures—many firms that fit the size requirements might be hesitant to enter the industry.

Beyond these specific problems lies a generic issue highlighted in chapter 17: A major product of first-generation synthetic fuel plants is information about the relationship of such a facility with its economic, physical, and sociopolitical surroundings, but this information is costly to acquire. A plant must be built and operated (or fail to operate) in order to secure it. Once this information is developed, however, most of it is freely available to all comers. Thus, no firm wants to go first. Everyone wants to follow, not to lead.

Many of these problems reinforce each other. If the expected cost of synthetic fuels were far enough below the price of nature-made alternatives, plants might be built despite technological and other uncertainties. Alternatively, if environmental effects were known to be benign and regulatory delays minimal, it might take a smaller potential profit margin to induce entrepreneurs to move forward. Consequently, each of these impediments need not be addressed by a particular policy. An instrument that promises to reduce financial uncertainty and increase expected return could be broadly effective by itself.

Required Financial Support

The financial support package needed for synthetic liquid facilities differs somewhat from that required by projects designed to supply high-Btu gas to natural gas pipelines. The variation arises from the different character of price regulation faced by the two industries. As regulated public utilities, the pipeline transportation and local distribution phases of the gas industry will be subject to cost-of-service regulation for the foreseeable future. This means that the cost of expensive supplies of synthetic gas would generally be paid for by consumers rather than by stockholders. The situation is very different for liquid fuels, where the price control and entitlements system in place in 1979 was not very effective in shifting risk to consumers and away from investors. Furthermore, the framework of our entire policy discussion here assumes that price controls on fuel would be ended.

Synthetic pipeline-quality gas. In its sales to gas distributing utilities, a gas pipeline system is allowed to recover the initial cost of the gas it has purchased or produced and also the costs of handling and transportation. Utilities in turn are allowed to recover those costs fully in the rates they charge final users. Since the cost of an increment to the gas supply from a synthetic gas plant would be averaged-in with the cost of all gas delivered, it would have a proportionately small effect on the gas rates charged final consumers. Thus, if an entrepreneur were authorized to build a plant under an "all events tariff,"[4] he could be (almost) sure that the cost of the plant would be recovered even if the cost of the gas it produces were above that of other gas on the market. His risk would be limited to the possibility that a market might not exist for his total gas supply at the higher average price induced by this high-cost addition.

---

[4] As implied, the plant is treated in this case like an integral part of the regulated firm. Its capital cost goes into the rate base (to earn the allowed rate of return), and its operating costs are part of the total cost of service. If separate corporate entities are involved, this treatment still permits the utility purchaser of the gas to include within its cost of service the full gas purchase expense and to pass it along to customers. Thus, the regulated firm is free to contract with its supplier to pay the full cost of the gas, whatever that might be.

Although an all events tariff was a substantial financial incentive at an earlier stage of the gas industry, it might be insufficient to induce firms to build the first few synthetic gas plants, plants that would prove out technology and provide other information important to making long-term energy decisions.[5] Two other elements might be required if the decision is made that they should be built.

The first of these policy supports is a nonrecourse loan guarantee, which would reduce exposure to the risk that the synthetic gas facility might never come on line as planned. If some factor caused a project to be abandoned, the cost of the project might drive the average cost of the other gas sold by the firm beyond a level that could be supported by the market. Thus, even an all events tariff might not induce firms to build synthetic gas plants;[6] but they might be willing to do so if the federal government guaranteed repayment of some portion of the loans taken out to build such plants. To be effective, this guarantee should be made without recourse to the other assets of the firm.

Guaranteeing a portion of the debt would reduce the cost of capital to the synthetic gas producer (and hence reduce the private cost of the gas produced).[7] The proportion of the debt capital to be guaranteed could

[5] Regulation of the field price of natural gas sold for resale in interstate commerce left gas underpriced relative to alternatives and created a shortage that existed from the late 1960s through 1978. Under those circumstances, firms would have been able to pass higher incremental gas costs forward without fear of lost markets; but this situation may not continue because of shrinking markets and narrowing margins between the average cost of gas and the cost of other fuels. The first reason for the shrinkage is that industrial consumers have reacted to the uncertainty of future gas supply by shifting to other fuels. Second, legislation now requires industrial gas consumers alone to bear most of the cost of incremental gas supplies, and fuel demand is price responsive in the industrial market. Finally, the electric utility market for gas is declining owing to competition with other fuels and to legislation. For example, new federal laws forbid new boiler use of gas, with only limited exceptions. The price of gas in the field markets has been rising rapidly and will continue to rise under legislation passed in 1978. Such increases reduce the gap between the cost of nature-made and synthetic gas, but they also reduce a gas firm's ability to spread the higher costs of incremental supplies over its total gas supply and still continue to find markets.

[6] Moreover, the consumers who had to pay the resulting tariffs would be bearing costs that might more equitably be ascribed to energy consumers as a whole. Thus a guarantee against the risks of failure might be appropriate on equity as well as expediency grounds.

[7] It is important to note that the total (private and public) cost of the gas is not changed by these varying financial arrangements. That cost depends on the present expected value of the resources absorbed in the project, and it does not depend on who bears the risk of failure. Similarly, of course, the proportion of debt or equity capital used does not affect the total cost of gas. For the private sector, the use of debt capital results in a tax deduction of interest payments, but payments to equity owners are not treated similarly. Use of debt rather than equity thus transfers some of the cost to taxpayers as a whole (and away from gas consumers), but it does not

be subject to competitive bid; and an upper limit (say, 75 percent) could be determined so that firms and their customers would still have a direct incentive in the successful operation of the plant.

The amount of planned capacity that would be supported in this manner could be limited to the quantity required to develop the economic and technical information needed for national policy planning purposes. It would also be desirable to structure the availability of loan guarantees by broad technology types, by locations, or by sources of hydrocarbons. This would ensure that a maximum amount of information was obtained.

In case a guaranteed loan project of this type were abandoned, the government could participate proportionately with noncovered lenders in proceeds from disposing of the facility. A new or reorganized firm might proceed to finish the synthetic gas plant—which might be made to pay if the acquisition price were low enough.

If public financial support beyond loan guarantees were required to get synthetic gas plants built in a timely manner, construction subsidies would be the preferred instrument. A construction subsidy (determined as a fixed amount per unit of gas production capacity) reduces the private cost of the capital facility, limits the risk exposure of the firm, and increases access to capital. However, it does not substantially lessen the incentive to build the facility expeditiously and economically, and to operate it efficiently. It spreads some of the cost of the plants to taxpayers as a whole rather than to just the consumers served by it.

A construction subsidy differs from the loan guarantee because it increases the chance of financial success rather than reducing the cost of failure. A subsidy program represents a certain cost to government rather that a contingent cost; and it offers a direct benefit to the firm (and its customers) whether things go right or wrong.

Synthetic liquid fuels. Financial incentives for synthetic liquids must be somewhat different from those for pipeline quality gas because of the different institutional arrangements under which the respective fuels may be sold. The output of a synthetic liquids plant must be sold at a price which is no higher than that commanded by nature-made fuels with the same characteristics. Purchasers of these fuels are not under the cost-plus regulation offered by the public utility approach. There is no captive market, and there is no reason for users of liquid fuel to average-in higher

---

change the quantity of resources used up in producing synthetic gas. As a matter of social decision making, it is the total cost of synthetic gas—not the private costs alone—that should be compared with the total cost of alternatives.

cost fuel from one source when that means that the cost of goods sold would be higher than those of competitors.

It is possible, of course, to use the power of government to force such a result. Each refiner could be required to purchase a given proportion of feedstock from synthetic fuel plants (with that proportion based on synthetic fuel capacity as compared with total feedstock input). If those obligations were subject to trade, a market in synthetic fuel use requirements would develop; and refiners who could use such fuel most inexpensively would be paid by others in the industry to do so.[8] Synthetic fuel producers would then have a market for their output, and they would be paid whatever price was necessary to induce them to produce it. The subsidy would be paid proportionately by all liquid fuels consumers.

Despite its potential effectiveness, this instrument may be fatally flawed by its ancillary effects and because it does not provide an adequate incentive for firms to minimize their costs. The ancillary effects would be to increase still more the potential for distortions in the energy industries caused by government intervention. The arbitrary allocation of benefits to some firms (by deciding which firms would be allowed to build which plants) is contrary to good government practice. Further, unless (and really, even if) government scrutinized costs intensively and monitored performance closely, there would be no way to ensure that fuels were produced efficiently. Finally, this instrument might make it more difficult to remove price controls; it would give them an excuse for permanency.

A preferable instrument is available in the purchase guarantee. Because the costs of synthetic fuels are expected to be above world market prices for some time to come, the purchase guarantee would solicit bids for fuels specified by generic technology, region, and feedstock. Under the program the government would accept delivery (at the bid price, but for resale at market prices) of fuel meeting agreed-upon specifications; and the firm would also be free to sell that fuel on the open market if the price were higher. The government would be obligated for the difference

---

[8] Prototypes for this arrangement are found in the Mandatory Oil Import Program (which set import quotas for then-cheaper imported oil between 1959 and 1973) and in the entitlements program from 1974 onward (which allocated among refiners the right to purchase cheaper domestic oil). The complexities of these programs, and other problems that have arisen with them, do not commend their imitation in the case of facilities producing synthetic liquids (see Douglas R. Bohi and Milton Russell, *Limiting Oil Imports*, Baltimore, Johns Hopkins University Press for Resources for the Future). However, until price controls on petroleum are removed completely, it would be desirable to provide synthetic liquids facilities with entitlement treatment that would give their products the world price of oil, as proposed by the Carter administration.

between the guarantee price and the world price, and this obligation would last for the life of the plant. The firm could lose on its investment if it should find that its bid on the price guarantee was too low; but it would receive protected profits if its cost stayed below the guarantee price. These two factors should induce fuel producers to bid realistically and to produce efficiently.

As in the case of synthetic gas, it may be necessary or desirable to provide loan guarantees for synthetic liquids plants. Loan guarantees could widen the range of firms which could enter the industry by making project financing more feasible and by lowering the size of the risk any one firm would undertake. They would also lower the cost of capital to the firm and hence reduce the price required before the project was profitable. By broadening the list of prospective entrants into the industry, a loan guarantee program could also lessen the concern that the program would tend to concentrate energy production in the hands of a few firms. Such guarantees would be particularly critical for the first series of plants built, with which the risk of noncompletion or of unforeseen complications is greatest. For later-generation plants, when technical and regulatory uncertainty is less, the loan guarantee program would be far less important.

Other Policy Support

We have identified four impediments to synthetic liquid and gas production that are only indirectly susceptible to remedy through financial instruments such as those suggested above. The problems concern resource availability, uncertainty about future environmental standards, failure to gain regulatory approvals even when standards are met, and failures to gain siting approval because of potential boomtown problems.

Availability of resources.   The federal government owns vast portions of the oil shale resource base and can make them available to prospective producers of synthetic liquids.[9] Chapter 18 discussed some of the diffi-

_____

[9] Each portion of the reserve may have a different value because of location, quality of the ore body, and so forth. Consequently, a bidding mechanism is required to allocate the different deposits among prospective exploiters, to capture the differential value for the taxpayers, and to ensure that different costs of shale oil from different firms do not simply represent different levels of indirect input subsidy from taxpayers. One complication is that the amount each firm bids depends on its expectation of receiving a subsidy for liquids production; but the subsidy it requires will reflect in part the cost of the shale input to its plant. Further, speculative holding of shale in anticipation of future oil price increases may lead to bids which do not

culties in enhancing coal production, but in the long run coal supplies should be no problem. As for other resources required—such as trained labor, equipment, and transportation facilities—no problems should arise from a systematic and orderly buildup of a synthetics program. By the time large commitments to synthetic fuel production become economic, industries will have had sufficient lead time to develop or expand such resources. A crash program to expand synthetic fuels rapidly, on the other hand, could face a number of restraints. Depending on its scale, it could exhaust available supplies of managerial skills, equipment production capacity, and labor skills, and overburden transportation. If priority were given to such a program it could disrupt output elsewhere in the economy with possibly serious results in some sectors, including energy production. Numerous bottlenecks could develop, all of which could be overcome, but only after delaying the project. Although some relief from such problems could be gained by importing equipment and skills from abroad, an undertaking of a magnitude designed to quickly replace a substantial portion of imported oil supplies would wrench the economy and inevitably be slower to bring to completion than would a more modest effort. Various measures could enhance availability of needed resources and could speed the projects to completion; willingness to adopt and pay for them would depend on the urgency with which the program was viewed.

Water availability may prove a difficult constraint to overcome. Water rights are already largely apportioned in the arid West, and there are growing regulatory restraints on diversions of water to industrial use even where these rights can be purchased. Early stages of the synthetic fuel industry in water-short regions are unlikely to strain regional availability, however, and firms seeking to build plants will be able to find adequate water supplies by choosing their locations carefully, so long as other constraints, such as the boomtown problem, do not restrict access to relatively water-rich sites.[10]

---

reflect differential value in efficiency but differences in expectations about the future value of the resource itself. Although this outcome may not be against the public interest in principle, it does give rise to an unpleasant image of private firms converting the public domain to private use. While these problems are very difficult to overcome, large sums are not involved. Thus, limiting the amount of land put up for lease (but making it larger than the amount required for the number of plants contemplated) and enforcing "due diligence" requirements on successful bidders may be sufficient to obtain an acceptable outcome.

[10] A larger program might require some interregional transfers to bring the water together with other inputs. Any sizable increase in water use by the energy industries will present institutional difficulties that will require time and effort to overcome.

Uncertainty about environmental regulation. Uncertainty about future environmental protection requirements is a serious impediment to private investment in synthetic fuel plants. Although especially applicable to shale oil facilities, difficulties may also be encountered with coal-based plants, even though conversion to gas or liquids may be the cleanest way to use coal. An effective policy for dealing with regulatory uncertainty is a so-called "hold harmless" commitment from the federal government. A hold harmless guarantee would state that for authorized plants, the cost of upgrading environmental protection devices required by a change in regulations would be covered (up to, say, 80 percent) by the federal government. In the event that the technology could not be made environmentally acceptable, the federal government would pledge to buy out the same proportion of the private firm's investment. Such a program would largely remove regulatory uncertainty as an obstacle to plant construction.

Facilitating environmental approvals. Another discouraging problem for potential synthetic fuel producers is the difficulty in getting timely environmental approvals and in avoiding obstruction of operations even when formal requirements are met. The problem of delay is well recognized; in part it flows from uncertainties as to the nature of the hazards and of the means to ameliorate them, but to some degree it is a product of the adversary system. Parties feel strongly about environmental issues, and procedural delays can be used as a tactic to forestall projects which might not be denied approval ultimately. There is understandable reluctance to override local concerns or to allow those agencies whose mission it is to protect the environment to be overruled in the interest of more rapid synthetic fuel production. No "quick fix" by statute or promulgation appears feasible, at least in the absence of a consensus that a national emergency exists. Nevertheless, the problem of delay could perhaps be ameliorated by promoting a climate for decision making that is less susceptible to emotional appeals, and by developing institutions that are less prone to paralysis through procedural attack.

Coping with siting problems. A major barrier to new synthetic fuel installations is fear of the boomtown problem. Boomtowns are problems when the costs they impose are not compensated and when their effects get out of hand because they are not treated in time.

The socioeconomic costs of synthetic fuel plants are concentrated at their locations. If taxing jurisdictions do not coincide with impact sites, offsetting benefits are not available to the parties affected and they may oppose synthetic fuel plants. This situation is not unique to energy developments, but the question has special force here because synthetic fuel plants are usually large in relation to the communities near which they might be located.

One solution is an equitable sharing of tax revenues and impact burdens. Often this requires either an enlargement of the taxing and spending jurisdiction or else creation of an equitable formula by which the revenues can be shared. The latter course appears more practical, and indeed moves are underway in several states to implement it. For example, Montana and Wyoming have earmarked almost 20 percent of their coal severance tax revenues to assist local communities in handling energy-related problems.

A more serious problem arises from the failure of revenue flows to accrue in time to make the early outlays necessary to meet expanded local responsibilities. Tax receipts lag behind the building of a new installation, while social capital expenditures must precede it if streets, schools, hospitals, and sewerage and water systems are to be adequate for the influx of construction and operating personnel. An inadequate tax base may leave localities unable to provide adequate fire, police, and social services as soon as needs arise. As a result, the quality of life deteriorates for previous citizens and new citizens find services inadequate. This specter joins physical degradation of the natural environment to produce the hostility to energy facilities that has been prevalent in the West. Except for those citizens who stand to benefit directly (landowners, the unemployed, and a few merchants), the prospects from development are mostly bad.

It is possible to lessen local problems by bridging the gap between prospective revenues and needed current expenditures. One effective instrument for accomplishing this might be a federal guarantee of the stream of property tax receipts from the energy facility. With such a guarantee, the local government could enter the capital market to borrow the money required to prepare for the coming population increase. The existence of the guarantee would assure lenders of repayment. It would also relieve the fears of the local community that it might be burdened by an infrastructure which it did not need and could not afford. By freeing local decision makers of the financial uncertainties that bedevil advanced planning, this program might also lessen the broader local opposition to installations. In that way, it might open for use preferable sites that otherwise would have been foreclosed.

Implementing Synthetics Programs

While research and development efforts have been proceeding (and some firms have announced projects on their own), the support necessary to bring to completion a full-scale liquid or gas project has not been forthcoming. Thus, efforts to obtain information on commercial-scale production of synthetic liquids and gases have not yet been successful. The country is even further from a program to produce significant quantities of fuel. The Synthetic Fuels Commercialization Program introduced by the Ford Administration was stymied in Congress, and the Energy Independence Authority (an entity proposed later which would have subsumed the former's responsibilities) similarly was rejected.

A number of factors conspired against the success of those initiatives. Their cost appeared excessive, their environmental impacts were not certain, the federal role seemed overwhelming, and even the states and localities in which they would be placed were unenthusiastic because of uncertainty about whether attendant socioeconomic problems could be managed. Most serious, perhaps, was the charge that these programs would enrich selected firms at the expense of taxpayers as a whole. The approaches suggested thus far in this chapter are responsive to some of these issues. The arrangement of incentives is designed to widen the field of firms which could compete and to make sure that government costs are minimized and that firms are not unjustifiably enriched.

The major issue still standing in the way of a synthetic fuels program is unwillingness to pay for it. To decision makers and the public, the benefits of the program have not appeared substantial enough to overcome its costs. Indeed, the output of such plants will likely cost more than nature-made fuels for some time to come, but there are also the less tangible benefits from such a program discussed above.

Viewed as a source of information and insurance rather than of fuel, a synthetics program could be promoted for its contribution to decision making. It could be very worthwhile if it prevented the premature abandonment of this country's huge natural gas distribution system, made possible an orderly (rather than disruptive) reduction in reliance on liquid fuels for transportation, or lessened the strain of a major energy supply disruption. An information and insurance focus would serve to limit the potential costs of the program. These purposes could largely be fulfilled with one-of-a-kind installations; all of them need not even be made to work. There need be no open-ended commitment to produce as much fuel as possible. The combination of recognizable direct benefits and prospective costs that are limited rather than open-ended might overcome the understandable reluctance of taxpayers to underwrite a technology that, on narrow economic terms, promises to be a drain on the nation's resources.

Increased Use of Solar Energy for Space and Water Heating

Increased use of solar energy enjoys much popular and political support as an option for meeting energy demands. From the wide array of potential enhanced applications of solar energy we have chosen to concentrate here on residential space and water heating. These technologies have attracted public enthusiasm and have potential for economic application.

Let us consider two possible levels of effort for a policy to enhance their use. The first would try to remove barriers which now handicap solar use by making it even less attractive than underlying economic realities warrant. The second would encourage solar use beyond the level that an efficient market would yield.

In the following discussion, we first identify the major institutional barriers to solar use and suggest ways to remove them. Next we investigate the economic handicaps under which solar space and water heating must compete owing to the underpricing of other fuels. Those handicaps may be more difficult to remove. Finally, we consider actions to promote solar uses which at present appear uneconomic. Such actions might be used to offset the underpricing of alternative energy sources if pricing reform is not achieved. Alternately, they could be a means of implementing environmental "premiums" for solar energy, as discussed in chapter 11.

Removing Institutional Barriers to Solar Use

Institutional barriers to increased use of solar energy clearly include: (1) the absence of general legal protection for solar incidence (sun rights); (2) lending policies that directly or indirectly discriminate against use of solar technologies; and (3) utility policies that limit availability of back-up service or make it excessively expensive. Other institutional barriers that are sometimes cited include inflexible and inappropriate building codes, zoning requirements, and restrictive labor practices; but our conclusion is that those problems are either less serious or are on their way to resolution.

Few jurisdictions provide legal protection against having solar collectors shaded by structures or vegetation on adjacent property. The issue is important, because access to the sun may conflict with the free enjoyment of space owned by neighbors. No common law doctrine protects a user of solar devices from shadows. Interference may actually be rare (because prospective use of adjacent property will be reasonably well known before solar equipment is installed), but the risk may retard installations by making potential users and lenders more cautious than necessary.

Rights to sunshine may be secured through private transactions in the purchase of easements, through public action that involves zoning or similar existing devices, or through specific legislation. Solar applications are affected by local conditions, so regulations promoting them should reflect local needs. Consequently, detailed federal legislation on this issue may be counterproductive, especially since most matters pertaining to real property lie under state or local aegis. Federal encouragement of state and local action, however, may be useful in overcoming inertia. Local efforts could be induced by predicating the location of federal facilities on the existence of solar access laws, by limiting availability of federal mortgage guarantees to jurisdictions that have such provisions in force, or by other similar indirect means.

Another barrier to solar space and water heating is posed by mortgage lending policies and practices. Several types of problems exist. Because of uncertainties about the resale value of solar-heated homes, lenders have tended to limit the size of loans to the cost of the home without the solar device—with the effect that higher down payments are required from those who want solar homes. Also, the rules of thumb used to determine the ability of borrowers to service loans are based on income levels; but these formulas have often not taken into account the lower prospective fuel bills in residences utilizing solar equipment or passive solar design. A homeowner who has lower fuel bills to contend with is better equipped to meet mortgage payments. Taken together, current lending policies make solar homes less easy to afford, and thus less attractive to buy than are conventional homes.

The federal government has powerful instruments to rectify this discrimination against solar space and water heating. First, it could explicitly authorize the inclusion of solar equipment in all home financing programs.

Second, it could relax restrictions on lending institutions for loans on properties that include solar equipment and even provide special incentives to lenders in the form of priority federal servicing for solar-associated loans. Third, it could promulgate standard procedures for evaluating loans and loan applicants to ensure that lenders take account of the energy savings from solar installations in assessing loan eligibility. Fourth, it could flatly prohibit discrimination against solar-equipped properties, although this provision could lead to serious enforcement problems. And finally, the government could subsidize loans for purchasers of solar equipment to be used in retrofitting existing structures or in new construction. As lenders learned to assess properly the impact of solar equipment on housing and commercial investments, such special federal programs would probably become unnecessary. But they would hasten the learning process and remove some distortions that now favor installation of conventional space and water heating.

Solar installations are seldom designed to supply all of the heat energy required by a home or commercial establishment. The intermittent nature of sunlight and the variation in energy requirements pose technically formidable problems of storage; and the capital investment necessary to meet peak demands might be prohibitively large anyway. Hence back-up service is required, and it can usually be provided most efficiently by conventional electric and gas utility service. The economic attractiveness of a solar system depends in part on the charge for this service.

The principle for proper ratemaking is that each utility customer should pay the marginal cost of service to him. Applying this principle to back-up service, however, is exceedingly difficult. It is not even clear whether the charge should be more or less than that for a residence with the same energy requirements but without a solar device. No rule of thumb is possible, because each location, type of customer, and utility system may differ in ways that change the marginal cost of back-up service. Moreover, if solar space and water heating becomes important, it may shift peaks and alter daily and annual load factors; and those changes in themselves would affect the marginal cost of back-up services. Solar space and water heating will be hindered, however, until such cost uncertainties are reduced. The Public Utility Regulatory Policies Act of 1978 encouraged state regulatory authorities to consider revising rate structure along marginal-cost pricing lines. Expediting these efforts could help to remove an important barrier to additional use of the sun; and, at the very least, proper rate reform should improve the efficiency with which energy and other resources are used.

Removing Preferences to Other Energy Sources

Perhaps the most important barrier to increased installation of solar space and water heating has been the preference given alternative sources of energy by underpricing them. Government regulation has depressed the price of natural gas and, since 1973 of petroleum at the wellhead. It has allowed rate-making standards that price gas and electric utility services below marginal cost. Other government policies supply subsidized capital to some utility systems (the Tennessee Valley Authority, the Rural Electrification Administration, and the various power authorities) and give special tax relief to others. Non-solar energy has also benefited from numerous other government actions, ranging from R&D directed toward nuclear power to the subsidy of barge transportation of coal and the furnishing of geological knowledge to the oil and gas exploration industry. Finally, as noted earlier, reliance on conventional energy sources imposes uncompensated external costs involving the environment, health and safety, and leads to potential economic disruption if the supply of imported petroleum and natural gas is interrupted. These costs are not reflected in the costs consumers bear as part of their direct energy bill, and this represents still another subsidy to conventional energy use.

Putting an end to the underpricing of conventional energy sources has been a recurrent theme in this study (specifically in chapter 17) and in most other discussions of energy policy, but results have been few. If the economic barriers to solar energy from such underpricing are to be removed, it may be necessary to introduce "balancing distortions." Implicit subsidies to conventional energy could be offset in many ways; and some of them will be discussed in the next section when we take up the matter of federal actions to "force" solar use beyond the level that would be achieved through private market incentives. However, removing barriers to solar use directly (rather than through price reform) would distort consumer choices between energy use and conservation and probably lead to more energy being used. In the long run it would lead to lower levels of national output.

"Forcing" Solar: The Federal Role

Solar energy is blessed with a cadre of enthusiasts who will stimulate the commercialization of this technology, but barriers to widespread use of solar space and water heating remain large and introduction of these

technologies may prove slow for some time to come. The economics of
solar energy are not particularly attractive, and no "quick fix" for the
institutional barriers—or removal of the subsidies to alternatives—
appears possible.

However, if national policy so dictates, a number of federal actions
could hasten growth in solar use. While the ultimate objective of all such
actions would be to reduce the relative cost of solar energy (as perceived
by the consumer), it is useful to divide policy instruments into those
which would reduce the actual costs of solar power and those which would
simply transfer part of its costs onto taxpayers and other citizens.

Instruments to reduce costs.   A major problem in massive solar penetration of the space- and water-heating market is uncertainty about the
prospective performance of solar devices. Performance standards are
badly understood if they exist at all; procedures for certifying equipment
are nonexistent or untrustworthy; and installation is of uncertain quality.
Consumers cannot be sure that the equipment is installed properly, will
work as advertised, or last as long as promised. The small firms that dominate the field are typically undercapitalized, and some may be unwilling
or unable to stand behind the systems they sell.

Programs to train building inspectors and others (architects, contrac-
tors, and the like) in the requirements of solar equipment installation and
in elements of the materials and designs involved could make an important contribution to increased use. They would give consumers added
assurance that building codes and other standards would be applied
correctly. Government-backed warranty programs, of course, would reduce uncertainty even further and thus promote consumer acceptance of
a product that might otherwise remain unused even though its economic
desirability had been demonstrated.

In reducing consumer costs, perhaps the most critical step of this type
would be the development, promulgation, and enforcement of standards
by which performance criteria could be judged. Although a danger of
misuse exists, it should be possible to develop and implement such procedures in a way that does not discourage novel and possibly superior
approaches to use of the sun. Findings would need to be adjusted for local
conditions, but the relative standings among different systems would be
important information for consumers. The model of EPA automobile
gasoline mileage testing is appropriate.

A side effect of creating uniform, measurable performance standards
could be to lower the costs of producing solar equipment. Firms could

design equipment to meet the market they wished to serve, knowing that competitors would face exactly the same performance tests. When coupled with a large-scale demonstration program, production facilities for standardized designs could be optimized and costs lowered. This process normally occurs in the later stages of product development, but perhaps the federal government could hasten the process for the solar industry.

A large-scale federal demonstration program would give assurance to manufacturers and installers that a market existed, it would allow for cost-reducing mass production, and it would serve to increase consumer confidence at the same time. Small federal buildings—homes on military bases, U.S. Department of Agriculture offices in rural communities, Federal Aviation Administration installations—could have solar equipment mounted by local purveyors. Increasing the size of the market would allow solar firms to expand to more nearly optimal size. Such a program would provide widespread test sites on which standards could be monitored, and it would also offer information and an example to local citizens. It could serve as a training ground for the enlarged cadres of building trades professionals required eventually for a major commitment to solar energy. Short courses and information programs aimed at practitioners could be conducted as an integral part of the construction and operation of such demonstration projects.

The demonstration program could also serve as a laboratory for further improvements in solar technology and performance. Research and development activities could be funded to improve the products as well as to find better techniques for integrating them into new and existing structures. Performance data collected could be applied to improving design and to guiding the formulation of incentives for broader private use of the same technologies. Finally, actual experience in living with and maintaining these installations could be digested into a form that prospective purchasers would find useful. Some processes are common to most of the solar water and space heating technologies, so the experience gained in the demonstration program could lessen costs for every potential purveyor of solar equipment and aid all in finding markets for their products.

Transferring solar costs to taxpayers. Solar use could also be increased if some of its costs were transferred to taxpayers, just as they have been in the past for conventional energy use (see discussion above). The transfer could come through subsidies to manufacturers that reduce the price of what they sell or through direct subsidies to consumers. Many instruments could be used. These include tax credits or deductions, subsidized loans, and various programs of expenditure. Ideally, the subsidy instrument should be neutral with regard to specific solar technologies, and it should minimize government intervention in final decisions. Instruments should not interfere with consumer incentives to minimize costs, should be self-policing or require a minimum enforcement effort, and should produce the maximum amount of fuel saving per dollar of taxpayer expenditure. This last criterion should be interpreted broadly: it should reflect any energy savings due to demonstration and research and development effects from the equipment installed.

Any subsidies should be obvious, so that their extent is clear to both beneficiaries and taxpayers. For example, rebates on capital equipment are direct in their action and would probably be easiest to administer and police. Subsidies extended through the tax system are popular because they hold down the size of budget outlays, but they are less open to public scrutiny and they bedevil the tax structure with tasks alien to the revenue function. In an era when marginal tax rates are attracting more and more concern, any further erosion of the tax base should be resisted unless a tax credit or deduction has very great advantages over some other instrument.

Further discussion of the pros and cons of different subsidy instruments is unnecessary here. Such discussions are widely available and the issues are reasonably well understood, but they have little to do with solar energy use per se. The important point to note is that if the federal government is to encourage the wider use of solar energy, a transfer of wealth might be required from citizens as a whole to those who meet a portion of their energy needs through solar-based water and space heating. Some transfer instruments are preferable to others, but not because solar energy is the function to be subsidized.

Subsidizing solar: A caution.   In the long run, subsidies can stifle technological progress and retard true commercialization. If state-of-the-art technologies find a market, some of the private incentive for further improvement is dissipated. The acceptable becomes the enemy of the better, because individual firms come to have a stake in present technology. Minor improvements will be made to stay ahead of the competition, but there is little motivation toward major steps away from a successful line of business. Once a basic design is established, it also becomes more difficult for federal research and development managers to support radically different approaches to the same problem. There is fear of appearing foolish, hesitation in seeming to second-guess prior decisions, concern about upsetting investment in the operating technology, and pressure to satisfy competing demands for funds to support marginal improvements in current practice (which have a good chance for immediate payoffs).

Subsidies can actually retard commercialization too, because the market is limited to the amount of subsidy available. Even if justified on private economic grounds, installations may be delayed if consumers believe that the government might bear part of the cost later on. (Home insulation activities apparently lagged while legislation authorizing an insulation tax credit for homeowners was under consideration.) Finally, the existence of a subsidy could sound a note of warning to consumers. Rather than reassure them, it might add to the uncertainty with which they approach this technology.

Ultimately, then, the maximum use of solar energy might be facilitated by foregoing any direct attempt to force solar devices on to the market prematurely. Funds used in demonstration projects and for installation subsidies could be used just as easily (and perhaps even more effectively) for fundamental research and development to support work on new approaches to use of solar energy. Then, as commercial potential developed, the solar industry could stand unsupported without institutional and bureaucratic drag—and without the constraints on imagination that may be imposed when subsidies are involved.

20 *Making Energy Choices*

The United States has substantial freedom of choice in shaping its energy future. The level of energy consumption can be varied, and the balance between environmental quality (including human health and safety) and other goals can be adjusted. The relative reliance on different energy forms and sources can be shifted, and so can the ratio of domestic to imported energy. Even the institutions through which decisions are made can be altered. But these choices are interrelated, they are complex, they are controversial, and, what makes them even more difficult, they are important. These characteristics have led to failure of the decision process in the past; the task is to improve that process for the future.

On a national level, political consensus in regard to energy policy has eluded three successive administrations. Energy issues have absorbed a disproportionate amount of attention, and have fostered suspicion and mistrust among elements of society. Part of the reason is that the facts required for decision making are often unknown or incomplete and outcomes of proposed actions are uncertain. In addition, energy issues have become emotionally charged and discourse on this subject has been dominated by extremes. There has been no generally accepted basis for evaluating alternatives . . . and no grand system by which choices can be legitimatized. Governing institutions based on majoritarian principles have bogged down in an issue that has no clear-cut choices. The need here is to specify the *degree* to which national policy should pursue *several* interrelated and potentially conflicting goals.

Three elements can contribute to lessening the conflict over energy policy:

- The first is improved knowledge about the facts of the energy situation, which includes the frustrating admission that uncertainty about some things is itself an important fact that no amount of shouting and recrimination will change.

536

- The second element is formulation of a "shared" world view within which energy choices can be made. Conflicting perceptions of energy's role are bound to persist, but there is still room for consensus if we recognize the mutual legitimacy of these perceptions and resolve that the essential core of each must not be violated.
- Finally, we need a decision process that all contending parties will respect and value sufficiently to protect, even when the outcome requires that original stands be modified.

Most of this book has been dedicated to the first of these elements—trying to get at the underlying facts. Chapters 1 and 15 dealt with the second element—the conflicting perceptions of socio- economic- politico-philosophical values which have generated so much unproductive heat in the national energy argument. Finally, we must turn to a discussion, necessarily incomplete, of approaches and processes by which argument might be converted into consensual action.

Legitimatizing an Approach to Energy Decisions

A number of energy policies have failed to achieve success or have even become untenable because of changes over the past few years. Taken together, those changes have been staggering: Energy prices have risen dramatically, an objective fact of major importance. In addition, the nation is now vulnerable to oil supply disruptions abroad, a matter with deep psychological as well as geopolitical and economic consequences. The relative weight placed on environmental quality has also shifted in the minds of most citizens, although to very different degrees. And the process by which energy options may be exercised has been altered by a more activist court system and a series of changes in legislation and in government institutions.

If so many shifts had not occurred, adjustment could have taken place within the existing decision system, and it could have retained a continuing legitimacy. In dealing with a multitude of issues that suddenly require simultaneous (and closely shaded) decisions, however, the political circuits have simply become overloaded. Citizens are not sure whom or what to trust, but it appears that they are losing faith in the market processes and other institutions which helped to carry out the necessary adjustments in earlier and less complex days. The skein of energy policies built up from decades of informal compromise and implicit mutual accommodation has come unwound.

Let us consider an illustration: In the energy context of an earlier era, if new information about harmful effects of emissions from coal combustion became available, a satisfactory compromise could perhaps have been reached between the urge to maintain lower energy costs (facilitating traditional economic growth) and the desire to protect or improve one aspect of environmental quality. For example, conversion from coal to oil might be required only for *new* plants and for those with fifteen years or more of economic life remaining. Costs would be increased by such an approach, but slowly; and air quality would improve too, also slowly. "Fine tuning" might induce still further narrowing of differences, perhaps by allowing *all* existing coal plants to continue operating on that fuel in exchange for general restrictions on the use of coal during atmospheric inversions. Finally, when an acceptable compromise was reached, any still-unsatisfied minority could be overruled by a general consensus that the compromise was reasonable.

But suppose that the legitimacy of economic growth as a goal is being challenged at the same time that the question of air quality versus energy cost arises. Suppose that oil is not available . . . that people are already rebelling against higher energy bills . . . that alternative energy production facilities are already being utilized heavily . . . and that environmental quality standards are undergoing repeated tightening as a result of new knowledge and changing preferences. Then no simple compromise is possible.

With these problems in mind, let us go back to the energy–environment tradeoff. There are a number of changes in energy policy which would improve the environment and also improve the prospects for economic growth (an example is the replacement-cost pricing of energy). Unless stymied by some other conflict—for example, with regard to the distribution of income—agreement on them should be possible once the facts are known.

The matter is not so easy when additional environmental quality can be obtained only by sacrificing some economic growth. There, the outcome will depend on the skills, preferences, and strengths of the parties involved and on antecedent conditions. What is required to *get any* agreement in this situation may be mutual recognition of *primacy* —that is, of which party can "legitimately" block an outcome. Then a side payment can be negotiated, and an outcome reached that is better than any feasible alternative. In terms more familiar to an economist, the issue is analogous to establishing "property rights" in an outcome. Without them, it is logically impossible to identify externalities and the party or parties to which payment is owed—and to reconcile conflicts.

The promise of this general approach can be seen in a policy now being implemented by the Environmental Protection Agency (EPA). "Primacy" is established by regulations which allow existing firms to continue to operate, but prevent additional pollution from being introduced into certain regions. But EPA will allow new polluters to enter if they can arrange to remove more pollution (the "offset" policy) from existing operations than the new installations would emit. Side payments are used to induce such reductions when the prospective entrant finds it worthwhile; the environment is improved and regional growth is not stymied.

This policy works because the crucial parties can be bound by their agreements, a condition that does not hold for all energy–environment decisions. Indeed, a small minority can hold up action through institutions such as the courts, through demonstrations, or even violence. Our institutions recognize that minorities are to be protected, and that intensity of preferences should be represented along with pluralities in the outcomes of policy dispute. Finally, though, decisions must be taken, and the larger the constituency for consensus the easier resolution becomes.

Detente in the multifaceted conflict over energy policy might be achieved through an approach that meets the *minimum* requirements for acceptability by all important groups, and thus creates an overall energy strategy which, while not the preferred path for *any* of them, is judged superior to some plausible outcomes by *all* of them. The "expansionist," for instance, must have some assurance that "adequate" energy (with its precise amount undefined) will be available on a continuing basis to meet the requirements of a "growing" (again undefined) economy. The "limited world" view, on the other hand, insists that (1) the use of resources (specifically, energy) be minimized and (2) the environment (as broadly defined) be strictly protected, with major irreversible damage avoided even at clearly extraordinary cost.[1] Once the major parties acknowledge the legitimacy of *all three* of these aims, and are willing to defend a process which yields them, a method opens up by which individual choices can be made. Specifically, the three "minimum requirements for acceptability" can provide guidance for establishing primacy for one position in many of the conflicts over energy. Then it is up to the proponents of other

---

[1] Another major interest is that of equity—concern for the fairness of outcomes. In this context, a minimum requirement for equity might be that the lowest income groups be protected from deterioration in their levels of living. This matter can best be dealt with outside the energy context, however, because threats to the well-being of the poor can come from many directions and can be addressed most easily and efficiently with general policy instruments. In this discussion, then, we ignore the equity component, even though we recognize its importance, on the grounds that if consensus can be reached on other conflicts, equity issues can be resolved. See, however, the discussion of equity issues in chapter 17.

positions to acquiesce or else to provide the side payments necessary to gain agreement. The hopeful message of the findings reported in this book is that the preconditions seem to exist for meeting these three irreducible goals. None need be sacrificed in pursuit of the others. Conflict over minimum requirements for each party is not inevitable.

The potential for success from recognizing the legitimacy of each party's minimum requirements and then seeking compromise on all else is shown by the National Coal Policy Project, which is now in its third year. It is an important example of a reasonably successful attempt to find agreement on concrete actions and policies even though there are conflicting attitudes toward degrees of environmental protection, resource conservation, and energy supply. Although the project deals with only one fuel source, it has operated within a context that recognizes the sweeping changes in our overall energy picture which were mentioned above.

The sixty or so individuals who are formal "participants" in the project are evenly divided among people who are active in environmental and in industrial (coal mining, iron and steel, pulp and paper, chemical, electric utility) activities and organizations. An initial set of findings and recommendations was published in a 1978 report entitled "Where We Agree."[2] A multi-party structure that attempted to address the overall problems of energy in all its forms would find it vastly more difficult to reach agreement, but the start made by the Coal Policy Project is significant and promising.

Paths Toward Consensus

On the energy supply side, our findings are that a number of potential sources of enhanced energy supply exist, and that the economic cost differences between them do not appear so great as to alter substantially the potential level of economic growth. This permits flexibility among supply options in case some must be foreclosed because of their environmental effects.

On the energy demand side, our findings are that widely different levels of energy consumption could be generally compatible with a level of economic growth in the range ordained by availability of other resources. Hence it will be possible to fulfill the expansionist's requirement that enough energy be available to support economic growth while meeting the

[2] *Where We Agree*, Report of the National Coal Policy Project, published in cooperation with the Center for Strategic and International Studies, Georgetown University, vols. 1 and 2 (Boulder, Colo., Westview Press, 1978).

conservationist demand that energy use be lessened substantially from what previously was thought to be the necessary minimum. The same *level* of energy use may satisfy *both* minimum requirements—so long as expansionists know that energy use can be expanded if that turns out to be necessary, and conservationists know that all feasible steps to reduce energy use are being taken. The statesmanlike aspect of achieving consensus comes in making it clear to all parties that this is not mere linguistic legerdemain, but an honest surrender of what each considers "surrenderable," without either sacrificing fundamentals or yielding to chaos that could cripple all.

The avoidance of major irreversible environmental damage from the acquisition and use of energy is, of course, consistent with the conservationist goal of lowering the rate of energy use. It need not conflict with assurance of an adequate energy supply as long as further supply options exist even after those which are judged dangerous to the environment have been rejected. Absolute safety cannot be guaranteed, but if prospects for major damage from any energy source could lead to that source's speedy replacement, it should be possible to mute resistance to a specific proposal.

Operationally, this approach to consensus suggests an overall energy strategy with a number of characteristics:

- A broad array of energy supply possibilities should be pursued, no one of which should be allowed to dominate. Multiple options for energy supply should be investigated and brought to fruition, even though prospective needs could be met less expensively by concentrating on a smaller group of the most promising technologies and sources. This implies a strong energy research and development drive at the national level, without restricting support and demonstration exclusively to the options which now appear least expensive on a dollars-and-cents basis. It means paying attention to some of the economically less promising energy sources to the extent that they appear to be more benign environmentally. It recognizes that this approach will lead to more expensive energy and to redundant expenditure, but it offsets that penalty with greater assurance that demands can continue to be met without sacrificing other basic aims.

- New technologies and practices to conserve energy should be developed, and existing conservation opportunities should be exploited fully. Federal involvement in research, development, and demonstration is called for, as is reform of energy pricing. Conservation would be given fresh market incentives by price decontrol, full incremental cost pricing, and energy taxes to compensate for such external costs as those imposed by the insecurity of foreign oil supplies. Devices such as energy efficiency standards would also have a logical place in this part of the strategy.

- This strategy implies an aggressive effort to discover *potential* harmful environmental effects from energy production and use, and a commitment to eliminate them when significant suspicion of serious danger can be supported. Exploration of basic environmental processes such as the formation of photochemical smog and of sulfates in the atmosphere is required in addition to research on such matters as the effects of low-level radiation or of CO_2 build-up. Equally important, institutional arrangements, such as the "hold harmless" policies considered earlier, need to be developed so that environmentalists can be assured that irresistible political opposition will not prevent an operation from being closed down when potential danger appears. For the same reason, some excess energy supply capacity should be supported (by public funds, as necessary).

In gaining environmentalist support for a broad-gauged energy policy, expenditures beyond those now considered "reasonable" might be required. For example, closing down nuclear power plants adjacent to population centers and banning new ones from such sites might prove to be necessary, as might placing some new nuclear plants underground or restricting their size. All coal-using plants may be required to utilize even more stringent postcombustion emission controls. And it may prove advisable to substitute new and more benign technology (such as, perhaps, fluidized bed combustion) for lower cost technologies to minimize effluents—at least for certain areas—in order to broaden the consensus of support. What the environmentalist must surrender in turn is the legitimacy of preventing "adequate" energy being made available—so that the expansionist can look to the future with some assurance.

An energy strategy based on arriving at consensus on energy supply adequacy, conservation, and environmental protection is not as neat as the way of thinking that has dominated sophisticated policy analysis over the past several decades. "Optimization" emphasized a careful comparison at the margin of benefits and costs, and its goal was to achieve the greatest level of satisfaction possible from the limited resources available. Since what constitutes "satisfaction" itself has been at issue, this approach has led to political dead ends. The attempt to optimize has meant policy paralysis. What is required instead is a commitment to do "good enough" everywhere—in terms of the overall performance of both our economy and our political system with regard to energy.

Living with Conflict—
Making Choices in a Divided Society

There are basic divisions in this society regarding energy. They involve disagreement about the kind of future people want, about the prospects for attaining different futures, and about the distribution of the benefits, costs, and risks from acquiring and using energy. The nature of these disagreements is much broader than those encompassed specifically within the energy sector, but the events which forced energy decisions to the fore have focused these conflicts on energy matters. Energy has become the testing ground for conflict over broader social choices.

We have examined numerous subjects over which conflict is waged. In public discourse they are often posed as questions of the morality of using nuclear power, the legitimacy of continued economic growth, the proper distribution of income, and to what extent human wants should be satisfied when they interfere with the preservation of environmental amenities, to mention only a few. In essence, value systems are in conflict. If contradictory value systems have no common elements or if the areas they occupy jointly are too narrow, conflicts of this sort can threaten the survival of a social system. That does not appear to be the case in this instance, but there is still room for tragedy if the conflicts we have described are mismanaged.

With regard to the conflict within the energy sector, the major basis for unity among conflicting value systems relates to the processes by which decisions are made and expressed. The social stability inherent in a "constitutional" political system is that the decision process is agreed upon prior to knowledge of the specific outcome of that process. All parties have a stake in preserving a process which they deem fair. In this country, the restraint of the majority when its views conflict with deeply held convictions of minorities is the key to the constitutional system. Limits on government, and hence on the use of force, are accepted by everyone because each wishes to be protected if, in the future, he finds himself in the minority. Thus, it is essential for energy expansionists, if they are in the majority, to protect the ability of small groups to obstruct particular additions to supplies, even though this means that disproportionate attention will be paid to a minority's preferences and extra expense may be necessary to meet them. Similarly, however, that majority must retain its ultimate ability to obtain from *some* source the energy that it believes is needed. Otherwise, the incentive for restraint—for living within the rules—is lost.

In political terms, this means that energy policies must be compatible with the minimum requirements we have outlined above. All parties to the energy debate can live with continued tension, but none can tolerate the prospect of a change which conflicts with fundamental precepts of its value system. Living with conflict implies avoidance of total victory or total defeat by any side. So long as there is hope that a process supported by all sides can yield a tolerable future, it is possible to proceed on the most critical matters while agreeing to disagree on others.

Index of Names

The letter n following a page number refers to material contained in a footnote.

Index of Subjects

Note: The letter *n* following a page number refers to material contained in a footnote.

Library of Congress Cataloging in Publication Data

National Energy Strategies Project.
Energy in America's future.

Includes index.
1. Energy policy—United States. 2. Energy
consumption—United States. 3. Power resources—
United States. I. Schurr, Sam H. II. Title.
HD9502.U52N3714 1979 333.7 79-2195
ISBN 0-8018-2280-7
ISBN 0-8018-2281-5 pbk.